Courtroom Dramas on the Stage

Courtroom Dramas on the Stage
Volume 2: The Twentieth Century

Amnon Kabatchnik

BearManor Media
2023

Courtroom Dramas on the Stage
Volume 2: The Twentieth Century

Published in the United States of America by:

BearManor Media

1317 Edgewater Dr #110
Orlando FL 32804

bearmanormedia.com

Printed in the United States.

Typesetting and layout by PKJ Passion Global

ISBN–979-8-88771-135-5

Courtroom Dramas on the Stage
Volume 2: The Twentieth Century

Amnon Kabatchnik

BearManor Media
2023

Courtroom Dramas on the Stage
Volume 2: The Twentieth Century

Published in the United States of America by:

BearManor Media

1317 Edgewater Dr #110
Orlando FL 32804

bearmanormedia.com

Printed in the United States.

Typesetting and layout by PKJ Passion Global

ISBN–979-8-88771-135-5

For

Adi and Jerry, Edan and Jennifer

CONTENTS

Interrogation

Lawyers and Judges Out of Court

Jury Room

Introduction

Even though the judicial jury's system prevailed in ancient Greece and Rome, plays produced as early as the fifth century B.C. illustrated the life-and-death power of the Gods of Olympus over the fate of the citizens. In Aeschylus's *Prometheus Bound* (480 B.C.), Zeus, the chief Greek deity, leashed his thunderbolts to dispatch the titan Prometheus to Hades for having stolen fire from the gods and handing it to mankind. In Sophocles's *Ajax* (c.444 B.C.), Athena, the Goddess of war and wisdom, who disliked the Greek hero Ajax, cast a spell over him, causing him to lose his mind and commit suicide by falling on his sword. In Euripides's *The Bacchae* (405 B.C.), when Pentheus, the young ruler of Thebes, cancelled the traditional rites of worship to Dionysus, the god of wine, Dionysus instigates the kingdom's women to get drunk, attack Pentheus in mass, strip his flesh from his ribs, and "play ball" with his carcass.

In addition to the absolute power wielded by the gods, kings too controlled the destiny of their inhabitants. The title character of Sophocles's *Antigone* (c. 442 B.C.) is a Theban princess who defied the edict of King Creon and stealthily buried her rebellious brother, who had died on the battlefield, his body exposed to the ravages of wild animals. The king condemns Antigone to be buried alive in a cave. *Thyestes* (60 A.D.), by the Roman Lucius Annaeus Seneca, features an avenging king, Atreus, who stabs and capitates the young siblings of his brother Thyestes for seducing his wife. During a royal banquet, Atreus gleefully informs Thyestes that he has munched on his own children and drank their blood.

Kings continued to dictate the fate of their inhabitants for centuries. In *Herod the Great* (c. 1554 A.D.), by England's The Wakefield Master, the king of Judea is advised by his counselors that a ruler will arise in the future from Bethlehem. Herod sends his soldiers to Bethlehem with an order to assassinate all boys who are two years old and younger. In Christopher Marlowe's *Edward II* (c. 1592 A.D.), the king avenges the murder of his male lover by executing two of his advisers. Several plays by William Shakespeare, including *The Tragedy of King Richard the Third* (c. 1593) and *Macbeth* (c. 1605), clarified how monarchs hired professional assassins to advance their cause.

In the seventeenth Century, the Spanish theater introduced mayors of small towns as the legal executioners of dastardly villains. In the nineteenth century, early American plays demonstrated how the colonist Councils condemned to death Native Americans. *Black Ey'd Susan* (1829), by England's Douglas Jerrold, created on stage the pomp and ceremony of a military trial.

The twentieth century was awash with more than two hundred courtroom dramas. Several of the playwrights were well known, among them Leo Tolstoy of Russia, W. Somerset Maugham of England, Arthur Miller of the United States, and Jean Genet of France. Many of the others are regrettably forgotten today. I have chosen about a hundred courtroom plays, the most innovative ones, for inclusion in this book, relating the plots, introducing the characters, marking the production data, and sketching biographies of playwrights, directors, and key actors.

The first scene of *Old Sleuth* (1902), a blood-and-thunder melodrama by the prolific Hal Reid, takes place in the lower Manhattan Police Court. The title character is a flamboyant, larger-than-life private detective, typical of the turn-of-the-century heroes who overcome sensational cliffhangers. The action moves to a number of settings, including a deserted graveyard, an East River saloon, the edge of Niagara Falls, and a railroad tunnel where two locomotives collide. The "Old Sleuth," whose name is Burt Brandon, dons various disguises, appearing as a woman dressed in black, a bearded sailor, a Jewish peddler, and an Italian hunchback, to name a few.

The climactic scene of *Madame X* (1908), by the French Alexandre Bisson, in which a mother charged with murder is unknowingly defended by her son, is most wrenching. John Galsworthy's *Justice* (1910) took aim at the flawed British justice system and led to the reform of England's prisons.

Bayard Veiller's *Within the Law* (1912) was rejected by most New York producers but when eventually staged, it became one of the great successes of the decade. The plot revolves around Mary Turner, a salesgirl in a department store, who is accused of stealing assorted merchandise. Though innocent, she is sent to prison for three years. Mary questions the fairness of the legal system and vows revenge.

The Mystery of the Yellow Room, a 1907 novel by Frenchman Gaston Leroux (author of *The Phantom of the Opera*), was adapted to the stage five years later. The case that unfolds in court is centered on a baffling attempted murder that took place in a bolted room with barred windows, while witnesses are stationed outside the door. The culprit is not to be found. How could he enter and exit the room?

On Trial (1914) by Elmer Rice introduced on stage a cinematic flashback. During the testimony of key witnesses, the lights dim, and the action shifts to various locales, relating the events that preceded the trial. The accused, Robert Strickland, has been charged with the fatal shooting of a prominent banker while robbing his safe. Strickland was caught red-handed with a smoking pistol in his hand.

Englishman George Pleydell used his experience as a court clerk to write an early legal novel, *The Ware Case*, in 1913, and two years later adapted it to by introducing "a junk heap of worn, irrelevant melodramatic devices" that "served only to confuse the audience." Nevertheless, Rand gave Woods credit for a gimmick that ended up making the play a hit: the jurors were selected from the audience and different short endings were written to accommodate the diverse verdicts. Rand also supported the casting of two performers: a young unknown actress, Doris Nolan, in the role of Karen Andre, who is accused of hurtling down from the roof of the Faulkner Building the body of Bjorn Faulkner, and Walter Pidgeon as Larry "Guts" Regan, a gangster in love with her.

Bernard Merivale's *The Unguarded Hour* (1935) focuses on a prosecuting counsel, Sir Francis Dearden, who is known for his ability to shatter witnesses at London's Old Bailey. Unexpectedly, Sir Francis finds himself a suspect in the murder of a famous aviator, Diana Lewis, who was found strangled in her Westminster flat. A string of coincidences — a matching description of the man who was seen leaving the crime scene, a bleeding wound, the lack of an alibi — convinced the police to arrest him. In a happy conclusion, Sir Francis returns to court with a softer, kinder demeanor.

Not unlike the prosecutor of *The Unguarded Hour*, the protagonist of *What Really Happened* (1936), by Marie Belloc Lowndes, is a hard, opinionated judge at the Old Bailey. In the case of the Crown versus Eva Raydon, who is charged with the poisoning of her husband, Justice Lenison advises the jury that the accusation is not unusual against a woman who wishes to marry her lover. The jury retires to consider the verdict and a flashback reveals what really happened.

Elsa Shelley's *Pick-Up Girl* (1944) unfolds in the modest courtroom of a New York juvenile court. Judge Bentley oversees the case of fifteen-year-old Elizabeth Collins, who fearfully admits to a first-time intimate relationship with a sailor on leave. It got her pregnant and she went through an abortion. Elizabeth claims that she hasn't been "familiar" with older men since then. The middle-aged Alexander Elliott was guided to her home by one of her friends, insisted on entering, and pushed her into the bedroom. Elizabeth is aware that a snooping neighbor called the police. Judge Bentley admonishes Elliott and tells him that he will soon be summoned to criminal court. The judge then calls in Elizabeth's parents, Mr. and Mrs. Collins, and reveals to them that a medical check concluded that Elizabeth has venereal disease. Elizabeth will be taken away from them, first to a hospital, later to the State Training School for Girls at Hudson. Mrs. Collins cries and blames herself for neglecting her daughter, but the judge says that "it's the fault of all of us . It's our indifference, our greediness, that's at fault. We don't realize that the *real* natural wealth in the world is in children."

The entire action of *Billy Budd* (1951), by Louis O. Coxe and Robert Chapman, is set aboard the British naval vessel *Indomitable* during the Napoleonic war. The sadistic master-at-arms, John Claggart, envies the sailor William Budd, who is liked by his ship mates. Claggart tells Captain Vere that "the sweet, vicious lad" is spreading unrest and rebellion among the crew. Vere orders an inquiry. Claggart denounces Billy to his face for "acting against the ship, the service, and the King." Shocked, Billy tries to respond. After gesturing and stammering, he hits Claggart, who staggers, falls, then lies still, dead. A court-martial convenes at Captain Vere's quarters. The officers vote for a self-defense acquittal, but Vere reminds them that since this is a wartime cruise, according to the Admiralty code, they have no choice but execute the man who fatally struck his superior officer. They sentence Billy to be hanged on board.

Arguably Agatha Christie's masterpiece, the three-act *Witness for the Prosecution* (1953) begins with the arrest of Leonard Vole, a likeable young man, for the murder of Miss Emily French, a middle-aged lady of means who had befriended him. French was found dead by a blow on the back of her head. The trial takes place at the Central Criminal Court, London — better known as the Old Bailey. The prosecution's case is strong, as bloodstains were found on Vole's jacket sleeves, a housekeeper testifies that she heard Vole's voice conversing with Miss French on that crucial evening, and the suspect's wife, Romaine Heilger, relates that her husband was not with her as he had maintained. The step-by-step progression of the case features several twists that were concocted ingeniously by the Queen of Crime.

Arthur Miller wrote a play — *The Crucible* (1953) — depicting the 1692 Salem witch trials, wherein the plot is a parable about McCarthyism of the 1940s and 1950s. A group of vindictive, seemingly possessed young girls, is regarded by church authorities as messengers of God who can point out the Devil's surrogate witches. Those named are clapped in jail, taken to court, and sentenced to hang.

In 1953, Herman Wouk adapted his massive Pulitzer-Prize-winning novel, *The Caine Mutiny*, into an exciting courtroom drama. The proceedings unfold at the General Court-Martial Room of the Twelfth Naval District, San Francisco, in 1945. Lt. Stephen Maryk is accused of mutiny in wartime for relieving from duty Lieutenant Commander Philip Francis Queeg, the captain of the *U.S.S. Caine*, Lt. Maryk contends that during a raging typhoon in the Pacific, Captain Queeg became numb with panic. In order to save the ship, he relieved the skipper of duty and seized control. The prosecutor John Challee summons to the witness stand several navy officers and builds up a strong case against Maryk. However, defense attorney Barney Greenwald turns the tables. In an intense cross-examination, he breaks down the self-assured Captain Queeg, who gradually disintergrates and ends up sobbing, a broken man. Lt. Maryk is exonerated, but during an acquittal party, attorney Greenwald hails the Queegs of the Navy for holding back the Nazis while the nation was preparing for war.

Inherit the Wind (1955), by Jerome Lawrence and Robert E. Lee, covers the historic "monkey trial" of Tennessee high school teacher John T. Scopes, who was accused of teaching Charles Darwin's Theory of Evolution in defiance of state law. The playwrights fictionalized the place and the characters but presented faithfully the highly intense clash between defense attorney Clarence Darrow (in the play, Henry Drummond) and prosecutor William Jennings Bryan (Matthew Harrison Brady) over a person's right to think.

The main character of Henry Denker's *Time Limit!* (1956) is Major Harry Cargill who is about to be court-martialed for treason. He is accused of betraying his fellow-Americans in a North Korean prison camp by cooperating with the enemy, making propaganda broadcasts against the United States. The court proceedings, enhanced by hard-hitting flashbacks, reveal harrowing events that took place in the prison camp and the reason why Cargill became the mouthpiece for the North Koreans.

Unlike the often grim proceedings that evolve in courtroom cases, *The Ponder Heart* (1956), by Joseph Fields and Jerome Chodorov, presents the case of Uncle Daniel Ponder, accused of killing his child bride, in the spirit of broad comedy. The play unfolds in the small Southern town of Clay. Uncle Ponder makes sure that during the trial his accusers get good seats in the front row, and congratulates his nemesis, Prosecutor Dorris R. Gladney, for delivering one of the most moving pleas he has ever heard. On a more serious note, Uncle Ponder describes how during a severe thunderstorm, his wife Bonnie Dee became literally frightened to death. He held her in his arms and could feel her heart beating fast, then stopping. That's exactly what happened, announces Uncle Ponder, the whole truth and nothin' but the truth. As expected, Uncle Ponder is found not guilty.

Nathan Leopold, age nineteen, and Richard Loeb, age eighteen, spoiled sons of Chicago millionaires, killed a fourteen-old boy to prove that they can commit a perfect crime. *Compulsion*, a 1957 play by Meyer Levin, reveals how the two cocky murderers (presented with changed names) failed in their scheme. A pair of designed spectacles, found in the vicinity of the corpse, serves as the key clue. The discovery of the instrument of death, a chisel with a taped blade, clinches the case. Defense attorney Jonathan Wilk (in real-life, Clarence Darrow) manages to convince the judge that the defendants' age and mental condition are mitigating circumstances. The verdict was life imprisonment instead of death.

The French playwright Jean Genet pits reality versus illusion in his drama *The Blacks* (1959). On an upper level there is a Court of Justice. Its members are a haughty Queen, her dwarfish Valet, a hanging Judge, a missionary Bishop, and an island Governor. They wear white masks, representing the dominant white race. Below them is a group of ordinary villagers, some of whom killed a white woman, an old drunkard. They'll reenact the crime step-by-step with the action revolving around a catafalque. The entire cast is Black. Reviewers were fascinated by "Mr. Genet's furious flights of language encompassing obscenity and purity, violence and tenderness, hatred and love," and declared that "*The Blacks* was the first sophisticated play about the racial question to be written with no taboos in its use of words, images or ideas."

Rashomon (1959), by Fay Kanin and Michael Kanin, goes back a thousand years ago to Kyoto, the ancient capital of Japan. A dangerous bandit named Tajomaru was arrested and taken to a Police Court for rape and murder. Tajomaru's testimony is visualized in the form of a flashback: a husband, Takehiko, is seen leading a white horse, on which his wife Kinume is riding, through the winding path of a forest. Tajomaru is enchanted by her exquisite face, attacks the husband and binds him to a tree. He then accosts the wife, who struggles fiercely, but gradually succumbs. Kinume pleads with Tajomaru to give her husband a chance to avenge her honor — and his own. Tajomaru unties Takehiko's bonds and a sword fight ensues, at the end of which the bandit plunges his weapon to its final conclusion. During the contest, the wife runs away. No, he didn't look for her, why should he. Three contrasting versions of the event are related by the wife, by the spirit of the husband via a medium, and by a witness, a woodcutter who claims to have watched the encounter from behind a bush. Peering through the play's melodramatic aspects is the issue What is True?

The Anderson Trial (1959), by Saul Levitt, is based on the official record of the 1865 trial of Henry Wirz, commandant of the notorious Confederate prison-of-war stockade at Andersonville, Georgia. Wirz was held responsible for the barbarous confinement of forty thousand Union soldiers without adequate shelter against the heat of summer and the cold of winter; that he did not provide the prisoners with sufficient food, clothing, or medical care, causing fourteen thousand of them to languish and die. Wirz insisted that the military code dictated that he obey orders, that he could not disobey, and that he had to keep his feelings to himself.

Conceived by Swiss playwright Frriedrich Duerrenmatt as a radio play and adapted to the stage by James Yaffe, *The Deadly Game* (1960) takes place in a secluded Alpine retreat, where three retired men of law — a judge, a prosecutor, and a defense attorney — relive their glory days by playing legal charades with stranded strangers. A fourth elderly gentleman, hovering in the background, has shared the municipality as its official hangman.

The Man in the Glass Booth (1967), by Robert Shaw, is based on the case of Adolf Eichmann, a Nazi colonel who fled to Argentina and lived there under an assumed name. In 1960 he was captured by Israeli Mossad agents and abducted to Israel, where he was tried for crimes against humanity, found guilty, and executed. *The Man in the Glass Booth* begins with the kidnapping of Arthur Goldman, a real estate tycoon in Manhattan, who is suspected of being Adolf Karl Dorff, a colonel in a unit of the S.S. Goldman is flown clandestinely to Israel. In a Tel Aviv courtroom, he is placed in a bullet-proof glass booth. Witnesses testify about the horrors of the concentration camps and the atrocities committed by the Nazis. Surprisingly, Goldman seems carefree and high-spirited at the conclusion of each testimony. The reason behind his gleeful disposition is revealed at the climax of the play.

Conduct Unbecoming (1969), by Barry England, unfolds in 1800s India. Edward Millington, a newly arrived second lieutenant, joins the British regiment. During an officers' ball, Millington feebly accosts the regiment's sweetheart, Marjorie Hasseltine, an attractive widow. He is taken aback when the lady accuses him of a much graver offence — an attempted rape. Millington is tried by a kangaroo court martial, where witnesses against him include the regiment's doctor, the Second-in-Command, the Mess Major, and Mrs. Hasseltine herself. The upcoming proceedings entail several twists.

Inquest (1970), by Donald Freed, covers the trial and execution of Julius and Ethel Rosenberg, who during the cold war were accused of delivering secret information about the atom bomb to Russian agents. Wken in 1970 the drama opened at the Music Box Theatre on Broadway, it featured images of newspaper headlines from the 1940s and 1950s on an upstage screen. The tone of the play is sympathetic to the Rosenbergs, and the last scene, taking place on death row at Sing Sing prison, is presented in harrowing detail.

The Trial of the Catonsville Nine (1971), by Daniel Berrigan and Saul Levitt, is inspired by the actual case of seven men and two women, all Catholics, who in 1968, at the height of the Vietnam War, entered the draft board in Catonsville, Maryland, snatched hundreds of recruitment files, brought them to a parking lot, and set them on fire with homemade napalm. They were arrested, tried, convicted, and sentenced to prison terms ranging from two to three-and-a-half years.

Execution of Justice (1984) by Emily Mann depicts the real-life double murder that was committed in San Francisco in 1978 : Dan White, a former member of the Board of Supervisors, shot and killed Mayor George Moscone and City Supervisor Harvey Milk. Emily Mann drew on the trial manuscript and published news reports. The play unfolds in quick episodes with images of Moscone and Milk projected on a white screen overhead. As Prosecutor Thomas F. Norman and Defense Attorney Douglas Schmidt are selecting the jury, a projected television reporter announces that "by all accounts, there are no blacks, no gays, and no Asians" on the jury, and "Dan White will certainly be judged by a jury of his peers." Defense Attorney Schmidt points out that Harvey Milk had been acting to prevent White's reappointment. White, asserts Schmidt, came from a vastly different lifestyle than Milk, "who was a homosexual leader and politician." Schmidt emphasizes, however, that the friction between White and his victims was a political fight over who controlled the city, not a hate-crime against a gay person. The prosecutor insists that these were deliberate, premeditated, and cold-blooded executions. The jury returns a guilty verdict of voluntary manslaughter. White was sentenced to seven years and eight months in prison, the maximum punishment for two counts of voluntary manslaughter. The lenient verdict led to rioting. On the screen are projected images of cars burning, City Hall being stormed, a line of police officers in riot gears.

Harper Lee's 1960 novel *To Kill a Mockingbird* was adapted to the stage in 1987 by Christopher Sergel. The play depicts a sensational crime that rocked the imaginative Maycomb, Alabama, in 1935. We see the proceedings through the eyes of Jean Louise Finch (nicknamed "Scout"), an alert six-year-old girl who tries to understand the web of racial undercurrents prevailing in the South. She and her brother Jeremy sneak to the balcony of a courtroom and watch their father Atticus, a lawyer, defend a young Black man, Tom Robinson, accused of raping a nineteen-year-old white woman, Mayella Ewell. In spite of Atticus' contention that evidence indicated that Mayella was beaten savagely by someone using his left hand, and that Tom Robinson's left hand was crippled, the jury, as expected, finds the defendant guilty. The kids are disappointed, but their aunt, Miss Maudie, tells them that their father was the only man in the area who could keep the jury out so long in a case like this. "Maybe we're taking a little step, a little step along the way," says Miss Maudie.

The main action of Aaron Sorkin's *A Few Good Men* (1989) takes place in a military courtroom at the United States Naval Base in Guantanamo Bay, Cuba. Marine Lance Corporal Harold Dawson and Private First-Class Louden Downey have been charged with murder in the second degree and conduct unbecoming a U.S. Marine. The victim, William Santiago, was an unpopular private in their platoon. Assigned to defend Dawson and Downey is Lieutenant Daniel A. Kaffee, a Harvard Law School graduate with no practical experience. In court, Kaffee finds himself pitted against Lieutenant Colonel Nathan Jessup, the formidable base commander, and gradually sheds his neophyte image.

The Laramie Project (2000) is a political docudrama created by New York's Tectonic Theatre Project under the helm of its artistic director, Moisés Kaufman. In 1998, company members traveled to Laramie, Wyoming, to interview townspeople regarding the murder of Matthew Shepard, a gay student at the University of Wyoming. On October 7, 1998, Matthew met with two local men, Aaron McKinney and Russell Henderson, at a popular bar and agreed to join them for a car ride. The duo pistol-whipped and tortured Matthew, tied him to a fence in a remote, rural area, and left him to die. Matthew was discovered eighteen hours later by a cyclist, but to no avail. He was pronounced dead at the hospital. McKinney and Henderson were arrested shortly thereafter. Four weeks after the homicide of Matthew Shepard, nine members of the Tectonic Theatre Project descended on Laramie and for the next year conducted hundreds of interviews. The material was eventually edited into a three-act play, with the trial of the case unfolding in the third act. Henderson pleaded "guilty" and was sentenced to life imprisonment. McKinney's defense team approached Matthew's parents, Dennis and Judy Shepard, and pleaded for their client's life, Dennis Shepard made a statement in court, announcing his hope that good may come out of evil. "This is the time to begin the healing process," said Shepard. "To show mercy to someone who refused to show any mercy. Mr. McKinney, I am going to grant you your life... May you have a long life, and may you thank Matthew every day for it."

* * *

A number of enterprising playwrights concentrated on causes leading to a crime, and kept the ensuing trial proceedings in the background, off stage.

In *The Living Corpse* (c. 1900), a drama by the Russian Leo Tolstoy, the plot rotates around a case of bigamy, when a wife mistakenly believes that her missing husband is dead and gets married again. In an off-stage trial, the judge rules that she must either give up her new husband or be exiled to Siberia.

The Red Robe (1900), by the French playwright Eugene Brieux, unfolds in the office of M. Vagret, a prosecuting attorney who is up for judgeship. To insure his promotion, Vagret introduces damaging information about the wife of a suspect in a murder case — and lives to regret it. *The Witching Hour* (1907), by Augustus Thomas, is also geared to political ambitions, when a recently promoted district attorney is found to be involved in the murder of Kentucky's governor. *The Witness for the Defense* (1911), by the English playwright A,E,W, Mason, focuses on Stella Ballantyne, who back in India had been charged with the murder of her husband, and acquitted. Now rumors of the case turn her into "the freak" of Little Bedding, Sussex. A local solicitor takes it upon himself to review the proceedings of the Indian courtroom. W. Somerset Maugham's *The Letter* (1927) unrolls on a plantation in the Malay Peninsula. As the curtain rises, Leslie Crosbie empties her six-chamber revolver into the prostate body of Geoffrey Hammond, her lover. Shedding crocodile tears, she tells a good friend, attorney Howard Joyce, that Hammond attempted to rape her. With Joyce's guidance, the trial of R. vs. Crosbie clears Leslie of any wrongdoing.

Playwright Maxwell Anderson wrote two plays about shoemaker Nicola Sacca and fish peddler Bartolomeo Vanzetti, who were indicted for the 1920 robbery and murder of a postmaster and his guard in Braintree, Massachusetts. They were found guilty despite contradictory evidence, and after seven years of incarceration, were executed on August 23, 1927. Anderson's *Gods of the Lightning* (1928) probes the crime and the trial with changed names, while *Winterset* (1935) depicts an imaginary aftermath, years later, when the son of one of the executed men crusades to clear his father's name.

Terence Rattigan's *The Winslow Boy* (1946) captures the real-life story of Ronnie Winslow, a thirteen-year-old cadet at an English naval academy, who is accused of stealing and cashing a five-shilling postal order. He is expelled. Ronnie's father, a banker, beleves the boy's pleas of innocence and wages a long struggle to clear his name. It becomes a national issue, debated in Parliament. Against all odds, the Winslow boy eventually defeats the Crown. William Faulkner's *Requiem for a Nun* (1951) depicts the case of Nancy Mannigoe, a Black domestic maid, who stands trial at a Mississippi courthouse. for smothering a baby girl in its cradle. She is found guilty and sentenced to death by hanging. The motive is revealed at the climax of the play.

* * *

Following are several plays that feature interrogation of suspects by the authorities which may or not lead to an indictment and trial.

In *The Third Degree* (1909), by Charles Klein, Howard Jeffries, an unhappy young man who is in the wrong place at the wrong time, confesses to murder after enduring a lengthy "third degree" questioning. *Darkness at Noon* (1951), adapted by Sidney Kingsley from Arthur Koestler's novel, unfolds in a Russian prison, where Ivanoff, the compound's warden, attempts to solicit a confession from one of the inmates, Rubashov, that he had been part of a plot to assassinate "the leader." A confession would result in a few years of jail instead of a death sentence. When writing *The Prisoner* (1954), England's Bridget Boland was inspired by the plight of Cardinal Jósef Mindszenty who crusaded in Hungary against the regime's plan to nationalize all Catholic schools. He was charged with treason and sentenced to life imorisonment. Following the 1956 revolution, Mindszenty was freed. *The Prisoner* unfolds in a gloomy jail room with barred windows. The Cardinal faces an Interrogator and the give-and-take between them is not unlike a chess game between two worthy opponents.

Paul Sevigne, a young examining magistrate, who has just been prmoted to a post in Paris, is the principle character of Marcel Achard's *A Shot in the Dark* (1961). His first case is seemingly a cut-and-dried murder. The prime suspect, Josefa Lantenay, is a parlor maid of a Parisian household. She was found unconscious, nude, and clutching a gun next to her dead lover, the chauffeur. As Sevigne interrogates Josefa, he realizes by her naive statetements that she could not be a murderess and turns his attention to her aristocratic employers. *In the Matter of J. Robert Oppenheimer* (1964), by the German playwright Heinar Kipphardt, goes back to the hysterical era of McCarthysm when in 1954 J. Robert Oppenheimer, "the father of the atomic bomb," was summoned to a congressional hearing regarding his security clearance. Kipphardt sifted through 3,000 typed papers before ondensing the records about Oppenheimer into a two-act, three-hour play. The time: April 12 -May 6, 1954. The place: Room 2022, Building T3, Atomic Energy Commission, Washington, D.C. When the curtain rises, Oppenheimer steps forward and introduces himself to the audience as a "Professor of Physics at Princeton." He explains that he has been summoned to answer questions put to him concerning his views, his associations, his actions, and the suspicion that he has been disloyal.

In John Pielmeier'd *Agnes of God* (1991), a court appointed psychiatrist, Martha Livingston, is assigned to determine the sanity of a young nun, Agnes, accused of strangling her own newborn baby. Through hypnotic interrogation, Livingston elicits from Agnes details of a tortured childhood by abusive parents and a confession by the simple-minded nun that she killed the baby girl to "give her back to God." The siring of the infant remains an enigma — could it have been God's, or that of a visiting priest, or a local field hand? *Death and the Maiden* (1991), by Ariel Dorfman, is the story of Paulina Salas, a South American married to a prominent lawyer. On their way to a beach home, they have a flat tyre, Doctor Roberto Miranda stops to help. They invite the Good Samaritan to spend the night. Upon hearing the doctor's voice, Paulina believes that he is the man who raped and tortured her fifteen years earlier as she lay blindfolded in a military detention center. Late at night, she slips into Roberto's bedroom, hits him with a blunt instrument, binds him to a chair, and gags him with her panties. Then she orders her shocked husband to serve as the doctor's defense attorney in "a trial."

* * *

I have included a few fascinating plays that feature lawyers and judges out of courtroom.

The Woman in the Case (1905), by Clyde Fitch, begins with a Manhattan dinner party, hosted by man-about-town Julian Rolfe and socialite Margaret Hughes in celebration of their weddeing. The mood of the evening is clouded by the recent murder of Philip Long, the best man. Margaret's mother enters clutching an evening newspaper that blazes the claim of a notorious vamp, Claire Forster, boasting publicly of an affair with Julian. At that moment, the police arrive with a warrant for Julian's arrest for the murder of Philip Long. Margaret is desperate, so a good friend, the lawyer George Thompson, steps in. *At Bay* (1913), by George Scarborough, introduces a crooked Washington, D.C. lawyer, Judson Flagg, who attempts to blackmail the daughter of the U.S. District Attorney and ends up sprawled across his desk with the sharp point of a paper knife in his heart. Another unsympathetic lawyer, Robert Harding of *The Law of the Land* (1914) by George Broadhurst, whips his young son cruelly and is shot by his wife.

John Willard's classic 1922 melodrama, *The Cat and the Canary*, begins in an isolated mansion on the Hudson, with the lawyer Roger Crosby reading the will of Cyrus Ganby West to a group of relatives. By the end of the first act, Crosby's body topples out of a closet. *The Leavenworth Case* (1936), by Basil Ring, adapted from Anna Katharine Green's early detective novel, launched the body-in-the-library subgenre. The victim is Horatio Leavenworth, a Fifth Avenue millionaire, who was shot dead before he could alter his will. The mansion doors have been locked for the night and the windows shuttered, so it appears that this is an inside job. A young lawyer, Everett Raymond, falls in love with one of the suspects and joins the police in the investigation of the case.

The tables have turned on the leading character of *Hanging Judge* (1952) by Raymond Masey. Sir Francis Brittain, a ruthless High Court jurist, finds himself accused of fatally poisoning a blackmailer. Perry Mason, the renowned literary attorney created by Erle Stanley Gardner, hero of numerous novels, movies and television series, defended a client on stage only once, in *A Case for Mason*, dramatized by William McCleery in 1967. The dastardly proceedings involve the theft of diamons and a murder by poison. Mason succeeds in defending the suspect in the case and unearthing the actual murderer, but here the events unfold out of court without the customary trial climax.

The action of Tim Kelly's *Curse of the Werewolf* (1990) commences in the sitting room of Gargoyle House, a spooky castle on a lonely New England island. The master of the estate, Algernon Snipes, is very arthritic and moves bent over, with the aid of two canes. The effect is of a spider or land crab walking. The play begins with a visit by Algernon's lawyer, Joan Tarbuckle, capable and self-assured, carrying an attache case. As the play progresses, Tarbuckle will be revealed as a greedy manipulator who cavots the estate. She will meet a premature doom, her corpse found in the lower part of a grandfather clock.

* * *

I began the subgenre of jury-room plays with *The Woman on the Jury* (1923) by Bernard K. Burns. Eleven men on the jury vote for the conviction of Grace Pierce, on trial for fatally shooting her lover for deceiving her after their child was born. The one woman on the jury, Betty Brown, who went through a similar experience, sympathizes with Grace and recommends acquittal. The action of Fred Ballard's *Ladies of the Jury* (1929) takes place in a New Jersey jury room, where the panel of twelve men and women deliberates the case of Yvette Yvet Gordon, an ex-chorus girl charged with the murder of her wealthy, elderly husband. Here too eleven members of the panel vote guilty, with one holdout – Mrs. Livingston Baldwin Crane, a high-society matron who is guided exclusively by intuition. Conversely, juror number 8 of *Twelve Angry Men* (1954), by Reginald Rose, analyses the evidence didactly before convincing eleven jurors that "there is reasonable doubt" in the case of a Black youth from the slums, who is charged with stabbing his father. The audience attending a production of *A Wicked Soul in Cherry Hill* (2022) is assigned to act as the jury, scaling the pros and cons of a real-life case of a rabbi accused of hiring an assassin to kill his wife.

* * *

In order to gain a historical perspective, I have kept potentially offensive elements intact and did not edit out sexism, racial prejudices, anti-Semitic slurs, or other derogatory content. The plays must be seen in their historical context, each a work of art that is shaped by its era.

Regrettably, only a few of the plays covered in this book are read and seen by today's public so I have described the plots with some length. Almost without exception, these courtroom dramas deserve scrutiny, study, and theatrical revival. I hope that this labor of love will rekindle interest in neglected playwrights and forgotten plays.

Old Sleuth (1902)

Hal Reid (United States, 1862-1920)

James Halleck Reid (who used the pen name Hal Reid) joined the golden group of melodrama playwrights who could whip up a four-act play in a week or less, then reap financial bonanzas when a dozen road companies performed their works simultaneously across the United States. Reid's first New York production took place in 1895. By 1911 he was credited with 117 titles, surpassing Owen Davis's claim to 112 original dramas, but falling behind Dion Boucicault's 400 titles.[1]

Typical of Reid's melodramas was *Old Sleuth*, produced at the dawn of the twentieth century It involved convoluted plots, wild happenings, humorous interludes, one-dimensional characters, flamboyant villains, and sensational cliffhangers.

Old Sleuth begins at lower Manhattan's Jefferson Market Police Court. George Washington Jones, a Black vagrant, is charged with disturbing the peace. Officer Jerry McDugan testifies that he found Jones asleep on a street corner and had to wake him up with his fist; he admits that he "trimmed him a bit" while in custody, leaving "black walnuts" on the "nigger's head."

Justice McDougal is unmoved by what seems to be customary police practice and intends to send Jones to the Island, but the detective Burt Brandon intervenes and offers to give the prisoner, if discharged, "work at once." The judge consents.[2]

Rene Ruthendale, Judge McDougal's next case, is charged with burglary. She is "elegantly dressed and very pale," but without legal representation. Detective Brandon measures Rene with his eyes and tells her, "I am a judge of criminals; I am sure you are innocent; I would stake my life upon it." He asks Justice McDougal to grant an adjournment "until such time as your honor set the case for preliminary hearing." The Judge allots a $5,000 bond, which Brandon pays.

Court is adjourned. Bayard Knight, Rene's accuser, described in the play's program as "A Royal Rogue," queries Assistant District Attorney Samuel Irving about Burt Brandon. "He is known as Old Sleuth the Detective," says Irving. "He is not old in years but experience. He is unquestionably the 'King of Detectives.' I don't like him, but he is a wonder."

Knight approaches Rene and asks to speak with her but Brandon points to the door: "Go, Bayard Knight. From this time, you are a marked man. I'll know you the next time I see you." Knight leaves. Brandon sends his urchin assistant, Mick Mullane, to follow him.[3]

Rene tells Brandon that by her "women's intuition" she feels she can trust him as a brother— "I will tell you all." She has a faint recollection of "once living in a grand home, surrounded by every luxury and elegance," and being kidnapped from her loving family as a small child. "It seems as if I had been snatched from Paradise and plunged into the horrors of hell itself," she says. A circus acrobat, Leon Leonardi, claimed to be Rene's father and as a child she performed in the ring with his troupe. One day, Bayard Knight came into the tent, presented himself as Rene's uncle, and demanded possession of the girl. Knight took good care of Rene, introducing her to New York society as his stepdaughter.

But one night Knight "threw aside his mask and told me that he loved me and tried to force me to become his wife. I escaped from the house and managed to hide for several days when yesterday we met face to face. It was then that he had me arrested on this false charge."

Brandon assures the distraught Rene that he will solve "the mystery" of her life. "You are the victim of some horrible villainy and by the memory of my mother, I swear to you to track it down, if it costs me my life," he states.

Brandon sends Rene out through a back exit. Knight returns and offers the detective $5000 "to clear out of this matter." Brandon laughs and says he will settle for nothing less than "one half of the stolen Ruthendale estate." Knight draws a pistol, but Brandon is "just a trifle quicker" in aiming his gun at Knight's head.

Knight: Damn you, Brandon. You are a great detective. I am only a plain citizen, but I will play this game with you to the bitter end.

Brandon: The game has just started. The end will be your death—or mine, for while I draw the breath of life, I am going to leave no stone unturned in this case—and I will try to prove to all the world that I deserve the name "Old Sleuth, King of Detectives."

The villain, the hero and the lady-in-distress are all set now for a series of chases and escapes.

The first encounter unfolds in a Sailors Lodging House on the East River, a setting complete with a dusty saloon floor, a wooden dock and a marooned boat. Knight has lured Rene to this forsaken den with a note, presumably signed by Brandon. He tells her that he intends to marry her and thus gain access to "an immense fortune." The maiden stamps her foot vehemently and shakes her head, no. She would rather die.

Knight motions to his underlings, Jack Heads, Brute Brune and Leon Leonardi, to tie the girl and lock her in a cabinet. They then raise glasses for a toast. Brandon enters disguised as a full-bearded sailor, accompanied by his assistant, Lady Kate, who is dressed in a Salvation Army outfit. Brandon levels a pistol and shoots the glass out of Leon's hand. "Damn you. Who are you?" asks Knight. "Old Sleuth, the Detective," declares Brandon and pulls off his beard. The sleuth could have forced the issue then and there, but since there are two more acts to follow, he retreats to the door, assuring Knight, "I'll land you where you belong if God lets me live," and exits, followed by Kate.

The action shifts to a graveyard at midnight. and George Jones is sent there by Brandon to keep watch, A long, mournful howl by a dog in the distance causes George to tremble and shake. "I got higgety and swelled in de haid," he whispers, "and I had to be a black sleuth, en now de time's come. I'm goin' to be a black cawpse."

Brandon arrives disguised as a woman. Entering a crypt, he discovers that the body implanted there is not that of Rene Ruthendale's.

In a corner of the graveyard, Knight and Leonardi are confronted by Lady Kate. She calls Knight "a thief, a woman stealer and perhaps a murderer," and reminds him of how he has wronged her. She levels a pistol at Knight's head. Leonardi strikes it out of her hand and grasps her throat. A woman dressed in black rushes in and knocks Leonardi flat with a punch. "Woman, who are you?" asks Knight. "I'm a woman by the name of Burt Brandon," says the detective as he throws off bonnet and veil.

Again, instead of escorting the brigands to the nearest police station, Brandon tells Knight that he can go— "but don't think that this means the end, for day by day, night by night, hour by hour, minute by minute, I shall be on your track like your own shadow."

The proceedings continue on the edge of Niagara Falls. For no discernible reason, Rene and Knight meet there. She calls him, "monster, monster, monster," and he chuckles, "Beauty and the Beast, eh?" She shouts, "the day of retribution is near at hand," and he promises to "put you into a barrel and send you over the falls to death."

Knight and Leonardi shove Rene into a barrel and saunter out, but not before she drops her handkerchief. Brandon and George enter swiftly and find Rene's handkerchief.

A barrel attached to an invisible wire is pulled quickly several times, then tumbles down. A duplicate barrel containing Rene is shot up when Brandon and George appear in a boat. They pull the barrel into the boat and release Rene.

In front of a ground row of rocks, Knight aims a pistol at Brandon and shoots. With a cry, the detective pitches forward out of the boat. George dives into the water after him. Knight grabs Rene and takes her ashore. George is seen holding Brandon up, hanging on to a rock.

The next setting is that of a private insane asylum in New Jersey. Dr. Jose Hilker, the head of the institution, is nervous. He has heard that Burt Brandon, the detective, is inquiring about Bayard Knight's patient, a young lady. Dr. Hilker tells his assistant, Ellen Mackay, that he means to tell Knight tonight to take his patient elsewhere.

George Washington Jones enters dressed in overalls; he has just been hired as a handyman. George goes to the engine room and stokes the furnace. Lady Kate passes through the guards with a fake note from Knight, meets Rene, whispers to her that she is "a woman detective working with Burt Brandon for your liberation," and reveals to the young girl that she is her mother.

The final scene transpires in a railroad tunnel. The fronts of two locomotives, with highlights glowing and smoke billowing, are pushed forward on rollers, accompanied by a whistling effect and a whirl of motors. Knight is discovered on one engine, Brandon on the other. Concealed stagehands push the "trains" so that it seems that the detective's train is gaining. Shutting off the engine, Brandon jumps over and tackles Knight with his fists. Knight breaks away and pulls out a pistol. "You'll never take me alive," he says, placing the weapon to his head, and firing. A startled conductor asks Brandon. "Who the devil are you, man?" "Old Sleuth, the Detective!" comes the answer, cheerfully, and the curtain descends.

* * *

Promoted as "The Melo-Dramatic Sensation of the Season" and "The Great Detective Play," *Old Sleuth* opened at the Music Hall in New York City on October 27, 1902. A press release by Mammoth Productions predicted that "the play is bound to create a profound impression in the hearts and minds of the audience. It produces a tale which is soul-stirring in its pathos and intensely dramatic in its tragic incidents… The portrayal of the various characters, the realistic, stupendous and most magnificent scene effects, the surprising mechanical devices and electrical displays, must be seen, the most illustrious pen being unable to give a fair description of the stirring and luxuriously equipped production. The cast, like a collection of precious stones, glitters and reflects the excellent quality thereof."

The title character was played by Hal Stephen. The reviewers nodded with approval, pointing out with awe that "during the evening Mr. Stephens portrayed no less than fourteen characters, among them a farmer, Hebrew peddler, drunken sailor, old darkey, young lady, an Italian hunchback and others equally varied."

* * *

Before writing plays, James Halleck Reid, a native of Kentucky, was a reporter in Cincinnati, Ohio, adding to his weekly stipend by acting as a walk-on with visiting theatrical companies.

"My object was to study audiences from the stage," he said, "to see what they would applaud, what they would laugh at, and what would make them cry… After eight years—in which I slowly graduated from super to actor—I began to write my first play." At the age of twenty-three Reid penned *La Belle Marie*, which earned a modest profit and incited him to discard his newspaper job and launch a playwriting career.

Reid ventured into New York with a melodrama, *Human Hearts*, which, under a new title, *Logan's Luck*, and using the moniker Hal Reid, was produced at the People's Theatre in the Bowery on June 3, 1895, for eight performances. It reverted back to the original title, *Human Hearts*, and was revived in Manhattan in 1895, 1896 and 1897. It also ran in the provinces for many years and was filmed in 1910 and 1922.

Human Hearts depicts a scheming city woman who marries a young westerner, the son of a wealthy farmer, for his money. When the father becomes suspicious of her intentions, the woman and her former lover, an ex-convict, kill him. The victim's son is accused of the murder, but the woman repents and confesses the truth.

A stream of popular successes followed; mostly sensational tear-jerkers peppered with elements of crime. *Knobs of Tennessee* (1899) tells the story of the Preston family who own a "moonshine" still in the Tennessee mountains, are raided by revenue officers, and go through a succession of setbacks before they unexpectedly discover valuable minerals on their land.

The Prince of the World (1901), co-written by Reid and his wife Bertha Belle Westbrook, is based on Biblical incidents. A notation in the program stated that "the authors offer an apology for any liberties taken with history for the sake of the drama." The Emperor, Caesar, falls in love with the Israelite Judith. When she rejects his advances, Caesar orders that she be thrown into a lion's den. In full view of the audience, Judith is placed in a cage surrounded by real lions. The beasts do not harm her.

Racial prejudice is the core of *At the Old Cross Roads* (1901). The protagonist is a Mississippi octoroon, Parepa, who endeavors to shield her daughter, Annabelle, from the knowledge of her mixed blood. Parepa has always claimed to be Annabelle's nurse. Annabelle is reared as a white girl, and is sent to a finishing school, returning an accomplished young lady. The white father, Dayton Thornton, keeps tormenting Parepa. One day, after he had struck her with a whip, she shoots him dead at the old crossroads. A coroner's jury declares it justifiable homicide and Parepa is acquitted. To pacify the era's audiences, it turns out that Parepa was not an octoroon, but white. Annabelle was not "tainted" with Negro blood after all.

Reid's varied themes include the clash between conservative parents and wayward children (*The Peddler*, 1902); the predicament of working girls under despotic and lecherous employers (*A Working Girl's Wrongs*, 1903); the contention of a will by disgruntled, violent, often homicidal would-be-inheritors (*A Midnight Marriage*, 1904); the deadly encounter for the possession of a gold mine (*At Cripple Creek*, 1904); the plight of abused children (*Nobody's Darling*, 1905); the search for the parents of abandoned infants (*The Little Organ Grinder*, 1907); the evils of alcohol (*Lured from Home*, 1905) and drugs (*From Broadway to the Bowery*, 1907); the charge of murder against an innocent person (*For a Human Life*, 1906); and tragic love triangles (*A Millionaire's Revenge*, 1906).[4]

Reid's melodramas are populated with white-collar schemers, dastardly foreigners and savage Indians. The heroine is tied to a post by the East River and left to drown, thrown into an icy millpond, or almost run over by an on-rushing Third Avenue trolley car. The hero has to duck the fusillade of bullets, the sling of arrows, and sticks of dynamite. The action rotates from hidden caves in the Kentucky mountains to Colorado mining camps to opium dens in lower Manhattan's Chinatown.

* * *

Hal Reid made his mark in the silent cinema as actor, writer, and director. In 1910, he participated in the film version of his hit play, *Human Hearts*. Two years later, he played the title roles in *Cardinal Wolsey* and *Rip Van Winkle*. Between 1910 and 1919, Reid appeared in and directed 20 features. Simultaneously, during that time span, he wrote more than 30 screenplays, many containing elements of crime and mystery.

Reid wrote, directed, and appeared in *The Deerslayer* (1913), adapted from J. Fenimore Cooper's novel. *Dan* (1914) is a Civil War drama in which the title character, a loyal slave bound to an aristocratic Southern family, sacrifices himself by taking the place of his master to be executed. *Time Lock Number 776* (1915) is a thriller about New York counterfeiters. During the climax, the heroine is locked in a time-locked vault and rescued from certain suffocation by the Secret Service.

Reid returns to his favorite theme of temperance in *Prohibition* (1915), a five-reeler, in which a jealous suitor coaxes his rival brother to drink, turning him into a hopeless lush, and for good measure also attempts to kill him. Another of Reid's recurring motifs is dissected in *Thou Shalt Not Kill* (1915)—the arrest and conviction of an innocent man on circumstantial evidence. Harry Meredith is seen holding a man who has been shot in his arms. Witnesses are convinced that he committed the murder. A tramp issues a deathbed confession, but it is too late—Harry has already been executed.

Also in 1915, Reid made a gritty documentary, *Leo M. Frank*, about a New York Jew who moved to Georgia, where he was employed as a schoolteacher. When one of his pupils, Mary Phagan, was found murdered, Frank was charged with the crime. Vitriolic anti-Semitism of the era overshadowed loose evidence and Frank was found guilty and sentenced to death. Georgia Governor John M. Slaton commuted the sentence to life imprisonment, but Frank was abducted from a prison train and lynched by a mob. "Though the film did not presume to decide upon Frank's guilt or innocence (the actual guilty party would not confess until nearly four decades later)," writes Hal Erickson, "Reid seized the opportunity to offer an eloquent plea against capital punishment."[5]

Embezzlement, kidnapping, drug addiction, and murder play a part in *Warning! The S. O. S. Call of Humanity* (1916). Politics, frame-up and murder mesh in *Mothers of Men* (1917). Sinn Fein activities, imprisonment, escape and a firing squad swirl in *For the Freedom of Ireland* (1920). Gangsters, crooked lawyers and sensation-seeking journalists are present in *Every Woman's Problem* (1921). A bootlegging gang secretly operates in the basement of *The Little Red Schoolhouse* (1923).

NOTES

1. Other prolific blood-and-thunder melodramatists of the era included Theodore Kremer, Charles E. Blaney, Lincoln J. Carter and Charles A. Taylor.
2. Jones becomes a sidekick of the detective, providing not only assistance but also broad comedy, a melodramatic fixture of the era's Black characters.
3. It was customary in melodramas of the era to incorporate among the dramatis personae a bright, courageous youth.
4. *A Millionaire's Revenge* was inspired by a real-life murder that took place on the roof of Madison Square Garden. On June 25, 1906, famous architect Sanford White was killed there by Harry Shaw, a socialite. Shaw pumped three bullets into White's head in front of shocked onlookers. To his arresting officer, Shaw said, "He deserved it. He ruined my wife."
5. Hal Erickson, *All Movie Guide*, www.allmovie.com

Madame X (1908)

Alexandre Bisson (France, 1848-1912)

The French drama *La Femme X*, by Alexandre Bisson, appeared in the three theater capitals of the world in successive years, beginning in Paris on December 15, 1908. Next came London (September 1, 1909), then New York (February 2, 1910). An overwhelming success, the play spawned more than half-a-dozen motion picture adaptations. The climactic scene, in which a mother charged with murder is unknowingly defended by her son, is perhaps the most wrenching in the annals of courtroom dramas.

In his English adaptation, titled *Madame X,* John N. Raphael divides the proceedings into a prologue and three acts. The prologue is set in Judge Lucien Fleuriot's study at Neuilly, near Paris.Dr. Chesnal, overseeing the care of the judge's little boy Raymond, assures the worried father that his son soon will recover. The doctor also feels that the judge needs to start taking better care of himself. He tells Fleuriot to eat more nourishing foods, exercise regularly and consider remarrying, so that he'll have a woman to look after him.The judge admits that, in fact, he is not a widower, as everyone has assumed, but that his wife, Raymond's mother, deserted him for a lover: "I am unhappy—very unhappy… I can think of nothing but her, in spite of myself!"

After the two men exit, Jacqueline Fleuriot unexpectedly arrives, concerned about her son's health, but soon relieved to learn from a servant that all "danger is over." When her husband finds her there in his house, he angrily orders her to leave. She falls to her knees: "Forgive! Forget! … I was mad! … I was so young! Twenty! Forgive me! I am sorry! Forgive me!... I cannot live without you, without my child!"

"Raymond thinks you are dead. . .!" Judge Fleuriot tells her. "You no longer exist for us." He pushes Jacqueline out and shuts the door.

Twenty years later, Jacqueline, ravaged by drink and drugs, lives in a rundown hotel with Frederic Laroque, a card shark. Laroque's unsavory associates, Perissard and Merivel, recognize an opportunity for blackmail. Grasping their intentions, Jacqueline rouses herself to insist: "I don't want my son to know that I am alive, don't you understand? … I don't want him to know that his mother has become what she is!" When Laroque maintains that he will pursue the matter, Jacqueline reaches in a drawer for a gun and fires three shots. Laroque whispers, "The jade," falls and dies.

Three months later, Perissard and Merivel arrive at Judge Fleuriot's house only to learn that he is away. Meanwhile, Raymond and his lover discuss their marriage plans. Helene is the daughter of M. Valmorin, the Procureur General, while Raymond is just launching his career as a lawyer. On the very next day, he is scheduled to present a final summation in the defense of his first and only client, a mysterious woman who refuses to talk to her counsel, and who is known only as Madame X.[1]

"Try to be moving, touching, pathetic," advises his father. But such stratagems will not be possible, Raymond reminds him, since the accused has given him no information with which to work. "Well, take advantage of her silence," suggests the judge. "Call her a victim of fate, heredity—anything you like—but win over the jury."

When an old friend, M.Noel, who, once, himself was in love with Jacqueline, drops by, Fleuriot tells him that, since Raymond is about to be married, he intends to reveal to his son the truth about his mother – "Who knows if he will ever forgive me? … He will think my conduct odious, monstrous, and he will condemn me!" At this point, Perissard and Merivel are shown in. They extract money for Jacqueline from Fleuriot, telling him she is penniless; he is thrilled to entrust it to them for her, elated by the news that she is still alive. "I will fetch her and bring her home," Fleuriot tells Noel. "I will surround her with care and tenderness, and she will forgive me."

At the Assize Court, Jacqueline is seated in the dock between two policemen. Weeping, she hides her face with a handkerchief. Fleuriot is presiding. Raymond, in his gown, examines a sheaf of papers. Twelve men file into the jury box. Among the spectators are Noel, Dr. Chesnel, Hélène, Perissard and Merivel. The prisoner is accused of an unprovoked murder.

On the witness stand, a policeman describes the scene of the crime: "I found the body of a man bathed in his blood. He had just been killed by revolver shots fired by a woman, his own wife, it appeared, the woman Laroque… She said it was to prevent him from committing an infamy, a shameful action, something abominable, which would have caused the unhappiness and despair of someone she loved… She has not opened her mouth since."

When Raymond is called to deliver his defense plea, Jacqueline suddenly realizes, to her horror, that her attorney is none other than her son. She cries out in shock and breaks into sobs.

Raymond: "… what makes the case more particularly touching is the mystery which surrounds it. Who is this woman who is weeping in despair? Whence does she come, and why did she kill the man with whom she was living? She alone could dissipate these obscurities and she refuses to do so… Why? In order to defeat the ends of justice? No, certainly not, for in such case she would speak, she would try to exonerate herself by clever lies—self-defense, madness, anything you like… Ought she to be punished for having put an end to the evil brute who threatened the happiness of someone she loved?"

Hearing this, Jacqueline rises, identifies Perissard and Merivel as the instigators of a blackmailing scheme, and they are arrested.

Judge Fleuriot recognizes his own wife.

The jury's verdict is "Not Guilty." But when Fleuriot gavels, Jacqueline shrieks, "No, no! ... I want to die! I want to die!" and drops to the floor in a faint.

Soon, Raymond is kneeling next to his client in the President's private chamber at the Palais de Justice: "My father has just told me all you have been through, my poor mother. But it is all over now! We will forget the unhappy days which have kept us apart so long." But it is too late. Jacqueline's heart stops beating.

Laments Dleuriot: "And she did not forgive me!"

(In the French original, following the jury's verdict, the court is cleared, and Raymond and Jacqueline enact their tender scene.The final words are Raymond's: "Too late—too late.")

* * *

In its earliest days as a crowd-pleasing melodrama, *La Femme X* was a vehicle for legendary actress Sarah Bernhardt, who brought it to Broadway in the original French during the 1910-1911 season. Simultaneously, its American production (which ran for 125 performances on Broadway at the New Amsterdam Theatre) starred Dorothy Donnelly. Noted the *New York Times* reviewer: "With tears flowing as freely as they did at the New Amsterdam last night, gondolas may soon be at a premium in Forty-Second Street."[2]

Madame X was revived in 1927 in London and played again in New York the same year. American road companies toured it all over the country, and two well-known actors, Alfred Lunt and John Ireland, starred in it at different times before going on to greater fame. *Madame X* was billed variously as "The Greatest Emotional Drama of the Age," "The Most Powerful Drama Ever Written," and "The Dramatic Sensation of Two Continents."

In 1910, J.W. McConaughy adapted *Madame X* as a novel. The play saw seven American film versions, all offering variations on the conclusion; in some, Raymond remains unaware of his relationship to his client. The actresses portraying the title role on celluloid were Jane Hading (1910), Dorothy Donnelly (1916), Pauline Frederick (1920), Ruth Chatterton (1929), Gladys George (1937), Lana Turner (1966, an Americanized reincarnation, in Technicolor), and Tuesday Weld (1981, an updated movie-made-for-television).

* * *

"Alexandre Charles Bisson wrote twenty-one plays in the period from 1873 until 1908 when he turned from the line of farces to the writing of *La Femme X*, the startling melodrama," stated his obituary in the *New York Times.*[3] Bisson's comedies, often penned with a co-writer, were generally woven around marital complications caused by an authoritative mother-in-law.

With the exception of *La Femme X,* Bisson touched upon crime elements only marginally. *Feu Toupinel*, adapted by William Gillette as *Mr. Wilkinson's Widows* (1895), is the story of a bigamist who gets into hot water with both his unknowing wives—and the law. *Disparu*!!! (1906) finds the Paris police investigating the affairs of a wealthy bachelor who courts his friends' wives by handing each a will leaving her his property while at the same time assuring her that he intends to blow out his brains. Bisson's celebrity as the author of *Madame X* led to invitations to write about the theater for *The Saturday Evening Post.*

Awards and Honors: Alexandre Bisson was elected a Chevalier of the Legion of Honor.

NOTES

1. The magazine *Tips and Tales* explained that "Madame X is a term taken from French legal nomenclature. It is given every woman prisoner who refuses to betray her real name. In this country and England, the term "Jane Doe" is applied. Were the prisoner a man he would be called "Monsieur X" in France, and "John Doe" here (*Tips and Tales*, New York, November 15, 1909).
2. *New York Times*, February 3, 1910.
3. *New York Times*, June 28, 1912.

Justice (1910)

John Galsworthy (England, 1867-1933)

John Galsworthy's *Justice*, "A Tragedy in Four Acts," took aim at the workings of the flawed British justice system. Its blows struck their target. The play was to influence public opinion and help lead to the reform of England's prisons.

The first act opens in the office of father-and-son solicitors James and Walter How, where Robert Cokeson, the managing clerk, admits a young woman, Ruth Honeywill, who has asked to see William Falder, the firm's junior clerk. Though such a personal meeting on the premises is irregular, he agrees.

Falder, Ruth's lover, assures Ruth he has purchased train tickets for that evening. She whispers that her husband is "on the drink again... He tried to cut my throat last night." They cling together passionately, then break apart as Cokeson reenters and Ruth leaves.

Unexpectedly, a financial irregularity is now discovered as the office accounts are gone over: there has been a forgery, money is missing, and the culprit, obviously, is Falder. Pleading for leniency, Falder wins the sympathy of the younger How, but James How insists that he be prosecuted. A detective from Scotland Yard is summoned, and Falder is taken away.

The setting for the second act is a courtroom, "crowded with barristers, solicitors, reporters, ushers and jurymen." The case for the Crown has just been concluded, and the counsel for the defense warns that "men like the prisoner are destroyed daily under the law... If the prisoner is found guilty, and treated as though he were a criminal type, he will, as all experience shows, in all probability become one. I beg you not to return a verdict that may thrust him into prison and brand him forever..."

Nonetheless, the jury returns a "Guilty" verdict, with the frail Falder sentenced to three years. While he is serving his time, it quickly becomes clear to prison officials that he is barely hanging onto his health and sanity. In a harrowing, wordless scene, Falder is shown caged in a cramped, dark cell. Suddenly, a banging sound is heard, started up by his fellow inmates, growing louder and louder, traveling from cell to cell, till it finally invades his space. Trembling from head to foot, he flings himself against the metal door, helplessly beating on it.[1]

After her lover is released, Ruth Honeywill pleads with James and Walter How to give Falder a second chance. The senior How is reluctant: "A gaolbird in the office? I don't see it." Still, he agrees to rehire him, but only on the condition that Falder renounce Ruth. Such a relationship offers the wrong kind of temptation, How explains, and will keep him from going straight. "I couldn't give her up. I couldn't! Oh, sir, I'm all she's got to look to. And I'm sure she's all I've got," is Falder's unhappy rejoinder.

How then tells Ruth she holds her sweetheart's fate in her hands. "I want to do the best for him," she says, indicating that she's ready to make the sacrifice demanded of her. At this moment a policeman appears to re-arrest Falder for failing, as a parolee, to report his whereabouts. As he drags Falder out, the young man, in despair, breaks free and throws himself down the stone stairs—to his death. The curtain falls.

* * *

Justice premiered simultaneously at the Royalty Theatre, in Glasgow, and at the Duke of York's Theatre, in London, on February 21, 1910. The latter production, directed by Harley Granville-Barker, featured Dennis Eadie (William Falder), Edmund Gwenn (Robert Cokeson) and Dion Boucicault (Mr. Justice Floyd). It ran for twenty-six performances. A reviewer, filing from London for the *Chicago Record-Herald*, pronounced it "an extremely strong play and an extremely depressing one"[2] In fact, the atmosphere shown onstage seemed so real to its English audiences that rumors spread claiming Galsworthy had served a six-month prison sentence for a minor offense to better achieve authenticity.

The play's first American performance was in Chicago in 1911, where it was presented by the Hull-House Players, a company formed at the famed settlement house and dedicated to mounting socially conscious works. It did not arrive on Broadway until five years later where, after try-outs in New Haven, Connecticut, and Boston, Massachusetts, it opened at the Candler Theatre on April 3, 1916. John Barrymore now played William Falder, although the part was different from anything the actor had attempted before. (The idea to cast matinee idol Barrymore in the unlikely role came from playwright Edward Sheldon, a friend of the producers.)

The *New York Times* offered this description of the opening night: "The members of the audience that packed the Candler will remember it all the days of their lives. They saw there a powerful realistic drama of the criminal law, profoundly moving in its direct appeal to the sympathetic, beautiful both in its fidelity to life and in its utter simplicity."[3] *Justice* continued there for 104 performances, at which point the company took it on tour.

Over the next four decades American revivals were mounted in Providence, Rhode Island (1922); in Boston, Massachusetts(1924); in Cincinnati, Ohio (1926); in New York (this time, in Yiddish, 1926); in Los Angeles, California (1931); in San Francisco, California (1937); and again in New York at the Equity Library Theatre (1947).

London revivals of *Justice* took place in 1922, 1928, 1932, and in 1935 (as part of a Galsworthy festival). In 1968, the play was resuscitated at the St. Martin's Theatre, in London. By now, however, the luster of the work and its creator had diminished, and the temper of the times was different. In the *Observer*, Ronald Bryden called Galsworthy"a second-class writer" and *Justice* "… a peculiarly ill-made play."[4] Playwright Hugh Leonard stated, "If *Justice* at one time generated fiery indignation in the collective bosom of the audience, today it is apt to induce smugness… not only is Galsworthy preaching to the converted, but they have all died long ago and gone to Heaven. These people in period costumes seem to have little to do with us."[5]

Justice was filmed in 1917 in England, directed by Maurice Elvey, starring Gerald du Maurier as Falder.

* * *

John Galsworthy was born in 1867 in Kingston Hill, Surrey, England, into an upper middle-class family. He was educated at Harrow and New College, Oxford, where he studied law. He never practiced but made use of courtroom scenes in many of his stories and plays.

Galsworthy admired Zola, Turgenev, Tolstoy, Maupassant, Dickens, Flaubert, and Kipling, among other literary giants. A chance meeting with Joseph Conrad while on a South Sea voyage convinced him to abandon jurisprudence and become a writer. His works consistently reveal sympathy for society's underdogs. Of his twenty novels, the linked series of books forming *The Forsyte Saga* remains the best known. A popular 2002 television dramatization of *The Forsyte Saga* (presented by England's Granada Television in thirteen episodes), rekindled interest in the British novelist, poet, and playwright.[6]

Galsworthy wrote twenty-one full-length plays and seven short ones. Those with suspense themes include *The Silver Box* (1906), about a charwoman unjustly accused of stealing; *The Mob* (1914), a political drama with a violent climax; *The First and the Last* (1921), portraying two brothers on opposite sides of the law; *Loyalties* (1922), a high- society drama of theft and blackmail that was selected by Burns Mantle as one of the Ten Best Plays of 1922-1923. Though subtitled "A Comedy in Three-Acts," *Windows* (1922) is the story of a young mother imprisoned for strangling her illegitimate baby, while *The Forest* (1924) is about financial misdealings in the City of London. *Escape* (1926) spotlights a respectable citizen sent away for manslaughter who makes a desperate break for freedom; it was selected by Burns Mantle as one of the Ten Best Plays of 1927-1928. Others with dark aspects are *The Sun*

(1919, first magazine publication; 1922, first stage production), depicting a triangular relationship with ominous overtones, and *The Show* (1925), relating a Scotland Yard investigation of the shooting death of a war hero.

Throughout the years, Galsworthy's stage output was both attacked and revered. "The plays of Mr. John Galsworthy have been persistently overpraised," claimed Clayton Hamilton in *The Bookman.*"Mr. Galsworthy is not a great playwright... Mr. Galsworthy lacks essentially a feeling for the theatre—a natural enjoyment of that spontaneous response which may be called forth from a gathered audience... The average spectator prefers to see a struggle between people who he is expected to like and people whom he is expected to dislike; he prefers to attend a play, as he attends a ball-game, with a pre-determined spirit to 'root' for one team against the other. This elemental human impulse, Mr. Galsworthy has chosen to ignore. His plays are destitute of heroes and villains."[7]

On the other hand, Robert McKnown, in *Theatre World*, opined: "It was realism, the gift of putting live people on the stage, that made Galsworthy a great dramatist...Galsworthy, alone in his generation, filled his plays with men and women we meet every day...There is a small but select company of dramatists who have raised the Theatre from its mid-Victorian depths and restored it to a position it has not occupied since the death of Shakespeare. No member of this company is more honored than John Galsworthy; no one has done more to deserve honor."[8]

Acting Edition: Samuel French, Inc. (in manuscript form).

Awards and Honors: John Galsworthy was nominated for knighthood in 1918, but declined the honor because he believed that writers should not accept titles; Order of Merit, 1929; D.Litt, Oxford University, 1931; Honorary Member, American Academy of Arts and Sciences, 1931; Nobel Prize in Literature, 1932 (Galsworthy contributed his Nobel Prize money to the trust fund of PEN, an international organization that he co-founded in 1924.)

NOTES

1. When Winston Churchill, Home Secretary at the time, saw the play, he was affected by the scene and reduced the allowable period of solitary confinement in England's prisons from nine months to four weeks.
2. *Chicago Record-Herald*, February 26, 1910.
3. *New York Times*, April 4, 1916.
4. *Observer*, London, April 2, 1968.
5. *Plays and Players*, April 1968.

6. The work was filmed previously by *MGM* under the title *That Forsyte Woman* (1949), and by *BBC Television* in 1967 (26 episodes).
7. *The Bookman*, May 1917.
8. *Theatre World*, March 1933.

The Confession (1911)

James Halleck Reid (United States, 1862-1920)

Under the moniker Hal Reid, James Halleck Reid wrote more than 100 sensational melodramas. In 1911 he signed his full name to *The Confession,* subduing his tone, omitting the traditional cliffhangers, and fleshing out the characters. *The Confession* is the story of a man accused of a murder he did not commit and of his brother, a Roman Catholic priest. The latter knows the real culprit by privilege of confession but believes he cannot reveal the truth.

The play begins at the rectory of "Our Lady of Mercy" church in Gloucester, Massachusetts. On stage are Mrs. Mary Bartlett, the mother of Reverend J.J. Bartlett and Thomas Bartlett; Rose Creighton, sweetheart of Thomas; the sexton Michael Grogan; and Patsey Moran, a boy from New York's Bowery, given here a haven.

It is the first day of John Bartlett's pastorate and Rose is decorating the room with branches and flowers. "To think that John has a parish at last," sighs Mrs. Bartlett contently, rocking by the fire.

Tom enters in a hunting suit, carrying a rifle and an empty game bag. He attempts to kiss Rose, but she turns away from him— "No. Tom, not when you've been drinking."

The playwright's message of temperance becomes rather clear when Rose lectures on the dangerous effects of liquor and gives Tom back her engagement ring, telling him he needs to choose between drink and her. Tom storms off.

A storm is brewing outside. The wind blows fiercely, accompanied by thunder, lightning, and rain. Enter Reverend J.J Bartlett, his arms full of holly branches. There is a rap on the door and "a tall, big man, rough-looking, dressed in a fisherman outfit, oilskins," bursts in, looks around furtively, and introduces himself as "Joseph Dumont—ah come Riviare, Saint Lawrence, Canada."

Dumont kneels and tearfully relates that he has killed a man—M'sieu Creighton, a friend of Father Bartlett. He shot Creighton because he came to Canada and ran away with Dumont's sister, Fanchette, "without the blessing of a priest." Now Dumont is asking for absolution.

Father Bartlett says, "You have committed a great sin. You took a life, gave it no time to prepare for Eternity… You must pray morning, noon, and night for forgiveness and for the soul of the man you have murdered… I am about to absolve you, but before doing so you must promise if the weight of your sin should fall upon another you will make reparation."

Dumont crosses himself, says "Qui, qui, qui. I promise," thanks Father Bartlett, and exits into the blizzard.

Tom Bartlett rushes in drenched and nervous, exclaiming, "God help us! There's been murder done!…Jimmy Creighton. Rose's brother… I am accused of it." Tom tells his shocked brother that after Rose has broken their engagement, he went to Johnson's saloon and drank heavily. He then got into a fight with Rose's brother Jimmy, it came to blows, they grappled out into the street. "When suddenly I heard a shot, and Jimmy dropped to the ground dead, and then I ran here as fast as I could to tell you. By the soul of our mother, I did not kill him!"

Father Bartlett has hardly a chance to react when there are knocks on the door. Police detective Andrew Strong steps in carrying Tom's rifle and arrests Tom for the murder of James Creighton. There are violent reactions from Rose ("My brother! My poor, poor brother! Dead—Dead!") and Mrs. Bartlett ("They can never make me believe that Tom killed Jimmy Creighton").

Tom swears his innocence. Rose believes him and asks that he give her back the ring. Strong leads Tom to the door. Father Bartlett attempts to stop them, then changes his mind. The sounds of the storm continue unabated as the curtain descends.

The next day, Joseph Dumont appears and, anguished, tells the priest that a letter from his Canadian sister has just arrived, informing him that she has not been seduced by James Creighton—they got married. "I keel M'sieur Creighton for noding," cries Dumont, "for noding." He squeaks, "I go—mais qui I go, I tell truth. I go for die. I go for de rope."

Then, trembling, he changes his mind: "De rope! She's choke... I not die, I not choke by de rope. I live! I go free… I go back to River St. Lawrence, Canada… you dare not tell. You dare not tell!" He points a finger at Father Bartlett and scurries out.

The third act unfolds six months later in a Preliminary Court, Gloucester, Massachusetts. The prisoner, Thomas Bartlett, pleads "Not guilty," and Judge John Peabody announces that "the burden of proof rests upon the State. Any citizen may be arrested and accused of crime, but the law presumes that he or she is innocent until they are proven guilty."

On the witness stand, Andrew Strong relates that he has found a rifle, with an inscription on it ("From John to Tom on his 21st. birthday") beside the body of James Creighton. Prosecutor E.P. Dustin calls for Joseph Dumont, who tells how he tried to pull apart the struggling men. He adds that he saw the prisoner shoot M'sieu Creighton with a rifle.

Defense attorney C.B.Blackburn takes over and surprises Dumont with the question, "Did you ever threaten in Canada to kill Creighton for taking your sister away? ... Is it not a fact that you came here, and settled here as a fisherman, until some dark night you could get a chance to kill Mr. Creighton?"

Blackburn calls Sexton Grogan to the stand and elicits from him the information that on the crucial night, Joseph Dumont arrived in the Rectory twice. Father Bartlett is sworn in, but when Blackburn queries, "Is it not a fact that Joseph Dumont came to the Rectory the first time to make a confession?" Bartlett responds, "I cannot answer that." The attorney reminds the priest that his client's life is at stake and that his mother "is sitting over there sobbing her soul away." Blackburn thunders: "If Joseph Dumont came to you in confession that night, what did he say?"

Father Bartlett refuses to answer, for he "would never betray the sacred confessional of the Roman Catholic Church," not even under duress.

Judge Peabody sums up the case by pointing out that the shooting was done with the rifle owned by the prisoner at the bar, that it is not denied by the defendant that there had been a quarrel, and that his garment was bloodstained—"My judgment, therefore, is that the prisoner, Thomas Bartlett, be remanded to jail and held for trial without bail on the charge or murder in the first degree."

The action shifts to a prison at Charlestown, Massachusetts. The playscript calls for "practical barred doors, real heavy iron locks and big keys—if the atmosphere of a prison is lost it will mean much to the detriment of the scene." We learn that Joseph Dumont, incarcerated for perjury, is in the jail's hospital with consumption, while Thomas Bartlett is to be hanged that afternoon at four o'clock. Andrew strong is now warden of the prison. He has already examined the scaffold.

At the Governor's office in Boston, Blackburn appeals that Thomas Bartlett's sentence be commuted to life-imprisonment— "I maintain, Your Excellency, that even if a man be found guilty in the first degree upon circumstantial evidence, mark you—circumstantial evidence alone—that he should not be hung... If the great state of Massachusetts had taken his life by mistake, as great as she is, she cannot give it back again."

The Governor responds: "You fail to present or even claim anything in the shape of new evidence... my duty is plain. Thomas Bartlett must hang today."

Enter Father Bartlett and Rose, supporting Mrs. Bartlett. The Governor asks Father Bartlett is there is anything he can say as to interfere with the execution of the law. The priest says, "Nothing." Mrs. Bartlett points at the figure of Justice embedded in the window and cries, "You're a blot upon the name of Justice... You cannot see the truth, you cannot see the light of day! A curse upon you, an old mother's curse! You've robbed me of my child! A curse, a curse upon you!"

Andrew Strong enters, half-dragging, half-carrying Joseph Dumont. Strong explains that Dumont "is so near death I dared not delay. I put him in an automobile and have brought him here."

Dumont falls in a heap on the floor. Father Bartlett kneels by him and with his thumb marks the sign of the cross on Dumont's forehead.

Strong: Go on, man, what have you to say? My God, it is too late! He is dead!

Father Bartlett: Oh, thou immaculate, thou eternal, thou Almighty, give him life, give him life! …

Dumont:(faintly): M'sieu le Governor—

(The Governor bends his ears to Dumont's lips. Nothing but a whisper is heard. Dumont's head falls.)

Governor: He is dead—but he did not die until he whispered to me that it was he who murdered Creighton. Thomas Bartlett is pardoned…

Father Bartlett: The Cross, the Cross! The hope of all humanity!

* * *

The Confession opened in New York at the Bijou Theatre on March 13, 1911. The *New York Times* reported that "the play, performed by an unusually well selected cast, visibly affected last night's audience and kept the majority of the women in tears."[1] The *Evening Post* maintained that "at least one-quarter of *The Confession* could be omitted, and enough of a fairly strong melodrama would be left to supply a rather tearful evening's entertainment."[2] The *Telegraph* applauded "neat and skillful" performances but sniffed at "a melodrama in the older use of the phrase."[3] The *Tribune* found the play "crude and melodramatic."[4]

Orrin Johnson, as Father Bartlett, and Theodore Roberts as Joseph Dumont, were showered with praise. Playwright Reid took over the part of Dumont during a run of fifty-six performances.

The Confession went on a lengthy tour. The *Toledo Times* gushed: "Swinging from tears to laughter, gripping the audience at every turn of its unusual plot, *The Confession* met with decided approval at the Auditorium last night."[5] However, when the play came to Philadelphia's Grand Opera House, the reviewer of the *Express* treated it with disdain: "Painted as it is, in broad, crude colors, and weakened in fiber by a great quantity of obvious sentimentality, this drama is reduced to little more than melodrama with everything turning out just as one would hope."[6]

Mumsey Magazine headlined its review "Cruelty to Audiences" and threw darts at "this direful concoction of dramatic horror… You may tell me that women love to weep at a play, but I cannot believe that anyone enjoys seeing such harrowing scenes as are set forth in the courtroom and prison episodes of *The Confession*. In the one, the mother of the prisoner wallows on the floor in a fit of hysterics; in the other, there is shown in all its biting realism the parting between a bride and her husband five minutes before the noose is to be placed around his neck. Small wonder that in Montreal a woman in a box is reported to have collapsed during the performance, and to have died before she could be removed from the theatre."[7]

The Confession was filmed in 1920 starring Henry B. Walthall (Father Bartlett) and William Clifford (Joseph Dumont). In 1927 it was re-released as *Confession*.[8]

NOTES

1. *New York Times*, March 14, 1911.
2. *New York Evening Post*, March 14, 1911.
3. *New York Telegraph*, March 14, 1911.
4. *New York Tribune*, March 14, 1911.
5. *Toledo Times*, Toledo, Ohio, September 16, 1912.
6. *Philadelphia Express*, January 28, 1913.
7. *Mumsey Magazine*, May 1911.
8. The theme of a priest abiding by the principles of the Church, preserving the inviolability of the confessional even when in possession of a penitent's guilt, or when an innocent person's life is at stake, was invoked in an earlier play, *The Cardinal* (1902), by Louis N. Parker. The plot of *The Cardinal* is similar to that of *The Confession*: Cardinal Giovanni de'Medici hears the confession of unscrupulous soldier Andrea Strozzi that he had stabbed the merchant Bartolomeo Chigi in the heart during an altercation over the latter's refusal to consent to Strozzi's plea for his daughter's hand. An inquiry points the finger at the Cardinal's younger brother, Giuliano, who was enamored with the maiden and whose dagger was found near the murdered man.

   Giuliano is arrested, brought to trial, and condemned to death. The Cardinal is unable to mention the confession. On the day of the execution, he sends a cordial invitation to Strozzi and manages to elicit from him a disclosure of guilt that is heard by witnesses.

   The motif of *The Confession* is repeated in Alfred Hitchcock's film, *I Confess* (1952), scripted by George Tabori and William Archibald from the French play *Dos Deux Consciences* (*Our Two Consciences*) by Paul Anthelme. Montgomery Clift enacts the role of Quebec's Father Michael Logan who is accused of a murder. The murder was committed by a man who confessed to Logan of the deed—and Logan remains silent despite having his own life on the line.

Boomerang (1947), adapted to the screen by Richard Murphy from an article, "The Perfect Murder" by Anthony Abbott, was inspired by a true event. It is the story of a Bridgeport, Connecticut minister who was shot to death by a parishioner who panicked after revealing his sins via confession. An innocent man is accused of the murder in this taut film directed by Elia Kazan.

Within The Law (1912)

Bayard Veiller (United States, 1869-1943)

When the modest drama *The Primrose Path* opened at the Majestic Theatre on May 6, 1907, and expired after sixteen performances, no one could have predicted that its author, Bayard Veiller, would rise to become one of the lions of Broadway with three milestone melodramas—*Within the Law* (1912), *The Thirteenth Chair* (1916), and *The Trial of Mary Dugan* (1927).

In his autobiography, *The Fun I've Had,* Veiller recounts how *Within the Law* was initially rejected by New York producers: "George Tyler did not like it. George Cohan was very definite about it. You can't do a play in which the heroine is a crook. And Mr. Frohman pretended to have read it. Anyway, it came back from his office with the usual little printed slip. Wagenhals and Kemper, old friends of mine, friends for years, handed it back sorrowfully and shook their heads. No, it would not do. And so it went down the list. Every manager in New York refused it. Finally, [William] Brady produced it."[1]

Prior to the New York presentation, *Within the Law* had tried out in Chicago, where it was a dismal failure. Consequently, Veiller sold his rights for a meager sum—not realizing the money to be accrued when the play developed into one of the great successes of the decade.

The plot of *Within the Law* revolves around Mary Turner, a salesgirl at the Emporium department store, who is accused of stealing assorted merchandise. The goods were found in her locker, stuffed in the pocket of her coat. Mary claims her innocence—and there are hints that another girl, Helen Morris, is the real culprit.

Edward Gilder, proprietor of the Emporium, who could have recommended to the court a suspended sentence, prefers to punish Mary as a warning to other employees.

Though *Within the Law* is primarily a rip-roaring melodrama, the playwright slips in some moral issues when Mary, prior to her imprisonment, confronts Mr. Gilder, lamenting the living and working conditions of the shop girls.

Mary: Do you know how we girls live? Of course, you don't. Three of us in one room doing our own cooking over a two-burner gas stove, and our washing and ironing evenings —after being on our feet for nine hours…

Gilder:What has that got to do with –?

Mary:And when you're sick and you have to stop work, what are you going to do then? Do you know the first time an honest girl steals, it's often because she needs a doctor or some luxury like that? And some of them do worse than steal; and they started straight, too, and wanted to stay that way…

Mary also questions the fairness of the legal system, complaining that she was saddled with an inexperienced lawyer, and thus not given a fair trial.

She vows revenge.

Act 2 takes place four years later. Following her incarceration, Mary is now surrounded by a few unsavory, but faithful, followers: Agnes Lynch is a confidence woman masquerading as a society matron; Joe Garson is an expert forger. Mary guides them in the commission of white-collar offenses kept scrupulously within the law.

As part of her revenge, Mary meets Gilder's son Richard and marries him.

Eddie Griggs, a crook known as "English Eddie" because of his immaculate social graces, comes to Mary and Garson with a scheme: a set of Gothic tapestries worth $300,000 are hanging on the walls of the Gilder mansion – easy plucking. Here is a chance to get even, says Garson, but Mary objects: it's out of their line; she won't be mixed up in anything that's outside the law.

However, unbeknownst to Mary, Garson joins Griggs to commit the burglary. During the break-in he discovers that the suave Griggs is actually a police informer who was sent by Inspector Burke of the New York constabulary to instigate the tapestry scheme in order to trap Mary Turner and catch her gang red-handed. Garson shoots Griggs with a revolver equipped with the new invention of a Maxim Silencer (its first use on the stage).

Attempting to save Garson, Mary informs the police that her husband Richard shot Griggs in self-defense, protecting his property. But the New York cops, who come across as brutal and amoral, trick Garson into a confession.

A penitent letter sent by Helen Morris establishes Mary's innocence of the Emporium theft. Remorseful, the elder Gilder makes amends with the long-suffering heroine. His son Dick envelops Mary with a passionate embrace as the final curtain falls.

* * *

"All the hints that Gaboriau, Anna Katherine Green and Sir Arthur Conan Doyle, not to mention the authors of *Arsene Lupin* and *Raffles*, have given to aspiring young crooks, may be considered hereafter as abridged information in face of Bayard Veiller's *Within the Law*," wrote critic Alexander Woollcott upon the opening of the show at the Eltinge Theatre on September 11, 1912. "How he dared have the play performed during the present demoralized condition of the police force is a matter he must settle with his own conscience."[2]

Jane Cowl won a personal triumph in the role of Mary Turner during the 541 performances of the Broadway show. "She *was* the girl; the illusion was absolute," declared Woollcott.[3] Ann Davis, Margaret Illington, Helen Ware and Clara Joel played Mary on tour, while Edythe Goodall performed the part at London's Haymarket Theatre, where it opened on May 24, 1913, for 426 performances, and in two short-run revivals in 1920 and 1924. "Goodall's acting in the first portion of the play is so strong that one hesitates to believe that the piece is the mere melodrama it ultimately proves to be," chirped"Jingle" in *The Bystander*.[4]

In Australia, *Within the Law* ran for 102 weeks. Paris, France, welcomed the play in 1918.

Within the Law was revived by the Chamberlain Brown Players in New York's Park Theatre in 1928. Violet Heming appeared as Mary Turner, supported by Claudette Colbert as Agnes Lynch, Robert Warwick as Joe Garson and Charles Ray as Richard Gilder. Reviewer Brooks Atkinson believed that "For present-day purposes Mr. Veiller's current *Trial of Mary Dugan* is vastly better entertainment. But, although *Within the Law* no longer retains its youth, it retains a good part of its vitality... Granted that the movement is slow, the fake robbery, the murder and the third degree in the last act still bring pleasure to the pure in heart who take their crime vicariously."[5]

Amused, the critic wrote, "Last evening, to the immense delight of the audience, the curtain rose too soon for the second act and Claudette Colbert found herself alone on the stage, shouting through an inanimate door, 'Mary, what are you doing? What are you doing, Mary, dolling up?' After two or three minutes they lowered the curtain and dispatched an armed posse to bring Mary back into the theatre."[6]

Within the Law was novelized by Marvin Dana in 1913. The play was made into a movie five times. The respective Mary Turners were Muriel Starr in a 1916 (lost) Australian rendition; Alice Joyce (1917); Norma Talmadge (1923); Joan Crawford in a 1930 version titled *Paid*; and Ruth Husssey (1939). *Within the Law* was telecast by *Broadway Television Theatre* on June 6, 1952, with Lola Montez.

* * *

Brooklyn-born Bayard Veiller was described as "a short, nervous chap, always in a hurry and infernally busy." At age sixteen, he left the College of the City of New York to work for a newspaper. He served as leg man on the *Star, World, Mail, Journal* and *Evening Post.* In turn, Veiller became an advance agent for touring theatrical productions. Stranded in Seattle, Washington, he quit the road and left for San Francisco, where he became a reporter for

The Examiner, The Chronicle and *The Bulletin.* There he met his future wife, Margaret Wycherly, an actress with Belasco's Alcazar Stock Company.

After their marriage in 1903, the Veillers came back East, and Bayard began dusting off ideas and writing plays. They lived mostly on Margaret's appearances in Yeats's dramas.

In 1887, Veiller submitted his first play to manager Augustin Daly, who returned it with the comment that he didn't know anyone could write a play as bad as that. Veiller's initial efforts on Broadway were a fiasco, but he remained undaunted. By his own account, he penned and destroyed no less than twelve plays.

Capitalizing on his experience as a police reporter and inspired by Alexandre Dumas' vengeance plot in *Monte Cristo,* Veiller scrawled *Within the Law.* "I finished the job in three weeks," Veiller told *Metropolitan Magazine.* "I wrote it for money. Up to that time I had made several contributions to art. The most notable of them was a superb thing which ran for one week, *The Primrose Path.*"[7]

"*Within the Law*, in its original form, was an attack on the jury system," said Veiller, "The jury had been out all night. Everybody was worn out with the long, tedious wait for the verdict. The jury filed in, sleepy, bleary-eyed, and cross. The proceedings were hurried as much as possible... The foreman in a weary voice announced the verdict 'guilty'. In a word, I showed the case of a girl who was being railroaded to prison in order that the judge might get away on a hunting trip and that everybody else concerned might hurry through with their work... I did not have to invent this. Such conditions actually exist and have existed for years. I knew the whole police and criminal courts situation backwards, thanks to my experience of several years as a reporter. I 'covered' police headquarters in New York for a long period before I took to playwriting."[8]

Acting Edition: *Within the Law* is included in *Famous Plays of Crime and Detection*, compiled by Van H. Cartmell and Bennett Cerf (Philadelphia: Blakiston, 1946).

NOTES

1. Bayard Veiller, *The Fun I've Had* (New York: Reynal & Hitchcock, 1941), 201.
2. *New York Times*, September 12, 1912.
3. *Ibid.*
4. *The Bystander*, London, June 11, 1913.
5. *New York Times*, March 6, 1928.

6. *Ibid.*
7. Despite the failure of *The Primrose Path* on Broadway, the drama, about the travails of a struggling young artist and his self-sacrificing wife, was filmed twice—in 1915 and in 1920 (as *Burnt Wings*), each a five-reel silent feature.
8. *Metropolitan Magazine*, June 1913.

The Secret Woman (1912)

Eden Phillpotts (England, India-born, 1862-1960)

Raw, primitive emotions mightily explode in the gray, northern quarter of Dartmoor when Ann Redvers, a simple farmer's wife, discovers that after twenty years of blissful marriage, her husband Anthony has fallen for another woman. Fiercely religious, Ann tells their son, Michael, that his father is "False—false as the first snake". Ann confides to Michael, her pet (a second son, Jesse, is closer to his father), how last night she saw with her own eyes, albeit from far away, Anthony embracing a young unidentified woman in the glen by the river.

Ann urges Michael to shoot the "thieving heron down the river". Her son hesitates, then exits with his gun. But later that day it is Ann who confronts Anthony at the edge of Harter Farm. The husband confesses, pleading, "Has no man ever loved two women true and tender? I love you with all my heart and soul. I'd die for you, and die laughin."

Ann is willing to forgive him, until Anthony begins to whistle "Widecombe Fair," the tune he hummed while waiting for his elusive date. Ann's demeanor changes into one of fury. The two sons appear just as she cries, "Lewd, pitiless wretch!" and flies at Anthony, striking the back of his neck with both hands.

He utters. "Ann!" then topples forward and disappears. There is a moment of silence before his body is heard striking the rocks beneath.

Ann wishes to be arrested for murder so that her soul may be saved, but her sons will not allow her to give herself up. At the inquest, Anthony's death is ruled an accident. A year passes. Jesse proposes to a neighbor's daughter, Salome Westaway, but the pretty maiden demurs:" I'm not the marrying sort. I must be free. There's a lot of the devil in me, Jesse."

During an unguarded moment, Jesse spills out that his father did not die accidentally but was struck by his mother "like the flash of lightening. He fell and the rocks in the riverbed killed him."

Salome collapses into the sofa: "Ann Redvers. There's only one thing that woman would have done murder for."

Salome decides to face Ann: "Know then, you cold-blooded, man-killing fiend! I—I was his secret woman… I loved every breath of his voice, every hair of his head… I worshipped him, I prayed to him. He was my sun, and air, and food…and all my light and joy you killed when you killed him. I'm his widow—not you. 'Tis you shall suffer now, you flint-hearted wretch. They'll put you away if there's justice in the world. I've given you up. Your time's short…"

However, Salome is cheated of vengeance when Ann says, "You poor, broken thing, I've prayed for this to happen night and day. And now 'tis come. Dark are the Lord's ways and wonderful." Upon the arrival of an inspector and two constables, Ann goes with them joyfully.

Salome reveals to Jesse that she was his father's mistress. Horrified and remorseful, Jesse shoots himself.

At Anne's trial, the jury had "a very great sympathy with the prisoner, because the woman pleaded guilty" and believed Ann when she said she never meant to kill her husband. The verdict—five years of penal servitude, but "if she's as good as gold in prison, they may let her free in less". No one knew who the other woman was; her name never came up during the court arguments. It is implied that Ann will "sing in clink, like a caged lark, now her soul be saved," and "spend her spare time on her knees praying for Jesse's soul."

And the secret woman? The play ends with Salome doomed to loneliness, staring into the dark of night through a window, singing—in a far away, gentle voice— "Widecombe Fair."

* * *

The Secret Woman was initially banned by the Lord Chamberlain unless certain passages were cut out. However, with the nomination of a new official, Lord Sandhurst, and in the face of mounting criticism by eminent men of letters (including Shaw, Masefield, Galsworthy, Barrie, and Pinero), the drama was licensed for six private performances at London's Kingsway Theatre beginning February 22, 1912.

In a wireless to the *New York Times*, reviewer Marroni Tranantinni asserts that "The play was listened to with deep attention. Beyond what one critic present spoke of as 'a certain luxuriance of language here and there,' no harm was found in it, and the general opinion was that the Censor, Mr. Brookfield, had been hyper-critical in refusing a license." Tranantinni also reported that "The critics are not impressed by the play, calling it 'intolerably dull,' 'unexhilarating,' 'somber,' and 'uninspiring.'"[1] Later revivals, both in London and on the radio, had a lackluster reception.

Nevertheless, more than a hundred years after its controversial premiere, *The Secret Woman* is still admired by many for its thematic stand against strict moral and religious codes, and for its treatment of the highly charged passions, physical and spiritual, of humble people.

Commenting about Phillpott's original novel on which the play is based, Waverly Girvan opines that "*The Secret Woman* may repel the timid and the conventional, just as the central waste of Dartmoor may itself repel the lover of nature in a softer mood. But an author who could have conceived and executed such a tragedy is not one whose name will easily be forgotten."[2]

* * *

Eden Phillpotts' first ambition was to become an actor. He attended classes, but "he could never properly control his legs on stage, so he ultimately abandoned the idea. His need for some form of self-expression persisted, however, so he took to writing."[3]

Phillpott's long, phenomenal literary career began with the publication of a poem in an amateur theatrical journal, and he was still writing at the age of ninety. His more than 250 books include novels, nonfiction, plays, and collections of short stories, poems, fables, and essays. Notable within the vast output are the twenty Dartmoor novels (a cycle beginning with 1898's *Children of the Mist,* culminating in 1923's *Children of Men*),The Human Boy series, and Phillpotts' several joint efforts with Arnold Bennett.

Phillpotts' foray into crime publication began with his first book—*My Adventure in the Flying Scotsman,* a collection of railway adventures—whose first edition is extremely rare (London, Hogg, 1888). His earliest novel, *The End of a Life* (1891), was concerned with murder. Over the years Phillpotts continued his detective fiction with eight short story collections and more than fifty novels. *The Gray Room* (1921), an ingenious locked-room mystery, is perhaps Phillpotts' masterpiece in the genre. Highly regarded are *The Red Redmaynes* (1923), *A Voice from the Dark* (1925), *The Mysterious Miser* (U.S. title *Jig-Saw,* 1926), *The Jury* (1927), *Found Drowned* (1931), *A Clue from the Stars* (1932), *Monkhood* (1939), and the mystery novels he penned under the pseudonym Harrington Next: *Number 87* (1922), *The Thing at Their Heels* (1932), *Who Killed Diana?* (U.S. title *Who Killed Cock Robin?* 1924), and *The Monster* (1925).

Mystery novelist John Rowland finds in Phillpotts' works "another quality, far deeper than is to be seen in the average piece of detective-fiction craftsmanship of the twentieth century... every detective novel written by Eden Phillpotts has a flavor of high tragedy. The author of *The Mother* and *The Secret Woman* cannot write of violent death without showing that in his view violent death is more than just material for an exciting puzzle-story. He is bound to stress the way in which murder is an aspect of fate. When a Phillpotts character is murdered in mysterious circumstances the reader does not feel that this is a mere matter of puppetry, manipulation of two-dimensional figures, the movement of cardboard characters in a toy theatre. His people are alive, his plots are never mechanical, his victims never mere animated dolls."[4]

Phillpotts' first play was *The Policeman,* a farce produced in 1888. By 1951, the prolific author had penned almost forty plays, some in collaboration with Jerome K. Jerome or Arnold Bennett, some co-written with his daughter, Adelaide, and a few adapted from his own novels. The most successful were the Devon comedies *The Farmer's Wife* (1916) and *Yellow Sands* (1926).

The few Phillpotts plays that made it to New York include *The Councilor's Wife* (1892), bittersweet fare about an embezzling, hypocritical bigamist whose villainy is unmasked by his young wife, and *The Shadow* (1922), wherein a man confesses falsely to murder, sacrificing himself so that the husband of the woman he loves will remain free

NOTES

1. *New York Times*, February 23, 1912.
2. Waveney Givran, Ed., *Eden Phillpotts: An Assessment and a Tribute* (London: Hutchinson 1953), 22.
3. *Ibid*, 12.
4. *Ibid*, 141.

The Mystery of the Yellow Room (1912)

Gaston Leroux (France, 1868-1927)

Gaston Leroux's novel, *le Mystere de la chamber jaune* (*The Mystery of the Yellow Room*), serialized in *L'Illustration* in 1907 and published in book form the following year, is an early "locked room" mystery and one of the genre's classics. The main character is an eighteen-year-old journalist, Joseph Rouletabille, a disciple of C. Auguste Dupin and Sherlock Holmes, who is able to solve baffling criminal cases by sheer deductive reasoning. Rouletabille continued to be the hero in eight sequels.

Leroux dramatized *The Mystery of the Yellow Room*—adding elements from 1908's *The Perfume of the Lady in Black*—as a five-act thriller.

The curtain rises on the Grand Ball at the Elysee Palace. A waltz is playing off stage. Rouletabille cajoles a gaggle of cynical *L'Epoque* reporters to mingle among the distinguished guests and gather tid-bits of gossip for the morning edition. Milling around are Professor Stangerson, a renowned scientist; his thirty-six-year-old daughter, Mathilde; and her fiancé, Robert Darzac, an assistant to the professor. Lurking in the background is the sureté inspector Frederic Larsan, celebrated for capturing the international criminal Ballmeyer several years earlier in America.

Rouletabille, who recently helped the police solve a murder by descending into the city's sewers to find the foot of a mutilated woman, tells Larsan jocularly, "Come, cheer up, Larsan. We shall work again together for God and for France."

Rouletabille intends to interview Mathilde Stangerson but upon approaching her is taken aback. The odor of the lady's perfume is familiar and brings back images of his childhood when as a tiny vagabond on the docks of Marseille he was visited sporadically by a woman dressed in black, with a thick veil.

Sinclair, a lawyer friend of Rouletabille, tells the young man that he caught "a glimpse" of his character— "behind all your gaiety… you hide a sorrowful heart." It was Sinclair who recommended to the editor of *L'Epoque*, a leading Paris newspaper, to take Rouletabille on as a page boy, and there he has progressed rapidly to the present position of "head of the reporting staff."

In another corner of the ball, Mathilde expresses to Robert Darzac her recurring fears that her late husband, a bandit who was arrested the morning after their wedding, is still alive. "For years I have felt his presence with me, years!" she says, trembling. "I have to repeat to myself, 'he's dead, he's dead.'"

The action shifts to Professor Stangerson's laboratory in Glandier, situated next to a thick forest. Mathilde locks herself in for the night in a small yellow bedroom while her father continues to work at his desk in the next room. Suddenly, Stangerson and Old Jacques, the butler, hear Mathilde screaming, "Help me! He's killing me!" followed by the loud noise of furniture being overturned and a gunshot.

Stangerson and Jacques bang on the door, and more servants rush in. They attack the door with their shoulders, and it gives way. They all gasp upon seeing Mathilde on the threshold, her nightgown stained with blood, her forehead bleeding profusely. She stands for a moment, then falls in a heap. No one else is in the room.

Mathilde is carried to the main house where a doctor decrees that she is out of danger. She tells the local magistrate, de Marquet, that "All of sudden, there was someone near me, clutching at my throat… I reached into the drawer, pulled out a revolver, and fired. I received a terrible blow on the head, it all happened so quickly. I know nothing more."

De Marquet is baffled. The yellow room was bolted from the inside and its windows are barred. There is no sign of entry on the walls, in the floor, in the ceiling, anywhere. How could the culprit enter the room and, for that matter, how could he exit unseen with witnesses stationed outside the door?[1]

Inspector Larsan searches the grounds and finds a pair of boots in the pond. They turn out to belong to Old Jacques. Rouletabille manages to outwit the guarding gendarmes and slides into the laboratory through the chimney, covered in soot. "Reporter for the *Epoque*, at your service," he tells the magistrate.

A battle of wits develops between Larsan and Rouletabille. The Inspector suspects that Robert Darzac is the guilty party while the reporter believes that "Darzac is an honest man."

Disguised as Professor Stangerson, Larsan enters Mathilde's room. He removes the wig and beard, and Mathilde is horrified to meet face-to-face with the man presumed to be dead—her husband, the criminal Ballmeyer. Larsan demands that she cancel her engagement to Darzac and elope with him. "You did love me once," he says. "Don't you remember our kisses, our caresses?" Mathilde protests. Larsan grabs her by the hair and forces her to drink a sleeping potion. When she loses consciousness, Larsan yells, "Darzac!"

Darzac runs into the room with a revolver in hand. Larsan calls for the gendarmes and orders, "Arrest that man… I surprised him in the very act of carrying Miss Stangerson off."

Convinced of Darzac's innocence and aware of the identity of the guilty party, Rouletabille travels by boat to America. He returns on the day of Darzac's trial. Mathilde disobeys her protective father and arrives, unexpectedly, at the Provincial Court of Assizes, where she testifies that Darzac is innocent. She points at Larsan, "It was him… Him!" Rouletabille takes the witness stand. He proposes the theory that when asleep in the yellow room, Miss Stangerson had a nightmare, got caught in the sheets, rolled over, dragging a pedestal with her, its marble edge striking her on the temple; the revolver she had placed on top of the side table also fell, and accidentally discharged.

During a court recess, Rouletabille urges Larsan to escape to Spain. "There is a car waiting for you," he says. "I have everything I need to convict you, documents, etc.… Your marriage to Miss Stangerson is void… you had been married several times before… you have no hold on her!... Leave!" The two men threaten each other with revolvers. Mathilde enters, calls Rouletabille "my son," and the stupefied Larsan realizes that he is Rouletabille's father.

Darzac is found innocent. Rumors spread that Larsan came into the office of the municipal district attorney, shot himself in the head and fell out the window. But La Souris, an *Epoque* reporter, tells Rouetabille, "For a man who killed himself, he was swimming quite well."

* * *

The Mystery of the Yellow Room premiered at the Ambigu-Comique Theatre, Paris, on February 14, 1912. Maxime-Lery played Rouletabille, Etievant played Larsan, and Leontine Massart played Mathilde Stangerson. The reviews were laudatory. Edmond See wrote in the *Gil Blas*: "This *Mystery of the Yellow Room* is a drama at once very entertaining and terrifying, rich in plot twists and turns and in sometimes unexpected *coup de theatre*."[2] Guy Launay (Leon Bloom) applauded in the *Matin*: "Mr. Gaston Leroux has carefully handled this surprising story with remarkable intelligence, accuracy and a sense of effect and surprise… I trembled, I cried, I laughed, and the reception was more than warm:"[3] Regis Gignoux opined in *Paris-Journal*: "The play has the qualities of a novel—new plotlines, subtle and checkered development, an extraordinary mix of observation and imagination."[4]And Robert de Flers cheered in the *Figaro*: "One of these extraordinary stories a la Edgar Allan Poe, in which mystery, anguish, and good humor combine in the most charming way."[5]

Translated into English by Hannaford Bennett, *The Mystery of the Yellow Room* opened at St. James's Theatre, in London, on May 26, 1920, featuring Arthur Pusey (Rouletabille), Franklin Dyal (Larsan), and Sybil Thorndike (Mathilde). It ran for ninety-three performances.

The Mystery of the Yellow Room was transferred to the screen as a silent feature in France (1913) and in the United States (1919). French talkie versions were made in 1931, 1949, 1965 and 2003. Rouletabille was also the protagonist of several movies based on *The Perfume of the Lady in Black* and on other Leroux novels in which the cub reporter proved himself as an intuitive detective. Radio, television, and comic strips were not far behind.

* * *

Other plays by Leroux produced in Paris include *La Maison des Juges* (*The House of Judges*), *L'homme qui a vu le diable* (*The Man Who Saw the Devil*), and *Alsace*.

The House of Judges, a three-act drama, premiered at the National Odeon Theatre on January 26, 1907. In this, his first play, Leroux explored the transformations and deviations of the notion of justice through three generations of Lamarque family of judges. Each of the acts focuses on a different case, probing a complicated web of morals, laws and agendas. Among the questions asked: Does a magistrate have the right to punish? Does society have the right to defend itself?

The Parisian critics were unanimous in their praise, calling *The House of Judges* "fascinating," "astonishing," "passionate," "disconcerting," and "as moving as any other theatrical masterpiece."

The Man Who Saw the Devil, which premiered at the Grand Guignol Theatre (home of horrors and broad farce) on December 17, 1911, combines elements of mystery and the supernatural. The Faustian plot revolves around a man whom Satan has given the infallible power of winning at cards in exchange for his soul. The critics called it "a beautiful piece of work" and "a play that makes one shiver and affects the viewer at the most profound level." It was reported that some members of the audience, overcome by emotion and panic, hurried out mid-performance.

Alsace, co-written by Leroux and Lucien Camille, was presented at the Rejan Theatre on January 10, 1913, with Mme. Rejan, a leading French actress, in the role of Jeanne Orbay, an exiled Alsacian who returns home to find her family and community divided between traditionalists who are still patriotic to Mother France and a new generation loyal to Germany (the province had repeatedly changed hands between countries). Jeanne's young son, Jacque, marries a German girl, but when he hears an unruly mob chant "Vive l'Allemagne!" he shouts back "Vive la France!" and is lynched.

The Lily (*Le Lys*), a romantic drama by Leroux and Pierre Wolff, was adapted, produced, and staged by David Balasco at New York's Stuyvesant Theatre on December 23, 1909. Nance O'Neill played the role of Odette de Maigny, an aristocratic woman whose forfeiture of innocence lost her a fiancé and her standing in society. Odette reconciles herself to a loveless life, but fiercely comes to the aid of her younger sister when she faces the same dilemma.

The Lily ran 164 performances. In London, the play opened at the Kingsway Theatre on February 23, 1911, for eighty-three showings. In 1926, it was filmed as a seven-reel silent feature with Belle Bennett as Odette.

* * *

Born in Paris, Gaston Louis Alfred Leroux gained a law degree in 1889 but turned his back on a legal career and became a newspaper reporter, first writing drama reviews, then courtroom events. He later penned exclusive interviews with celebrities, and eventually became a roving correspondent across Europe, Asia, and Africa.

Influenced by Edgar Allan Poe and Arthur Conan Doyle, Leroux began to write detective stories. His more than thirty novels, published at the rate of one or two a year,embrace romance, fantasy, and horror.

Jean-Marc and Randy Lofficier relate in *Shadowmen* that "Leroux's literary idols being Alexandre Dumas and Paul Feval, it was no surprise that he was equally comfortable chronicling extravagant tales of murder, revenge, masked men, swooning women, mysterious dwarves and secret societies meeting in underground caverns."[6]

A series criminal, Cheri Bibi, is the protagonist of five novels and several movies. John Gilbert portrayed Bibi in 1931's *The Phantom of Paris.*

Leroux's most enduring work is the novel *The Phantom of the Opera* (1910). Erik, a mysterious, ghostly figure residing in the catacombs of the Paris Opera House, is obsessed with a young, beautiful singer, Christine Daae. When the managers of the opera house refuse to cast Christine in a leading role, Erik sends the ceiling's chandelier plunging down during a performance.

Masquerading as Poe's Red Death, Erik abducts Christine and takes her to his lair. While playing on the piano his composition *Don Juan Triumphant*, Christine unmasks him and is horrified by his disfigured face.

Christine's lover, Raoul de Chagny, and Ledoux, a retired Persian chief of police, enter the subterranean passages in search of Christine but are imprisoned by Erik in a torture chamber. Christine offers to marry Erik to save Raoul's life. Moved by her sacrifice and her true love for the young man, Erik releases them and remains alone, in his underground cavern, until his death.

The Phantom of the Opera was filmed in the United States in 1925, with Lon Chaney portraying the title role.[7] Claude Rains, Herbert Lom, Maximilian Schell, Robert England, and Charles Dance donned the mask of Erik in various remakes. Loosely based on the Leroux story are the feature *Phantom of the Paradise* and the made-for-television *The Phantom of Hollywood*, both filmed in 1974.

There have been many stage adaptations of *The Phantom of the Opera*, notably by Arthur Kopit, Ken Hill, Gene Traylor, and John Kenley and Robert Thomas Noll, but the triumphant one is the musical version composed by Andrew Lloyd Webber with lyrics by Charles Hart. It opened at Her Majesty's Theatre, London, on October 9, 1986, under the direction of Harold Prince. Starring Michael Crawford and Sarah Brightman, it became a smash hit, and moved on to New York's Majestic Theatre on January 26, 1988. There, it mushroomed into the longest running attraction ever on Broadway, concluding its 35-year run in April 2023. An overlong and over-produced 2004 motion picture version of the musical, directed by Joel Schumacher and featuring Gerald Butler and Emmy Rossum, was a failure.[8]

Awards and Honors: Gaston Leroux's novels *The Mystery of the Yellow Room* (1907) and *The Perfume of the Lady in Black* (1908-9) are included in the Haycraft-Queen Definitive Library of Detective-Crime-Mystery Fiction.

NOTES

1. The "impossible" situation in a crime scene was invented by the father of the detective story, Edgar Allan Poe, in *The Murders in the Rue Morgue*, 1841 (throttled bodies found in the chimney of a locked room). Prior to Leroux, the technique was utilized by Israel Zangwill in *The Big Bow Mystery*, 1892 (a victim with a cut throat is discovered in a shuttered bedroom), and by Arthur Conan Doyle in *The Story of the Lost Special*, 1898 (the disappearance of a train from a railroad line guarded at both ends).

    Among the better known, and fiendishly ingenious, practitioners of the hermetically sealed puzzles were English authors Edgar Wallace, Margery Allingham, E. C. Bentley, Anthony Berkeley, G. K. Chesterton, and Agatha Christie. American writers who concocted impossible predicaments include Melville Davisson Post, Ellery Queen, S.S. Van Dine, and John Dickson Carr/Carter Dickson, the foremost exponent of the "locked room" mystery.

    On stage, locked-room murders were depicted in *In the Next Room* (1923), dramatized by Eleanor Robson and Harriet Ford from Burton E. Stevenson's 1912 novel, *The Mystery of the Boule Cabinet*; *The Canary Murder Case* (1928) adapted by Walton Butterfield and Lee Morrison from S. S. Van Dine's 1927 novel of the same name; *Alibi*, aka *The Fatal Alibi* (1932) by Michael Morton, based on Agatha Christie's 1926 novel, *The Murder of Roger Ackroyd*; *The Locked Room* (1933) by Herbert Ashton. Jr.; and *Busman's Honeymoon* (1936) by Dorothy L. Sayers and Muriel St. Clare Byrne.

2. Quoted in the journal, *L'Illustration Theatrale*, Paris, March 23, 1912.
3. *Ibid.*
4. *Ibid.*
5. *Ibid.*
6. Jean-Marc and Randy Lofficier, *Shadowmen* (Encino, California: Black Coat Press. 2003), 263.
7. "It is likely that *Phantom of the Opera* would have become as neglected as Leroux's other works had it not been selected as a vehicle for Lon Chaney and filmed by Universal in Hollywood," wrote George Perry, a film editor for the *London Sunday Times*, in *The Complete Phantom of the Opera* (New York: Henry Holt and Company, 1987, 30-31). "Leroux lived long enough to enjoy the renewed fame the film brought him in his last years... On 15 April 1927, at the age of fifty-nine, he died unexpectedly from the effects of an acute attack of uraemia after an operation."
8. Frederick Forsyth, bestselling author of *The Day of the Jackal* and *The Odessa File*, wrote a sequel to Leroux's work, *The Phantom of Manhattan* (1999).

On Trial (1914)

Elmer Rice (United States, 1892-1967)

In 1913, just as Elmer L. Reizenstein was admitted to the New York State bar, he resigned his post as managing clerk at the law offices of House, Grossman and Vorhans and began to write a play. He completed *According to the Evidence* in the spring of 1914 and, ignorant of conventional procedure, left copies of the manuscript with the receptionists of two producers—Arthur Hopkins and Edgar Selwyn (the latter, a year earlier, had mounted the successful Bayard Veiller courtroom melodrama, *Within the Law).* Hopkins responded first and within a week twenty-one-year-old Reizenstein found himself knocking on the threshold of Broadway—he signed a contract and received an advance fee of $500.

Hopkins insisted on major rewrites. "The original story indeed had been thrown away," wrote Rice in his autobiography, *Minority Report.* "And so had every character, situation, and line of dialogue in the original. Only the framework remained intact. It was still a murder trial, and within the encompassing courtroom scenes the plot elements were still disclosed in an inverted time sequence."[1]

Hopkins assigned the option to the producing firm of George M. Cohan and Sam H. Harris, among Broadway's foremost managers, and the play, now called *On Trial,* entered the grinding process of casting and rehearsal.

On Trial was considered revolutionarybecause it introduced cinematic flashback. The main setting is that of a courtroom, covering two days in a murder trial. During the testimony of several key witnesses, the lights dim, and using two joined platforms that pivot on-and-off stage, the action shifts to other locales, informing viewers of events that preceded the trial.

The accused, Robert Strickland, has been charged with the murder of Gerald Trask, a prominent banker who had come to Strickland's aid in financial matters. Strickland had repaid Trask a loan of $10,000 in cash but is accused of entering the banker's home at night with an accomplice, robbing the safe containing the money, and, when interrupted, shooting Trask to death. The accomplice escaped with the money while Strickland was caught red-handed with a smoking revolver in his hand.

On the witness stand, Trask's widow, Joan, tells how she entered the living room and saw Strickland shoot her husband. Flashbacks picture Joan struggling in the dark with an intruder who disappears at the corner of the room; Strickland enters through a window; the telephone rings; Trask stumbles in from his bedroom and switches on the light; Strickland shoots him twice; Trask falls dead; his secretary, Stanley Glover, rushes in with a heavy stick, hitting Strickland's arm with a crushing blow.

The defendant's counsel, Mr. Arbuckle, calls to the stand Strickland's wife, May. The scene transfers to a hotel room in Great Neck, New York, where we learn that prior to her marriage to Strickland, Trask had lured May to a hotel with a false promise of matrimony. Recently, tells May, "He recognized me and threatened to tell Robert everything… He demanded that I come to his house at Long Branch the next day. I begged for mercy. I went down on my knees to him. He wouldn't even listen to me. He said he would ruin Robert and make a pauper of him. I was mad with fear. I didn't care for myself, I only thought of Robert and my baby… I had to save them… Then Robert found out… Can't you understand? He didn't go there to rob; he didn't take the money. Robert's not a thief. I am to blame. The fault is all mine."

The jury members are sympathetic. They intend to vote for acquittal. But the foreman, Trumbull, is holding out. He understands Strickland's fury regarding the womanizing cad and feels for May Strickland and their little daughter. If he had been placed in similar circumstances, he probably would have done the same—but he is not convinced that Strickland went to Trask's house solely because of his wife. He is inclined to think that Strickland also went there to rob the safe.

Trumbull reminds the jurors that according to the testimony of secretary Glover, Strickland had the combination of the safe written on a card that he attempted to destroy. "There's only one reason why Strickland should attempt to destroy that card, gentlemen," asserts Trumbull, "and that is to wipe out the evidence that would be bound to convict him."

The jury recalls Stanley Glover who repeats under oath that after hitting Strickland with a stick, the intruder fell on the floor, raised himself on the right elbow and with his left hand attempted to tear a card. However, Arbuckle calls to the stand the police physician, Dr. Morgan, who testifies that after being struck "a terrible blow with a heavy cane," Strickland's wrist was badly fractured, his hand was totally paralyzed, and "he couldn't have moved the arm or the hand a fraction of an inch."

Confronted with the doctor's testimony, Glover admits that he stole the money. Two officers drag him into custody. The jury agrees that Strickland is innocent, and he takes his wife into his arms.

* * *

On Trial previewed in Stamford, Connecticut on August 14, 1914, and opened at New York's Candler Theatre five days later. The *New York Times* stated that "Mr. Reizenstein has done his work well," that "his first work has the manner and fascination of a good detective story," and that "he has reproduced with singular success the very manner of our courtrooms."[2]

Other critics applauded a "a triumph of dramatic construction." Burns Mantle believed *On Trial* to be "one of the noted dramas of the American theatre" and selected it as one of the ten best plays of the decade.[3]

On Trial ran 365 performances, went on tour, and crossed the Atlantic, opening at London's Lyric Theatre on April 29, 1915, raising its curtain for 174 showings. The *London Post* reported that the play "had as enthusiastic reception as any play this season."[4] The *London Times* was also complimentary.

On Trial was filmed in 1917, 1928 and 1939,and earned novice playwright Reizenstein well over $100,000 in royalties.

* * *

For the next half-century, Reizenstein wrote thirty-five plays under the name Rice, establishing himself as a foremost American dramatist. His crime-tinged works include *Find the Woman* aka *For the Defense* (1919), *It Is The Law* (1922), *The Adding Machine* (1923), *The Mongrel* (1924), *Cock Robin* (1928), *Street Scene* (1929), *See Naples and Die* (1929), *We, the People* (1933), *Judgment Day* (1934), *Flight to the West* (1940), *The Grand Tour* (1951), and *Cue for Passion* (1958).

Rice leaned on his legal background when penning *Find the Woman,* a courtroom drama about a young district attorney prosecuting the woman he loves for murder, and he used flashbacks again in *It is the Law,* in which he dramatized a novel by Haden Talbot. The action revolves around a fiendish plan hatched by a spurned suitor to implicate his rival in a murder he himself has committed.

The Adding Machine is an expressionistic drama about a smalltime clerk who is fired from his job after twenty-five years of service and kills his boss.

The protagonist of *The Mongrel,* adapted from the German of Herman Bahr, is a forester who killed the dog of an old neighbor and finds himself targeted for deadly revenge.

Rice teamed with famed playwright Phillip Barry on *Cock Robin,* a mystery melodrama in which "the murder was to be cleverly committed in full view of the audience, without their being aware of it."[5] In a duel scene of a play-within-a-play, the lead actor is shot with a presumed prop gun loaded with blank cartridges and falls dead.

Street Scene is a Pulitzer Prize-winning drama unfolding in a squalid New York neighborhood. A boorish, jealous husband fatally shoots his wife and her lover. In *See Naples and Die,* a deposed Russian prince is assassinated by East European agents. In *We, the People,* a radical student is accused of shooting to death a police officer during a rally. Though innocent of the crime, he is found guilty and sentenced "to be hanged by the neck until you are dead." *Judgment Day* is a political, anti-Nazi courtroom drama that unfolds at the Palace of Justice in a capital of Southeastern Europe. The entire action of *Flight to the West* takes place aboard a Pan-American transatlantic clipper on two successive days in July 1940. A dozen passengers have taken the trip from Lisbon to New York, and, in *Grand Hotel* style, the focus shifts from character to character as people are flung together within the confined quarters. One of the passengers is a Russian spy who is exposed by a snoopy American newspaperwoman.

The protagonist of *The Grand Tour* is a lonely Connecticut schoolteacher who, upon her father's death, inherits $60,000 and decides to travel first-class to the Continent. On the deck of an ocean liner she meets and falls in love with a banker from Minnesota, but soon finds out that he has embezzled a large amount of money from his bank to maintain a standard of living beyond his means.

Set in Southern California, *Cue for Passion* incorporates events that resemble Shakespeare's *Hamlet.* A young student returns home to find that his father has been killed, presumably in an earthquake, and that his mother has remarried an old beau, the family lawyer.Successful plays without criminal motif by Elmer Rice include *The Left Bank (1931),* focusing on two bohemian, mismatched American couples living in Paris; *Counsellor-at-Law* (1931), depicting the personal and professional tribulations of a rags-to-riches Manhattan lawyer; and *Dream Girl* (1945),in which the romantic manager of a bookstore flees from reality into a fantasy world, imagining herself as a prostitute on the city's streets, a murderess on the dock, and a Broadway star.

Rice came full circle in his last play, *Court of Last Resort* (1965), returning to matters of law and jurisprudence that had launched his career in 1914's *On Trial.*

Awards and Honors: Critic Burns Mantle selected *On Trial* as one of the ten best plays of the decade in *The Best Plays of 1909-1919.*

NOTES

1. Elmer Rice, *Minority Report* (New York: Simon and Schuster, 1963), 108.
2. *New York Times,* August 20, 1914.
3. Burns Mantle and Garrison P. Sherwood, editors, *The Best Plays of 1909-1919* (New York: Dodd, Mead and Company, 1943), 202.
4. Quoted in the *New York Times,* May 16, 1915.
5. Elmer Rice, *Minority Report* (New York: Simon and Schuster, 1963), 227.

The Ware Case (1915)

George Pleydell (England, 1868-1956)

Capitalizing on his experiences as a court clerk, George Pleydell penned an early legal novel, *The Ware Case*, in 1913, and two years later adapted it to the stage.

Pleydell read the play to Gerald du Maurier and Frank Curzon, managers of Wyndham's Theatre in London, and within a few hours they accepted it as a vehicle for du Maurier to star in and direct.

Pleydell remembers the rehearsals as "a wonderful and delightful experience in every way…for the first time I had the opportunity to watch Gerald du Maurier as a producer. He was at the zenith of his strength in those days. He was a fine director of his stage…He was a most charming and accomplished actor. I make bold to say that until now no one has filled his place."[1]

When Pleydell described to du Maurier the physical layout of the Old Bailey for the trial scene, with the prisoner's dock on the spectators' right, the judge on the left, and Counsel facing the audience, "who therefore would make the fourth wall and become the jury," the actor-director exclaimed, "A great idea, Phew! My word! It's never been done."[2]

The action of *The Ware Case* begins at "the old grey oak-paneled lofty Library at Wilbury House, Middlesex, Sir Hubert Ware's country residence… The whole appearance of the room is suggestive of wealth and good taste and is typical of a fine old English mansion." Sir Hubert is "a handsome man of about thirty-five, exceedingly well groomed, debonair, and fascinating in manner." Sir Hubert is also a gambler and philanderer, and heavily in debt. His long-suffering wife, Magdalen, "a very attractive woman of twenty-five," is willing to stand by him but tells Sir Hubert, "There's no love in it. Not an atom. You've killed that."

At the end of the first act, Lady Ware's wealthy brother, Eustace Ede, is found drowned in the estate's pond. There is a bruise on his forehead, likely caused by a struggle with an assailant. The gardener, Henson, claims that he glimpsed in the vicinity a well-dressed man. The coroner's verdict is "Willful murder against a person or persons unknown."

Magdalen inherits Ede's fortune and pays all of her husband's debts. This suggests a motive and Sir Hubert is arrested. The trial commences a few months later at the Central Criminal Court, London, with the audience serving as jury.

Sir Hubert has had pneumonia in prison but, though pale and haggard, is deemed fit for examination on the stand. The attorney-general, Sir John Murless, punctures Ware's alibi at the time of the crime, establishes that the accused was near the bathing-shed, and submits into evidence two books found in his possession, *French Crimes* and *The Farm Pond Murder*, the latter being "a story strangely similar to the one we're investigating." Sir Hubert admits with a weary smile that it has been his habit to read "that sort of thing…I was steeped in crime."

The attorney-general continues his attack by presenting a signet-ring found by the police when dragging the pond— "The doctor swore that the bruise and mark on Eustace's forehead could have been made by a blow from a hand wearing that ring." Sir Hubert contends that "three days after the catastrophe" he lost the ring when he went down to the lake and bathed.

Though there is no doubt he is an amoral cad, the prisoner's seemingly candid responses and wry sense of humor win the sympathy of the jury, and a verdict of "not guilty" is received.

Sir Hubert returns home a complete physical wreck, and his wife guides him to a settee. Overcome with emotion, she gushes that the "past is buried" and that a new start is ahead of them. In a surprising twist, Sir Hubert breaks down and confesses, "I did it!...I did it! His weak, mean, useless face was there! I struck at it! That was all…no more…" Sir Hubert then swallows a tablet and falls to the ground, dead.[3]

* * *

The Ware Case opened at Wyndham's Theatre, London, on September 4, 1915, during World War I. Pleydell reports that in the midst of one performance there was a zeppelin raid. Bombing thuds come nearer and nearer and the audience became restless. Du Maurier told his company to raise their voices high— "They did so, almost to a shout. The audience remained stock still. There was no semblance of a panic which at all costs had to be saved. The thuds ceased. The act reached its end. The curtain fell. And there was a burst forth of a mighty 'call' from the thousand people there, an unusual demonstration… It was a terrific ovation that the public gave them… Led by Gerald, the company came right down to the footlight and clapped their hands at the audience."[4]

The Ware Case ran in London for 209 performances. The play opened at New York's Maxine Elliott Theatre on November 30, 1915, staged by Bertram Harrison, featuring Lou-Tellegen, a French actor residing in the United States, as Sir Hubert. The critics were lukewarm. All agreed that the first three acts had "little dramatic action," but the fourth and last demonstrated "greater theatrical vitality." The *Sun* pointed out that "rarely has the secret been more carefully concealed than in this piece."[5] The *American* called *The Ware Case*" an unusual drama" and "a queer success."[6] *Theatre Magazine* declared, "This is not a good play," but adjudged the trial scene "well presented and stimulating."[7] *The Ware Case* lasted 47 performances in New York.

King George V and Queen Mary chose *The Ware Case* to be presented for one matinee performance (Adelphi Theatre, London, June 25, 1924) to raise money for a Pension Fund for Actors and Actresses. The all-star cast included—in leading and small roles—du Maurier, J. Forbes-Robertson, Ernest Thesiger, Arthur Wontner, Edmund Gwenn, Leslie Banks, Herbert Marshall, and C. Aubrey Smith. *The Ware Case* was revived twice more on the West End: at Wyndham's Theatre, October 18, 1924, for 161 performances, and at the Regent Theatre, November 10, 1928, for 12 performances.

"It appears to be the first time that a playwright has taken full advantage of the natural drama arising from a hard-fought legal case," writes James Harding in *Gerald du Maurier, the Last Actor-Manager*, "and although the idea has been used again several times, *The Ware Case* inaugurated a fashion."[8]

The Ware Case was filmed in England three times: as a silent in 1917, directed by Walter West, with Matheson Lang in the role of Sir Hubert Ware, and in 1928, directed by H. Manning Hayes, featuring Stewart Rome as Sir Hubert. A talkie was made in 1938, directed by Robert Stevenson, starring Clive Brook. Here the action gets under way at the trial scene. The jurors begin to review the evidence and the events leading up to this moment are shown in flashbacks. "This is a good job from almost every angle," wrote *Variety*, "adaptation, direction, casting and photography."[9]

* * *

George Pleydell Bancroft's parents were prominent nineteenth-century actors who also managed the Old Prince of Wales's Theatre in London. Young George literally grew up on the knees of the era's stars. He knew Henry Irving and Ellen Terry and was nurtured by the plays of Victorien Sardou and T.W. Robertson.

Pleydell became a barrister but led a double existence by writing plays and acting on stage. He performed in Anthony Hope's *The Prisoner of Zenda* (1896), A.W. Pinero's *The Princess and the Butterfly* (1897), and Shakespeare's *As You Like It* (1897).

Hovering between the stage and the law, in 1905 Pleydell accepted an offer by actor Herbert Beerbohm Tree to be the administrator of his new school for acting, the Academy of Dramatic Arts (later the Royal Academy of Dramatic Arts). Among the first students was Reginald Owen, who later played both Sherlock Holmes and Dr. Watson and became a mainstay character actor in Hollywood.

In 1913, Pleydell was appointed to the honored position of Clerk of Assize for the Midland Circuit, serving there until 1946. He recounts in *Stage and Bar* that upon attending "a big trial at the Old Bailey," he watched a prisoner acquitted with cheers. "I was convinced of his guilt. I couldn't help thinking how dramatic it could be if, to the accompaniment of those cheers when the judge discharged him, the prisoner had told the court he had 'done it.' And there was the genesis of a novel and a play that I began to write not long afterwards. I called it *The Ware Case*. If I hadn't heard that trial, I never should have written it."[10]

NOTES

1. George Pleydell Bancroft, *Stage and Bar* (London: Faber and Faber, 1939), 231-232.
2. *Ibid*, 234.
3. Similar denouements that turn a court's verdict upside-down – ironic criticisms of the legal procedure – are found in Henry Wade's novel *The Verdict of You All* (1926); Agatha Christie's short story *Witness for the Prosecution* (1933), which she adapted for the stage in 1953; and Robert Traver's novel *Anatomy of a Murder* (1958), dramatized by Elihu Winer the following year.
4. Bancroft, 236.
5. *New York Sun*, December 1, 1915.
6. *New York American*, December 1, 1915.
7. *Theatre Magazine*, January 1916.
8. James Harding, *Gerald du Maurier, the Last Actor-Manager* (London: Hodder & Stoughton, 1989), 93.
9. *Variety*, December 14, 1938.
10. Bancroft, 179-180.

An American Tragedy (1926)

Patrick Kearney (United States, 1894-1933)

Theodore Dreiser's massive novel, *An American Tragedy,* was adapted for the stage by Patrick Kearney in a cohesive step-by-step format that clearly and intelligently pictures the rise and fall of Clyde Griffiths, a victim of society, weak, confused, selfish and ambitious.

A short prologue introduces the shabby Griffiths family—Asa, Elvira and their four children—praying and chanting through the streets of Kansas City, Missouri. Young Clyde, hymn book in hand, joins them but his heart is not in it .He feels embarrassed as passersby poke fun at the "religious nuts."

The action shifts to the palatial home of Samuel Griffiths in Lycurgus, New York. Having just returned from a business trip to Chicago, Samuel, founder of the thriving Griffiths Collar and Shirt Company—and a sharp contrast to his brother, Asa—reports to the family that he has met his nephew Clyde, a hotel bellhop, has decided to give him a chance, and invited him to relocate to their town in New York.

Samuel's young, peppy daughter, Bella, is curious, but her vain brother Gilbert is jealous at the notion of being rivaled by a relative his own age and embarrassed at Clyde's humble background.

Clyde is introduced to the Lycurgus branch of the family and is grateful for his job as foreman at the collar factory. Beautiful Sondra Finchley arrives for dinner and the mutual attraction between her,and handsome Clyde is obvious. However, Clyde is not invited to stay for dinner. The Griffiths keep distance between them and "the bell-hop." Virtually ignored by his uncle's family, Clyde makes friends with Roberta Alden, an employee at the factory, and asks her out so persistently that she finally agrees to meet him secretly one night.

Sandra Finchley includes Clyde in her social circle—to the chagrin of Gilbert. Invited to a whirl of prominent parties, Clyde has trouble coping with Roberta's complaints of neglect. He is concerned that if it becomes known, the clandestine affair could cost him his job and jeopardize his new standing in the community. When Roberta reveals that she is pregnant, Clyde takes her to a country physician, but the doctor refuses to perform the abortion for moral reasons.

Roberta insists that Clyde marry her and threatens public exposure. Since Sondra has just declared her love to him, Clyde is desperate. A newspaper story about an accidental death at Pass Lake plants an idea in his mind: "What if Roberta and I were in a canoe and it overturned..." Following a tortured inner struggle, Clyde takes Roberta to a lakeside inn in the Adirondacks for a two-week premarital rendezvous. They register under an assumed name, and he rents a rowboat. The play version skips Dreiser's descriptive bay scene of how Clyde's courage fails, Roberta leans toward him, he pushes her away while fumbling with a camera, and the boat capsizes. Roberta screams for help, Clyde swims ashore, thankful that he has not really killed her; or has he?

Instead, the play immediately moves on to a house party given by Sondra. Clyde attends, "looking awful sick.... so worried and unhappy." It is not long before the sistrict attorney of Cataraqui County, Orville Mason, apprehends Clyde, tells him that love letters written by Roberta were found in his bureau, and with the horrified Sondra watching, Mason and his deputies handcuff Clyde and lead him away.

The play now assumes a surreal tone, played in front of a black cyclorama. Pinpointed by baby spots, Clyde reveals the complete truth to his lawyer, Alvin Belknap, insisting that he did not strike Roberta intentionally. Belknap tells Clyde that the jury would never believe him and concocts a defense of temporary insanity.

Prosecutor Mason, aiming to advance his political career via this cause clèbre, tinges the evidence by having his laboratory expert testify that the victim's hair got caught in the fatal camera. The novel's incriminating testimony by 127 witnesses at court, covering every detail of Clyde's activities before and after his arrest, is compressed in the play into a battle of wits between prosecutor Mason and defense attorney Belknap. Only Clyde takes the stand.

Clyde maintains his innocence until Mason exhibits a camera, and Roberta's hair mounted on cardboard. The jury finds the defendant "guilty of murder in the first degree."

The last scene of Kearney's adaptation takes place in Sing Sing's death house. While the Dreiser original has Sondra send a letter to Clyde professing her loyalty, the playwright devises a meeting between the two in his cell. "I have suffered... too .... Clyde," she whispers. "Oh, Sondra, I want to live. I want to live," he says. In the final moments, a Guard slits the inside of Clyde's trousers and Reverend Duncan McMillian marches with him, praying, toward the electric chair, as the twenty-three-year-old prisoner is executed for a crime he did not commit.

* * *

An American Tragedy opened at the Longacre Theatre on October 11, 1926, staged by Edward Goodman, with Morgan Farley, Miriam Hopkins, and

Katherine Wilson enacting, respectively, Clyde, Sondra, and Roberta. The *New York Times* critic believed that "the dramatization begins slowly and somewhat uncertainly, proceeds a bit jerkily, when the emotional power of Dreiser's story begins to gain the upper hand. The fourth and final act plays upon the emotions frankly and magnificently."[1] J. Brooks Atkinson, in a follow up *Times* piece, scoffed at "long stretches of the drama, contributing nothing essential to the story, arbitrary and hackneyed," but pointed out that the "the pungency of Dreiser somehow seeps through."[2] *An American Tragedy* ran 216 performances.

The drama went on the road the following year with movie actor Leslie Fenton as Clyde Griffiths, and was revived at the Waldorf Theatre, New York, on February 20, 1931. The 137 performances were directed by George Greenberg, featuring Roy Hargrave, Dorothy Watson, and Ruth Nugent in the lead roles. The *New York Times* complained about the leisurely pace of the action and was not willing to forgive the cast member who stepped before the curtain and said, "that the 'mechanism' to speed the scene changes had broken down."[3] A London production, staged by Raymond Massey, lasted for only one performance.

Erwin Piscator and Lena Goldschmidt adapted *An American Tragedy*, under the title *Case of Clyde Griffiths*, as a Greek tragedy, with a chorus standing in the orchestra pit interpreting the social significance of the drama. This abstract version, in which the characters are separated into workers and capitalists, was successfully mounted in Europe, but received little audience response in New York when it opened at the Ethel Barrymore Theatre on March 13, 1936. Despite Brooks Atkinson's endorsement in the *New York Times*— "the Group Theatre has admirably staged it"[4] — the play lasted only nineteen performances. Lee \Strasberg coached Alexander Kirkland as Clyde, Margaret Barker as Sondra, Phoebe Brand as Roberta, and Morris Carnovsky as the speaker. Suporting roles were played by future luminaries Jules (John) Garfield, Luther Adler, Elia Kazan, Sanford Meisner, and Robert Lewis.

The Metropolitan Opera of New York City presented the world premiere of *An American Tragedy* on December 2, 2005, with music by Tobias Picker and libretto by Gene Scheer. The leading roles were sung by Nathan Gunn (Clyde Griffith), Patricia Racette (Roberta Alden), and Susan Graham (Sondra Finchley). Francesca Zambello directed. Instead of being placed in the twenties, the opera goes back two decades to the time of the real-life Gillette/ Brown murder case.

An American Tragedy was adapted for the screen twice by distinguished directors. Josef von Sternberg cast Philips Holmes, Sylvia Sidney, and Frances Dee in a 1931 version; twenty years later, George Stevens chose Montgomery Clift, Elizabeth Taylor and Shelly Winters as the ill-fated triangle in a remake titled *A Place in the Sun.* It won six Academy Awards — Best Direction, Screenplay, Cinematography, Score, Film Editing, and Costume Design.

* * *

Patrick Kearney's contributions to the Broadway stage include *A Man's Man*(1925), revived as *A Regular Guy* (1931), depicting the trials of a lower middle class couple anxious to leap from rags to riches but beaten by a blustering conman; *Elmer Gantry* (1928), adapted from the Sinclair Lewis novel, telescoping spectacular incidents in the career of a roguish evangelist; and *Old Man Murphy* (1931), co-written with Harry Wagstaff, a comedy about a newly immigrated, streetwise Irishman who aids his son's mayoral campaign and tames a domineering daughter-in-law.

Theodore Dreiser (1871-1945) tried writing for the stage—unsuccessfully. A one-act play titled *The Girl in the Coffin* (1918), part of a bill presented by the Washington Square Players at the Comedy Theatre, unfolds in a mill town during a strike. The *New York Times* described the proceedings: "The center of the stage is occupied by the coffined corpse of a girl who has died as the result of what was presumably an illegal abortion. Her father, William Magnet, one of the leaders in the strike, is raging for the blood of his daughter's unknown lover. His comrades call for him to come and speak at an all-important meeting, but he is determined to spend the night with the girl's body. Finally Chief Ferguson appears and pleads with him... Magnet conquers his mood and goes out to speak to the strikers. It then transpires that Ferguson was the dead girl's lover."[5]

A four-act tragedy by Dreiser, *The Hand of the Potter* (1921), produced Off Broadway by the Provincetown Theatre, is thematically similar to *An American Tragedy*. It is concerned with a young Russian-Jewish immigrant, Isadore Berchansky, who rapes and murders an eleven-year-old and commits suicide when captured.

Sandhog (1954), a ballad in three acts by Early Robinson and Waldo Salt, is based on Dreiser's short tale, *St. Columba and the River*, which was inspired by the story of an Irish immigrant hired to dig a tunnel beneath New York's North River in the 1880s. The scene unfolds through dialogue, song, and dance.

Dreiser, recognized as a major American author of the twentieth century and a foremost exponent of the naturalistic school of fiction, never completed his high school education. Following a succession of menial jobs in Chicago, he launched a journalistic career, and in 1890 published his first controversial novel, *Sister Carrie.* Dreiser's novels include *Jennie Gerhardt* (1911); the *Trilogy of Desire—The Financier* (1912); *The Titan* (1914); *The Stoic* (published posthumously in 1947): *The Genius* (1915); and *The Bulwark* (1946). He is also the author of four volumes of short stories, four travel books, four essay collections which mix politics and social commentary, two biographies, a book of poems, and one of plays (*Plays of the Natural and Supernatural*, 1916, containing *The Girl in the Coffin*, *The Blue Sphere*, *Laughing Gas*, *In the Dark*, *The Spring Recital*, *The Light in the Window*, and *Old Ragpicker*).

"It is in *An American Tragedy* that Dreiser extends his abilities as a novelist and thinker further than he was able to do before or after," writes James Lundquist in *Encyclopedia of World Literaturein the 20th Century*. "As Dreiser worked the story out, threading his way through the tangle of melodrama, subconscious symbolism, and the private obsessions of the public mind, he comes up with a book, whatever its faults (lengthiness, dated vocabulary, silly dialogue), that explains how such murders happen and why they happen so often in the United States."[6]

Acting Edition: Samuel French, Inc. (in manuscript form).

Awards and Honors: *An American Tragedy* is an entry in *The Howard Haycraft-Ellery Queen Definitive Library of Detective-Crime-Mystery Fiction.*

NOTES

1. *New York Times*, October 12, 1926.
2. *New York Times*, October 24, 1926.
3. *New York Times*, February 21, 1931.
4. *New York Times*, March 14, 1936.
5. *New York Times*, December 4, 1917.
6. Leonard S. Klein, editor, *Encyclopedia of World Literature in the 20th. Century*, volume 1, (New York: Frederick Ungar Publishing Company, 1981), 588.

Caponsacchi (1926)

Arthur Goodrich (United States 1878-1941)

Robert Browning's monumental 1868 to 1869 poem, *The Ring and the Book* (twenty thousand lines published originally in four volumes), was inspired by a sensational court case in Rome of 1698. Surprisingly, the poet, whose half-a-dozen attempts to write for the stage all but failed, did not recognize the theatrical potential of the wrenching crime tale. It was a young lady from Washington, D. C., Rose A. Palmer, who discerned that promise and in the early 1920s wrote a letter to Walter Hampden, suggesting that the character of Giuseppe Caponsacchi was tailor-made for him. The distinguished actor turned the matter over to his brother-in-law, Arthur Goodrich, who had been an admirer of Browning ever since his undergraduate days at Wesleyan.

Goodrich, the author of seven books during 1905 and 1916, and of three plays which were mounted on Broadway with various degrees of success, undertook the assignment with relish. In an Afterward of the published Goodrich-Palmer drama, Clayton Hamilton asserts,

"The technical difficulties of the task would have daunted any other dramatist that I have ever been privileged to meet. In the first place, Browning had retold his intricate and puzzling seventeenth century murder story from a dozen different points of view; the opportunity of observing the material under the changing lights of such a psychological kaleidoscope had offered him, indeed, the basic project of his poem. But, in the theatre, a story must be told unfalteringly from a single point of view. Since Mr. Hampden was pre-destined to appear in the part of Caponsacchi, the point of view to be selected by the dramatist was, obviously, that of the warrior-priest, the soldier-saint, who occupies far less of Browning's attention, in his epic rendering, than the villain of the story, Guido Franceschini."[1]

Told from Caponsacchi's angle, the action unfolds in flashback as the monk relates to three Vatican judges the events that led to the stabbing death of Pompilia and her parents by Count Guido. The playwrights had to rewrite many sequences in which Caponsacchi is not present and, therefore, could not be privy to their contents.

Pope Innocent XII makes an appearance during a prologue and shares with the captain of papal guard his puzzlement as to whether Guido had reason to kill his wife. The Pope hides behind a curtain as the trial commences and Caponsacchi tells his story.

Eleven months earlier, in March 1697, during a masked carnival, Count Guido Franceschini and his friend, the knave governor of Arezzo, had met slyly on a street corner. Guido related to the Governor his disdain for his wife Pompilia, who is "Soft, clinging, innocent, and tasteless."

Pompilia's parents, Pietro and Violnate, now plan to return to Rome and ask Guido for the five thousand liras in gold they had deposited with him for safekeeping. Guido draws his sword and accuses them of seeking to plunder him. Pietro and Violante leave to seek help. Guido whispers to the governor that a murder during the Carnival may never be solved.

He stalks his in-laws, but they are saved by the young, popular Canon Caponsacchi and his friend Canon Conti who have been masquerading as fortunetellers among the throng. A physical tussle ensues between Caponsacchi and Guido, concluding with the count sprawled on the ground and Conti calmly sitting on his stomach.

The Archbishop informs Caponsacchi of the good news that he will be assigned to Rome. Later that day, Caponsacchi spots Pompilia from a distance, their eyes meet, and the priest is stricken: "She's like a Raphael." He gazes helplessly as Guido drags Pompilia away roughly.

Count Guido concocts a plan—his maid Margherita is sent armed with messages, presumably from Pompilia, begging the priest to deliver her from a sadistic mate. Caponsacchi and Pompilia meet in the shadows of the gate. Pompilia reveals to him that she is with child. Caponsacchi promises to take her with him to Rome that very night.

On the road to Rome, at the Inn of Castlenuovo, Guido and his guards arrive on horseback to warn the landlord that a carriage is about to arrive, and that its departure must be delayed until morn. Guido offers the landlord a few silver pieces if he swears that the travelers stayed all night in the same room. Guido brings forth a packet of letters, supposedly written by Caponsacchi and Pompilia, and asks the landlord to plant them in the room.

When Caponsacchi and Pompilia enter the inn, the priest and the duke engage in a sword duel. With a twist of the wrist Caponsacchi sends Guido's rapier flying. Guido falls on his knees pleading for his life. Capponsacchi withdraws his sword. The guards arrive stealthily and seize Caponsacchi. Bound, he and Pompilia are herded to Rome, accused by Guido as adulterers. During a hearing in a Vatican Courtroom, the judges, flaunting a package of letters, aggressively inquire how Pompilia could write "filth like this."

Caponsacchi insists that the letters are a forgery, considering that Pompilia cannot even write. The Judges place Pompilia "under her parents' watchful eye."

Guido knows that with his new-born child comes all the family's wealth, once his wife and her parents are out of the way. On Christmas Eve, Guido and four ruffians invade Pietro's home. He sadistically forces Pompilia to watch as he stabs both Pietro and Violante. His men surround and pierce Pompilia who dies in Caponsacchi's arms.

In the epilogue we return to the Papal Court. Caponsacchi has ended his sad testimony. Guido claims that it is all false, an attempt by Caponsacchi to save himself and incriminate him. The three Judges ask Caponsacchi to produce witnesses, but his friend Canon Conti was called back to Arezzo on some trumped-up cause, and poisoned. The judges, indecisive, somewhat afraid and hypocritical, intend to exempt Count Guido from blame, but the Pope steps out from behind the curtains, declares that the truth is plain, and orders the beheading of Count Guido and his four men. Guido pleads for his life and struggles with the guards but is dragged out screaming. The Pope calls Caponsacchi "my valiant warrior priest," and bids him to find "new courage" and dedicate himself to "make the world better."

* * *

Walter Hampden toured with the play, initially called *The Ring of Truth*, prior to changing its title to *Caponsacchi* and bringing it to his own Manhattan playhouse on October 26, 1926. Hampden produced, staged and starred in the title role. The *New York Times* critic found in *Caponsacchi* "a straight story of villain, hero and heroine… One knows always whom to hate and whom to love… When Browning prevails, it is all quite convincing, but when the two adapters set themselves to writing blank verse—some of it is even rhymed—the resulting combinations of words are not always happy."[2]

Despite the lukewarm review, the costume melodrama pleased theater-goers, ran for 271 performances, and was revived in 1928 and 1929. An opera with a libretto by Goodrich and music by Richard Hageman, produced in Germany in 1932 and at New York's Metropolitan Opera House in 1937, follows the play's proceedings judiciously.

* * *

Arthur Frederick Goodrich fiddled with crime in a few additional plays. *The Joker* (1925) depicts the dilemma of young, irresponsible Dick Hamill who is suspected of stealing a large amount in bonds from the office, and—with his wife's faith to sustain him—sets out to clear his name and unmask the real thief. A 1929 new version of Sir Edward Bulwer Lytton's historical drama of court intrigue, *Richelieu,* featured Walter Hampden as the crafty cardinal who outwits his enemies at every turn. *A Journey by Night* (1935), adapted by Goodrich from the German *A Trip to Pressburg* by Leo Perutz, cast James Stewart in the role of a Viennese bank clerk who embezzles money to elope with his brother's former wife.

Goodrich's other offerings to Broadway consisted of comedies of manners. His first produced play was *Yes or No* (1920), in which two women, one an uptown socialite, the other a tenement dweller, talk a young wife out of eloping with another man by sharing with her their domestic experiences. *So This Is London* (1922) throws satirical darts at English and American customs by mating the son of a Yankee shoe manufacturer and the daughter of a blue blood Londoner. Charles Coburn starred in *The Plutocrat* (1930), based on a Booth Tarkington novel, as an American tourist who travels with his family to North Africa and, to the chagrin of his wife, becomes fascinated with a French vamp. *The Perfect Marriage* (1932) unfolds during the celebration of a golden anniversary when Bernard and Suzanne Catalan discover each other's past indiscretions, forgive each other, and return to their blissful ways. *Caponsacchi* remains Arthur Goodrich's most substantial contribution to the stage.

* * *

Renowned English poet Robert Browning (1812-1889) was encouraged by thespian William Charles MacReady to become a dramatist. However, lacking theatrical fire—an astonishing flaw from the Victorian generally considered unsurpassed by any poet since Shakespeare—most of his plays never reached the stage and the three that did fizzled: *Stafford* (produced 1837), *Pippa Passes* (1841), *King Victor and King Charles* (1842), *The Return of the Druses* (1843), *A Blot in the 'Scutcheon* (produced 1843), *Colombe's Birthday* (1844, produced 1853), *Luria* (1846), *A Soul's Tragedy* (1846), *In a Balcony* (1855), and an adaptation of Aeschylus' *Agamemnon* (1877).

A drama by Rudolf Besier, *The Barretts of Wimpole Street* (London, 1930), depicts the turbulent courtship and eventual elopement of Elizabeth Barrett and Robert Browning.[3]

Acting Edition: D. Appleton and Company.

Awards and Honors: Theatre Club gold medal for Best Play of the Year, 1926

NOTES

1. Arthur Goodrich and Rose A. Palmer, *Caponsacchi*, (New York: D. Appleton and Company, 1928), 180.
2. *New York Times*, October 27, 1926.
3. Katharine Cornell and Brian Aherne portrayed Elizabeth Barrett and Robert Browning in *The Barretts of Wimpole Street* on Broadway

during 1931, 1935, and 1945. There were touring engagements of the play throughout Italy, France and the Netherlands, and it was produced in makeshift theatres for American soldiers abroad. *The Barretts of Wimpole Street* was transferred to the screen twice by Metro-Goldwyn-Mayer—with Norma Shearer and Fredric March in 1934, Jennifer Jones and Bill Travers in 1957. A musical version of the play, titled *Robert and Elizabeth*, starring Keith Michell and June Bronhill, played in London in 1964.

Chicago (1926)

Maurine Watkins (United States, 1901-1969)

Drawing from her experience as a cub court reporter for the *Chicago Tribune*, Maurine Watkins wrote the first draft of *Chicago* as a class assignment in a drama course tutored by Professor George Pierce Baker at Yale University. An embellished version was optioned by veteran producer Sam Harris, who engaged George Abbott to stage the "satirical comedy" for a December 30, 1926, opening at New York's Music Box Theatre. Overnight, the twenty-five-year-old novice playwright found herself to be the toast of Broadway with a hit show that ran for 172 performances.[1]

Chicago begins with a bang when Roxie Hart, a beautiful married chorus girl, described as a Raphael angel with a touch of Medusa, accuses her sugar daddy of betraying her with another woman and promptly shoots him to death with her pearl-handled .32 revolver.

The ensuing investigation is conducted by Police Sergeant Murdock, who boasts to the news reporters that the emergency call came at 9:30, and in less than an hour an arrest was made and a confession signed. He accentuates his name, Sergeant Charles E. Murdock, insisting on his middle initial.

The confession was signed by Roxie's husband, Amos, who gallantly took the blame when Roxie tells him that the victim, Fred Casely, was a burglar she shot in self-defense. However, upon learning the truth about Roxie's adultery, Amos recants, and Roxie, hysterical, admits that she shot Casely out of jealousy, and was proud of it.

Roxie is held in the women's ward of the Cook County Jail amidst tabloid hoopla coining her "the prettiest woman ever charged with murder in Chicago." Jake, a reporter on *The Morning Gazette*, tells Roxie that she is getting something money can't buy—front-page advertising. Her face will be known from coast to coast.

Chicago continues to throw biting satirical darts at media mongers, carnivorous lawyers, and opportunistic politicians. "God, if I can only hang that woman!" prays an ambitious assistant state attorney as he poses for press pictures.

In prison, Roxie meets various inmates on Murderess Row, including Velma, a dark, quiet woman in her late thirties, who denies killing her husband for his insurance. Soon the two women launch a fierce competition for the media spotlight. When a cynical press photographer requests to see Roxie's "million-dollar knees," she charmingly crosses her legs. Jealous of the attention that Velma gets when her trial commences, Roxie feigns fainting and upon recovery she claims, sobbing, that she is pregnant. Of course, this is fodder for front-page news.

Roxie's counsel for the defense is Billy Flynn, a little man with a Napoleon complex, who collects his fee in advance, and dismisses Roxie's coy advances with a flat statement that he is not interested in her looks, age, or sex; she means just one thing to him: $5,000.

Flynn's gambit is to gain public sympathy for his client. He will concoct the story of her life: a Southern belle educated at the Sacred Heart, her parents dead, her fortune swept away, a lovely, innocent child, bewildered by the mad whirl of a metropolitan city.

Chicago's satirical edge is sharpest when Flynn coaches Roxie how to behave in court. He instructs her to throw her head back, nobly; never to look at the jury, and instead seek the eyes of her husband. Flynn wants the jury to know that her husband wants her back, hoping they'll wish to play Cupid and reunite the young, expecting couple.

When Roxie's trial commences, carnival atmosphere prevails in court. Newsreel cameras keep grinding, Klieg lights throw their eerie glare. Roxie draws everyone's eyes with a low-cut dress, shining hair, petal pink cheeks, rosy parted lips, and white hands clasped to her breast. It all works: on the witness stand she appears to be an innocent and honest girl. Softly, Roxie relates that she was willing to go out with Fred Casely only because of a quarrel with her husband Amos.

Flynn asks the jury to give Roxie "another chance." The jury complies: Roxie is found not guilty. The cameras are popping flash, bang! flash, bang! This is Roxie's big moment—she squeals, kisses the judge, the court stenographer, anybody within reach. She mounts the counsel table and begins her carefully rehearsed speech, when three pistol shots are heard from an adjacent corridor, accompanied by a woman's shriek. A police whistle sounds outside. The reporters and the crowd fling around and break for the door.

Roxie attempts to stop them but no one pays attention. Flynn, the only one left behind, says: "Forget it, you're all washed up!" The journalists, photographers, and policemen reenter, clustered around a weeping, defiant girl who killed her lover and his wife. The reporters have a new front-page story. Their cameras grind.

* * *

The *New York Times*' morning-after reviewer, J. Brooks Atkinson, found in *Chicago* a "tawdry story" laced with "racy dialogue."[2] In a follow up piece, Atkinson assured "Play-goers with no Alma Mater" that they too "will enjoy the robustious burlesque of Miss Watkins' satire on the customs and manners of criminals in Chicago."[3]

George Jean Nathan picked *Chicago* as the first play to be published in *The Theatre of Today* series, and in his preface, complimented Maurine Watkins for "The caricature she has contrived with an uncommon dexterity... her play is an eminently worth-while affair, its roots in verity, its surface polished with observation and humorous comprehension."[4] According to Nathan, "*Chicago* is American to the core,"[5] and perhaps this is the reason why the play was received poorly in Berlin ("The all important final scene flopped down and lay there lifeless"),[6] and in London ("This story of the trial and acquittal of a Chicago murderess has a flat monotony that produces only boredom and disgust").[7]

Chicago toured successfully in Detroit, Boston, Chicago, and Los Angeles. It was filmed in 1927 with Phyllis Haver (Roxie), Julia Faye (Velma), and Robert Edelson (Flynn) – deviating from the original concept and focusing on the plight of Roxie's husband, Amos Hart (Victor Varconi), who at the end declares that he is through with his straying spouse and finds comfort in the arms of Katie (Virginia Bradford), an understanding woman who does not appear in the play. In a remake more akin to the stage work, scripted by Nunnally Johnson and directed by William Wellman, Ginger Rogers portrayed the title role in *Roxie Hart* (1942), co-starring Adolphe Menjou as her manipulating lawyer.

Chicago got a new lease on life when converted into a musical in 1975, with book by Fred Ebb (1932-2004) and Bob Fosse (1927-1987), lyrics by Fred Ebb, and music by John Kander (b. 1927). The adaptation follows the original play quite judiciously, enhancing the satirical barbs with the introduction of a master of ceremonies and such mocking numbers as "Cell Block Tango" (in which the murderous female inmates croon "He Had It Coming, He Only Had Himself To Blame") and "We Both Reached For The Gun" (wherein Roxie assures news reporters that she'd give her life to bring him back).

The jazzed-up version of *Chicago* premiered at the Forty-sixth Street Theatre on June 3, 1975. The critics' reception was mostly enthusiastic. Douglas Watt, in the *Daily News*, called the musical "Bold, cynical and stylish as can be."[8] Leonard Probst of *NBC-TV* found *Chicago* to be "a highly stylized, highly polished razz-ma-tazz musical"[9] *Cue Magazine's* Marilyn Stasio advised her readers that the show "propositions you with forbidden pleasure, dangerous beauty. It's all about evil, and it's irresistible."[10] *Newsweek*'s Jack Kroll admired the direction and choreography—"In a high-pressure stream of brilliantly staged, bitingly funny scenes, Bob Fosse paints a world of grotesquely gay corruption,"[11] while T. E. Kalen of *Time Magazine* was taken by "the erotic poetry in motion that uncoils whenever Gwen Verdon (Roxie

Hart) and her sister in crime, Chita Rivera (Velma Kelly), do their solos and duets."[12]

There were a few dissenting voices. Clive Barnes of the *New York Times* declared, "never in the history of the Broadway theatre has so much been done by so many for so few final results."[13] *The Christian Science Monitor's* John Beaufort concluded, "For all of its flamboyance, talent, and super-directed energy, *Chicago* wound up seeming hollow, melancholy, and abrasively alienating."[14] Kevin Sanders of *WABC-TV* announced, "The show has no unifying theme. It has no center."[15] Still *Chicago* became the toast of New York, garnering 898 performances.

Twenty years later (and seventy years after the presentation of the original Watkins play), the musical *Chicago* was revived—in a concert rendition—at Manhattan's City Center, followed (on November 14, 1996) by a full-scale, enormously successful, production at the Richard Rodgers Theatre, starring Ann Reinking, who also choreographed the show in the vaudevillian style of Bob Fosse. A motion picture followed, scripted by Bill Condon, and directed by Rob Marshall, an energetic concoction enhanced by jump-cut editing and cynical, on-the-mark performances by Renee Zellweger (Roxie), Catherine Zeta-Jones (Velma), Richard Gere (Flynn), and Queen Latifah (a prison matron) – winning an Oscar as Best Picture of 2002 and for Supporting Actress (Zeta-Jones), Film Editing, Art Direction, Costume Design, and Sound. Jerry Springer, the tabloid television host, played Billy Flynn for six weeks in a 2009 London revival of the musical.

* * *

The promise engendered by Maurine Dallas Watkin's original *Chicago* fizzled when her next play, *Revelry*, based on a controversial novel about the corrupt regime of President Warren G. Harding by Samuel Hopkins Adams, received mixed reviews while trying out in Philadelphia and even contemptuos ones upon opening in New York's Masque Theatre on September 12, 1927, for a forty-eight-performance run.

Watkins achieved notable success as a screenwriter. *Up the River* (1930), directed by John Ford, had Spencer Tracy and Warren Hymer as convicts escaping from prison, coming to the aid of a blackmailed couple (Humphrey Bogart and Claire Luce), and returning "up the river" in time to win the prison's annual baseball game. A remake was shot in 1938. *Party Girl* (1932), with Loretta Young, focused on compulsive gambling, while *The Strange Love of Molly Louvain* (1932), based on Watkin's unpublished play *Tinsel Girl* (copyrighted 1931), pictured the travails of a cigar counter girl, portrayed by Ann Dvorak, who gets in trouble with the police. *Professional Sweetheart* (1933) starred Ginger Rogers as Glory Eden, a radio celebrity, who rebels against the sponsor's insistence that she lead a pristine existence; Glory refuses to sign her new contract until she is allowed "to sin and suffer." *Search for Beauty*, featuring the odd combination of Larry "Buster" Crabbe (the Flash Gordon of the celebrated serials) and Ida Lupino, spotlights the behind-the-scenes shenanigans of a beauty contest. The romantic comedy *Libeled Lady* (1936), nominated for a Best Picture Oscar, depicts the desperate efforts by the *New York Evening Star* to avoid a $5 million suit for a false story on an heiress (Myrna Loy). *The Star people* (Spencer Tracy, William Powell, and Jean Harlow) utilize any and all means to change the heiress's mind. The film was remade in 1946 under the title *Easy to Wed*, featuring Esther Williams, Van Johnson, Lucille Ball, and Keenan Wynn. *I Love You Again* (1940) is the story of an amnesiac con man (William Powell) who settles in Habersville, Pennsylvania, marries a beautiful socialite (Myrna Loy), and becomes a pillar of the community.

Acting Edition (of the musical version): Samuel French, Inc.

Awards and Honors: The original play—A top-ten selection in *The Best Plays of 1926-1927* ("Just before New Year's Maurine Watkins' *Chicago* startled the town into applause and laughter, scoring one of those immediate hits that frequently punctuates a theatre season and gives it color.")[16]

The musical version—A top-ten selection in *The Best Plays of 1975-1976* ("The most popular new musical of the season… stylishly colorful.")[17]

The musical version (1996 revival)—winner of five 1997 Antoinette Perry Awards: Best Revival of a musical; Leading Actor in a musical—James Naughton (Billy Flynn); Leading Actress in a musical—Bebe Neuwirth (Velma Kelly); Lighting Design—Ken Billington; Choreography—Ann Reinking; Direction of a musical—Walter Bobbie.

Fred Ebb, Bob Fosse, and John Kander were each inducted into The Theatre Hall of Fame for outstanding contributions to the American theatre. Fred Ebb and John Kander are recipients of Kennedy Center Honors, 1998.

NOTES

1. According to Thomas H. Pauly in his introduction to *Chicago*'s publication by Southern Illinois University Press, Maurine Watkins's Radcliffe application indicates that she was born on July 27, 1896, and "by the time she applied to Yale School of Drama, she had already moved her birth date back to 1898 and thereafter regularly led people to believe that she was younger than she actually was."
2. *New York Times*, December 31, 1926.

3. *New York Times*, January 9, 1927.
4. Maurine Watkins, *Chicago* (New York: Knopf, 1927), vii, viii.
5. *Ibid*, viii.
6. Quoted in *New York Times*, December 5, 1927.
7. Quoted in *New York Times*, March 14, 1935.
8. *Daily News*, June 4, 1975.
9. *NBC-TV*, June 4, 1975.
10. *Cue Magazine*, June 16, 1975.
11. *Newsweek*, June 16, 1975.
12. *Time Magazine*, June 16, 1975.
13. *New York Times*, June 4, 1975.
14. *The Christian Science Monitor*, June 6, 1975.
15. *WABC-TV*, June 3, 1975.
16. Burns Mantle, ed., *The Best Plays of 1926-1927*, (New York: Dodd, Mead and Company, 1927), 12.
17. Otis Guernsey Jr., ed., *The Best Plays of 1975-1976*, (New York: Dodd, Mead and Company, 1976), 13.

The Trial of Mary Dugan (1927)

Bayard Veiller (United States, 1869-1943)

Having established himself as an important voice in the annals of mystery plays with *Within the Law* (1912) and *The Thirteenth Chair* (1916), Bayard Veiller came up with yet another major contribution—the era's most famous courtroom drama.

When *The Trial of Mary Dugan* premiered at New York's National Theatre on September 19, 1927, the entire playhouse was converted into a tribunal. Uniformed policemen loitered in the lobby. A threatening court summons was inserted into the program. Attendants directed the audience to their seats. No curtain divided the auditorium from the courtroom setting before the play began, or during the two intermissions.

Fifteen minutes prior to the start of the play, cleaning women dusted the judge's podium and the witness chair. The court clerk, interpreter, and stenographer took their places. Newspaper reporters and photographers rushed in to claim strategic spots. The district attorney and his assistant entered with briefcases and displays. Various witnesses were herded into a special area.

The court clerk boomed, "Court attention! Hear ye, hear ye, hear ye. All ye who have business draw near, give attention and ye shall be heard." Judge Nash walked in and took the bench. The clerk rapped twice, and all were seated. The lights in the auditorium dimmed.

The prisoner, Mary Dugan, an attractive woman of about thirty, was ushered in by a guard. A crowd surged after her but was pushed back by the court bailiff. The clerk rapped sharply to restore order, and Mary took her place beside the defense attorney.

It soon became evident that the spectators were to serve as jury. "Everything about the performance conspired to delude the audience into expecting the customary juror's fee after the verdict," wrote J. Brooks Atkinson in his *New York Times* review.[1]

"May it please the Court," said district attorney Galway, and the trial commenced.

Mary Dugan, a "Follies" dancer, is accused of stabbing to death, in a pique of temper, her sugar daddy, Edgar Rice, a married business tycoon. Galway has summoned medical examiners, police inspectors, chorus girls, and the victim's wife, Gertrude, as prosecution witnesses. He also displays enlarged photographs of Rice, clad in pajamas, and of the accused, in a blood-stained nightgown, staring at the dead body.

Things look bad for Mary Dugan when she dismisses veteran attorney, Edward West, and engages her young, inexperienced brother, Jimmy, to take over the defense. It is his first court case, but Jimmy proves to be worthy of the task. After continuous wrangling between the lawyers, Jimmy exhibits to the court a three-dimensional dummy of the victim and demonstrates that, by the position of the stab wounds, the murderer had to have been left-handed.

A surprising twist reveals that Mrs. Rice had a lover of her own—none other than Dugan's former defense attorney, Edward West. He is called to the stand. Critic Atkinson describes the climactic moment of the play: "Suddenly the attorney for the defense (Mary's brother Jimmy) tosses the knife to a witness (West). Caught off guard, the witness automatically catches it with his left hand. Play and performance prepare for this incident so craftily and quicken it with such general excitement throughout the court room that it penetrates the audience like a knife thrust of its own."[2]

At the end, the "not guilty" verdict came from a voice in the audience.

* * *

Six years before Perry Mason first turned the tables in court, saved an innocent party from the gallows, and exposed the least likely murderer in *The Case of the Velvet Claws* (1933), Bayard Veiller achieved the feat in *The Trial of Mary Dugan.*

The play ran for 437 breathless performances with Ann Harding as the accused Mary Dugan and Robert Cummings as her nemesis, Police Inspector Hunt. Hollywood then beckoned the two talented actors, but they were not cast in the duo movie versions—Norma Shearer enacted the title role in MGM's first straight all-dialogue picture, 1929's *The Trial of Mary Dugan*, supported by veteran thespians, H.B. Warner, and Lewis Stone, under Bayard Veiller's direction; Laraine Day took over the role in a 1940 remake, in which Robert Young played her lawyer brother, and Tom Conway the prosecutor. Norman Z. McLeod directed.

The Trial of Mary Dugan was also filmed in France (1930), Spain (1931), and Germany (1931). The play was adapted to Yugoslavian television in 1961.

Staged by Guthrie McClintic, *The Trial of Mary Dugan* was presented at the Queen's Theatre, London, on March 6, 1928, with Genevieve Tobin in the title role. The *New York Times* reported "an enthusiastic reception" and a curtain speech by playwright Veiller, in which he told the audience, "I have come 3,000 miles to be in London tonight… I would willingly have crawled that distance over broken glass to hear your generous applause."[3] Mary Dugan was acquitted at the end of 310 performances.

Betty Bowden played the role in a London revival that commenced on August 1, 1938, at the Regent Theatre (twelve performances), and Betsy Blair was Mary at the Savoy Theatre, July 2, 1958 (seventy-seven performances).

The Trial of Mary Dugan was produced at Reinhardt's Berliner Theater in June 1928. "It was a mighty overwhelming triumph," dispatched C. Hooper Trask to the *New York Times*. "American art has conquered Berlin."4 In September, 1928, the courtroom drama was shown at the Vigszinhaz Theatre in Budapest.E.P. Jacobi wired, "*The Trial ofMary Dugan* is a distinct hit… *Mary Dugan* appears to be just the right blend of romance, thrill, honest craftsmanship and brilliant playableness to suit European palates."5

The Trial of Mary Dugan was novelized by William Almon Wolff. Published by Doubleday, Doran, and Company in 1928, the narrative is told from the point of view of a character who does not exist in the play—Steve Barrow, ace investigative reporter for the *Star*. The courtroom happenings commence half-way through the 335-page volume.

* * *

Brooklyn-born Bayard Veiller was described as "a short, nervous chap, always in a hurry and infernally busy." At age sixteen, he left the College of the City of New York to work for a newspaper. He served as legman on the *Star, World, Mail, Journal* and *Evening Post.* In turn, Veiller became an advance agent for touring theatrical productions. Stranded in Seattle, Washington, he quit the road and left for San Francisco, where he became a reporter for *The Examiner, The Chronicle* and *The Bulletin.* There he met his future wife, Margaret Wycherly, an actress with Belasco's Alcazar Stock Company. After their marriage in 1903, the Veillers came back East, and Bayard began dusting off ideas and writing plays. At that time, they lived on Margaret's appearances in Yeats' dramas.

In 1887, Veiller submitted his first play to manager Augustin Daly, who returned it with the comment that he didn't know anyone could write a play as bad as that. Veiller's initial efforts on Broadway were a fiasco, but he remained undaunted. By his own account, he penned and destroyed no less than twelve plays.

Capitalizing on his experience as a police reporter and inspired by Alexandre Dumas' vengeance plot in *Monte Cristo,* Veiller scrawled *Within the Law*, the story of a department store salesgirl who, though innocent, is sent to prison for stealing assorted merchandise.

In his autobiography, *The Fun I've Had,* Veiller recounts how *Within the Law* was initially rejected by New York producers. "George Tyler did not like it. George Cohan was very definite about it. You can't do a play in which the heroine is a crook. And Mr. Frohman pretended to have read it. Anyway, it came back from his office with the usual little printed slip. Wagenhals and Kemper, old friends of mine, friends for years, handed it back sorrowfully and shook their heads. No, it would not do. And so, it went down the list. Every manager in New York refused it. Finally, (William) Brady produced it."[6]

Prior to the New York presentation, *Within the Law* had tried out in Chicago, where it was a dismal failure. Consequently, Veiller sold his rights to producer Brady for a meager sum—not realizing the money to be accrued when the play developed into one of the great successes of the decade.

Following *Within the Law*, playwright Bayard Veiller huffed and puffed on Broadway with a few inconsequential efforts—until he came up with another milestone melodrama, *The Thirteenth Chair*, which raised its curtain at the Forty-eighth Street Theatre in New York on November 20, 1916, and packed the house for 328 shivering performances. The plot revolves around a stabbing murder committed during a séance conducted by a celebrated medium.

Bayard Veiller continued to pen plays and film scripts—with mixed results. *Damn Your Honor*, a comedy he co-wrote and co-staged with Becky Gardiner, was produced at the Cosmopolitan Theatre in New York on December 30, 1929. Set on the isle of Baratavia, the hero, La Tour, a swashbuckling nineteenth-century buccaneer, steals the jewels and the heart of Cydalys Waring, the Governor's wife, but he left audiences untouched; the show closed after eight performances.

Veiller's next venture, *That's the Woman,* opened at the Fulton Theatre on September 3, 1930. Here, Richard Norris is accused of murder on circumstantial evidence. Norris refuses to divulge his alibi—Margaret Erskine, alluring and married—but at the eleventh-hour Erskine goes to court to save her lover. *That's the Woman* ran for twenty-nine performances.

On the West Coast, in MGM studios, Veiller co-scripted three criminous motion pictures in 1932: *Arsène Lupin,* starring John Barrymore as the French gentleman-burglar and Lionel Barrymore as his sûreté hunter; *Night Court,* in which Walter Huston portrayed a crooked judge; and *Unashamed,* with Helen Twelvetrees playing a society girl whose testimony acquits her brother on trial for murdering her paramour.

Acting Edition: Samuel French, Inc. (in manuscript form).

NOTES

1. *New York Times*, September 20, 1927.
2. *New York Times*, October 9, 1927.

3. *New York Times*, March 7, 1928.
4. *New York Times*, June 24, 1928.
5. *New York Times*, September 30, 1928.
6. Bayard Veiller, *The Fun I've Had* (New York: Reynal & Hitchcock, 1941), 201.

The Bellamy Trial (1928)

by Frances Noyes Hart (United States, 1890-1943) and Frank E. Carstarphen (United States, 1871-1952))

Frances Noyes Hart's tour de force novel *The Bellamy Trial* (1927), inspired by New Jersey's real-life Hall-Mills murder case, unfolds within a county courtroom, as seen through the eyes of a pair of young reporters. Its play adapters, Mrs. Hart, and Frank E. Carstarphen, a former assistant district attorney, dispensed with the characters of the newspaper rookies but preserved the unity of judicial locale—the courthouse of Rosemont, New York.

The prisoners at the bar are Stephen Bellamy and Susan Ives, accused of having murdered Bellamy's wife, Madeleine, because she presumably had an affair with Ives' husband. Madeleine had been found in the gardener's cottage of Governor Thorne's estate fatally stabbed.

Amid constant sparring by the aggressive prosecuting attorney Farr and watchful counsel for defense Lambert, an array of witnesses are sworn in. Doctor Paul Stanley, who performed the autopsy, testifies that Mrs. Madeleine Bellamy's heart was punctured by some sharp instrument—a knife, he thinks. In response to the prosecutor's questions, Dr. Stanley asserts that the knife passed between the victim's ribs easily, and that a woman could have struck the blow.

That bit of evidence seems to have been directed against Susan Ives but is actually an unnoticed clue which points to the real murderer.

Melanie Cordier, a governess employed by the Ives, states that on the night of June 19 she heard Mrs. Ives telephoning Mr. Stephen Bellamy, asking him to pick her up. Orsini, the Bellamy's handyman, affirms that on that day he saw, through the upstairs window, Mr. Bellamy and Susan Ives driving away in the master's car. A neighbor, Elliot Farwell, one of Susan's former beaus, recalls warning her that her husband was making a fool of himself with Madeleine Bellamy, and that they were meeting each other secretly at the governor's cottage at Orchards. However, Mrs. Daniel Ives, Patrick's mother, insists on the stand that her son and daughter-in-law are a happy couple.

Defense counsel Lambert addresses the jury declaring that the case against Susan Ives and Stephen Bellamy is so slight that a stronger one could be made against half a dozen people who have been paraded in court that day. Lambert calls Stephen Bellamy to the stand. The accused relates that Sue Ives called him, saying that it is essential for them to meet at once. He drove over to meet her. She confided to him that his wife Madeleine has gone to meet her husband Pat at Orchards. She assumed that they're having an affair, and that they've been using the gardener's cottage for a rendezvous. Bellamy states that he and Sue Ives drove around for some time, then he took her home and returned to his own home at dawn.

Prosecutor Farr pursues his case by summoning to the stand fingerprint specialist Doctor Gabriel Barretti. He identifies a set of prints on the surface of a brass lamp found in the gardener's cottage as those of Susan Ives.

Lambert counters by swearing in Patrick Ives. Ives maintains that he loves his wife fervently and devotedly. He explains that the late Mrs. Bellamy was blackmailing him about passionate letters he had written to her prior to his marriage to Susan. Patrick insists that he had not gone to the cottage on that fateful night.

Lambert calls Sue Ives to the stand. She confides that an acquaintance, Mr. Farwell, told her that Pat, her husband, was having an affair with Madeleine Bellamy, and that Madeleine was going to meet him that evening. She called Steve to take her there. When they got in, they found Madeleine dead. Steve said that it doesn't make any difference how innocent they are, if it's ever known that they were in that room tonight. They got into the car and Steve drove her home.

An unexpected voluntary witness is sworn in. Mr. Randolph Phillips recounts that he, a married man and a high school teacher, while frolicking with a young pupil at the Thorne estate on the night of June 19, heard from inside the cottage a woman saying, "You wouldn't dare touch me—you wouldn't dare!" Scuffling followed, then a short, sharp scream and a crash. The teacher and his companion were just coming around the corner of the cottage when they saw a car turning in form the main drive, and a man and a woman got out and went to the front door. He recognized them - Mr. Stephen Bellamy and Mrs. Patrick Ives.

During a recess, Mrs. Daniel Ives corners defense counsel Lambert and confesses that about a month ago she realized that there was "something between Madeleine and Pat." Carrying her rose basket, she went to the cottage with the intent of persuading Madeleine to leave her son alone for the sake of the security and joy of two little babies—her grandchildren. Madeleine laughed that little wicked laugh of hers, said, "Now get this straight—I don't care whether your precious babies die in the gutter," put both hands on Mrs. Daniel's shoulders, and pushed her hard, so hard that the old woman stumbled and fell on her knees. She dropped the basket, and all the things in it fell out on the carpet. There on the flowered carpet, just in reach of her hand, something was shining—it was a little knife that she'd used to cut the dead wood out so that the live roses would grow better. She stood up with the knife in her hand. Madeleine screamed, caught at the table when she fell, and it made a dreadful crash. After a minute, says Mrs. Daniel Ives, she went out of the room and across the meadow to the garden gate.

The foreman of the jury declares Stephen Bellamy and Susan Ives not guilty.

* * *

The Bellamy Trial premiered at Boston's Copley Theatre on August 19, 1928.

The *Boston Herald* reviewer, in a special to the *New York Times*, found *The Bellamy Trial* "a drama of exceptional strength. It moves steadily forward in almost unbroken continuity. The interest of the audience is held in masterly fashion… here is a play which deserves to rank with two other famous dramas of similar character, *Within the Law*, and *Madame X*."[1]

E.E. Clive both directed and acted in *The Bellamy Trial*, portraying defense counsel Lambert with Fred Eric as prosecutor Farr, the duo returning to court in the Broadway show, at the Forty-eighth Street Theatre, on April 22, 1931, for sixteen performances. Critic J. Brooks Atkinson was perturbed by "an insufficiently rehearsed company. *The Bellamy Trial* seemed overburdened with detail and monotonous in the unfretted style of its narrative, but it is doubtless more interesting than the actors permitted it to be… the performance as a whole is as casual as a street corner conversation. That is no way to play murder. Murder is a nervous game."[2]

Monte Bell scripted and directed for MGM a 1929 silent movie of *The BellamyTrial*. The film was partially reshot for talking sequences. The boy and girl reporters of the original novel were resurrected for the motion picture version. Flashbacks illustrated the courtroom testimony. Charles Middleton, who a few years later would become (in)famous as Ming the Merciless in the *Flash Gordon* serials, played the district attorney, confronting Charles Hill Mailes as the defense counsel.

The Bellamy Trial was serialized in *Saturday Evening Post*, 1927, becoming a runaway bestseller in book form later that year. Frances (Newbold) Noyes Hart penned two more crime novels: *Hide in the Dark* (1929), wherein a group of jolly youngsters gather on Halloween for a game party, which degenerates into bitter feuds and a murder, but culminates with the solving of a ten-year-old mystery. This novel popularized the parlor game Murder. *The Crooked Lane* (1934) is told from the point of view of a Viennese police official visiting Washington D.C., combining romance and scientific detection.

Hart also wrote a volume of short tales, *Contact and Other Stories* (1923); a non-genre novel—*Mark* (1913); and a duo of nonfiction books, *My A.E.F.: A Hail and Farewell* (1920), and *Pigs in Clover*, aka *Holiday* (1931).

Hart's reputation rests on *The Bellamy Trial*, called by Barrie Hayne in *Twentieth Century Crime and Mystery Writers*, "the best of all crime novels told within the format of a court procedure."[3]

Acting Edition: Samuel French, Inc. (in manuscript form).

Awards and Honors: *The Bellamy Trial* is an entry in *The Howard Haycroft-Ellery Queen Definitive Library of Detective-Crime-Mystery Fiction*, and in the *Sunday Times' 100 Best Crime Stories*, selected by Julian Symons.

NOTES

1. *New York Times*, August 20, 1928.
2. *New York Times*, April 23, 1931.
3. John Reilly, Ed., *Twentieth Century Crime and Mystery Writers* (New York: St. Martin's Press, 1980), 745.

ken bottle and comments how strange it is that there were no fingerprints on the bottle's neck. He then presents a pair of woman's rubber gloves and a white nightgown, found wet at the bottom of the soiled clothes hamper. "Why did you try so desperately to wash that blood away – before you called the police?" booms the lawyer for the prosecution. Helen breaks down. "I did it!" she confesses, "to be free."

The last episode takes place in a prison cell. An impersonal Priest is going through the ritual of prayer. A barber cuts a patch from Helen's hair. Helen's mother comes along the passageway. At first, the Young Woman refuses to talk to her, calling her mother "a stranger," but she relents and embraces her mother through the bars, asking her to take care of her child. Two guards grab Helen by the arms and lead her down the passageway, followed by the Priest. The Young Woman calls out, "Somebody!Somebod –" and her voice is cut off. Curtain.

* * *

Directed by Arthur Hopkins and designed by Robert Edmund Jones, *Machinal* opened at New York's Plymouth Theatre on September 7, 1928. The critics were enthusiastic. "Cruelly beautiful and affecting," chirped Gilbert W. Gabriel.[1] "Biting and often deeply moving," applauded Robert Littell. "There is great warmth and courage in *Machinal* beneath the bitter, imprisoned despair."[2] "A strangely-moving shadowy drama," stated Brooks Atkinson. "*Machinal* is fraught with a beauty unfamiliar to the stage."[3]

Robert Benchley wrote in *Life* magazine that "the whole drama had been stirring in its simple and episodic forward march," and that he found in the bedroom scene "as delicate and lovely an idyl of illicit love as we remember seeing for a long long time."[4]

The cadre of reviewers praised Zita Johann in the role of the Young Woman and Clark Gable as The Man. Hollywood beckoned both actors.[5]

Machinal proved to be too somber for the general public and closed after ninety-three performances.

Thirty-two years later, in 1960, *Machinal* was revived impressively, for seventy-nineshowings, at Off Broadway's Gate Theatre, directed by Gene Frankel, featuring Dolores Sutton (Helen Jones), Vincent Gardenia (George H. Jones), and Gerald O'Loughlin (the Man). Brooks Atkinson, in the *New York Times*, asserted that the play "lost nothing through the years. It is still fascinating. Essentially, it is the story of a frightened, colorless young woman who is caught in the machinery of a large city that grinds out an endless series of stupid crises and actions."[6] Atkinson continued his love affair with *Machinal* in his book, co-authored with Albert Hirshfeld, *The Lively Years 1920-1973*: "By mixing realism with expressionism Miss Treadwell touched a live nerve in the deadened city she was writing about, and found the one weak point in the technique of expressionism – total objectivity and detachment. Everything that happens in *Machinal* is cruel or contemptible. But Miss Treadwell, being on the side of the damned, made a rueful, touching play out of forbidding materials."[7]

It has taken thirty more years for *Machinal* to be revived again in New York. Michael Greif directed the drama at Off Broadway's Public Theatre in 1990 with Jodie Merkell as the Young Woman. Critic Frank Rich welcomed the arrival of the 1928 Broadway play which "dramatizes urban America as an unrelenting assembly line, carrying the blank but thrashing heroine from one cruel way station to the next as if she were a lost lamb being led to the slaughter." Rich admired the playwright's "deadpan tone that keeps both sentimentality and ideological boilerplate at bay… Treadwell strips everything bare, from dialogue to characterization to narrative, as she pours out her fable in the streamlined cadences of a modernist hallucination."[8]

Machinal was first performed in Great Britain under the title *The Life Machine* in 1931. The *London Times* critic was taken aback by the death-row scene, but otherwise found the play "expressive and beautifully clean-cut."[9] Other reviewers were offended by the play's sexual content. *The Life Machine* was withdrawn after six performances.

Machinal was revived in England under its original title in 1993 at the Royal National Theatre, directed by Stephen Daldry and starring Fiona Shaw as the Young Woman. The show was a great success.[10]

San Francisco's American Conservatory Theatre performed *Machinal* in 1997, and four years later, the drama was re-staged at Off Broadway's Ohio Theatre. Led by Jessica Claire as Helen Jones, half-a-dozen actors played multiple roles. "*Machinal* retains a timeless fascination," wrote reviewer Lawrence Van Gelder.[11]

* * *

Born in California, Sophie Treadwell developed an interest in theater at the University of California, where she devoted her junior and senior years to acting. Upon graduation, she went to Los Angeles, played in stock, and sang in vaudeville. After serving as a war correspondent from 1916 to 1918, Treadwell became a protégé of Mme. Helena Modjeska (1844-1909), assisting the famous actress in writing her memoirs. That's when she first tried her hand at playwriting. Her first play, *Gringo* (1922), is the story of an American named Chivers who has been mining gold in Mexico. His half-breed daughter, Bessie, is kidnapped by the bandit Tito. Chivers raises enough money to ransom Bessie, only to find that she has fallen in love with the rogue and refuses to leave him.

Treadwell contributed several more plays to Broadway. Helen Hayes portrayed the title role in *Loney Lee* (1923), a comedy about a Kansas girl, the star of her high school plays, who goes to New York determined to reach Broadway and is soon disillusioned. Hayes dropped out of the play after a trial run in Atlantic City. Two years later, now called *O, Nightingale*, it came to Broadway's Forty-ninth Street Theatre, for twenty-nine performances, featuring Martha Bryn.

Treadwell's *Ladies Leave* (1929) is a drawing-room comedy about a restless married woman who flees to Vienna in search of true love. *Lone Valley* (1933) spotlights a golden-heart prostitute who inherits an isolated ranch in the southwest and gets entangled with a rancher and a farm hand who are competing for her favors.

Plumes in the Dust (1936) tells the familiar story of a haunted alcoholic poet. Henry Hull portrays Edgar Allan Poe from his youth in 1826 until his death in 1849. The drama shows how Poe angers his foster father, John Allan of Richmond, because of gambling debts at school, and is ordered out of the house. Poe then marries thirteen-year-old Virginia Clemm, has some success as an editor and writer, but is soon found by his friends dying in a Baltimore hospital. Directed by Arthur Hopkins, *Plumes in the Dust* previewed in Princeton, New Jersey, and moved to New York's Forty-sixth Theatre on November 6, 1936. It failed to gain favor from critics or audiences and closed its doors after only eleven performances.

Treadwell's last Broadway offering was the drama *Hope for a Harvest* (1941), presented by the Theatre Guild, starring Fredric March and Florence Eldridge. When Carlotta Thatcher (Eldridge) returns from Europe to her family ranch in California's San Joaquin Valley, she finds that the American farmers have degenerated into lethargy while the immigrant farmers from Japan and Italy are hard-working and successful. Carlotta takes it upon herself to energize her former lover, Elliott Martin (March), and the people around them. Before the final curtain comes down, there is hope for both a better harvest and racial tolerance. The rural drama garnered lukewarm reviews and lasted thirty-eight performances.

Machinal remains Sophie Treadwell's sole important and enduring play.

Acting Edition: Nick Hern Books, London.

Awards and Honors: A top-ten selection in Burns Mantle's *The Best Plays of 1928-1929.*

Sophie Treadwell's *Hope for a Harvest* was a top-ten selection in *The Best Plays of 1941-1942.*

NOTES

1. *New York Sun*, September 8, 1928.
2. *New York Evening Post*, September 8, 1928.
3. *New York Times*, September 8, 1928.
4. *Life*, September 28, 1928.
5. Born in Hungary, Zita Johann (1904-1993) emigrated to the United States in 1911. During the 1930s, she appeared in seven motion pictures, working with such distinguished directors as D.W. Griffith, Howard Hawks, and Karl Freud. Johann is mostly remembered for her double roles of Princess Ankh-es-en-amon and Helen Grosvenor in the classic horror movie *The Mummy* (1932), co-starring Boris Karloff. She retired to work in the theater, but returned for a final screen appearance, as a librarian, in the 1986 horror film *Raiders of the Living Dead*. Johann died at the age of 89 in Nyack, New York. It is reported that her ashes were scattered in a stream in upstate New York.

   Clark Gable (1901-1960), the son of an Ohio oil-well driller, was a high school dropout. At seventeen, Gable was inspired to become an actor. He toured in stock companies and was rigorously coached by an acting teacher to lower his high-pitched voice and become more natural. Excelling on Broadway as the Man in *Machinal* and as "Killer" John Mears in John Wexley's *The Last Mile* (1930), Gable was signed by MGM and found himself paired with stars Joan Crawford, Norma Shearer, Greta Garbo, and Jean Harlow. On a loan to Columbia Pictures, Gable appeared in Frank Capra's *It Happened One Night* and won a Best Actor Oscar in 1934. A succession of popular pictures earned Gable the title of "King of Hollywood." Among his better roles were Fletcher Christian in *Mutiny of the Bounty* (1935) and Rhett Butler in *Gone with the Wind* (1939). Gable's last film was Arthur Miller's *The Misfits*, directed by John Huston. He died in Los Angeles, California, in 1960, of a heart attack.
6. *New York Times*, April 8, 1960.
7. Brooks Atkinson and Albert Hirshfeld, *The Lively Years 1920-1973* (New York: Association Press, 1973), 70.
8. *New York Times*, October 16, 1990.
9. *London Times*, October 16, 1931.
10. A year later, in 1994, director Stephen Daldry helmed another immensely successful revival – J.B. Priestley's *An Inspector Calls*.
11. *New York Times*, March 21, 2001

No Other Tiger (1928)

A.E.W Mason (England, 1865-1948)

A.E.W. Mason adapted his sprawling 1927 novel, *No Other Tiger*, to a three-act play unfolding in five locales in two countries, France, and England. The curtain rises on the Court of Assize in Grenoble, France. Three judges in scarlet robes with black satin facings are seated at the dais. The stage is populated by twelve jurors and a crowd of spectators. In the dock stands Archie Clutter, an Englishman, and beside him are two sergeants-de-Ville in dark blue uniforms.

In response to a series of queries by the presiding judge, Clutter testifies that he was invited by the Greek Andreas Eleuteros to his Alps chateau for a week of shooting chamois. During a card game he caught the Comte de Rozart cheating and realized that he was lured to the chateau for a rigged game. When he confronted de Rozart, four other card players seized him, and the Comte repeatedly slapped his face. Clutter became enraged, snatched a champagne bottle, and shattered it on the Comte's head, killing him.

On the witness stand, Eleutheros testifies that "Clutter's strength was monstrous," and that he was "fighting like a wild beast." The prisoner's wife, Elizabeth Clutter, an attractive woman of thirty, testifies that her husband never hit her. However, Clutter's Burmese servant, Mauny H'La, claims that his employer has a volatile temperament.

The avocat général, Henri, addresses the jury and calls the defendant "a beast of the jungle." He demands the death penalty for "a barbarous crime." The defense attorney, Lorolle, points out that the accused is a young officer with a blameless record of service, and argues that he is being victimized by malignant rogues who "looked for a sheep to shear, but found a tiger."

The jury finds Clutter guilty of manslaughter but not premeditated murder. Clutter is sentenced to twenty years of hard labor in the Cayenne penal colony.

The second scene takes place eight years later in the London home of Elizabeth Clutter. Elizabeth confides to her friend Corinne, a professional dancer, that she is terminally ill and gives Corinne an envelope stuffed with 40,000 pounds "to hold in trust for Archie – if he still lives."

Word comes that Archie Clutter plans to escape from Cayenne. Corinne and her Spanish lover, Leon Battchilena, a struggling pianist, solicit the help of Elizabeth's valet, Mauny H'La, to switch Elizabeth's sleeping draught with poisonous disinfectant.

The second act begins at a private room in a Soho restaurant. Clutter and fellow escapee Hospel Roussencq have been hiding at the back of the restaurant for two months. We learn that they escaped Cayenne after being picked up by a tramp steamer which was short on hands. Lady Ariadne Ferne will host a party at the restaurant tonight and Clutter and Roussencq plan to masquerade as waiters. Among the guests are Ariadne's dearest friend, Corinne, and her companion Leon, "a perfectly divine pianist."

Corinne and Leon are shocked to hear from the world-traveler Colonel Strickland that during a Burmese hunting party, Mauny H'La was found dead, and it is rumored that he was murdered by the escapee Archie Clutter.

Later that night, Clutter stealthily enters Corinne's bedroom, wakes her up, throttles her scream, puts the telephone out of reach, and tells her that he tore the truth out of Mauny H'La before "braining" him and knows that they killed his wife. H'La paid with his life. From Corinne he wants the money left for him.

The third act moves to a secluded chateau near Avignon, France, the summer home of Ariadne Ferne. While the Lady and her beau, Strickland, are attending the circus, Clutter and Roussencq enter through a window. They surprise Corinne as she comes down carrying a dressing case, ready for travel. The two escaped felons conduct a mock trial, with Clutter putting a lampshade on his head and Roussencq playing the role of the avocat général. They blame Corinne for treachery and murder, demanding the death penalty. They intend to bind Corinne when the sound of an approaching car is heard. After a few minutes, Lady Ariadne and Colonel Strickland enter and turn on the lamp. Clutter throws a knife at Strickland, and it strikes the side of the staircase. The Colonel draws a revolver and fires. Clutter rocks on his feet and crashes to the floor. While Strickland is checking the body, Roussencq escapes. Strickland flings open a side door and is aghast at the sight of Corinne hanging from the chandelier.

* * *

No Other Tiger was first performed at the Opera House in Leicester, England, on October 8, 1928. The thriller came to London's St. James's Theatre on December 26, running for fifty-two performances. The cast included Dennis Neilson-Terry (Archie Cutter), Wilfrid Hyde-White (the avocat général), J.S. Carré (Hospel Roussencq), Gladys Black-Roberts (Elizabeth Clutter), and Mary Glynne (Corinne).

The reviews were mixed. The *Daily Telegraph* scowled, "This is crude stuff," while the *Daily Mail* cheered, "the best thriller we have had for many months."[1]

* * *

Born in Camberwell, London, Alfred Edward Woodley Mason was a student at Dulwich College and read literature at Oxford University. When joining the Oxford Dramatic Society, he further developed his passion for the stage. Degree in hand, he was hired by a touring repertory company as an actor.

Returning to London, he went to work as a journalist, served as a Liberal Member of Parliament and was encouraged to keep writing by such friends as Oscar Wilde and Anthony Hope. Writing would soon be his full-time occupation. Mason's first novel appeared in 1895, and he went on to publish more than thirty popular potboilers in a variety of genres, the most famous of which is the adventure novel *The Four Feathers* (1902). His most enduring hero, however, is M. Hanaud, a detective with the French Sûreté, who made his debut in 1910's *At the Villa Rose* and appeared in four more books. During World War I, Mason lied about his age in order to serve in the Royal Marine Light Infantry and also worked with British Naval Intelligence.

Mason "made ample use of the psychological element—and in doing so, was in advance of his time."[2] His plays with suspense elements include melodramas taken from his fiction, such as *The Witness for the Defense* (1911), *At the Villa Rose* (1920), *Running Water* (1922), and *The House of the Arrow* (1928). He died at the age of eighty-three, while at work on a biography of the celebrated seventeenth-century British admiral, Sir Robert Blake.

Awards and Honors: *At the Villa Rose* (1910) is included in the *Howard Haycraft-Ellery Queen Definitive Libraryof Detective-Crime-Mystery Fiction.*

NOTES

1. Both reviews quoted in *Play Pictorial*, December 26, 1928.
2. Daniel P. King, *Twentieth Century Crime and Mystery Writers*. ed. John M. Reilly (New York: St. Martin's Press, 1980), 1017.

The Silent Witness (1930)

by Jack de Leon (England, 1897-1956) and Jack Celestin (England, 1892-1949)

Jack de Leon and Jack Celestin, collaborators of several West End thrillers, came up in 1930 with their standout, *The Silent Witness.*

The play begins with young Anthony Howard arriving home at about midnight, sinking into a chair, and mopping his brow. When his parents – Sir Austin Howard and Lady Mary – return from the theatre and rebuke him for not joining them, the overwrought Tony blurts out that he killed a girl, choked her with his own hands, a little after eight o'clock.

The lights fade out to a flashback at Doreen Smith's apartment in Bloomsbury. Tony lets himself in with a key. Doreen sashays from the bedroom scantily dressed. She is startled – "I didn't expect you." Tony buries his head on her breast and mumbles that he wants to marry her. He insists on giving her a &25 check payable to cash, which his father had given him.

Enter Carlo Montforte, using his key. Tony inquires about Carlo, and Doreen confesses that he is her husband. Shocked and angry, Tony orders Carlo out – "This is my flat; I pay for it." The Spaniard leaves, smirking. A high-voltage quarrel ensues between Tony and Doreen, climaxing with him seizing her by the throat, tightening his fingers. Doreen slides down in front of the couch. Tony stares at her face, shocked at what he's done, grabs his coat and rushes out.

Back at the Howard home Tony is sobbing. Austin pours him a drink and asks a few questions. It seems that no one saw Tony enter or leave the Bloomsbury flat, except the victim's husband. But Austin fears that the police will trace Tony through some clue or other and concocts an alibi. When the doorbell rings, Austin firmly instructs his son to tell everyone that he was at the theatre with them. He sends Tony upstairs. Inspector Robins of Scotland Yard is ushered in. The Inspector exhibits a check signed by Sir Austin and a calling card with his name – both found at the crime scene. After grilling Austin, Robins places the barrister under arrest.

The second act plays out at the Old Bailey three months later. Austin Howard is at the dock. His hair has gone grey, and he looks pale and aged. The counsel for the defense, Sir John Lawson, parades witnesses who can help determine that Doreen died between 8:00 and 9:20 p.m. He then calls to the stand a taxi driver and a theatre porter who testify that the accused was attending a show on the evening of September 8. Upon cross-examination, the counsel for the crown, Arthur Drinton, presents a seating plan of the theatre for that date in which seats No. D-10 and D-11 are crossed-out, but No. D-12 is not. A check of the stubs collected by the attendant verifies that D-12 is missing. Drinton declares that the tickets and plan prove that Sir Austin wasn't at the theatre that night. Sir Austin squirms and, highly hysterical, cries that he cannot stand this any longer and that he admits to killing Doreen Smith. A young man jumps up from his spectators' seat and shouts, "No, no, no. You can't convict that man. It wasn't him." A security guard grabs the intruder by the shoulder and drags him out.

The third act takes place at the Scotland Yard office of Inspector Robins. Tony Howard comes in, blurts that his father has been shielding him, and details the events of September 8. Robins advises Tony that he is struck by an inconsistency in his confession – the body of Doreen Smith was not found on the floor but on the couch. The Inspector sends for Lady Howard and Carlo Montforte, Doreen's husband, and orders police to bring prisoner Howard. When all are assembled, Robins calls in the fellow who interrupted the court proceedings, Howard Ward, and instructs him to narrate a statement he had signed earlier that day. Ward, a petty criminal, says that he met Doreen seven months ago in Brighton and used to visit her often. On the evening of September 8, he came over about a quarter to six for "kanoodling," making love. Doreen knew that in Brighton he had a sea-side booth where he used to write visiting cards and copy signatures.

Fade-out, and fade-in to Doreen's flat. Ward enters – "Hello, Duckie." They drink and kiss. She tells him about a "big coup." In a couple of days she shall have a signature for him to copy on somebody else's bank account; a kid, an awfully stupid one at that. The doorbell rings. Doreen opens the door. It is Austin Howard. Sir Austin gives her his card. Horace excuses himself and goes into the bedroom.

Doreen will give up Tony for &1,000. Sir Austin writes her a check, says that he expects Doreen to break with his son immediately, and leaves.

Back at Scotland Yard, Ward states that Doreen gave him the check for cashing. He and Doreen were "kanoodling" in the bedroom when Tony Howard arrived and had his spate with Doreen. Ward was hiding in a cupboard when Carlo Montforte made an appearance.

In a flashback to the Bloomsbury flat, Doreen is discovered lying on the floor. Tony babbles and scurries out. Before Ward can leave, Carlo Monforte enters and begins to ransack drawers. Doreen rises slowly, feebly sits on the couch, and utters, "I was just nearly murdered." Carlo keeps searching, asking for her money. Doreen snaps that she is aware that Carlo is married and threatens to sue him for bigamy. He suddenly grabs her by the throat and forces her down the couch.

As the lights come back to the Scotland Yard office, Ward relates that he silently and fearfully witnessed how Carlo choked Doreen. Carlo slowly raises his gun and points it at Ward. Austin clutches the weapon and forces it up into the air. The gun discharges. Inspector Robins and a uniformed sergeant seize Carlo and coerce him out. Austin, Mary, and Tony embrace as the curtain descends.

* * *

An early draft of *The Silent Witness*, entitled *The Man in the Dock*, previewed at London's "Q" Theatre on November 26, 1928. The revised version premiered at the Comedy Theatre on April 4, 1930, with Malcolm Keen as Sir Austin, running for 197 performances. A West End repeat, featuring Derek Cotter, played at the Regent Theatre, May 23, 1931, for twelve performances. In the U.S., *The Silent Witness* warmed up at the Broad Street Theatre, Newark, New Jersey, for a short run that began on February 16, 1931, and moved to Manhattan's Morosco on March 23, 1931. It was staged by Harry Wagstaff Gribble with a revolving stage that contributed smooth transitions.

The Silent Witness won the praise of reviewers. "A good example of its kind," chirped Arthur Ruhl. "It is crisply written, for the most part, gets away to a flying start, and is well played." Ruhl praised Lionel Atwill in the role of Sir Austin as "forceful and at ease throughout," and Fortunio Bonanova's Carlo as "a suave and debonair Spanish villain."[1] Brooks Atkinson found the authors of *The Silent Witness* "artful dodgers" and lauded "a good, bewildering evening among gilded sons, blackmailers, forgers, light-minded ladies and dour representatives of the law."[2] Gilbert W. Gabriel believed that the play "was chockfull of baffle and clashing brains and handsome climaxes, and gave me, I must say, the best time I've had in a court-room since the days of Mary Dugan."[3] Richard Lockridge admired a work "written with some urbanity, its characterization going a little deeper than is common in such affairs."[4]

The Silent Witness ran for eighty performances. Lionel Atwill went with the play to the Selwyn Theatre, Chicago, Illinois, in 1931, and reprised the role of Sir Austin in a faithful 1932 film adaptation, making his talking picture debut.

* * *

Other crime plays by Jack de Leon and Jack Celestin that were produced in London include *The Man at Six, Line Engaged, House of Danger*, and *Crime on the Hill. The Man at Six* (1928) unrolls in "The Chestnuts," a Gothic manor near Kingston, England, during a foggy evening. The owner of the abode, old Elizabeth Rowson, has disappeared. Chief Inspector Dawford of Scotland Yard, celebrated private sleuth Campbell Edwards, and Sybil Vane, an operative of the Vane's Detective Agency, arrive on the scene to investigate. Stolen jewelry, a secret passage, a time-bomb, and the murder of the household servant partake in the tense proceedings. At the end, in a series of surprises, no one turns out to be who he or she is supposed to be.

The lead character of *Line Engaged* (1934) is David Morley, the young author of popular suspense novels and son of divisional detective-inspector Sam Morley of Scotland Yard. David falls in love with Eva Whiston, the good-looking wife of sadistic Gordon Whiston.When Gordon is found shot to death in his study, David Morley becomes the prime suspect, but it turns out that the culprit is Eva's mother.

House of Danger (1930) is about a peaceable young man who finds his cozy flat invaded by various kinds of crooks and meets the challenge with aplomb, while *Crime on the Hill* (1933) is a prussic acid case with multiple suspects.

In 1945, De Leon directed the West End production of *Laura*, dramatized by Vera Caspary and George Sklar from Caspary's classic novel. Celestin scripted for British cinema *The Crimes of Stephen Hawke* (1936), in which the title character is a respectable money lender by day and a cruel serial killer, "The Spinebreaker," by night; and *Jury's Evidence* (1936), picturing a lone juror's stand to prove the innocence of the defendant in a murder trial.

NOTES

1. *New York Herald Tribune*, March 24, 1931.
2. *New York Times*, March 24, 1931.
3. *New York American*, March 24, 1931.
4. *New York Evening Sun*, March 24, 1931.

They Shall Not Die (1934)

John Wexley (United States, c. 1903-1985)

Following his socially conscious plays *The Last Mile* (1930), and *Steel* (1931), John Wexley came up with yet another controversial drama, *They Shall Not Die*, which he based on the transcript of the Scottsboro Boys criminal trial. The playwright changed names and locales, but otherwise constructed a fair replica of the tragedy.

The play begins in the sleepy Southern town of Cookesville, Alabama, which is energized by a fistfight between several homeless white boys and a group of black youngsters aboard the freight train from Chattanooga, Tennessee. The sheriff's posse ushers the youths into two segregated steel-barred cells at the Matchachubbe County jail (in real life, Morgan County). Also riding the train were two white girls—the haughty Virginia Ross (in reality, Victoria Price), who proudly boasts of being the "hottest gal in Chattanoogie", and the drab Lucy Wells (Ruby Gates).

The community's prejudices rear their heads when Deputy Sheriff Trent and District Attorney Mason decide to bribe the girls into claiming that they were raped. Simultaneously, they beat a confession from the Black kids, aged thirteen to nineteen. Soon a lynch mob surrounds the jail but Trent and Mason, shrewdly political, insist on legal proceedings.

The nine Black youths are sentenced to death after a quick trial, but the state's Supreme Court orders a new hearing. A famous New York criminal attorney, Nathan G. Rubin (actually, Samuel S. Leibowitz), is engaged by the National Labor Defense Committee to represent them.

In the Dexter County courtroom (replacing Decatur), crowded with white spectators, Rubin demolishes the credibility of the prosecutor's star witness, Virginia Ross. He also calls on the medical examiner, Dr. Thomas, to testify that there was no physical evidence of rape, proving that so-called eyewitnesses have been lying. He himself is threatened by hostile spectators who sneer at him with anti-Semitic innuendo.

At the climax of an electrifying court scene, a remorseful Lucy Wells makes an unexpected appearance and exposes the frame-up. However, when the jury files out, its members can be heard laughing. Attorney Rubin springs up defiantly and swears that he will not rest until making sure that these "boys" are found innocent. Curtain.

* * *

They Shall Not Die opened at New York's Royale Theatre on February 21, 1934, to a spate of favorable reviews. "It is a play of terrifying and courageous bluntness of statement," wrote Brooks Atkinson, "thoughtfully developed, lucidly explained and played with great resolution."[1] John Anderson proclaimed the endeavor an "engrossing drama!"[2] F. Raymond Daniell, leading news correspondent of The *New York Times*, who attended the Scottsboro Trials, asserted, "When the curtain fell on *They Shall Not Die*, I experienced a sensation the theatre never had given me before… I had seen reality in grease paint, history which the footlights only faintly distorted… details have been faithfully reproduced… Mr. Wexler is writing for the theatre and not for a newspaper, which helps to explain why his work will be remembered long after the work of journalists has crumpled to dust."[3]

Among the men of letters who endorsed *They Shall Not Die* were Theodore Dreiser, S. N. Behrman, and Robert Benchley. The large cast, portraying sixty-four speaking roles as well as hobos, soldiers, townspeople, reporters, jury members, court guards and court audience, included thespians who would leap into distinguished movie careers, notably Claude Rains as defense counsel Rubin, Ruth Gordon as Lucy Wells, Dean Jagger as Lucy's boyfriend, Thurston Hall as the Judge, and Tom Ewell in a variety of small roles.

Philip Moeller directed, and Lee Simonson designed the settings for a play that ran only sixty-two performances. "Alas! The great public does not want to be harrowed," bemoaned Brooks Atkinson,[4] Nevertheless, *They Shall Not Die* became an archetype for courtroom docu-dramas.

Acting Edition: Samuel French, Inc. (in manuscript form).

Awards and Honors: A top-ten selection in *The Best Plays of 1933-1934* ("a cohesive and moving dramatic entertainment").[5]

NOTES

1. *New York Times*, February 22, 1934.
2. *New York Evening Journal*, February 22, 1934.
3. *New York Times*, March 4, 1934.
4. *New York Times*, March 11, 1934.
5. Burns Mantle, ed., *The Best Plays of 1933-1934* (New York: Dodd, Mead and Company, 1934), 203.

Judgment Day (1934)

Elmer Rice (United States, 1892-1967)

Elmer Rice wrote, produced, and directed *Judgment Day*, a political, anti-Nazi courtroom drama which unfolds at the Palace of Justice in a capital of Southeastern Europe. Lydia Kuman, the patriotic wife of Alexander Kuman, a revolutionary leader; George Khitov, a fiery spokesman for the outlawed People's Party; and Kurt Schneider, a half-witted, drug-addicted trigger-man, are accused of conspiring to overthrow the National Government and attempting to assassinate the Minister-President of the state, Grigori Vesnic. Prosecutor Wolfgang Bathory demands the death penalty.

During a one-week trial, five judges—some independent, some puppets of the dictator — cross-examine witnesses, most of whom were prompted to lie for the prosecution. Constantine Parvan, private secretary to Vesnic, describes how Madame Kuman and Kurt Schneider were received by the Minister-President in his office and how "Schneider drew a pistol from his pocket… fired twice and the bullets struck our leader in the chest and in the shoulder… He fell to the floor. I seized Schneider's arm and wrestled the pistol from him. People rushed into the room and took the assassins into custody."

Prosecutor Bathory tells the court that "for weeks the Minister-President has hovered precariously between life and death." He was eventually declared to be out of danger.

Vassili Bassaraba, a waiter, testifies that on the evening before the assassination attempt, "Monsieur Khitov, and Madame Kuman, and the German gentleman" were seated at the Café Danube, whispering among themselves, and he saw Khitov hand Schneider a pistol.

Dr. Stambulov, the defense attorney, calls to the stand the Italian opera Diva, Madame Giulia Crevelli and she rebuts Bassaraba's testimony by declaring that Schneider could not have been at the Café Danube because he came to her apartment at five o'clock in the afternoon and remained there "until next morning, that's how long."

The judges are split on the verdict. The wounded ruler, Vesnic, enters in a wheelchair and demands "an immediate sentence of death for the assassins." Rebels headed by Alexander Kuman invade the courthouse. The eldest and noblest judge, Count Leonid Slatarski, fires point-blank at Vesnic then turns the revolver on himself.

* * *

The premiere of *Judgment Day* took place at New York's Belasco Theatre on September 12, 1934, Rice relates in his autobiography that in order "to emphasize the extravagant and sinister character of the proceedings," he "pitched the performances high, aiming at the emotional response from the audience." "That's exactly what I got. There were cheers and applause throughout the opening-night performance, and a demonstration at the end. But there was still the press to be reckoned with, so I did not allow myself to become too jubilant," Rice wrote.[1]

Rice's premonition proved disastrously correct. "A pretty clumsy play," sniffed Brooks Atkinson. "...No one can tell on short notice whether Elmer Rice intends it as melodrama, cartoon or burlesque, for all those impressions swirl madly through it."[2] Percy Hammond objected to "a wild phantasmagoria of theatrical hysterics."[3] John Mason Brown lamented, "The sad news for this evening is that in *Judgment Day* Mr. Rice seems to have taken a vacation from his customary skill—and from his sense of humor...a propagandist melodrama which is at times almost as funny and as old-fashioned as *The Drunkard*."[4]

But several reviewers liked *Judgment Day*. Richard Lockridge stated, "Elmer Rice has written a play to make your hair and your sympathies stand on end... It is a thrilling, stirring play, making the old Belasco ring with high words, and lighting it with an author's fine fury."[5] Arthur Pollock called it "a swell melodrama... the writing of it is crafty, concise, and sure... *Judgment Day* is a first-class 'show.'"[6]

Rice had to fight to keep a play running. He moved the production to a theatre that had a cut-rate policy, waved his royalties, and managed to raise the curtain of *Judgment Day* for ninety-three performances. In London, the play opened at the Strand Theatre on June 2, 1937, where it ran for 116 showings and was reviewed at the Phoenix Theatre on November 21, 1939, for ninety more. Fear and censorship prevented the performances of *Judgment Day* in the Continent. The play resonated in Israel, however, where the Ohel Theatre of Tel Aviv presented it—with great success—in a Hebrew translation by M. Bogdanoviski, May 1938.

NOTES

1. Rice, Elmer, *Minority Report* (New York: Simon and Schuster, 1963), 338.
2. *New York Times*, September 13, 1934.
3. *New York Herald Tribune*, September 13, 1934.
4. *New York Evening Post*, September 13, 1934.
5. *New York Sun*, September 13, 1934.
6. *Brooklyn Daily Eagle*, September 13, 1934.

Night of January 16th (1935)

Ayn Rand (United States, Russia-born, 1905-1982)

The prominent New York producer A. H. Woods, who had scored big with *The Trial of Mary Dugan* in 1927, brought to the boards another courtroom drama, *Night of January 16th*, eight years later.

Initially called *Penthouse Legend*, Ayn Rand's play was first presented by the British actor E. E. Clive at the Hollywood Playhouse in the fall of 1934, then called *Woman on Trial*. It had a modest run. When A. H. Woods secured the production rights, he used his contractual prerogative to rename the manuscript *Night of January 16th* and changed it extensively.

The playwright's aim was an in-depth study of the rise and fall of a ruthless, yet charismatic financial mogul based on the real-life career of the late "Match King," Ivar Kreuger (1880-1932).

A battle between Rand and Woods developed. According to Rand, Woods "was famous as a producer of melodramas, some of which have been good, some dreadful. Melodrama was the only element of my play that he understood, but he thought that there wasn't enough of it. So, 'to liven it up,' he introduced, in small touches, a junk heap of worn, irrelevant melodramatic devices that clashed with the style, did not advance the action and served only to confuse the audience—such as a gun, a heat test to determine its erased serial number, a flashy gun moll, etc.... Woods actually believed that only guns, fingerprints and police matters could hold an audience's attention, but 'speeches' could not."[1]

Nevertheless, Rand gave Woods credit for a gimmick that ended up making the play a hit: the jurors were selected from the audience and different short endings were written to accommodate the diverse verdicts.

Rand also supported the casting of a young unknown actress, Doris Nolan, in the role of the accused, Karen Andre, and of Walter Pidgeon as Larry "Guts" Regan, a gangster in love with her. "The rest of the play's history was hell," states the playwright.[2]

The play begins with an instruction by Judge Heath for the court clerk to draw a jury. The clerk steps forward with a list in his hand, and addresses the audience, telling the viewers that they are the panel from which the jury will be selected to try the case. As he calls a name, the juror steps up on stage and receives instructions from Judge Heath. The jury, often composed of celebrities (Jack Depmsey served on opening night, September 16, 1935), is sworn in, seated, and only then the lights in the auditorium are dimmed and the play commences.

Judge Heath requests the jurors to listen to the testimony carefully. They are to determine whether the defendant, Karen Andre, is guilty or not guilty of the murder of Bjorn Faulkner. Her fate rests in their hands.

District attorney Flint rises to present an opening statement. He begins by a reminder that on the 16th of January, near midnight, a man came hurtling down from the Faulkner Building. The district attorney goes on to state that the body was identified as that of Bjorn Faulkner, the bankrupt financier, who had hoped to start all over with his new bride, Nancy Lee, only daughter of philanthropist John Graham Whitfield. Flint drives the point that two weeks after his wedding Faulkner dismissed his mistress-secretary, Karen Andre, who must have nourished smoldering hatred and revenge in her heart. On the night of January 16th, says Flint, Bjorn Faulkner did not kill himself. He was murdered, murdered by delicate and capable hands that threw him down, from a great height, to crash into the pavement.

Flint calls to the stand a succession of witnesses supplying impressive circumstantial evidence, immoral implications, and eyewitness reports. Most damaging is the testimony of a private detective, engaged by Faulkner's wife to shadow the accused, who states that he saw Andre hoisting a man's body on the parapet and pushing him over with all her strength, down into space.

The Faulkner housekeeper sneers that the secretary had an affair with the boss from the beginning of her employment. Nancy Lee Faulkner declares that her husband pointed to Karen Andre as the cause and symbol of his darkest years and dismissed her for a new start. Her father, the distinguished Mr. Whitfield, affirms that Faulkner had no reason to commit suicide. According to the district attorney, there is no escaping the conclusion that the abandoned Karen shot Faulkner and pitched his body off the skyscraper.

Defense Attorney Stevens counters with witnesses of his own: a handwriting expert, a former secretary of the deceased, and the accused herself, building up the case of a broken tycoon whose only choice is suicide.

A surprising twist reveals that the mangled corpse found on the street was not that of Faulkner. Karen confesses that she did throw a man's body off the penthouse. But she claims that the body was dead before she threw it, and it was not Bjorn Faulkner. The suicide was staged by Faulkner himself, who wanted to be officially dead. Karen's boyfriend, Larry Regan, stole the body of a gunman, 'Lefty O'Toole,' who was shot by rival gangsters. O'Toole's height, measurements, and hair resembled Bjorn's. He was the man she threw off the penthouse.

Karen, maintaining that she was not a jilted lover but a devoted secretary, describes the elaborate plan of exchanging the identities between Faulkner and the dead O'Toole. Then Regan is called to the stand, and he discloses that following the events of January 16th, Faulkner was murdered, indeed, but by underworld figures hired by none other than his father-in-law John Graham Whitfield, who promptly denies the charge as "fantastic."

On the heels of a balanced summation by the defense and the prosecution, the bailiff escorts the jury out for deliberation. The stage is blacked out. One by one, pin spotlighted, the various witnesses repeat the most significant portions of their testimony—a quick succession of contradicting statements, presenting both sides of the case. The jury returns. The bailiff instructs the prisoner to rise and face the jury.

The actors are ready with two different verdicts: not guilty, in which case, the prisoner is discharged by the judge; or guilty, whereupon the defense attorney will tell the judge that he wishes to file an order of appeal.

According to the stage manager of the Broadway production, who kept a tally, during the six-month run of the play the verdicts were 3 to 2 in favor of acquittal.

* * *

Night of January 16th commenced in Philadelphia's Chestnut Street Opera House on September 10, 1935. The tryout performance yielded a positive reaction by Linton Martin of the *Inquirer*, who found the play filled with "tricky criss-cross currents."[3] Opening in New York's Ambassador Theatre six days later, Brooks Atkinson of the *Times* concluded, "It is routine theatre with the usual brew of hokum."[4] Still, the courtroom drama ran for 235 performances and crossed the Atlantic to captivate London (Raymond Massey was a member of the jury on opening night, September 29, 1936). The reviewer of the *London Times* acclaimed Phoebe Foster's "tense and beautiful performance as the accused," and the *Telegraph* critic, W. A. Darlington, confidently predicted "audiences would flock to the play."[5] However, *Night of January 16th* ran for only twenty-two performances.

A reading of *Night of January 16th* by Nathaniel Branden took place in New York's Atlantic Hotel on June 16, 1936. The Cecil Howard Stock Company revived the play at Off Broadway's Cherry Lane Theatre, April 24, 1940. The jury, recruited from students of New York law schools, brought in the verdict of not guilty. Another Off-Broadway presentation reverted to Ayn Rand's original title, *Penthouse Legend*, opening at the McAlpin Rooftop Theatre, February 23, 1973, running for thirty performances. Throughout the years there were road companies and summer stock productions galore, and many presentations across Europe. The play has been performed on radio and twice made for television.

Night of January 16th was adapted for the screen in 1941 with Robert Preston, Ellen Drew, Nils Asther, Rod Cameron, and Cecil Kellaway. Leonard Maltin felt that the "Hit Broadway play receives lackluster screen treatment; a talky and uninspired whodunit."[6] Ayn Rand called the movie version "another horror story. I had nothing to do with its screen adaptation. There is nothing of mine in that movie, except the names of some of the characters and the title. The *only* line of dialogue from my play which appears in the movie is: 'The court will now adjourn till ten o'clock tomorrow morning.'"[7]

A 1932 motion picture, *The Match King*, directed by Howard Bretherton, is another fictionalized account of entrepreneur Ivar Kreuger, portrayed by Warren William.

* * *

Ayn Rand's only other play to reach Broadway was *The Unconquered*, adapted from her novel, *We the Living*. It depicts a grim existence in the Soviet Union. The drama begins with the unsettling sight of a room that has obviously been searched. We soon learn that Leo Kovalesky, an aristocrat whose father, an admiral, was executed for "treason," is being stalked by the secret police.

The Unconquered opened at the Biltmore Theatre on February 13, 1940, but despite the efforts of producer-director George Abbott, designer Boris Aronson, and a top-notch cast, the show was lambasted by the critics and closed after only six performances.

Two other plays by Rand, each with criminous ingredients, were rarely produced but are included in 1986's *The Early Ayn Rand*, edited by Leonard Peikoff. *Ideal* (1934) is the story of Kay Gonda, a Hollywood star, who is suspected of shooting an affluent friend, Granton Sayers. Kay was the last person to see the victim alive and since has vanished from sight. Kay's secretary, Miss Terence, is puzzled by the disappearance of five letters from the actress's fan mail. Each of the letters is then projected on a screen, followed by a series of vignettes, in which Kay Gonda visits her devoted admirers, one by one, relates to them that the police are searching for her, and asks for help. The various fans – a small businessman, a radical sociologist, an artist, an evangelist, a playboy count – react to the situation in less-than-honorable ways. In the final scene, it is revealed that Granton was not murdered; he committed suicide due to financial ruin and the fact that Kay refused to marry him. In October 1959, *Ideal* received its first – and only – performance at the Melrose Theatre in Los Angeles.

Think Twice (1939) is a three-act, ripe murder mystery. The action takes place in the plush estate of Walter Beckenridge, a stately, gray-haired man, a benevolent and altruistic inventor. His Connecticut laboratory houses radioactive elements and cosmic rays. On Beckenridge's fiftieth birthday, his wife Helen hosts a party for friends and associates. Through snatches of conversation, it soon becomes clear that by his generosity, Beckenridge wields power overall. When he is shot to death off stage in the garden, district attorney Gregory Hastings uncovers various suspects, all with burning motives.

The arrow of guilt seems to be pointing at Beckenridge's colleague, Steve Ingallis. Ingallis's fingerprints are found on the murder weapon, a cigarette of his brand lies in the grass by the body, his handkerchief hangs on a tree branch nearby, and he has no alibi whatsoever. But Hastings believes that the too-obvious clues were planted by Serge Sookin, a Russian spy with a foolproof alibi. A spin at the end turns the tables, exposing Ingallis as the culprit committing "the sloppiest and most obvious murder – and that is why it will be the perfect crime."

* * *

Ayn Rand (real name Alissa Rosenbaum) was born in St. Petersburg, Russia (now Leningrad), and graduated from the University of Petrograd in 1924. Two years later she immigrated to the United States, landing in Hollywood, where she found employment as a movie extra. Rand moved to New York in 1929, serving in the wardrobe department of RKO Pictures. During the 1930s she began her career as a screenwriter for Paramount, Universal and Metro-Goldwyn-Mayer.

A prolific author of novels, non-fiction and short stories, Rand is best known for her negatively reviewed, but best-selling, *The Fountainhead* (1943), the story of an idealistic architect, Howard Roark, battling the compromises of society, and *Atlas Shrugged* (1957), which rotates around various characters' rejection of suffocating government rules. Both books promote Rand's Objectivist philosophy. In follow-up dissertations – notably *The Virtue of Selfishness* (1965) and *Capitalism: The UnknownIdeal* (1966) – Rand continued to expound on what she called "rational selfishness": "My philosophy, in essence, is the concept of man as a heroic being, with his own happiness as the moral purpose of his life, with productive achievement as his noblest activity, and reason as his only absolute."

In addition to her own scenario of the film *The Fountainhead* (1949), Rand's more realized motion pictures are 1945's *You Came Along* and *Love Letters*. Rand was in the midst of penning for television a mini-series based on her novel *Atlas Shrugged*, when she died at the age of seventy-seven in 1982.

Two biographical treatments about Ayn Rand were made for television: the two-hour-and-twenty-minute documentary *Ayn Rand: A Sense of Life* (1997), written and directed by Michael Paxton; and Showtime's Emmy winning *The Passion of Ayn Rand* (1999), based on Barbara Branden's 1986 memoir, with Helen Mirren and Peter Fonda (as Rand's husband, Frank O'Connor). Among the various books about Rand are *Who Is Ayn Rand?*

(1962) and *My Years with Ayn Rand* (1999), both by Nathaniel Branden, a lover and disciple of the author. The Ayn Rand Institute, in Marina del Rey, California, was founded in 1985 to promote Rand's philosophy of Objectivism.

Acting Edition: Signet, New American Library.

Awards and Honors: An Ayn Rand first-class postage stamp was issued by the U.S. Postal Service in 1999.

NOTES

1. Ayn Rand, *Night of January 16th* (New York: Signet, New American Library, 1971), 8-9.
2. *Ibid*, 8.
3. *New York Times*, September 10, 1935.
4. *New York Times*, September 17, 1935.
5. *New York Times*, September 30, 1936.
6. Leonard Maltin, *2002 Movie and Video Guide* (New York: Signet, New American Library, 2001), 975.
7. Ayn Rand, *Night of January 16th* (New York: Signet, New American Library, 1971), 14.

The Unguarded Hour (1935)

Bernard Merivale (England, 1882-1939)

Sir Francis Dearden, KC., is a renowned prosecuting counsel, admired for his uncanny ability to shatter witnesses on the stand and win difficult cases. He is the front-runner for the position of attorney general.

Inside the court at the Old Bailey, Sir Francis cross-examines the prisoner Metcalf, accused of murdering his wife Phyllis in the scenic English Lake District. Tearfully, Metcalf insists that at the plateau of the Eagle Rock his ailing wife accidentally fell from the summit to the ravine below. There was a lady there who heard him warning Phyllis to stay away from the edge of the precipice. He cannot describe the lady—"All women wear much the same nowadays, and they all look the same age"—but Metcalf remembers that she had a silver wheatsheaf in her hat.

Sir Francis pooh-poohs Metcalf's statement and reminds the court that despite the fact that "England has been ringing with the story of this woman," she has not come forward and obviously does not exist. Sir Francis clinches his case when pointing out that a month prior to the fatal event, Mr. Metcalf took out a short-term policy on his wife's life for &3000.

The curtain now rises on the library of Dearden's home in Queen Anne's Gate. Colonel William Mason, head of the Special Branch at Scotland Yard, congratulates Yvonne Dearden on her thirtieth birthday. But Yvonne—tall, slender with dark hair and blue eyes—complains that she spent a miserable day sitting in court and watching Frank prosecuting that poor man. Mason asserts that her husband has only been doing his duty to get a conviction, but Yvonne remains troubled as he seems to have changed into a person without emotion.

Francis enters, dressed for dinner, with his hand bandaged and tells them that he pinched his finger on the door of the car. Yvonne confronts him, maintaining that he may have had a wonderful case according to the letter of law, but she believes, as do hundreds of people, that Metcalf is an innocent man.

Colonel Mason chides Francis for seeming to be two different people, but Francis laughs it off, claiming that he is paid to be Mr. Hyde when on the job. He offers Mason a labeled, Hungarian cigarette, which he bought while strolling near the Embankment, and insists that the chain of evidence in the Metcalf case is complete. Mason reflects that it might have been a series of coincidences, that there are times when all the stars in their courses are fighting against one, that everyone at times has an unguarded hour when everything is against him, but he is oblivious of the pitfalls. Suppose it was Metcalf's unguarded hour, and unfortunately for him, it synchronized with his wife's accident.

The telephone rings. It is a call for the Colonel. Diana Lewis, the famous aviator who has just returned to London from a much-touted world flight, was found strangled to death in her Westminster flat. Francis had defended Lewis a while back when she was accused of purloining a frock, and they have kept in touch. Unexpectedly, he now finds himself a suspect in her murder. A tall, broad-shouldered, distinguished-looking man was seen entering Diana's building. On the floor next to the victim a knife smeared with blood was found—she probably tried to defend herself. The Prosecutor's arm has a fresh, bleeding wound. A bottle of Green Chartreuse, 150 years old, purchased earlier in the day by a man fitting Francis's description was located in the murder room, as well as a stub of a Hungarian cigarette. Francis states that he had been walking along the Embankment but cannot prove his whereabouts between five and six that afternoon.

Francis calls the mounting evidence nothing but a string of coincidences. Adding to his distress is Yvonne's accusation that he is no longer a kind man, but a hard and callous prosecutor. She threatens to leave him.

In a happy windup, a contrite Francis returns to court to sink his own case against Metcalf, and prove to Colonel Mason that, though innocent, he too was ensnared by circumstantial evidence. His statement restores tranquility at home.

* * *

Bernard Merivale adapted *The Unguarded Hour* from the Hungarian of Ladislaus (Laszlo) Fodor, which was based on the German *Kopf in der Schlinge* by Otto Bastian. Early versions of the play were tried out at the Majestic Theatre in Brooklyn, New York, 1932 (titled *Circumstantial Evidence*), and the Montclair Theater, New Jersey, 1933 (titled *Between Five and Six*). Renamed *The Unguarded Hour*, the drama opened at Daly's Theatre in London on July 31, 1935, with Godfrey Tearle in the role of Sir Francis, and moved to several playhouses for 140 performances. Critic Charles Morgan called it "an ingeniously contrived but emotionally unpersuasive story."[1] A year later, *The Unguarded Hour* was adapted to the screen by Howard Emmett Rogers and Leon Gordon, directed by Sam Wood. Franchot Tone and Loretta Young were cast as the Deardens. A major change in the plot situated Lady Dearden as the elusive witness in the Metcalf case. An added character was blackmailer Hugh Lewis, (played by the oily Henry Daniell) who turns out to be the murderer.

The Unguarded Hour was presented by the Pasadena Playhouse in Pasadena, California, on April 4-15, 1939, and adapted for a CBS Lux Radio Theatre broadcast on December 4, 1944, featuring Robert Montgomery, Laraine Day, and Roland Young.

* * *

After graduation from St. John's College, Bernard Merivale wrote twelve plays, most with elements of crime. In 1925, he teamed with Brandon Fleming on a farcical melodrama, *None But the Brave.* The protagonist, Eric Tankerdown, is an idle nerd who inherits the estate of an aristocratic British uncle and has to fend for himself against pompous, vulturous relatives who fabricate a murder to entrap him.

Merivale allied with Arnold Ridley, author of the popular *The Ghost Train*, on two stage thrillers: *The Wrecker* (1927), depicting a series of devastating train wrecks orchestrated by an elusive saboteur, and *The Flying Fool* (1929), pitting an aviation sleuth against a band of jewel brigands.

Mystery Cottage, a 1936 tongue-in-cheek one-act play by Merivale, tells the adventure of four young girls who escape a summer rain by going into a desolate house situated on the Suffolk Coast, where they wrongly believe that they are endangered by a serial killer.

Merivale joined forces with Jeffrey Dell in adapting from the Hungarian of Ladislaus (Laszlo) Fodor, the comedy thriller *Blondie White* (1937), focusing on a high-society author of sensational melodramas who helps Scotland Yard solve the murder of a night-club hostess.

For the silver screen, Merivale wrote *Condemned to Death* (1932), a crime drama based on the 1931 play, *Jack O'Lantern*, by George Goodchild, a prolific British mystery novelist.[2] Arthur Wontner, taking a respite from his duties as filmdom's Sherlock Holmes, played Sir Charles Wallington, a severe judge, who sentences an arch criminal to the gallows. The villain, Tobias Lantern, hypnotizes the judge into killing the jurors responsible for his conviction. To fulfill the task, Sir Charles assumes a dual personality and masquerades as a mysterious figure who hires hoodlums to do his bidding. At the conclusion, a Scotland Yard inspector permits Sir Charles to commit suicide rather than face public disgrace. Directed by Walter Forde, no prints of *Condemned to Death* have survived.

Acting Edition: Samuel French, Inc. (in manuscript form).

NOTES

1. *New York Times*, August 25, 1935.
2. George Goodchild (1888-1969) utilized a number of pseudonyms to write dozens of mysteries between the teens of the twentieth century and the 1960s. In 1916, Goodchild novelized *The Barton Mystery*, a play by Walter Hackett. The recurring sleuth in numerous novels and short story collections by Goodchild is Chief Inspector McLean of Scotland Yard.

What Really Happened (1936)

Marie Belloc Lowndes (England, France-born, 1868-1947)

Ten years after its publication in 1926, Marie Belloc Lowndes adapted her novel *What Really Happened* to the stage. Lowndes kept the overall structure of the novel, framing the story with proceedings at the Old Bailey in London at the beginning and end. In the prologue, Justice Lenison sums up for the jury—ten men and two women—the case of the Crown versus Eva Raydon, charged with the murder of her husband. Heavily slanted against the accused, the judge declares that the charge is not unusual for a woman who wants to wed her lover. The jury retires to consider the verdict and a flashback illustrates what really happened.

Mrs. Eva Raydon is lovely, outgoing, extravagant, and child-like. She married Birtley Raydon, a wealthy businessman, with some trepidation, since her heart belonged to Army Officer Jack Mintlaw, but Jack was penniless and seemingly without prospects. As the years passed, Eva found herself content in a cozy Mill House home, spending much of her allowance on the latest fashions. Even the animosity of old Mrs. Raydon, Birtley's mother, did not cloud Eva's cheerful and care-free life.

Chief among the Raydons' household servants is Adelaide Strain, a widow raising a ten-year-old son, Gilly. Adelaide is devoted to Eva.

Jack Mintlaw, who has gone to Canada and prospered there, returns to town. Eva rushes to meet him, clandestinely and innocently. When Birtley refuses to pay Eva's latest dressmaker bill, Jack loans her &3,000.

Clouds begin to gather when, under the influence of his sour mother, Birtley gives Adelaide notice. The housekeeper unsuccessfully begs him to change his mind for the sake of her son. Sitting by the window, Adelaide hears from the garden how Eva pleads with Birtley on her behalf. She also hears the husband's retort: "Mrs. Strains's not worth more than her keep, and never has been .... And don't talk to me about her boy. I hate the sight of him. Unnatural, pompous little prig!"

Adelaide takes an envelope out of her evening bag, opens the flap, pours powder into a tumbler, and stirs the mixture. Birtley Raydon comes in from the garden, asks for his ginger beer, takes the tall glass, drains it, and walks up the stairs. Adelaide watches him, absorbed in sensations of terror and anguish.

The family practitioner, Dr. Durham, is ready to sign the death certificate but old Mrs. Raydon insists on a postmortem. Her son was in perfect health, she says, and she desires to know the reason of his sudden death.

They find fourteen grains of arsenic in the body of Birtley Raydon. Police Inspector Plimmer and his staff sergeant arrive at the Raydon home with an "attitude." Plimmer believes that women—even the best of 'em—are as artful as a bagful of monkeys, bless 'em! Following the interrogation of the befuddled, shocked Eva, regarding the events of September 3 and the check for &3,000 from Jack Mintlaw, Plimmer concludes that "she's cooked her goose." Soon Eva is arrested on the charge for the murder of her husband.

The play's epilogue reverts the proceedings back to Court. Awaiting the jury's verdict, Sir Joseph Molloy, the defense counsel, is gravely concerned about Mr. Justice Lenison's summation, which was dead against his client. Little Gilly pulls a small revolver out of the coat pocket of his mother." Is it for me?" he asks. Mrs. Strain seizes the weapon and puts it back in the pocket—"Yes, Gilly, it's for you—and me..." She submits a letter to Sir Joseph, to be read after the verdict is announced, but snatches it back when the jury returns and its foreman declares, "Not guilty."

When the commotion subsides and Eva Raydon leaves the courthouse with her arms round Adelaide Strain, an admiring barrister tells Sir Joseph that he will never have a bigger feather in his cap than the one he won today. Sir Joseph responds with a chuckle and expresses his belief that his client got away with it.[1]

What Really Happened was shown at the Duke of York's Theatre, London, on September 13, 1936, for one performance.

* * *

Marital infidelity results in violent consequences in two dramas by Belloc Lowndes, *The Key* and *With All John's Love*, both copyrighted in 1930.

In *The Key*, twenty-four-year-old Ruby Aschcott, described as "exceedingly beautiful," is married to Jacko Aschcott, aged sixty-seven, an affluent businessman. Jacko, intensely jealous, keeps Ruby on a tight leash in their home on the outskirts of London. Ruby complains to a family friend, the widow Blanche Clyde, that she is Jacko's slave, buried alive, and is not allowed to go anywhere.

Blanche mischievously introduces Ruby to young Edward Thwing, a smooth womanizer who sweeps the naive wife off her feet. Edward gives Ruby a key to his rooms in King's Office Row and a tryst develops between them, lasting many months.

One day Ruby enters Edward's flat and finds another woman with a latch key of her own. Saucy, "modern" Betty Berwick introduces herself as

Edward's paramour and mockingly advises Ruby to run away, like a good little girl, and get another lover, as Edward is damn sick of her. Ruby backs out of the room, but soon returns, kicks off her shoes, picks up a coil of rope lying on the chest, fashions it into a wide noose, creeps behind Betty, slides the noose over her head, and draws it tight.

When Ruby learns that Edward is suspected of murdering Betty and may be facing the gallows, she slips a letter-of-confession into the hands of Edward's guardian and shoots herself.

As *The Second Key*, the play was produced at London's Arts Theatre on October 2, 1935, running four performances.

The romantic triangle of *With All John's Love* involves an elderly, rich businessman – John Eascott; his young, "extremely attractive" mistress – Emmy Chart; and her live-in beau, a clerk – Joe Crickling. A snoopy charwoman reveals to Joe that Emmy is being set up by her lover in a fashionable apartment. Joe sees red, stabs Emmy to death "again and again in a frenzy-like," and turns the knife on himself, fatally.

* * *

Yet another good-looking woman is the lead character in Belloc Lowndes' thriller, *Her Last Adventure*. Eva Bude, a beautiful young widow, is a buyer for a big wholesale house. Eva confides to her friend, Nellie Hayward, that even though she is fond of her frequent escort, John Welbeck, now and again, in the last few years, she had met a man by chance who has fallen for her. Each of her romantic adventures was like a page torn out of a fairy tale, says Eva, and admittedly she now longs for another adventure, one last adventure, before settling down to respectability – forever.

Eva meets Don Juan James Malton in a first-class railway carriage. James tells her boldly that she is the loveliest thing he has ever seen. Soon Eva agrees to visit him at his old home, The Folly, some miles from Dover, where she spends the night. It is stormy outside—thunder, lightning, heavy rain. Suddenly they hear from below the sound of a falling piece of furniture. In a state of abject horror, James gets a revolver. Eva calms him, offering to go down to see who it is; she has never been afraid "of man or devil."

In a cobwebbed basement, Eva encounters a limping man and a little Cockney girl. They say they thought the house was empty, so took shelter during the storm. Eva brings them a tray of food and walks about in disdain, commenting on the bad smell permeating the basement.

Eva finds out the source of the peculiar odor when a few days later she is visited by Superintendent Eaton of Scotland Yard. Eaton informs her that a pair of vagrants reported to the Dover police their discovery of a dead woman's body in the basement of The Folly, and it has been determined that the victim was James Malton's wife. The police "weren't sharp enough," says the Superintendent, to stop Malton from poisoning himself with a concealed dose of strychnine. Eva tells John Welbeck that they will not wait any longer but get a special license and be married quietly tomorrow,

Her Last Adventure opened at the Ambassadors Theatre, London, on March 30, 1936, for seven performances.

* * *

Two of Lowndes's more celebrated novels—*The Chink in the Armour* (1912) and *The Lodger* (1913)—were adapted to the stage by Horace Annesley Vachell. *The Chinkin the Armour* dramatization, called *The House of Peril*, depicts a cunning murder plot hatched by an unscrupulous, sinister German couple against a very young, very naïve, and very wealthy English widow, who is barely saved at the last curtain. It opened at the Queen's Theatre in London on March 8, 1919, for 105 performances, and was filmed in 1922.

The Lodger dramatization was titled *Who Is He*? —the tale of a mysterious gentleman who rents the attic of a Bloombury rooming house and may, or may not, be the notorious Jack the Ripper. Henry Ainley played the role at London's Haymarket Theatre, December 9, 1915, for 157 performances. Lionel Atwill took over at New York's Maxine Elliott Theatre on January 8, 1917, for fifty-six performances, which were presented under the original title, *The Lodger.*

The Lodger was filmed in 1926 by Alfred Hitchcock, and again in 1932 as *The Phantom Fiend* in the U.S., and in 1944 and 1954 as *Man in the Attic.*[2] More than half a century later, in 2009, David Ondaatje wrote and directed a new movie version of *The Lodger*, shifting the proceedings to modern Los Angeles.

* * *

Marie (Adelaide) Belloc was born in St. Cloud, France, in 1868. Her parents moved to England when she was four years old. The sister of renowned man of letters Hillaire Belloc, Marie began writing at sixteen and became a professional author at twenty. In 1891 she married Frederic Lowndes, a journalist for the *London Times.*

A perfectionist who rewrote painstakingly, Marie still managed to produce forty-four crime books, eleven main-stream novels, seven volumes of short stories, a few non-fiction studies, including *Noted Murder Mysteries* under the pseudonym Philip Curtin, seven plays, and four autobiographical works.

In addition to *The Lodger*, several other criminous novels by Lowndes were converted to the screen. *Letty Lynton* (1931) was inspired by the 1857 Glasgow, Scotland trial of young Madeleine Smith, accused—and acquitted—of poisoning her lover. *Letty Lynton* was filmed by Metro-Goldwyn-Mayer in 1932 with Joan Crawford and Robert Montgomery.[3] In 1947, Universal-International made *The Story of Ivy*, under the title *Ivy*, featuring Joan Fontaine as an ambitious, amoral woman who poisons her spouse to advance her social position.

Virginia Macdonald, in *Twentieth Century Crime and Mystery Fiction,* asserts that Marie Belloc's "significant contributions to the genre share a sensitive understanding of women's problems, a modern sensibility, a concern with the psychology of crime, especially motive. They focus on ordinary persons involved in sudden violence, people 'enmeshed in a web of tragic circumstances' involving jealousy, greed, sudden love or sexual entanglements, and failure to communicate."[4]

NOTES

1. Marie Belloc Lowndes pictured inquests and trials realistically - and cynically - in several of her novels: *The Terriford Mystery* (1924), *Letty Lynton* (1931), *The Chianti Flask* (1934), *Motive* aka *Why It Happened* (1938), and *Lizzie Borden* (1939).
2. In 1903, prior to Lowndes's *The Lodger*, German playwright Frank Wedekind (1864-1918) penned *Die Büchse der Pandora (Pandora's Box)*, depicting a troubled, sexually driven heroine, Lulu, who ends up a victim of Jack the Ripper. Another dramatization of Lowndes's novel, by Patrick Prior, was presented at the Dukes Theatre, Lancaster, England, November 3-25, 2000.
3. MGM had to defend itself in a noted plagiarism suit when the two authors of a play entitled *Dishonored Lady* accused the motion picture company of basing the movie *Letty Lynton* on their work, not on Lowndes' novel. *Dishonored Lady*, by Margaret Ayer Barnes and Edward Sheldon, was produced at New York's Empire Theatre on February 4, 1930. It starred Katharine Cornell in the role of Madeline Cary, a Manhattan socialite who poisons her Argentinean lover when planning to marry a titled Englishman. In *Lady*, Cary is tried and acquitted. The courts first exonerated MGM of the charge but after seven years of legal maneuvers, the decision was reversed and the judgment favored the plaintiffs, who were awarded more than half a million dollars. Another screen adaptation of *Dishonored Lady* was filmed by MGM in 1947, starring Hedy Lamarr and Dennis O'Keefe. The actual Glasgow case

was depicted by David Lean in 1950, with Ann Todd as the poisoner *Madeleine.*

4. John M. Reilly, ed. *Twentieth-Century Crime and Mystery* (New York: St. Martin's Press, 1980), 969.

Blind Man's Buff (1936)

Ernst Toller (Germany, 1893-1939) and Denis Johnston (Ireland, 1901-1984)

A poet, essayist and dramatist, Ernst Toller was an influential Expressionist writer, creating a symbolic reality and using non-naturalistic stage techniques. In his first play, *Die Wandlung* (*Transfiguration*, 1919), Toller explored the dilemmas of assimilation of Jews in Germany and urged the abolition of war. The characters represent types rather than individuals and the action unfolds in short tableaus — a device Toller would use in many of his later plays.

Toller continued to pen dramas using universal themes. In his introduction to *Seven Plays by Ernst Toller*, Toller chastises the writers and artists who "forgot" that their task was "to serve the eternal powers of life—truth, justice, joy, beauty, freedom, the mind and the spirit," and asserts that "the plays collected in this volume are social dramas and tragedies. They bear witness to human suffering, and to fine yet vain struggles to vanquish this suffering."[1]

Unlike most of Toller's plays, his *Die blinde Göttin* (*The Blind Goddess*, 1934), adapted by Irish playwright Denis Johnston under the title *Blind Man's Buff* (1936), is a realistic, straightforward murder yarn. The play scrutinizes human foibles and criticizes the judicial system.

The first scene takes place at Dr. Chavasse's house in a small rural Irish town. There are two interior doors on each side of the hall—one leading to a sitting-room, the other to a consulting room. The curtain rises on the maid, Mary Quirke, listening intently at the door of the consulting room. The doctor's young daughter, Laura, skips in playing with a ball. Mary rebukes Laura, reminding the little girl that her mother is lying sick in the next room. The doorbell rings. It is Dominick Mapother, a talkative, philosophizing farmer who has come for medicine for his sick cow. Mary warns him to keep his voice down, explaining that the mistress, Mrs. Chavasse, is near death.

A concerned Dr. Chavasse calls a former lover, Dr. Anice Hollingshead, to rush over to help, as his wife Elizabeth is sinking fast. Mary and Mapother hear as the two doctors inject the patient with camphor, listen to her heart with a stethoscope, and finally conclude that "there's nothing more to be done—she's dead."

Dr. Chavasse comes out with an ashen face and can hardly listen to Mapother, who pleads for "an elixir" for his "unfortunate cow." It seems that the bottle of medicine prepared for him is missing but little Laura admits that she took the bottle for her Teddy bear and it's in her dolly's pram. Chavasse asks Laura to give the bottle to the farmer and consults with Anice about the cause of his wife's death. Anice believes that Elizabeth died of cyanide poisoning, no doubt self-administered. Chavasse confides that despite their deteriorating relationship, Elizabeth wouldn't agree to a divorce or separation, and was working herself into a complete breakdown.

At that moment of sorrow and confusion, Mary demands to know what happened to her mistress, and hints that she knows "some things that may interest the police." When Sergeant Carey arrives on the scene, Mary insists that he look into Dr. Chavasse's desk drawer where he'll find a batch of love letters written by Dr. Hollingshead to Dr. Chavasse and accuses them of murdering her mistress.

A month later, at the Central Criminal Court in Dublin, Dr. Chavasse stands accused of homicide. In the witness box, the farmer Mapother amuses the spectators as he rhapsodizes about his beloved, sick cow. Dr. Anice Hollingshead testifies that in the past she had an affair with the accused but "that was over and done with." She believes that Elizabeth Chavasse, a neurotic with suicidal tendencies, took her own life, and that the maid, Mary Quirke instigated the investigation out of "spite and venom." However, the love letters found in Dr. Chavasse's desk are produced in court as proof of motive, and the fact that no medicine bottle was found near the body negates the theory of suicide. Chavasse is found guilty. His death sentence is commuted to life imprisonment.

The third act unfolds at the State Solicitor's office. Prosecutor Liam Poer receives Anice Hollingshead, listens patiently to her plea on behalf of Chavesse, but insists that she has not provided any proof of the doctor's innocence. It is only when Mapother arrives for reimbursement of his expenses as a witness, that a new element enters the case. Mapother bemoans the death of his cow and mentions the black bottle of medicine that was given him by Dr. Chavesse's child. He still has the bottle "standing on a shelf in the byre, a monument to the selfishness and indifference of mankind."

Now that the medicine bottle has been found, Prosecutor Poer believes that Elizabeth Chavesse took her own life. He reopens the case and Dr. Chavesse is released. The doctor returns home and is greeted warmly by Anice. Observing Chavesse mistreating his daughter, Anice has a change of heart. She tells the doctor that she loved him when he was being wronged, when he faced heavy odds, but now no longer loves him. There was a time, she says, when she loved him so much that she could have killed his wife. With that sense of guilt, she leaves, and the curtain falls.

* * *

Blind Man's Buff was first performed with great success at the Abbey Theatre in Dublin on December 28, 1936. The drama was directed by Hugh Hunt and designed by Tanya Moiseiwitsch. Arthur Shields, soon to become a Hollywood fixture, played Frank Chavesse, Eileen Crowe portrayed Anice Hollingshead, and F.J. McCormick enacted Dominick Mapother.

Staged by John Fernald, *Blind Man's Buff* came to London's Arts Theatre on September 23, 1938, for several performances, featuring Bernard Lee, later "M" in the James Bond movies, as Dr. Chavesse. Dennis Price enacted the role in a 1953 revival that ran at the St. Martin's Theatre, London, for fifty-three showings.

* * *

The son of a Jewish merchant, Ernst Toller was born in East Prussia and educated at the universities of Heidelberg, Munich, and Grenoble. He was wounded in the trenches during World War I and became a fervent pacifist. He joined political organizations, including the Communist Party, and served several jail sentences for subversion.

Most of Toller's dramas reflect his political views and are tinged with violence. *Masse-Mensch* (*Man and the Masses*) was written in 1919 in the prison-fortress of Niederschoenenfeld. In a dark cell, Toller feverishly wrote the play in two-and-a-half days until, he states, "my fingers, clammy and trembling, refused to serve me."[2] Interweaving dream sequences with visionary abstracts of reality, *Man and the Masses* spotlights an upper-class woman who leads a revolutionary strike. Her husband, a state employee, complains that she is "crippling" his career. When the woman remains loyal to her cause, the husband leaves home.

"The masters build their palaces, while our brothers rot in the trenches," grumble workers who ignore the woman's pleas for non-violence. A bloody confrontation ensues and many of the strikers are killed by volleys of machine guns. The woman is imprisoned. Her comrades hatch a plan to free her, but because it would kill a guard, she rejects this route to freedom. "If I took but one human life," she says, "I should betray the Masses… No man may kill men for a cause." The woman remains in her cell and is executed.

Translated by Louis Untermeyer, *Man and the Masses* was produced in 1924 at London's New Theatre with Sybil Thorndike as The Woman (four performances), and at New York's Garrick Theatre with Blanche Yurke (thirty-two performances).

Die Maschinensturmer (*The Machine Wreckers*) unfolds in London and Nottingham, and spans between 1812 and 1815. The play is inspired by the historical Luddite revolt of 1815 in Nottingham in the wake of industrialization. Strike workers attack a weaving factory, destroy its machinery, and beat to death one of their leaders, who advocates peaceful resistance. The drama was first produced by famed director Max Reinhardt in Berlin in 1922 and was shown all over Europe. It reached London in 1923 and New York in 1937.

Toller's *Feuer aus den kesseln* (*Draw the Fires*!) is dedicated "To the memory of the sailors Köbis and Reichpietsch who were shot on the 5th of September, 1917." The play chronicles the events on the German battleship *Prinzregent Luitpold* during the Battle of Jutland in 1916. Several sailors complained of the harsh treatment inflicted by their officers and as a result were accused of high treason, tricked into confession, and condemned to the firing squad. *Draw the Fires*! was performed in Berlin in 1930, and in London five years later.

Hoppla! Wir leben! (Hopla! Such Is Life! 1935) mixes live action with cinematographic images. The play begins in a large prison cell where six revolutionaries are awaiting execution. The warden, Rand, enters and declares that five of them have been granted clemency; the sixth prisoner, Wilhelm Kilman, is to remain. The revolutionaries go their way, believing that Kilman will be shot. Eight years later, they find that Kilman has not only been released but has become an important administrator in the government. Under his command are "first-class spies" tracking dissidents. When one of his former cellmates, Karl Thomas, accuses Kilman of being a traitor to the cause and the common man, Kilman brushes him off, declaring that "the mob is impotent" and that "power brings responsibility."

Kilman is elevated to the position of prime minister. Karl Thomas plans to kill Kilman in the private room of a restaurant, but a disgruntled student gets there first and fatally shoots him. "Because he's a Bolshevist, because he's a revolutionary, because he's sold our country to the Jews," explains the student to Karl Thomas as he flees the scene. Thomas is accused of the murder and is sent to prison. The last scene unfolds simultaneously in several cells where the prisoners learn that the real murderer of Kilman has been caught. But it is too late for Karl Thomas. He had earlier torn a strip of a bed sheet, fastened it to the door-hook, climbed on a stool, and hung himself.

Toller had to leave Germany when the Nazis took over. He went on lecture tours in Europe and America, campaigned against Franco in Spain, and spent a short period of time as a writer in Hollywood. Sorrowful of world affairs on the threshold of World War II, and despondent when his wife, twenty-five years his junior, left him, Toller hung himself in a New York hotel in May of 1939. He was only forty-five years old.

A play about Ernst Toller, entitled *Toller*, by Tankred Dorst, was produced in Milan, Italy, by the Piccolo Teatro in 1971. The drama focuses on the playwright during the failed 1919 rebellion in Bavaria.

* * *

(William) Denis Johnston was born in Dublin into a family of lawyers. He was educated at Andrew's College in Dublin, Merchiston Castle School in Edinburgh, and Harvard Law School in Cambridge, Massachusetts. While working as a barrister in Dublin, Johnston got involved in theatrical activities. He submitted his first play, *Rhapsody in Green*, to the Abbey Theatre but the typescript was returned to him with the notation, "The Old Lady says 'No!'" written on it, a reference to Artistic Director Lady Gregory. The play was produced at the Gate Theatre in 1929, using this remark as its title.

Stylistically, Johnston was influenced by Ernst Toller, whom he admired. His best known play is *The Moon in the Yellow River*, an absurdist, symbolic satire about an electrical engineer, Dobelle, who zealously keeps his hydroelectric station outside Dublin functioning. Blake, a revolutionary, tries to blow up the generator and is shot. F.J. McCormick enacted Dobelle and Denis O'Dea portrayed Blake in the original Abbey Theatre production (1931), roles played by Claude Rains and Henry Hull on Broadway the following year.

Johnston joined the board of the Gate Theatre, where two of his plays were mounted: A *Bride for the Unicorn* (1933), a drama of complex symbolism, and *Storm Song* (1934), a comedy about a film director.

In the late 1930s Johnston joined the BBC in Belfast as a radio producer and moved to London to work in the new medium of television. But he continued to write plays with a message. Like *Blind Man'sBuff*, Johnston's *The Golden Cuckoo* (1939) attacks the blindness of the legal system, which is not concerned with guilt or innocence, but with appearances.

During World War II, Johnston served as a war correspondent for BBC. The campaign in Africa, which he admired, and the concentration camp at Buchenwald, which shocked him, were experiences he recorded in the autobiographical *Nine Rivers from Jordan* (1953). In 1948, Johnston moved to New York, where he worked as a freelance author for the Theatre Guild. He also began teaching at Mount Holyoke, Amherst, and Smith colleges in Massachusetts. In 1956, Johnston returned to his quest for societal justice in by penning *Strange Occurrence on Ireland's Eye*, a reworking of *Blind Man's Buff.*

Acting Edition: Random House (together with Ernst Toller's *Pastor Hall*).

Awards and Honors: Denis Johnston was awarded the OBE (Officer of the British Empire) in 1948. He received honorary degrees from the University of Ulster and Mount Holyoke College.

NOTES

1. Ernst Toller, *Seven Plays by Ernst Toller* (New York: Liveright Publishing Corporation, 1936), ix.
2. *Ibid*, 111.

Johnny Belinda (1940)

Elmer Harris (United States, 1878-1966)

The time is 1900. The place is Prince Edward Island, off the coast of Nova Scotia. The action unfolds in a bleak little village perched on a cliff.

It is a semi-primitive environment. Hard-bitten Scotch-Irish farmers live in houses made of weather-beaten shingles, with tall peaked roofs to shed the weight of winter snow. The farmers divide their time between fishing and tilling the stubborn soil.

The curtain rises on a street corner. Among the key characters who pass by are the newly arrived Dr. Jack Davidson, a young and kind man; the hypochondriac Mrs. Lutz; the sniffy, gossipy Mrs. McKee, the "first lady" of the community; Locky McCormick, the village Lothario; and Stella Maguire, who is enamored with him.

The scene moves to Grist Mill, a property belonging to the gruff widower Black McDonald. Dr. Davidson pays McDonald a visit and meets Black's deaf-mute daughter, Belinda. She is barefoot, in a ragged dress, scooping grain from a sack into the hopper.

Dr. Davidson learns that the villagers consider Belinda mentally retarded and refer to her as "the dummy." He suggests that McDonald send Belinda to a school for the deaf in Montreal. The farmer insists that he needs Belinda to fulfill her daily chores. Davidson undertakes to teach Belinda sign language and gradually the pair develop a close rapport.[1]

During a party that takes place in the grounds of Grist Mill, Locky McCormick corners Belinda in a barn and despite her protestations, he seizes her around the waist, forces her on a pile of sacks, and rips open her dress. Locky holds Belinda powerless as the curtain comes down.

Months lapse. Belinda gives birth to a baby boy, Johnny. Locky McCormick marries Stella, and no one is aware that he is the father of Belinda's child. Malicious gossip mongers label Dr. Davidson the father. When Black McDonald learns the truth, he intends to "blow Locky's guts out," but Davidson calms him down and offers to marry Belinda.

During a heavy storm, Black McDonald is struck by lightning and dies. Locky arrives unexpectedly, accompanied by Mrs. McKee. Mrs. McKee says that she represents "the good ladies in the village," and exhibits a signed petition to let Locky and Stella adopt Belinda's child, thus taking him away from "the brazen hussy."

Slowly, Belinda realizes what is happening. When she tries to block Locky from entering the baby's room, he slaps her face and yanks her away from the door. Belinda gets a gun, slips two shells into the chamber, and exits after Locky. Off stage we hear Locky yelling, "Dummy, don't!" followed by the sound of a shot.

The last scene of the play unfolds in a courtroom. Stella, Locky's widow, causes a sensation when she testifies that Locky had confided to her that he was the father of Belinda's baby. Defense Counsel McVail asserts that Belinda was merely trying to protect her child.

The climactic sequence of the trial – and the play – occurs when Belinda is called to the stand and Dr. Davidson signs the judge's queries. Belinda responds with hand movements of her own. Davidson translates, relating to the judge Belinda's emotional statement that she loves her boy "better – than – my life," and that she shot Locky because she was afraid that "he – would – hurt – my – child."

The judge orders that the child be returned to his mother and dismisses the case. A matron brings the baby. Belinda rushes from the dock, takes the boy lovingly in her arms, and utters, "John-ny!" Jack Davidson is shocked and delighted. Belinda takes his hand and they saunter out together.

* * *

Johnny Belinda opened at the Belasco Theatre in New York on September 18, 1940. Most of the critics were unhappy. "An overdose of melodrama," complained Sidney B. Whipple.[2] "An evening at once lugubrious and hackneyed," sniffed John Mason Brown.[3] "It is shameless in its sentimentality… just trash," pounced Richard Watts, Jr.[4] Brooks Atkinson guffawed at a play containing "seduction, child-birth, death by lightning, murder by shot-gun, a snowstorm, a Canadian Mounted in scarlet uniform and a court room scene… Elmer Harris has exhausted the art and craft of the drama."[5] Only Burns Mantle supported "a good old-fashioned emotional evening in the theatre."[6]

In spite of the negative reception, *Johnny Belinda* ran for 321 performances. A successful road company production traveled across the U.S. during 1941-1942. A Yiddish adaptation was mounted at the Parkway Theatre of Brooklyn, New York, in 1942, and the Wimbledon Theatre in England produced *Johnny Belinda* ten years later.

A musical version of *Johnny Belinda*, with book by Mavor Moore and music by John Fenwick, premiered on July 1, 1968, at the Charlottetown Festival in Canada. Subsequent productions were seen in Toronto, Montreal, and Ottawa. A television adaptation of the musical, called *Belinda*, was telecast by the CBC on March 9, 1977.

The Charlestown Confederation Centre for the Arts, located in Charlottetown, Prince Edward Island, resuscitated Elmer Harris's play in the summers of 1998 and 2000. Several American amateur companies presented *Johnny Belinda* at the dawn of the twenty-first century.

In 1948, Warner Brothers transferred *Johnny Belinda* to the screen. Jean Negulesco directed a moody, compelling film, highlighted by Jane Wyman's sensitive portrayal of Belinda McDonald. The movie took some liberties: Belinda's father confronts seducer Locky McCormick, and during a tussle, Locky pushes Black off a cliff to his death. Stephen McNally, who plays Locky, appeared (as Horace McNally) in the original Broadway production in the role of Dr. Jack Davidson. *Johnny Belinda* was nominated for eleven Academy Awards, including Best Picture, Screenplay, Director, and Cinematography. Jane Wyman won for Best Actress.

Johnny Belinda was aired as a radio play by the CBC in 1950. The play was adapted to television by NBC in 1958, with Julie Harris (Belinda), Christopher Plummer (Dr. Davidson), Victor Jory (Black McDonald), and Rip Torn (Locky McCormick). ABC televised *Johnny Belinda* in 1967, featuring Mia Farrow, Ian Bannen, Barry Sullivan, and David Carradine. Warner Brothers remade *Johnny Belinda* in a 1982 television movie, starring Rosanna Arquette, Richard Thomas, Roberts Blossom, and Dennis Quaid.

* * *

Elmer Blaney Harris was born in Chicago in 1878. After a fire destroyed his father's broom factory, the family moved to Oakland, California. In 1898, Harris began to study acting at the University of California, Berkeley, where he wrote and acted for his school's Skull & Keys club.

Harris's theatrical activities attracted the attention of Phoebe Apperson Hearst, the mother of William Randolph Hearst. With her financial backing he traveled to England, where he mingled with renowned actors and producers; to France, where he joined Benoit Constant Coquelin's company; and to Germany, where his first play – *Tempesta* – was produced in Hamburg.

In 1905, Harris returned to California. He lectured on Shaw and Ibsen, wrote articles and drama critiques, served as a reporter for the *San Francisco Call-Bulletin*, and, with a group of fellow writers, established an artists' colony in Carmel-by-the-Sea.

Harris began penning plays in 1907 and soon found himself writing for both the stage and the cinema, dividing his efforts between the East and West coasts. For Broadway, Harris wrote *The Offenders* (1908), a melodrama about political corruption; *Sham* (1909), a farce throwing barbs at the hypocrisy of high society; a series of domestic comedies in the late 1920s and early 1930s;

and the drama *The Man Who Killed Lincoln* (1940), focusing on actor John Wilkes Booth.

In Hollywood, Harris contributed original screenplays and adaptations for major studios.At United Artists, he wrote scripts for Mary Pickford and Douglas Fairbanks. For Columbia Pictures, he drew up the story for Frank Capra's first film, *The Matinee Idol* (1928).

Harris's crime-oriented movies include *Father and Son* (1929), *Young Sinners* (1931), *Cross Country Cruise* (1934), *Looking for Trouble* (1934), *Let 'em Have It* (1935), and *The Three Wise Guys* (1936).

In 1934, Harris wrote the screenplay for *The Inner Silence*, the story of a deaf- mute woman who is raped by the town thug on Prince Edward Island. It was the genesis of *Johnny Belinda.*

Acting Edition: Dramatists Play Service.

NOTES

1. Playwright Harris suggests that groups contemplating a production of *Johnny Belinda* should familiarize themselves with sign language invented by the eighteenth-century French priest, the Abbe de l'Epee.
2. *New York World-Telegram*, September 19, 1940.
3. *New York Post*, September 19, 1940.
4. *New York Herald Tribune*, September 19, 1940.
5. *New York Times*, September 19, 1940.
6. *Daily News*, September 19, 1940.

Native Son (1941)

Paul Green (United States, 1894-1981) and Richard Wright (United States, 1908-1960)

Paul Green and Richard Wright turned the latter's best-selling 1940 novel, *Native Son*, into a ten-scene play that was mounted on Broadway by the Mercury Theatre in 1941.

We first meet the lead character, Bigger Thomas, a bitter, rebellious twenty-year-old African American, in a rat-infested one-room apartment, located in the crowded Black Belt of Chicago's south side. Bigger shares the small dwelling with his mother, Hannah, middle-aged, tired, and worn; his sister Vera, a timid sixteen-year-old; and his brother Buddy, an eager and spunky boy of twelve.

There is good news as the play opens. Miss Emmet, a kindly and efficient social worker, arrives to tell Bigger that she found a position for him. The landlord, Mr. Dalton, needs a chauffeur. She has told Mr. Dalton that Bigger has spent time in a reform school for stealing automobiles, but Mr. Dalton, always interested in placing his jobless tenants, will accept Bigger despite the young man's checkered past.

The scene ends on an ominous note: A signal whistle comes up from outside the window. Bigger calls his cronies Jack and Ernie to wait for him. He pulls out from under the bed a wooden box, unlocks it, takes out a pistol, crams the weapon into his coat, and quickly goes out. Hannah gazes worriedly after him as the lights fade out.

Scene 2 takes place on a sidewalk in front of Ernie's Kitchen Shack. Bigger meets his pals, the short and pudgy Jack Hanson, and Gus Mitchell, a small guy wearing his cap turned around like a baseball catcher. They huddle in whispers, hatching a plan to rob Blum's pawnshop. They speculate that there should be at least $150 in the cash register.

Clara Mears, an attractive Black girl, sashays in, carrying a package. She admonishes Bigger for failing to show up the night before and coaxes him for a date that night. Gus sneezes twice and says fearfully, "That's a sign o' bad luck!" Bigger scolds him for being "a superstitious nigger."

Scene 3 unfolds in Henry G. Dalton's breakfast room. His blind wife, Ellen, and his private detective, Jeff Britten, are present when Dalton interviews Bigger. Dalton goes over Bigger's file and notices that Bigger's father was killed in a Mississippi race riot when the applicant was five years old.

Bigger tells him that he has a driver's license and that he can handle any kind of car. As Bigger is questioned, the sound of an automatic furnace turning itself on is audible. Bigger is told that one of his duties will be to stoke the furnace and clean out its ashes.

Soon Bigger meets the Dalton's neurotic daughter, Mary, who bluntly declares, "I'm the pampered daughter and heiress to all of the Dalton millions." She orders Bigger to light her cigarette and tells him that tonight he will drive her to a political rally of a special friend, Edward Max, who is running for district attorney.

Scene 4 begins with a giggling Mary Dalton pulling a reluctant Bigger into her bedroom. She is heavily intoxicated. Bigger, dressed in his chauffeur's uniform, pleads, "Lemme go, Miss Dalton. This ain't my job." Mary falls suddenly into his arms. Frantic, he drags her to the bed. From the hallway comes Mrs. Dalton's voice, "Mary – is that you, Mary?" and the door opens. Mrs. Dalton's tall form is visible, standing in a white dressing gown. Bigger, petrified, watches the blind woman move farther into the room, and backs noiselessly. "Mary, are you asleep?" asks Mrs. Dalton. She reaches the bed, fumbles for a coverlet and spreads it over Mary's feet. She turns back towards the door and a low sigh of relief passes through Bigger's lips. Mrs. Dalton wheels about. Instinctively, Bigger picks up a pillow and pushes it into Mary's face. Her hands move, clawing helplessly at his arms. He holds the pillow against her, anxiously watching Mrs. Dalton. After a moment, Mrs. Dalton exits silently, closing the door behind her.

Bigger is momentarily relieved, but then stares down at Mary, touches her, and trembles violently, realizing that she is dead. The hum of the furnace is heard from below. The sound grows louder as Bigger rushes through the door carrying Mary's body in his arms.

The curtain rises on Clara Mears' kitchenette apartment. In the street outside a chorus sings a Christmas carol. Bigger tells Clara that the daughter of his employer is missing. She is wild enough, says Bigger, to elope with a lover. Why not make it seem like she has been kidnapped. We can cash in, says Bigger, we can ask for $10,000. They got millions – won't miss it.

He gets his gloves from his coat pocket, puts them on, and chuckles, "That dumb detective can look for fingerprints, but he won't find any." Clara sobs and attempts to stop him, but Bigger begins to write, "Sir: we got your daughter – say nothing to the police – the ransom price is –" The lights dim.

At the basement of the Dalton's home, detective Britten and a lynx-eyed, middle-aged newspaperman named Jed Norris are milling around. Peggy MacAulife, the Dalton housekeeper, orders Bigger to stock the furnace. He picks up the coal shovel but makes no move to stir up the fire. Mr. Dalton enters and tells Britten and Norris that his daughter has been kidnapped.

Someone left a ransom note under the front door, demanding $10,000. Dalton tells Norris that if he can publish in the *Tribune*, he will pay the ransom.

Norris watches Bigger as he reaches out to open the furnace door, then backs off. Norris moves closer and taunts Bigger to shake the pile of ashes down. Fearful, Bigger plunges the shovel into the bank of glowing, red-hot ashes. A puff of dust sails out and settles about the room. Norris lifts a charred object from the ashes, and says, "It's a piece of bone." He picks up a bit of rounded metal and identifies it as an earring. Bigger stumbles out, and Norris tells Britten, "You'd better catch him. He raped and killed Mary Dalton and burned her body in the furnace!"

Bigger hides in an empty room on the top floor of an abandoned apartment house. He hears a siren and grips his gun tightly. Clara enters with a bag of food. She tells him that his picture is on the front pages and that a reward of $25,000 has been offered for his capture.

Bigger tells Clara that he never meant to kill anyone, that it was an accident. He just pushed the pillow over Mary's mouth to keep her from talking. Clara pleads with Bigger to give himself up. Suddenly, a bright light floods into the room. A heavy pounding is heard from below. "You set 'em on me, you bitch!" screams Bigger. He grabs Clara and holds her protectively in front of him. Shots ring out and she sags in his arms, dead. He shoots at the door and keeps firing as the scene fades out.

In the city courtroom, district attorney David Buckley calls the defendant "a sub-human killer" and demands the death penalty. Defense attorney Edward Max declares that the press, radio, even the authorities have inflamed public opinion against the prisoner from the very beginning and pleads for Bigger on the basis of the young man's deprived upbringing and racial suffering. "In this courtroom today not only Bigger Thomas is on trial but our American civilization," argues Max, asking the judge to spare Bigger's life.

The lights come up on a death row cell. Hannah, Vera, and Buddy have said their good-byes and leave sobbing. Attorney Max assures Bigger that because of him justice and freedom are nearer. The door of the execution chamber opens, and light streams out. Bigger pushes off the hands of the guards, straightens his shoulders and goes defiantly toward the light. The guards follow. The door closes behind them. From the death cell comes the hum of the deadly dynamo that puts the end to Bigger's short and troubled life.

* * *

Directed by Orson Welles, *Native Son* premiered at the St. James Theatre in New York City on March 24, 1941. Canada Lee played the confused, defiant Bigger Thomas. The critics were sharply divided. Brooks Atkinson applauded "a powerful drama."[1] Burns Mantle believed it to be "the most sensational of this season's dramas."[2] Sidney B. Whipple found here "a relentless, cruel and compelling document that holds the listener in its emotional grip long after the curtain has descended."[3]

On the other hand, John Anderson called *Native Son* an "uneven play... overwrought with a sort of monotonous hysteria, phony in its argument and finally tiresome."[4] Richard Watts, Jr. concluded that the "drama is considerably less impressive than the book from which it is derived."[5]

There was unanimous praise for Orson Welles' intermissionless "dynamic" staging, James Morom's "grimly imaginative sets," and Canada Lee's "clean, honest, driving performance of remarkable versatility."

Native Son ran for 114 performances. The play was revived at the Majestic Theatre on October 23, 1942, with Canada Lee reprising the role of Bigger Thomas for eighty-four performances. A somewhat revised version of the drama was produced by the Carolina Playmakers for the dedication of the Paul Green Theatre at the University of North Carolina in Chapel Hill, on September 29, 1978.

In 2000 and 2002, an adaptation of Richard Wright's novel by Christopher McElroen was presented by the Classical Theatre of Harlem. Anita Gates of the *New York Times* called the production "admirable," performed by an ensemble "uniformly good."[6]

Despite being twice the age of Bigger Thomas, Richard Wright himself portrayed the title role of *Native Son* in a 1951 screen version of his novel. He was supported by Willa Pearl Curtis as Mrs. Hannah Thomas, Ruth Robert as Mrs. Ellen Dalton, and Jean Wallace as Mary Dalton. A 1986 remake cast Victor Love (Bigger), Oprah Winfrey (Mrs. Thomas), Carroll Baker (Mrs. Dalton), and Elizabeth McGovern (Mary Dalton).

Acting Edition: Samuel French, Inc.

Awards and Honors: A top-ten selection in *The Best Plays of 1940-1941*.

NOTES

1. *New York Times*, March 25, 1941.
2. *Daily News*, March 25, 1941.
3. *New York World-Telegram*, March 25, 1941.
4. *New York Journal American*, March 25, 1941.
5. *New York Herald Tribune*, March 25, 1941.
6. *New York Times*, February 20, 2002.

Pick-Up Girl (1944)

Elsa Shelley (United States, Russia-born, c.1905-1968)

First called *Elizabeth vs.You and Me*, Elsa Shelley's *Pick-Up Girl* is a courtroom drama dealing with war-time juvenile delinquency. Shelley, an actress married to playwright Irving Kaye Davis, became interested in the issue of restless female adolescents who were making themselves available to servicemen on leave. She put a great deal of time into researching the alarming social dilemma, attending court room trials and visiting reform schools. She offered the materials to her husband to fashion into a play, but Davis suggested that she first try it herself. Shelley's manuscript made the rounds of Broadway producers and was finally accepted by famed producer Michael Todd.

The entire action of *Pick-Up Girl* unfolds in the sparse courtroom of a New York juvenile court. Judge Bentley, "a keen-eyed, stern-looking man" of great sensitivity, is at the desk signing documents. The judge does not wear the customary robes, but a well-tailored business suit instead. Mrs. Busch, a middle-aged probation officer, is at a table below the judge's platform. Miss Porter, the court stenographer, "a spinster lady of about forty," is sorting papers at another table behind the witness chair.

The case in motion is that of fifteen-year-old Elizabeth Collins, "a golden-haired, baby-faced girl, with a beautiful maturing figure." She is brought in by a uniformed policeman and turned over to Mrs. Busch, who guides her to a chair. Elizabeth, still very much a teenager, is obviously bewildered and scared.

Police Officer Owens is the first witness called, recounting how he answered a complaint about an act of immorality that might take place that night. Owens took position across the street from the apartment house in question. Soon after, a man and a boy entered the apartment. When the boy left, Owens went in.

Three young children were asleep in a bedroom. No parents were around. In another bedroom, Owens found Mr. Alexander Elliott, wearing only his undershirt, and the girl Elizabeth Collins stark naked. He ordered them to dress. Owens arrested Elliott, who was arraigned and held for a felony count, and the girl, who was placed in the detention home.

Judge Bentley questions Alexander Elliott, who admits to being forty-seven-years-old and insists that he was not aware that Elizabeth was only fifteen. He also claims that it was her who threw herself at him. The judge admonishes Elliott and tells him that he will soon be summoned to criminal court.

Next the Judge calls for Ruby Lockwood, "a coarse-looking girl of sixteen, blonde, stylishly dressed, a fur around her shoulders; loud makeup, sexy, impudent in every look and gesture." Ruby testifies that Elizabeth met Elliott at a party and has no doubt that Elizabeth "schemed" to meet Elliott, even though she, Ruby, told all the girls "to lay off him." Elizabeth double-crossed her by attempting to hook her man.

A middle-aged, nervous Mrs. Marti testifies that she lives in the same house as the Collins family. She is a widow supporting herself and her son Peter by dressmaking. Peter studies the violin, and "everybody said he should become a great violinist like Heifetz." She was the one who had registered a complaint about Elizabeth Collins. Her son is fond of Elizabeth and insists on being friends with her. Elizabeth, who used to be "a sweet girl," has recently become friends with Ruby Lockwood, "a bad girl," and has completely changed. Two weeks ago, late at night, she overheard Elizabeth and her rough friend Larry planning a night visit by a Mr. Elliott. It was then that she decided to call the police.

Elizabeth's parents are questioned next. Mrs. Collins testifies that she is the mother of four children, Elizabeth being the oldest. Both of the Collins are presently working, she as a cook for a theatrical couple, he in a shipyard in California. Elizabeth has been helping with the housework and looks after her younger siblings. Mrs. Collins admits that Marti told her that Elizabeth was hanging out with Ruby, but she told Mrs. Marti to mind her own business. Mrs. Marti was always "squeaking about someone or other."

Judge Bentley calls for Elizabeth. She relates that she began running around with Ruby when she needed a dress for her graduation dance. Ruby loaned her a dress and then, one night, took her for a walk down Broadway to Times Square. They stood at West Forty-third Street, where two sailors from the merchant marine asked that they join them for dinner at The Park Inn. After dinner Elizabeth took a room with one of the sailors, Jerry, dizzy with drinks. That was the first time she had had intimate relations with a man, says Elizabeth, and it got her pregnant. Ruby took her to get an abortion and Jerry paid the bill.

Mrs. Collins weeps silently and Mr. Collins crumples his hat in his hands. Elizabeth insists that she hasn't been "familiar" with older men since then. She and some girl friends went out with them only for such fun as ice cream and cake. She didn't want Alex Elliott to come to her house but the boy Larry insisted and she had to open the door for them because they kept ringing the bell and she didn't want the kids to wake up. After Elliott sent Larry for a bottle, he started to make passes, pushed her into the bedroom, and pulled off her robe.

During a recess, Peter Marti suggests to Elizabeth that if the judge sends her to jail, they will run away. He tells her to ask to go the ladies' room where there's a window. In his violin case there is a long scarf. By tying one end to the water pipe Elizabeth can let herself out the window and down to within jumping distance of the yard. Peter will be waiting for her and before anyone will miss them, they'd be far away.

Judge Bentley calls Mr. and Mrs. Collins and reveals to them that a medical check concluded that Elizabeth has venereal disease. The judge informs them of his decision: Elizabeth will be taken away from them, first to a hospital, then to the State Training School for Girls at Hudson. Mrs. Collins, crying, blames herself for neglecting her daughter, but the judge says that "It's the fault of all of us. It's our indifference, our greediness, that's at fault. We don't realize that the *real* natural wealth in the world is in children."

When Elizabeth hears that she is to be taken away, she falls apart, but Judge Bentley assures her that with some help she will be a credit to her community, her country, her parents – and herself. Peter is standing by the door waiting for her to ask for permission to go to the bathroom. Yet instead, Elizabeth asks the judge permission to return something her friend gave her.

Elizabeth opens her pocketbook and gives Peter his scarf. He frantically tries to give it back to her, but she promises that while away she'll be thinking about how *much* he wanted to do for her.

Mrs. Busch and Elizabeth pass through the hall door. Peter stands staring after them as the curtain falls.

* * *

Pick-Up Girl opened at New York's 48th Street Theatre on May 3, 1944, directed by Roy Hargrave, featuring William Harrigan as Judge Bentley and Pamela Rivers as Elizabeth Collins. Most of the critics appreciated the restrained presentation of a volatile topic. "A candid and sincere play," wrote Herrick Brown.[1] "It is admirably acted, cleverly directed and often movingly written," stated John Chapman.[2] "It's the most effective trial play I've ever seen, with the possible exception of *The Trial of Mary Dugan*," exclaimed Robert Garland.[3] "I'd say this play is perfect in every way—in concept, in characterization, in thematic progression, in observation of court procedure, in realism, in the acting, the staging, the costuming and the setting, in mood, emotional depth, taste and intelligence," gushed Burton Rascoe.[4]

On the other hand, Lewis Nichols found *Pick-Up Girl* "talky, often dull and, on the occasion when it changes pace, it lunges over into a shrill hysteria."[5] "Elsa Shelley's play is grimy exhaustive," sighed Howard Barnes.[6] "It is aping facts rather than achieving truth… what Miss Shelley does invent on the side seems all too concocted," scoffed Louis Kronenberger.[7]

Pick-Up Girl ran for 198 performances. Peter Cotes, soon to be known as the director of Agatha Christie's mega hit *The Mousetrap*, staged *Pick-Up Girl* in 1946 in London, where it was seen by Queen Mary and moved from a club theatre in Notting Hill into the West End, running 170 performances.

ITV Television Playhouse aired *Pick-Up Girl* in 1957. Three years later it was adapted to the screen as *Too Young to Love* with Thomas Mitchell as Judge Bentley and Pauline Hahn as Elizabeth Collins.

* * *

Elsa Shelley, born in Russia, grew up in America. She went to school in New York and took extension courses at Columbia University. Shelley's parents wanted her to be a musician, but she decided upon an acting career. Her breakthrough came in 1928, when she appeared with Ethel Barrymore in *The Lady of the Camelias*, as Juliet to Walter Hampden's Romeo, and in feature roles in the musical *Veils*, the melodrama *Caravan*, and Edgar Wallace's thriller *Sign of the Leopard*. In 1930, Shelley performed a one-woman dramatic monologue, *Courtesan*, written by her husband, Irving Kaye Davis.

Following her success as a playwright with *Pick-Up Girl*, Shelley penned two more plays for Broadway, but none had the same impact. *Foxhole in the Parlor* (1945) featured Montgomery Clift as a former soldier afflicted by a trauma caused by his war experiences. The drama ran for forty-five performances. *With a Silk Thread* (1950), which Shelley also directed, starred Claire Luce as a jealous, neurotic actress. It lasted thirteen performances.

Acting Edition: Gorgi Books

Awards and Honors: A top-ten selection in *The Best Plays of 1943-1944*. In 1945, Elsa Shelley was awarded the Scroll of Merit by the New York University School of Education for service to youth in playwriting.

NOTES

1. *New York Sun*, May 4, 1944.
2. *Daily News*, May 4, 1944.
3. *New York Journal-American*, May 4, 1944.
4. *New York World-Telegram*, May 4, 1944.
5. *New York Times*, May 4, 1944.
6. *New York Herald Tribune*, May 4, 1944.
7. *PM*, May 4, 1944.

Anne of the Thousand Days (1948)

Maxwell Anderson (United States, 1888-1957)

Anne of the Thousand Days is Maxwell Anderson's verse-and-prose prequel to *Elizabeth the Queen* (1930) and *Mary of Scotland* (1933). A play of memory, it begins in the year 1536 when Anne Boleyn, the second wife of Henry VIII, is imprisoned within the Tower of London, musing as to whether or not she is slated for execution: "Would he kill me? Henry? The fool? The great fool, kill me?" She is reminiscing about her thousand days of star-crossed romance with the King of England, captured in the form of sequential fade-outs.

Henry's mistress of many years was Mary Boleyn. But now the impetuous monarch desires her younger sister Anne, who is engaged to Lord Henry Percy, Earl of Northumberland. When the maiden's father, Thomas Boleyn, attempts to intervene, Henry tells him curtly:

> I am younger than you. I am younger than Wolsey.
> I am younger than many dukes and earls and peers.
> But I am the King of England. When I pray God answers.
> I will not have this questioned.

Henry woos Anne as "a doubting, hoping, tremulous man", but she fires back:

> I've seen you too close
> and known you too long. I've heard what your couriers say,
> and then I've seen what you are. You're spoiled and vengeful,
> and malicious and bloody...

Anne's resistance fans the king's passion. He explains to Anne that the marriage to Catherine, his brother's widow, was forced upon him for political reasons— "I've never loved her. I should never have married her. There's a curse on the marriage. We cannot have sons. Our sons are born dead. There is no male heir to the English crown because of this accursed union... yet because of the church, I remain Catherine's husband". Anne insists,

> If you will marry and make me
> Queen of England

I will give you boys in plenty,
but I will take nothing less.

Henry places Anne in York Palace—the beginning of a volatile, love-hate relationship between two willful, ambitious, brutish people with few scruples. The reluctant Anne sets a high price for her consent, but Cardinal Wolsey informs the king "The Pope will not annul your marriage to Catherine." Henry maintains, "There must be a divorce this year. Nan is with child—and her child must be heir to the throne". Wearily, Wolsey says, "I have marshaled cardinals and bishops like storm troops to assail the Pope's position. I have tried from every angle, from every direction, with money, influence, and temporal power. I have run my head against this wall like a bull in a stone barn—till there's blood dripping in my eyes and I'm worn out." It is Thomas Cromwell, the king's cunning adviser, who informs Henry of an old, forgotten law "that makes it treason to acknowledge any higher authority than the will of the king. The church in England must grant the king a divorce if he wishes it. To maintain that the Pope may govern the king in such a matter—or in any matter—is traitorous and punishable by death… At one stroke you could obtain your divorce and make yourself the wealthiest monarch in Europe. The monasteries of England are richer than the gold mines of the new world. Quarrel with Rome, set yourself the head of the English church, and these riches are yours." Henry makes a decision: "The alter of St. Paul's will stand ankle-deep in blood. The shop-keepers will mop blood from their floors—but it must be done…" The king marries Anne and sends many of his friends to the block, including Sir Thomas More.

Henry is bitterly disappointed when he learns that Anne has borne not a boy but a little daughter— "and her name's to be Elizabeth." Now that feisty Anne has mellowed into a loving wife and mother, the king turns his affections towards lady-in-waiting Jane Seymour. False witnesses are threatened and tortured into admitting carnal affairs with Queen Anne. In a chamber trial conducted by Cromwell, she is adjudged guilty and sentenced to the gallows. Henry offers exile to Anne and daughter with the condition that she signs a nullification of their marriage, but Anne chooses the executioner's axe, preserving for Elizabeth a succession claim to the throne.

According to John Chapman, "*Anne of the Thousand Days* was a triumph of skill and perseverance… For, at the beginning of its tryout, *Anne* looked pretty hopeless. Witnesses found it cumbersome, and it needed an extraordinary amount of work—work which took time and increased the losses on the road."[1] When the play arrived at Manhattan's Shubert Theatre on December 8, 1948, it was greeted with hosannas by the critics: "Fascinating and absorbing… a literate, rewarding and stirring evening in the theatre"—Robert Coleman;[2] "A sonorous, robust and panoplied drama… much more than a historical pageant; it is profoundly compassionate"—John Chapman;[3] "Broadway and Maxwell Anderson have another 'should-see' attraction to their credit"—Robert Garland;[4] "A vivid and frequently soaring chronicle"—Ward Morehouse;[5] "A work to be cherished... a richly rewarding experience"—Howard Barnes;[6] "An old hand at scribbling about Kings and Queens, Maxwell Anderson has written one of his most stirring dramas"—Brooks Atkinson.[7] The sole dissenter, Richard Watts Jr., was untouched by "the conflict between a selfish, brutal, stubborn monarch and a shrill, shrewish and equally selfish woman."[8] Much praise was heaped on Joyce Redman and Rex Harrison in the leading roles, director H.C. Potter, designer Jo Mielziner, and costumer Motley. *Anne of the Thousand Days* ran for 286 performances.

The drama was transformed to the screen in 1969 under the direction of Charles Jarrott—145 minutes of historical pomp in Panavision, winning a costume Oscar for Margaret Furse. Richard Burton and Genevieve Bujold enacted Henry and Anne, ably assisted by Anthony Quayle as Cardinal Wolsey and John Colicos as counselor Cromwell. Henry's first wife, Catherine, who is only a shadow figure in the play version, appears here in the flesh, enacted by Irene Papas, defying the King— "I will live and I will die your wife and the Queen." The movie ends with the beheading of Anne as little Elizabeth walks away from the cameras to the sound-track echo, "She will be a great Queen."

Henry VIII was also portrayed in the cinema by Oscar-winning Charles Laughton—*The Private Life of Henry VIII* (1933), and on BBC-TV by highly acclaimed Keith Michell—*Henry VIII and His Six Wives* (1973). Richard Leech played Henry VIII in the London stage production of Robert Bolt's *A Man for all Seasons* (Globe Theatre, July 1, 1960), Keith Baxter on Broadway (ANTA Theatre, November 22, 1961), and Robert Shaw in a 1966 motion picture—depicting the clash between the monarch and Sir Thomas More (Paul Scofield in all three versions, garnering a Tony and an Oscar as Best Actor).

Acting Edition: Dramatists Play Service.

Awards and Honors: a top-ten selection in *The Best Plays of 1948-1949* ("A distinguished drama—the best I think, of all of Mr. Anderson's investigations of the loves of Kings and Queens.") [9]

NOTES

1. John Chapman, ed., *The Best Plays of 1948-1949*, (New York: Dodd, Mead and Company, 1949), 88.

2. *Daily Mirror,* December 9, 1948.
3. *Daily News,* December 9, 1948.
4. *New York Journal-American,* December 9, 1948.
5. *The Sun,* December 9, 1948.
6. *New York Herald Tribune,* December 9, 1948.
7. *New York Times,* December 9, 1948.
8. *New York Post,* December 9, 1948.
9. John Chapman, ed., *The Best Plays of 1948-1949* (New York, Dodd, Mead and Company, 1949), 12.

Lost in the Stars (1949)

Book and Lyrics: Maxwell Anderson (United States, 1888-1959), Music: Kurt Weill (Germany/United States, 1900-1950)

Based on the 1948 novel *Cry, the Beloved Country* by Alan Paton and told against a backdrop of racial strife in South Africa, *Lost in the Stars*, subtitled "A Musical Tragedy," is the poignant saga of a middle-aged, dignified Zulu Christian minister who leaves his humble village dwelling near Ndotsheni, Natal, in search of his erring son. Stephen Kumalo sings longingly about his son, Absolom, who has migrated to the metropolis Johannesbur

At the train station, Stephen is greeted warmly by Arthur Jarvis, a white acquaintance, who, in turn, is rebuked by his father James, a plantation Englishman, for speaking to a Black man. But Arthur holds his ground, insisting that he has friends among the Zulus. The chorus imitates an approaching train, "Clink, clink, clickety," and the passengers go aboard.

In the big city, Stephen doggedly pursues his son. He is unaware that in a distant, sleazy dive, Absalom is being coaxed by two delinquents, Johannes, and Mathew, to join them in the robbery of a house "that is never locked." Absalom is reluctant, but here is an opportunity to be "a new man—not somebody's dumb ox," and to get his sweetheart, Irina, into a better place than Shanty Town. Mathew insists that Absalom bring a gun— "If you're scared to carry that cheap revolver of yours, you're no use to us." At night, the three young men, with handkerchiefs over their faces, enter the plush Jarvis home. A servant confronts them, and Johannes strikes him with an iron bar. Arthur Jarvis runs into the doorway, and Absalom, frightened, fires his gun. The chorus chants a song of "Murder in Parkworld!"

James Jarvis mourns the death of his son. He finds bitter irony in the killing of an advocate of Negro equality by a Negro. Jarvis tells parole officer Eland that Blacks should be treated by "a stronger hand and a firm policy." Eland objects to blaming a whole race by the action of one misguided person.

Absolom is arrested. Eland takes Stephen to his son's cell. Absalom confesses to his father that he killed the white man. Dazed, Stephen sings the title song about a God who seemingly has gone away and people who are lost in the stars.

In court, Johannes and Matthew deny their involvement and are discharged. Absalom refuses to lie, admits to firing the fatal shot, and is condemned "to be hanged by the neck until he is dead."

On the eve of Absalom's execution, Stephen addresses his congregation with painful resignation, admitting to simmering doubts about the choice of good versus evil; he is not sure of his faith, he is lost. However, James Jarvis arrives unexpectedly at Stephen's home, tells him that he heard his speech, and realized they share the same grief. Perhaps something positive can come out of their terrible loss. He urges Stephen to stay in Ndotsheni — Let them be neighbors. Let them be friends. Stephen consents.

And as the clock strikes four, Absalom's execution time in Johannesburg, Jarvis goes to the mournful Stephen and puts an arm around him.

* * *

Lost in the Stars, staged by Rouben Mamoulian and designed by George Jenkins, premiered at the Music Box on October 30, 1949. The critics were split. An enthusiastic reception came from Brooks Atkinson, who wrote that "Out of a memorable novel has come a memorable musical drama,"[1] and Walter Kerr, who believed that the play "has excitement, flavor, heart and a stern authority."[2] Ward Morehouse saw "a colorful and soaring musical show. Let's be grateful for it,"[3] and John Chapman lauded "a magnificently pictorial and emotion-stirring theatre."[4]

Naysayers included Robert Garland, sniffing that "there is too much of words and music, production and direction, scenery and costumes."[5] Richard Watts Jr. said that "There is, indeed, very little lacking in *Lost in the Stars* save inspiration,"[6] and Robert Coleman complained that the musical "lacks the distinction one expects from the joint efforts of Maxwell Anderson, Kurt Weill and Rouben Mamoulian."[7] *Lost in the Stars* ran for 273 performances.

The reviewers hailed Todd Duncan, enacting Stephen Kumalo, and Leslie Banks as James Jarvis. When *Lost in the Stars* was transformed to the screen in 1974, director Daniel Mann cast Brook Peters and Paul Rogers in the roles.

Cry, the Beloved Country was filmed powerfully twice—in England, 1951, adapted by Alan Paton from his novel and directed by Zoltan Korda, with Canada Lee and Charles Carson; and in the U.S., 1995, scripted by Ronald Harwood, directed by Darrel James Roodt, starring James Earl Jones and Richard Harris.

A 1956 verse stage adaptation of *Cry, the Beloved Country* became the initial laboratory project of the late Lucille Lortel's innovative matinee series at Off Broadway's Theatre de Lys.

The first Maxwell Anderson-Kurt Weill collaboration was *Knickerbocker Holiday* (1938). Following the success of *Lost in the Stars,* the pair began working on another musical, *Twain on the River*, based on Mark Twain's *Tom Sawyer, Huckleberry Finn*, and *Life on the Mississippi*. Weill's death in 1950 curtailed the project.

* * *

Alan Paton was founder and National Chairman of the Liberty Party in South Africa until it was forced out of existence by the Nationalist government. Among his books about the beautiful and tragic South African landscape are *Too Late the Phalarope* (novel, 1935); *The Land and People of South Africa* (social study, 1955); *Tales from a Truthful Land* (short stories, 1961); *Sponono* (play, 1965); *Instrument of Thy Peace* (meditation, 1968); and *Towards the Mountain* (autobiography, 1980).

Perusal Material: The Rodgers and Hammerstein Organization.

Awards and Honors: A top-ten selection in *The Best Plays of 1948-1949* ("Probably no other team but the son of the preacher [Maxwell Anderson] and the son of the cantor [Kurt Weill] would have been inspired to make a musical theatre piece of so sweeping a work of fiction.")[8]

NOTES

1. *New York Times,* October 31, 1949.
2. *New York Herald Tribune,* October 31, 1949.
3. *The Sun,* October 31, 1949.
4. *Daily News,* October 31, 1949.
5. *New York Journal-American,* October 31, 1949.
6. *New York Post,* October 31, 1949.
7. *Daily Mirror,* October 31, 1949.
8. John Chapman, ed., *The Best Plays of 1949-1950* (New York: Dodd Mead and Company, 1950), 146.

A Pin to See the Peepshow (1951)

F. Tennyson Jesse (England 1888-1958) and H.M. Harwood (England, 1874-1959)

F. Tennyson Jesse and H. M. Harwood, a husband-and-wife team on several light-hearted thrillers, were in a grimmer mood when adapting to the stage the former's 1934 novel, *A Pin to See the Peepshow,* a fictional account of a real-life love triangle murder. Twenty-eight-year-old Edith Thompson had a successful London millinery store when in 1921 she attached herself to Frederick Bywaters, a shipping clerk eight years her junior, and together began planning the elimination of Thompson's stodgy, bossy husband, Percy. On the evening of October 3, 1922, Percy Thompson was found stabbed to death on a side road. The relationship between Edith and Frederick was soon established, damning correspondence between them was unearthed, and bloodstains were discovered on young Bywaters' jacket. The lovers were found guilty and on January 9, 1923, they were hung.[1]

The play version of *A Pin to See the Peepshow* unfolds in two acts divided into thirteen scenes. Beginning in spring 1916, we follow Julia Almond, whose youthful ambition is "going into a shop, a dress shop." Julia's querulous mother disapproves, but the nineteen-year-old girl interviews for the position of apprentice at a fashionable dress shop and is hired.

By the winter of 1920, Julia has been promoted, and regularly travels to Paris as a buyer. To get away from her drab home, she marries a middle-aged neighbor — Herbert Starling, a commissioned officer in His Majesty's Forces. Soon Julia realizes that they have nothing in common, and the fact that her salary is larger than Starling's is a constant source of irritation and bickering.

Julia soon meets a young sailor, Leonard Carr, and they fall in love. When Starling is found dead in a town square, his skull fractured, the relationship between Leonard and Julia is revealed. Letters written by Julia, found on Leo's ship, expressing the wish that her husband be "out of the way," are deemed incriminating enough to charge them with murder. Both are found guilty and condemned to hang.

The last few prison scenes are harrowing: Julia screams, tries to climb the green wall of her cell. She grabs at it with her nails, nearly mad. A doctor injects her with morphine. Two matrons converse quietly, one of them expressing the playwright's maxim that Julia is conceivably innocent: "I like her. I don't think she's bad... She got caught up in something like people being caught up in machinery, and it was stronger than she was." Julia is eventually led to the scaffold, supported by the female prison officers and accompanied by the Governor, Doctor, Hangman, and Chaplain. The cell remains empty. After a pause, the sound of the trap dropping is heard. Blackout.

* * *

A Pin to See the Peepshow was refused a license by the Lord Chamberlain. So the play was shown privately in a London theatre club — in May of 1951 — under the direction of Peter Cotes (who had staged the initial production of Agatha Christie's *The Mousetrap*). Two years later, Cotes mounted *A Pin to See the Peepshow* at New York's Playhouse, casting his wife, Joan Miller, in the role of Julia Almond, and Roger Moore (later Agent 007 in several James Bond movies) as Leonard Carr.

The critics were unhappy. "A tepid play," frowned Brooks Atkinson. "In tedious details it chronicles the misadventures of a highly romantic lady."[2] Richard Watts Jr. complained of "a slow-starting and decidedly commonplace murder play"[3] Robert Coleman scoffed at "a sordid, awkward and dull drama."[4] While John Chapman pouted, "It may be that truth is duller than fiction, after all."[5]

Most reviewers admired Miller's "arsenal of technical equipment," but some believed that it was "rather a mannered performance," needing "occasional restraint." The show opened, and closed, on September 17, 1953.

A Pin to See the Peepshow was adapted to British television in 1973, shown in four episodes, with Francesca Annis as Julia Almond and John Duttin as Leonard Carr.

* * *

Fryn Tennyson Jesse, the daughter of a clergyman and a great-niece of the poet laureate Alfred, Lord Tennyson, began her career as a painter and book illustrator but shifted to writing as a reporter and book-reviewer for *The Times* of London. During World War I she was a correspondent for the British Ministry of Information.

Jesse once wrote, "My chief passion is murder," a zeal manifested in her non-fiction studies, short stories, novels and plays. In *Murder and Its Motives* (1924, revised 1958), Jesse asserts, "Most criminals are great egoists and inordinately vain, but the two qualities are found in excess in murderers." Jesse edited several volumes in the *Notable British Trials* series, including the cases of Madeleine Smith, Timothy John Evans, and John Reginald Halliday Christie, all published in 1957. Jesse's collection, *The Solange Stories* (1931), fea-

tured a French girl, the daughter of a police scientist, who is "gifted by nature with an extra spiritual sense that warned her of evil."

In collaboration with her husband, playwright Harold Marsh Harwood (1874-1959), Jesse created several crime-oriented dramas. *The Black Mask,* a one-act play, is a three-character affair, unfolding in the kitchen of James Glasson's house in a small Cornish village. Years ago, a nearby mine collapsed, leaving James with a scarred face and one eye. Since then, he has been covering his warped features with a straight black mask. Even his wife Vashti – fierce-eyed and black-haired – does not have the nerve to look at his countenance.

When James pretends to go to the village for medicine, William Strick, Vashti's handsome lover enters, and she is soon cuddled in his arms. James suddenly returns, Vashti escapes to the upstairs bedroom, and, after a fierce struggle, James plunges a knife into William's back. Vashti believes that it is her Willie climbing up the dark stairs. As James reaches the door, he pulls his mask off and enters the bedroom. There is a moment's silence, and then wild screams of terror, rising in intensity, as the curtain falls.

The Black Mask was presented by the Princess Players of New York as part of their seasonal repertoire, premiering September 27, 1913. The play opened at London's Garrick Theatre on August 9, 1915, for nine performances, and was revived on the West End in 1919, 1933 and 1936.

* * *

Jesse and Harwood's *How to be Healthy Though Married* is justly dedicated to "Each Other With a Pinch of NaHCO 3." But the chemical used by the play's main character, the French Madame Blanchard— "a brilliant, tempestuous creature of twenty-nine"—in an attempt to dispose of her elderly husband Jacques, is the potent arsenic. Or so she thought. For weeks Claire Blanchard has been mixing Jacques' medicine with doses of white powder mailed to her clandestinely by her young lover, Leon Mercier. Upon Jacques' demise, the widow will inherit his vast estate and be free to unite openly with Leon.

Alas, Monsieur Deschanel, the Procureur de la Republique, discovers the scheme through a mix-up at the post office and summons the lovers to his office. When Deschanel warns them, "In France the *attempt* to murder is a crime punishable by death," Claire crumples, but Leon bursts out laughing. "Arsenic nothing!" he titters. "All I sent her was bicarbonate of soda… All the time she imagines the poor man is fading away before her eyes, whereas, as a matter of fact, he never was so well in his life. It's cured his indigestion. He eats like a horse, and is fit as a fiddle."

An analysis of the powder verifies Leon's contention. He lightly explains that he has never intended "to put my head under the guillotine." Claire, her vanity wounded, is enraged. "Come, Madame," says Deschanel. "Be thankful you have been prevented from committing a terrible crime." But Claire is inconsolable: "Crime—crime? What crime was I committing, compared with what this man has done? —Killing my heart and soul! Making a mockery of me! He's a criminal! A miserable coward who hadn't the courage to kill like a man."

Daschnel will allow Claire to go back to her husband, but cautions: "This time there must be no more lovers." Claire, still hurt, assures the prosecutor, "After this I shall never *speak* to a man again. I *hate* them—*hate* them!" She returns home and when we next see her, eighteen months later, "she has lost her look of smoldering enmity towards the world, and indeed seems the most prosperous and content of women."

How to be Healthy though Married opened at London's Strand Theatre on May 25, 1930, for a single performance.

Non-criminous plays by Jesse and Harwood include *Billeted* (1919), in which, during World War I, a fifty-year-old army colonel, James Preedy, and half-his-age Penelope Moon discover that age does not matter when the heart flutters; *Quarantine* (1924), a romantic comedy about an Englishman, Tony Blunt, who finds his true love during a week's quarantine in the Bahamas; and *The Pelican* (1926), a sentimental drama about an English woman, Wanda Heriot, who sacrifices her happiness for the sake of her illegitimate son.

Harold Marsh Harwood was a prolific playwright and sought-after director. From 1919 to 1930 he leased the Ambassadors Theatre, a small playhouse in West Street, London. He teamed with Robert Gore-Browne, the author of several highly-regarded detective novels, on the plays *Cynara* (1930), a drama of infidelity with tragic consequences, and *King, Queen,Knave* (1932), an adventure melodrama encompassing monarchy, revolution, patriotism and betrayal in an imaginary European country, the Republic of Carmania. Harwood collaborated on the screenplay of *Queen Christina* (1933), a historical drama starring Greta Garbo as the Swedish queen who abdicated for love.

Awards and Honors: F. Tennyson Jesse's *The Solange Stories* (1931) was selected by Ellery Queen for inclusion in *Queen's Forum: A History of the Detective-Crime Story as Revealed in the 106 Most Important Books Published in the Field Since1845.*

NOTES

1. Francis Iles's *As for the Woman* (1939) is also a fictional account of the Thompson-Bywaters case. The plays *Spellbound* (1927) by Frank Vosper

and *Leave Her to Heaven* (1940) by John Van Druten are based on the same real-life murder.

2. *New York Times*, September 18, 1953.
3. *New York Post*, September 18, 1953.
4. *Daily Mirror*, September 18, 1953.
5. *Daily News*, September 18, 1953.

Billy Budd (1951)

Louis O. Coxe (United States, 1918-1993) and Robert Chapman (United States, 1919-2000)

Herman Melville began his novella *Billy Budd* in 1888 and completed it three years later. It was published posthumously in 1924. In 1947, two novice playwrights, fans of Melville since their student days at Princeton, embarked upon a dramatization of the incidents aboard *H.M.S. Indomitable* in August 1798. "We saw in *Billy Bud* a morality play...a story of good, evil, and the way the world takes such absolutes," say the authors. "We will look far before we find another theme of equal interest or vitality."[1]

The entire action of the play is set aboard the British naval vessel *Indomitable* during the Napoleonic war. The master-at-arms, John Claggart, a malevolent sadist, insists that Enoch Jackson, an ailing sailor, climb up the ladder to the mainmast and Jackson falls to his doom. Claggart lies to the ship's captain, Edward Fairfax Vere, about ordering Jackson aloft. The next target of the master-at-arms is William Budd, a handsome, guileless, newly recruited foretop man, described fondly by the sailors a "half man, half child" and nicknamed "Baby."

"I want Billy on report," says the master-at-arms. But to Claggart's chagrin, Billy distinguishes himself during an encounter with a French frigate and is promoted to captain of the foretop. Jenkins, a bitter sailor, stalks Claggart with a knife, but Billy intervenes. A scuffle ensues, during which Billy wrestles the weapon from Jenkins. Saved by Billy, Claggart simmers even more and tells Captain Vere that "the sweet, vicious lad is dangerous... spreading unrest and rebellion in the crew."

Vere, doubtful of the accusation, orders an inquiry. The master-at-arms denounces Billy to his face for "acting against this ship, this Service, and the King," threatening the officers with murder, and bent on urging other men to mutiny.

Shocked, Billy tries to respond, but an impediment in his speech yields only incoherent sounds. After agonized dumb gesturing and stammering, Billy hits Claggart, who staggers, falls, then lies still, dead.

A court-martial convenes at Captain Vere's quarters. The officers vote to render a self-defense acquittal, but Vere reminds them that since this is a wartime cruise, according to the Admiralty code, they have no choice but put to death a man who fatally struck his superior officer. They sentence Billy to be hanged.

At dawn the men are called. When they realize that Billy is to be executed, they rush the deck, but Billy shouts out fervently, with no trace of a stutter, "God bless Captain Vere!" He climbs quickly up the ropes and out of sight. Officers and mates, in deep breathless consternation, stare overhead as the curtain falls.

* * *

Louis O. Coxe and Robert Chapman presented *Uniform of Flesh* at ANTA's Experimental Theatre on January 29, 1949, for seven performances, and kept embellishing the text from a "strict poetic form, austere in tone and structure," to one with "dramatic incident, contrapuntal conflict, and realistic speech."[2] Reverting to Melville's original title, *Billy Budd* opened at the Biltmore Theatre on February 10, 1951, under the direction of Norris Houghton.

It garnered split verdicts. Brooks Atkinson wrote, "Louis O. Coxe and Robert Chapman have made a horrifyingly candid drama" out of Melville's novel, and their play "has size and depth as well as color and excitement."[3] William Hawkins found *Billy Budd* "a striking parable about the existence of right and wrong in humans… unquestionably memorable theatre."[4] Richard Watts Jr. acclaimed, "a remarkably sensitive and absorbing play that has the courage to raise an austere moral problem and face it on a high emotional and intellectual level."[5] Naysayers included John McClain, who stated that *Billy Budd* was "only casually convincing at best."[6] Bert McCord believed that "the argument is too diffused and the language too confused to create or even maintain any suspense."[7] Robert Coleman opined, "the action runs aground on metaphysical shoals."[8] John Chapman scoffed, "I should have been emotionally enthralled. Instead, I thought Billy was silly."[9]

The all-male cast of *Billy Budd*, headed by Dennis King as Captain Vere, Torin Thatcher as Claggart, and Charles Nolte in the title role, and with Jeff Morrow, James Daly and Lee Marvin lending support, was applauded by the reviewers. Nevertheless, the grim drama would have closed soon after its opening had it not been for a good Samaritan, producer-director Herman Shumlin, who had no stake in the production but paid for a display advertisement in the *New York Times* expressing his admiration for the artistry of *Billy Budd*. The cast members volunteered to take wage cuts, and *Billy Budd* chugged along for 105 performances, coming within two votes of winning the 1950-1951 New York Drama Critics Circle Award as the best play of the season (Sidney Kingsley's *Darkness at Noon* got the prize with ten votes, *Billy Budd* was close with eight).

Billy Budd was revived by the Masques at Off Broadway's Rooftop Theatre on May 3, 1955. Arthur Gelb declared the play "compelling and absorbing."[10] Still another resuscitation of *Billy Budd* took place at the DeWitt Clinton

Adult Center, the Bronx, on February 27, 1959, before embarking on a borough tour. The Trinity Square Repertory Company, in Providence, Rhode Island, adapted the Melville novel, under Adrian Hall's direction, on March 3, 1969. A musical version, entitled *Billy*, with book by Stephen Glassman, music and lyrics by Ron Dante and Gene Allen, opened—and closed—at New York's Billy Rose Theater on March 22, 1969. Most of the critics savaged the effort: "A book that reduces the Herman Melville story to the level of pulp adventure" (Clive Barnes);[11] "It is the clumsiest and most childish grasp for Melville that I have yet seen" (Martin Gottifried);[12] "It is a noisy and physically energetic musical drama in which the sound and fury signify virtually nothing" (Richard Watts Jr.).[13]

Retitled *The Good Soldier*, the Coxe-Chapman play was presented at the Lyric Theatre, in the Hammersmith borough of London, on April 4, 1956, for twenty-one performances. Philip Bond portrayed Billy Budd, Leo McKern enacted Claggart, and Sean Connery appeared as one of the sailors.

Music lovers may be comforted by Benjamin Britten's 1951 masterful opera *Billy Budd* (libretto by E.M. Forster and Eric Crozier). A phonograph record is available with tenor Peter Pears, Britten's life companion, in the role of Captain Vere. The Dramatic Publishing Company, Chicago, published in 1969 a one-act condensation of the Melville novella by James M. Salem.

Billy Budd was transformed effectively to the screen in 1962,produced/directed/cowritten by Peter Ustinov, who also starred as Captain Vere. Terence Stamp made his film debut in the title role, for which he was nominated for an Academy Award. Robert Ryan played Claggart.

* * *

Herman Melville (1819-1891), an old sea dog, began his literary career with *Typee (*1846), loosely based on his adventures in the Marquesas Islands, followed by *Omoo* (1847), *Mardi* 1849), *Redburn* (1849), and *White Jacket* (1850), all involving ocean travel. In 1851, Melville published *Moby Dick*, the great whaling epic. *Moby Dick* was dramatized by Howard Rodman (1955), Orson Welles (1955), Philip Hanson (1961), and Christopher Martin (1970).

Other stories by Melville that have been converted to the stage include 1853's *Bartleby*– with a score by William Flanagan, libretto by James Hinton Jr. and Edward Albee (1961) — and 1855's *Benito Cereno,* adapted by poet Robert Lowell (1964).

Melville's output may be found in *Romances of Merman Melville* (1928), *The Shorter Novels of Herman Melville* (1928), *Collected Poems of Herman Melville* (1947), *The Complete Stories of Herman Melville* (1949), The *Portable Melville* (1952), and in two all-encompassing volumes printed by The Library of America (1982, 1983). *The Letters of Herman Melville* was published by Yale University Press in 1960. The two standard biographies are *Herman Melville* by Leon Howard and *The Melville Log* by Jay Leyda, both appearing in 1951. *Melville, His World and Work*, by Andrew Delbanco, was published in 2005.

Adapter Louis O. Coxe wrestled with the problem of good versus evil again in *Witchfinders* (Provincetown Playhouse, May 10, 1956), setting the scene during the Salem, Massachusetts witch hunt.

Acting Edition: Dramatists Play Service.

Awards and Honors: A top-ten selection in *The Best Plays of 1950-1951.*

NOTES

1. Louis O. Coxe and Robert Chapman, *Billy Budd* (New York: Hill and Wang, 1962, 88-90.
2. *Ibid*, 90.
3. *New York Times*, February 12, 1951.
4. *New York World-Telegram*, February 12, 1951
5. *New York Post*, February 12, 1951.
6. *New York Journal-American*, February 12, 1951.
7. *New York Herald Tribune*, February 12, 1951.
8. *Daily Mirror*, February 12, 1951.
9. *Daily News*, February 12, 1951.
10. *New York Times*, May 4, 1955.
11. *New York Times*, March 24, 1969.
12. *Women's Wear Daily*, March 24, 1969.
13. *New York Post*, March 24, 1969.

Witness for the Prosecution (1953)

Agatha Christie (England, 1890-1976)

Agatha Christie's masterpiece is arguably *Witness for the Prosecution*, a three-act play she expanded from a short story included in the collection *The Hound of Death* (1933). Her research embraced the perusal of the *Famous Trials* series and the study of the British judicial system.

In her autobiography, Christie cheerfully states, "One night at the theatre stands out in my memory especially: the first night of *Witness for the Prosecution*. I can safely say that that was the only first night I have enjoyed."[1] The Queen of Crime recounts how she had to fight, tooth-and-nail, for the triple-twist ending: "Nobody liked it, nobody wanted it, everyone said it would spoil the whole thing… I don't often stick out for things, I don't always have sufficient conviction, but I had here. I wanted that end. I wanted it so much that I wouldn't agree to have the play put on without it."[2] In the original short story, the resolution allows the murderer to get away with the crime, while in the play he escapes legal justice but does not go unpunished.

The action begins at the Temple Chambers of Sir Wilfrid Robarts, Q.C. Mr. Mayhew, a middle-aged solicitor, escorts a likeable, friendly young man, Leonard Vole. Leonard, looking slightly worried, informs Sir Wilfrid that he may be arrested for murder any minute. It's the case of Miss Emily French, he explains, which has been widely reported in the press—a middle-aged lady living alone but for an elderly housekeeper, in a house in Hampstead, found hit on the back of the head, killed.

Leonard relates that he met French a few months before. She dropped her parcels in the middle of Oxford Street and he managed to get her to the curb safely when "a bus was almost on top of her." A grateful Miss French invited Leonard to visit her and they struck up a warm friendship.

Leonard admits airily that he is broke. The murdered woman was well off and left all her assets to Leonard. Therefore, Leonard's wife, Romaine, warned that the authorities may suspect him of the foul deed and suggested that he hire a lawyer.

On the fateful evening of October 14, Leonard had a cup of coffee and played cards with Miss French until 9 p.m. At 9.30, the housekeeper, Janet Mackenzie, returned to the house and heard somebody talking with Miss French. "It wasn't me," claims Leonard, confident that Romaine, a devoted wife, will confirm his story.

A Scotland Yard Inspector enters with a warrant and Leonard is taken away. Sir Wilfred and Mayhew are impressed favorably by the young suspect who does not seem to realize the danger of his position. Romaine Vole arrives and confides that Leonard is not really her husband. They went through "a form of marriage" in Berlin so that Leonard could get her out of the Russian zone and bring her to England. To the chagrin of the attorneys, Romaine, "cool as a cucumber," is not very reassuring about Leonard's alibi.

The proceedings now shift to the Central Criminal Court, London—better known as the Old Bailey. Before the bewigged, stern Mr. Justice Wainwright, the jurors are sworn in and the Clerk intones the indictment. Prosecutor Myers, Q.C., describes the circumstances of the case and calls to the stand Detective Inspector Robert Hearne, who negates the theory of a robbery in conjunction with the murder and emphasizes that bloodstains were found on Vole's jacket sleeves. Dr. Wyatt, a police surgeon, takes the stand and affirms that Emily French was coshed to death between the hours of 9.30 and 10 p.m. Finally, Janet Mackenzie, a dour Scotswoman, the housekeeper of the victim, testifies that she heard Mr. Vole conversing with Miss French on the eve of October 14. She also relates that later that night she found her mistress dead, and that neither she nor Miss French were aware that the prisoner was married.

Sir Wilfred shakes Mackenzie's testimony when he cross-examines her in a low voice, proving that she is in need of a hearing apparatus and could not be relied upon to distinguish Leonard's voice from behind closed doors. Sir Wilfred also produces a sharp-edged French vegetable knife, explaining that the stains on Vole's sleeve were caused by a nasty cut obtained when the accused was carving a loaf of ham.

Tension vibrates in court when the prosecutor calls "Romaine Heilger." Romaine asserts that her marriage to the accused is not valid and that she is willing to testify against him. She relates that her husband was not with her as stated, but didn't return until after 10 p.m., with blood on his sleeve, telling her that he killed Miss French. "When it is murder," says Romaine, "I cannot come into Court and lie and say that he was there with me at the time it was done. I cannot do it."

In rebuttal, Sir Wilfrid calls the accused to the witness box. Leonard insists that he reached home at "twenty-five minutes past nine," that his clothes were not smudged with blood, and that he had no knowledge of the terms of Miss French's last will— "I didn't kill her. I've never killed anybody. Oh God! It's a nightmare. It's some awful, evil dream."

Back at chambers, Sir Wilfred and solicitor Mayhew discuss the status of the case when "a rather common young woman, violently and crudely made-up, her blonde hair falling over one side of her face, flamboyantly but cheaply dressed," is ushered in. In a shrill cockney accent the woman offers to sell them letters, written by that wicked Jezebel who gave evidence at court—letters "that might do the prisoner a bit of good." The woman haggles for fifty pounds, gets twenty, takes out a packet of letters from her shabby handbag, and throws them on the desk. "What have you got against Romaine Vole?" asks Sir Wilfred. The woman dramatically swings the desk lamp so that it glows on her face and pushes her hair to reveal a slashed, scarred cheek. Bitterly she explains that Romaine stole her chap, and when she found them together, her ex-lover cut her up with a razor.

The woman thrusts her disfigured face towards Sir Wilfred: "Want to kiss me?" He shrinks back. As the men turn to examine the letters, she quietly slips out of the room.

At the Old Bailey, the next morning, Sir Wilfrid offers in evidence letters from Romaine Heilger and calls her to the stand. "Do you know a certain man whose name is Max?" he asks. Romaine starts violently, hesitates, and then answers: "Certainly not." Sir Wilfrid picks up a letter and quotes: "My beloved Max… An extraordinary thing has happened. I believe all our difficulties may be ended."

Romaine interrupts, denying that she wrote the letters, but Sir Wilfrid continues: "The old lady I told you about has been murdered and I think Leonard is suspected… His alibi depends on me. Supposing I say he came home much later… If Leonard is convicted of murder, I could come to you safely and we could be together for always… Your adoring Romaine."

Stonily, Romaine admits to writing the letter. The Jury finds Leonard Vole not guilty.

A policeman suggests that Romaine wait in the courthouse for a while to avoid the crowd riled up against her. Mayhew congratulates Leonard on being free—and rich. Sir Wilfrid warns Romaine that proceedings for perjury will be launched shortly. Measuring her balefully, the barrister tells Romaine that since their first meeting he made up his mind to beat her at her "little game. And, by God, I've done it. I've got him off—in spite of you."

In the ensuing conversation it turns out that Romaine and the woman selling the letters are one and same. Romaine wanted the jury to dislike and mistrust her, to believe that she was lying when she was testifying against Vole. In a cockney accent, Romaine says, "So now you know the whole story, Mister—like to kiss me?"

Sir Wilfrid is thunderstruck: "Couldn't you just trust me? We believe, you know, that our British system of justice upholds the truth. We'd have got him off." Romaine utters slowly: "I couldn't risk it. You see, you *thought* he was innocent…" Sir Wilfrid interrupts with quick appreciation: "And you *knew* he was innocent. I understand." Romaine responds: "But you do not understand at all. I *knew* he was *guilty.*"

The Duchess of Crime still has another trick up her sleeve. A young, strawberry blonde girl rushes in, embracing Leonard. Romaine is puzzled.

Leonard flings off all disguise of manner and says with coarse brutality: "She's fifteen years younger than you are." He laughs and moves towards Romaine menacingly: "I've got the money. I've been acquitted, and I can't be tried again, so don't be shooting off your mouth, or you'll just get *yourself* hanged as an accessory after the fact."

Leonard turns to the girl and kisses her as Romaine picks up a knife from the exhibit table. She says calmly, "I shall not be tried as an accessory after the fact. I shall not be tried for perjury. I shall be tried for murder—the murder of the only man I ever loved." She stabs Leonard in the back.

* * *

Produced by Peter Saunders and directed by Wallace Douglas, *Witness for the Prosecution* previewed at the Theatre Royal, Nottingham, on September 28, 1953, and opened at London's Winter Garden Theatre a month later, for a run of 458 performances. David Horne portrayed Sir Wilfrid Robarts, with Derek Blomfield as Leonard Vole and Patricia Jessel as Romaine. In New York, the play raised its curtain at Henry Miller's Theatre on December 16, 1954, and enjoyed a run of 645 performances. The Broadway replica was staged by Robert Lewis and featured Francis L. Sullivan (Sir Wilfrid), Gene Lyons (Vole), and Patricia Jessel, recruited from the London production for the role of Romaine.

Critic Robert Coleman found Miss Jessel "electrifying as the wife, as menacing as a cobra one moment and as frantic as a lioness at bay the next."[3] The reviewers unanimously showered superlatives on the play, such as "a decisive knockout," "a platinum-plated whodunit," and "theatrical skullduggery at its peak," while gingerly skipping around the punchy denouement.

Equity Library Theatre of Manhattan revived *Witness for the Prosecution* in March 1966, and Off Off Broadway's Wonderhorse Theatre did the same in August 1975. The straining requirement of thirty cast members did not deter the Oakland University Professional Theatre Program, Rochester, Michigan from presenting *Witness* in 1975, nor the Old Globe Theatre of San Diego, California, in 1980; Studio Arena Theatre, Buffalo, New York, 1982; Players State Theatre, Coconut Grove, Florida, 1983; and New CenturyPlayers, Milwaukee, Oregon, 2015.

A splendid motion picture version, directed by Billy Wilder, was made in 1957, with the stellar cast of Charles Laughton (Sir Wilfrid), Tyrone Power (Leonard), and Marlene Dietrich (Christine instead of Romaine). A facsimile of the Old Bailey courthouse was built in Hollywood on the Samuel Goldwyn lot where much of the action was shot. The publicity department drummed up the surprise ending, and a great deal was made of a huge poster hung outside the studio requesting everyone entering to sign a pledge "not to reveal any of the secrets relating to the film's electrifying climax." *Witness of the Prosecution* received six Academy Award nominations: Best Picture, Best Director (Wilder), Best Actor (Laughton), Best Supporting Actress (Elsa Lanchester), Best Sound, and Best Film Editing—but won none.

* * *

Born in Torquay, Devon, Agatha Mary Clarissa Miller (1890-1976) was raised reading detective stories. Gaston Leroux's *The Mystery of the Yellow Room*, a sealed-room classic, Robert Barr's *The Triumphs of Eugene Valmont*, a pioneering volume of humorous sleuthing, and Marie Belloc Lowndes' creation of French investigator Hercules Popeau were among her treasured literary influences. During World War I, Agatha married Archibald Christie, a dashing Colonel in the Royal Flying Corps. While working in the Volunteer Aid Detachment Hospital, she gained knowledge of drugs and poisons, information that came in handy later in her books. Agatha had not planned to be a writer. In fact, Agatha's first novel was written as a response to a challenge by her sister, Madge. *The Mysterious Affair at Styles* (1920) introduced Hercule Poirot, the diminutive Belgian detective who was destined to rival the popularity of Sherlock Holmes.

In her second novel, *The Secret Adversary* (1922), Christie plotted an adventure tale in which the leading characters, Prudence Cowley, known to her friends as Tuppence, and Thomas Beresford, her beau, pursue an elusive man who plots to overthrow the British government.[4] Successive novels in the early 1920s introduced the recurring characters of Colonel Race and Superintendent Battle of Scotland Yard. In 1926 came the tour de force *The Murder of Roger Ackroyd*, which made Christie a household name.

Following the publication of *The Murder of Roger Ackroyd*, Agatha herself became a headline mystery. On December 3, 1926, the celebrated author did not return home. Her frost-covered car, a green Morris, was found alongside a dirt road with the lights still on. On the seat were a brown fur coat and a small dressing case that had burst open, scattering clothing and some papers, including an out-of-date driver's license in her name. Agatha's disappearance caused a sensation. Was she the victim of foul play? Did she commit suicide? Or was it merely an audacious publicity stunt? A nationwide search was launched immediately.

Author Gwyn Robyns, in *The Mystery of Agatha Christie* (1978), asserts that in order to understand the circumstances of the bizarre case it is important to learn that "It had been a traumatic year for Agatha Christie." Her mother had died after a severe illness, and her marriage had deteriorated.

Kathleen Tynan, in *Agatha* (1978), provides an imaginary scenario about the author's disappearance: Preoccupied with the painful realization that she was losing her husband to a beautiful rival, the shy, sensitive author withdraws into herself—and drops out of sight. Tynan's speculative narrative attempts to penetrate the psyche of a woman betrayed. How will this accomplished mystery writer, plotter of intrigue and creator of suspenseful incidents, react? Will she remain passive, or will she direct her talents towards sinister revenge?[5]

Agatha returned home after eleven days—claiming temporary amnesia. Two years later the Christies were divorced. In 1930, Agatha Christie married Max Mallowan, an archeologist. By accompanying him on digs to the Middle East, Agatha discovered exotic source material for such books as *Murder in Mesopotamia* (1936), *Death on the Nile* (1937), *Appointment With Death* (1938), *Death Comes as the End* (1945), and *They Came to Baghdad* (1951).

It is widely perceived that only the Bible and the plays of Shakespeare have sold more copies than Agatha Christie's murder mysteries. "In a career that spanned over half a century," writes popular-culture czar Peter Haining, "she published in all 78 crime novels, 19 plays (of which seven are adaptations of her books), six romantic novels under the pen-name Mary Westmacott, and four non-fiction titles… it is true to say that Agatha Christie is the most widely published writer of any time and in any language, and the royalties deriving from her books alone now run in excess of two million pounds every year."[6] Haining calls attention to the energetic productivity and high achievements of Dame Christie in the world of entertainment—on stage, in films, and on radio and television: "This contribution amounts to at least 20 major theatrical productions on both sides of the Atlantic (not to mention a vast number of touring productions and repertory performances); two dozen films for the cinema; in excess of 50 radio programs; and an even larger number of individual stories and serials for both British and American television."[7]

Agatha Christie died peacefully at her home in Wallingford, Berkshire, on January 12, 1976, at age eighty-five.

Acting Edition: Samuel French, Inc. (in manuscript form).

Awards and Honors: Agatha Christie became a Fellow, Royal Society of Literature, in 1950. She was awarded the C.B.E. (Commander, Order of the British Empire) in 1956, and made a D.B.E. (Dame Commander, Order of the British Empire) in 1971. She was president of England's Detection Club (1954) and recipient of the Mystery Writers of America Grand Master Award (1955). D.Litt: University of Exeter, 1961.

NOTES

1. Agatha Christie, *An Autobiography* (London: Collins, 1977), 514.
2. Christie, *An Autobiography*, 514.
3. *Daily Mirror*, December 17, 1954.
4. Tuppence and Tommy will return in Christie's novels *Partners in Crime* (1929), *N or M?* (1941), *By the Pricking of My Thumbs* (1968), and *The Postern of Fate* (1973).
5. *Agatha* was filmed by Director Michael Apted in 1979, featuring Vanessa Redgrave in the title role, Timothy Dalton as the fickle husband, and Dustin Hoffman as an American reporter, Wally Stanton, who tracks Agatha Christie down to a seaside hotel. Decades later, Agatha's disappearance gained renewed interest and scrutiny in two speculative books: *The Mystery of Mrs. Christie* (2021) by Marie Benedict and *The Christie Affair* (2022) by Nina de Gramont.
6. Peter Haining, *Agatha Christie—Murder in Four Acts* (London: Virgin Books, 1990), 11.
7. Haining, *Agatha Christie*, 11-12.

The Crucible (1953)

Arthur Miller (United States, 1915-2005)

During the Cold War, when America and Russia were involved in a mighty clash, there arose fear in the United States that Communism was threatening the American way of life. In the late 1940s and into the 1950s, Senator Joseph McCarthy of Wisconsin headed the House Un-American Activities Committee. HUAC held hearings and conducted wide-range investigations of suspected Communists. Author Arthur Miller, who in his plays championed the cause of the common man, was called to appear before the HUAC on May 21, 1956. He denied that he was a Communist, freely admitted that he attended certain meetings and refused to name others who had been present. By 373 votes to 9 the House of Representatives found Miller in contempt of Congress, and he was blacklisted by Hollywood. The ruling was reversed by the courts in 1958. There is little doubt that his drama *The Crucible*, about the 1692 Salem witch trials, is a parable about McCarthyism.

The curtain rises on Reverend Samuel Parris's house in Salem, Massachusetts in the spring of 1692. It is a stark interior with a black back drop and sparse, wooden furniture – "the mood must be one of high mystery, impending revelation." The minister is kneeling at the bedside of his ten-year-old daughter, Betty, who is strangely ill. Word comes from the town's doctor that he cannot discover an appropriate medicine in his books. Dr. Griggs believes that the cause of Betty's malady is "unnatural."

Abigail Williams, the Reverend's strikingly beautiful seventeen-year-old niece, is an orphan who was brought up in his home. She tells her uncle that she, Betty, and several of their girl friends danced in the forest but insists that it was "only sport" and no witchcraft was involved.

Enter Mrs. Ann Putnam, "a twisted soul of forty-five, a death-driven woman, haunted by dreams." She has buried seven babies and wants to know about Betty's illness so as to compare it to her daughter Ruth's symptoms. She believes that "there are hurtful, vengeful spirits layin' hands on these children." Ann's husband, Thomas Putnam, arrives and declares that no doubt there is a murdering witch among the town folks.

Upstairs, by Betty's bed, several girls meet and compare notes on how much Reverend Parris knows about their dancing naked in the woods. The timid Mary Warren is scared to death that they will be named as witches and hung. The presumably sick Betty sits up and accuses Abigail of drinking blood as a charm to kill farmer John Proctor's wife. Abigail slaps Betty's face and warns the girls to keep mum about their frolicking.

John Proctor and Abigail meet, and we learn that they have had a romantic liaison. Abigail tells Proctor that she has been waiting for him every night, but he insists that he never committed himself to an on-going relationship. Abigail now speaks angrily, calling Proctor's wife Elizabeth "a cold sniveling woman."

Reverend John Hale, a ruddy, bright young man from the town of Beverly, arrives carrying half a dozen heavy books "weighted with authority." He tells a gathering of community people that "in these books the Devil stands stripped of all his brute disguises. Here are all your familiar spirits – your witches that go by land, or air, or by sea; your wizards of the night and the day."

Hale attempts to communicate with the ill Betty, but she fails to respond. When Hale asks Abigail what happened in the forest, she accuses the household slave, Tituba, of making Betty drink blood. The shocked slave, realizing that she may be hanged as a witch, opts to "confess" and distributes the blame by suggesting that the Devil has many surrogate witches. Betty rises and soon she, Tituba and Abigail cry out names of town people they saw "with the Devil." The curtain of the first scene descends on their hysterical, frenzied name calling.

The second scene takes place at John Proctor's farmhouse. As Proctor and his wife converse, we learn that four judges were sent to Salem from Boston, headed by a deputy-governor, and that there are fourteen women in jail awaiting trial. A band of girls led by Abigail Williams, seemingly possessed, howl and fall to the floor, the person they mention is clapped in jail for bewitching them.

Mary Warren, the young servant who works for the Proctors, enters and weakly informs them that there are now thirty-nine prisoners to be tried. Goody Osburn confessed that she made a compact with Lucifer and has been sentenced to hang by the deputy-governor. Mary says that she is an official of the court and as such she's expected to be there every day. Proctor is on the verge of whipping the girl, when Mary points at Elizabeth and declares that she saved her life today. She cannot reveal who accused Elizabeth, for she's sworn to secrecy. Pompously, Mary strides off to bed. "Abigail wants me dead," says Elizabeth. "She thinks to take my place."

There is a knock on the door. It is Reverend Hale, who seems different now, drawn. There is a sense of guilt about him as he relates to the Proctors that he has just come from Rebecca Nurse's home. The Proctors are shocked to hear that Rebecca has been charged with the murder of Ann Putnam's seven babies. Elizabeth dismisses the notion that a pious seventy-year-old woman like Rebecca has trafficked with the Devil.

The rumble of an upcoming wagon is heard. From it comes the clerk of the court, Ezekiel Cheever, with a warrant from the deputy-governor for Elizabeth's arrest. Proctor rips the warrant, picks his gun up and points it at Cheever. Elizabeth presses the rifle down and says that she must go as ordered. She is chained and taken away. Hale attempts to calm Proctor: "The court is just." The farmer cries: "Little crazy children are jangling the keys of the kingdom, and common vengeance writes the law!" Hale is shaken and greatly disturbed.

The second act begins at night in the woods, where John Proctor, holding a lantern, meets Abigail and warns her that if she does not withdraw her accusation against Elizabeth, he will confess in open court that they have committed adultery, a deadly sin in this strict religious community. But to his terror, Abigail calmly promises to save him from himself.

In the forbidding, high-beamed anteroom of the General Court, one can hear the examination taking place in an adjacent courtroom. Salem Judge Hathorne and Deputy- Governor Danforth are mercilessly cross-examining Martha Corey. They are clearly suspicious of her hobby of reading fortunes. Giles Corey, Francis Nurse and John Proctor ask Danforth to receive their depositions on behalf of their respective wives, but Danforth will not allow anyone to tamper with his authority. He does not accept depositions and has no doubt that the voice of Heaven is speaking through the accusing children. He has sent nearly four hundred sinners to jails from Marblehead to Lynn, and upon his signature, seventy-two have been condemned to hang. He knows where his duty lies.

Proctor submits to Danforth a paper signed by more than ninety friends and neighbors, declaring their good opinion of Elizabeth, Rebecca Nurse and Martha Corey. Danforth hands the paper to Cheever and orders him to issue a warrant for every person who signed the petition. Reverend Hale tries to counsel moderation and casts doubt at the accusations claimed by the girls. Danforth asks Cheever to go into court and bring the children.

Proctor introduces Danforth to his frail witness, Mary Warren, who weakly states that the girls' finger pointing was nothing but pretense. Mary is then confronted by Abigail, Mercy Lewis, Susanna Walcott and Betty Parris. Abigail cunningly becomes marvelously indignant as she listens to Mary's confession and with the support of Judge Hathorne, Reverend Parris and the officious Cheever, becomes haughty and threatening, and suddenly goes into a frightened, trance-like state. The girls join her, shivering and moaning; Mary falters, reduced to whimpery hysteria. Proctor cannot take more of this and ruins himself by accusing Abigail of lechery – "She thinks to dance with me on my wife's grave." He and Giles Corey are taken off to jail.

The last scene unfolds three months later in a cell in a Salem jail. The window is barred, and by a light effect, a bar-like image is produced on the floor and faces of the actors. Danforth, Hathorne and Cheever enter, the latter carrying a dispatch case and a flat wooden box containing writing materials. They talk of Reverend Hale's return to Salem, praying with Rebecca Nurse and Martha Corey. They wonder if Hale preaches in Andover, where the court was overthrown and there is outright rebellion.

Parris walks in — gaunt, sweating, frightened. He reveals that his niece and her young friends are gone and are now aboard ship. He is concerned, for news of Andover has broken here, and there may be a riot. As a matter of fact, upon opening his door to leave the house, a dagger clattered to the ground, a warning for him. He suggests the postponing of hanging for a time. But Danforth will not budge. He will hang whoever dared to rise against the law.

Hale enters, exhausted and sorrowful. He, too, begs Danforth for more time - no one has yet confessed. Danforth decides that the court's best chance of obtaining a confession lies with John Proctor; his pregnant wife might soften his resistance.

The jailer, Hopkins, ushers in Elizabeth and removes her chains. She is now heavy with child, gaunt and pale, but still shows amazing strength of character. Hale pleads with her to prevail upon her husband to confess—let him lie, but live, as life is God's most precious gift. Elizabeth responds quietly, "I think that be the Devil's argument." Proctor is brought in from his three months' incarceration in a dungeon—filthy, bearded, his eyes misty. He halts inside the doorway and catches sight of Elizabeth. The emotion flowing between them prevents anyone from speaking for an instant. Hale begs the judges to leave the Proctors alone. Danforth sweeps out, his retinue following.

The Proctors clasp hands. Elizabeth tells John that their boys are being well taken care of by friends. None of their group has confessed to witchery. Giles Corey died under cruel torture. John tells his wife that he is thinking of making a confession. She weeps, "I cannot judge you, I cannot." The judges return and Proctor says that he will have his life. Danforth, elated, asks him to sign a confession; it will be posted upon the church door. Under protest, Proctor signs, but when asked if he has seen other prisoners in the company of the Devil, he says that he'll not sell out his friends and tears his confession. He embraces his wife and is led out. Hale asks Elizabeth to plead with John to change his mind, but she says firmly, "He have his goodness now. God forbid I take it from him."

A drum roll is heard. It heightens in intensity as the curtain falls.

* * *

Staged by Jed Harris and designed by Boris Aronson, *The Crucible* premiered at New York's Martin Beck Theatre on January 22, 1953. The leading roles were played by Arthur Kennedy (John Proctor), Beatrice Straight (Elizabeth Proctor), Madeleine Sherwood (Abigail Williams), Jenny Egan (Mary Warren), Walter Hampden (Deputy-Governor Danforth), and E.G. Marshall (Reverend John Hale). It is reported that a mesmerized opening-night audience greeted *The Crucible* with nineteen curtain calls. However, the morning-after reviews ran the gamut of opinions. John Chapman applauded "a strong production, splendidly acted and strongly written."[1] Robert Coleman cheered "a rip-roaring melodrama about the historic witch trials in Salem, Mass… It should spellbind those who relish real drama, conflict and impassioned action."[2] William Hawkins found the play "big and bold and very theatrical."[3] Richard Watts Jr. appreciated "a drama of emotional power and impact… a hard-biting and effective play … written with feeling and indignation."[4]

The naysayers included Walter F. Kerr, who appreciated the playwright's "shrewd theatrical gifts," but believed that the drama was a "mechanical parable," catering to the "intellect, not the heart."[5] Brooks Atkinson felt that "it may be that Mr. Miller has tried to pack too much inside his drama, and that he has permitted himself to be concerned more with the technique of the witch hunt than its humanity."[6] John McClain sighed, "I was not greatly moved by anything that had happened… I never felt myself part of the proceedings."[7]

There was general consensus that Jed Harris has directed the play "with great force and precision," and that Boris Aronson "succeeded in creating some dour New England settings." Kudos were handed to Arthur Kennedy, "at his rare best as the farmer who must live or die for honor," and Walter Hampden, "as the stern and unrelenting magistrate who sends the blameless to the gallows."

The Crucible ran for 197 performances. Translated into Hebrew by Aharon Amir, it was presented by the Habimah Theatre of Israel in 1954.[8] Adapted by Marcel Aymé under the title *Les Sorcières de Salem* (*Witches of Salem*), the play reached Paris in February 1955 to great fanfare by the *Figaro* critic and his colleagues. The theatre reviewers of London also warmly welcomed *The Crucible* when it opened on April 9, 1956, at the Royal Court Theatre, directed by George Devine, who also appeared as Deputy-Governor Danforth, featuring Michael Gwynn (John Proctor) and Kenneth Haigh (Reverend John Hale), and introducing future stars Mary Ure (Abigail Williams), Joan Plowright (Mary Warren) and Alan Bates (jailer Hopkins). *Theatre World Annual* stated, "Mr. Miller portrays with uncanny insight the rising tide of mass hysteria inaugurated by a group of adolescent girls hitherto repressed by a stern, joyless puritanism, and said now to have consorted with the Devil in the woods nearby."[9] The play, however, ran for only thirty-two performances.

The Crucible was revived at Off Broadway's Martinique Theatre on March 11, 1958, directed by Word Baker, with Michael Higgins (John Proctor), Barbara Harris (Elizabeth Proctor), Ford Rainey (Deputy-Governor Danforth), and Ann Wedgeworth (Abigail Williams). The long-running production, amassing 571 performances, was called by Lewis Funke of the *New York Times* "provocative, stimulating, and, most of all, an inspiring creation."[10] Simultaneously, the drama was presented with great success by the Horseshoe Stage Theatre of Hollywood, California, with Dwight Frye, star of Universal's horror films, as Reverend Samuel Parris.[11]

In 1964, a somewhat revised version of *The Crucible* was presented by Eva Le Gallienne's National Repertory Theatre at Broadway's Belasco Theatre. Critic John Chapman of the *Daily News* felt that the passage of time had not been kind to the play and it "now seems a rather juvenile and stereotyped exercise in dramatics."[12] But other reviewers were awed. "A brilliant revival," wrote Judith Crist. "*The Crucible* now glows as it never has before."[13] Howard Taubman asserted that "Arthur Miller's play retains the fury of its intensity and its pride in the inviolability of man's dignity and honor."[14] Norman Nadel pointed out the play's "timelessness," and complimented director Jack Sydow for his "earnest and urgent" staging.[15] John McClain singled out set designer Peter Larkin for employing "some bleached beams and other bits of crude driftwood to suggest the environs of early New England, with extremely good effect."[16] The entire cadre of critics applauded actors Farley Granger and Anne Meacham as the Proctors, and Thayer David in the role of Deputy-Governor Danforth. The revival was shown for sixteen performances during the month of April, in repertory with Anton Chekhov's *The Seagull.* A year later, in 1965, The Long Wharf Theatre in New Haven, Connecticut, was founded and as its inaugural production presented *The Crucible.*

Across the Atlantic, England's National Theatre mounted *The Crucible* at the Old Vic on January 20, 1965, under the direction of Laurence Olivier. "A stunning production," said reviewer B.A. Young in a dispatch to the *New York Times*, adding special kudos to actors Colin Blakely (John Proctor), Robert Lang (Reverend John Hale), Joyce Redman (Elizabeth Proctor), and Pearl Prescod (the slave, Tituba).[17] Scholar Martin Esslin, in *Plays and Players*, called the production "a gripping and moving experience" and hailed its "triumphant demonstration of genuine ensemble acting."[18] The National Youth Theatre of Great Britain revived *The Crucible* on September 16, 1982, for a week's run.

New Yorkers had several more opportunities to see *The Crucible.* In 1972, the play was presented by the Repertory Theatre of Lincoln Center, directed by John Barry, designed by Jo Mielziner, featuring Robert Foxworth (John Proctor), Martha Henry (Elizabeth Proctor), Pamela Payton-Wright (Abigail

Williams), and Aline MacMahon (Rebecca Nurse). In 1991, Tony Randall's National Actors Theatre produced *The Crucible* at Broadway's Belasco Theatre, garnering mixed reviews. *USA Today* called the show "a searing success,"[19] and *New York Newsday* found it "ablaze with first-rate actors making powerful theatre,"[20] but the major critics had strong reservations, throwing darts at director Yossi Yzraely for failing "to mold the actors into a solid ensemble"[21] and instructing them "to perform at an emotional, hand-wringing level that takes the play straight toward melodrama."[22] Frank Rich scoffed at "actors who tend to saw the air with their hands, thump their chests and declaim to the Belasco's two balconies." He was particularly unhappy with two stars: Martin Sheen in the role of John Proctor, "looking more like Daniel Boone than a New England farmer... in a vocally constricted performance of sloppy emotions and knee-jerk righteous indignation;" and Michael York as Reverend John Hale who "is allotted but a single (and weepy) note... and looks here as if he stepped off a Dutch Masters cigar box." The critic was also irked by the drama's villains who, "with the exception of Fritz Weaver's majestically malevolent Deputy-Governor Danforth, are routinely presented as snarling, physically unattractive screamers."[23]

The Crucible ran for thirty-one performances. The following year, 1992, the play was revived at Broadway's Virginia Theatre, directed by Richard Eyre. "Playing husband and wife under moral siege during the Salem witch trials, Liam Neeson and Laura Linney bring a transfixing heat to Richard Eyre's otherwise merely sweaty revival," said the *New York Times*. "Mr. Eyre is far less confident in overseeing the rest of his large and exasperatingly uneven cast, or in making a worthy old war horse of a play gallop like a young stallion."[24] The production ran for 103 showings.

The most revived play in the Arthur Miller canon, *The Crucible* was produced in May 2009 by Actors Co-op of Hollywood, California, directed by Marianne Savell, who, according to the *Los Angeles Times*, after a rocky first act, "hits her stride in the more intimate second act encounter between flawed hero John Proctor and his steadfast wife Elizabeth."[25] In January 2010, the drama was mounted by Off-Off Broadway's Manhattan Theatre Source, staged by Jessica Solce; and in March, by Off-Off Broadway's The Old Stone House, helmed by Claire Beckman.

The world premiere of an opera based on the play, with libretto by Bernard Stambler and music by Robert Ward (who won a Pulitzer Prize for his composition), took place at the New York City Center on October 26, 1961. A radio adaptation, featuring Donald Houston as John Proctor and Donald Wolfit as Deputy-Governor Danforth, was aired by London's Radio Four in May 1970. A 1956 French motion picture, adapted by Jean-Paul Sartre and directed by Raymond Rouleau, starred Yves Montand and Simone Signoret as the Proctors while a 1996 movie, scripted by Arthur Miller and directed by Nicholas Hytner, featured Daniel Day-Lewis (John Proctor), Joan Allen (Elizabeth Proctor), Winona Ryder (Abigail Williams), and Paul Scofield (Deputy-Governor Danforth) and was nominated for several Academy and Golden Globe Awards.

The Crucible was televised in 1959 by UK's ITV Play of the Week with Sean Connery in the role of John Proctor and Susannah York as Abigail Williams. In 1965, it was seen on Spain's Estudio 1 with Francisco Piquer and Gemma Cuervo in those roles, and on Norway's television with Tom Stokke and Liv Ullmann as the Proctors. Don Taylor directed in England a 1980 television replica.

* * *

Arthur Miller was born in New York City in 1915. His father, Isadore Miller, was a successful ladies-wear manufacturer who lost his fortune during the Great Depression. The family's struggle to make ends meet left its mark on young Arthur and later influenced his writings. After graduating from high school in 1932, Miller worked for two years in an auto parts warehouse to earn money for college, and in 1934 he enrolled at the University of Michigan, where he twice won the Avery Hopwood award for playwriting.[26] He received his B.A. degree in 1938 and returned to New York, joining the Federal Theatre Project and writing radio scripts for such programs as "The Cavalcade of America" and "The Columbia Workshop." For "Theatre Guild on the Air" he adapted Ferenc Molnar's *The Guardsman* and John Cecil Holm's *Three Men on a Horse*.

In 1944, a Hollywood studio hired Miller to tour Army camps and gather material for the war movie *The Story of GI Joe*. That same year he had his first play produced at Broadway's Forrest Theatre, *The Man Who Had All the Luck*, about a small-town prosperous businessman who becomes obsessed with the idea that some disaster awaits him. It lasted for only four performances. His next effort was far more successful: *All My Sons*, a domestic drama about an upper-middle-class family whose existence turns into a nightmare when it is discovered that the much-loved father, Joe Keller, supplied defective equipment to the Army Air Force, causing the death of twenty-one pilots (Coronet Theatre, January 29, 1947, with Ed Begley as Keller—328 performances; London, Lyric Theatre, May 11, 1948, with Joseph Calleia—148 performances; filmed 1948 with Edward G. Robinson). Miller followed *All My Sons* with his masterpiece, *Death of a Salesman*, a cornerstone of modern American drama. It is the story, revealed in flashbacks, of an aging traveling salesman, Willy Loman, who is peremptorily fired, and in an act of devotion to his family, commits suicide so that, with his insurance money, they can rid themselves of debt and make a new start (Morosco Theatre, February

10, 1949, with Lee J. Cobb as Loman—742 performances; Phoenix Theatre, London, July 28, 1949, with Paul Muni—204 performances).

Miller took a stand against the corruption of authority in his adaptation of Henrik Ibsen's drama *An Enemy of the People* (Broadhurst Theatre, December 28, 1950, with Fredric March and Florence Eldridge—thirty-six performances) and in 1953's *The Crucible.* Then came *A View from the Bridge*, in which a married Brooklyn dockworker, Eddie Carbone, falls in love with his adopted eighteen-year-old niece, Catherine. When Catherine plans to marry the young and handsome Rodolpho, an illegal Sicilian immigrant, Eddie's jealousy drives him first to accuse Rodolpho of being a homosexual, and then to betray him and a cousin, Marco, to the immigrant authorities. Marco avenges the exposure by confronting Eddie on the waterfront and stabbing him to death (Coronet Theatre, September 29, 1955, with Van Heflin as Eddie—149 performances; Comedy Theatre, London, October 11, 1956, with Anthony Quayle—219 performances; Off Broadway, Sheridan Square Playhouse, January 28, 1965, with Robert Duvall—780 performances).

In 1964, the newly formed Lincoln Center Repertory presented two plays by Miller at the ANTA-Washington Square Theatre: *After the Fall* is a stream-of-consciousness drama in which Quentin, a successful lawyer, strives to determine the extent of his guilt in relation to people who shaped his life, particularly the three women to whom he committed himself. The play brought Miller a storm of criticism, for critics noted the resemblance between his recently deceased second wife, the actress Marilyn Monroe, and Maggie, the blond-wigged, drug-addicted protagonist in the play, and accused him of defiling Monroe's image (January 23, 1964, with Jason Robards, Jr. as Quentin; Barbara Loden as Maggie—208 performances). *Incident at Vichy* is the story of a group of several men and a boy of fifteen, all suspected of being Jews, who wait in a barren room to be interrogated in Vichy, France, in 1942 (December 3, 1964 – thirty-two performances).

Miller's last significant play was *The Price*, wherein two brothers, Victor and Walter Franz, meet after their father's death to dispose of the family's furniture, and clash with mutual accusations (Morosco Theatre, February 7, 1968, with Pat Hingle and Arthur Kennedy– 429 performances). Miller's later plays—among them, *The Creation of the World and Other Business* (1972), a comedy based on the Old Testament, featuring Adam, Eve, Cain and Abel; *The Archbishop's Ceiling* (1977), a drama set behind the Iron Curtain; *The American Clock* (1980), an episodic play unfolding during the Great Depression; *Danger! Memory!* (1987), about the danger of remembering and the danger of forgetting; and *Broken Glass* (1994), the story of a Jewish married couple living in Brooklyn in 1938, and the effect upon them of the Kristallnacht (Night of Broken Glass) in Nazi Germany—were not well received, and he took to denounce Broadway as obsessed with commerce and greed.[27]

Miller also wrote essays, novels, short stories and a 1987 autobiography, *Timebends: A Life.*[28] He was married three times: In 1940 to his college sweetheart Mary Grace Slattery, from whom he was divorced in 1955; the following year he married Marilyn Monroe, and they were divorced in 1960; two years later, he married Swedish photographer Ingeborg Morath, who died in 2002. When Marilyn Monroe was his spouse, he wrote for her the screenplay of *The Misfits* (1961), a brooding story about over-the-hills cowboys in the Nevada desert, in which she co-starred with Clark Gable and Montgomery Clift under John Huston's direction. Miller's sister is the actress Joan Copeland, and his daughter is the filmmaker Rebecca Miller, who is married to the actor Daniel Day-Lewis. Miller died at his home in Roxbury, Connecticut, of congestive heart failure, on February 11, 2005, at the age of 89. Broadway theatres dimmed their marquee lights at curtain time in his memory.

Acting Edition: Dramatists Play Service.

Awards and Honors: Winner of the 1953 Tony Award as Best Play, and a top-ten selection in *The Best Plays of 1952-1953*.
Miller's *All My Sons* was a top-ten selection in 1947, won two Emmy Awards, and took the New York Drama Critics' Circle Award. Miller's *Death of a Salesman* (1949) won the triple crown of the Pulitzer Prize, the New York Drama Critics Circle Award, and the Tony. The fiftieth anniversary production of the play received the Tony and Drama Desk Awards for Best Revival of a Play, as did the Roundabout Theatre's production of *A View from the Bridge*. Miller was the recipient of a 1999 Tony for Lifetime Achievement. Off Broadway's Signature Theatre Company dedicated its 1997-1998 season to his plays.

Miller garnered the National Association of Independent Schools Award in 1954, an American Academy of Arts and Letters Gold Medal in 1959, the National Medal of Arts in 1993, the National Book Foundation 2001 Medal for Distinguished Contribution to American Letters, Japan's 2001 Praemium Imperiate for lifetime achievement in arts, Spain's Principe de Asturias Prize for Literature as "the undisputed master of modern drama" in 2002, and the Jerusalem Prize in 2003.

Miller was International President of PEN, London and New York, 1965-1969, and a member of the American Academy of Arts and Letters since 1971. He held honorary doctorate degrees from the University of Michigan, Harvard University and Oxford University, and he received the Creative Arts Award from Brandeis University.

A 1998 survey by Britain's Royal National Theatre of more than eight hundred playwrights, directors, actors, and critics chose Arthur Miller as the best playwright of the twentieth century. Although Samuel Becket's *Waiting for Godot* was selected as the century's best play, Miller wound up with two plays in the top ten, *Death of a Salesman* at number two and *The Crucible* at number six.

NOTES

1. *Daily News*, January 23, 1953.
2. *Daily Mirror*, January 23, 1953.
3. *New York World-Telegram*, January 23, 1953.
4. *New York Post*, January 23, 1953.
5. *New York Herald Tribune*, January 23, 1953.
6. *New York Times*, January 23, 1953.
7. *New York Journal-American*, January 23, 1953.
8. In addition to its 1954 Habimah Theatre production, *The Crucible* was mounted two more times in Israel – by the Haifa Municipal Theatre in 1970, a highly theatrical interpretation of the play with an emphasis on pictorial tableaus, and by the Be'er Sheva Municipal Theatre in 1991.
9. *Theatre World Annual*, 1956.
10. *New York Times*, March 12, 1958.
11. Dwight Frye (1899-1943) etched notable movie characterizations as Fritz, the hunchbacked, sadistic tormentor of the Monster in *Frankenstein*, and mad, fly-eating Renfield in *Dracula*, both films released in 1931. On Broadway, in 1933, he played the sympathetic Chinese murderer Ah Sing, who is unmasked by Honolulu police sergeant Charlie Chan in Earl Derr Biggers' *Keeper of the Keys*. That same year he enacted at the Alcazar Theatre of San Francisco the role of the double-faced Lord Lebanon in Edgar Wallace's *The Case of the Frightened Lady* (aka *Criminal at Large*). In the late 1930s, Frye portrayed Dan, the baby-faced killer, in a Los Angeles, California production of Emlyn Williams' *Night Must Fall*.
12. *Daily News*, April 7, 1964.
13. *New York Herald Tribune*, April 7, 1964.
14. *New York Times*, April 7, 1964.
15. *New York World-Telegram*, April 7, 1964.
16. *New York Journal-American*, April 7, 1964.
17. *New York Times*, January 20, 1965.
18. *Plays and Players*, March 1965.
19. *USA Today*, December 12, 1991.
20. *New York Newsday*, December 6, 1991.
21. Howard Kissel, *Daily News*, December 11, 1991.
22. Edwin Wilson, *The Wall Street Journal*, December 20, 1991.
23. *New York Times*, December 11, 1991.

24. *New York Times*, May 31, 2002.
25. *Los Angeles Times*, May 8, 2009.
26. Avery Hopwood (1884-1928) was a prolific and popular author of many Broadway comedies, farces and musicals during the first quarter of the twentieth century. His most memorable achievement was the 1920 classic melodrama *The Bat*, on which he collaborated with Mary Roberts Rinehart, an adaptation from her 1908 novel, *The Circular Staircase.*
27. Though it received mixed reviews in New York, *Broken Glass* won the 1995 Olivier Award for best play in London.
28. *The Theatre Essays of Arthur Miller*, edited by Robert A. Martin and published by Viking Press in 1978, collects articles, prefaces and interviews published in books, newspapers, and magazines over a thirty-year period. Edited by Christopher Bigsby with an introduction by Harold Clurman, Viking also published in 1971 *The Portable Arthur Miller*, a comprehensive overview of Miller's contributions to the stage, and in 2001, a slim volume by Miller, *On Politics and the Art of Acting*, analyzing the thespian skills of Ronald Reagan, Bill Clinton, JFK, and FDR.

The Caine Mutiny Court-Martial (1953)

Herman Wouk (United States, 1915- 2019)

Herman Wouk took a portion of his sprawling 1951 Pulitzer Prize-winning novel, *The Caine Mutiny,* and turned it into a pulsating courtroom drama.

The time is February 1945. The scene is the General Court-Martial Room of the Twelfth Naval District, San Francisco. Lt. Stephen Maryk is accused of mutiny in wartime, for "willfully, without proper authority, and without justifiable cause" relieving from duty Lieutenant Commander Philip Francis Queeg, the captain of the *S.S. Caine.*

Lt. Maryk's contention is that during a raging typhoon in the Pacific he believed that Captain Queeg lost his faculties and became numb with panic. In order to save the ship, he relieved the skipper of duty and seized control.

During the first act, prosecutor John Challee summons to the witness stand Navy officers and experts, building up a strong case against Maryk.

In the second act, Maryk's defense attorney, Barney Greenwald, turns the tables. In a grueling cross-examination he proves that the captain of the *S.S. Caine* was a petty tyrant and paranoid coward. Throughout a rambling account of stolen strawberries, a missing icebox key, and incomplete officers' logs—the outwardly self-assured captain gradually disintegrates and ends up trembling and sobbing, a broken man.

Lt. Maryk is exonerated, but playwright Wouk has one more arrow in his shaft. During an acquittal party, a drunk, tormented Barney Greenwald hails the Queegs of the Navy for staving off the Nazis while the nation was preparing for war. He lashes out at Maryk's friend, Lt. Thomas Keefer, as "The guy who started the whole idea that Queeg was a dangerous paranoiac," and instead of helping the sick captain, inflamed a mutiny that yanked out of action the *S.S. Caine,* a minesweeper, when it was most needed in the hottest part of the war.

* * *

The Caine Mutiny Court-Martial was first presented at the Granada Theatre in Santa Barbara, California, on October 12, 1953. After sailing around the country for more than three months, the play, under the direction of Charles Laughton, anchored in New York's Plymouth Theatre on January 20, 1954, docking there for 415 performances. It won unanimous raves from the critics: "Mr. Wouk's drama has some of the unforced inevitability for a tragedy," stated Brooks Atkinson, "It is remarkably well-planned and it is written neatly."[1] Walter Kerr pointed out that the play "builds to a second-act climax of such hair-raising intensity that you are sure nothing, and no one, can ever top it. Someone then proceeds to top it… *The Caine Mutiny Court-Martial* is a thrilling achievement."[2]

Richard Watts, Jr. expressed similar sentiments, "*The Caine Mutiny Court-Martial* is provocative and arresting."[3] John Chapman added, "It is enormously compelling and exciting;"[4] William Hawkins agreed, "A brilliantly exciting drama about heroes under stress… the drama's full impact hits like dynamite;"[5] and Robert Coleman urged his readers to "rush to the Plymouth Theatre box-office immediately… an arresting, absorbing and completely fascinating evening of theatre."[6]

The all-male cast, headed by Henry Fonda as Greenwald, John Hodiak as Maryk, and Lloyd Nolan as Queeg was saluted enthusiastically.

The courtroom drama opened at London's Hippodrome on June 13, 1956, with Lloyd Nolan directing and repeating the role of Captain Queeg. It ran for 132 performances.

Almost thirty years later, a revival of *The Caine Mutiny Court-Martial* was mounted at the Hartman Theatre in Stamford, Connecticut, on May 5, 1983, on its way to Broadway's Circle in the Square Uptown. "Holds its own admirably," wrote John Beaufort.[7] "Wouk's words have lost none of their power," echoed Joel Segal.[8] "Strong stuff," agreed Clive Barnes.[9] The play, staged by Arthur Sherman, featured Jay O. Sanders (Maryk), Michael Moriarty (Queeg), and John Rubinstein (Greenwald). It ran for 213 performances.

Charlton Heston directed, and starred as Queeg in a highly acclaimed London production in 1984. Heston later brought the show to the Kennedy Center's Eisenhower Theatre in Washington, D.C.

The Caine Mutiny Court-Martial was revived at Broadway's Gerald Schoenfeld Theatre on May 7, 2006, in a disappointing production that ran for only seventeen performances. Charles Isherwood of the *New York Times* called it "torpid" and "plodding," performed by a "blandly efficient cast," and directed "with metronome in hand by Jerry Zaks."[10]

A top-notch 1954 movie version of *The Caine Mutiny,* scripted by Stanley Roberts and directed by Edward Dmytryk, starred Humphrey Bogart as Captain Queeg, Van Johnson as Lieutenant Maryk, Fred MacMurray as Thomas Keefer, and Jose Ferrer as Defense Attorney Greenwald.

In 1988, Robert Altman directed an effective made-for-television version of *The Caine Mutiny Court-Martial* for CBS, with Eric Bogosian as Greenwald, and Brad Davis as Queeg.

* * *

Herman Wouk was born in the Bronx in 1915, the son of Russian-Jewish immigrants. In 1934, he received his Bachelor of Arts degree at Columbia University, where he majored in comparative literature and philosophy. In college, Wouk edited the humorous *Columbia Jester* and wrote several varsity shows.

Between 1935 and 1941, Wouk worked as a radio writer and producer. In 1942, he enlisted in the Navy and served for three years as a deck officer on the destroyer *U.S.S. Zane* and as an executive officer on the *U.S.S. Southard.* While on duty in the Pacific, Wouk began to write his first novel, *Aurora Dawn*, a satire about radio advertising.

Wouk's play *The Traitor* was produced on Broadway in 1949. It is a Cold War story of a young nuclear scientist who believes that the only way to stop catastrophe is to let the Russians in on the secret of the atomic bomb.

Among Wouk's best-selling novels are *Marjorie Morningstar* (1955), the chronicle of a Jewish girl who, to the chagrin of her traditional family, wishes to become an actress, and *Youngblood Hawke* (1962), a critique of the publishing world, based on the life of Thomas Wolfe. The epic *The Winds of War* (1971) and *War of Remembrance* (1978) focus on a family of naval heroes before and after the Japanese attack on Pearl Harbor. Judaism is the main factor in *Inside, Outside* (1985) while *The Hope* (1993) and *The Glory* (1994) tell the story of the land of Israel. In 2010, at the age of ninety-five, Wouk published the brief *The Language God Talks*, described by Louisa Thomas of *Newsweek* magazine as "an unusual work – partly a quick trip through developments in cosmology, partly an episodic memoir, partly an essay on faith and science."[11]

Herman Wouk died in his sleep in his home in Palm Springs, California, on May 7, 2019, at the age of 103.

Acting Edition: Samuel French, Inc.

Awards and Honors: A top-ten selection in *The Best Plays of 1953-1954. The Caine Mutiny Court-Martial* was the Drama Critics Circle runner-up in the category of Best Play (the winner was *Teahouse of the August Moon* by John Patrick).

Herman Wouk received the Pulitzer Prize for his novel *The Caine Mutiny* (1952); the Columbia University Medal of Excellence (1952); the American Academy of Achievement Golden Plate Award (1986); the U.S. Navy Memorial Foundation Award (1987); the Guardian of Zion Award (1998); and the Library of Congress Award for Lifetime Achievement (2008).

NOTES

1. *New York Times*, January 21, 1954.
2. *New York Herald Tribune*, January 21, 1954.
3. *New York Post*, January 21, 1954.
4. *Daily News*, January 21, 1954.
5. *New York World-Telegram*, January 21, 1954.
6. *Daily Mirror*, January 21, 1954.
7. *Christian Science Monitor*, May 11, 1983.
8. *WABC-TV-7*, New York, May 5, 1983.
9. *New York Post*, May 6, 1983.
10. *New York Times*, May 8, 2006.
11. *Newsweek*, April 9, 2010.

Inherit the Wind (1955)

Jerome Lawrence (United States, 1915-2004) and Robert E. Lee (United States, 1918-1994)

The historic "monkey trial" of Tennessee high school teacher John T. Scopes, accused of teaching Charles Darwin's theory of evolution in defiance of state law, was dramatized by Jerome Lawrence and Robert E. Lee in a rousing fashion. *Inherit the Wind* was first presented at the Dallas Theatre on January 10, 1955. Later that year, on April 21, it opened to great fanfare in New York's National Theatre for a whopping run of 803 performances.

"The authors of *Inherit the Wind* have followed the outline of the trial very closely and have not neglected its humorous aspects," wrote critic John Chapman in the *Daily News*, "but they have done much more than manufacture a documentary. They have made a play which, in addition to abundantly satisfying the desires of a theatergoer, stirs the mind."[1]

The events that took place in Dayton, Tennessee, during the scorching July of 1925 are the genesis of the play. The playwrights fictionalized the place and the characters but remained faithful to the titanic clash between defense attorney Clarence Darrow (in the play, Henry Drummond) and prosecutor William Jennings Bryan (Matthew Harrison Brady) over a person's right to think.

The drama unfolds in the makeshift courthouse of Hillsboro. Matthew Harrison Brady basks in the idolization of the fundamentalist townspeople. Henry Drummond's defense is steamrolled by a strict judge. No specialists or scientists are allowed to submit evidence. Drummond changes tactics and receives permission to summon a witness who is a Scripture expert, none other than Matthew Harrison Brady. Brady is delighted to take the stand, consumed with righteousness, confident of himself as the champion of the people. There are loud "Amens" and much applause from the spectators.

The courtroom duel between Drummond and Brady is the high point of *Inherit the Wind*. Drummond picks up a copy of Darwin's *Origin of Species* but the Judge decrees that he will confine his questions to the Bible. Drummond tosses Darwin's volume on the counsel table and gets a copy of the Bible. He solicits from Brady his belief that "Everything in the Bible should be accepted, exactly as it is given there." Drummond queries Brady about the story of the whale swallowing Jonah, about Joshua making the sun stand still, and Brady insists, "I have faith in the Bible."

Drummond and Brady continue to parry about various biblical segments, drawing heated reactions from the Hillsboro audience. At last, the judge resorts to his gavel: "Colonel Drummond, the court must be satisfied that this line of questioning has some bearing in the case." Brady says calmly that he is willing to endure "Mr. Drummond's sneering, disrespect, and contempt for all that is holy." Heated, Drummond insists that he finds the individual human mind holy, that an idea is a greater monument than a cathedral. When Brady insists that people should not abandon faith, for faith is the most important thing, Drummond counters with, "Then why did God plague us with the power to think?" and points out that the power to reason is the one faculty that lifts human beings above other earthly creatures.

Gradually, the crowd slips away from Brady and aligns itself more and more with Drummond.

Drummond points at teacher Cates and roars, "This man wishes to think!" He then displays a rock about the size of a tennis ball and asks Brady how old he thinks the rock is. Brady lamely jokes that he is more interested in "the Rock of Ages than in the Age of Rocks." Drummond relates that according to experts the rock is at least ten million years old. Brady dismisses the notion, asserting that the rock could not be more than six thousand years old; he argues that a careful computation of the ages of the prophets as set down in the Old Testament proves that "the Lord began the Creation on the 23rd of October in the year 4,004 B.C. at 9 a.m."

Drummond pounces sarcastically, demanding to know if that was Eastern Standard, Rocky Mountain, or perhaps Daylight-Saving time. Brady loses his equanimity, becomes confused, and begins to stutter. Relentlessly, Drummond continues to lunge at a deflated Brady until he breaks him completely. The astonished crowd shifts its support to the defendant.

The teacher, Bertram Cates, is found guilty but his light sentence – a fine of one hundred dollars – punctures the mighty Evolution Law. Bending history but achieving a touchy climax, the playwrights picture Brady attempting in vain to address his once-faithful flock. Alas, all focus is drawn away from him, and, quivering, Brady falls, dying.

A cynical Baltimore reporter, E.K. Hornbeck (H.L. Menkin), eulogizes Brady as "a Barnum-bunkum Bible-beating bastard." Drummond's reaction is surprising. He admonishes Hornbeck for forgetting that Brady was once "a giant" who got lost because he was looking for God too high up and too far away.

Left alone, Drummond intends to put Darwin's *Origin of Species* in his brief case when he notices the Bible on a desk. He picks it up, and weighs the two books, one in each hand. Smiling, he slaps the books together, inserts them both in the briefcase, and ambles off into the sunset.

* * *

Most of the critics greeted *Inherit the Wind* with hosannas. "An effectively provocative chronicle drama," wrote Richard Watts, Jr.[2] "The town has a hit that is distinguished and challenging," stated William Hawkins.[3] "The new arrival is at its tense best during the trial episodes," asserted Robert Coleman. "These hold the interest in a vise-like grip. It is something like that memorable one in *The Caine Mutiny Court-Martial*. It has drive, suspense, and color. "[4]

Paul Muni's portrayal of Henry Drummond won plaudits from the entire cadre of reviewers. "There's a whale of an old-fashioned, free-swinging, suspender-snapping fight going on at the National, and Paul Muni wins it," declared Walter F. Kerr. "In the rich, raucous, rough-and-tumble second act in the courthouse, he gets hold of the role like a starved hound of magnificent ancestry and shakes it till the feathers fill the room."[5] John McClain gushed, "Hold up your count, Mr. Auditor, we've got a whole flock of new votes for the best performance of the year. Paul Muni, returning to the stage after a long and unauthorized absence, has just brought in a large plurality for his superb delineation of Clarence Darrow."[6] Even Lewis Funke, who dissented from his brethren and found *Inherit the Wind* "lacking in suspense" and "only intermittently compelling," credited Mr. Muni with "a magnificent performance."[7]

Kudos were also showered on Ed Begley as Brady, Tony Randall as Hornbeck, Karl Light as Cates, Bethel Leslie as Rachel, and Staats Cotsworth as Rachel's fundamentalist father, Reverend Jeremiah Brown. Paul Muni won the 1956 Tony Award for Best Actor, Ed Begley won the Tony as Best Featured Actor, and Peter Larkin got the nod for his scene design. Director Herman Shumlin was nominated. [8]

Inherit the Wind did not replicate its New York success when it came to London's St. Martin's Theatre in 1960, running for sixty-nine performances.

The play was revived on Broadway in 1996, directed by John Tillinger, featuring George C. Scott as Henry Drummond and Charles Durning as Matthew Harrison Brady (forty-five performances), and in 2007, staged by Doug Hughes, with Christopher Plummer as Drummond and Brian Dennehy as Brady (100 performances).

Stanley Kramer directed an engrossing movie version of the play in 1960, starring Spencer Tracy (Drummond), Fredric March (Brady), and Gene Kelly (E.K. Hornbeck). A radio rendering was aired in 1965. Television adaptations were broadcast in 1965, with Melvyn Douglas and Ed Begley winning Emmy Awards for their performances as Drummond and Brady; in 1988, with Jason Robards and Kirk Douglas; in 1999, with Jack Lemmon and George C. Scott, the latter now switching roles, playing Brady.

* * *

Both Jerome Lawrence and Robert Edwin Lee were born in Ohio—Lawrence in Cleveland in 1915, Lee in Elyria in 1918. Both inherited an interest in writing from their mothers—a poet and a teacher, respectively. Both excelled at top learning institutions; Lawrence graduated from Ohio State University and the University of California at Los Angeles, Lee from Northwestern University in Chicago and Ohio Weslyan. Both served as consultants to the Secretary of War during World War II, and it was there that they met and cofounded Armed Forces Radio.

The first play that Lawrence and Lee wrote together was the book for the 1948 musical *Look, Ma, I'm Dancing!*, directed by George Abbott and choreographed by Jerome Robbins, cheerfully spotlighting behind-the-scenes escapades of a traveling ballet company. Their next Broadway venture was *Inherit the Wind*. They continued their collaboration on ten additional dramas, comedies and musicals that were produced in New York, including the book and lyrics for *Shangri-La* (1956), based on the novel *Lost Horizon* by James Hilton, about a group of strangers stumbling into a utopian Tibetan land; *Auntie Mame* (1956, London 1958, filmed 1958; revived 2004), based on the autobiographical novel by Patrick Dennis, in which young Patrick is indoctrinated by his flamboyant aunt to become as free-spirited as she is; and *The Gang's All Here* (1959), depicting the corrupt administration of President Warren Harding.

The protagonist of *Only in America* (1959), based on a book by Harry Golden, is a Lower East Side New Yorker who moves to North Carolina and publishes his first book. *A Call on Kuprin* (1961), aka *Checkmate*, based on a novel by Maurice Edelman, is a suspense melodrama in which an American tourist in Russia helps a friend escape from the police state. *Diamond Orchid* (1965), aka *Sparks Fly Upward*, pictures the rise and fall of an obscure radio actress who becomes the First Lady of a Latin-American country but is not accepted by the social and intellectual elite of the nation.

Lawrence and Lee wrote the book and lyrics of *Mame* (1966), an enormously successful musical comedy (1508 performances; filmed 1974; revived 1983), based on their play, *Auntie Mame*. They also wrote the book of *Dear World* (1969), a musical inspired by Jean Giraudoux's play, *The Madwoman of Chaillot*, a fable about an old woman who saves Paris from the scheme of greedy prospectors who plan to tear up the city in order to unearth an oil field. *The Incomparable Max* (1971), drawn from two stories by Max Beerbohm, is about a poet who makes a pact with the devil, and a young man who can see into the future. *First Monday in October* (1978; filmed 1981), is a pre-Sandra Day O'Connor comedy-drama about the first woman appointed to the Supreme Court of the United States and her clash with the chauvinistic all-male body.

Plays penned by Lawrence and Lee that were performed outside of New York include the early 1970s *The Crocodile Smile*, in which a beautiful French woman is in love with two inspired comedians and agrees to marry the "better actor," instigating a rivalry between them to prove their superiority; *Jabberwock*, subtitled, "Improbabilities lived and imagined by James Thurber in the fictional city of Columbus, Ohio;" and *The Night Thoreau Spent in Jail*, a dramatization of biographical incidents in the life of author-poet-naturalist Henry David Thoreau.

Lawrence and Lee's last collaboration, seen at the Missouri Repertory in Kansas City in 1994, was *Whisper in the Mind*, recounting an imaginary meeting between Benjamin Franklin and the eighteenth-century hypnotist Frank Anton Mesmer.

In addition to their important contribution as playwrights, Lawrence and Lee left an indelible mark as co-founders of the American Playwrights Theatre and as committed educators who taught and lectured extensively in the field. Lee served as an adjunct professor of playwriting at UCLA for twenty years. Lawrence was a visiting professor at Ohio State, New York, and Baylor Universities. Ohio State University houses The Jerome Lawrence and Robert E. Lee Theatre Research Institute.

Acting Edition: Dramatists Play Service.

Awards and Honors: a top-ten selection in *The Best Plays of 1954-1955.* Winner of the Donaldson Award, the Outer Critics Circle Award, and the Variety Critics Poll Award both in New York (1955) and London (1960).

Jerome Lawrence and Robert E. Lee earned two George Foster Peabody Awards for distinguished achievement in broadcasting (1949, 1952). They received a Lifetime Achievement Award from the American Theatre Association (1979), the Ohioana Award, keys to the City of Cleveland, an Ohio State Centennial Medal, the Ohio Governor's Award, a Cleveland Play House Plaque, a Pegasus Award, the Moss Hart Memorial Award for plays of the Free World, and a U.S. State Department Medal. In 1984, Lawrence and Lee received the Writers Guild of America Valentine Davies Award for contributions to the entertainment industry. In 1990, they were inducted into the Theatre Hall of Fame and named Fellows of the American Theatre. Among other recognitions, Lawrence and Lee were the recipients of honorary doctorates from the College of Wooster and Ohio State University.

NOTES

1. *Daily News*, April 22, 1955.
2. *New York Post*, April 22, 1955.
3. *New York World-Telegram*, April 22, 1955.

4. *Daily Mirror*, April 22, 1955.
5. *New York Herald Tribune*, April 22, 1955.
6. *New York Journal-American*, April 22, 1955.
7. *New York Times*, April 22, 1955.
8. Paul Muni (1895-1967) was born Meshilem Meier Weisenfreund in Lvov, Poland (now Lviv, Ukraine). His parents, Jewish actors, took the boy to America in 1902 and joined New York's Yiddish theatre. Muni made his stage debut at the age of twelve, joind the Yiddish Art Theatre, and in 1926 made his first appearance on Broadway in *We Americans*, portraying an elderly Jewish man. Hollywood beckoned. In 1932, Muni appeared in two milestone crime films: as the mobster Antonio Camonte in Howard Hawks' *Scarface*, and as James Allen, an innoicent man victimized by the justice system, in Mervyn LeRoy's *I Am a Fugitive from a Chain Gang*. Muni's wide variety of screen roles included the lawyer Johnny Ramirez in *Bordertown* (1935); coal miner Joe Radek in *Black Fury* (1935); the famous French scientist in *The Story of Louis Pasteur* (1936); farmer Wang in *The Good Earth* (1936); the title role in *The Life of Emile Zola* (1937); the Mexical leader Benito Juarez in *Juarez* (1939); Pierre Esprit Radisson, the founder of a trading company in *Hudson's Bay* (1941); Erik Torensen, a Norwegian fighting the Nazis, in *Commandos Strike at Dawn* (1942); Professor Joseph Elsner, mentor of Chopin, in *A Song to Remember* (1945); Eddie Kagel, a murdered convict who is sent back to earth by the Devil as a respected judge, in *Angel on My Shoulder* (1946); and Dr. Sam Ableman, a kind Brooklyn family doctor, in *The Last Angry Man* (1959). Muni was niminated for an Academy Award five times, winning once for *The Story of Louis Pasteur*.

   Prior to *Inherit the Wind*, Muni added to his slaurels highly regarded Broadway appearances as ex-convict Benny Horowitz in George Abbott's *Four Walls* (1927); the lawyer George Simon in Elmer Rice's *Counsellor-at-Law* (1931); King McCloud, who confronts a gang of gamblers in Maxwell Anderson's *Key Largo* (1939); Tevya, a concentration camp survivor in Ben Hecht's *A Flag is Born* (1946); and Tony, a Napa Valley winegrower, in Sidney Howard's *They Knew What They Wanted* (1949, revival).

Time Limit! (1956)

Henry Denker (United States, 1912-2012)

Major Harry Cargill is about to be court-martialed for treason. He is accused of betraying his fellow Americans in a North Korean prison camp by cooperating with the enemy, making propaganda broadcasts, and confessing falsely that the United States unleashed germ warfare.

The Major admits that he is guilty and offers no defense. But a zealous judge advocate in charge of the case, Lt. Col. William Edwards, is not satisfied and insists on digging deeper. *Time Limit!* centers on Edwards' investigation as he interrogates a few former POWs. Their accounts are related via flashbacks.

Edwards' superior, Major General Joseph Connors, whose son died in a Korean stockade, declares that it is an "open-and-shut" case of betrayal. But Edwards persists. Following an interview with Cargill's wife, Mary, Edwards remarks to his secretary, WAC Corporal Jean Evans, that Cargill seems to be two men—and the man his wife described would not have committed treason.

The breakthrough in the case occurs when Edwards and Evans notice that various witnesses used identical phrases when presenting the Korean events; they all said, "it happened suddenly" and described a disease as "an acute case of dysentery," "bacillary dysentery," and "dehydration." None said "a bad case" or "a violent case," muses Edwards, always "an acute case."

By the end of the second act, in a harrowing flashback, we learn that it was General Connor's son who cracked under pressure and informed on his fellow prisoners. The American captives cast lots in choosing an executioner, and against Cargill's protestations ("This is a cold-blooded murder"), young Connors is strangled while the group sings a rousing chorus of "Caissons" to drown out his screams.

In a shattering scene that elevates *Time Limit!* from a mere thriller to the realm of provocative ideas, General Connors learns the bitter truth about his son. At first the general refuses to believe it, but he later insists that he cannot forgive cowardice, not even in his own son. Edwards attempts to convince him that everyone has his limit and that there is no crime in being human.

Major Cargill then reveals his motive in collaborating with the enemy. Upon the killing of young Connors, the commander of the camp, furious, addressed Cargill as the ranking officer and threatened that unless he cooperated, all eighteen men would be tried for murder and executed. To him, says Cargill, eighteen men—their wives, their families—seemed important. He just gave the Koreans everything they wanted, everything.

Edwards appreciates the fact that Cargill initially didn't defend himself, reluctant to involve the men. However, General Connors believes that no matter the circumstances, anyone who gives aid or comfort to the enemy is a traitor. He feels sorry for Cargill, for everything that happened to him, for having been through the horrors of a prison camp, but no man is exempt, not his son, not anyone. The fact remains: he helped the enemy. That is the code of conduct. Their job is to obey rules, not remake them.

Edwards tells the general that if Cargill is tried, he will volunteer to defend him.

* * *

The passage of time has eroded some of the impact generated by *Time Limit!* when it premiered at the Booth Theatre on January 24, 1956. The New York critics were enthusiastic. "Out of a sample case of prison camp treason, the authors of *Time Limit!* have written a stunning drama," stated Brooks Atkinson. "They have taken a look at a horrifying wartime situation that cannot be resisted, and they have asked some searching questions about it that cannot be dismissed."[1]

John Chapman found the play "a crisp, tightly fashioned, suspenseful thriller about a brain-washing job in Korea and what happens afterward."[2] William Hawkins coined *Time Limit!* "a bombshell of human endurance."[3] John McClain assured his readers that "It seems fairly safe to say there's a new hit in town… My wife said she enjoyed it immensely—and I think you'll agree with her."[4] Richard Watts Jr. peppered his review with superlatives: "*Time Limit!* is a taut and striking topical melodrama with disturbingly thoughtful overtones… An extremely moving and unsettling play…Another excellent drama has come to town."[5] Robert Coleman declared, "*Time Limit!* is a gripping drama about what makes men break under pressure… An absorbing and exciting experience in the theatre. It is an intelligent and thoughtful appraisal of some of the issues which our Army, and nation, must face."[6]

The sole dissenter was Walter F. Kerr: "Why, then, does *Time Limit!* seem to thin out along the way, to approach its roaring climax with a kind of waning sense of responsibility?... *Time Limit!* has taken a robust whack at the barbed wire that tangles men's minds. But when it cuts through, it does not cut quite clean."[7]

In his introduction to the *Best Plays of 1955-1956*, Louis Kronenberger suggests that an "uneasy blend of truth and theatre reduced the value and blurred the integrity of *Time Limit!*... The debate asks at what point cracking up might be forgivable, and how far a moment of capitulation must cancel out a lifetime of loyalty. It asks finally whether Communist brainwashing tactics may not call for revised standards of judgment – and justice. In asking such questions, *Time Limit!* offered, beyond scenes that proved vibrant and tense, a nice new twist from a thriller. What cost its distinction was its commonplace writing; what reduced its importance was it letting a serious theme too often defer to a lurid plot; what blurred its point was having Cargill, even when he turned traitor, act from such worthy motives. This last maneuver meant salvaging the play's hero at the cost of jettisoning its problem."[8]

Guided by director Windsor Lewis, the acting ensemble of *Time Limit!* was unanimously hailed. Atkinson: "As the inquiring Judge Advocate, Arthur Kennedy gives another one of those performances that are simple in outline but that represent concentrated emotion."[9] Kerr: "Richard Kiley, as the suspect man who is willing to take any punishment meted out to him, shapes the rising tension with shrewd skill."[10] McClain:"In the uniformly superb cast… Thomas Carlin, a most promising neophyte, who plays the unhappy Lt. George Miller; Allyn McLerie, most decoratively filling the uniform of a WAC corporal and Harvey Stephens lending dignity in the role of the major general."[11]

McClain also compliments designer Ralph Alswang, who "has contrived a set which can switch from an office in an Army post to a Korean prison compound by the flick of a switch."[12]

Time Limit! ran for 127 performances.

Scripted by Henry Denker, an effective movie version of *Time Limit!* was directed by Karl Malden in 1957, featuring Richard Widmark (Lt. Col. William Edwards), Richard Basehart (Major Harry Cargill), Carl Benton Reid (Maj. General Joseph Connors), Dolores Michaels (WAC Corporal Jean Evans), and June Lockhart (Mary Cargill).

* * *

Born in New York City in 1912, Henry Denker received his Law Qualifying Certificate from New York University in 1931 and his doctorate in 1934. A member of the New York State Bar Association, Denker penned another stirring courtroom drama – *A Case of Libel* (1963), based on the book *My Life in Court* by Louis Nizer. The action, unfolding mostly in New York County's Supreme Court, is rooted in the once-famous Quentin Reynolds-Westbrook Pegler lawsuit. Denker also probed legal system machinations in a number of best-selling novels, notably *My Son, the Lawyer* (1950), *Error of Judgment* (1979), *Judge Spencer Dissents* (1986), *Labyrinth* (1990), *Doctor on Trial* (1992), *This Child Is Mine* (1995), and *Clas$$ Action* (2005).

Denker's best play is arguably *A Far Country* (1961), a poignant depiction of Sigmund Freud's first critical psychoanalysis case, that of young Viennese Elizabeth von Ritter who had lost the use of her legs after the death of her father.[13] The playwright's contributions to the stage include a number of comedies whose topics range from the generation gap (*What Did We Do Wrong?*) to the love affair between two senior citizens (*The Second Time Around*), to the cementing of a stormy relationship between a Jewish widower in a wheelchair and his African-American therapist (*Horowitz and Mrs. Washington*).

For radio, Denker wrote *Radio Reader's Digest* (CBS, 1943-1946) and was writer, director and producer of *The Greatest Story Ever Told* (ABC, 1947-1957). For television, he originated the series *False Witness* (NBC, 1939), wrote *Give Us Barabbas* (Hallmark Hall of Fame, NBC, 1961), produced *The Man Who Wanted to Live Forever*, aka *The Only Way Out Is Death* (1970), the supernatural tale of an isolated medical research center catering to eternal youth, and penned *A Time for Miracles* (1980), a chronicle of the life story of America's Elizabeth Bayley Seton who, as Mother Seton, was canonized in 1975.

For the cinema, Denker immersed himself in crime: he penned the screenplays for *The Hook* (1962), about a psychopathic serial killer who has a hook in place of one of his hands; *Twilight of Honor* (1963), in which a young lawyer defends a black-jacket rebel accused of murder; *Judgment: The Court Martial of Lt. William Calley* (1975), spotlighting the man responsible for the My Lai massacre during the Vietnam War; and *Outrage!* (1986), still another trial case, the tale of an idealistic attorney who defends a client accused of killing the man who allegedly raped and murdered his daughter.

Acting Edition: Samuel French, Inc.

Awards and Honors: Henry Denker's *A Far Country* was a top-ten selection in *The Best Plays of 1960-1961*. As author-director of the religious radio series *The Greatest Story Ever Told*, Denker received the Peabody Award, the Christopher Award, the *Variety* Showmanship Award, and the Brotherhood Award from the National Conference of Christians and Jews.

NOTES

1. *New York Times*, January 25, 1956.
2. *Daily News*, January 25, 1956.
3. *New York World-Telegram*, January 25, 1956.
4. *New York Journal-American*, January 25, 1956.
5. *New York Post*, January 25, 1956.

6. *Daily Mirror*, January 25, 1956.
7. *New York Herald Tribune*, January 25, 1956.
8. *The Best Plays of 1955-1956* (New York: Dodd, Mead and Company, 1956), 15,16.
9. *New York Times*, January 25, 1956.
10. *New York Herald Tribune*, January 25, 1956.
11. *New York Journal-American*, January 25, 1956.
12. *Ibid.*
13. Years later, *A Far Country* still proved to be both suspenseful and thought provoking when it was presented, under my direction, at Stanford University and, in a Hebrew translation, at the Zavit (Angle) Theatre in Tel-Aviv, Israel.

The Ponder Heart (1956)

Joseph Fields (United States, 1895-1966) and Jerome Chodorov (United States, 1911-2004)

Uncle Daniel Ponder has a heart as big as the sky. He doesn't meet a person without giving him something. Uncle Daniel inherited a fortune from his father, which he keeps distributing among the villagers of Clay, a small Southern town, and to newcomers who cross his path. His niece, Edna Earle, cannot stop him from dispensing with his suits of clothes, calves, pigeons, a goat, a Shetland pony, a cow pasture, a cypress cistern, a field of Dutch clover, even his own cemetery plot. But now the man with "the sweetest disposition in the world" is being tried for the murder of his wife.

Joseph Fields and Jerome Chodorov based *The Ponder Heart* on a story by Eudora Welty (1909-2001) that was published in 1953 in *The New Yorker* and reprinted the following year by Harcourt, Brace and Company. The Fields-Chodorov adaptation focuses on a claim by the backwoods family of Bonnie Dee Peacock, goaded by an ambitious district attorney, that Uncle Daniel killed his child bride during a thunderstorm. In the whimsical spirit of *Alice in Wonderland,* Uncle Daniel escorts his accusers to the trial so that they "get good seats in the front row," congratulates his nemesis, Prosecutor Dorris R. Gladney, for "one of the most movin' and beautiful pleas I ever heard to a jury," insists on taking the stand against advice by counsel, and invites Gladney to grill him.

In a flashback, we meet his late wife Bonnie Dee, a seventeen-year-old simple-minded waif whom he encountered at a candy store. She marries her suitor so she can stay in bed as late as she pleases at the Ponder Hill House, lick pistachio ice cream cones, and admire the shiny dishwashing machine.

Uncle Daniel claims proudly, "I just married the sweetest little doll on two feet," while the bride is described by Edna Earle as someone who "could sit all day and try to figure out how the tail of the C got through the L in the Coca-Cola sign."

Back at the County Courthouse, Mr. Gladney equates the case to *Othello,* and casts Uncle Daniel as Dr. Jekyll and Mr. Hyde. The local boys retort by squirting the prosecutor with water pistols. Judge Waite, chomping on a cigar, his feet on the desk, permits the accused to leave the premises to stretch his legs.

On the witness stand, Uncle Daniel gives away all his assets: a trust fund in Edna Earle's name, his big house up on the hill to the Peacocks, the Studebaker to his dear friend, Miss Teacake Magee, and to Judge Waite, the pickup truck. All his possessions, says Uncle Daniel, give him only trouble.

Uncle Daniel describes how during a severe thunderstorm, Bonnie Dee was literally frightened to death. He pulled the girl from under the sofa, held her in his arms, and could feel her heart beatin' like a frightened rabbit. She took her last breath in his arms, "an' blew off like one of those little dandelion puffballs like we used to tell time by." That's exactly what happened, declares Uncle Daniel, the whole truth and nothin' but the truth. As expected, by the Clay townsfolk and by the New York audience, Uncle Daniel is found not guilty.

* * *

The Ponder Heart opened at New York's Music Box on February 16, 1956. The morning-after reviewers admired David Wayne as Uncle Daniel, Sarah Marshall as Bonnie Dee, Una Merkel as Edna Earle, Will Geer as District Attorney Gladney, and John McGovern as Judge Waite, but they were split on the merits of the play. The yessers included Walter F. Kerr, who lauded "a bubbling spirit beneath its lazy graces;"[1] Brooks Atkinson, who found the play "original, charming and funny;"[2] and Richard Watts Jr., who considered it "one of the funniest and most engaging of the season's comedies."[3]

The naysayers were Robert William Hawkins, who believed that "*The Ponder Heart,* for all its attractions, is not about anything much;"[4] John McClain, who objected to "a plot that wears thin. We see what's coming down the pike, and we don't much care;"[5] and Robert Coleman, who called it "a frail vehicle."[6] *The Ponder Heart* beat for 149 performances.

The Ponder Heart was not converted to the silver screen, but in 1964, West Germany's television adapted the play to television under the title *Angeklagter: Onkel Daniel*, with Rudolf Platte playing the title role.

* * *

In 1955, Eudora Welty's *The Ponder Heart* was awarded The Howells Medal of the American Academy of Arts and Letters. Welty was a notable novelist and short story writer, whose output includes *A Curtain of Green* (1941), *The Robber Bridegroom* (1942), *The Wide Net* (1943), *Delta Wedding* (1946), *Golden Apples* (1949), *The Bride of Innisfallen* (1955), *The Shoe Bird* (1964), *Losing Battles* (1970), *The Optimist's Daughter* (1972), *The Eye of the Story: Selected Essays and Reviews* (1977), and *The Collected Stories of Eudora Welty* (1980).

Native New Yorkers Joseph Fields and Jerome Chodorov found each other in Hollywood, where they began their collaboration on crime riddled

The Gentleman from Louisiana (1936), a yarn about horse-race fixing, and *Reported Missing* (1937), in which planes are sabotaged by a gang of robbers. Among Fields-Chodorov's notable movies are *Two Girls on Broadway* (1940), with Lana Turner and Joan Blondell; *Dulcy* (1940), a comedy based on the Broadway hit by George S. Kaufman and Marc Connelly; *Louisiana Purchase* (1941), a Bob Hope vehicle; and *Man from Texas* (1948), a Western adventure founded on the play *Missouri Legend* by Elizabeth B. Ginty.

Fields and Chodorov's first Broadway play, *Schoolhouse on the Lot* (1938), spoofed filmland intrigue. A succession of generally successful productions included *My Sister Eileen* (1940), a dramatization of Ruth McKenney's stories about the misadventures of two Ohio sisters in Greenwich Village; *Junior Miss* (1941), an adolescent comedy extracted from the *New Yorker* sketches by Sally Benson; *The French Touch* (1945), depicting the patriotic zeal of Parisian actors during the Nazi occupation; *Wonderful Town* (1953), the musicalization of *My Sister Eileen; The Girl in Pink Tights* (1954), a musical taking place following the Civil War in the theatrical district of New York; and *Anniversary Waltz* (1954), a domestic comedy of marital discord.

On his own, Jerome Chodorov contributed material to the review *Alive and Kicking* (1950); wrote the book for the Coney Island musical *I Had a Ball* (1964); penned the comedy *Three Bags Full* (1966), about a womanizing sports goods tycoon; drafted the book for the Los Angeles tryout of *Dumas and Son* about the great French writer(1967); revamped the Viennese operetta *The Great Waltz* (1970); tinkered on the road with a Claudette Colbert vehicle, *A Community of Two,* during the 1973-74 season; and, with Mark Bramble, adapted the John O'Hara-Richard Rodgers musical *Pal Joey* (1978).

Chodorov's sentiment for suspense was expressed in his film adaptation of Earl Stanley Gardner's *The Case of the Lucky Legs* (1935), his Broadway direction of Alec Coppel's mystery-comedy *The Gazebo* (1958), and his penning, with Norman Panama, of *A Talent for Murder* (1982), starring Claudette Colbert and Jean-Pierre Aumont.[7]

Joseph Fields's solo work encompasses *The Doughgirls* (1942), a comedy unfolding in wartime, overcrowded Washington; and *I Gotta Get Out* (1947), about a gang of bookies setting up shop in the kitchen of a trusting Long Island matron. With Anita Loos, Fields wrote the book for the successful musical *Gentlemen Prefer Blondes* (1949), going back in time to the flapper days of the 1920's; with Peter De Vries, he penned *The Tunnel of Love* (1957), poking fun at expecting wives and unwed mothers; with Oscar Hammerstein II, he adapted the novel by C.Y. Lee for the musical *Flower Drum Song* (1958), a romance set in San Francisco's Chinatown.

Fields staged on Broadway Arthur Miller's *The Man Who Had All the Luck* (1944) and William Marchant's *The Desk Set* (1955).

For the cinema, Fields wrote the screenplays of many B Movies during the 1930s and 1940s. He incorporated crime elements into *Lightning Strikes Twice* (1934), *Waterfront Lady* (1935), *The Walking Dead* (1936, with Boris Karloff on a revenge quest), *Grand Jury* (1936), *Reported Missing* (1937), *The Girl and the Gambler* (1939, based on the play *The Dove* by Willard Mack); *The Spellbinder* (1939), *Two Thoroughbreds* (1939), and *Phantom Raiders* (1940, featuring Walter Pidgeon as sleuth Nick Carter).

Other motion pictures scripted by Fields include *Annie Oakley* (1935), starring Barbara Stanwyck as the legendary sharpshooter; *A Night in Casablanca* (1946), with the Marx Brothers confronting a ring of Nazi spies; and *The Farmer Takes a Wife* (1953), a period musical romance enlivened by Betty Grable.[8]

Acting Edition: Samuel French, Inc. (in manuscript form).

Awards and Honors: A top-ten selection in *The Best Plays of 1955-1956*: "Beguiling entertainment… a nice light pastel daffiness about it, a way of making things look delightfully woozy through wrong-prescription rose-colored glasses."[9] Jerome Chodorov and Joseph Fields wrote the book of *Wonderful Town*, the 1953 Tony Award winner for Best Musical.

NOTES

1. *New York Herald Tribune,* February 17, 1956.
2. *New York Times,* February 17, 1956.
3. *New York Post,* February 17, 1956.
4. *New York World-Telegram,* February 17, 1956.
5. *New York Journal-American*, February 17, 1956.
6. *Daily Mirror*, February 17, 1956.
7. Jerome Chodorov's older brother, Edward Chodorov, was also a playwright, author of the nerve-wracking *Kind Lady* (1935).
8. Joseph Albert Fields was the son of vaudevillian Lew Fields and the brother of writers/lyricists Herbert and Dorothy, who collaborated on musicals composed by Richard Rodgers, Cole Porter, George Gershwin, and Irving Berlin and penned the libretto and lyrics of *Redhead* (1959), a Broadway musical murder mystery set in a waxworks museum in 1880s London.
9. Louis Kronenberger, ed., *The Best Plays of 1955-1956* (New York: Dodd, Mead and Company, 1956), 8.

Compulsion (1957)

Meyer Levin (United States, 1905-1981)

Nathan Leopold, age nineteen, and Richard Loeb, age eighteen, spoiled sons of Chicago millionaires, conspired to kill a fourteen-year-old boy, Bobby Franks, for the thrill of it. Intellectually brilliant, the two collegiates set out to commit the perfect crime. When caught and brought to trial, the counsel for the defense, Clarence Darrow, convinced the judge that the heinous act was rooted in a pathologically compulsive, uncontrollable urge, so instead of the chair, Leopold and Loeb were condemned to life imprisonment.

Author Meyer Levin based his 1956 novel, *Compulsion*, on the 1924 Leopold-Loeb *cause célèbre* trial, following the facts of the case closely, while changing names. A year later he reenacted the event in a sprawling dramatization of twenty explicit scenes with fifty-one intense characters.

During the tryout preparations for the opening of *Compulsion* on Broadway, a feud ensued between author Levin and producer Michael Myerberg. According to behind-the-scenes mavens, it was Robert Thom who inked the final rendition of the play (billed in the program as the "Producer's Version"). Whoever wrote it, *Compulsion* captures what Brooks Atkinson of the *New York Times* calls the "morbid, horrible, degenerate, odious" elements of the case.[1]

The action zigzags through various locales. A prologue takes place in a prison cell, where Sid Silver, a middle-aged journalist, interviews Judd Steiner (Loeb), who, after being incarcerated for thirty years, is now eligible for parole; his partner Artie Straus (Leopold) died in jail. "We believed we could be gods," says Judd. "Gods! With power over life and death!"

A flashback transfers us to a river embankment where a murder has just been committed. Judd and Artie hide the body in a concrete sewer cistern — "It's as good as Edgar Allan Poe," chuckles Artie.

In order to sidetrack the police, the cocky young murderers send a ransom note to the victim's family and go out to celebrate in a speakeasy.

Artie and Judd keep reassuring one another that "our minds are superior; we must win," but two mistakes cause their downfall. A pair of spectacles found in the vicinity of the corpse was too big to fit the murdered boy, so it is concluded that they must have been dropped by the culprit; eventually the glasses are tracked to Judd. And an analysis of the ransom note leads the police to Judd's portable typewriter, where an identical "p" is out of line. The discovery of the instrument of death, a chisel with a taped blade, clinches the case against the killers.

Compulsion ruminates upon Judd's idolation of Artie and their homosexual relationship. Judd confesses to Dr. McNarry, Director of the Washington Hospital for the Mentally Diseased, that he completely identified himself with Artie, would even watch with envy the food Artie ate and the drink going down his throat.

Defense Attorney Jonathan Wilk (Darrow) decides to have the pair plead guilty before a judge alone and present the accused mental condition as a mitigating circumstance. The trial of Illinois State versus Judah Steiner, Jr. and Arthur Straus, accused of the willful kidnapping and murder of Paulie Kessler (Franks), pits prosecution and defense psychiatrists against each other. Questions of juvenile delinquency and capital punishment are also subject of the courtroom battle.

The judge's verdict, chiefly in consideration of the defendants' age, was life imprisonment instead of death.

* * *

Compulsion premiered at the Ambassador Theatre on October 24, 1957, to a mixed critical reception. John Chapman called the play "overpowering for a good stretch of the way — a story of crime to make the blood run cold."[2] Robert Coleman found the script "rough, raw and gripping... It is melodramatic meat for those with strong stomachs... It is as fascinating to watch as a cobra, head puffed up with venom, ready to strike. It is like sinking into a jazzed-up replica of *Dante's Inferno*."[3] John McClain greeted *Compulsion* as "the most ambitious production of the new season, generally a bounteous and brilliant exploration of the facts in the case, legal and psychological."[4]

Walter Kerr was less enthusiastic: "*Compulsion* lacks the dramatic shape to sustain, and pull together, its many virtues. ... The materials are interesting, if coldly clinical; the incidental excitements are often real; the end result is a mammoth labyrinth from which no identifiable play emerges."[5] Frank Aston concluded, "Among the shortcomings are its great length and lack of suspense. You can't sit on the edge of your seat wondering how it will come out when everyone has known the answer these last 33 years—not for three hours you can't"[6] Richard Watts Jr. believed that "*Compulsion* talks itself into ineffectuality."[7]

Brooks Atkinson praised Peter Larkin's "stunning unit set in which a monstrous bridge presses down on the drama with a weight that is remorseless and sinister," and hailed the performances: "Roddy McDowall and Dean Stockwell play the two boys brilliantly—Mr. McDowall gay, antic and arrogant; Mr. Stockwell crushed, weak, gloomy."[8] In a follow-up article Atkinson bemoaned that the play "lasts more than three hours, which is a long time to be steeped in crime, perversion and morbidity…If *Compulsion* were a serious work of theatre art, these actors could endow it with wisdom and beauty. They are less mechanical than the play in which they are appearing."[9]

Compulsion ran for 140 performances on Broadway. It was adapted to the screen in 1959, under Richard Fleischer's direction, with Dean Stockwell repeating the role of Judd, Bradford Dillman as Artie, and Orson Welles as attorney Wilk.

Other plays inspired by the Leopold-Loeb case include Patrick Hamilton's *Rope* (1929), filmed by Alfred Hitchcock in 1948, featuring John Dall and Farley Granger as the youthful murderers;[10] John Logan's *Never the Sinner*, which premiered in Chicago in 1985, played in Adelaide, Australia in 1994, opened in London in 1990, and ran successfully Off Broadway in 1997; George Singer's *Leopold and Loeb*, produced by Off Broadway's Emerging Artists Theatre Company in 1997; *Thrill Me* (2003), with book, lyrics and music by Stephen dolginoff, whose conceit is that Nathan Leopold left behind the incriminating glasses purposefully, counting on a verdict of life imprisonment and thus having the fickle Richard Loeb all to himself forever; and *Dickie and Babe* (2008), written and directed in Hollywood, California by Daniel Henning after three years of immersing himself in court transcripts, medial reports and other documents related to the case.

* * *

Born in 1905, Meyer Levin emerged from one of the crime-riddled sections of Chicago to become a reporter for the *Chicago Daily News* and a contributor to the literary magazine *The Menorah Journal* at the age of eighteen. When twenty-four, he drew on his experiences and published his first novel, *The Reporter*. In 1931, Levin wrote the novel *Yehuda*, about the tribulations of farmers on a kibbutz in Palestine. Six years later he examined assimilation among Chicago's second-generation Jews in *The Old Bunch*, regarded by some as his best novel.

In the 1930s, when ten steel mill strikers were shot down, Levin campaigned against Chicago police brutality and covered the event in *Citizens*, a 1940 novel admired by Ernest Hemingway.

During World War II, Levin made documentary films for the U.S. Office of War Information and became a war correspondent for the Jewish Telegraphic Agency. After the war he went to Palestine, joined the Haganah underground, and in 1947, a year before the creation of the state of Israel, he made two films in Hebrew: the drama *Bayit Avi* (*My Father's House*), about a boy's search for his parents, who disappeared after being held in a concentration camp, and the documentary *Lo Tafhidenu* (*The Unafraid*), also known as *The Illegals*, an account of a ship that smuggled Jewish escapees from war-torn Europe.[11]

Levin's *Compulsion* (1956), the chronicle of the Leopold and Loeb case, was the first "documentary novel," a style later used in Truman Capote's *In Cold Blood* and Norman Mailer's *The Executioner's Song*. Mailer referred to Levin as "one of the best American writers working in the realistic tradition."

Levin penned a powerful trilogy dealing with the Holocaust: *Eva* (1959), *The Fanatic* (1963), and *The Stronghold* (1965). His historical novels *The Settlers* (1972) and *The Harvest* (1978) are concerned with early pioneering life in pre-Israel Palestine.

In 1951, Levin became aware of "*The Diary of Anne Frank*" and conceived it as a play and movie. His dramatization was accepted for production but suddenly the producers decided that it was "unstageworthy" and mounted on Broadway an adaptation of the diary by Frances Goodrich and Albert Hackett. It became a big hit and spawned a major motion picture. Levin launched a twenty-year legal battle to have his rejected version performed, and told the agonizing story in *The Obsession* (1974).[12]

Levin also wrote a series of non-fiction books about Judaism and its philosophy and composed an illustrated Haggadah for the Passover ceremony.

Acting Edition: Dramatists Play Service (in manuscript form).

Awards and Honors: The novel *Compulsion* was given a Special Edgar Allan Poe Award by the Mystery Writers of America in 1957.

NOTES

1. *New York Times*, October 25, 1957.
2. *Daily News*, October 25, 1957.
3. *Daily Mirror*, October 25, 1957.
4. *New York Journal-American*, October 25, 1957.
5. *New York Herald Tribune*, October 25, 1957.
6. *New York World-Telegram*, October 25, 1957.
7. *New York Post*, October 25, 1957.
8. *New York Times*, October 25, 1957.
9. *New York Times*, November 3, 1957.
10. In addition to the movie versions of *Rope* (1948) and *Compulsion* (1959), the low-budget, black-and-white *Swoon* (1992) was also inspired by the Leopold-Loeb story.
11. In 1978, Meyer Levin described what became of the passengers of the *Un-afraid* in a thirty-eight-minute short made in the United States.

12. The saga of Mayer Levin's painstaking lobbying for his version of *The Diary of Anne Frank* is accounted in the play *Compulsion* by Rinne Groff, presented February 1 to March 13, 2011, at Off Broadway's Public Theatre. Mandy Patinkin played a fictionalized version of Levin.

The Blacks (1959)

Jean Genet (France, 1910-1986)

Jean Genet called his play *Les Nègres* (*The Blacks*) "a clown show." Using a play-within-a-play structure, *The Blacks* continued Genet's recurring device of pitting reality against illusion to critique contemporary civilization, already established in *Le Balcon* (*The Balcony*, 1957).

The curtain is drawn to reveal a backdrop curtain of black velvet and several tiers of different heights. On an upper level there is the Court of Justice, composed of a haughty Queen, her dwarfish Valet, a hanging Judge, a missionary Bishop, and an island Governor. Below them is a group of ordinary villagers who weave in and out of a variety of impersonations. The entire cast is Black. Those of the Court wear white masks, representing the dominant white race, and are an extension of the white audience in the theatre.

In the center of the stage is a catafalaque—a raised platform—covered with a white cloth, decorated with bouquets of flowers. Four Black men and four Black women are dancing a minuet to Mozart's "Don Giovanni." The men's evening clothes are worn with brown shoes; the ladies' costumes—heavily spangled evening gowns—suggest fake elegance, the height of bad taste. As they dance, they pluck flowers from their lapels and bodices and lay them on the catafalque.

A garish neon light fades up on the Court. The Queen wears a sad white mask with a drooping mouth. A royal crown is on her head, a scepter in her hand. The Valet wears a striped waistcoat and carries a towel on his arm. The Governor wears a uniform and is holding a pair of field glasses. The Judge wears a scarlet robe, while the Bishop is clad in a white cape and pectoral cross.

The dancers bow ceremoniously to the Court. One of the men, Archibald Absalom Wellington, introduces himself to both the Court and audience, and continues to name the other dancers. The Queen cuts him short and abruptly asks the Bishop, "Are they going to kill her?" The Bishop is taken aback: "But Madam—she's dead!"

Archibald and the group prepare to present to the Court a ritual, a ceremony, in the form of a trial for murder. He and his friends killed a white woman, an old drunkard who used to squat on a pile of rags at the entrance of the village bridge. They'll reenact the crime step-by-step.

The Black villagers light cigarettes and arrange themselves in a circle. Alarmed, the Governor whispers, "They're going to cook her and eat her!"

The Bishop urges the Court members to pray. The Court becomes even more alarmed when the villagers proclaim that they also did away with a milkman, a postman, a seamstress and a government clerk.

The villagers decide to shift their attention to the rape and murder of a young, attractive woman. The local vicar, Samba Graham Diouf, dons a blond wig, a pair of white gloves, and a crude cardboard carnival mask representing a laughing white woman with big, rosy cheeks. He stands in front of the catafalque, facing the audience and knitting a pink helmet. A villager stealthily enters a bedroom lit dimly by moonlight and tells the Court: "The husband arrived too late. He'll find only his wife's corpse, disemboweled and still warm."

A person representing the Newport News announces that the murderer will "certainly be executed." The Queen, Judge, Bishop, Governor and Valet leave to discuss the case and its verdict. They reenter drunk, hiccoughing and laughing. The Judge declares," One can't hold all of Africa responsible for the death of a white woman. Nevertheless, there's no denying the fact that one of you is guilty… He killed out of hatred. Hatred of the color white." The Judge adds that it doesn't matter who among the villagers committed the crime; a Negro's a Negro, and any Black man will do to break his limbs and put his neck into the noose.

Nrs. Felicity, militant, confronts the Court with a warning that "everything is changing. Whatever is gentle and kind and good and tender aill be black. Milk will be black, sugar, rice, the sky, doves, hope, will be black..."

Suddenly several firecrackers explode off-stage, and their sparks are seen against the dark background of the set. The Black villagers, who were squatting, stand up, draw revolvers, and shoot. One by one, the Governor, Judge, Bishop, Valet and Queen fall, forming a heap in the middle of the stage.

But soon the five "dead" characters rise, take off their masks, and bow. Archibald announces to the audience that the performance has come to an end. The opening measures of "Don Giovanni" are heard. With an adieux to the spectators, the entire cast dances the minuet around the white-draped catafalque with which the play began.

* * *

The Blacks was first performed on October 28, 1959, at the Théatre de Lutèce in Paris. The play was directed by Roger Blin, who went on to stage English-speaking productions of the play in Cambridge, Cardiff and London, the latter opening on May 30, 1961, at the Royal Court Theatre. The Lord Chamberlain insisted on removing "blatantly shocking" words, but the critics remained harsh. Kenneth Tynan appreciated the theme— "a timeless struggle between the ins and the outs" – but felt that the play "drowns in a flood of prose poetry... Genet's mind moves from image to image, never from an idea to idea."[1] Other reviewers called the production "pointless," "weary," "obscure," and "reeling."

Across the Atlantic, *The Blacks* came to Off Broadway's St. Marks Playhouse on May 4, 1961, featuring a luminous cast of Black actors destined for greatness on stage and screen: Roscoe Lee Browne (Archibald Absalom Wellington), Raymond St. Jacques (Judge), Maya Angelou Make (Queen), Charles Gordone (Valet), and James Earl Jones, Cynthia Belgrave, Cicely Tyson, Godfrey M. Cambridge, and Helen Martin as some of the prominent villagers. Gene Frankel directed. The team of designers included Kim E. Swados (set), Patricia Zipprodt (costumes and masks), and Lee Watson (Lighting). Howard Taubman of the *New York Times* wrote: "There is no mistaking the fierce motif that courses through M. Genet's furious flights of language encompassing obscenity and purity, violence and tenderness, hatred, and love... In *The Blacks*, M. Genet is not only a moralist of high indignation but also a prophet of rage and compassion."[2]

The Blacks had a whopping run of 1,408 performances. In 1963, the company traveled to Montreal, Canada for two showings at Her Majesty's Theatre. The play was produced at the Mark Taper Forum in Los Angeles in 1962, and again in 1970. In 1964, *The Blacks* was presented at the West Berlin Festival, at the Venice Biennial, and in Darmstadt, West Germany, with white players in blackface. Additional showings of *The Blacks* were undertaken by the Seattle Repertory Theatre, Seattle, Washington (1969) and by the Black Repertory Theatre at the Kennedy Center, Washington, D.C. (1973).

In 2002, a localized version of *The Blacks* was produced in Israel, replacing African-Americans with Palestinians. The Classical Theatre of Harlem mounted the play in 2001-2002, 2002-2003 (winning four Obie Awards), and 2008, establishing the group as one of Off Broadway's most innovative companies. In 2007, *The Blacks* was revived at the Theatre Royal, Stratford East, London.

Louis Kronenberger asserts in *The Best Plays of 1960-1961* that "*The Blacks* was the first sophisticated play about the racial question to be written with no taboos in its use of words, images or ideas."[3]

Scholar Joseph T. Shipley writes: "No more violent attack on white supremacy and 'superiority' has been staged than this savage clownerie, to use the author's term, by the lifelong rebel, Jean Genet."[4]

* * *

Born on December 19, 1910, Jean Genet was the illegitimate son of a Parisian prostitute. He was orphaned at seven months and was brought up in a Public Assistance institute. At the age of seven, he was placed with a foster family.

At thirteen, he stole money from his foster parents and began a life splattered with crime. At fifteen, he was sent to a reformatory.

Young Genet joined the Foreign Legion, deserted, and spent time in prison for petty theft and homosexual prostitution. At age thirty-two, while serving a life sentence, he wrote *Our Lady of the Flowers*. His handwritten manuscript was smuggled out of prison and came to the attention of André Gide, Jean Cocteau, and Jean-Paul Sartre, who lobbied vigorously for a pardon. Dozens of writers and artists petitioned for Genet's release and in 1948 he was pardoned.

Genet's five novels and five plays expressed sympathy for society's dispossessed. His background as a beggar, thief, male prostitute, pornographer, and convict fed his writings. His first books were partially autobiographical. *Notre-Dame-des-Fleurs* (*Our Lady of the Flowers*, 1944, revised 1951) unfolds in a prison cell, where an inmate imagines that he is free to roam the streets of Paris in the company of homosexuals and criminals. The protagonist of *Miracle de la Rose* (*Miracle of the Rose*, 1946, revised 1951) is an adolescent who is sent from a reformatory to prison and eventually to the scaffold.

As a playwright, Genet was influenced by Luigi Pirandello's constant juggling of illusion and reality and by Antonin Artaud's Theatre of Cruelty. Genet's first play, *Haute Surveillance* (*Deathwatch*), was probably written in 1944 but not performed until 1949. Professor Richard N. Coe writes that the play takes us to "the world of prisons and symbols, flowers and criminals... *Haute Surveillance* is the technical name for the peculiarly sadistic form of detention that French criminal law prescribes for its condemned prisoners awaiting execution."[5] The entire action takes place in one narrow, claustrophobic prison cell, in the course of a single afternoon. Three men are confined in the cell: Lefranc, a petty burglar; Maurice, an adolescent delinquent; and Green Eyes, a killer facing the death penalty (his real name is never revealed). Under the watchful eyes of a sadistic guard, the three prisoners compete to prove their machismo; the two small-time criminals vie for the favor of the tough murderer. The death-fixated bickerings, recriminations, and clashes reach a climax when Lefranc, aiming to be exalted as a bona fide killer, attacks Maurice and strangles him.

The first American production of *Deathwatch* was mounted by five Harvard students in Cambridge, Massachusetts in 1957. The following year, *Deathwatch* was presented at off Broadway's Theatre East, directed by Leo Garen, with the high-powered cast of Vic Morrow (Lefranc), George Maharis (Green Eyes), Harold Scott (Maurice), and Stephen Gierasch (The Guard). David Amram provided incidental music. Critic Louis Calta of the *New York Times* found it "a generally static, drab and occasionally obscure psychological drama on the peculiar workings of the criminal mind... M. Genet's unwholesome subject falls flat. It lacks the necessary theatrical impact."[6] Nevertheless, the play ran for seventy performances.

England's Foco Novo Theatre Company produced *Deathwatch* under the direction of Roland Rees at the Birmingham Repertory Theatre in February 1985, launching a tour that reached the Young Vic in London two months later. The reviews were mostly positive. Nina-Anne Kaye applauded "a still shocking, mordant piece of theatre," and direction and design "which powerfully convey the menace and sexual tension locked within the cell."[7] Andrew Risik admired a production "spare and compelling" and believed that "in the main, the tension and vigor of the piece are admirably sustained."[8]

Genet's *Les Bonnes* (*The Maids*) was inspired by the real-life case of Christine and Léa Papin, sisters and domestic servants who savagely beat their mistress and her daughter to death in Le Mans, France in 1933. In its day, the Papin case was as sensational as the Lizzie Borden axe murders, the Lindbergh kidnapping, the killing of JonBénet Ramsey, or O.J. Simpson's alleged double murder. The crime was grisly – the victims' eyes were gouged, and their bodies mutilated. During the trial, the murderous sisters were revealed to be lovers, locked in an incestuous relationship. They were dubbed by the press "the monsters of Le Mans." The gruesome event has fascinated French writers and scholars ever since.

A ninety-minute one act, *The Maids* unfolds in Madame's elegant bedroom. The maids Claire and Solange Lemercier indulge in make-believe games, take turns playing their glamorous, young employer, and express loathing of their lowly station in society, coupled with an intense loathing of their Madame. Solange tells Claire how she entered Madame's bedroom at night intending to strangle her, but she lacked the strength to follow through. The sisters vow to murder their mistress, then "carry her off to the woods, and under the fir trees cut her to bits" and "bury her beneath the flowers." They decide to put ten phenobarbital tablets in Madame's tea.

The plan fails, with Madame rushing out to meet her lover, who has been accused of theft and has just been granted bail. Instead of tea, she'll have champagne at the Hong Kong bar. The two sisters are temporarily speechless. Claire puts on an apron. It is Solange's turn to impersonate Madame. She orders Claire to kneel and strikes her viciously. She then orders Claire to drink the tea. They will both escape servitude. Claire will die by poison and Solange will be accused of murdering her.

The Maids was first performed at the Theatre de l'Athènèe, Paris, on April 19, 1947. Louis Jouvet produced and directed. London saw *The Maids* in French at the Mercury Theatre and at the Royal Court Theatre in 1952, and in English, at the New Lindsay Theatre club, four years later. The American premiere of *The Maids* took place at Off-Off Broadway's Tempo playhouse in 1955. In 1963, the play was revived at Off Broadway's Sheridan Square Playhouse, by the Dallas Theatre Center, and broadcast by London's BBC's Third Programme. A notable production of *The Maids* was mounted in 1969 by the Spanish Nuria Espert Company, directed and designed by Victor Garcia, who staged the play ritualistically on a steeply raked platform inclined towards the public. It ran in Barcelona for 500 performances and went on tour to Austria, Italy, France, Yugoslavia, and Iran.

The Maids continued to enthrall audiences on world stages throughout the twentieth century and beyond. Off Broadway groups have produced it repeatedly. In 1993, the Classic Stage Company presented *The Maids* with an all-male cast, as Genet originally intended; the Chocolate Factory Theatre did the same thing in 2005. An all-female cast followed a month later at the Bouwerie Lane Theatre in a Jean Cocteau Repertory production that shifted the proceedings to 1947 Los Angeles. In 2006, the Jean Cocteau produced *Maids x 2*, a back-to-back presentation of the play on the same evening – one with the three characters played by women, the other by men. The female version was fairly straightforward while the male rendering was staged in the round and partially in the raw.

The Maids was filmed in the United Kingdom in 1974, starring Glenda Jackson (Solange), Susannah York (Claire), and Vivien Merchant (Madame).

The scene of Genet's *Le Balcon* (*The Balcony*) is Irma's luxury brothel, where ordinary men escape their mundane existence by masquerading as judges, bishops, and generals, and play-act perverse games. Lust, sex and sadism have a field day. Meanwhile, outside in the streets of the city, a revolution is taking place. Soon the patrons of the "house of illusion" become involved.

Translated by Bernard Frechtman and directed by Peter Zadek, *The Balcony* was first performed in 1957 at London's Arts Theatre Club, a private meeting place that enabled the production to circumvent the Lord Chamberlain's ban on public showings of the play. Subsequent productions of *The Balcony* were staged by Hans Lietzau in Berlin (1959), Peter Brook in Paris (1960), Leon Eppin in Vienna (1961), Erwin Piscator in Frankfurt (1962), Roger Blin in Roterdam (1967), Victor Garcia in Sao Paulo (1969), Terry Hands in London (1971), the Picolo Theatre in Milan (1976), and the Royal Shakespeare Company in London (1977).

The first American production of *The Balcony* was presented by Off Broadway's Circle in the Square in 1960, directed by José Quintero and designed by David Hayes. The large cast included some major thespians of the era's Off-Broadway scene – Nancy Marchand as Irma, the Madame with a heart of gold; Roy Poole as a Gestapo-like police chief; Arthur Malet as a masochistic judge; Sylvia Miles, Salome Jens and Grayson Hall as kinky trollops. The show ran for 672 performances.

The Balcony continued to be produced on both sides of the Atlantic. Richard Schechter directed an "updated" version of the play for The Performance Group in New York City in 1979. Terry Hands translated, staged and lighted a rendering shown at London's Barbican Theatre in 1987. It was described as "limp and placid" by the reviewer of *Plays and Players.*[9] Off Broadway's Jean Cocteau Repertory revived the play in 1999. "In this production," wrote critic J.R. Bruckner in the *New York Times*, "the director, Eve Adamson, has made it a psychological puzzle, handing on to the audience much of the task of supplying meaning."[10] Manhattan's Medicine Show Theatre reincarnated *The Balcony* in 2007.

A 1963 motion picture version of *The Balcony*, scripted by Ben Maddow, featured Shelley Winters as Madame Irma. Peter Falk, Lee Grant, Jeff Corey, Kent Smith, Leonard Nimoy, and Ruby Dee played the brothel's sadomasochistic clientele. In 2002, France's Aix-Eu-Provence Festival premiered an opera, *Le Balcon*, composed by Peter Eotvos. "High-spirited, jazz-touched, and in a sense, straight in its treatment of the original play, by Jean Genet," wrote Paul Griffiths in the *New York Times.*[11]

Les Paravents (*The Screens*), first performed at Berlin's Schlossparktheatre in 1961, unfolds during the Algerian revolution. The action revolves around a pair of outcasts – an Arab couple who barely survive as thieves. *Saintete*, a ninety-minute play written by Genet in the mid-1950s and translated as *Elle*, was produced posthumously by Off Broadway's Zipper Factory in 2002. It pokes fun at the insatiable lust for fame by celebrities, centering on the Pope posing for publicity pictures. Alan Cumming portrayed the pontiff wearing roller skates and a tiara marked "P." Critic Donald Lyons wrote in the *New York Post* that "Genet sets out to show, in this short, would-be shocking spectacle, that the institution of the papacy is a conscious, cynical imposition of arbitrary symbols designed to awe." Lyons found *Elle* a "coarse satire made worse by a trendy adaptation of the text and a campy production."[12] The play ran for fifteen performances.

In the 1970s, Genet joined the causes of Algerian immigrants in France, the Black Panthers in the United States, and Palestinian refugees in Lebanon. He developed throat cancer and died in 1986 in a hotel room in Paris. He is buried in the Spanish cemetery in Larache, Morocco.

Acting Edition: Samuel French, Inc.; Grove Press

Awards and Honors: Jean Genet's *The Balcony* received an Obie Award in 1961. *The Screen* was a top-ten selection in *The Best Plays of 1971-1972*. Genet's work earned him the Grand Prix des Arts et Letters in 1983.

NOTES

1. *New York Herald Tribune*, June 1, 1961.
2. *New York Times*, May 9, 1961.
3. Louis Kronenberger, ed., *The Best Plays of 1960-1961* (New York: Dodd, Mead and Company, 1961), 44.
4. Joseph T. Shipley, *The Crown Guide to the World's Great Plays* (New York: Crown Publishers, Revised and Updated Edition, 1984), 249.
5. Richard N. Coe, *The Vision of Jean Genet* (New York: Grove Press, 1968), 226.
6. *New York Times*, October 10, 1958.
7. *City Limits*, London, April 12, 1985.
8. *Time Out*, London, April 25, 1985.
9. *Plays and Players*, September 1987.
10. *New York Times*, November 19, 1999.
11. *New York Times*, July 9, 2002.
12. *New York Post*, July 25, 2002.

Rashomon (1959)

Fay Kanin (United States, 1917-2013) and Michael Kanin (United States, 1910-1993)

About a thousand years ago, at the edge of the Rashomon Gate in Kyoto, the ancient capital of Japan, a Buddhist Priest, tired and defeated, sat on the stone floor, near a meager bonfire. "The gate," says a production note, "fell into bad repair and became a decayed relic with an unsavory reputation, a hideout for thieves and a dump for unclaimed corpses." It was raining hard on this "crumbling and deserted edifice."

A woodcutter, his handmade axe stuck in his belt, comes running through the rain and asks the Priest if the rumor of his going away is true. The Priest acknowledges that the "savagery of men toward one another" is beyond his understanding. A wigmaker enters, with hair stolen from cadavers, and asks about the recent sensational murder. The woodcutter relates that he was the one who found a man's body in the woods, behind a clump of bamboo shoots, next to a woman's sedge hat, with a veil on it, dangling from a brush. He tore his legs and arms running to the police.

The cynical wigmaker, eager for details, learns from the woodcutter that the victim was a samurai warrior who had been run through with a sword, his frightened wife was found lost in the woods, and the culprit – accused of rape and murder – was arrested. "It's Tajomaru," says the woodcutter, "the most dangerous bandit in this part of the country." The Priest, haltingly, joins the conversation and relates that he had been present when Tajomaru was questioned.

Tajomaru's account at the police court is visualized in the form of a flashback. The husband, Takehiko, is seen leading a small white horse, on which his wife Kinume is riding, through a winding path in the forest. A breeze flutters among the leaves, blowing the woman's veil. Tajomaru, who was lounging about, is fascinated by her exquisite face. "In that first moment," says the bandit, "I made up my mind to take her. Even if I had to kill the man."

After a struggle, Tajomaru binds the husband to a bamboo stump, then accosts the wife. Kinume struggles wildly, but gradually succumbs, her hand moving along Tajomaru's back to clasp him in a reciprocating embrace.

Later, Kinume pleads with Tajomaru, "At least, give my husband a chance to avenge my honor – and his own." Tajomaru unties Takehiko's bonds. A fierce sword fight ensues, at the end of which the husband stumbles and the bandit plunges his weapon downward to its fatal conclusion. During the contest, the wife runs away. No, says Tajomaru, he didn't look for her. She was just a woman, after all.

Three contradictory versions of the event are related by the wife, by the spirit of the dead husband via a medium, and by the woodcutter.

Kinume describes how following the rape she released her husband's bonds, but he kept looking at her with cold, silent disdain. Desperate and angry, she must have fainted. When she came to, she found her husband dead, the sword in his breast. It was then that she realized that she had killed him. She ran into the woods, deeper and deeper, tried to drown the sight of herself in the river. But even the river scorned her.

Takehiko, speaking from the dead, accuses Kinume of submitting to Tajomaru willingly, and requesting the bandit to slay her husband – "As long as he lives I'll always be his wife. I can never be completely yours. Kill him. Kill him! Kill him!" Tajomaru, disgusted, cuts the husband's rope, and the wife flees. Takehiko is left alone, his eyes filled with tears – a man whose hopes are shattered, his pride gone. He draws the sword, raises it above his breast, and thrusts it into himself. "I sank down, down into the blackness of space," says Takehiko through the medium.

The woodcutter claims to have watched the event from behind a bush and insists that "none of their stories are true. They lied – all of them." His tale unfolds in broadly comic strokes. As both men decide to leave the woman behind, she lashes at her husband for being a coward and at the bandit for being a small, cheap imitation of himself with exaggerated reputation.

The two men are now impelled to prove their mettle. The wife smiles with triumphant satisfaction as they assume en garde positions. A sword duel follows – a spineless, bloodless pantomime filled with slapstick pratfalls. After a while, the husband stumbles and is impaled by his own weapon.

Rashomon winds up on an optimistic note. A baby is left crying by the gate. The woodcutter says that even though he has six children at home who are sometimes hungry and cold, he will take the baby with him; there is little enough, but how much can such a small mouth eat? This glimmer of man's goodness revitalizes the downcast Priest. His face is now at peace. The rain has stopped, and he finds the air clean and sweet. "The Rashomon," says the Priest, "Somehow, it's no longer so fearsome – with all its crows, and corpses and jackals. Even out of its crumbling ruins can come – life."

* * *

Piercing through the play's melodramatic aspects is the issue "What is Truth?" When *Rashomon* opened on January 27, 1959, at New York's Music

Box, critic Richard Watts, Jr. pointed out its theme: "How much do motives of fear, pride and self-interest cause one to see what one wants to see?"[1]

Brooks Atkinson asked, "What is the truth? Is the bandit a brute or a romantic figure? Is the wife a woman of modesty or a strumpet? Is the husband a man of honor or a coward? Truth has many sides according to the witness, for the witness sees what he wants to see and tells what he wants the world to believe." Atkinson praised the authors of the play, saying that "Mr. and Mrs. Kanin preserved the integrity of the theme; the writing is reserved and passionless;" the director, Peter Glenville, who "has transmuted the material into a perfectly imagined microcosm of sound, color and movement;" the thespians who "act their suitable parts with subtlety, conciseness and unfailing skill;" and the entire enterprise: "pure art of the theatre. No one need despair of a commercial theatre that can deal in exclusive materials with so much delicacy, expertness, and charm."[2]

John McClain saluted the all-star cast: "Rod Steiger, the brawny and bellowing bandit, gives a performance of enormous strength and persuasion in contrast to Claire Bloom's fragile and fluttering efforts as an ex-domestic who has wed the aristocrat. But it is Oscar Homolka, playing a cynical and disreputable wigmaker (his product comes straight from the grave) who has been assigned most of the best lines and he has a merry time for himself. Akim Tamiroff is convincing as the woodcutter-witness and Noel William is a suitably proud and disdainful Samurai."[3]

The sole dissenter among the morning-after reviewers was John Chapman of the *Daily News*: "*Rashomon* is a pretentious bore – overwritten, overset, overacted and overdirected. Now and then it gets so far over in one department or another that it is ridiculous, and in these brief moments it is fun – which is not what the authors intended."[4]

Rashomon ran for 159 performances.

Many community theatres and university drama clubs found this philosophical excursion to the ancient Far East a worthwhile endeavor. *Rashomon* does not require the sumptuous sets and costumes of the original Broadway production to create a magicaland thought-provoking ambience. But it has taken almost three decades for the play to be revived in New York. Off Broadway's Roundabout Theatre presented *Rashomon* with an all-Asian cast in 1988.

Theatre Works of Silicon Valley, California, included *Rashomon* in the company's 1990-1991 season. The Shaw Festival of Niagara-on-the-Lake, Ontario, Canada, presented *Rashomon* in 1996. The play triggered a hub of activity at the turn of the twenty-first century with productions mounted by the Rude Guerilla Theatre Company in Santa Ana, California (1999); Pan Asian Rep in uptown Manhattan, New York (2001); and the Blunt Theatre Company in downtown Manhattan (2004). The Golden

West College Theatre, Huntington Beach, California, offered *Rashomon* in 2009.

Rashomon was adapted by the Kanins from two stories by Ryunosuke Akutagawa (1892-1927), "Father of the Japanese short story." The same stories served as the basis for Akira Kurosawa's 1950 masterful motion picture, Oscar winner as Best Foreign Film. The movie catapulted Toshiro Mifune, in the role of the notorious bandit, and Machiko Kyo, as his raped victim, to international fame. "The film's very title has become part of our language," states Leonard Maltin in his annual *Movie and Video Guide*.[5]

A lackluster U.S. remake, *The Outrage* (1964), directed by Martin Ritt, had Paul Newman as a Mexican bandit who allegedly rapes Claire Bloom while her husband Laurence Harvey helplessly stands by.

Rashomon was transferred to television by America's Play of the Week in 1960, featuring Ricardo Montalban as the bandit and Carol Lawrence as the wife, and by British BBC the following year, with Lee Montague and Yoko Tani.[6]

* * *

Fay Mitchell Kanin was born in New York City and raised in Elmira, New York, where she attended the private Elmira College. She wrote items for the *Elmira Star-Gazette* and edited the college yearbook. When visiting her grandmother, who lived in the Bronx, Kanin saw a matinée of Robert E. Sherwood's *Idiot's Delight*, starring Alfred Lunt and Lynn Fontanne, and decided to devote herself to the theater.

Kanin spent her senior year at the University of Southern California and after graduation was hired by RKO Pictures as a story editor at $75 a week. It is there that she met Michael Kanin, a writer in the B unit, and soon they got married. Their first team effort was *Sunday Punch* (1942), a bitter-sweet comedy about the misadventures of a group of fledging boxers living in a boarding house. Many other collaborative projects followed, with Michael, who was trained as an artist, providing a visual sense, and Fay concentrating on character and dialogue.

Among the Kanins' films were *My Pal Gus* (1952), a domestic comedy starring Richard Widmark; *Rhapsody* (1954), with Elizabeth Taylor torn between two musicians; *The Opposite Sex* (1956), a comedy-with-music inspired by Clare Boothe Luce's *The Women*; *Teacher's Pet* (1958), about a hard-knuckled newspaper editor, played by Clark Gable, who pretends to be a student in a class conducted by journalism teacher Doris Day; *The Right Approach* (1961), in which a group of young bachelors living together in the Hollywood Hills find their peaceful existence shattered upon the arrival of an ambitious, ruthless newcomer (Frankie Vaughan) who will stop at nothing on his way to fame as a singing star.

The Kanins detoured to Italy for *Swordsman of Siena* (1962), a swashbuckling adventure, and to West Germany for the comedy *Mein oder Dein* (*Mine or Yours*, 1964).

For the Broadway stage, Fay Kanin wrote the comedy *Goodbye, My Fancy*, and her husband produced it at the Morosco Theatre in 1948. The protagonist is a liberal Congresswoman who returns to her alma mater as an honorary visitor and clashes with the rigid trustees. *Goodbye, My Fancy* ran for 446 performances at the Morosco Theatre and was filmed in 1951 with Joan Crawford. *His and Hers*, by both Fay and Michael Kanin, is the story of a husband-and-wife playwriting team who after a succession of failures dissolve their marriage and they each start writing a new play. When the plays end up rather similar, the two find themselves in court suing each other for plagiarism. The 1954 comedy ran at the Forty-sixth Street Theatre for seventy-six performances.

Suggested by Arthur Schnitzler's *The Affairs of Anatol*, the Kanins wrote the book for the *The Gay Life* (aka *The High Life*), with music by Arthur Schwartz, lyrics by Howard Dietz, highlighting the romantic escapades of a notorious ladies' man in turn-of-the-century Vienna. The musical premiered at the Shubert Theatre in 1961 and ran for 113 performances.

On her own, Fay Kanin wrote the book for the 1985 musical *Grind*, picturing a burlesque theatre with an ensemble of both black and white performers, in Chicago of 1933. Though directed by master Hal Prince and featuring the powerhouse cast of song-and-dance man Ben Vereen and slapstick comic Stubby Kaye, the reviews were mixed, and the show closed after seventy-one performances, losing its entire $4.75 million investment.

In the early1970s, Fay Kanin began to focus on made-for-television movies. Her efforts include *Heat of Anger* (1972), about the relationship between an older woman and a younger man, both lawyers; *Tell Me Where it Hurts* (1974), centered on a group of women who get together to exchange ideas; *Hustling* (1975), the story of a prostitute who recounts her past to a reporter; *Friendly Fire* (1979), the Emmy-winning drama of a mother who discovers that her son was killed by friendly fire in Vietnam; *Fun and Games* (1980), covering sexual harassment in the workplace; and *Heartsounds* (1984), dealing with a married couple coping with heart disease.

Fay Kanin was elected president of the Academy of Motion Picture Arts and Sciences in 1979 and held the position for four terms until 1983. She also served as president of the Screen Branch of the Writers Guild of America, was a member of the board of directors of the American Film Institute, and a member of the board of governors of the Academy of Motion Picture Arts and Sciences.

* * *

Michael Kanin, the older brother of writer/director/producer Garson Kanin, was born in Rochester, New York. He began his show business career writing and acting in Catskill resort shows and worked as a commercial artist. In 1939 he was signed to a screenwriting contract by RKO Pictures. A year later he married RKO colleague Fay Mitchell.

Several B movies penned by Michael Kanin were tinged with elements of crime. *Panama Lady* (1939) featured Lucille Ball as a saloon dance-hall girl who gets entangled with a gun smuggler and ends up facing lethal danger in the jungles of Ecuador. In *They Made Her a Spy* (1939), a patriotic secret service girl infiltrates a ring of saboteurs.

Classier efforts by Kanin included *Anne of Windy Poplars* (1940), a sequel to *Anne of Green Gables*, in which a schoolteacher in a small Canadian town becomes prey to the local gossips. *Woman of the Year* (1942), directed by George Stevens, about rival reporters, was the first of the Spencer Tracy-Katharine Hepburn comedies. *The Cross of Lorraine* (1943) centered on a group of French soldiers who were prisoners of war during World War II.[7]

Kanin served as producer of *A Double Life* (1947), in which Ronald Colman enacted an obsessed thespian who loses himself when playing Othello and strangles Desdemona on stage. Colman won the Oscar for his portrayal, as did Miklos Rosza for Original Score.

Kanin's sole directing assignment was the modest *When I Grow Up* (1951), in which Bobby Driscoll played a young boy who feels neglected and intends to run away from home, but leafing through his grandfather's diary he gains a new understanding of his elders and changes his mind. Kanin's last movie script, in collaboration with Ben Starr, was *How to Commit Marriage* (1969), a Bob Hope-Jackie Gleason-Jane Wyman comedy that rotates around an adopted baby.

Acting Edition: Samuel French, Inc.

Awards and Honors: Michael Kanin and Ring Lardner, Jr. shared an Academy Award for the screenplay of *Woman of the Year* (1942). Fay and Michael Kanin were nominated for an Academy Award and a Writers Guild of America Award for their screenplay of *Teacher's Pet* (1959). Fay Kanin won the American Bar Association Gavel Award for *Heat of Anger* (1972). Fay won a Writer of the Year Emmy for *Tell Me Where It Hurts* (1974). Fay's *Hustling* was nominated for an Edgar for Best Television Feature and for an Emmy for Outstanding Original Teleplay (1976). Fay's *Friendly Fire* won an Emmy for Outstanding Drama/Comedy Special ((1978). Her *Heartsounds* was nominated for an Emmy, and *Grind* was nominated for a Tony (both in 1985).

NOTES

1. *New York Post*, January 28, 1959.
2. *New York Times*, January 28, 1959.
3. *New York Journal-American*, January 28, 1959.
4. *Daily News*, January 28, 1959.
5. *Leonard Maltin's 2008 Movie Guide* (New York: Signet, 2007), 1122.
6. In 2005, playwright-composer Michael John LaChiusa based his musical *See What I Wanna See* on the same short stories by Rynosuke Akutagawa, moving the proceedings from ancient Japan to modern New York. On a stroll through Central Park, a married couple is accosted by a brash thief who rapes the wife and murders the husband. Or does he? The conflicting accounts of what happened raise doubts.
7. Four decades after the making of the film *Woman of the Year*, a Broadway musical version, with book by Peter Stone, music by John Kander and lyrics by Fred Ebb, based on the screenplay by Michael Kanin and Ring Lardner, Jr., was presented at the Palace Theatre, starring Lauren Bacall and Harry Guardino, running 770 performances.

The Andersonville Trial (1959)

by Saul Levitt (United States, 1911–1977)

Based on the official record of the 1865 trial of Henry Wirz, commandant of the most notorious Confederate prisoner-of-war stockade, *The Andersonville Trial* raises the issue of passive moral conviction among military men who blindly obey the inhumane orders of their superiors.

During a hearing in Washington, D.C., Wirz was held responsible for the deaths of fourteen thousand Union soldiers. The president of the court was General Lew ("Ben Hur") Wallace.

The indictment, announced at the beginning of the play, specifies that Henry Wirz, who was in charge of the Confederate prison at Andersonville, Georgia, kept in barbarous confinement forty thousand federal soldiers without adequate shelter against the burning heat of summer and the cold of winter; that he did not provide the prisoners with sufficient food, clothing, or medical care, causing 14,000 of them to languish and die; that he instructed the prison guards stationed near the walls of the prison stockade to fire upon and kill any prisoner who might pass beyond that barrier; that he used bloodhounds to hunt down, seize, and mangle escaping prisoners of war; that through these various causes he brought about the deaths of fifty federal soldiers; and that through direct order and/or by his own hand he brought about the murder of thirteen prisoners, their names unknown.

The judge advocate, Lt. Col. N. P. Chipman, presents a parade of witnesses to relate harrowing accounts of maltreatment, hunger, lack of shelter, and a bare existence under "cruel and inhuman rules." The prosecution witnesses include a Southern official assigned to inspect the Georgia prison camp; a medical officer; the owner of a plantation adjacent to the compound, who testifies that he heard Wirz boast that he had killed more Yankees in Andersonville than Lee at Richmond; a former Andersonville inmate, who witnessed dogs tear up his companion; and another captive, who saw Wirz empty his revolver into a fellow prisoner.

Wirz's defense counsel, Otis H. Baker, artfully parries many of the accusations and demonstrates in court that Wirz, who had an injured shoulder, could not pull a trigger. Against counsel's advice, Wirz insists on taking the stand. He declares that the military code dictated that he obey orders, that he could not disobey, and that he had to keep his feelings to himself.

Prosecutor Chipman retorts that he shudders for a world that would let total obedience murder people instead of saving them, and the president of the court agrees. Wirz is found guilty of all charges and condemned "to be hanged by the neck till he be dead, at such time and place as the President of the United States may direct."[1]

* * *

Saul Levitt first wrote *The Trial of Captain Wirz* for a 1957 television episode on *Climax!,* with Everett Sloane in the title role and Charlton Heston as prosecutor Chipman. Levitt's expanded version, now called *The Andersonville Trial,* opened in New York at the Henry Miller Theatre on December 29, 1959. Most of the critics greeted it with kudos. "Saul Levitt has written a striking and effective courtroom drama about a famous case in American history," stated Richard Watts Jr. "He has offered a provocative study of the moral issues involved in the conflict between man's obligation to authority and his conscience."[2] Frank Aston asserted, "Mr. Levitt has turned up a hell-raising heart searcher."[3] John Chapman found *The Andersonville Trial* "the best courtroom play since *The Caine Mutiny Court-Martial,*"[4] while Walter Kerr promised the audience "a whale of an evening."[5]

On the other hand, Robert Coleman described the play as "a worthy attempt that doesn't come off,"[6] and Brooks Atkinson felt that "the theatre was triumphing over truth by being consistently ingenious, showy and planned."[7]

The reviewers unanimously praised director José Ferrer and actors George C. Scott (Judge Advocate Chipman), Albert Dekker (Defense Counsel Baker),[8] Herbert Berghof (defendant Wirz), and Russell Hardie (General Wallace), who held court for 179 performances.

The Andersonville Trial was a success in Berlin in 1960 but was not welcome in the American South, where Captain Wirz was, and perhaps remains, a hero. Shows were cancelled in Atlanta and Birmingham for fear of protests. The play did not have a major production in the South until Theatre Atlanta's production in 1967.

Early in the twenty-first century, *The Andersonville Trial* was revived by the Finlandia University Community Theatre in Hancock, Michigan (2005), Off-Broadway's The Actors Company Theatre (2008), and the Flint Youth Theatre in Flint, Michigan (2010).

In 1970, George C. Scott directed a made-for-television movie of *The Andersonville Trial,* with William Shatner stepping into the role of the prosecutor. Produced by the Public Broadcasting Service, it was a star-studded affair featuring Richard Basehart as Henry Wirz, surrounded by Cameron Mitchell, Buddy Ebsen, Albert Salmi, Jack Cassidy, Whit Bissell, and Martin Sheen.

The Andersonville Trial was presented on television in Belgium (1962), West Germany (1972), and the former Yugoslavia (1975).

The dire events at the Confederate POW camp (1861–1865) were also captured in 1996's *Andersonville*, a 200-minute television miniseries based on Mackinlay Kantor's 1955 Pulitzer Prize–winning novel of the same name, scripted by David W. Rintels and directed by John Frankenheimer, with Jan Triska as Henry Wirz.

* * *

Saul Levitt was born in Hartford, Connecticut, the son of a hatmaker. He studied at Morris High School in the Bronx and the College of the City of New York. He was planning on a career in engineering but in 1934, when he was twenty-three, his first article was published in the magazine *American Mercury* and he shifted direction. During World War II, Levitt served as a radioman in the Air Force. Because of injuries suffered in a vehicle accident, he was reassigned to *Yank Magazine*, the army's weekly publication.

In the 1940s, Levitt pursued a writing career as a freelancer and novelist. Following *The Andersonville Trial*, he focused his creativity on television, where between 1953 and 1967 he contributed episodes to *You Are There*, *Climax!*, *Ivanhoe*, *Decoy*, *The Untouchables*, *Westinghouse Presents*, and *Judd for the Defense*.

In 1967, Levitt collaborated on the screenplay of *A Covenant with Death*, in which an innocent man, convicted as a murderer, kills his hangman. Four years later, Levitt teamed with renowned pacifist Father Daniel Berrigan on *The Trial of the Catonsville Nine*, a courtroom drama about the priest's raid of a local Vietnam-era draft board in Catonsville, Maryland, setting its files on fire. It was presented under the auspices of the Phoenix Theatre at the Lyceum Theatre. Subsequently, Levitt and Berrigan joined forces on the screenplay of *The Trial of the Catonsville Nine*.

Acting Edition: Dramatists Play Service.

Awards and Honors: A top-ten choice in *The Best Plays of 1959–1960* (in spite of some misgivings by editor Louis Kronenberger: "The play offered an evening that had much in its favor in both theme and treatment, that had both effective bursts of eloquence and genuine bouts of theatre. At the same time the play lacked a certain cleanness of impact; it pounded Saul Levitt too hard in places, it stretched out too long. . . Vivid in so many of its parts, the play did not altogether satisfy as a whole.")[9]

Saul Levitt won an Emmy Award for Outstanding Writing Achievement in Drama for 1970's television adaptation of *The Andersonville Trial.* The show won an Emmy for Outstanding Single Program.

NOTES

1. Henry Wirz was the only man tried and executed for war crimes committed during the Civil War.
2. *New York Post*, December 30, 1959.
3. *New York World-Telegram*, December 30, 1959.
4. *Daily News*, December 30, 1959.
5. *New York Herald Tribune*, December 30, 1959.
6. *Daily Mirror*, December 30, 1959.
7. *New York Times*, December 30, 1959.
8. Born in Brooklyn, New York, Albert Dekker (1905–1968) made his professional debut with a Cincinnati stock company in 1927. The following year, he played several small roles in the Broadway production of Eugene O'Neill's *Marco Millions*. A decade of theatrical performances followed, including the parts of Baron von Gaigem in 1930's *Grand Hotel* and editor Hovstad in 1937's *An Enemyof the People.* Dekker migrated to Hollywood and appeared in some seventy films from the 1930s to the 1960s. His most memorable roles were villainous: a mad scientist in the horror movie *Dr. Cyclops* (1940), a vicious hitman in the film noir *The Killers* (1946), a shady dealer in atomic fuel in the whodunit *Kiss Me Deadly* (1955), and an unscrupulous detective in the western *The Wild Bunch* (1969). On May 5, 1968, Dekker was found dead in his Hollywood home. It was reported that there were no signs of forced entry, but money and camera equipment were missing.
9. Louis Kronenberger, ed., *The Best Plays of 1959–1960* (New York: Dodd, Mead, 1960), 12.

The Deadly Game (1960)

James Yaffe (United States, 1927–2017)

In a secluded Alpine retreat, three retired men of law—a judge, a prosecutor (Gustave), and a defense attorney (Bernard)—relive their glory days by playing legal charades with stranded strangers. Mr. Howard Trapp, a brash, self-assured American traveling salesman, finding shelter here during a blizzard, agrees to humor his hosts by joining their parlor game.

"Just like in the movies, huh?" laughs Trapp. "'Where were you on the night of the murder?'" The judge smiles and assures him that their game is not so melodramatic. The prosecutor states that law is the exercise of logic and precedent; melodrama plays no part in it whatsoever.

However, *The Deadly Game* is brimming with melodrama. The setup of an isolated chalet during a night of whistling winds and heavy snow is reminiscent of *The Cat and the Canary*, *Seven Keys to Baldpate*, *The Mousetrap*, and many other unblushing stage shockers. A sense of unease creeps in when the initially amused Mr. Trapp, during a lavish dinner, learns more about the planned diversion. The Judge relates that their game is rather unusual. The three hosts undertake their former jobs in a law court. They reenact the famous trials of history: the trial of Socrates, the trial of Joan of Arc, the Dreyfus Affair. Gustave presents the evidence for the prosecution, Bernard presents the evidence for the defense, and the Judge of the court arrives at a verdict and delivers the appropriate sentence.

Trapp laughs and says that this "intellectual sort of game" might be fun. The Judge remarks that even though it is challenging to recreate famous trials of history, it is even a greater challenge to have a real person stand before their court. A month ago, he relates, they had a most interesting case. During a snowstorm, a former mayor of the province found his way to the house just as they were finishing dinner. It was a delicious meal. The poor man was unlucky to miss it. He was convicted of poisoning his first wife, and they sentenced him to hang. Naturally he was upset, but the law is the law.

The vibes of foreboding increase when at the end of act I Trapp is somberly accused of the murder of his former chief, the late Mr. Foster, and when he finds out that a fourth elderly gentleman, who has been hovering in the background, has served the municipality as its official hangman.

The prosecutor doggedly pursues the murder theory and elicits from Trapp that he was anxious to get ahead in the world by replacing the late Mr. Foster, that Foster had a dangerous heart condition, and any shock might kill him, and that he deliberately carried on an affair with Foster's wife. The prosecutor maintains that Trapp intentionally spread the word about the illicit liaison, making sure that the cuckolded husband heard of it— "You struck the fatal blow, just as surely as if your hand had wielded a knife!"

The Deadly Game carries on the cynical theme that Düerrenmatt planted in *The Visit*, showing us that humanity is corrupt, that each of us is capable of committing a major crime, that it is a dog-eat-dog world. The facts may be against Mr. Trapp, says the defense attorney in his summation. He did hate his chief and coveted his job; he did make love to his chief's wife, confessed the affair to his bitter rival and ultimately caused the late lamented Foster's death by heart failure; but *in his mind* Trapp committed no murder. He started off with no grand plan which he then cunningly and cold-bloodedly set into motion; he proceeded rather by fits and starts. In this respect, declares the defense attorney, the defendant is not much different from the rest of mankind. He is *unconscious* of the implication of what he does. Granted, his behavior is mean, selfish, and ignoble. But it is also human—overwhelmingly, devastatingly human—and therefore worthy of pity, compassion, and forgiveness.

The prosecutor responds by disagreeing that the world is a battlefield occupied by unthinking, unfeeling savages. He refuses to believe it. Men do not *all* behave like brutes, but the brute is *in* us all, fighting to take control of us. The purpose of this court is to fight this brute who lies hidden inside every man, to help in a small way to stamp it out, by stamping out those individuals who have allowed it to turn them into destroyers of their fellow men. Howard Trapp is just such a destructive force, asserts the prosecutor, and demands that Trapp will pay for his crime with his life.

A few days later, Helen Trapp arrives on the scene and is told by a sympathetic trio that her husband's death was an accident: he drank a bit too much, grew somewhat confused, and rushed out into the storm. In the dark, he couldn't possibly have seen the precipice before he fell over it.

In an ironic fade-out, Helen accepts their invitation to stay for dinner. As she is offered "a very special brand" of cognac, the attorney says: "You know, it's been so long since we entertained a lady in this house, it will really be quite a novelty." And after dinner, adds the Judge, they'll think of something to amuse her, to take her mind of her troubles. Perhaps some little parlor game. . .(The curtain slowly falls.)

* * *

The Deadly Game was initially conceived by Swiss playwright Friedrich Duerrenmatt in 1955 as a radio play—*Die Panne* (*The Breakdown*). Two years later it was adapted by James Yaffe for an episode on the American television series *Suspicion*, featuring Boris Karloff as the Judge and Gary Merrill as the traveling salesman. Subsequently, Yaffe converted it to the stage. The play was first presented at the Longacre Theatre, New York City, on February 2, 1960, to generally favorable reviews.

"Better news in the theatre for a change," wrote John Chapman. "*The Deadly Game* is a tidy, literate, well-staged and well-acted piece of dramatic make-believe."[1] Frank Aston found the play "A collegebred hair raiser. . . Under William Gaskill's adroit direction, all this grim jesting turns into an adult delight."[2] Richard Watts Jr. stated: "Anyone who saw the Lunts in *The Visit* knows the Swiss Friedrich Duerrenmatt's chilling ability to present his sardonic view of sin and punishment in terms of ironic melodrama. *The Deadly Game* captures his disturbing vision of human weakness and implacability with fidelity. . .The Duerrenmatt sense of the world's evil makes *The Deadly Game* coldly haunting."[3]

John McClain and Robert Coleman savored the play with mixed feelings. "*The Deadly Game* will not be one of the season's standouts, but it will enhance Mr. Duerrenmatt's status as an original and creative contributor to the modern theatre," concluded McClain.[4] "*The Deadly Game* is only intermittently gripping, though it has the potentialities for a real hair raiser," inferred Coleman. ". . . It's a play for pessimists, for those who like to watch a cat toying with a mouse. The blood in Duerrenmatt's veins must be as cold as the glaciers of his native land."[5]

The two drama deans Walter Kerr and Brooks Atkinson were disappointed. "What turns the thread of the evening inside out, I think, is an unexpected pair of theatrical vices," lamented Kerr. "The first of these is a curious lack of subtlety. Though our hearty American is supposed to be thick headed he is so conveniently quick to convict himself out of his own mouth that the very fun of the game is dissipated. Once the trial is under way, his inquisitors have much too easy a time of it. The second, and much more important, tactical error is an air of smugness that begins to hover about the Duerrenmatt vision."[6] Atkinson was more caustic: "The exposition is in the conventional style of parlor melodrama. When Mr. Yaffe finally gets to the trial, he does not write with much distinction. Although the moral issues are provocative, they are not dramatized with force. With the harshness of *The Visit* fresh in mind, *The Deadly Game* seems like commercial fiction."[7]

The entire cadre of critics, including the naysayers, complimented the cast of players. Atkinson said: "Pat Hingle vigorously describes the brassiness, cleverness and callousness of the traveling salesman."[8] Kerr wrote: "The three wise owls who glower at Mr. Hingle are all handsomely feathered. Max Adrian, the prosecutor, exposes all of his teeth in a deadly-nightshade smile and tosses his carved jester's head with a splendid arrogance. Claude Dauphin, preening himself whenever he scores a point on behalf of the client he is charged to defend, is the very picture of arthritic enthusiasm. Ludwig Donath's judge is soberly and quietly horrifying, in a fatherly way."[9]

The Deadly Game stopped playing after thirty-nine performances. London had a somewhat longer run during the 1966–1967 season.

A slightly revised version of *The Deadly Game* was presented Off-Broadway at the Provincetown Playhouse on February 13, 1966, and ran for 105 performances. An added character, Nicole, a maid at the Swiss abode, contributes some glamour to the gray proceedings. Howard Trapp flirts with her quite outrageously, foreshadowing the revelation of his affair with the boss's wife, a key factor in the "guilty" verdict.

The Deadly Game was televised in India (1971), called *Silence! The Court Is in Session*; as a 1972 Italian/French production, named *The Most Wonderful Evening of My Life*, starring Alberto Sordi, Michel Simon, Charles Vanel, Claude Dauphin, and Pierre Brasseur; and in the United States (1982), with George Segal as Howard Trapp, interrogated by Trevor Howard, Robert Morley, and Emlyn Williams.

California's Hillbarn Theatre of Foster City resuscitated *The Deadly Game* in February 2001, as did The Long Beach Playhouse in January 2008.

* * *

James Yaffe was born in 1927 in Chicago, Illinois, to a middle-class Jewish family. He attended Yale University from 1944 to 1948, graduating summa cum laude. In 1948 he began to contribute episodes to television's Studio One. During the 1950s and 1960s he wrote for *The United States Steel Hour*, *The Elgin Hour*, *The Defenders*, *The Alfred Hitchcock Hour*, and *The Nurses*.

Beginning with 1953's *The Good-for-Nothing*, Yaffe published several novels, often capturing the milieu of his upbringing. That same year he began penning crime stories for the *Ellery Queen Mystery Magazine*. Following *The Deadly Game*, Yaffe came up with two more plays of suspense, *Ivory Tower* (1969) and *Cliffhanger* (1985).

Ivory Tower, cowritten with Jerome Weidman, is a courtroom drama that played in various resident theatres but has not reached New York. The protagonist, Simon Otway, a famous American author who lived in Paris during World War II, is accused of treason for calling on the invading Allied forces, in several radio broadcasts, to lay down their arms and stop the bloodshed.

Like Henry Wirz of *The Andersonville Trial* a decade ago, Otway ignores his attorney's advice and insists on taking the stand. The proceedings, heretofore too highbrow and lacking in dramatic fireworks, now shift gears to an intense confrontation between Otway and prosecutor Harold Gutman. By the end of a grueling cross-examination, the renowned writer begins to crack and eventually, with agonized tears, admits that his broadcasts caused the death of American soldiers.

The *Citizen-Journal* of Columbus, Ohio, poses the question "Did he or did he not intentionally commit treason? . . . Simon Otway, the central figure, is so overwhelming in detail, so articulate, that he becomes the unwitting artist-on-trial and the ultimate victim of his own character. The trial brings about a kind of catharsis—a mind-bending recognition of his real motives." The *Ann Arbor [Michigan] News* found *Ivory Tower* an "intense, absorbing courtroom drama with pace, style, force and purpose."

Unlike *The Deadly Game* and *Ivory Tower*, James Yaffe's *Cliffhanger* is a conventional, old-fashioned comedy-thriller. It is the bittersweet tale of Henry Lowenthal, a gentle small-college philosophy professor, who in a moment of fit seizes a bust of Socrates and with it strikes the vindictive, ruthlessly ambitious chairperson of his department, Edith Wilshire. The panicky Henry and his wife Polly attempt to dispose of the body, but complications arise when a rather odd student, Melvin McMullen, witnesses the action and threatens exposure unless the professor elevates his F grade. "If I flunk your course," says Melvin, "my father will kill me!"

Intimidated, goaded, and losing his head again, Henry picks up the bust of Socrates and prepares to smash Melvin's head. However, in a surprise twist it turns out that Edith Wilshire was not killed when hit by the professor; she only lost consciousness. It was Melvin who did her in. "It was the wrong time to ask her about my grade, I guess. She laughed at me. . . She just kept laughing. . . I picked up this rock and I hit her."

Henry Lowenthal is appointed chairman of the philosophy department.

Cliffhanger was first produced at the Alliance Theatre in Atlanta, Georgia, then presented by the Lamb Theatre in New York City on February 7, 1985. Vintage Theatre, at the Glass Center of Corning, New York, included *Cliffhanger* in its Summer of Suspense '96 series. The box-office gross exceeded those of such classics as *Ten Little Indians* and *Dial "M" for Murder*. Pennsylvania's Bristol Riverside Theatre mounted *Cliffhanger* in August 2004, while Broadway Onstage Live Theatre of Eastpointe, Michigan, produced the play in January 2005.

One hopes that the deadly events of *Cliffhanger* are not autobiographical, but it should be noted that since 1968 James Yaffe has been a member of the Department of English, and since 1981 Director of General Studies, at Colorado College in Colorado Springs. Yaffe's series character, Mom, introduced in the *Ellery Queen Mystery Magazine* and catapulted to hardcover in *A Nice Murder for Mom* (1988), followed her son Dave from the Bronx out to Mesa Grande, Colorado, where the quick-witted Jewish mother solves crime cases over Sunday brunches and homemade chicken soup.

Shades of *Cliffhanger*, the focal point of *A Nice Murder for Mom* is the simmering rivalry between two college professors until it reaches a deadly level. A subsequent novel, *Mom Doth Murder Sleep* (1991), reveals that the hallowed community theatre is nothing but a cesspool of intrigue, mayhem, and bloodshed. The seventy-five-year-old sleuth gets entangled with the murder of an actor in a production of *Macbeth*. There are several other novels in the series, published by St. Martin's Press. The complete "Mom" short stories are collected in *My Mother, the Detective*, published in 1997 by Crippen and Landru.

Acting Edition: Dramatists Play Service.

Awards and Honors: A top-ten selection in *The Best Plays of 1959–1960*. James Yaffe received a National Endowment for the Arts award for drama in 1968.

NOTES

1. *Daily News*, February 3, 1960.
2. *New York World-Telegram*, February 3, 1960.
3. *New York Post*, February 3, 1960.
4. *New York Journal-American*, February 3, 1960.
5. *Daily Mirror*, February 3, 1960.
6. *New York Herald Tribune*, February 3, 1960.
7. *New York Times*, February 3, 1960.
8. *New York Times*, February 3, 1960.
9. *New York Herald Tribune*, February 3, 1960.

Settled Out of Court (1960)

William Saroyan (United States, 1908-1981) and Henry Cecil (England, 1902-1976)

It may seem truly surprising that William Saroyan, the Pulitzer-Prize-winning dramatist whose writings epitomize American life in his native Fresno, California, appears within the covers of a book dedicated to courtroom trials. Even more surprising, he co-wrote a thriller that is singularly English in environment, plot and characters.

But there is no mistake. Saroyan joined Henry Cecil, a British county court judge and prolific detective-story writer, in dramatizing Cecil's 1959 novel, *Settled Out of Court*, a credit missing from most, if not all, bibliographical listings of Saroyan's works.

The three acts of *Settled Out of Court* unfold in the study of Sir George Halliday, a High Court judge. The room is described as "impressive in its mixture of spaciousness and solidity." There are double doors leading to the hall and staircase. A window overlooks the grounds. The walls are lined with bookcases full of law books. In an alcove are a China cabinet and a grandfather clock.

When the curtain rises, Sir Halliday, a distinguished old man, is posing in wig and gown for his portrait. Charles Brandy, more-or-less the same age as Sir George, is painting at an easel, working slowly and thoughtfully. Soon Sir George gets up, stretches, and crosses to his desk for a cigarette. Brandy puts down his palette and brushes. As they relax smoking, Brandy asks Sir George what he thinks about when he sits on the bench, dressed in his robes, and if he ever sympathizes with "the poor chap in the dock."

Sir George states that if the man is innocent, he'll get off, 999 times out of a thousand —though, admits the judge, "laws made by man must be fallible; mistakes must occasionally occur."

The doorbell rings, and the housekeeper, Mrs. Parsons, ushers in a man wearing a policeman's uniform. "Judge Halliday, I presume," he says, and introduces himself as "officer Banks." The play now casts off its cozy beginning when suddenly officer Banks draws a revolver, orders the judge to sit on the settee, and blows a whistle.

A tall man enters from the hall. He tells the judge that his name is Mr. I — for the ninth letter in the alphabet, he explains, as this is his ninth "production" as an international crook. Mr. I declares, "Your house has been seized and occupied;" other members of the gang enter and search the rooms. Mrs. Parsons is ordered to stay in the kitchen. Judge Halliday is astonished to learn that Charles Brandy, the artist who has painted his portrait, is Mr. I's henchman.

Enter Angela Walsh, the attractive daughter of Lonsdale Walsh, a man sent to prison for murder by Judge Halliday. Walsh had been found guilty of causing the death of his business associate, Thomas Barnwell, by running him down with a car. Angela tells the judge that the witnesses at her father's trial have been coaxed to come to the judge's home. She intends to conduct a "retrial" and prove that they were lying and that her father is innocent.

The assembled witnesses prove to be a motley group. Josephine Barnwell, the widow of the victim, "a handsome woman with a great deal of physical appeal," complains that she was lured to an ambulance by the false message that her young brother had been taken to the hospital and was dangerously ill. Harold Allwinter, a young, soft-spoken artist, was conned with an offer to paint Sir George Halliday's portrait. He is curious about the judge's chauffeur—how did he get that terrible scar from the top of his forehead to the bottom of his neck? Miles Hampton, a bit-part film actor, believes that he was cast in a movie. Mrs. Meadows, "a very large lady," was told that she won a hefty sum in a football pool. Herbert Adams, "a little fellow of the streets," thought that the two coppers who accosted him in Hyde Park were taking him to a police station. He demands to know, "What's the charge?"

Lonsdale Walsh enters, dressed in a torn prison uniform. He tells his daughter that "apart from a little difficulty in getting over the wall, everything was perfect."

Sir George: The police will be searching for you in every corner of the country.

Walsh: I'm sure they will—except here. Your house is the safest place for me, don't you think?

Walsh tells the judge that he was convicted on perjured evidence. He would like to re-examine the case and prove that there was a miscarriage of justice at his trial. The judge vehemently objects, but changes his mind when Walsh promises to give himself up whatever the verdict.

Lonsdale Walsh acts as his own attorney and cross-examines the witnesses. Harold Allwinter testifies that he saw Barnwell come out of a house and start to cross the road. Suddenly, a very fast car seemed to come from nowhere and struck him flat. He saw the car drive off, but didn't see the face of the driver, didn't think of getting the car's license tag number — but he is certain that it was a premeditated murder.

"Has it occurred to you that the driver of the car might not have seen him?" asks Walsh. He instructs Angela to take a small container of black pepper from her briefcase and have Allwinter sniff it. Allwinter is overcome and sneezes. During the sneeze, Walsh crosses away, making a point of the fact that the artist did not see him move.

The widow, Josephine Barnwell, testifies that her late husband and Thomas Walsh were not on speaking terms before he was killed; they were fighting for control of one of the biggest companies in the country, Midland Consolidated. Her husband had filed a motion to remove Walsh from the company's board.

Miles Hampton and Herbert Adams relate that prior to the death of Thomas Barnwell, they were sitting on a bench in Hyde Park. A man came along wearing a bowler hat, a black jacket, and striped trousers. He walked down the path, says Hampton, and threw a newspaper into the litter basket. Adams got up, retrieved the newspaper and started to read. Both Hampton and Adams noticed that the newspaper was curiously mutilated. Parts of it had been torn out. The man also dropped a pigskin glove by the litter basket. After reading of the car homicide, an account that included an item about a missing glove, they went to the police.

The last witness, Mrs. Meadows, admits that her late husband, Kenneth Meadows, was a hardened criminal with many previous convictions and jail time. Knowing that he had a short time to live, Meadows went to the police and later testified at the trial, that three days before Barnwell was killed, Walsh approached him with an offer of a hundred pounds to drive his car over a man. Meadows refused. He died a few days after the trial ended. Walsh categorically denies that he was the one who spoke with Meadows.

Judge Halliday tells Walsh that so far he hasn't produced "one little, iota, scintilla of additional evidence. All you say is that you were framed. Anyone can say that."

However, when Walsh interrogates Miles Hampton again, with machine-gun pace, the actor breaks under the rapid grilling, and admits to being paid for his testimony. One by one, the witnesses admit that they had succumbed to bribes by Josephine Barnwell and had provided false testimonies at trial.

Sir George is now persuaded that a grave miscarriage of justice has taken place and that Lonsdale Walsh is innocent of the crime. Thomas Barnwell was probably killed accidently, and it was made to look to be murder afterward.

Mr. I and his band depart. Walsh corners Josephine Barnwell and assures her that there is no evidence that she is the one who framed him. Messrs Hampton, Adams and company wouldn't dare speak out, for they're involved themselves. "You'd have been amused if you could have seen me collecting the little fellows and rehearsing them in their parts," chuckles Josephine.

In a surprising twist, Walsh admits to Josephine that he actually drove the homicidal car himself. There is nothing she can do about it, for no one will believe her. He tells her that he now intends to take a trip around the world.[1]

Walsh cheerfully says "good-bye" and moves towards the double doors. "No, Lonsdale, not quite good-bye," intones Josephine. He may not see her again, but she shall certainly see him. Wherever he goes, somewhere, sometime, he'll have to cross a road.

* * *

Settled Out of Court opened at London's Strand Theatre on October 19, 1960. Nigel Patrick directed and played Lonsdale Walsh. The *New York Times* reported that "the newspaper critics differed only in the intensity with which they disliked it."[2] The *Times of London* said, "Mr. William Saroyan is named in the program as Mr. Cecil's co-adapter, but of the American's easily identifiable thumb-mark there is not a trace."[3] Critic Robert Muller of the *Daily Mail* concurred: "What but dire and undeserved poverty could have persuaded Saroyan to lend his gifts, not alone his name, to the concoction of this dusty clutter of a play which calls itself a 'comedy thriller.'"[4] Bernard Levin of the *Daily Express* called *Settled Out of Court* "a surprisingly preposterous play… ludicrous even within its own terms of reference."[5]

However, disagreeing with the London critics, the public clamored to see *Settled Out of Court,* and the play ran for the best part of a year.

* * *

Born in London in 1902, Henry Cecil Leon was educated at St. Paul's School, London; King's College, Cambridge; and Gray's Inn, London. He was called to the bar in 1923. During World War II he served in the Middle East. In 1949 he was appointed a county court judge, a position he held until 1967. He was chairman of the British Copyright Council from 1973 to 1976, the year he died.

Cecil used his legal expertise as inspiration for his twenty-five novels, three volumes of short stories, eight plays, half-a-dozen radio dramas, and several television episodes. In his writings, he often attempted to prove that the law is an ass, poking fun at the British legal system.

For the stage, he coadapted, with Ted Willis, one of his most celebrated novels, 1955's *Brothers in Law,* for an opening at the New Theatre, Bromley, in February 1957. *Brothers in Law* relates the experiences of a young barrister, Roger Thursby, during his first year in chambers. Also in 1957, the book was made into a film by the Boulting Brothers, Roy and John, starring Ian Carmichael as Roger. Five years later, *Brothers inLaw* was converted into a television series, featuring Richard Briers. In 1970, Briers reprised the role in a long-running radio program.

Cecil teamed with Felicity Douglas and Basil Dawson to dramatize his 1960 novel, *Alibi for a Judge*, in which Mr. Justice Gerald Carstairs cannot make up his mind whether Lesley Burford is lying in an attempt to save her husband from a ten-year prison sentence, or whether she is telling the truth by supplying him with an alibi. *Alibi for a Judge* premiered at the Savoy Theatre, London, on August 5, 1965, with Andrew Cruickshank as the judge and Amanda Grinling as Lesley. Reviewer John Russell Taylor of *Plays and Players* sniffed: "Why this mish-mash took three writers to compile from one book I cannot imagine; maybe it is just a classic demonstration of too many cooks spoiling the broth."[6] However, the play was chosen by J.C. Trewin to be included in his *Plays of the Year*, and ran for more than 300 performances. Two years later, Cecil, Douglas and Dawson collaborated on another dramatization of a Cecil novel, 1954's *According to the Evidence*, scoring a 260-performance run. The play featured Ambrose Low, a former criminal, and Colonel Brain, an ex-army officer, recurring Cecil characters, combine forces to get the murderer of a murderer acquitted.

In 1970, Cecil's dramatization of his 1967 novel *A Woman Named Anne* played at West End's Duke of York's Theatre. This "courtroom comedy" is about a trio of foxy lawyers who grill the title character in a divorce case with a string of questions about her secret love life. Reviewer Peter Ansorge of *Plays and Players* reported that he left the theatre "feeling that everyone involved would have had a much better time on a big dipper or inside a little cinema, or even in the dock of a real-life divorce court."[7]

Cecil was also the author of the nonfiction guides for the layman, *Brief toCounsel* (1958, revised 1972), *Know about English Law* (1965, revised 1974), and *The English Judge* (1970, revised 1972). His autobiography, *Just within the Law*, was published in 1975. His manuscripts are housed at McMaster University, Hamilton, Ontario, Canada.

"Mystery literature abounds with excellent writers who, because they are stereotyped as 'mystery writers,' fail to acquire the larger audience they deserve," writes Donald J. Pattow in the *St. James Guide to Crime & Mystery Writers*. "Henry Cecil is one of these writers. Cecil wrote a number of works, of which almost all manage to keep a fine balance; while they are thoughtful and thought-provoking, they maintain a healthy view of society's more curious foibles. Though one might not always agree with Cecil's views, he is always provocative and entertaining… though he is obviously very knowledgeable about law and the legal system, he is never (well, almost never) pedantic. Though he has strong feelings, they are tempered with a humaneness and humor that are rare today."[8]

* * *

William Saroyan was born in Fresno, California, to Armenian immigrants. His father died when he was three, and Saroyan was placed in an orphanage in Oakland, California. He grew up supporting himself with odd jobs and was self-educated. He began his writing career with articles published in *Overland Monthly* and short stories that appeared in the Armenian journal, *Hairenik*. Many of his stories were based on his childhood experiences among the Armenian-American fruit growers of the San Joaquin Valley. The short story collection *My Name is Aram* (1940, about a young boy and his immigrant family, became an international bestseller.

Saroyan made his breakthrough with *The Daring Young Man on the Flying Trapeze*, published in *Story* magazine in 1934, the tale of a young writer trying to survive during the Depression. He continued to write rapidly and intensely, drinking and gambling away much of his earnings. Some of his essays depicted the people he had met on travels in Europe, such as Finnish composer Jean Sibelius, playwright George Bernard Shaw, and actor-director Charlie Chaplin.

In 1939, Saroyan had his first plays produced on Broadway: *My Heart's in the Highlands*, a comedy about a young boy and his Armenian family, set in Fresno, California (Guild Theatre, April 13, 1939—forty-four performances), and *The Time of Your Life*, a character study set in a San Francisco waterfront saloon (Booth Theatre, October 25, 1939—185 performances), which won both the Pulitzer Prize for Drama and the New York Drama Critics Circle Award. Staged by Eddie Dowling, the cast included several actors who would migrate to Hollywood: William Bendix, Celeste Holm, Gene Kelly, Curt Conway, Edward Andrews, and Tom Tully. The play was revived in New York in 1955, featuring Franchot Tone, Biff McGuire, John Carradine, Myron McCormick, John Randolph, and Clifton James; in 1969, with McGuire, James Broderick and Philip Bosco; and in 1975, with Nicolas Surovy, Kevin Kline, Patti LuPone and David Schramm. It was adapted to the screen in 1948, starring James Cagney, supported by William Bendix, Wayne Morris, Jeanne Cagney, Broderick Crawford, and Ward Bond.

Other Broadway productions by Saroyan include *Love's Old Sweet Song*, a screwball comedy of mistaken identities taking place in 1939 Bakersfield, California at the start of World War II (Plymouth Theatre, May 2, 1940 – forty-four performances); *The Beautiful People*, written, produced and directed by Saroyan, about an alcoholic father living with his adolescent son and daughter in a decaying mansion on San Francisco's Red Rock Hill (Lyceum Theatre, April 21, 1941—120 performances); and *Get Away Old Man*, a satire about Hollywood (Cort Theatre, November 24, 1943—thirteen performances).

Saroyan's poignant one-act play, *Hello, Out There* was accompanied by G.K. Chesterton's *Magic* as a double bill presented at the Belasco Theatre on

September 29, 1942, for forty-seven showings. The protagonist of *Hello, Out There* is a Young Man who is held in the jail of a small Southern town for an alleged rape. He enlists a local maid, who is sympathetic to his plight, to help him escape, so that they can run away to San Francisco together. However, his victim, her husband and their friends arrive at the jail to lynch him. Famed director James (*Frankenstein*) Whale directed a forty-one-minute film version of *Hello, Out There* in 1949. The film was never released because its producer, Huntington Hartford, was dissatisfied with it. *Hello, Out There* was televised by BBC-TV on March 17, 1950.

In the early 1940s, Saroyan worked in Hollywood on the screenplay of *The Human Comedy*, a slice-of-life drama taking place in a small Californian town during World War II. The focus is on young Homer Macauley, a telegraph messenger, who witnesses the joys and sorrows of his neighbors. Homer was played by Mickey Rooney, and the typical Macauley family was enacted by Jackie "Butch" Jenkins, Fay Bainter, Ray Collins, Van Johnson, and Donna Reed. ,It is reported that Louis B. Mayer, head of MGM, balked at the film's length and removed Saroyan from the project. Saroyan then turned the script of *The Human Comedy* into a novel. The novel served as a basis for a Broadway musical (Royale Theatre, April 5, 1984 — twenty previews and thirteen performances).

Saroyan's last play of note was *The Cave Dwellers*, set in an abandoned theatre on the lower East Side of New York, populated by homeless, down-on-their-luck men and women (Bijou Theatre, October 19, 1957—ninety-seven performances). The manuscripts of Saroyan's plays are housed at Stanford University.

Saroyan died in Fresno in 1981 at the age of seventy-two. The cause was prostate cancer. Half of his ashes were buried in California, and the remainder in Armenia at the Pantheon.

Acing Edition: Samuel French, Inc. (in manuscript form).

Awards and Honors: William Saroyan's *The Time of Your Life* was a top- ten selection in *The Best Plays of 1939-1940*. It also won the 1940 Pulitzer Prize for Drama and the New York Drama Critics Circle Award.

NOTES

1. The unexpected turnaround ending is reminiscent of George Pleydell's classic *The Ware Case* (novel, 1913; play, 1915), wherein the protagonist, Sir Hubert Ware, accused of the murder of his wife's brother, gains the sympathy of the jury (and the audience) as a victim of circumstances,

and is found not guilty. Prior to the final curtain he confesses to the deed.

2. *New York Times*, October 20, 1960.
3. *Times of London*, October 19, 1960
4. *Daily Mail*, October 19, 1960.
5. *Daily Express*, October 19, 1960.
6. *Plays and Players*, October 1965.
7. *Plays and Players*, April 1970.
8. Jay P. Pederson, ed., *St James Guide to Crime and Mystery Writers*, 4th edition (Detroit, MI: St. James Press, 1996), 164.

Daughter of Silence (1961)

Morris L. West (Australia, 1916-1999)

At the end of a quick prologue, a young woman named Anna Albertini crosses the village square of San Stefano and knocks on the door of Mayor Rosati's home. Without a word she fishes a pistol from her handbag and shoots him in the chest.

Daughter of Silence is set in the Province of Tuscany, Italy, a decade after World War II. The courtroom drama revolves around the question of why a nineteen-year-old girl killed the buffoonish mayor of a small, quiet town. It turns out to be an act of revenge. At the age of eight, Anna witnessed the rape and execution of her mother, falsely accused of collaborating with the enemy.

On a deeper level, according to Walter Kerr in the *New York Herald Tribune*, the author is determined "to peel its bloodthirsty surface away until every last social, legal and moral implication of the insane act is uncovered."[1]

An inexperienced lawyer, Carlo Rienzi, undertakes Anna's defense in an attempt to prove himself before his capricious, unfaithful wife, Valeria, and become free from the shackles of his domineering father-in-law, Alberto Ascolini, a famous legal authority. "You have no hope at all of winning," says Ascolini. "Your first case! They'll butcher you for a summer holiday and I'll be there to watch it!"

Carlo faces numerous obstacles, including a hostile police force and a conspiracy of silence by the villagers. However, he manages to call witnesses who reveal the victim's shady past: Father Bonifacio testifies that many of Gianbattista Rosati's actions were dictated not by the needs of the war but by a desire for private vengeance or private gain. Ignazio Carrese, Rosati's number two, relates that the late mayor was mad at the "Moschetti bitch," once exclaiming, "Nobody slaps Rosati and gets away with it!"

"Who killed Rosati—this woman, or a child of eight?" asks Carlo in court.

In his summation, he requests "a minimum penalty . . . on the grounds of partial mental infirmity." The president of the court agrees and sentences Anna to serve a sentence of three years in a medical institute.

In an unexpected, unnerving ending, Anna reverts to her mad quest for vengeance by attacking Carlo: "You killed her! You killed my mother!" The guards rush in and carry her out. On a mellower note, Valeria makes amends with the distraught lawyer, and they proceed to give their marriage another try.

* * *

Daughter of Silence, dramatized by Morris L. West from his novel, opened at the Music Box Theatre on November 30, 1961, to a gamut of opinions. Robert Coleman raved: "It's an intelligent drama . . . an arresting, stirring vehicle . . . Here is a literate and exciting excursion into the world of illusion. Don't miss it."[2] Norman Nadel scoffed: "*Daughter of Silence* is too predictable to generate much suspense. . . . It would take a combination of rewriting, recasting and redirecting, with only Oliver Smith's sets retained intact, to lift this new drama to mediocrity."[3] Positive reactions were expressed by Howard Taubman, who called it "a richly satisfying drama,"[4] and John Chapman, who called it "a distinguished play."[5] Less receptive were Richard Watts Jr., who found it "powerful but a little dissatisfying,"[6] and John McClain, who theorized, "And, as the book takes form as a play, it seems the author has been caught between two themes."[7]

Emlyn Williams as Ascolini, Rip Torn as Carlo, Joanne Linville as Valeria, and newcomer Janet Margolin as Anna stirred audiences for thirty-six performances.

* * *

Morris Langlo West was represented on Broadway earlier in 1961 via a faithful adaptation by Dore Schary (1905–1980) of his novel *The Devil's Advocate* (1959), a religious thriller.

Born in St. Kilda, Victoria, West graduated from the University of Melbourne in 1937, worked as a teacher in New South Wales and Tasmania, and spent twelve years in a monastery of the Christian Brothers. In 1941 he left without taking his final vows, got married, and enlisted in the Royal Australian Air Force. He left Australia in 1955 to write, lived in Austria, Italy, and the United States, was the Vatican correspondent for the *Daily Mail*, and finally returned to Australia in 1980.

West won international acclaim with a succession of worldwide best sellers, including *Children of the Shadows* (1957), *Navigator* (1976), *The World Is Made of Glass* (1983), *Master Class* (1988), *The Lovers* (1993), and the Vatican Trilogy: *The Shoes of the Fisherman* (1963; filmed 1968), *The Clowns of God* (1981), and *Lazarus* (1990).

His novels of intellectual suspense are comprised of *The Big Story* (U.S. title *The Crooked Road*, 1957; filmed 1965), *The Second Victory* (U. S. title

Backlash, 1958; filmed 1986), *Ambassador* (1965), *The Tower of Babel* (1968), *Summer of the Red Wolf* (1971), *The Salamander* (1973; filmed 1981), *Harlequin* (1974), *Proteus* (1979), *A West Quartet, Four Novels of Intrigue and High Adventure: The Naked Court, Gallows on the Sand, The Concubine, Kundu* (1981), and *Vanishing Point* (1996).

West contributed pulsating TV episodes to UK's *Armchair Theatre* (1958) and *ITV Television Playhouse* (1961) and to Australia's *Whiplash* (1961). In 1989 he penned the thriller *Cassidy* for Australian television.

West died of a heart attack in 1999 in Clareville, New South Wales, while working on his novel *The Last Confession*, about Giordano Bruno, an Italian philosopher who in 1600 was burned at the stake for heresy by the Roman Inquisition. West has long been fascinated with the figure of Bruno. In 1970, West's blank-verse play, *The Heretic,* on the same subject, was produced in London, and in 1998 he converted it into a libretto for an opera. West's family published the unfinished novel in 2000 without editing, letting the reader imagine how the story might have ended.

Acting Edition: Samuel French, Inc.

Awards and Honors: Morris L. West was appointed chairman, Council of the National Library of Australia. In 1959 he was awarded the James Tait Black Memorial Prize for *The Devil's Advocate.*

NOTES

1. *New York Herald Tribune*, December 1, 1961.
2. *New York Mirror,* December 1, 1961.
3. *New York World-Telegram*, December 1, 1961.
4. *New York Times*, December 1, 1961.
5. *Daily News*, December 1, 1961.
6. *New York Post*, December 1, 1961.
7. *New York Journal-American*, December 1, 1961.

Sequel to a Verdict (1962)

Philip Dunning (United States, 1890-1968)

In 1954, the British playwright-journalist Ludovic Kennedy wrote the drama *Murder Story* as a protest against capital punishment, which he called "legal killing." Eight years later, American Philip Dunning came out with the courtroom drama *Sequel to a Verdict*, also condemning the practice.

The action of the play takes place in an imaginary Connecticut town, Nortonberg, in the 1920s. On trial is Otto Ludwig Grossmeir, a carpenter accused of kidnapping and murdering an infant girl. The newspapers deemed it "the crime of the century." The circumstances of the case are reminiscent of the Charles Lindbergh tragedy. In that case, Charles August Lindbergh, Jr., baby son of aviator Charles Lindburgh, was abducted from his crib in a New Jersey home on March 1, 1932. A ransom note was left behind, peppered with spelling mistakes and grammatical errors. Two months later, the body of the toddler was discovered a short distance from the Lindbergh home. After a two-year investigation, Bruno Richard Hauptmann was arrested and charged with the crime. The 1935 trial culminated with the death penalty. Hauptmann, who proclaimed his innocence to the very end, was executed by electric chair on April 3, 1936, but the author made a special note in the published edition of *Sequel to a Verdict*, declaring that "the court trial is purely imaginary" and that "all the characters are fictitious and have no relation to any person living or dead."[1]

State Attorney Floyd Warren, "forceful and ambitious and just a bit of a show-off," calls to the stand the first witness for the prosecution – the grieving mother of the dead infant child, Mrs. Brundage, who testifies that she, her husband Frank, and the nursemaid, Abbie Lee, found the baby's crib empty. Frank Brundage, an architect, relates how he came upon a ransom note on the windowsill of the room. Prosecutor Warren exhibits the note to the jury members, emphasizing that the dollar mark is after the numbers (50,000$), and that the hand-written message is riddled with misspellings – "anyding" instead of "anything;" "gut" instead of "good;" "singnature" instead of "signature."

State Trooper Rouls testifies that he saw dirt tracks leading from the window toward the crib, and that there were footprints on the soft ground outside, next to a ladder.

Prosecutor Warren summons an array of witnesses, including the nursemaid Lee, who confirms the evidence given by her employers; a neighbor of the Brundages, Adolph Nockheiser, who testifies seeing the accused in the neighborhood on the eve of the kidnapping; a handwriting expert, Andrew Campbell, who verifies that the writing on the ransom note matches Grossmeir's scribbling in his account book; Department of Justice Agent Daniel Knapp, who reveals that he found the ransom money hidden in a shoe box under the wooden floor of Grossmeir's garage.

Defense Attorney Martin calls upon Otto Ludwig Grossmeir to rebut the prosecution's case. A carpenter by trade, the defendant denies that he built the ladder that was used to enter the baby's room and says in derision: "It looks like a musical instrument of some kind, to me." Grossmeir insists that an acquaintance, Emil Spitzer, asked him to store the shoe box before leaving for Europe, and he never knew that it contained money. At a police station on Greenwich Street, Brundage's neighbors could not identify him in a lineup.

In his summation, Counsel Martin maintains that the kidnapping was an inside job. He points out that there are six rooms on the second floor of the Brundage home and scoffs, "How in the name of heaven could any stranger know exactly the window that led to the nursery?" And, argues Martin, "Why didn't the baby cry? Why didn't the dog bark?" However, the jury finds the defendant guilty, and Judge Pritchart sentences Grossmeir to death in the electric chair.

In a short epilogue, a Story Teller addresses the audience with the notion that "maybe it's time to abolish capital punishment. There might be some better way – anyhow think it over."

* * *

Philip Hart Dunning began his theatrical career as a performer. At an early age he left his Meriden, Connecticut home to join a carnival show as a magician's assistant. He sang and danced in vaudeville, and appeared in stock and in New York in the early 1920s. He also managed a Marilyn Miller musical before finding himself a celebrated dramatist with the 1926 melodrama *Broadway*, which he cowrote with George Abbott. *Broadway*, a potpourri of cabaret entertainment, gangland territorial war, and true love blossoming in the midst of sleaze, ran for 603 performances. In 1932, Abbott and Dunning teamed on *Lily Turner*, picturing the romantic escapades of a circus barker's wife, and coproduced the Ben Hecht-Charles MacArthur hit comedy *Twentieth Century*.

Dunning followed *Broadway* with another speakeasy melodrama, *Night Hostess* (1928), interweaving illegal gambling, racketeering and murder, all taking place in the bustling "Little Casino." *Night Hostess* ran for 117 performances, introduced Katherine Hepburn (billed as Katherine Burns) in a small role as a hostess, and was filmed in 1930 under the title *The Woman Racket*.

Dunning's *Sweet Land of Liberty* (1929) also unfolds in a shady night club operating on bootlegging and "protection" payoffs. Two liquor dealers witness the shooting of a federal prohibition agent and find themselves in hot water when they agree to tell what they saw to the grand jury. *Kill That Story* (1934) exposes crooked newspaper deals. In *Page Miss Glory* (1934), James Stewart played a hustling promoter who submits a composite photo of Hollywood beauties to a contest for "the most beautiful girl in America," wins the award, and then has to produce the girl. Complications ensue when a pair of petty criminals mistake a hotel chambermaid for the non-existent celebrity and kidnap her for ransom. *Page Miss Glory* was filmed in 1935.

Acting Edition: Dramatists Play Service.

NOTE

1. Philip Dunning, *Sequel to a Verdict* (New York: Dramatists Play Service, 1962), 3.

A Case of Libel (1963)

Henry Denker (United States, 1912-2012)

Inspired by the once-celebrated Quentin Reynolds-Westbrook Pegler lawsuit (as recounted in Louis Nizer's first chapter of the 1961 book *My Life in Court), A Case of Libel* is about an ace war correspondent's litigation against a widely syndicated columnist. The names have been changed, but the facts remain true to the real-life case.

The correspondent, Dennis Corcoran, a political liberal, and columnist Boyd Bendix, a right-winger, had once been friends. The relationship sours when Corcoran reviewed a biography of Bendix, titled *Hangman on Horseback*, which, albeit favorable, points out his faults and eccentricities. Bendix retaliates with a barrage of poisonous columns, questioning Corcoran's patriotism, accusing him of being a war profiteer, and branding him a "drunken, immoral, yellow-bellied degenerate" who engages in sexual vulgarities of all sorts.

Corcoran asks famed attorney Robert Sloane (a fictional name for Louis Nizer) to represent him. Sloane warns him of the danger in taking on the most powerful news syndicate in the world, arguing that it has millions to spend and batteries of the best lawyers on retainer. But Corcoran insists that he is not going "to run and hide."

Reluctantly, Sloane agrees to take the case. In court, a battle royale develops between him and Paul Cleary, Bendix's defense counsel. When Boyd Bendix takes the stand in his own defense, Sloane subjects him to a grueling cross-examination about sex and politics. The clash reaches its boiling point when Sloane waves sheets of paper and quotes passages from articles by Corcoran. Bendix charaterizes the quotes as Red propaganda, Communist inspired, not realizing that midway Sloane has begun to quote statements from his own writings.

Sloane coaxes Bendix to declare that the writer of the articles is without a doubt a Communist. Sloane brandishes the papers and submits in evidence "certain writings from the columns of Boyd Bendix!"

The verdict is predictable.

Defendant News International is ordered to pay the plaintiff Dennis Corcoran punitive damages in the sum of $500,000, and Boyd Bendix is to pay him $100,000.

* * *

A Case of Libel, staged by Sam Wanamaker, opened at New York's Longacre Theatre on October 10, 1963. It featured Van Heflin as attorney Sloane, John Randolph as plaintiff Corcoran, Larry Gates as columnist Bendix, and Sidney Blackmer as defense lawyer Cleary.

The reception by the critics was mostly positive. John McClain began his review with a dissertation on the role of courtroom dramas in world theatre "since the first time Portia haggled with Shylock over a pound of Antonio's prime filet" and concluded that "Henry Denker made good use of all these elements in fashioning *A Case of Libel*... This is engrossing stuff, and Mr. Denker has endowed it with the proper amount of hokum...There are a reasonable number of tricks of the trade, employed by the dedicated counsel for the plaintiff, but in the final summation it comes down to the fact that the defendant has been irresponsible in his research and is hence threatening the freedom of the press."[1]

Richard Watts Jr. found "Henry Denker's documentary dramatization of the trial frank in its partisanship, detailed in its report, and, of course, you know how it is going to turn out, but it has the almost inevitable effectiveness of courtroom dramas on the stage and provides the emotional satisfaction of seeing justice score a triumph."[2]

"Despite its periodic flaws, *a Case of Libel* is suspenseful, even if you know how it will turn out," wrote Norman Nadel. "Most of the dialogue—tracing back to Nizer, Pegler, Reynolds and the others in the true case—has an impact and a vividness that set this play above the run of courtroom dramas."[3] Howard Tuabman numerated flaws and virtues in *A Case of Libel*, concluding; "If you're a soft touch for courtroom drama, as I am, and if you enjoy seeing an extremist get his comeuppance, as I do, you should find *A Case of Libel* lively theatre, especially when it warms up to its business."[4]

Walter Kerr hailed the performances of several actors: "Mr. Heflin does not win by a show of power. He wins by fiddling... He is splendid;" "Mr. Blackmer is gracious. Mr. Blackmer is genial. Mr. Blackmer is fun;" "You will hate Mr. Gates, which is to say he is very good."[5]

In the negative corner was John Chapman, who stated bluntly, "There is a lack of suspense in *A Case of Libel*... In Denker's play—and Denker is a lawyer as well as a dramatist—it is certain that the plaintiff has been libeled before the stage trial begins. So there isn't much for an audience to do but listen as the evidence is carefully built—and I think the audience has reached its decision many scenes before the unseen jury delivers its verdict in the courtroom in the Longacre;"[6] Robert Coleman said: "*A Case of Libel* suffers somewhat from being too literal. As George Kelly once pointed out, life itself can be unconvincing behind the footlights."[7]

Henry Denker, a member of the New York bar, had scored previously with the hit military-court drama *Time Limit!* (1956). The civil suit of *A Case of Libel* drew spectators for 242 performances and was adapted to television in 1968 (with Lloyd Bridges as Dennis Corcoran, José Ferrer as Boyd Bendix, and Van Heflin repeating his role of Robert Sloane), and in 1984 (with Gordon Pinsent, Daniel J. Travanti, and Edward Asner).

Acting Edition: Samuel French, Inc.

NOTES

1. *New York Journal-American*, October 11, 1963.
2. *New York Post*, October 11, 1963.
3. *New York World-Telegram*, October 11, 1963.
4. *New York Times*, October 11, 1963.
5. *New York Herald Tribune*, October 11, 1963.
6. *Daily News*, October 11, 1963.
7. *Daily Mirror*, October 11, 1963.

Blues for Mr. Charlie (1964)

James Baldwin (United States, 1924-1987)

James Baldwin's *Blues for Mr. Charlie*[1] begins with a murder. The curtain rises on a dark stage and we hear a shot. Lights come up slowly on Lyle Britten as he looks around, bends down, and picks up the body of Richard Henry. As he carries Henry off, Lyle mumbles, "And may every nigger like this nigger end like this nigger—face down in the weeds."

Lyle Britten is a white grocery-store owner in a small town, circa the 1960s. Richard Henry was a young, rebellious African-American musician who went North, became a junkie, kicked the habit, and returned home. The murder scene will be repeated several times as the play progresses through a series of flashbacks in which the action moves between past and present.

A skeletal set divides the proceedings between Whitetown and Blacktown. The action among the whites takes place on one side of the stage, the action among the blacks on the other. The church is divided by an aisle. The courthouse is segregated.

Reverend Meridian Henry, the father of Richard, returns home from a rally, accompanied by his students. They are exhausted, disheveled, wounded. They carry placards bearing such statements as "Freedom now;" "One man, one vote;" "We want the murderer." Pete, a militant student, wonders how the authorities will explain "what Richard's body was doing in them weeds." Reverend Henry says that he'll not rest "until they bring my son's murderer to trial," but the student Lorenzo complains that "the cops ain't going to protect us," and reminds the reverend that the suspected killer, Lyle Britten, once killed another black man and "the sheriff just shoveled the body into the ground and forgot about it."

A friendly white man, Parnell James, editor of the local newspaper, enters and informs the group that a warrant has been issued for Lyle's arrest. Juanita Harmon, lover of the deceased, pooh-poohs the possibility that Lyle will be convicted.

In Whitetown, Parnell pays a visit to Lyle's home. Lyle is playing with his infant son, whom he soon hands over to his wife, Josephine, for a change of diapers. Parnell tells Lyle that he'll soon be arrested, for according to the testimony of Joel Davis, otherwise known as Papa D, the owner of the local juke joint, Lyle was the last person to see Richard alive. Lyle says calmly that he is not concerned; Richard was probably killed by "some other nigger—they do it all the time."

In a flashback, Richard tells his grandmother, Wilhelmina Henry, of his suspicion that his late mother did not fall down hotel steps by accident but was pushed by a white man. Grandma Henry maintains that the steps were slippery and that her daughter fell. "You can't start walking around believing that all the suffering in the world is caused by white folks," she states. Richard contends that "the only way the black man's going to get any power is to drive all the white men into the sea." He takes a small sawed-off pistol from his pocket and announces, "This gun goes everywhere I go."

At Papa D's tavern, Richard, Juanita and Pete sit at a table. Over loud music, Juanita tells Richard, who has been away in New York for eight years, that Lyle Britten shot a black man a few years back and nothing was done about it. Pete explains that the victim was Bill Walker, whom everybody called Old Bill. Bill's wife, "a pretty little thing," was coveted by Lyle. Following Bill's death, his wife disappeared, went North somewhere. Richard chats about his New York experience, living in bohemian Greenwich Village, and describes his conquest of "a whole gang of white chicks." Richard exhibits girls' pictures and says, "I take their money and they love it." Papa D comes over nervously and requests that Richard put the pictures away. As they eat and drink, Richard confesses that he was addicted to dope, got busted, but has since recovered.

Richard and Juanita go to the dance floor when Lyle Britten enters and crosses to the counter. He gets cigarettes out of the machine, watches the dancers for a moment and on the way out jostles Juanita. Richard and Lyle stare at each other. Lyle apologizes and exits.

In a shift to the present, Parnell advises Reverend Henry that circumstantial evidence is not reliable and there's no proof that Lyle Britten killed Richard. He has known Lyle for many years and he does not believe that he is a wicked man. The truth will come out in the trial. However, Henry feels that the jury will never convict Lyle.

In church, Reverend Phelps assures Lyle that he is supported by every white person in town. A member of the congregation, Ellis, complains that there is an attempt "to put niggers on the jury." Parnell opines that this is only fair as the town's population is 44 percent black. Josephine Britten corners Parnell and asks him about the rumors that her husband lusted after Old Bill's wife and that's why he shot the old man. She's puzzled about the attraction of white men to women of color. Parnell confides to Josephine that when he was eighteen years old he fell in love with an adolescent black girl, Pearl. One day they were sitting in the library kissing, when Pearl's mother came in. The mother didn't say a word, took her daughter by the hand, and they left. He never saw Pearl again. Her mother sent her away. If he ever found Pearl again he'd marry her.

Josephine becomes agitated: if Lyle felt that way about Old Bill's wife, he could have shot him, and if he could have killed Old Bill, he could also have killed Richard.

That evening Parnell goes to Lyle's store and asks him point blank about Willa Mae, Old Bill's wife. Lyle, a little inebriated, admits that he had a liaison with Willa Mae, who was much younger than her sixty-year-old husband. At first, he took her by force but later "she liked it as much as me." Lyle believes that it was Papa D who told Old Bill of the affair. He noticed that the old man began looking at him murderously. Parnell prods Lyle for more details, but Lyle says nothing.

A crucial flashback unfolds in the Britten store. Lyle is hammering nails in the back, fixing the baby's carriage, and Josephine is minding the store when Richard and his friend Lorenzo enter from the road and purchase two bottles of coca cola. "That will be twenty cents," says Josephine. Richard says that all he has is a twenty-dollar bill. Josephine calls Lyle, who enters carrying the hammer. A quarrel ensues, leading to a physical confrontation. As Lyle raises the hammer, Richard grabs his arm and knocks Lyle down. Richard chuckles, "Now, who do you think is the better man? Ha-ha! The master race!" He points at Josephine and smirks: "You let me in that tired white chick's drawers, she'll know who's the master!" He walks out laughing, followed by Lorenzo.

The proceedings now take place in the courtroom, two months later. Attending the segregated hearings are black and white townspeople, the jury, journalists, photographers. Scattered about are television cameras and microphones. The judge's chair is center stage, the witness stand downstage. The playwright suggests that each witness be revealed behind a scrim when called. The testimonies are supported by flashback episodes.[2]

The first witness called by the state is Josephine Britten, wife of the accused. She relates the incident in which Richard Henry came to the store to buy two cokes. "He acted like he was drunk or crazy or maybe he was under the influence of dope," she says, and adds that Richard pushed himself against her "real close and hard," behaving "like an animal." When her husband, Lyle, came to her rescue, Richard and his friend jumped on him and knocked him down. She and Lyle decided not to report the incident because there was already so much trouble in town. On the morning of August 24, the day Richard was found dead, she and her husband were at home.

The clerk calls Joel Davis to the stand. Davis ("Papa D") testifies that Lyle and Richard clashed face-to-face in his juke joint, after which he never saw the boy again, and he has no doubt that Lyle killed him. Juanita Harmon concurs. By the time she persuaded Richard to take her away "from this terrible place," it was too late. Lyle killed him – "like they been killing all our men, for years, for generations!" Wilhelmina Henry denies that her grandson carried a gun or that he was ever under the influence of hard drugs. Under cross-examination, Reverend Meridian Henry rejects the supposition that his son was a pimp, dope addict, and rapist. Editor Parnell James testifies of his awareness that racial dynamics have been greatly strained of late, but to his knowledge the black population has not armed itself. As to the accusation by Mrs. Britten of Richard's misbehavior, it may be, says Parnell, that she misconstrued the boy's actions – he has been in the North for a long time, his manner was free and bold.

After deliberating, the foreman of the jury announces, "Not guilty, Your Honor," and there's cheering in Whitetown. Lyle is congratulated and embraced. The stage is taken over by reporters, photographers, townspeople. Slowly they file out until only a few people remain on stage. Reverend Henry approaches Lyle and asks, "Did you kill him? … What was the last thing my son said to you – before you shot him down—like a dog?" A flashback illustrates the final encounter between Lyle and Richard on the road outside Papa D's joint. Lyle demands that Richard apologize for insulting his wife the other day. Richard refuses and Lyle insists, producing a gun. Richard flashes with anger, calls Lyle "sick," and goes into a tirade about white women. Lyle shoots. Richard cries "Juanita! Daddy! Mama!" and falls.

The play ends on an ominous note when Reverend Henry says to his students, "You know, for us, it all began with the Bible and the gun. Maybe it will end with the Bible and the gun." He announces that he has kept Richard's gun in the pulpit, under the Bible.

* * *

Blues for Mr. Charlie was the first Broadway play to express Black militancy.[3] Produced by the Actors Studio, it opened at The ANTA Theatre on April 23, 1964. Burgess Meredith directed a glittering cast that included Rip Torn (Lyle Britten), Ann Wedgeworth (Josephine Britten), Al Freeman, Jr. (Richard Henry), Percy Rodriguez (Reverend Meridian Henry), Rosetta Le Noire (Mother Henry), Diana Sands (Juanita), Pat Hingle (Parnell James), and future stars Ralph Waite and Jon Don Baker in small roles. Scenery and lighting were designed by Feder.

The morning-after reviewers were divided. Leonard Harris lauded playwright Baldwin for refusing "to create abstract symbols, Negro or white. All his people have blood, and when that blood spills, it makes you want to cry rather than picket." Harris also commended the technique of maneuvering "movements forward and backward in time" with ease and lucidity. "His dramatic situation is lively and builds in intensity," wrote Harris.[4] Howard Taubman also liked the use of "a free form which weaves in and out of the present

and the past" in a play penned "with fire of fury in its belly, tears of anguish in its eyes and a roar of protest in its throat."[5]

On the other hand, Richard Watts Jr. believed that "the play's technique, which includes flashbacks and occasional speeches and meditations directly aimed at the audience, hasn't been quite mastered… It makes for initial confusion… Mr. Baldwin remains essentially a novelist."[6] John McClain asserted that "the civil rights issue is certainly the most important problem facing our nation today and I'm afraid that James Baldwin's *Blues for Mr. Charlie* doesn't have the size to advance the cause appreciably… For reasons which I found difficult to understand, most of the story is told in reverse, or certainly in the most confusing order… It seemed a cumbersome way to tell a plot which could just have easily followed a chronological pattern."[7] John Chapman admired Baldwin's hopes for "harmonious life between colored and white people," but believed that the playwright's methods as a dramatist were "oddly anachronistic… *Blues for Mr. Charlie* has been couched in the scenery-chewing terms of the turn of the century… As the play digs into a rather obvious story of Southern justice, it doesn't dig in a straight line; it zigs and zags and meanders through a series of flashbacks and flashforwards which makes it difficult to remember whether a certain character is supposed to be dead or alive."[8]

The production elements were universally admired. Walter Kerr applauded "a few most intelligently used geometric designs under the ghostly spill of light magnetically arranged by Feder" and declared that "Burgess Meredith has directed superbly."[9] The cast was hailed by the entire cadre of critics.

Blues for Mr. Charlie ran for 148 performances. In summing up the theatrical season in New York, Otis L. Guernsey, Jr. wrote in *The Best Plays of 1963-1964*: "Instead of presenting us with a well-behaved Negro who is unjustly killed by a bigoted white man, Mr. Baldwin offers us a young militant, who, on returning South from New York, feels compelled to assert himself by using bad language and publicly mocking and insulting the whites… One feels that this man, Richard, is the natural reaction to a long period in which previous generations of Negroes persisted up a blind alley of patience and hope. That generation is represented by Richard's father, the Reverend Meridian Henry, who now finds himself questioning Christianity."[10]

Blues for Mr. Charlie came to London in 1965 and drew a hostile reaction from the critics. The *Times of London* said that the playwright was "exchanging creative writing for demagogic oratory" and that the Actors Studio's company "far from deepening the play, were broadening and coarsening it even more."[11] The *Financial Times* complained that "throughout the whole first act the players gave a display of uniformly bad acting."[12] The *Daily Mail* called the Actors Studio display of method acting "a sorry disappointment."[13] Lee

Strasberg, the artistic director of the Actors Studio, said at a press conference that "the unclarity was partially our fault, partially the author's."

* * *

James Arthur Baldwin was born to a poor family in Harlem, New York, in 1924. His adoptive father, David Baldwin, was a preacher. Baldwin attended DeWitt Clinton High School in the Bronx, where he wrote for the school magazine. At the age of fourteen, Baldwin joined the Pentecostal Church and became a child preacher, but at seventeen he turned away from his religion and moved to Greenwich Village, a bohemian neighborhood in Manhattan. He studied at the New School and began writing essays, book reviews, and short stories.

A homosexual, Baldwin became disillusioned by American prejudice against blacks and gays, and in 1948 departed for Paris, France, where he was soon embedded in the cultural radicalism of the Left Bank and contributed articles to various literary magazines, most notably *Zero: A Review of Literature and Art.*

During the 1950s, Baldwin published his autobiographical novel, *Go Tell It on the Mountain* (1953); a first collection of essays, *Notes of a Native Son* (1955), the title referring to his mentor Richard Wright, author of the novel *Native Son*; and a second novel, *Giovanni's Room* (1956), controversial due to its homoerotic content. In the 1960s, Baldwin wrote mainly about the restive civil rights movement. His lengthy essay *No Name in the Street* discussed the assassination of his personal friends Medgar Evers, Malcolm X and Martin Luther King, Jr. In the 1970s, Baldwin penned two novels, *If Beale Street Could Talk* and *Just Above My Head,* advocating the importance of nurturing black families, and a series of essays offering provocative studies of American society through an analysis of various motion pictures, including *A Tale of Two Cities, You Only Live Once, Dead End, Rebel Without a Cause, The Birth of a Nation, In the Heat of the Night, In This Our Life, The Defiant Ones, Home of the Brave*, and *Guess Who's Coming to Dinner*. In the 1980s, Baldwin concluded his literary career with a nonfiction book, *The Evidence of Things Not Seen,* covering the Atlanta Child Murders. He focused on the two-year period 1979-1981, during which at least twenty-eight African Americans were murdered in Atlanta, Georgia.

Politically, Baldwin aligned himself with the ideals of the Congress of Racial Equality (CORE). In 1963, along with prominent figures like Harry Belafonte and Lorraine Hansberry, Baldwin met with then Attorney General Robert F. Kennedy to voice the concerns of the Black community. He appeared at the Civil Rights March in Washington, D.C. on August 28, 1963, accompanied by Belafonte, Sidney Poitier, and Marlon Brando.

Among Baldwin's associates and friends were fellow writers Langston Hughes and Maya Angelou, singer Nina Simone, and French painter Philippe Derome.

Besides *Blues for Mr. Charlie*, Baldwin's only other contribution to the Broadway scene was the drama *The Amen Corner*, previously produced at Howard University (1953) and at the Robertson Playhouse in Los Angeles, California (1964). It arrived at the Ethel Barrymore Theatre on April 15, 1965. The protagonist of *The Amen Corner* is Margaret Alexander, the pastor of a small church in Harlem. Margaret loses her son, husband and congregation before realizing that in her fervent devotion to the service of God, she neglected her duty to her family. Bea Arthur enacted Sister Margaret. Frank Silvera produced and directed. Howard Taubman said in the *New York Times*, "The structure of the play is elementary. The characterization is halting, and points are made obviously and repetitively," but the critic asserted that the play "throws some light on the barrenness of the lives of impoverished Negroes who seek surcease from their woes in religion."[14] *The Amen Corner* ran for eighty-four performances and, headed by Claudia McNeil in the role of Sister Margaret, went on an extensive tour to Vienna, Paris, Zurich, Amsterdam, Rotterdam, Munich, Turin, Milan, Budapest, Tel Aviv, and the Edinburgh Festival in Scotland.

Baldwin died on November 30, 1987, from esophageal cancer in Saînt-Paul de Vence, France. He was buried at the Ferncliff Cemetery in Hardsdale, near New York City. More than twenty years later, in 2010, Pantheon Books published *The Cross of Redemption*, a 300-page assembly of previously uncollected Baldwin speeches, book reviews, lectures, letters, and essays. Reviewing the book in the *Los Angeles Times*, Professor of English Lynell George writes of Baldwin: "Language—written and spoken—was his blade, and it was his balm."[15]

Acting Edition: Samuel French, Inc.

Awards and Honors: In 1987, the National James Baldwin Literary Society was founded. In 1992, Hampshire College in Amherst, Massachusetts, established the James Baldwin Scholars program. In 2002, scholar Molefi Kete Asante included Baldwin among the *100 Greatest African Americans: A Biographical Encyclopedia.*

NOTES

1. Mr. Charlie was an early 20th century phrase used by African Americans to refer to Southern whites.

2. The first play to illustrate the testimony of court witnesses via flashbacks was *On Trial* (1914) by Elmer Rice. The device, considered revolutionary at the time, has been used sporadically ever since.
3. On March 24, a month prior to the Broadway opening of *Blues for Mr. Charlie*, another explosive play with racial overtones, LeRoi Jones's one-act *Dutchman*, was presented at Off Broadway's Cherry Lane Theatre. *Dutchman* pictures an incident taking place in a New York subway. Lula, an attractive thirty-year-old white woman flirts with Clay, a studious Black man ten years her junior, arouses him by dancing sensuously in the subway car, taunts him about his skin colo, and then, unexpectedly, pulls out a knife and stabs Clay to death. Jennifer West and Robert Hooks portrayed Lula and Clay under Edward Parone's direction.
4. *New York World-Telegram*, April 24, 1964.
5. *New York Times*, April 24, 1964.
6. *New York Post*, April 24, 1964.
7. *New York Journal-American*, April 24, 1964.
8. *Daily News*, April 24, 1964.
9. *New York Herald Tribune*, April 24, 1964.
10. Otis L. Guernsey, Jr., ed., *The Best Plays of 1963-1964* (New York: Dodd, Mead and Company, 1964), 7.
11. Quoted in *New York Times*, May 5, 1965.
12. Quoted in *New York Times*, May 5, 1965.
13. Quoted in *New York Times*, May 5, 1965.
14. *New York Times*, April 16, 1965.
15. *Los Angeles Times*, August 22, 2010.

Hostile Witness (1964)

Jack Roffey (England, 1926-1969)

While not on a par with such milestone courtroom dramas as *On Trial* (1914), *The Trial of Mary Dugan* (1927) or *Witness for the Prosecution* (1953), *Hostile Witness* rewards its viewers with colorful glimpses of the pomp and ceremony of the British judicial system, the unusual dilemma of a famous barrister finding himself accused of murder, and a last-minute surprise resolution.

Hostile Witness premiered in Brighton, England, in 1964, moved to London in 1965, and came to New York in 1966, starring Ray Milland as Simon Crawford, Q.C., a no-nonsense lawyer. Crawford is a widower. Some months ago, his daughter Jill was killed by a hit-and-run driver. In his grief, Crawford swore that he would find the driver and kill him

Allegedly, the driver was a neighbor, Judge Anthony Gregory, who is found lying dead on the floor of his study with a knife in the chest. Crawford maintains that someone attacked him that night, on the way home, and knocked him out by bashing the back of his head. However, Crawford is incriminated by overwhelming physical evidence. His fingerprints are found on the fatal weapon, scrapings from the dead man's nails show fibers and threads identical with his overcoat, patches of blood on the coat correspond with the blood group of the deceased, Group A.

Crawford's defense attorney, Sir Peter Grossman, counters the prosecution's witnesses with a theory of his own: Suppose someone was waiting in the shadows that night for Crawford to return home, and hit him on the back of his head as he was about to open his front door. Suppose he or she then carried or dragged him into the judge's house where the judge was already lying dead—or alternatively brought the necessary objects out into the mews—pressed Crawford's hands round the knife with which the old man had been killed, then scraped the dead man's hands down the coat Crawford was carrying, so that fibers and threads from it lodged beneath the torn nails. In that case blood would have been transferred onto the coat itself for all to see. Would not the scientific evidence available in those circumstances be identical with the scientific evidence now being produced by the Crown?

When Crawford insists on calling a witness to establish his alibi, Sir Peter withdraws from the case. Crawford undertakes his own defense with the help of his junior assistants, but his alibi is shattered by the calculation of Daylight Savings time.

Just when the situation seems hopeless, and Crawford's team believes that "he hasn't a ghost of a chance," a connection is established to a past case of a convict named John Logan who, before being taken to prison on an armed robbery charge, pointed at Mr. Justice Gregory and at prosecuting counsel Mr. Crawford and threatened to kill both of them. Crawford cannot recall what Logan looked like, but he remembers that the man was color blind. That's what led to his arrest. The driver of the geaway car was injured by an enemy's bombing raid, so Logan drove the car himself. Being color blind, he drove through a red light and was stopped by the police. It was only a routine stop, but they saw the injured driver in the back—and that was that.

Logan's affliction is instrumental in identifying him when Crawford summons his chief of staff, Charles Milburn, to the stand. Milburn delivered to chambers a letter in an envelope typed in red and admits that he is color blind. Under Crawford's pounding cross-examination, Milburn makes a crucial slip of the tongue when he blurts that he could not be Logan, as Logan is dead. Crawford jumps at him with the query, "How do you know that Logan is dead?"

Milburn breaks down and admits that he is Logan. He became a clerk in Crawford's chambers and for years studied his employer and Judge Gregory. When Crawford's daughter was killed in a car accident, he saw his opportunity.

"That is the case for the Defense," says Crawford, and the curtain descends.

* * *

Hostile Witness opened at the Music Box Theatre in New York on February 17, 1966, and was greeted with hostility by critics Douglas Watt, who found it "so rickety and inept a piece of playwriting that the bubbles have turned to vinegar long before the payoff, which is, of course, merely arbitrary,"[1] and John McClain, who sniffed, "This is a singularly sad occasion… I'm afraid it will take a hung jury to save it from early execution."[2]

Other critics, however, welcomed the play. "Jack Roffey's *Hostile Witness* is strictly courtroom fun and games of the don't-you-believe-it-for-a-moment variety, and as such it's pleasantly tricky entertainment," wrote Walter Kerr.[3] "Sturdy and serviceable… has the necessary cliff-hangers at curtain times and the necessary credible twist at the end," stated Stanley Kauffman.[4]

Hostile Witness ran on Broadway for 157 performances. In his introduction to the Samuel French acting edition, playwright Jack Roffey maintains that "stock companies and amateurs are the life-blood of the theatre," but the sixteen speaking roles, courtroom extras, three sets, and wigs and gowns, place this play beyond reach of most shoe-string troupes.

Jack Roffey penned the screenplay of *Hostile Witness*. The movie was distributed in 1968, with Ray Milland directing and repeating his stage role as Simon Crawford. Roffey also collaborated on the scripting of the whodunit *Eight O'Clock Walk* (1953), about a London taxi driver, played by Richard Attenborough, who is accused of murdering a little girl.

During the 1950s and 1960s, Roffey, a real-life court official, contributed numerous suspenseful episodes to the British television series *Boyd Q.C.* (1956-1964), in which barrister Richard Boyd, a counterpart of the American Perry Mason, appeared in court as counsel for the defense. Notable among Boyd's cases were *By Gas: That's Murder*, *The Open and Shut Case*, *Nylon Spells Murder*, *Thread of Evidence*, and *The Case of the Lazy Eye*. Simultaneously, Roffey had three criminous plays produced in London: *No Other Verdict* (1953), *Night of the Fourth* (1956) and *Justice is a Woman* (1966), the latter starring Flora Robson as a Queen's Counsel called upon to defend an English boy accused of murder.

Acting Edition: Samuel French, Inc. (in manuscript form).

Hostile Witness is also included in *10 Classic Mystery and Suspense Plays of the Modern Theatre* edited by Stanley Richards (New York: Dodd, Mead and Company, 1973).

NOTES

1. *Daily News*, February 18, 1966.
2. *New York Journal-American*, February 18, 1966.
3. *New York Herald Tribune*, February 18, 1966.
4. *New York Times,* February 18, 1966.

The Man in the Glass Booth (1967)

Robert Shaw (England, 1927-1978)

The Man in the Glass Booth, a psychological thriller about guilt and redemption, is based on the case of Adolf Eichmann, a Nazi colonel referred to as "the architect of the Holocaust." After World War II Eichmann fled to Argentina and lived there under a false identity. In 1960 he was captured by Israeli Mossad agents and abducted to Israel, where he was tried for war crimes and crimes against humanity. He was found guilty and executed by hanging in 1962 in Ramla, Israel.

The Man in the Glass Booth raises its curtain on a palatial penthouse in Manhattan, the residence of Arthur Goldman, a real-estate tycoon. French windows open to a roof garden full of statues and artificial trees. The city's towers are seen in the background. Servants come up in a noiseless in-house elevator carrying priceless paintings, a butler pours Goldman his morning coffee, and a secretary enters with the New York dailies. It is November 20, 1964, Goldman's fifty-second birthday, and he plans to go to the opera that evening, escorting a duchess.

Goldman is charming, eccentric, and sure of himself, but he keeps waving a pistol about, perhaps awaiting some danger. Curiously, when the thing he fears comes, he tosses the pistol into a tropical fish tank.

A flower man arrives in the elevator, unloads artificial flower plants, and leaves. He soon returns with two young men, guns in their hands. They are followed by a stout woman, Mrs. Rosen, who is obviously their leader. "You are Adolf Karl Dorff," says Mrs. Rosen, "a colonel in the Einsatzgruppen, the mobile killing unit of the SS." Goldman does not deny the accusation. The young men, Israeli agents, search the apartment and frisk Goldman. One of them hits him in the stomach and he spits out a capsule of poison. He offers them a million dollars "hard cash" and raises it to three, then seven, then eight million.

The second act takes place in a Tel Aviv cell. Outside a peephole stands a guard. Inside, it is hot. Goldman, dressed in prison clothes, sits on the bed. Mrs. Rosen faces him. "Why did you pretend to be Jewish? Who killed Arthur Goldman?" she asks. In a jocular mood he admits to being Adolf Karl Dorff and requests to be allowed to wear his SS uniform at the pending trial.

During a blackout, the cell changes into a courtroom. A guard leads Goldman to a bullet-proof glass booth. The presiding judge, the prosecutor and Mrs. Rosen are seated at scattered tables. Goldman seems carefree and high-spirited as witnesses relate the horrors of the concentration camps and the atrocities committed by the Nazis. At the conclusion of each testimony, Goldman claps sardonically. Insisting that he conduct his own defense, he switches on a microphone from within the booth and relates with glee how in the camps he personally sought out the Jews who were spirited and rebellious, the ones who "smelled of freedom," and shot them. He also declares his admiration for Hitler: his generals lost him the war; his subordinates were unworthy; Hess was mad, Goering reviled, Himmler rejected. But the Fuehrer was loved, says Goldman, loved to the end— "Sieg Heil! Sieg Heil!"

The verdict "guilty" seems inevitable until an old woman in the auditorium rises and says quietly, "This man is not Dorff." The Judge allows the woman, Mrs. Lehman, to take the witness stand. She testifies that the man on trial was never a Nazi but is in fact a Jewish survivor of the concentration camps. She describes how towards the end of the war, Colonel Dorff was shooting people methodically in the neck, then throwing the twisted bodies into the snow. When Russian soldiers entered the camp on horseback, Mrs. Lehman reports, Dorff dropped his gun and fell to his knees. "We all ran and tore at Dorff," says Mrs. Lehman. "We tore him to pieces."

After a long silence, Mrs. Rosen enters the glass booth and undoes Goldman's cuffs. He comes out of the booth and embraces Mrs. Lehman. "Why did you do it?" asks a perplexed judge. He posed as a Nazi war criminal, explains Goldman, in order to present the enemy as he really was—evil and unrepentant. As a former concentration camp inmate, he seeks to tell the world about the Nazi horrors to make sure they are never forgotten, to ensure continuing vigilance against repetition. He is willing to sacrifice his own life to that end.

Goldman returns to the glass booth, snatches the door key, and locks himself inside. He takes off his Nazi uniform. The guards and the court officials surround the booth and examine it, not knowing how to get the man out. They attempt to dislodge him by tilting the booth, hoping to pry him loose from underneath, but their efforts fail. He can never be dislodged, says the playwright, he can only be remembered. The lights fade.

* * *

Adapted by Robert Shaw from his own novel and directed by Harold Pinter, *The Man in the Glass Booth* opened at West End's St. Martin's Theatre on July 27, 1967. The London reviewers next morning offered varied interpretations of Arthur Goldman's self-sacrifice and generally faulted the play for obscurity. Reviewer Thomas Quinn Curtiss wrote in a dispatch to the *New York Times* that Robert Shaw "delivered a fascinating if enigmatic play which benefits from the exacting direction of fellow playwright Harold Pinter, and from a masterly performance by Donald Pleasence in the central role."[1]

The American critic Walter Kerr attended the opening night of *The Man in the Glass Booth* on his way to the Chichester Festival and, he wrote, could not detach this "calculated grotesque" from his mind. He was fascinated by the character of the Jewish financier who is "imperious, coddling, oily, fearful, garrulous in a fake Brooklyn accent, cheerfully unreasonable... It so happens that I was more taken up with the play, and readier to forgive its intellectual uncertainties and occasional theatrical gaucheries than most of the London daily reviewers."[2]

John Russell Taylor, in *Plays and Players*, stated that he liked Robert Shaw's play "for precisely the qualities that most of the critics seemed to find against it, ... I liked it because it does not let itself become a play about the Jewish problem, Nazi guilt, the ethics of genocide, sadism as a way of life, or any of the other abstract notions which seem to be hovering in the wings... Anyone (well, more or less) can present a thesis of sorts. But to create a character as complex, surprising and, in spite of everything, as convincing as Goldman – that is something else again… if to experience magic in the theatre you are willing to accept a little mystery, this would be very much what you have been looking for."[3]

The Man in the Glass Booth ran for 151 performances and failed to become a commercial success. When the play was exported to New York's Royale Theatre on September 26, 1968, the reception by the critics was mixed. Richard Watts Jr. found it "A fascinating play… a play of striking theatrical effectiveness… a work of notable dramatic originality."[4] Leonard Harris believed it to be "Dramatically Viable… excellent drama,"[5] Walter Kerr pointed out "the fanciful flourishes of titillating melodrama: unidentified strangers in elevators, men stealthily opening forbidden safes, revolvers dropped into fish tanks."[6] Clive Barnes liked "a fantastically effective vehicle for the bravura acting of Donald Pleasence and the subtly virtuoso directing of Harold Pinter."[7]

Negative assessments came from John Chapman, "It came to be an undramatic bore to me last night,"[8] and Martin Gottfried, "The story is basically pulp fiction… a crudely written and badly boring gimmick play."[9]

The Man in the Glass Booth ran for 268 performances. Jack Warden replaced Donald Pleasence on March 31, 1969. The play was filmed in 1975, directed by Arthur Hiller and starring Maximilian Schell in an Academy nominated performance as Arthur Goldman. Off Broadway's Jean Cocteau Repertory revived *The Man in the Glass Booth* in 1998. Reviewer Wilborn Hampton wrote in the *New York Times*, "The play is no less harrowing today than it was three decades ago, and the admirable Cocteau revival is a taut staging that Eve Adamson, the director, gradually builds in intensity to its final explosion of malevolence, with the accused in the dock reveling in murders he committed."[10]

* * *

Robert Archibald Shaw was born in Westhoughton, Lancashire, England, in 1927. As a boy, he was an accomplished athlete, competing in rugby, squash and track events. The first play he saw was *Hamlet* in 1944 with Sir John Gielgud in the West End. He studied for the stage at the Royal Academy of Dramatic Art and, in 1948, embarked upon a career as an actor. He gained experience in regional theatres throughout England, notably with the company at Stratford-on-Avon. In 1951 he joined the Old Vic, where he played Cassio in *Othello* and Lysander in *A Midsummer Night's Dream.* In addition to several lauded performances in the West End, Shaw appeared on Broadway as Aston in Harold Pinter's *The Caretaker* (1961-1962) and as Möbius in Friedrich Duerrenmatt's *The Physicists* (1964-1965). He distinguished himself on the screen as a SPECTRE assassin in the James Bond film *From Russia with Love* (1963); a relentless German Panzer officer in *Battle of the Bulge* (1965); a young Henry VIII in *A Man for All Seasons* (1966), for which he was nominated for the Academy Award as Best Supporting Actor; General George Armstrong Custer in *Custer of the West* (1967); the Spanish conqueror Francisco Pizarro in *The Royal Hunt of the Sun* (1969); Lord Randolph Churchill in *Young Winston* (1972); a ruthless mobster in *The Sting* (1973); a sadistic subway-hijacker in *The Taking of Pelham One Two Three* (1974); an obsessed shark-hunting fisherman in *Jaws* (1975); the Sheriff of Nottingham in *Robin* and *Marian* (1976); a treasure hunter in *The Deep* (1977); and an Israeli Mossad agent in *Black Sunday* (1977).

As a writer, Shaw published his first novel, *The Hiding Place*, in 1960, and followed it with the novels *The Sun Doctor* (1961), *The Flag* (1965), *The Man in the Glass Booth* (1967) upon which he based his play, and *A Card from Morocco* (1969). His second play, *Cato Street*, about the 1820 Cato Street conspiracy, was produced by the Young Vic in London in 1971, starring Vanessa Redgrave and Bob Hoskins.

Shaw married three times and had ten children. His second wife was the actress Mary Ure. A heavy drinker most of his life, Shaw died of a heart attack in Ireland in 1978 while filming *Avalanche Express.* His remains were cremated, and his ashes scattered near his home in Ireland.

Acting Edition: Samuel French, Inc.

Awards and Honors: A top-ten selection in *The Best Plays of 1968-1969. The Man in the Glass Booth* was nominated for a Tony Award as Best Play in 1969.

NOTES

1. *New York Times*, July 29, 1967.

2. *New York Times*, August 27, 1967.
3. *Plays and Players*, October 1967.
4. *New York Post*, September 27, 1968.
5. *WCBS-TV*, September 26, 1968.
6. *New York Times*, October 6, 1968.
7. *New York Times*, September 27, 1968.
8. *Daily News*, September 27, 1968.
9. *Women's Wear Daily*, September 27, 1968.
10. *New York Times*, February 25, 1998.

Conduct Unbecoming (1969)

Barry England (England, 1932-2009)

Time: late 1800s. Place: the anteroom of a British regimental officers' mess in India. Playwright Barry England, who served in the Far East for two years as a subaltern, creates a military environment steeped in tradition and honor. Or so it seems.

The play begins with the arrival of two second lieutenants for a three-month probationary period with the regiment. Edward Millington, son of a much-honored general, turns out to be a drunkard and womanizer. He also has no intention of passing muster. "There is a ship, the *Doric Castle*, which sails to England in almost exactly three months to the day from now. I intend to be on her," he flippantly relates to his mate, the earnest Arthur Drake, who hopes to make the regiment his lifelong career.

During an officers' ball, Millington feebly accosts the regiment's sweetheart, Marjorie Hasseltine, an attractive widow. But the lady accuses him of a much graver offense—an attempted rape and the slashing of her backside with a saber.

Millington is set to be tried by a kangaroo court-martial under the presidency of the Adjutant, Captain Rupert Harper, who assigns Drake to be the defending officer. The adjutant tells Drake that it is necessary to go through the motions but adds that "it is very much a *fait accompli*." Drake says that he will do his best to defend Millington.

Millington is cynical about the proceedings, but Drake insists that he will get a fair trial. It soon becomes evident that the playwright's accusation of "conduct unbecoming" is not targeted at the cad Millington, but at the regiment's society of seasoned, code-honored officers and gentlemen. To their chagrin, Drake manages to puncture holes in the evidence of a succession of witnesses, including the regiment's doctor, Maurice Pratti; the second-in-command, Major Lionel Roach; the mess major domo, Pradah Singh; and Mrs. Hasseltine herself.

Drake proves that the widow was attacked a second time, by someone other than Millington, more viciously, on the evening in question. Millington is exonerated but there remains the question of the attacker's identity. Suspicion shifts from one officer to another and the suspense mounts until the final curtain when it turns out that the culprit is Major Roach. The motive is somewhat incongruous and less than convincing: Roach has a split personality, assaulting local women during his "Hyde" periods.

In a reversal, Millington stays with the regiment, while Drake, disillusioned, decides to submit his resignation.

* * *

Conduct Unbecoming was very successful when it originated at the Theatre Royal in Bristol (May 20, 1969) and then transferred to the Queen's Theatre in London (July 10, 1969). Critic John Spurling admired a play "complete with questions of honor, dark psychological undertow, class distinction and a liberal spicing of melodrama." Spurling applauded the visual "feast of scarlet jackets, jodhpurs, boots and spurs," and hailed playwright England as "a born story teller" who "tells his racy story without hollow pretensions," but "in just the way he finds it needs to be told."[1]

However, upon the arrival of *Conduct Unbecoming* to New York's Ethel Barrymore Theatre on October 12, 1970, the reviewers were sharply divided.

John Chapman hailed the play: "The tardy Broadway drama season got off to a rousing start last evening with the production of an English import, *Conduct Unbecoming*. It's like Kipling, but not as sloppy... absorbing entertainment."[2] Clive Barnes stated, "Quite a wonderful example of its genre. It is a whodunit, a why-he-did-it and a where-it-was-done of quite unusual interest and quality."[3] John J. O'Connor applauded, "It can't miss... super, absolutely super."[4] And John Schubeck cheered, "*Conduct Unbecoming* is the kind of stage dynamite that makes going to a play worthwhile."[5]

Among those who found *Conduct Unbecoming* less becoming was Walter Kerr, who lamented, "Its trouble is that it doesn't know it's 100 years out of date... There may even be a rule about stage thrillers: Not everything important can take place out on the lawn, to be reported third-hand; something of the mystery must take place in front of us."[6] Martin Gottfried sniffed, "The mystery is solved in a series of melodramatics so ludicrous that one can only wonder about the English audiences who made this play a success on the West End and about Roger Stevens, the American producer who imported it... this is the most preposterous, trite, ancient and boring production—a replica of the properly obsolete—that I have ever seen or could (not) imagine seeing."[7] Leonard Harris did not mince words on *WCBS-TV*: "If there is one saving grace to this British drama, and I don't know if there is, but if there is, it is the reassurance that bad English plays, even hits, can be every bit as bad as bad American plays... *Conduct Unbecoming*, with its frothy overacting, is dismal and heavy amateurism—a closet full of spiffy uniforms brought out to dress up a play with the dimensions and brain of a pea."[8]

Undaunted by the savagery of the naysayers, Otis L. Guernsey Jr. selected *Conduct Unbecoming* as one of the ten best plays of 1970-1971: "A colorful tale of warped values among the British officer caste of an Indian regiment in Her Majesty Queen Victoria's Imperial Army in the late 1800s... there are fibers of reality running through what is ostensibly a simple theatrical tale of suspense in a highly colorful setting."[9]

Staged effectively by Val May with a large ensemble of scarlet-clad lancers going through pomp-and-ceremony rituals, *Conduct Unbecoming* ran on Broadway for 144 performances. A 1975 British movie version, filmed in Islamabad, Pakistan and directed by Michael Anderson, featured an all-star cast that included Richard Attenborough, Michael York, Trevor Howard, Christopher Plummer, Stacy Keach, and Susannah York.

* * *

Barry England was raised in a Roman Catholic home and studied at Downside School. Following a stint in the army, he enrolled at the Royal Academy of Dramatic Arts as a playwright. The first of his plays to be produced was *End of Conflict* (1961), a drama about British soldiers serving in the Far East. England's second play, *The Big Contract* (1963), dealt with business shenanigans.

England scored big with his 1968 novel, *Figures in a Landscape*, the story of two prisoners of war who escape in an unnamed totalitarian country. They make their way through 400 miles of harsh weather in a territory rife with enemy soldiers. Critics hailed England's gritty prose and called the book "a brilliant achievement." The novel was adapted to the screen in 1970, directed by Joseph Losey, starring Robert Shaw and Malcolm McDowell.

During the 1950s and 1960s, England contributed episodes to the British television series *Armchair Theatre* and *Play of the Week*. German television presented his play *End of Conflict* in 1965.

He married actress Diane Clare (1938-2013). with whom he had two children. They remained married until his death in 2009.

Acting Edition: Samuel French, Inc.

Awards and Honors: A top-ten selection in *The Best Plays of 1970-1971*.

Barry England's 1968 novel, *Figures in a Landscape*, was nominated for the Booker Prize.

NOTES

1. Otis L. Guernsey Jr., ed., *The Best Playsof 1969-1970* (New York: Dodd, Mead and Company, 1970), 67.
2. *Daily News*, October 13, 1970.

3. *New York Times*, October 13, 1970.
4. *Wall Street Journal*, October 13, 1970.
5. *WABC-TV*, October 12, 1970.
6. *Sunday Times*, October 25, 1970.
7. *Women's Wear Daily*, October 13, 1970.
8. *WCBS-TV*, October 12, 1970.
9. Otis L. Guernsey Jr, ed., *The Best Plays of 1970-1971*, 13.

Inquest (1970)

Donald Freed (United States, 1932-)

One of the most enduring controversies of the cold war era is the trial and execution of married couple Julius and Ethel Rosenberg as Soviet spies. At the time, the Manhattan Project was the name given to the top-secret effort of Allied scientists to develop an atomic bomb. The Rosenbergs were accused and found guilty of delivering notes and charts of a crucial high explosive lens mold to Russian agents.

Playwright Donald Freed was inspired by Walter and Miriam Schneir's 1965 book, *Invitation to an Inquest*, when penning *The United States vs. Julius and Ethel Rosenberg*, a docudrama about the "Atom Spy Ring." The play had its world premiere at the Cleveland Playhouse, the oldest resident professional theatre in the country, in 1969. It ran for nine weeks to full houses but when the play (now called *Inquest*) came to New York the following year, director and cast were replaced.

When the audience entered the lobby of the Music Box Theatre, they were greeted with a sign: "There will be no curtain calls." Under Alan Schneider's direction, there was no curtain, and no intermission. The play began with frozen images on an upstage screen, including a picture of Hiroshima's victims and portraits of Senator Joe McCarthy and the FBI's J. Edgar Hoover, as well as a statement: "Every word you will hear or see on this stage is a documented quotation or reconstruction from events." Throughout the play, faces, occurrences, and newspaper headlines from the late 1940s and early 1950s were projected on a background composed of eighteen panels.

The action progresses on two platforms—one representing a courthouse, the other an interior of Julius and Ethel Rosenberg's home. While the case against the Rosenbergs is in progress, flashbacks revert back to incidents in the couple's personal life. The audience is the jury; dialogue is directed to them.

The sympathy of the playwright is clearly with the defendants. Irving H. Saypol, the United States Attorney for the Southern District of New York, and his prosecutor assistant, Roy Cohn, are bullies. Presiding Judge Irving R. Kaufman is supercilious. The State's witnesses, David Greenglass and Harry Gold, come across as moustached villains.

On the other hand, Julius and Ethel Rosenberg (shrewdly cast by sympathetic actors George Grizzard and Anne Jackson) and their defense attorney

Emanuel Bloch (portrayed by likable James Whitmore) are presented in positive, humane terms. Domestic sequences picture the Rosenbergs as a couple of lower middle-class Jews from New York's Lower East Side. We see them as loving parents to two sons, we see Julius playing chess, Ethel singing operatic arias. Both are bewildered by their fate.

"The charge is conspiracy to commit espionage," declares Judge Kaufman. In his opening remarks, Prosecutor Saypol assures the jury that the evidence will show that the loyalty and the allegiance of the Rosenbergs was not to the United States but to Communism, both national and international, and that they stole, through Ethel's brother David Greenglass, who was stationed in Los Alamos, "the one weapon that might well hold the key to the survival of the nation"—the atomic bomb.

Emanuel Bloch pleads with the jury not to be influenced by the prevalent hysteria of the times and asks for "a fair shake in the American way."

Act I is largely devoted to the testimonies of David Greenglass and Harry Gold, who had previously pleaded guilty to their own roles in the case before becoming the chief witnesses for the prosecution. Greenglass, Ethel Rosenberg's brother, testifies that his brother-in-law, Julius, asked him to write up anything he knew about the atomic bomb. Julius told him that the Russians would pay for his schooling and showed him a console table hollowed out to fit paraphernalia for photographic purposes. He gave Julius a sketch of a lens mold. Jello box sides served as a code of identity among the parties of the ring. He held up one piece of a Jello box and Harry Gold exhibited a matching piece when they first met.

In his cross-examination, defense attorney Bloch elicits from Greenglass that he was a business partner of Julius Rosenberg and they often quarreled.

Ruth Greenglass, David's wife, testifies that Julius Rosenberg confided to her that sharing the atomic bomb information with the Russians, an ally at the time, would likely prevent one nation from using the bomb as a threat against another. Rosenberg asked for physical descriptions of the project at Los Alamos, said Ruth, as well as the number of people employed there, including scientists.

Harry Gold, already convicted of espionage and serving a sentence of thirty years in a federal penitentiary, testifies that he served as liaison between a Russian spy, Anatoli Yakovley, and David Greenglass, contacting the latter in Albuquerque, New Mexico, introducing himself with a matching piece of cardboard.

In the second act, Emanuel Bloch calls Julius Rosenberg to the stand. The accused, New York born and thirty-three years old, denies any involvement with espionage, asserts that he is "heartily in favor of our Constitution and Bill of Rights," and maintains that he does not owe allegiance to any other country. When prosecutor Saypol queries whether Julius or his wife Ethel have been members of the Communist Party, Rosenberg refuses to answer on the grounds that it might incriminate him.

Ethel Rosenberg, on the stand, also denies any espionage activities and insists, "Neither of us is guilty."

In his closing statement, Emanuel Bloch emphasizes that the entire case against the Rosenbergs lacks any kind of meaningful physical or documentary evidence but relies on oral testimony by a shady David Greenglass and his "dolled up, arrogant" wife.

Irving Saypol points out that the case is one of the most important ever submitted to a jury in the United States, and declares that "the F.B.I. is never duped."

The foreman of the jury appears from the audience, mounts the stage, and announces that Julius and Ethel Rosenberg are "guilty as charged." Judge Kaufman sentences the Rosenbergs "to the punishment of death."

The last scene of the play takes place on death row at Sing Sing prison. Images of Jean-Paul Sartre, Albert Einstein and the Pope appear on the screen, asking for clemency, while Dwight D. Eisenhower states that he will not intervene in the matter.

The final moments are described in harrowing detail. The Rosenbergs, their heads shorn, are offered their last meal. Other prisoners stand frozen. Guards arrange the execution area. Enter a matron, a marshal, an electrician, and two doctors. A Rabbi intones, "The Lord is my shepherd, I shall not want" and continues with the reading of the Psalm as Julius Rosenberg is led in, pauses for a moment to give the Rabbi his spectacles, and is strapped to the electric chair by two guards. The cathode is adjusted, the helmet lowered on the head to make contact with the shaven spot. Three electric charges dim the lights. The doctor approaches, opens Julius's shirt, listens, and pronounces him dead. The body is placed on a gurney and is wheeled out. Ethel Rosenberg enters, along with a prison matron and the same ritual of death is repeated. The Rabbi intones the Hebrew lament for the dead.

Emanuel Bloch addresses the audience with a mournful comment that his biggest mistake was "underestimating the capacity for cynicism and evil in high places."

The tantalizing question remains: were the Rosenbergs guilty or not guilty of espionage? Were they traitors, or the victims of a shameful episode in American history, fed by Cold War tensions, anti-Communist hysteria, and a touch of anti-Semitism?

* * *

The New York critics greeted *Inquest* with mostly negative assessments. Douglas Watt called *Inquest* "a disturbing document, as it was meant to be," but "nevertheless, I found it often tiresome theatre," a drama that "falls inescapably into the category of a propaganda play, thus demeaning it subject."[1] Richard Watts believed that "Mr. Freed is stacking the cards to advance his point," thus "does no service to the disputed memory of the Rosenbergs. It could make many suspect they were guilty."[2] Martin Gottfried sniffed: "The script is so choppy, its editing so abrupt, there is such emphasis on minor matters and such skimming on major ones, the transitions are so sudden and elementary matters are so ignored that you simply can't keep the story straight."[3]

Clive Barnes, however, called *Inquest* "one of the most gripping courtroom dramas of my experience,"[4] and the television reviewers were positive: Edwin Newman of *NBC-TV4* thought that the play was "slow to start, but finally chilling and disturbing."[5] John Bartholomew Tucker of *WABC-TV7* stated, "It's probably the most shattering thing I've seen all year on Broadway."[6]

Inquest ran for twenty-eight performances.

Perhaps by coincidence, almost simultaneously with the incubation and performances of *Inquest*, another docudrama about the Rosenbergs, Alain Decaux's *Les Rosenberg ne doivent pas mourir* (*The Rosenbergs Shall Not Die*), was produced in Paris during the 1968-1969 season. The play argued the innocence of the executed Americans.

Four decades later, in 2007, the case of Julius and Ethel Rosenberg was revisited in *The Brother*. The title refers to Ethel's brother David Greenglass, a collaborator of the Rosenbergs who informed on them and got off with only ten years in prison. Playwright Sam Roberts utilized information from now-declassified files. *The Brother* premiered at Chicago's Theatre Building.

In 1965, Walter and Miriam Schneir published the 500-page *Invitation to an Inquest*, in which they claimed that Julius and Ethel Rosenberg were "punished for a crime that never occurred." The book further accused the U.S. government of orchestrating a political frame-up of the Rosenbergs. In the mid-1990s, upon the release of intercepted Soviet wartime cables, the Schneirs changed their conclusions, now believing that the couple had lied, and that Julius had indeed stolen military and industrial secrets. This shift is documented in Walter Schneir's *Final Verdict*, a slim book published posthumously by Melville House in 2010 (Walter Schneir died in 2009; Miriam Schneir completed the book).

* * *

Born in Chicago to a middle-class Jewish family and raised by a stepfather who was a successful merchant of military gear, Donald Freed has had multiple careers as playwright, novelist, screenwriter and actor. In the 1950s and

1960s, he appeared in various television programs, including *Medic*, *Official Detective*, *Target*, *Men in Space*, and *Checkmate*.

In the 1970s, Freed worked as an investigative reporter for the Citizens Research and Investigation Committee. His findings led to writing numerous articles on the assassinations of John F. Kennedy, Robert Kennedy and Martin Luther King, and the events surrounding the Watergate scandal. His subsequent books were politically engaged and often dealt with true crime incidents. Among them were *Agony in New Haven: The Trial of Bobby Seale, Ericka Huggins, and the Black Panther Party* (1973); *Death in Washington: The Murder of Orlando Letelier* (1980), implicating the CIA in the murder of the Chilean diplomat; and *Killing Time* (1996), cowritten with Raymond P. Briggs, an inquiry into the O.J. Simpson double-murder case of Nicole Brown Simpson and Ronald Goldman.

In 1978, the infamous Jim Jones engaged Freed to help in the matter of alleged plots by intelligence agencies against the Peoples Temple of Jonestown, Guyana. Freed concluded that there was a "massive conspiracy" against the Temple. On November 18, 1978, more than 900 Temple members committed mass suicide in Jonestown.

Freed also wrote several screenplays based on real-life events. *Executive Action* (1973), cowritten with Dalton Trumbo and Mark Lane and starring Burt Lancaster and Robert Ryan, portrays the assassination of John F. Kennedy as a conspiracy. *Secret Honor* (1984), written with Arnold M. Stone and directed by Robert Altman, features Philip Baker Hall as President Richard M. Nixon in a fictional account that follows his disgraceful exit from the White House. *Of Love and Shadows* (1994), adapted by Freed from a novel by Isabel Allende, tells the story of a magazine editor living under the yoke of the Pinochet dictatorship in Chile.

Among the many plays penned by Freed, notable are *American Iliad*, in which Richard Nixon, dying, looks back at his life. His reminiscences include glimpses of John F. Kennedy, J. Edgar Hoover and Marilyn Monroe; *Alfred and Victoria*, an interpretation of the sensational scandal in which Vicki Morgan, the notorious mistress of Alfred Bloomingdale, sued the scion of the department store family for palimony; *Circe and Bravo*, set in the President's lodge at Camp David; *The Quartered Man*, the story of the last day in the life of a spy, George C. O'Connor, in Central America.

In *Veteran's Day*, three veterans—shell-shocked, injured, decorated—meet just before a ceremony to honor them. *Child of Luck* is a cynical view of American politics, depicting a scandalous political campaign for the presidency. *Hamlet (In Rehearsal)* pries into the Shakespearean masterpiece in the form of a play within a play. *The Death of Ivan Ilych* is based on the novella by Leo Tolstoy. Writer James Joyce and his wife Nora go through a vaudevillian give-and-take in *Is He Still Dead?* as they attempt to flee Nazi-occupied

France in 1940. *Patient #1,* set in a futuristic secret psychiatric unit hidden in the Florida Everglades, focuses on a confrontation between a psychoanalyst and former President George W. Bush. *The White Crow: Eichmann in Jerusalem* pits an interrogator against the Nazi butcher Adolph Eichmann who escaped to Argentina, was unearthed by the Israeli Mossad in 1960, and was finally brought to Israel for trial.

Freed was described by radical historian Studs Turkel as "the most political and pertinent of all U.S. playwrights."

Freed's novels are also topical. *Spymaster* (1980) narrates the saga of a Yale graduate who goes through the shady world of espionage in many fronts until he finally becomes the director of Central Intelligence. *The China Card* (2003) is a novel of international intrigue set against the backdrops of Washington, Moscow, and Peking. *Every Third House* (2005) incorporates fictional court transcripts, prison letters and FBI memorandums into the life story of an imaginary Black Panther leader.

Freed served as artist in residence at the Workshop Theatre, University of Leeds, England (2006-2008) and as playwright in residence at York Theatre Royal (2007-2008), where he established a working relationship with Harold Pinter. He has also been playwright in residence at Dennison University, Ohio, and has taught creative writing at the University of Southern California for twenty-two years.

Acting Edition: Samuel French, Inc. (in manuscript form).
Awards and Honors: Donald Freed was the recipient of three Rockefeller Foundation Awards; two Louis B. Mayer Awards; The Unicorn Prize; The Gold Medal Award; The Berlin Critics Award; NEA award for "Distinguished Writing;" Hollywood Critics Award; PEN Literary Prize for Best Drama 2006 - *The Devil's Advocate*, a play set on Christmas Eve during the 1989 U.S. invasion of Panama.

NOTES

1. *Daily News*, April 24, 1970.
2. *New York Post*, April 24, 1970.
3. *Women's Wear Daily*, April 24, 1970.
4. *New York Times*, April 24, 1970.
5. *NBC-TV4,* April 23, 1970.
6. *WABC-TV7*, April 23, 1970.

The Trial of the Catonsville Nine (1971)

Daniel Berrigan (United States, 1921-2016) and Saul Levitt (United States, 1913-1977)

Daniel Berrigan was born in Virginia, Minnesota and grew up in Syracuse, New York. He began his Jesuit training in 1939 and after thirteen years of study entered the priesthood. He was active in community work in African American and Puerto Rican neighborhoods of New York City, and with his brother Philip (1923-2002) became passionately involved in civil rights and antiwar activities. In 1968, at the height of the Vietnam War protests, the brothers were joined by seven additional Catholic activists as they entered the draft board in Catonsville, Maryland, took 378 recruitment files, brought them to the parking lot, and set them on fire with homemade napalm.

The seven men and two women involved were arrested, tried, convicted, and sentenced to prison terms ranging from two to three-and-a-half years. After all appeals failed, the Berrigan brothers went underground. In 1970 Daniel was captured in Rhode Island by Federal agents and was sent to serve his term in Federal prison in Danbury, Connecticut.

Daniel Berrigan wrote the play *The Trial of the Catonsville Nine* in free verse. Saul Levitt adapted it into prose dialogue, basing his version on the transcripts of the trial, as he did with his 1959 courtroom drama *The Andersonville Trial.*

The time: Monday, October 7, 1968. The place: United States District Court for the District of Maryland. The curtain rises on Father Daniel Berrigan standing at a pulpit-like reading desk with the other eight defendants silhouetted behind him. Berrigan addresses the audience, reminding them of "that little business of pouring blood on draft records" (the defendants behind him pantomime the burning of the draft files).

Marshals enter carrying an American flag. Prosecution and defense attorneys follow and cross to their desks. Jury members take their seats in the jury box. The judge explains to the jury that this is an action of the United States against the nine defendants for seizing and burning records of the local draft board at Catonsville, Maryland. The Defendants plead not guilty. Marshals bring in trash burners and boxes of charred ash—the evidence.

A prosecution witness, Mrs. Boyle, a matronly office clerk, describes how the intruders entered the draft board offices, went straight to the cabinets, emptied the drawers of 1-A classification files into a trash burner, and took them outside to be incinerated. David Darst, one of the defendants, testifies that the records were burned using "a very crude form of napalm—two parts gasoline, one part soap flakes."

One by one the defendants are called to the stand. They identify themselves as priests, nuns, divinity students, and ghetto teachers. They worked for the betterment of human condition in Uganda, Guatemala, Yucatan, Mexico, the Dominican Republic, and in skid row areas of Chicago and New Orleans. They felt it was their duty to deal with the immorality of the Vietnam War. They joined vigils and demonstrations in Washington, D.C., and made a decision to protest the war by pouring their own blood on draft files, "in order to illustrate our horror over blood being shed in Vietnam," and destroying records "which are potential death certificates."

"There is a higher law we are commanded to obey," testifies the accused George Mische. "It takes precedence over human laws." Mary Moylan, one of two women among the accused, declares that as a nurse, her duty is "to preserve life… To pour napalm on pieces of paper is certainly preferable to using it on human beings." The other female defendant, Marjorie Melville, agrees, insisting that there are moments when opposition needs to turn into action.

Philip Berrigan states that the defendants do not believe that they have committed a crime. They violated the law, but their motive was to illustrate genocide in Vietnam and corruption at home. His brother, Daniel, testifies that in 1968 he received an invitation from the government of North Vietnam to bring home three captive American airmen and witnessed the horrors of war firsthand.

With great passion Father Berrigan exclaims, "The time is past when good people can remain silent…How many indeed must die before our voices are heard?"

In his summation, the prosecutor contends that the case is simply a matter of taking government property, throwing flammable material on it and burning it beyond recognition. If people are entitled to be acquitted by virtue of their sincerity or conviction, then, according to the same logic, should not the people who commit other crimes also be entitled to acquittal?

The defense attorney for the Catonsville Nine maintains that this is a unique case, sharing the historic meaning of other great contests of law—such as the trials of Socrates and Jesus. As to the burnt records, this is not a question of driving licenses "or licenses to operate a brewery," but records that directly affect life and death on a mass scale—life and death to young men.

The judge instructs the jury to decide the case not on the basis of conscience but solely on the basis of facts presented in court by both sides. The voice of the foreman of the jury is heard on a recorded tape as he announces the verdict: "Guilty."

* * *

Directed by Gordon Davidson and presented without an intermission, *The Trial of the Catonsville Nine* was first produced by the Center Theatre Group of Los Angeles at the Mark Taper Forum, then brought to New York by Off Broadway's Phoenix Theatre on February 7, 1971. Key roles were played by Ed Flanders (Daniel Berrigan), Michael Kane (Philip Berrigan), and William Schallert (Judge). Sam Waterston, Richard Jordan and Nancy Malone enacted three of the defendants. "The play grew on you like a fine painting of an historical event," wrote Otis L. Guernsey Jr. in *The Best Plays of 1970-1971*. "It had scant physical action but increasing sympathy for everyone caught in this moral and legal cobweb… Staged in a church which huddles near the travertine ostentation of the Lincoln Center complex, here was a piece of highly effective theater for our time, as relevant as a body count."[1]

The Trial of theCatonsville Nine ran for 130 performances and moved to Broadway's Lyceum Theatre on June 2 for twenty-nine additional showings. The transfer triggered some cast changes, with the better-known Biff McGuire, James Woods, Michael Moriarty and Josef Sommer taking over some of the parts.

The Trial of the Catonsville Nine came back to the Mark Taper Forum in Los Angeles on June 17, 1971, for fifty-four performances. John Stix staged the play for Baltimore's Center Stage, opening on October 31, 1971, featuring Ward Costello, John Newton, Roger DeKoven and Earle Hyman, running for twenty-three showings. On February 3, 1972, *The Trial* commenced at the Studio Arena Theatre in Buffalo, New York, for twenty-four performances.

Also in 1972, Gregory Peck produced an eighty-five-minute film version of the play. He recruited Gordon Davidson to direct and several members of the original production to reprise their roles. That same year, *Der Prozeb gegen die neun von Catonsville* was broadcast on German television. In 1975, the play was televised in what was then Yugoslavia.

More than three decades later, with wars in Iraq and Afghanistan, *The Trial of the Catonsville Nine* was still deemed relevant. In 2009, the play was reincarnated by the University of Maryland at the Clarice Smith Center for the Performing Arts, and by the Actors' Gang Theatre, helmed by Tim Robbins, in Culver City, California. Reviewer Charlotte Stoudt of the *Los Angeles Times* opined that "the Actors' Gang presents a lucid, impassioned revival of this free-verse courtroom drama," but added: "Despite the *Law and Order*-style sound cues used to button each scene, *Cantonsville* isn't exactly riveting courtroom theatre. While one is humbled by the Nine's moral rigor, the play is more sermon than debate."[2]

Later in 2009, the Actors' Gang traveled with *The Trial of the Catonsville Nine* to the Brisbane Festival in Brisbane, Queensland, Australia. On that occasion, Father Daniel Berrigan joined the cast.

Acting Edition: Samuel French, Inc.

Awards and Honors: a top-ten selection in *The Best Plays of 1970-1971*. Father Daniel Berrigan won the Lamont Poetry Award in 1957 and was nominated for a National Book Award in 1969. Saul Levitt's drama *The Andersonville Trial* was a top-ten selection in *The Best Plays of 1959-1960*.

NOTES

1. Otis L. Guernsey Jr., ed., *The Best Plays of 1970-1971* (New York: Dodd, Mead and Company, 1971), 25-26.
2. *Los Angeles Times*, February 19, 2009.

The Runner Stumbles (1976)

Milan Stitt (United States, 1941-2009)

Milan Stitt fashioned his courtroom drama, the *Runner Stumbles*, on a 1911 trial in Michigan, in which a Roman Catholic priest was accused of murdering a nun. The play was conceived in 1965 at the Yale School of Drama, then developed, tenaciously, during the next decade in a Boston University playwright's workshop at the Berkshire Theatre Festival (1971), a showcase at the Manhattan Theatre Club (1974), and a performance at the Hartman Theatre in Stamford, Connecticut (1975). Finally, it opened at Broadway's Little Theatre on May 18, 1976.

On a practically bare stage, the action of *The Runner Stumbles* unfolds in a jail cell, then moves to the courthouse. Flashbacks take place in Father Rivard's home. A similar technique was utilized in other plays based on real-life trials—*Nine Pine Street, Compulsion, A Case of Libel, Time Limit,* and *The Andersonville Trial*—but in Stitt's drama the flashback scenes are fleeting and kaleidoscopic, prompting Martin Gottfried of the *New York Post* to complain of "awkward writing and construction."[1]

Father Rivard is a maverick priest relegated to a parish in a rural, predominantly Protestant area of Michigan. The arrival of Sister Rita, a young, vivacious nun, ignites forbidden feelings. The priest lets Sister Rita reside at the rectory, and, to the dismay of his housekeeper Mrs. Shandig, a converted, devout Catholic, priest and nun fall in love.

Unable to curb their emotions, tension builds between Father Rivard and Sister Rita. Frustrated, he treats her harshly. In a moment of deep despair, the priest exclaims, "I hate God. I hate God. I want to kill God. I always wanted to kill," and he commences to choke Sister Rita. When the nun is found dead the next morning, Father Rivard is charged with her murder.

The priest's court-appointed lawyer, Toby Felker, is a novice who has "never argued an actual trial before." But at the end of the play, as aptly described by Douglas Watt in the *Daily News*, the lawyer "pulls a rabbit out of the hat."[2] Felker calls Mrs. Shandig to the stand and elicits from her an unexpected confession. Sister Rita was evil, says Mrs. Shandig. The Sister was not strangled to death by Father Rivard, but she deserved to die. She found the sister wiggling on the ground, making noises. She went to get a shovel and hit the snake's head. Then everything was peaceful.

Father Rivard walks free, and Mrs. Shandig is arrested, only to commit suicide in jail. "Banged her head against the wall till she died," relates Felker to the priest at the conclusion of a melancholy, dark play about lost souls caught in the web of hierarchical despotism.

* * *

The Runner Stumbles met with mixed reviews. Mel Gusow of the *New York Times* was taken by the play's "strong, emotional impact,"[3] and the *Wall Street Journal's* Edwin Wilson proclaimed that it "offers its own excitement—a mystery story, an exploration of psychological and moral problems, a whirlwind of strong passions, and excellent acting."[4] However, Douglas Watt stamped *The Runner Stumbles* as "a whodunit that exhausts a listener's interest in the outcome long before it arrives."[5]

The play stumbled along for 191 performances. It has had numerous regional productions over the years, notably by the Actors Theatre of Louisville in November 1978, running for seventeen performances. Off-Broadway's The Actors Company Theatre revived *The Runner Stumbles* in the fall of 2007; the Harold Washington College, Chicago, Illinois, in the spring of 2008; and the Port City Playhouse of Muskegon, Michigan, in the summer of 2009. In October 2009, Birmingham City University presented the UK premiere of the play.

The Runner Stumbles was transferred to the screen by Stanley Kramer, starring Dick Van Dyke (Father Rivard), Kathleen Quinlan (Sister Rita), Maureen Stapleton (Mrs. Shandig), and Beau Bridges (lawyer Felker). It was Stanley Kramer's last film. It opened to negative reviews and failed to be a commercial success.

* * *

Milan Stitt was born in Detroit, Michigan, in 1941. He studied for the priesthood at Albion College but dropped out, later enrolling at the University of Michigan and earning a bachelor's degree in 1963. Three years later he received an MFA from the Yale School of Drama. He held various writing and publicity jobs before founding Circle Repertory Company, an Off-Broadway incubator for playwrights. In charge of Circle Rep's development program, he served as dramaturge to budding playwrights Arthur Kopit, Albert Innaurato, Lanford Wilson, Paul Zindel, and David Mamet. At Circle Rep he wrote for Christopher Reeve the drama *Back in the Race*, in which the descendant of a distinguished American family returns to his now ramshackle ancestral summer home determined to fathom the unsettling legacy of his forefathers and exorcise ghosts of the past.

Stitt was chair of the playwriting program at Yale University from 1987 to 1993. He also taught dramatic writing at Princeton University, The University of Michigan, and New York University. In 1997 he was appointed head of the dramatic writing program at Carnegie Melon University. For television, Stitt penned teleplays and miniseries, notably *The Gentleman Bandit* for CBS (1981) and *Long Shadow* for PBS's American Playhouse (1996). He was a member of the Dramatists League, Writers Guild of America, P.E.N., the Eugene O'Neill Society, and the National Academy of Television Arts and Sciences.

Stitt died in 2009 of liver cancer at St. Vincent's Hospital in New York City.

Acting Edition: Dramatists Play Service.

Awards and Honors: A top-ten selection in *The Best Plays of 1975-1976* ("The year's outstanding Broadway drama," according to editor Otis L. Guernsey Jr.)[6]

NOTES

1. *New York Post*, May 19, 1976.
2. *Daily News,* May 19, 1976.
3. *New York Times,* May 19, 1976.
4. *Wall Street Journal,* May 19, 1976.
5. *Daily News*, May 19, 1976.
6. Otis L. Guernsey Jr., ed., *The Best Plays of 1975-1976* (New York: Dodd, Mead, 1976), 3.

Cause Célèbre (1977)

Terence Rattigan (England, 1911-1977)

In 1946, renowned playwright Terence Rattigan wrote *The Winslow Boy*, a drama based on the real-life case of George Archer-Shee, a young cadet at an English naval academy who was accused of stealing and cashing a five-shilling postal order. He was expelled. His parents waged a stubborn campaign to clear George's name in a case that caused a furor in England prior to World War I. Some dismissed it as an idiotic crusade; others hailed the "Cause Célèbre" as a milestone in protecting the honor and rights of the individual.

Three decades later, in 1977, Rattigan penned another courtroom drama based on an actual case—*Cause Célèbre*—re-creating the Alma Rattenbury-George Wood trial of 1935, the first double lawsuit in English history. In it, each defendant tried to exonerate the other by taking complete blame. Alma Rattenbury was an attractive thirty-eight-year-old composer of popular songs who had married an elderly, retired businessman, Francis, and subsequently entered into a sexual liaison with her eighteen-year-old handyman, George Wood. Francis Rattenbury was beaten to death with a wooden mallet, and both Alma and George were charged with the murder.

The case of a "scarlet woman" who had led a young man astray became a 1935 cause célèbre. The jury of the Central Criminal Court at the Old Bailey in London found Rattenbury innocent of the charge of murder, and she was released. Wood, however, was found guilty and was sentenced to be hanged. Convinced that her young lover was to die on the gallows, Alma Rattenbury stabbed herself with a knife. A few weeks later, Wood was reprieved, and his sentence commuted to life imprisonment. By the 1950s he was released.

"It had always been pure raw material for a Rattigan drama, and he knew it," writes Geoffrey Wansell in *Terence Rattigan*. "But he did not simply want to re-create the events of the trial. He would use the case as another opportunity to explore the English attitude to sex, to emotions, and the reactions of reticence and fear both regularly prompted."[1]

The setting of *Cause Célèbre* is a composite, with different areas of the stage used to represent different locales during the unfolding action. In general, the central area is furnished as a sitting-room used by both the Rattenbury Villa Madeira in Bournemouth, a seashore resort town in South England, and the Davenport apartment in Kensington, an affluent borough of West London. The area down-right represents the Old Bailey, while down-left is a prison cell. The action is juggled between present court proceedings and flashbacks of past events. Changes of locale are achieved through lighting.

When the curtain rises, the stage is in darkness except for spots pinpointing Alma Rattenbury, Edith Davenport, and the Clerk of the Court who announces that Alma Victoria Rattenbury is charged with the murder of Francis Mawson Rattenbury on March the twenty-eighth, nineteen hundred and thirty-five. Alma pleads "Not Guilty." The spots fade and the lights come up on a Kensington flat, where Mrs. Edith Davenport tells her younger sister Stella that she has just received an official summons for jury service. Alma also confides that she's determined to divorce her husband, John, an employee at the Home Office and a habitual womanizer. Their young son, Tony, who adores his father, will be hurt, but her mind is set.

The lights cross-fade to the Rattenbury villa. George Wood, seventeen, stands by the door, taking off his bicycle clips. He tells Irene Riggs, a maid, that he came about the advertisement for a houseboy. Alma Rattenbury interviews George at length and seems to be taken with him. When her sickly, cantankerous husband, "Ratz," returns from a walk and settles into his usual armchair, Alma vouches for young Wood and he gets the job.

Back at the Davenport flat, Tony rushes in with a newspaper and tells his mother that "Mrs. Rattenbury and Wood battered old Rattenbury on the head so hard they completely mashed his skull." The article conjectures that the defense will maintain that Wood was doped on cocaine and Mrs. Rattenbury was drunk. Edith Davenport expresses her belief that the more mature Mrs. Rattenbury ought to be lynched.

In prison, Alma Rattenbury is allowed to wear her own clothes. Her wardress, Joan Webster, is a gruff-voiced, rather-forbidding young woman. O'Connor, Alma's lawyer, arrives for a consultation, accompanied by Montagu, his junior assistant. Alma reaffirms her statement to the police, in which she contended that she was the one who picked up a mallet and hit her husband. O'Connor responds by telling her that Wood told investigators where the mallet would be found, hidden in the garden, and it was found exactly there, with his fingerprints all over it. Alma is taken aback for a moment, but she still insists, her voice firm and unwavering, "I killed Ratz alone and George had nothing to do with it."

Montagu harshly describes the strength and ruthlessness of the three mallet strikes that spilled the brains of the victim, and Alma begins to sob helplessly.

In darkness, we hear mob cries outside the courthouse: "Kill her!" "Hang her!" "Hanging is too good for her!" "Give her the cat!"

In a small cell, Casswell, George Wood's lawyer, dismisses his client's claim that he killed Mr. Rattenbury when under the influence of cocaine. During a quick cross-examination Wood cannot identify the color of the drug and is ignorant of the fact that it is called snow because it is white. Wood's only defense, says Casswell, is to testify that the older Alma Rattenbury made him do it. Wood refuses his lawyer's advice. He wants to live, but he's not going to betray the only woman "I've ever had, and the only one I've ever loved."

In Act 2 we learn that Edith Davenport was selected to be a member of the jury in the Rattenbury-Wood murder trial. The jury appoints her forewoman because her father was a judge. Edith's sister, Stella, informs her that the bookmakers are giving three-to-one odds for conviction.

At the Old Bailey, Police Sergeant Bagwell testifies for the prosecution that after receiving a call from the local hospital saying that all attempts to revive the deceased had failed, he presented himself at the Villa Madeira. Time? Two forty-seven a.m. There was a lot of commotion inside. The gramophone was playing full blast and the female prisoner, attired in a nightdress, was imitating bullfighting with her bed jacket. A flashback visualizes the event at the villa: Alma Rattenburg taking a hefty swig from an almost empty bottle, and drunkenly greets Sergeant Bagwell with a shriek of joy. She approached him sensually. The Sergeant turns the gramophone off and questions Alma. She says that her husband wanted to die, gave her a mallet, and dared her to kill him. She did.

Back on the witness stand, the Sergeant concludes his testimony by expressing his disgust at the behavior of a woman whose husband had been brutally killed only a few hours earlier. Defense Attorney O'Connor asks the Sergeant if he has ever heard of hysteria and the effect of alcohol on a shocked system.

The only witness for the defense is Alma Rattenbury herself. O'Connor elicits from her the information that prior to her union with Francis Rattenbury ("Ratz"), she was married twice and had a child with her second husband. Francis was her third husband, and they were married for eight years and have a son, John, now six. It was not a happy marriage. Francis was – well – stingy. They had constant quarrels about money. For several years they had lived in separate rooms. Yes, for two years she was having "regular sexual intercourse" with John Wood, the houseboy. They often went to hotels, where John "loved being waited on and called sir," and where she gave him such presents as silk pajamas and a new suit.

"Now we come to Sunday, the day of the murder," says O'Connor, and the lights fade up on the Villa Madeira sitting room. Alma, in her dressing gown, helps Rattenbury down the stairs and settles him in his armchair. They make plans to go on a trip and visit their friends, the Jenks. Wood appears at the top of the staircase, in his shirt sleeves. He calls Alma in a commanding tone to come upstairs, "Now!" She climbs up the stairs and Wood, forcefully, grabs her wrist. He demands to know why the bedroom was locked – was she making love to her husband? Alma dismisses the notion. He calls her "you lying bitch," and slaps her face. Alma warns Wood that if he ever does this again, she'll order him out of the house for good, and sends him to the kitchen to help with supper.

In the morning, we dimly see the slumped body of Francis Rattenbury in the armchair. Upstairs, Alma is in bed in pajamas, reading. Wood enters and climbs in beside her. He begins to cry and hesitantly tells her that he "hurt Ratz badly." Alma runs down the stairs, lets out a loud scream and staggers with shock. Irene, the housekeeper, comes out of her room, and Alma sends her to fetch Dr. O'Donnell. Rattenbury's body suddenly slumps onto the floor. Wood approaches and whispers that he had to do it – "he was stealing you away from me."

Back in court, prosecutor Croom-Johnson pounds Alma with the suggestion that she dominated "a boy of seventeen." A turning point occurs when Alma lets it slip that she and Wood sometimes made love in her bedroom while little John was asleep in the same room. The prosecutor kept emphasizing the point in his summation, calling Alma "a self-confessed liar, self-confessed adulteress, self-confessed seducer of a tender youth of seventeen… a boy young enough to be her son." In his turn, attorney O'Connor points out to the jury that even though they may feel a "natural disgust" for the defendant, that sense *must not* sway them to convict her of the crime of murder.

Alma and Wood are standing on the dock when jury forewoman Davenport reads Wood's verdict of "Guilty, with a rider to recommendation of mercy," and Alma's verdict of "Not guilty." The court is flooded with a storm of booing, hissing and shouts of "Shame." The judge announces that Wood will be "taken from this place to a lawful prison, and thence to a place of execution, and that you there be hanged by the neck until you are dead."

George Wood is taken away. Alma Rattenbury is discharged. Her maid, Irene, greets her with enthusiasm, slips on a large pair of horn-rimmed glasses, and they follow a policeman to a side exit.

The lights cross-fade to Edith Davenport's flat. Stella confronts her sister about the verdict. Edith confides that as forewoman she sat at the head of the table. Each person spoke up and she took the votes down. There were initially five for guilty, six for not. Her vote, not guilty, made it seven-five—"Then all the others gave way." Stella asks, "For God's name, why?" Edith pours herself a large, neat whiskey and says, "Because she was innocent … of murder."

The Lights fade up on a coroner—a little man sitting at an insignificant desk, reading aloud from a folder a statement from a parish laborer: Walking across a meadow along a stream, he watched a lady stab herself five or six times before he could get to her and stop her.

The coroner looks up at an unseen court of inquiry and remarks that if Mrs. Rattenbury lived only a few more days, she would have heard of the reprieve accorded to George Wood by the Home Secretary.

* * *

Initially titled "A Woman of Principle," *Cause Célèbre* began as a radio drama broadcast by BBC in October 1975. When premiering in London's Her Majesty's Theatre on July 4, 1977, the program—just as it had done for *The Winslow Boy* — contained a disclaimer: "This play is based on a famous case, but the characters are all fictitious." Rattigan wanted Dorothy Tuttin for the role of the doomed Alma Rattenbury, but Glynis Johns was cast.

Ill with Cancer, Terence Rattigan came to London for the July 4, 1977 opening of *Cause Célèbre,* knowing it would be his last first night. The play was still running at the time of Rattigan's death on November 30, 1977, achieving 282 performances. The American debut of *Cause Célèbre* took place at the Ahmanson Theatre in Los Angeles on October 12, 1979. Anne Baxter portrayed Alma Rattenbury for fifty-one performances.

Teamed with Hector Bolitho, Rattigan had previously penned an additional work with criminous elements—*Grey Farm,* depicting a tortured, possessive father, James Grantham, who, afflicted with murderous urges, fights against the impulse to kill both his son and the son's fiancée, finally strangling a blackmailing maid and shooting himself. Oscar Homolka played Grantham in this forgotten Rattigan melodrama that opened in New York's Hudson Theatre on May 3, 1940, and lasted thirty-five performances.

* * *

Terence Mervyn Rattigan began his theatrical career as a member of the Oxford University Dramatic Society. His first play, *First Episode* (1933), co-authored with Philip Heimann, unfolds in the living room of an undergraduate dormitory. Following the incubation of five unproduced efforts, through which young Rattigan learned his craft, came *French without Tears* (1936), a comedy about a flirtatious student who toys with her male classmates. The play scored big and played in London for over 1000 performances. A few successive comedies had hefty runs, and then, in 1946, Rattigan's first serious drama, *The Winslow Boy*, enhanced his reputation as master of the "well-made," neatly constructed play.

Rattigan returned to weighty themes in a series of plays which were first performed in London and then made the New York scene: *The Browning Version* (1948), a one-act about an embittered school master, Andrew Crocker-Harris, who is feared by his students, despised by his peers, and betrayed by his wife; *The Deep Blue Sea* (1952), in which a middle-aged woman, rejected by her lover and unable to face her husband, attempts to commit suicide before a doctor friend saves her life and restores her courage; *Separate Tables* (1954), a double bill set in a drab seaside residential hotel where the guests are lonely, desperate and in need of redemption; *Ross* (1960), depicting, in sixteen scenes, the mystical life of T. E. Lawrence (Lawrence of Arabia); *Man and Boy* (1963), the story of a ruthless tycoon who lets nothing stand in his way;[2] *A Bequest to the Nation* (1970), picturing the affair between Admiral Nelson and Lady Hamilton.

Rattigan comedies that came to New York include *First Episode* (1934); *French Without Tears* (1937); *While the Sun Shines* (1944); *O Mistress Mine* (1946); *The Sleeping Prince* (1956; musical version, *The Girl Who Came to Supper,* book by Harry Kurnitz, music and lyrics by Noel Coward, 1963); and *In Praise of Love* (1974).

Distinguished directors who tackled Rattigan plays included, in London, Anthony Asquith, Lawrence Olivier, John Gielgud, and John Dexter; in New York, Margaret Webster, George S. Kaufman, Michael Redgrave and Fred Coe; both in London and New York, Alfred Lunt, Glen Byam Shaw, Peter Glenville, and Michael Benthall.

Rattigan's canon was graced by a Who's Who of the theatre: Charles Boyer, Rex Harrison, Alec Guinness, Trevor Howard, Eric Portman, Stanley Baker, Roland Culver, Francis L. Sullivan, Michael Wilding, Jeremy Brett, Kenneth More, Laurence Olivier, John Mills, Paul Scofield, Maurice Evans, the Lunts, Vivien Leigh, Margaret Leighton, Peggy Aschcroft, Martita Hunt, Margaret Sullavan, Julie Harris, Barbara Bel Geddes, Nancy Kelly, and Jessica Tandy.

For the cinema, Rattigan concocted twenty-one screenplays, often in collaboration, including adaptations of his own *French without Tears* (1939), *The Winslow Boy* (1948), *While the Sun Shines* (1950), *The Browning Version* (1951), *The Deep Blue Sea, The Man Who Loved Redheads, Who is Sylvia?* (1955), *The Prince and the Showgirl, The Sleeping Prince* (1957), *Separate Tables* (nominated for an Academy Award, 1958), and *A Bequest to the Nation* (1973), as well as scripting the notable motion pictures *The Avengers* (1942), *The Way to the Stars* (1945), *Brighton Rock* (1948), *Breaking the Sound Barrier* (1952), *The V.I.P.'s* (1963), *The Yellow Rolls-Royce* (1964), and *Goodbye Mr. Chips* (1969). Rattigan adapted Dickens' *A Tale of Two Cities* for radio in 1951 and contributed five original plays to television.

In *Great Writers of the English Language*, Leonard R. N. Ashley perceives: "His best works will long be studied as models of playwriting and also as mirrors of the times. Rattigan can capture the social outlook of a whole period in *Cause Célèbre* (or the cause célèbre of *The Winslow Boy*) … He can make folly funny and pathos poignant and what some would dismiss as "a purely theatrical experience" deeply moving and quite unforgettable."[3]

The *London Times* obituary described Rattigan as "an emerging influence on the English theatre" and "one of the leaders of the twentieth century stage in what has come to be known as the Theatre of Entertainment... he wrote some of the most enduring narrative plays of his period, designed for a 'commercial' theatre and using traditional techniques Pinero and Henry Arthur Jones would have recognized."[4]

Critic Michael Billington commented in *The Guardian*: "It was often assumed that Rattigan was simply a purveyor of good middlebrow entertainment... Yet his whole world is a sustained assault on English middle-class values: fear of emotional commitment, terror in the face of passion, apprehension about sex. In fact, few dramatists this century have written with more understanding about the human heart than Terence Rattigan."[5]

Acting Edition: Samuel French, Inc.
Awards and Honors: Rattigan's *The Winslow Boy* - Ellen Terry Award, 1947; New York Drama Critics Circle Award as Best Foreign Play, 1947-1948; a top-ten selection in *The Best Plays of 1947-1948*. Other Rattigan top-ten entries in the *Best Plays* yearbook: *O Mistress Mine*, 1945-1946, and *Separate Tables*, 1956-1957. Rattigan was appointed Commander, Order of the British Empire (CBE) in 1958, and knighted in 1971.

NOTES

1. Geoffrey Wansell, *Terence Rattigan* (London: Fourth Estate, 1995), 383.
2. *Man and Boy* was revived by Off-Broadway's Roundabout Theatre Company in October 2011, with Frank Langella as a shadowy, Romanian-born oil magnate who clashes with a son who worships and detests him. While acknowledging "Mr. Langella's personal triumph," critic Ben Brantley called it a "lesser Rattigan work... an uneasy mix of daring plot gimmicks and synthetically silky dialogue" (*New York Times*, October 10, 2011).
3. James Vinson, ed., *Great Writers of the English Language: Dramatists* (New York: St. Martin's Press, 1979), 490.
4. *London Times*, December 1, 1977.
5. *The Guardian*, London, December 1, 1977.

Nuts (1980)

Tom Topor (United States, Austria-born, 1938-)

Newspaperman Tom Topor utilized psychiatric cases at New York's Bellevue Hospital as a springboard for *Nuts*, a courtroom drama about inmate Claudia Faith Draper, who is intent on proving herself mentally fit to stand trial for slaughter-in-the-first degree rather than being institutionalized indefinitely. Claudia, a high-priced hooker, believes that eventually she will be able to prove herself innocent of killing a violent client.

The court action takes place on the seventh floor of Bellevue. Frank Macmillan, representing the district attorney's office of New York County, claims that two examining psychiatrists found the defendant to be unfit to stand trial. Dr. Herbert Rosenthal, the unit chief of the hospital's prison ward, testifies that following a series of examinations the patient was diagnosed as a paranoid schizophrenic, severely out of touch with reality, dangerous to herself and others.

Claudia's bewildered mother, Rose, states on the witness stand that after divorcing Claudia's father and marrying Arthur Kirk, her daughter's behavior changed: she started to keep to herself, treated Kirk as if he had the plague, and acted as if she didn't trust anyone. During cross-examination of the self-assured Arthur Kirk by Claudia's court-appointed lawyer, Aaron Levinsky, it becomes evident that the stepfather abused his stepdaughter: "I washed her, and I dried her, and I sprinkled her, and I dried her, and I sprinkled her all over with talcum… young skin, soft, you touched it, you felt you were touching something magic."

Pugnacious and sardonic, Claudia Draper takes the stand in the third act of *Nuts*, relating her story of a tortured childhood, an unhappy marriage, an abortion, irregular income as a massage therapist, and enrollment at New York's University's Law School paid for by offering "favors" to men. She gets a hundred dollars for "a straight lay," says Claudia, a hundred for "a hand job," a hundred for "head" and a hundred and fifty for "rimming." Claudia insists that she knew what she was doing "every goddam minute" and is responsible for her behavior." I won't be nuts for you," she declares. Judge Murdoch concurs: "I will remand the defendant to the custody of the Commissioner of Corrections to await trial on the felony charge of manslaughter in the first degree."

Ultimately, Claudia makes peace with her parents; in the 1987 motion picture version, however, Claudia solely reunites with her mother, a more persuasive conclusion. Coscripted by Topor and directed by Martin Ritt, the all-star cast included Barbra Streisand in, arguably, her best screen performance as Claudia, Richard Dreyfuss as defense attorney Levinsky, Robert Webber as the prosecutor, Maureen Stapleton as Mother Rose, Karl Malden as stepfather Kirk, Eli Wallach as a hostile psychiatrist, and James Whitmore as Judge Murdoch.

A Recorder's announcement notifies us that "on June 15th, 1979, Claudia Faith Draper was tried in the State Supreme Court, New York County, on a charge of manslaughter in the first degree" and acquitted.

* * *

Off-Off-Broadway's Theatre at St. Clements presented a workshop draft of *Nuts* in June 1974. On February 23, 1980, WPA Theatre offered a revised version under Steve Zuckerman's direction, a production that was cosponsored by Universal Pictures and moved to Broadway's Biltmore Theatre on April 28, 1980. The critics hailed Anne Twoney as Claudia (the actress won a *Theatre World* Award for her "outstanding" performance) but were sharply divided regarding the merits of the play. "A slashing courtroom drama… *Nuts* is a play that bares its teeth right from the start and plunges forward through three terse acts," wrote Douglas Watt[1], while Frank Rich called the play "a courtroom melodrama without suspense, a moral debate without passion, a soap opera with more laughs than tears… a mess."[2] Clive Barnes hailed *Nuts* as "quite simply terrific, old time, belt them in the aisles, the guts and if necessary the kidneys, theatre,"[3] but Christopher Sharp believed that "while the play may not be nutty it is very foolish."[4] Joel Siegel announced that "Tom Topor knows his way around a courtroom…He's just opened one of Broadway's best plays of 1980;"[5] simultaneously, Dennis Cunningham complained that *Nuts* "is rather long on the craft of putting a play together, is woefully short on creating characters… *Nuts* certainly has its heart in the right place, but not, however, its head."[6] The play ran for ninety-six performances.

Nuts garnered steam during the first decade of the twenty-first century with productions at the Altarena Playhouse in Alameda, California (2004); the Raven Playhouse in North Hollywood, California (2008); and the Lee Center for the Performing Arts in Alexandria, Virginia (2010).

* * *

Tom Topor, born in Vienna, Austria, in 1938, was brought to London in 1939 and came to New York ten years later. He earned his BA degree at Brooklyn College in 1961. He began his writing career as a reporter for the Peterson,

New Jersey *Morning Call*, the *New York Times*, the *New York Daily News*, and mostly the *New York Post*, for which he covered police stations, courtrooms, and hospitals. He simultaneously pursued his interest in theatre as actor, director, stunt man, and playwright.

In 1969, Topor followed his calling as a playwright with several one-act plays staged Off-Off-Broadway. *Answers* depicts a suspect interrogated at the headquarters of Homicide South in Manhattan for a crime about which he claims to know nothing (WPA Theatre, June 8, 1972). *But Not For Me* is about the odd things that people do, or don't do, for love (Theatre at Noon, May 10, 1976). *Romance: Here to Stay* focuses on a husband and wife who prove to be hopelessly inept bank robbers (Theatre of the Riverside Church, December 1, 1978).

For television, Topor scripted and directed *Judgment* (1990), based on the real-life story of a Louisiana priest accused of molesting young parishioners; penned *Perfect Murder, Perfect Town* (2000), a mini-series inspired by the murder of six-year-old JonBenét Ramsey; collaborated with Norman Mailer on *American Tragedy* (2000), a teleplay focused on attorney Johnnie Cochran's defense of O.J. Simpson; served as creative consultant on *The Glimpse of Hell* (2001), in which a Navy officer, in charge of a gun turret on the battle ship USS Iowa, becomes the scapegoat of higher-ups' ineptitude when an explosion destroys the turret and kills forty-seven sailors; and teamed with other writers on adapting Nelson DeMille's novel, *Word of Honor* (2003), wherein the Army recalls an ex-lieutenant to stand trial for a massacre committed by his platoon in a Hue hospital.

For the silver screen, Topor wrote *The Accused* (1988), in which rape victim Sarah Tobias (played by Jodie Foster), enraged at the light sentence her attackers received, prods a female prosecutor, Kathryn Murphy (Kelly McGillis), to charge those who encouraged the men who gang raped her in a sleazy roadhouse. Foster won a Best Actress Academy Award, a Golden Globe Award, and a National Board of Review Award for her portrayal.

Acting Edition: Samuel French, Inc.

Awards and Honors: a top-ten selection in *The Best Plays of 1979-1980* ("*Nuts* was for two of its acts, the most gripping courtroom session in years and a survivor of its weaker third.")[7] Tom Topor won the Writers Guild of America Award for his script of the 1990 made-for-television film, *Judgment*.

NOTES

1. *Daily News*, April 29, 1980.

2. *New York Times,* April 29, 1980.
3. *New York Post,* April 29, 1980.
4. *Women's Wear Daily,* April 30, 1980.
5. *WABC-TV7,* April 28, 1980.
6. *WABC-TV12,* April 28, 1980.
7. Otis L. Guernsey Jr., ed., *The Best Plays of 1979-1980* (New York: Dodd, Mead, 1980), 15.

Execution of Justice (1984)

Emily Mann (United States 1952-)

On November 27, 1978, Dan White, a former member of San Francisco's Board of Supervisors, shot and killed Mayor George Moscone and gay City Supervisor Harvey Milk. White was charged with two counts of murder, but was instead convicted on two counts of voluntary manslaughter and sentenced to seven years and eight months in prison. Less than five years later, he was paroled. White subsequently committed suicide, gassing himself in his own garage.

In writing her docudrama *Execution of Justice*, Emily Mann drew on the trial transcript, published news reports, and interviews related to the notorious case. She also incorporated into the proceedings projected images of San Francisco scenes and audio dialogue from the Oscar-winning film *The Times of Harvey Milk* (1984).

The play unfolds in quick episodes. Act 1 is titled "Murder." The curtain rises on a bare stage. Images of Milk and Moscone are projected on a white screen overhead, accompanied by hot, fast music. A video depicts Dianne Feinstein, the President of the San Francisco Board of Supervisors, as she tearfully announces that Mayor Moscone and Supervisor Milk have been killed. A shaft of light illuminates Dan White praying on his knees next to a church window. His wife, Mary Ann, runs in breathlessly and crumples when he says, "I shot the Mayor and Harvey."

The lights change. A policeman articulates the atmosphere in which the killings occurred, illustrating his point by confronting a nun in drag, Sister Boom Boom, who is heavily made up and sashays on spiked heels. The cop complains of a city "stinkin' with degenerates," populated with "shaved-head men with tight pants, chains everywhere, French-kissing on the street… It's disgusting… Dan White showed you could fight City Hall."

The trial of the People of the State of California versus Daniel James White commences. Prosecutor Thomas F. Norman and Defense Attorney Douglas Schmidt are selecting the jury. Joanna Lu, a television reporter, declares on camera that "by all accounts, there are no blacks, no gays, and no Asians" on the jury, and that "most of the jurors are working and middle-class Catholics… Dan White will certainly be judged by a jury of his peers."

The defendant has entered a plea of not guilty to each of the charges. Prosecutor Norman addresses the audience, and it soon becomes clear that the auditorium spectators are called upon to serve as jurors. Norman presents defendant White – a war veteran, a decorated fireman, a respected ex-policeman – as a conscientious member of the Board of Supervisors who had resigned because of personal financial pressures. Then, when he wanted to withdraw his resignation and return to that post, Major Moscone and Supervisor Milk objected. On November 27, White went to City Hall carrying his police .38, entered by a window to avoid the metal detector at the front door, and walked into the mayor's office. Upon learning that he wasn't going to be reappointed, he shot Moscone four times, went to Milk's office and, reloading, put five or six bullets into Milk. He then called his wife and arranged to meet her at the cathedral. He went from there to the police station to give himself up.

Defense Attorney Schmidt points out that throughout his adulthood, Daniel White had suffered from a mental disease – "depression, sometimes called manic depression or uni-polar depression." Financial stress and his underlying mental illness culminated in his resignation on November 10, 1978. When he asked for his job back, he was given the runaround and finally learned from a television interviewer that his request had been denied. The mayor ignored more than a thousand petitions on his behalf. Furthermore, White believed that Harvey Milk had been acting to prevent his reappointment. Schmidt emphasizes that White came from a vastly different lifestyle than Milk "who was a homosexual leader and politician." Dan White, says Schmidt, deeply believed in the traditional American values of family and home.

Schmidt asserts that it was "not particularly unusual" for White to take his .38 caliber revolver with him when he went to City Hall. Dan White was an ex-policeman; for him to carry a gun was "common practice." Besides, he added, White's life was threatened continuously by the White Panther party and other radical groups.

Prosecutor Norman calls to the stand several witnesses who were at City Hall on the fateful day; they identify Dan White as the person who entered the building through a window and went into the mayor's office; gunfire was heard. White later came out, proceeded down the hall, and entered Harvey Milk's office; five or six shots rang out and White left the building.

The action detours to the office of homicide Inspector Frank Falzon. White, sobbing, says that he's been under "an awful lot of pressure lately" – financial pressure, family pressure. He found out that Supervisor Milk was working against him. He is not sure why he took his gun with him that morning. When the mayor told him that he was not going to be reappointed, "he was all smiles… Then I, I just shot him, that was it, it was over." White relates that he then went to Harvey Milk's office. "He started kinda smirking… I just got all flushed, and, and hot, and I shot him." He left and called his wife to meet him at St. Mary's cathedral. There he told her what occurred. She was horrified but said she loved him and would stick by him. She came with him to the Northern Police Station.

Act 2 is titled "In Defense of Murder." The trial continues with Defense Attorney Schmidt examining Inspector Falzon and other witnesses who have known White for years. They testify about White's distinguished career as a fire fighter, police officer, and city supervisor. Joseph Freitas, Jr., a former district attorney, believes that the friction between White and his victims was a political fight over who controlled the city, not a hate-crime against a gay person.

The defense then brings in several psychiatrists to testify as to the defendant's state of mind. The first, Dr. Jones, concluded that White was "enraged and anxious and frustrated in addition to his underlying depression." Dr. Blinder asserts that White became increasingly frustrated by what he perceived to be corrupt behavior at City Hall. Gradually, White began to abandon his usual program of exercise and good nutrition and started gorging himself on junk foods; he couldn't sleep, was dazed, confused, had crying spells, stopped shaving, became increasingly ill, and wanted to be left alone.

When the mayor put his arm around him, continues Dr. Blinder, seemingly concerned about White's future, the defendant felt "as if I were in a dream." He started to leave and then inexplicably turned around and like a reflex drew his revolver. "He had no idea how many shots he fired," says Dr. Blinder. "The similar event occurred in Supervisor Milk's office." Dr. Blinder approaches the jury: "In susceptible individuals, large quantities of what we call junk food, high sugar content food with lots of preservatives, can precipitate anti-social and even violent behavior."

The most emotional moment in court occurs during the testimony of Dan White's wife, Mary Ann, who speaks about their courtship, their life together, and the fateful morning of November 27. As Mary Ann stumbles off the stand, her husband, softly sobbing, shields his eyes.

The background screen depicts a candlelight march dedicated to the memory of Harvey Milk, and a funeral attended by mourners, headed by Mayor Moscone's wife.

Attorney Schmidt sums up for the defense, contending that even though Dan White is guilty, it is the degree of his responsibility and his state of mind that is at issue. "Heat of passion fogs judgment," declares Schmidt, "makes one act irrationally… It was a man broken, shattered… Something happened to him, and he snapped." Schmidt asks the members of the jury to come up with the verdict of "voluntary manslaughter, nothing more, nothing less," and points out that White, his child, and his family will have to live with the deed for the rest of their lives.

Prosecutor Norman states that the evidence laid before the jury *screams* for a ruling of murder in the first degree. Dan White brought a gun to City

Hall with extra cartridges; he went around the corner, and climbed through a window; he appeared, according to witnesses, to be calm as he approached the Mayor's office; he shot the Mayor twice in the body, then shot him in the head twice more; he reloaded his gun, went across the hall and "put three bullets into Harvey Milk's body, two more delivered to the back of his head." Norman insists that these were deliberate, premeditated, and cold-blooded *executions*.

The Jury returns a guilty verdict of voluntary manslaughter.

A television reporter relates on camera that Dan White was sentenced to seven years and eight months in jail, the maximum sentence for two counts of voluntary manslaughter. The lenient verdict led to rioting by homosexuals and their sympathizers. On the screen are projected images of a riot – angry faces, police cars burning, City Hall being stormed, a line of policemen in riot gear. Then another image appears on the screen: Execution of Justice. A gavel echoes, and the curtain descends. [1]

* * *

Emily Mann began writing *Execution of Justice* on a commission from San Francisco's Eureka Theatre in 1982. The play was first produced on March 8, 1984, by the Actors Theatre of Louisville, Kentucky, eliciting a positive nod from reviewer Holly Hill who called it an "epic drama." [2] *Execution of Justice* was subsequently produced by Baltimore's Center Stage; Theatre Cornell in Ithaca, New York; Seattle's The Empty Stage; Arena Stage in Washington, D.C.; the Abbey Theatre in Houston, Texas; Berkeley Rep; San Jose Rep; and the Guthrie Theatre of Minneapolis, Minnesota.

Mann directed and Ming Cho Lee designed *Execution of Justice* when it opened at New York's Virginia Theatre on March 13, 1986. The lead actors were John Spencer (Dan White), Mary McDonnell (Mary Ann White), Peter Friedman (Douglas Schmidt), and Gerry Bamman (Thomas F. Norman). Stanley Tucci, Wesley Snipes. Donal Donnelly, and Earl Hyman appeared in several small roles.

The play received mostly negative reviews. Douglas Watt called it "an interminable play" that "executed the audience… it induces practically unrelieved tedium… In Mann's and the designer's hands the stage is so filled with gimmickry that the result is distracting and often incoherent." [3] Clive Barnes opined that "the proceedings lack suspense" and did not ignite "outrage… and this kind of play, about justice's miscarriage, either fires one with a sense of outrage or, in the final count, fails." [4] Conversely, Ron Cohen believed that *Execution of Justice* "succeeds in striking fashion… It's a big, horrific play, but Mann, as both playwright and director, moves with sureness and balance through much of it… The 22-member company turn in a uniformly strong performance... *Execution of Justice* would validate any Broadway season with an insightful seriousness of purpose." [5]

The play ran for twelve performances. [6]

Early in 2011, a bill was introduced for approval by the California Legislature to mandate schools to teach gay history. Harvey Milk, one of the first openly gay elected officials in the United States, may take a prominent place in the state's history books.

* * *

Emily Betsy Mann was born in Boston, Massachusetts on April 12, 1952. Her father was a professor of American history, first at M.I.T., then at Smith College, and finally at the University of Chicago. Her mother was a remedial reading specialist. Playwright, director and actress, Mann staged productions at such top resident companies as the Tyrone Guthrie Theatre in Minneapolis; the Cincinnati Playhouse; the Brooklyn Academy of Music; the American Place Theatre in New York; the Actors Theatre of Louisville; the Hartford Stage Company; and the Mark Taper Forum in Los Angeles.

In 1990, Mann was appointed Artistic Director of the McCarter Theatre in Princeton, New Jersey, where she staged more than thirty productions, including the world premieres of Christopher Durang's *Miss Witherspoon*, Theresa Rebeck's *The Bells*, Steven Dietz's *Last of the Boys*, and Nilo Cruz's *Anna in the Tropics*, a 2003 Pulitzer Prize-winner. Notable plays helmed by Mann at the McCarter were *The Glass Menagerie* and *Cat on a Hot Tin Roof*, both by Tennessee Williams, *The Matchmaker* by Thornton Wilder, *All Over* by Edward Albee, and *The Tempest* and *Romeo and Juliet* by William Shakespeare.

As a playwright, Mann carved a reputation by penning documentary dramas she called "theatre of testimony," beginning with *Annulla Allen: Autobiography of a Survivor* (1977), based on interviews she conducted with a Polish Jewess who escaped a Nazi concentration camp by pretending to be Aryan. *Still Life* (1980) is a distillation of interviews with three characters from Minnesota who speak directly to the audience – Mark, an ex-marine and Vietnam veteran; Cheryl, his wife, mother of his children; and Nadine, his friend, a divorced artist. "It is about violence in America," writes Emily Mann. "The Vietnam War is the backdrop to the violence at home... I have been obsessed with violence in our country since the 1960s." [7] *Having Our Say: The Delany Sisters' First 100 Years* (1995) tells the saga of two black centenarian sisters, while *Greensboro: A Requiem* (1996) covers the murder of young communists by the Klu Klux Klan. *Mrs.Packard* (2007) dramatizes how in 1861 the Reverend Theophilis Packard had his wife committed to a psychiatric hospital because of a disagreement as to how to raise their children.

The indefatigable Mann also adapted and directed August Strindberg's *Miss Julie* (1993), Federico Garcia Lorca's *The House of Bernarda Alba* (1997), Isaac Bashevis Singer's *Meshugah* (1998), and Anton Chekhov's *The Three Sisters* (1992), *The Cherry Orchard* (2000), *Uncle Vanya* (2003), and *The Seagull* (2008).

Mann is a member of the Dramatists Guild and serves on its Council.

Acting Edition: Samuel French, Inc.

Awards and Honors: *Execution of Justice* won the HBO New Plays USA Award, the Helen Hayes Award, and the Bay Area Critics Award. The play was nominated for a 1986 Drama Desk Award for Outstanding New Play and is a top-ten selection in *The Best Plays of 1985-1986.*

Emily Mann's *Still Life*, which opened Off Broadway under her direction in 1981, won six Obie Awards, including Distinguished Playwriting and Distinguished Directing. Mann's 1995 Broadway production of *Having Our Say* was nominated for a Tony Award for Best Play and Best Direction; the play won a Joseph Jefferson Award as well as an NAACP Award. Mann's numerous awards include a Guggenheim, NEA Playwrights Fellowship, CAPS Award, McKnight Fellowship, a Dramatists Guild of America Hull-Warriner Award, and the Rosamond Gilder Award for Outstanding Creative Achievement in the Theatre. In 2002, Mann received an Honorary Doctorate of Arts from Princeton University.

NOTES

1. Dan White was paroled after five years in 1984. The following year he was found dead of carbon monoxide poisoning in the garage of his wife's home in San Francisco, California.
2. Otis L. Guernsey Jr., ed., *The Best Plays of 1983-1984* (New York: Dodd, Mead, 1984), 60.
3. *Daily News*, March 14, 1986.
4. *New York Post*, March 14, 1986.
5. *Women's Wear Daily*, March 14, 1986.
6. *Milk* (2008), a biographical motion picture about the life of Harvey Milk, written by Dustin Lance Black and directed by Gus Van Sant, starred Sean Penn in the title role and Josh Brolin as Dan White. The film earned high praise and garnered eight Academy Award nominations, including Best Picture. It won for Best Acting in a Leading Role (Penn) and Best Original Screenplay (Black).
7. Emily Mann, *Testimonies: Four Plays* (New York: Theatre Communications Group, 1997), 34.

Never the Sinner (1985)

John Logan (United States, 1961-)

On May 21, 1924, nineteen-year-old Nathan Leopold and eighteen-year-old Richard Loeb, students at the University of Chicago, kidnapped a friend, Bobbie Franks, killed him, then attempted to extract a ransom from Franks's parents. Obsessed with Nietzsche's "superman" theory, Leopold and Loeb believed that they had committed the perfect crime. But they hadn't: Leopold dropped his designer glasses at the scene of the crime and the police quickly traced them. The investigators also found the typewriter on which the ransom note had been typed. Leopold and Loeb were tried, defended by renowned attorney Clarence Darrow, found guilty, and sentenced to life imprisonment. Loeb was killed in a prison brawl in 1936. Leopold was paroled in 1958; he died in Puerto Rico in 1971.

In an introduction to the published play *Never the Sinner*, playwright John Logan recounts that in 1977, when he was attending high school in Millburn, New Jersey, he had an after-school job shelving books at the local public library. The blood-red binding of *Compulsion* by Meyer Levin caught his eye, and upon reading the book he couldn't shake the story from his mind: "Why did they do it? Why would two young men with every advantage in the world decide to murder an innocent fourteen-year-old boy? What were the demons lurking behind Loeb's flashing good looks? Behind Leopold's saturnine intellect? Those questions stayed with me – and stimulated my continued work on the play – for the past twenty years."[1]

When a senior in the theatre department at Northwestern University, Logan took a playwriting course "on a Lark." In class, he began to write a play about Leopold and Loeb. As the fates would have it, the Northwestern Library Special Collection was home to the Elmer Gertz Collection; Gertz was Leopold's parole attorney and amassed a large volume of information on the case. "So," writes Logan, "the gates were unlocked, and the pages spilled forth."[2] He buried himself in a stream of intimate letters between Leopold, Loeb and Darrow, in full trial transcripts, and in psychiatric reports, police statements, and newspaper accounts.

The first version of *Never the Sinner* was produced at Northwestern in 1983 at the end of Logan's senior year. On opening night, the play ran for three hours and had almost twenty characters, including Clarence Darrow's wife and Mrs. Franks. A revised, condensed version that had seven actors was produced at the Stormfield Theatre, Chicago in 1985, running just over two hours. In 1990, *Never the Sinner* was presented at the Playhouse Theatre in London, staged by Geoff Bullen. "With the tenacious support of Terry McCabe, who directed the first professional Chicago production… the committed work of actors like Donna Powers Branson in Chicago and Dennis O'Hare and Ben Daniels in London," relates Logan, "I tried to shape the spine of the play so that it charted more elegantly the intricate ebbs and flows of the relationship between Leopold and Loeb."[3]

In 1994, *Never the Sinner* was offered at the Space Theatre in Adelaide, Australia, staged by Rob Crosner. Three years later, in the summer of 1997, the play was presented by the Signature Theatre in Arlington, Virginia. The Signature production came to New York under the sponsorship of the National Jewish Theatre on December 1, 1997. Critic D.J.R. Bruckner of the *New York Times* called *Never the Sinner* "a remarkable play… based on years of research, including some sealed family archives."[4] The production subsequently reopened at Off Broadway's John Houseman Theatre on January 24, 1998. Ethan McSweeny directed and Lou Stanari designed the highly regarded show. The cast was headed by Jason Patrick Bowcutt (Nathan Leopold), Michael Solomon (Richard Loeb), and Robert Hogan (Clarence Darrow). In shaping the play to its final form, Logan admittedly "cannibalized" the ideas of talented producers, directors, designers, and actors.

The action of *Never the Sinner* unfolds in short vignettes that rotate, back and forth, from court proceedings to flashbacks leading to the murder of Bobby Franks. Three court reporters function as a chorus to relate the progression of the case and the nation's hypnotic involvement in the "trial of the century." It soon becomes clear that the audience will serve as the jury.

Leopold, "dark and brooding" and Loeb, "bright and airy" are led in handcuffs to their place in the courtroom. "The People of the State of Illinois versus Nathan Leopold, Jr. and Richard Loeb for the crime of murder," announces the bailiff, and Judge John R. Caverly takes his seat. Reporter 1 exclaims that "Clarence Darrow, Attorney for the Defense, entered the courtroom loaded down with weathered law books." Reporter 2 declares, "State's Attorney Robert Crowe stalked in – a slick symphony of sinewy ambition."

As the court proceedings begin, glimpses of the past reveal Leopold and Loeb's fascination with Nietzsche's theory of the *Ubermensh*– the *Superman* – who "is aloof to the petty concerns of mankind" and "is exempt from the laws that bind the common run of humanity." Loeb, who calls Leopold "Babe," leads him in a waltz and spins him around the stage while suggesting that the two of them "live up to their exalted potential and stun the world."

In court, state's attorney Crowe describes how the accused, two young men with "expensively cut suits" and "slicked back hair," cruised the streets of Kenwood in search of their victim. "Consider their smiles as they seduced little Bobby Franks into the car," barks Crowe. "As they pulled shut the door and mercilessly beat him to death. As they pushed him into that sewer." Crowe wishes "to tear those superior smirks from their faces" and asks for "the extreme penalty, for death."

A flashback describes Loeb and Leopold hatching a plan to stop a passerby in Lincoln Park, pretend to have guns in their coats' pockets, and rob a man's wallet. Loeb is obviously the leader; Leopold is at first reluctant, but after Loeb's sneer, "You're pathetic. Some Superman," Leopold agrees to go along.

They elevate their scheme from robbery to kidnapping and murder. Callously, they consider killing one of their fathers but discard the idea. Who among their student friends is a natural, ideal target? Finally, Leopold says, "Leave it to fate! Why don't we just cruise the Harvard School area and take whomever fits us." Loeb likes the idea, grabs Leopold's face and kisses him passionately, almost violently, and races off.

In court, psychologist Dr. White testifies, to hushed, mesmerized spectators, about a pact made between the accused men: "Leopold would take part in crimes primarily to accommodate Loeb, and Loeb would take part in sexual acts primarily to accommodate Leopold."

The reporters announce: "Body of boy found in swamp!" "Kidnapped rich boy found dead!" "Bobby Franks found dead in marshes!" "All city hunts for killers! Police call crime the strangest and most baffling in Chicago history!" "Al Capone Declares: Organized crime not responsible for Franks' murder!"

In a flashback sequence, Loeb and Leopold peruse a newspaper story about a pair of spectacles found near Bobby Franks' body. Loeb angrily admonishes Leopold for carelessly dropping his "fucking glasses" at the scene of the crime.

The unique hinges of the spectacles lead police to Leopold. Confronted with this evidence, Leopold and Loeb confess their crime. A flashback pictures Loeb and Leopold cruising in a "car" - three plain wooden chairs are used to suggest the vehicle. Leopold is driving. They stop to observe a neighborhood baseball game. Bobby Franks emerges from the playground and walks toward his home. He's alone. Leopold and Loeb pull up beside Franks and offer him a lift. Inside the car, without any warning, Loeb and Leopold smash the boy twice over the head with a chisel. Loeb lets out a savage scream as he batters Franks and drags his body to the back seat. Leopold recoils from the splattered blood and whispers, "My God! My God!" Loeb explodes into giggles, expresses joy at committing the deed "within a block" of Franks' home, and gushes, "Everything turned out beautifully; it was a work of art."

Clarence Darrow meets Loeb and Leopold in the jail's anteroom and asks them to confide the story of Franks' murder – and the lights fade out.

Act 2 continues to mingle past incidents and present court proceedings. A grim scene pictures the two protagonists pushing the body of Bobby

Franks into a culvert on the marshes. Loeb wipes mud and blood from his clothes while Leopold stands still, looking down at the dead boy. "The acid didn't work," says Leopold anxiously, but Loeb assures him that it doesn't matter, that no one will find the corpse "in this god forsaken spot." They plan to send a ransom note to Franks' parents.

In court, Darrow throws a bombshell by changing his clients' plea to "Guilty on all counts." He informs Judge Caverly that he will present testimony regarding the mental state of the accused that will explain – not justify – their actions. "The darkest recesses of the human mind are in question here," announces Darrow. "We must take that fact into account to arrive at a just verdict of punishment." Reporters 1, 2, and 3 note the change of plea with exclamation marks. However, Reporter 2 states that "foxy Mr. Darrow might be outfoxed yet, as Judge Claverly is popularly known as a 'Hanging Judge.'"

Prosecutor Crowe, who demands the death penalty, and Defense Attorney Darrow go through a series of clashes. "They're boys, Bob. Boys. And they're scared," says Darrow. Crowe retorts: "You want to throw away the law? If we do that, what will we have left?" The verbal duel climaxes with Darrow calling Crowe "a cold bastard," and the prosecutor sallying, "and you are a blind old man." Darrow softens his tone: "I could look at them like you do, Bob. I could damn these boys for what they did… I can see the sin in all the world. And I may well hate that sin, but never the sinner."

In their separate jail cells, Leopold and Loeb are interviewed by reporters. "That killing was an experiment," says Leopold. "It is just as easy to justify such a death as to justify an entomologist in killing a beetle on a pin!" And Loeb remarks coolly, "I know I should be sorry I killed that young boy and all, but I just don't feel it." The reporters remain speechless.

In the jail yard, Leopold and Loeb sit watching a baseball game. "If they hang us – would they do that together? At same time?" asks Loeb. Leopold nods, "Probably. They have two gallows here, side by side." Loeb mutters, "Then I hope they hang us."

In court, Dr. White testifies that despite the defendants' intelligence, their emotional development has been arrested "somewhere under the age of ten."

In his summation, Crowe demands the death penalty as the one proportional to the turpitude of the crime: "Hang these heartless 'supermen'! Hang them!" Darrow, however, claims that the boys were not in their right minds when they committed the crime, "*because they were made that way*. Because somewhere, somehow, in the infinite processes that go into the making of a boy or a man something … *slipped*."

In the jail anteroom, Leopold and Loeb await the verdict. They look at each other.

Leopold: Dick, why did we kill Bobby Franks?
Loeb: I don't know.

Leopold: I don't know either... We're not Supermen, are we?
Loeb: No. I guess not.

Reporter 1 announces: "September 10th – Dickie and Babe escape the noose. Judge's Verdict: Life Plus Ninety-Nine Years."

* * *

D.J.R. Bruckner of the *New York Times* found John Logan's play "remarkable... Other plays, and movies and books about the case have tended to foreground the sex; Mr. Logan treats it as fairly normal and concentrates on the personalities of the men and on the moral environment they lived in, with a result that the world is uglier and the killers somehow colder and more sinister than ever... Michael Solomon's Loeb is brutal and sentimental at once; manipulative, impulsive, devious... Jason Patrick Bowcutt has a trickier assignment in Leopold, who has to move from thrill to horror to wonder so fast and often that you question his sanity."[5]

Playwright Logan has a different take on the two murderers: "In the end, I feel great pity for Leopold and Loeb... To say that Leopold and Loeb were 'monsters' is too easy. To say that they were 'evil' is too facile... Leopold and Loeb were human beings. Just like the rest of us. They were tormented. They were brutal. They lacked any true moral, ethical compass. They could not find their way in our sunlit world, so they embraced the darkness. In that darkness they had each other. The real provocation of Leopold and Loeb is that we all could, given some unkind twists of fate and character, be them."[6]

* * *

In addition to *Never the Sinner*, other plays inspired by the Loeb-Leopold case include *Rope* (1929) by Patrick Hamilton; *Leopold and Loeb* (1997) by George Singer; *Thrill Me* (2003), a musical with book, lyrics and music by Stephen Dolginoff; and *Dickie and Babe* (2008) by Daniel Henning.

Englishman Patrick Hamilton (1904-1962) is remembered today mostly for his 1938 play *Gaslight* aka *Angel Street* and his 1941 Jack the Ripper novel *Hangover Square* – both filmed effectively in memorable motion pictures. *Rope* was Hamilton's first play. The action unfolds continuously on the first floor of a house in Mayfair, a fashionable neighborhood in London. The apartment is shared by Wyndham Brandon and Charles Granillo, Oxford students and lovers. When the curtain rises, the living room is completely darkened save for the pallid gleam from a lamplight in the street below. Silhouetted are the figures of Brandon and Granillo, bending over a chest, working intensely, when suddenly the lid of the chest falls with a bang. The two young men sink exhausted into armchairs and light cigarettes. Against the two pinpoints of light, they begin to converse. We learn that they have just strangled, by rope, young Ronald Kentley, a fellow undergraduate, deposited his body in the chest, and are expecting Ronald's father, his aunt, and several friends to come around for supper. For an extra thrill, the guests will be seated around the chest. "This is the complete story," says Brandon, "The complete story of a perfect crime."

They switch on a lamp. Brandon is tall and blond; Granillo, slim and dark. Brandon goes to switch on the light in the hall and returns fuming, his eyes blazing, holding a slip of blue paper in his hand. He castigates Granillo for neglecting to find a Coliseum ticket that dropped from their victim's pocket. The ticket later becomes the clue that leads to the downfall and capture of the two murderers.

Directed by Reginald Denham, an authority on stage suspense,[7] *Rope* played at West End's Ambassador Theatre in 1929, featuring Brian Aherne and Anthony Ireland as Brandon and Granillo, ran for 131 performances, and later that year came to New York's Masque Theatre, under the title *Rope's End*, for 100 showings. The *New York Times* found it "a novel diversion of pure morbidity."[8] Alfred Hitchcock brought *Rope* to the screen in 1948, featuring John Dall and Farley Granger as the youthful killers who are uncovered by their former professor, enacted by James Stewart.[9]

George Singer's *Leopold and Loeb* is an episodic, less-than-profound play that was produced by Artists Theatre Company at Off Broadway's 28th Street Theatre under Renee Philippi's direction, with Brian Weiss as Leopold and Marc Palmieri as Loeb. Reviewer D.J.R. Bruckner recounted that playwright Singer "focuses on the killers' convoluted and mostly unspoken sexual passions… but the dialogue so rigorously prevents both characters from revealing any self-awareness, that viewers are likely to conclude that evil really is banal."[10]

The action of Stephen Dolginoff's musical *Thrill Me* is book-ended between a prologue and an epilogue that take place in a Chicago pardon conference room. The year is 1958 and it is the fifth hearing for prisoner Nathan Leopold. As Leopold responds to queries by voice-over committee members, flashbacks picture his submissive relationship – psychologically and physically – with Richard Loeb, a charismatic Nietzsche disciple. Step by step Loeb draws Leopold into a crime spree motivated by a sense of superiority, capped by the fatal stabbing of a young boy in a remote, wooded area. Their perfect crime is botched by Leopold dropping a pair of prescription glasses at the scene of the crime. At the conclusion there is a twist: It is Stephen Dolginoff's theory that Leopold left the incriminating glasses behind purposely, counting on the pair's verdict of life imprisonment and thus having the fickle Loeb forever to himself.

Thrill Me has only two characters, Leopold and Loeb, so we are told, not shown, by word and song, such events as the execution of the murder, the police investigation, and the trial. The erotic relationship between the two protagonists is heightened with long kisses at the end of several scenes.

Thrill Me was first produced by a non-Equity troupe under the direction of Martin Charnin of *Annie* fame. The ninety-minute musical, containing sixteen songs, was presented for six performances at New York's 2003 Midtown International Theatre Festival. Christopher Totten played Nathan Leopold and Matthew Morris enacted Richard Loeb. In 2005, *Thrill Me* was revived for a limited run by Off Broadway's York Theatre Company, staged by Michael Rupert, featuring Matt Baur (Leopold) and Doug Kreeger (Loeb). Reviewer Frank Scheck of the *New York Post* opined that the Leopold-Loeb case "seems to resist musicalization… While, thankfully, the tragic subject matter isn't trivialized, it results in a ponderous, tedious evening, the most endearing aspect of which is its brevity."[11]

Thrill Me came to Hollywood, California in 2008, a production mounted by the Havok Theatre Company at the Hudson Backstage. Critic Steven Mikulan complimented director Nick DeGruccio for knowing "the difference between thrill and shock," and keeping the evening "from lapsing into Grand Guignol."[12] Kathleen Foley found Stewart W. Calhoun and Alex Schemmer, who played Leopold and Loeb, respectively, "so convincingly boyish that they resonate not as mere monsters, but as kids trapped in an escalating game of triple dare… they deliver wrenching performances that force us to care, almost in spite of ourselves."[13]

In March 2008, Daniel Henning directed his own play, *Dickie and Babe*, for the Blank Theatre Company of Hollywood, California, a production running simultaneously, two blocks away, from *Thrill Me*. According to David No of the *Los Angeles Times*, Henning "has set an ambitious if strangely academic goal for himself – to tell the Leopold and Loeb story as objectively as possible, minimizing conjecture and dramatic embellishments."[14] Not unlike John Logan before him, for three years Henning immersed himself in court transcripts, medical reports, letters and other documents, and pulled out verbatim dialogue from historical records. He even visited the Chicago neighborhood where the killers lived and retraced their path.

Books about the Leopold-Loeb case include *The Amazing Crime and Trial of Leopold and Loeb* (1924) by Maureen McKernan; *Life Plus 99 Years* (1958) by Nathan Freudenthal Leopold; *A Handful of Clients* (1965) by Elmer Gertz; *The Crime of the Century* (1975) by Hal Higdon (reprinted in 1999 under the title *Leopold and Loeb: The Crime of the Century*).

A low-budget but highly stylized motion picture, *Swoon* (1992), depicts the execution of the crime, the investigation, the trial, and the final fate of the two killers. *Swoon* was scripted and directed by Tom Kalin and starred Daniel Schalachet (Loeb) and Craig Chester (Leopold).

* * *

John Logan was born in San Diego, California, in 1961. The youngest of three children, he grew up in California and New Jersey before moving to Chicago to attend Northwestern University, where he graduated in 1983. Following *Never the Sinner*, Logan wrote *Hauptmann* (1986), about the German immigrant Bruno Richard Hauptmann who was convicted of kidnapping and murdering the Lindbergh baby; *Riverview*, (1991), a musical melodrama set at Chicago's famed amusement park; and *Red*, the story of artist Mark Rothko that opened at London's Donnar Warehouse in December 2009, ran for two months, and transferred to Broadway for a limited run, winning the 2010 Tony Award for Best Play.

In 1996, Logan penned *Tornado!*, a made-for-TV movie about storm chasers. Three years later, he concocted another television contribution, *RKO 281*, examining the struggle of young Orson Welles in making the greatest American film of all time, *Citizen Kane*. At the end of the 20th century, Logan began writing and producing feature movies in a gamut of genres. *Bats* (1999) is a horror flick about hordes of mutated killer bats attacking a Southwestern community. *Any Given Sunday* (1999) covers the world of pro football. *Gladiator* (2000) is a spectacle of ancient Rome. *The Time Machine* is an adaptation of the H.G. Wells classic and *Star Trek: Nemesis* is an impressive entry in the series – both science-fiction films made in 2002. *Sinbad: Legend of the Seven Seas* (2003) was called by Leonard Maltin an "entertaining animated blend of adventure, fantasy, comedy and romance as bad-boy Sinbad takes on a noble mission to save his boyhood friend – the prince."[15] *The Last Samurai* (2003) depicts a clash of cultures as an American cavalry officer arrives in 1876 Japan to train the emperor's soldiers, while *The Aviator* (2004) is a screen biography of billionaire Howard Hughes who sets out to conquer Hollywood. *Sweeney Todd: The Demon Barber of Fleet Street* (2007) is a stylized, brooding adaptation of the Stephen Sondheim-Hugh Wheeler musical about a vengeful barber in nineteenth-century London. *Coriolanus* (2011), inspired by Shakespeare's tragedy, follows the blood-splattered path of a centurion who was exiled from Rome and is returning as the head of an army to take his revenge on the city. *Rango* (2011) is a computer-animated family film about a pet chameleon who wanders into an old western town, presents himself as a tough drifter, becomes sheriff, and encounters gun-slinging outlaws, bank robbers, and a crooked mayor. *Skyfall* (2012) centers on James Bond trying to scuttle a plot on MI6. In *Spectre* (2015), Bond uncovers the existence of a sinister organization named SPECTRE. *Genius* (2016), is a biographical sketch of Thomas Wolfe. *Alien: Covenant* (2017) is a science fiction adventure that follows the crew of a colony ship landing on an uncharted planet and encountering a monstrous alien.

In 2015-2016, Logan created the TV Series *Penny Dreadful,* for Showtime, a series that goes back in time to the Golden Age of Hollywood in the 1930s, peppered with ghastly crimes, racial tensions, and Nazi conspiracies.

Acting Edition: Samuel French, Inc.; The Overlook Press.

Awards and Honors: John Logan won the 1999 Writers Guild of America Best TV Adapted Writing for *RKO 281*. He was nominated for a 2000 Academy Award and a BAFTA Award for Best Original Screenplay, *Gladiator.* In 2004, he was nominated for an Academy Award, a BAFTA Award, and a Writers Guild of America Award for Best Original Screenplay, *The Aviator.* In 2010, Logan won a Tony Award for Best Play for *Red*. Two years later, he garnered an Annie Award from the International Animated Film Society for Writing in a Feature Production for *Rango* (*Rango* also won Academy, BAFTA, and Annie Awards for Best Animated Feature Film).

NOTES

1. John Logan, *Never the Sinner* (Woodstock, New York: The Overlook Press, 1988), 12.
2. *Ibid*, 13.
3. *Ibid*, 15.
4. *New York Times*, December 2, 1997.
5. *New York Times*, December 2, 1997.
6. John Logan, *Never the Sinner* (Woodstock, New York: The Overlook Press, 1988), 16.
7. Among the thirty plays that Reginald Denham directed on Broadway were the criminous *Suspense* (1930), *Ladies in Retirement* (1940), *Suspect* (1940), *Guest in the House* (1942), *The Two Mrs. Carrolls* (1945), *Portrait in Black* (1947), *Dial "M" for Murder* (1952), *Sherlock Holmes* (1953), *Bad Seed* (1954), and *Hostile Witness* (1966).
8. *New York Times*, September 20, 1929.
9. Patrick Hamilton was contracted to pen the screenplay of *Rope*, Alfred Hitchcock's first picture filmed in color. The director's conceit was to shoot it without cuts, unraveling continuously in the apartment where the murder is committed. The task was too strenuous for Hamilton, who was replaced, successively, by Hume Cronyn and Arthur Laurents. A synopsis of Patrick Hamilton's *Rope* and *Gaslight*, the plays' production

data, and critics' evaluation can be found in Amnon Kabatchnik, *Blood on the Stage, 1925-1950* (Lanham, Maryland: Scarecrow Press, 2010).
10. *New York Times*, June 4, 1997.
11. *New York Post*, June 9, 2005.
12. *LA Weekly*, February 1-7, 2008.
13. *Los Angeles Times*, February 1, 2008.
14. *Los Angeles Times*, January 27, 2008.
15. *Leonard Maltin's 2011 Movie Guide* (New York: Plume, 2010), 1252.

To Kill a Mockingbird (1987)

Christopher Sergel (United States, 1918-1993)

Harper Lee's 1960 novel *To Kill a Mocking bird* won the Pulitzer Prize, has been translated into ten languages, sold well over thirty million copies in the United States and abroad, and continues to be widely taught in secondary schools. It also became an effective motion picture – and was faithfully adapted to the stage by Christopher Sergel.

The play depicts the events that rocked imaginary-yet-real Maycomb, Alabama, in 1935, through the inquisitive eyes of Jean Louise Finch (nicknamed "Scout"), an alert, forthright six-year-old tomboy. Together with her older brother, Jeremy ("Jem") and their friend Charles Baker Harris ("Dill"), Scout tries to understand the web of racial undercurrents then prevailing in the South.

Motherless, Scout and Jem are being raised by their father, Atticus, a reserved, quietly impressive lawyer who does what he considers just. The children are disappointed that their father won't play touch football or show them how to shoot their air rifles. Calpurnia, a capable Black housekeeper, helps discipline the siblings. Neighbors on the sleepy street include wise Maudie Atkinson, gossipy Stephanie Crawford, cranky Mrs. Dubose, and reclusive Arthur Radley ("Boo"), considered insane and dangerous.

Rumor has it that when Boo was in his teens, he took up with some bad fellows from Old Sarum. They were arrested on charges of disorderly conduct, disturbing the peace, and using abusive language in the presence of a female. Boo Radley was released to his father, who shut him up in the house; Boo has not been seen for fifteen years.

Atticus agrees to defend a young Black man, Tom Robinson, accused of raping a nineteen-year-old white woman, Mayella Ewell, whose large family resides by the town dump. Her father, Bob Ewell, hopes that the pending trial will make him an important community man. Scout asks Atticus, "what's rape?" pouts that the kids at school snicker at his defending "niggers," and confides that most people think he is doing something wrong. Atticus explains that the one thing that does not abide by majority rule is a person's conscience.

The play pictures some of the novel's memorable moments: Atticus shooting a rabid birddog as the children learn that their father was "the deadest shot in Maycomb County;" the lynch mob surrounding the county jail, confronted by Atticus and swayed by the unexpected interference of little Scout to return to their home; and the centerpiece of the drama, the trial. Scout, Jem and Dill sneak into the balcony of the courtroom and sit among the Blacks to watch the trial proceedings.

On the stand, Bob Ewell testifies that upon arriving home he found Tom Robinson raping his daughter. During cross examination Atticus has Ewell sign his name on an envelope, establishing him as left-handed. Young Dill understands: "Her *right* eye was blackened so it had to be someone left-handed."

Mayella, sworn in, insists that the "nigger yonder" took advantage of her and calls anyone who doesn't believe her "a yellow stinking coward."

Led by Atticus, Tom Robinson states that Mayella invited him into the house to fix an old door. Once inside, says Robinson, she jumped at him, hugged him, kissed his cheeks. He tried to leave but Mayella got in his way, blocking his path to the door. He tried to push her aside just as Mr. Ewell hollered through the window. He ran away.

In spite of Atticus' contention that circumstantial evidence indicated that Mayella Ewell was beaten savagely by someone who used his left hand, and that Tom Robinson's left hand was crippled, the jury, as expected, finds the defendant guilty. When Atticus leaves the courthouse, the balcony spectators rise to their feet. Miss Maudie tells the disappointed kids that their father was the only man in the area who could keep the jury out so long in a case like this. He didn't get an acquittal, but he got something. "Maybe we're taking a little step, a little step along the way," says Miss Maudie.

Atticus plans an appeal, but word comes that Tom Robinson, despondent, made a feeble attempt to escape from the Enfield Prison Farm only to be gunned down by the guards. Gaining respect for their father and affected by the dramatic events that will influence the rest of their lives, Scout and Jem still have one more crucial experience in store: After a costume party for the town children in the school auditorium, they are viciously attacked by Bob Ewell as they walk back home.

Unexpectedly, Boo Radley comes to their rescue. There is a struggle in the dark, after which Boo carries the injured youngsters home. In the morning, Ewell is found dead. Sheriff Heck declares that "Bob Ewell fell on his knife. He killed himself. Let the dead bury the dead."

As the stage lights dim, Scout wonders how Boo Radley, with all the bad stories about him, turned out to be *real* nice. Her father responds affectionately: "Most people are, Scout – when you finally see them."

* * *

To Kill a Mockingbird was transformed to the screen in 1962. Robert Mulligan directed a richly textured motion picture that earned Academy Awards for Horton Foote's screenplay and Gregory Peck's performance. The play was later adapted from the novel by Christopher Sergel, who was granted special permission to do so from Harper Lee. Producer-director Chris Hayes embellished Sergel's version when the drama toured regional theatres in the United Kingdom for nine months, before playing seven months at the Mermaid Theatre, London, in 1987. Four years later in the United States, director Robert Johanson of the Paper Mill Playhouse, Milburn, New Jersey, helped shape the final form of the play (with George Grizzard as Atticus).

A perennial favorite with provincial theatre audiences, *To Kill a Mockingbird* was presented during the 1990s by Denver Center Theatre, Denver, Colorado; ESIPA, Albany, New York; Wisdom Bridge Theatre, Chicago, Illinois; Actor's Theatre Series, Fullerton, California; Repertory Theatre of St. Louis, St. Louis, Missouri; Hippodrome Theatre Inc., Gainesville, Florida; Syracuse Stage, Syracuse, New York; Alabama Shakespeare Festival, Montgomery, Alabama; Fulton Opera House, Lancaster, Pennsylvania; Foothill Theatre, Nevada City, California; Great American History Theatre, St. Paul, Minnesota; Alliance Theatre, Atlanta, Georgia; Tennessee Repertory Theatre, Nashville, Tennessee; Montana Repertory, Missoula, Montana; and the Hanger Theatre, Ithaca, New York.

London saw two revivals of *To Kill a Mockingbird* in 1992. In 1997, it was filmed for the second time, directed by Scott Jacoby and Matt Moses, with Evan Nisenson portraying Atticus Finch. Matthew Modine starred as Atticus Finch in a 2009 production presented by Hartford Stage in Connecticut. The Lex Theatre of Hollywood, California offered the play during January-February 2011.

A new stage adaptation of *To Kill a Mocking bird*, by Aaron Sorkin, opened at Broadway's Shubert Theatre on December 13, 2018, with Jeff Daniels as Atticus Finch and Celia Keenan-Bolger as Scout. While some reviewers criticized liberties taken by Sorkin, the assessment was generally positive. Prior to the opening, $22 million were made in advance ticket sales at the box office.

During production, the show was involved in two legal disputes — one with the Harper Lee estate, the other against licensed productions of the Christopher Sergel adaptation. The issues were resolved but on March 12, 2020, *To Killa Mockingbird* had to close doors due to the Covid-19 pandemic. The play resumed performances on October 5, 2021, at the Shubert Theatre with the original two lead actors, Daniels and Keenan-Bolger, and a cadre of replacements. However, more than a year later, the *New York Times* of December 3, 2022, reported "further courtroom drama over *To Kill a Mockingbird*: the latest twist in a series of disputes about theatrical adaptations of the novel. In 2019, the producers of a Broadway adaptation of *To Kill a Mocking bird* [by Aaron Sorkin] provoked outrage by seeking to prevent a group of small theatres around the country from staging an earlier dramatization of the novel. Now the tables have turned: The publisher of the earlier adaptation [by Christopher Sergel] is seeking to block the Broadway version from being staged at a wide variety of venues." The legal tussling continues.

* * *

Except for two years spent on a schooner in the South Pacific and a year spent in the African bush, Christopher Sergel's entire life was devoted to playwriting and publishing. New York credits include dramatizations of Sherwood Anderson's *Winseburg , Ohio*, depicting life beneath the surface of a small town (Broadway's National Theatre, February 5, 1958 — thirteen performances), and John G. Neithardt's *Black Elk Speaks*, an account of the conquest of the West from the perspective of a Sioux spiritual leader (Off-Broadway's Entermedia Theatre, March 12, 1981 — six performances).

Sergel also convrted to the stage *The Mouse That Roared*, based on Leonard Wibberly's novel (Woodstock Academy, Woodstock, Connecticut — March 29, 1963,) and *Pillow Talk*, from the screenplay by Stanley Shapiro and Maurice Richlin (Concordia State Teachers College, Seward, Nebraska — February 14, 1963).

Other adaptations by Sergel include Kurt Vonnegut Jr's *Who Am I This Time?* and *Welcome to the Monkey House*; Hildegarde Dolson's *We Shook the Family Tree*; Sally Benson's *Meet Me in St. Louis*; Phil Strong's *State Fair*; Bel Kaufman's Up the Down Staircase; S. E. Hinton's *The Outsiders*; Christopher Morley's *Kitty Foyle*; James Hilton's *Lost Horizon*; and Frank Gilbreth and Ernestine Gilbreth Carey's *Cheaper by the Dozen*.

From television, Sergel borrowed Arthur Hailey's *Flight into Danger* and the series *Get Smart*, originally created by Mel Brooks and Buck Henry. The prolific playwright also adapted *Fame*, basing his stage treatment on the screenplay by Christopher Gore.

Sergel's output is available through the Dranatist Publishing Company, Chicago, founded by his great-uncle in 1885 and run by the Sergel family ever since. Sergel served as president of the company from 1970 until his death in 1993.

* * *

Nelle Harper Lee was born in 1926 in the small town of Monroeville, Alabama, the daughter of a lawyer. The youngest of four children, Lee befriended a schoolmate, Truman Streckfus Persons, who later became known as Truman Capote.

At five years old, Lee was deeply affected by a 1931 trial in the Alabama town of Scottsboro. Nine young Black men were charged with the rape of two white women, and despite flawed testimony, the all-white jury found the men guilty and sentenced them to death. The convictions were repealed in subsequent trials and all but one of the accused were freed. The Scottsboro case inspired Lee's *To Kill a Mockingbird.*

Lee attended the all-female Huntington College in Montgomery (1944-1945) and studied law at the University of Alabama (1945-1949). She relinquished a position as a reservation clerk with Eastern Air Lines in New York City in order to devote herself to writing. In 1959, she worked as a research assistant for Truman Capote when he investigated the brutal murder of the Clutter family in Holbombe, Kansas, described starkly in his *In Cold Blood.*[1]

In 1960, J.B. Lippincott Company published *To Kill a Mockingbird.* To commemorate the novel's fiftieth anniversary in 2010, filmmaker Mary McDonagh Murphy produced the documentary *Hey, Boo.* A companion volume, *Scout, Atticus and Boo,* published by Harper, features Murphy's interviews with celebrities about the effect of Lee's book. Among the interviewees are Tom Brokaw, Andrew Young, and Oprah Winfrey. Lee herself refused to be interviewed for the book and did not accept an offer by Winfrey to appear on her television show. Lee has not spoken publicly about *To Kill a Mockingbird* for more than half a century.

In July 2015, Lee published her second novel, *To Set a Watchman,* which was written before *To Kill a Mockingbird* and portrays the later lives of its characters. Lee lived quietly in her hometown of Monroeville, Alabama, where she died in her sleep in the morning of February 19, 2016, aged 89.

Acting Edition: The Dramatic Publishing Company.

Awards and Honors: Harper Lee – Pulitzer Prize for Fiction, 1961; Alabama Library Association Award, 1961; Brotherhood Award of National Conference of Christians and Jews, 1961; Best Sellers Paperback of the Year Award, 1962 – for *To Kill a Mockingbird.* In 1966, President Lyndon Johnson named Lee to the National Council of the Arts. She has received several honorary doctorates since then. In 1999, *To Kill a Mockingbird* was voted "Best Novel of the Century" by Library Journal. In 2005, Lee received the Los Angeles Public Library Literary Award. Two years later, President George W. Bush awarded her the Presidential Medal of Freedom, the highest civilian award in the United States. In the summer of 2010, in honor of the fiftieth anniversary of the publication of *To Kill a Mockingbird,* the publisher, HarperCollins, announced plans to issue four more editions of the novel, each with a different cover, and helped to organize parties, readings, scholarly discussions, and movie screenings.

NOTES

1. Harper Lee is a key character, portrayed by Catherine Keener, in the biographical movie, *Capote*, 2005. Lee was also played by Tracy Hoyt in the TV movie *Scandalous Me: The Jacqueline Susann Story* (1998), and by Sandra Bullock in the film *Infamous* (2006).

Beyond Reasonable Doubt (1987)

Jeffrey Archer (England, 1940-)

When Lord Jeffrey Archer's courtroom drama *Beyond Reasonable Doubt* opened in London in late September 1987, the production followed the best-selling author's sensational libel suit. Lord Archer had taken the *Daily Star,* a tabloid, to court for a story alleging that he had spent the night with a prostitute. The jury delivered a verdict in Archer's favor to the tune of half a million pounds.

But, to the surprise – and perhaps disappointment – of the first-night audience at London's Queens Theatre on September 22, 1987, *Beyond Reasonable Doubt* was not concerned with libel but with murder. Worse, the play's jury is persuaded to reach an incorrect verdict.

The first act of *Beyond Reasonable Doubt* takes place in the Central Criminal Court (The Old Bailey). The curtain rises on Mr. Justice Tredwell addressing the jury (i.e., the audience): "The case has already attracted much lurid publicity," says the judge. He instructs the viewers to concentrate on the evidence, and adds, "It is you and you alone who will decide if Sir David Metcalfe is guilty or not of murder."

The prosecutor, Anthony Blair-Booth, states that the indictment revolves around "the deliberate, non-accidental cold killing of Lady Millicent Metcalfe by the defendant, her husband." It gives him no pleasure, says Blair-Booth, to appear for the Crown against a man who was "an ornament of the Bar." However, continues the prosecutor, distressing as it is, the Crown will present a case which will prove, beyond reasonable doubt, that Sir David Metcalfe did willfully murder his wife in the early hours of March 24. Earlier that evening the two of them had quarreled; later, Sir David grasped the opportunity to "deliberately and knowingly" administer a lethal overdose of the drug Cyclotoxelix toLady Metcalfe.

Blair-Booth calls to the stand Detective Chief Inspector Richard Travers who testifies that the Metcalfe's housekeeper, Eileen Rogers, came to the Wimbledon police station and stated that she had witnessed Sir David poison his wife. He had put a Cyclotoxelix pill in her tea though he must have known that Lady Metcalfe had already taken the medication only a few hours earlier.

Sir David, who has elected to represent himself, cross-examines Inspector Travers.

Sir David: Inspector, if I had killed my wife in the manner indicated by the Crown, surely, I could have destroyed the evidence quite simply by having her body cremated?
Inspector Travers: Most criminals think they're cleverer than the law. That's usually how we catch them.

Blair-Booth calls housekeeper Rogers. She testifies that Sir David has a violent temper and "can always pick a quarrel over the slightest thing." On the fateful evening he came home drunk and hit Lady Metcalfe. Later, she saw him drop a red pill she takes only once a week into the Lady's tea. Upon cross-examination, Sir David produces three full pill bottles from the shelf on the dock. He asks Mrs. Rogers to identify the color of the pills in each bottle; she is wrong each time.

The next witness is the Metcalfe's family doctor, John Weeden, who ascertains that upon examining Lady Metcalfe's body in the early hours of March 24, he concluded that she died of natural causes. In an answer to Blair-Booth's query, Dr. Weeden explains that any excess of the drug Cyclotoxelix could prove fatal. He had prescribed the drug to Lady Metcalfe for Lymphosarcoma – cancer of the lymph glands. He adds that she was in considerable pain for the last fourteen months of her life.

Blair-Booth calls Lionel Hamilton, a solicitor, who testifies that Lady Metcalfe left a will bequeathing the bulk of the estate – just over one million pounds – to her husband.

That concludes the case for the prosecution. Sir David takes the stand and lets his junior counsel, Robert Pierson, question him. On the night in question he was awakened by a noise that seemed to come from downstairs, discovered that his wife was not at his side, ran down the steps, and found Millicent lying on the drawing-room floor. He picked her up and helped her to the sofa. She was badly shaken by the fall and asked for tea. He went to the kitchen immediately. When he returned with the tea, the pain had obviously become much worse. Millicent had two pill bottles in her hands and was fumbling with one of them, trying to open it. She handed the vials to him and asked him to put a pill in her tea. He did. He was concerned with his wife's condition and cannot remember the color of the pill. Millicent seemed to slip into a restful sleep. Later, he realized that she had started to grow cold and he could no longer hear her breathing. He called Dr. Weeden, who came within the hour and confirmed his worst fears. And, no, contrary to the housekeeper's testimony, he and his wife never quarreled. The only things they ever disagreed about were Dylan Thomas and cricket.

Blair-Booth cross-examines Sir David and elicits from him the information that preceding his wife's death, he had "a run of rather bad luck" and owed stockbrokers Gilbert and Goddard two hundred and eighty-one thousand pounds. Blair-Booth declares that Sir David found an easy way out, a chance to clear himself of embarrassing debts and an ailing wife. If it weren't for the courageous Mrs. Rogers, Sir David may have committed the perfect murder, he concludes.

The lights fade to a spot on the Judge, who addresses the audience-jury with the instruction, "If the evidence does not satisfy you beyond reasonable doubt you will bring a verdict of 'Not Guilty,' but on the other hand, if it does, your verdict, however unpalatable it may be – must be 'Guilty.'" The lights come up again and the Clerk of the Court faces front: "Mr. Foreman, do you find the prisoner, Sir David Metcalfe, guilty or not guilty of murder?" Everyone on stage stares fixedly at the audience as the curtain descends.

Act 2 is composed of a series of flashbacks showing what really happened. The lights fade up on the Metcalfe home in Wimbledon. Lady Metcalfe, in her late forties, and her housekeeper, Mrs. Rogers, are preparing a "pre-trial dinner party" – Sir David is set to defend Beverley Cutts, a woman who stabbed her lover seven times with a rusty pair of scissors. Theguests are Lionel Hamilton, an old solicitor, and Robert Pierson, David's junior counsel. They reminisce about their earlier cases – the Halford murders; Humphries Ascott, "the arson killer;" Lang, "the hatchet murderer;" Charles McCulloch, "the body in the freezer;" and Alice Campbell, charged with "theft, adultery, perjury, blackmail and attempted murder."

The conversation shifts to their nemesis – Anthony Blair-Booth. Young Pierson learns that the prosecutor had proposed to Millicent before she consented to marry Sir David, so the rivalry between them is not only professional but personal. The telephone rings. Sir David speaks to his broker and gets some bad news.

Later that evening, after the departure of their guests, Lady Metcalfe suffers a painful attack and collapses in a chair. She wearily tells her husband that there's no use fooling themselves – "we are talking of months at best." Mrs. Rogers enters, carrying a tray with a glass of water and a bottle of pills. "You must take your once-a-week pill tonight, my lady," she says. Lady Metcalfe swallows the pill and Sir David guides her to the stairs.

A week later, on the evening of March 23, Sir David enters the drawing room and sees his wife lying on the floor. He helps her to the sofa and she asks for tea. He exits to the kitchen and returns with a cup. She hands David a bottle of pills. Mrs. Rogers appears on the stairs and observes David drop a pill into the tea, then sit next to his wife. Mrs. Rogers exits upstairs. David sobs, "Millie, please… don't go yet."

The last scene unfolds two weeks after the trial. Sir David is standing by the desk with his back to the audience. The doorbell rings and Lionel Hamilton enters. He rebukes Sir David for living "like a hermit" since the verdict. He notices a bottle of red pills on the table and Sir David explains that the police returned them. Hamilton attempts to cheer up his subdued friend and mentions an upcoming case, an "extraordinary" one, of a boy who killed his mother, having dabbled in black magic.

Sir David says that the case is tempting but he cannot return to the Bar – because he *did* kill his wife. No, it was not an accident caused by exchanging pills. He deliberately mixed Millicent's tea with a red pill – that's what she wanted, and he couldn't refuse her. He had the pleasure of beating Blair-Booth, but he knew it would be his last appearance in court. He asked Hamilton to come to his house because he thinks he should know the truth – the whole truth. Shortly before Hamilton arrived, says Sir David, he took a fatal dose of three Cyclotoxelix pills with a glass of wine.

Hamilton reaches slowly for the phone and dials 999 as the lights slowly fade and the curtain falls.[1]

* * *

Beyond Reasonable Doubt premiered at the Queens Theatre, London, on September 22, 1987. It was directed by Robert Gilmore and designed by Tim Goodchild. The main roles were portrayed by Frank Finlay (Sir David Metcalfe), Wendy Craig (Lady Metcalfe), Jeffrey Wickham (Anthony Blair-Booth), and Andrew Cruickshank (Mr. Justice Tredwell). Critic Kenneth Hurren of *Plays and Players* slammed the drama as "pretty awful," found the flashbacks "irrelevant padding," and lamented the "total lack of elements of plausibility."[2]

Despite the negative critical reception, *Beyond Reasonable Doubt* ran for more than 600 performances. The play's box-office bonanza may be attributed to the notoriety of the playwright's successful libel action against the *Daily Star*.

A second courtroom drama by Archer, *The Accused*, premiered at the Theatre Royal, Windsor, England on September 26, 2000, and had a nine-week regional tour before anchoring at the Haymarket Theatre, London, on December 5. Archer himself played the title role of Patrick Sherwood; a doctor charged with fatally poisoning his wife. Sherwood pleads "Not Guilty." At the end of the trial, the audience is assigned the role of jury, voting on Sherwood's guilt or innocence. The play was savaged by the critics. Benedict Nightingale of the *New York Times* opined that as soon as Archer's Doc Sherwood enters the witness box, the play "creaks monotonously along, like a wooden crate dragged down a corridor."[3] *The Accused* ran for eight weeks.

Art imitated life again, for simultaneously Archer was accused of perjury related to the 1987 case. The formal charges came hours before the opening night of *The Accused*. In July 2001 he was convicted of "perjury and perverting the course of justice." The jurors determined that he had asked two

friends to provide a false alibi and compensated them for it during the *Daily Star* trial. A diary filled with bogus dates preserved by Archer's secretary served as the smoking gun. Archer was sentenced to four years and served half of his sentence. While incarcerated, he wrote the three-volume memoir *A Prison Diary*.

* * *

The son of a printer, Jeffrey Howard Archer was born in 1940 London and brought up in Somerset. He was educated at Wellington School and Brasenose College, Oxford, where he excelled in sports and was president of the Athletic Club. Archer ran the 100 yards in 9.6 seconds for Great Britain in 1966.

After leaving school, Archer trained for a while with the army and the police, then became a physical education teacher in several prep schools. He enrolled at Oxford and garnered an academic qualification in teaching. There have been claims that Archer provided false evidence of his academic qualifications to gain admission into Oxford. He was also plagued with rumors of financial wrongdoing during that period. However, that did not deter Mary Weeden, a chemistry student at St. Anne's College, Oxford, from marrying Archer in July 1966.

Soon thereafter, Archer entered politics and was elected to the Greater London Council, serving as a Conservative councilor from 1967 to 1970. At the age of 29, he was elected Member of Parliament (MP) for the Lincolnshire constituency of Louth. His ideology was to the left of the Conservative Party, and he rebelled against some of the party's policies, voting against restoring capital punishment, for example. In 1985 he was appointed deputy chairman of the Conservative Party by Margaret Thatcher but the following year he was forced to resign. This came on the heels of a scandal caused by an article in *The News of the World* that charged Archer with paying a "vice-girl."

Archer's books are peppered with heroic feats and crime elements. His first novel, *Not a Penny More, Not a Penny Less*, was published in both the Umited States and England in 1976 and was an instant success. The plot revolves around shady business deals and stock manipulation. His second novel, *Shall We Tell the President?* (1977), is a thriller depicting a plot to assassinate Edward Kennedy. His third, *Kane and Abel* (1979), tells the story of two men – one Polish, an illegitimate son of a Gypsy, the other a rich and privileged Bostonian. Their paths cross and they become bitter enemies, each determined to destroy the other. The book became an enormous bestseller, spawned two sequels, and was made into a television mini-series by CBS in 1985.

The following year, Granada TV screened a ten-part adaptation of Archer's *First Among Equals*, the saga of four ambitious MPs and their quest to become Prime Minister. *A Matter of Honour* (1986) is a tale about a letter that was never opened by the receiver, only to be passed to his son after his death. The opening of the letter changes the family's lives forever. *As the Crow Flies* (1991) begins in the east end of London at the turn of the twentieth century and follows the rags to riches career of Charles Trumper who, as a youth, ran a fruit cart. He eventually became the owner of some of the most successful businesses in England. *Honour Among Thieves* (1993) is a political thriller in which Saddam Hussein's emissaries steal the American Declaration of Independence and the CIA is on the hunt to recover the document. Israel's Mossad and New York' mafia get involved in the action. *The Fourth Estate* (1996) depicts the battle royale between media barons Rupert Murdoch and Robert Maxwell to control the British newspaper market.

In *The Eleventh Commandment* (1998), the chief of the CIA secretly orders the assassination of an international array of adversarial political figures. The proceedings move from the White House to the St. Petersburg hideaway of a Russian mafia boss. *Sons of Fortune* (2003) is the tale of Hartford, Connecticut twins who were separated at birth and grew up without knowing about the other. Eventually, both decide to run for governor of Connecticut. The truth surfaces when a car accident reveals that they share the same rare blood type.

Vincent Van Gogh's last painting, worth $70 million, is the MacGaffin of *False Impression* (2005), a twisty mystery novel that includes information about the September 11 attacks on New York and takes a breathtaking journey through several countries before the resolution. *The Gospel According to Judas* (2007), co-written with Frank Moloney, presents the events of the New Testament through the eyes of Judas Iscariot. *A Prisoner of Birth* (2008) is a contemporary retelling of Alexandre Dumas' *The Count of Monte Cristo.* Danny Cartwright, arrested for murder in an orchestrated plot by four friends, escapes from prison and unleashes his revenge upon the men who framed him. *Paths of Glory* (2009) is a controversial novel in which Archer supports the claim that George Mallory, an Englishman whose body was found in 1999 at 26,760 feet, was the first to conquer Mount Everest – before Sir Edmund Hilary. *Next in Line* (2022) features Archer's series detective, Scotland Yard's Chief Inspector William Warwick, as he is entrusted with protecting the royal family.

Highly regarded short story collections in which Archer plays a cat-and-mouse game with the reader include *A Quiver Full of Arrows* (1980), *A Twist in the Tale* (1989), *Fools,Knaves, and Heroes* (1989), *Twelve Red Herrings* (1994), *The Collected Short Stories* (1997), *To Cut a Long Story Short* (2000), *Cat O'Nine Tales* (2006), *And Thereby Hangs a Tale* (2010), *The New Collected Short Stories* (2011), *Tell Tale* (2017), *The Short,the Long and the Tall* (2020).

The indefatigable author has also published children's books, history chronicles, and various non-fiction yarns, Archer's forty-two works have been published in ninety-seven countries and translated into thirty-three languages, with combined sales passing 275 million copies.

Acting Edition: Samuel French, Ltd.

Awards and Honors: Jeffrey Archer was made a life peer in 1992; despite his criminal conviction at the Old Bailey, he retains the title of Lord.

NOTES

1. The verdict of "not guilty" awarded to a person charged with murder and later discovered to be guilty also occurred at the climaxes of *The Ware Case* (1915) by George Pleydell, *Witness for the Prosecution* (1953) by Agatha Christie, and *An Anatomy of Murder* (1959) by Elihu Winer (based on the 1958 novel by Robert Traver).
2. *Plays and Players*, November 1987.
3. *New York Times*, January 7, 2001.

M. Butterfly (1988)

David Henry Hwang (United States, 1957-)

On May 11, 1986, the *New York Times* announced that "a former French diplomat and a Chinese opera singer have been sentenced [in Paris] to six years in jail for spying for China after a two-day trial that traced a story of clandestine love and mistaken sexual identity... Mr. [Bernard] Bouriscot was accused of passing information to China after he fell in love with Mr. Shi [Pei Pu], whom he believed for twenty years to be a woman."[1]

American playwright David Henry Hwang utilized the account for his play *M. Butterfly*, changing names, adding characters, and creating fictional incidents.

From his sparsely furnished Parisian prison cell, in 1988, Rene Gallimard, sixty-five, breaks through the fourth wall and shares with the audience somewhat disordered, distorted recollections of an affair that began forty years earlier when he was on a diplomatic mission to China. In Peking he met Song Liling, an opera star, whom he calls "Butterfly, the Perfect Woman." Gallimard compares his experience to that of Benjamin Franklin Pinkerton, an American naval officer whose ship docks at the harbor of Nagasaki, Japan, the hero of Giacomo Puccini's opera *Madame Butterfly*. Pinkerton meets, marries, and has a child with a local geisha girl, Cio-Cio-San – "her friends call her Butterfly" – only to leave her behind and return to the United States, The distraught Cio-Cio-San commits suicide.

At the age of thirty-one, shy and introverted Gallimard married an older woman, Olga, whose father was the French ambassador to Australia. Gallimard was faithful to his wife for eight years until the day when, as a junior-level diplomat in Peking, he attended a private reception at the German ambassador's house, where Song Liling sang the death scene from *Madame Butterfly*. "Here was a Butterfly with little or no voice," relates Gallimard to the audience," but she had the grace, the delicacy... I wanted to take her in my arms – so delicate, even I could protect her, take her home, pamper her until she smiled."

Smitten with Song, Gallimard begins to attend the opera regularly. Song eventually invites Gallimard to her apartment, greets him wearing a sheer dressing gown, and mumbles, "I am your Butterfly." He kisses her roughly, starts to caress her, and opens her gown. "No, let me keep my clothes," she whispers, but promises to please him. He turns off the lamp.

Act 2 begins at Gallimard and Song's flat on the outskirts of Peking. Gallimard confides to the audience that over the years 1961 to 1963 they had settled into a domestic routine. Song would prepare a light snack and then, "ever so delicately," would please him with her hands and mouth. Gallimard is promoted to the rank of vice-consul, in charge of coordinating a revamped intelligence division. Song begins to express interest in her lover's work and asks about what is happening in Vietnam. Did the American president, John F. Kennedy, sign an order to bomb North Vietnam? When will the bombardment start? What cities are being targeted?

Song turns out to be a spy working for the Red Chinese government. She reports to her female supervisor, Comrade Chin, that the Americans will increase troops in Vietnam to 170,000 soldiers and 11,000 advisors. The United States will allow the Vietnamese generals to stage a coup and assassinate President Diem.

One evening, an inebriated Gallimard says that he wants to see Song naked. She demures but he insists. He crosses the room and grabs Song by the waist. He releases her, transfixed, when she utters, "I'm pregnant." Upon her next meeting with Comrade Chin, Song tells her that she needs a baby. When her lover told her to strip, she took a chance. If she can present him with an Asian baby with blond hair – he'll be hers for life!

Gallimard tells Song that he'll divorce his wife, marry her, and eventually they'll move to France. Song declines, for Gallimard is a diplomat with a skyrocketing career; what would happen if he divorced his wife to marry a Communist Chinese actress?

In 1966 Gallimard is sent home to France. In Paris, he confesses to Olga that he has had a mistress for eight years and now wants a divorce. Olga says, "I hope everyone is mean to you for the rest of your life," and leaves.

Comrade Chin orders Song to travel to Paris, renew her contact with the diplomat, and continue compiling weekly reports of useful information. Song connects with Gallimard and they resume their relationship.

Act 3 unfolds fifteen years later. The lights come up on Song standing in front of a mirror, removing a wig and a kimono. It's revealed that Song is a man wearing a well-cut suit. The action shifts to a courthouse. On the witness stand, Song testifies that at his urging, Rene Gallimard got a job as a courier, handling sensitive documents. Rene had photographed them and would then pass them to the Chinese embassy. When the judge asks whether Gallimard knew that he was a man, Song responds: "You know, Your Honor, I never asked."

Music from *Madame Butterfly's* "Death Scene" blows over the house speakers when Song confronts Gallimard, removes his clothes, and asks the Frenchman to admit that he still adores him. But Gallimard coolly asks him to leave.

In his prison cell, in 1988, Gallimard bemoans, "Love warped my judgment, blinded my eyes." He wavers between reality and fantasy. Dancers appear and help him get into Song's kimono, whiten his face, redden his lips. They hand him a dagger and he set himself in a hara-kiri position, the Japanese ritual of self-disembowelment. In an ironic reversal of the Puccini opera, it is not Song who commits suicide but Gallimard, who has finally realized that he has been the exploited Butterfly.

* * *

The original title of the play was *Monsieur Butterfly* but David Henry Hwang's wife persuaded him to emphasize the ambiguities of the situation. *M. Butterfly* opened at Broadway's Eugene O'Neill Theatre on March 20, 1988. John Dexter directed. John Lithgow portrayed Rene Gallimard and B.D. Wong enacted Song Liling. Critic Frank Rich found *M. Butterfly* "a visionary work that bridges the history and culture of two worlds... One must be grateful that a play of this ambition has made it to Broadway." But the critic also had some misgivings, scoffing at repetitions, a preaching tone, and "overly explicit bouts of thesis mongering."[2] Clive Barnes raved: "It enriches, it fascinates, it offers thought to feed on."[3] Edwin Wilson saluted playwright Hwang for having "something to say and an original, audacious way of saying it... he ingeniously has woven together a real-life story and events from Puccini's opera *Madame Butterfly*."[4] David Henry admired Eiko Ishipka's "marvelous design" [of set and costumes], John Dexter's "excellent staging," and John Lithgow's "forceful performance as Rene Gallimard."[5]

Negative reactions were expressed by Jack Kroll, who maintained that "at every level the play defies belief,"[6] and Joel Siegel, who commented, "The story is so bizarre everyone's first reaction is: How could it happen? And in two and a half hours the playwright doesn't tell us."[7]

M. Butterfly won Tony Awards for Best Play, Best Director (John Dexter), and Best Featured Actor (B.D. Wong) as well as Drama Desk Awards in the same three categories. The play was further nominated for a Pulitzer Prize. It ran for 777 performances. David Dukes, Anthony Hopkins, Tony Randall, and John Rubinstein took over the part of Gallimard at various times. An audio recording of the play was produced by the Los Angeles Theatre Works with Lithgow and Wong reprising their roles.

Revivals of *M. Butterfly* were presented at Arena Stage, Washington, D.C.(2004); Philadelphia Theatre Company, Philadelphia, Pennsylvania (2007); and Guthrie Theatre, Minneapolis, Minnesota (2010). The play also ran for a year in London's West End and has been produced in more than three dozen countries to date.

A Russian motion picture based on *M. Butterfly* was made in 1990, directed by Roman Viktyuk, with Kazakh tenor Erik Kurmangalie in the title role. Three years later, Hwang scripted an American version which featured Jeremy Irons (Rene Gallimard) and John Lone (Song Liling). The movie was shot by director David Cronenberg in Budapest, Hungary.

* * *

David Henry Hwang was born in Los Angeles, California, in 1957. He was raised in San Gabriel, a suburb near Pasadena, by his father, a banker who grew up in Shanghai, and his mother, a piano teacher reared in the Philippines. Hwang graduated from Stanford University in 1979 with a BA degree in English and enrolled at the Yale School of Drama. He briefly studied playwriting with Sam Shepard and Maria Irene Fornes.

Hwang's early works focused on the role of Chinese Americans in the modern world. His first play, *FOB*, depicts the contrasts and conflicts between established Americans and new immigrants. The play premiered at the Stanford Asian American Theatre Project in 1979 under the direction of the author and was further developed at the National Playwrights Conference of the Eugene O'Neill Center. Its professional debut took place at Off Broadway's Joseph Papp Public Theatre on June 8, 1980. The following year, the Public Theatre presented Hwang's *Family Devotions*, a drama concerned with West-East clash within three generations of an Americanized Chinese family living in a Los Angeles suburb. The play was nominated for a Drama Desk Award.

Rich Relations is the story of a wealthy WASP family and the damage inflicted from parent to child, with many religious overtones. The play was first shown by Off-Broadway's Second Stage Theatre on April 21, 1986.

Golden Child relates the struggles of a nineteenth-century Chinese family confronting westernization. The drama premiered at the Joseph Papp Public Theatre on November 19, 1986, directed by James Lapine. A revised version was tried out in California and Singapore and opened at Broadway's Longacre Theatre on April 2, 1988. It was nominated for a Tony Award as Best Play.

Hwang's adaptation of Henrik Ibsen's *Peer Gynt*, a poetic, symbolic fantasy that deals with the degeneration of the human soul and the redeeming power of love, streamlined the complicated, episodic original and added many contemporary references. The work was commissioned by the Trinity Repertory Company in Providence, Rhode Island, where it debuted on February 3, 1998.

Tibet Through the Red Box is an adaptation of the chldren's book by Peter Sis about a boy growing up in Prague in the 1950s. The play was commissioned by the Seattle Children's Theatre, where it opened on January 30, 2004.

The protagonist of *Yellow Face* is the author himself. Partly autobiographical, *Yellow Face* is a satire that raises questions of how politics and media function in society and what America really stands for. The play opened at the Joseph Papp Public Theatre on December 10, 2007. It won an Obie Award and placed Hwang as a finalist for the Pulitzer Prize. *Chinglish*, a comedy about the misadventures of an American businessman hoping to make his fortune in China, raised its curtain at Broadway's Longacre Theatre on October 27, 2011. Much of the dialogue is delivered in Mandarin, accompanied by supertitles in English, purposely mistranslated. Ben Brantley of the *New York Times* found the device of "merrily mutilated" language, "the principal source of this production's mirth." However, the critic remained dissatisfied: "While David Korins' nifty revolving set is meant, I think, to summon the whirligig dizziness of farce, *Chinglish* only rarely achieves the sort of momentum that sends audiences into the ether. Even when its characters are floating helplessly on the wings of unhinged words, this play feels too solidly grounded for its own good."[8] Despite the fact that *Chinglish* received generally favorable reviews and was named the number one new American play of 2011 by *Time Magazine*, box office sales were modest, and the comedy ended its run after 128 performances.

Short plays by Hwang include *The Dance and the Railroad*, which describes a strike in a coolie railroad labor camp in the mid-nineteenth century. Commissioned by the New Federal Theatre and presented at the Joseph Papp Public Theatre on July 16, 1981, the play was a finalist for the Pulitzer Prize for Drama. It was also produced on television by the ABC Arts channel, winning a CINE Golden Eagle Award. *The House of Sleeping Beauties* focuses on Japanese author Yasunari Kawabata, a 1968 Nobel Prize winner, and how he came to write a novella of the same name. The one-act was produced at the Joseph Papp Public Theatre on November 6, 1983, accompanied by Hwang's *The Soul of a Voice*, a ghost story inspired by Japanese folk tales and Noh theatre.

As the Crow Flies depicts the double life of an African American maid living in a Chinese home in Los Angeles. The playlet premiered at the Los Angeles Theatre Center on February 16, 1986, double-billed with Hwang's *The Sound of a Voice*. *Bondage* deals with issues of racial stereotypes by placing a fully disguised man and woman in a sadomasochistic parlor, playing out sexual games. The play premiered at the Actors Theatre of Louisville on March 1, 1992, featuring B.D. Wong and Hwang's wife, Kathryn Layng. Four years later, the Actors Theatre of Louisville presented Hwang's *Trying to Find Chinatown*, a playlet covering dilemmas of racial identity by pitting an Asian street musician against a Caucasian man who claims Asian American heritage. The violinist is not aware that the white man was adopted by Asian-American parents. Also penned in 1996, a ten-minute piece by

Hwang, *Bang Kok*, concerns two businessmen who share stories of prostitution in Thailand. In the climax, one of the men confesses to his friend that he has contracted AIDS. *Merchandising*, commissioned in 1999 by the Actors Theatre of Louisville's Humana Festival, tells of two filmmakers who lament the failure of their picture and the nature of marketing in Hollywood. *Jade Flowerpots and Bound Feet* is centered on a Caucasian woman who passes herself off as a minority to sell a book to a major publishing company. The play premiered on November 5, 2001, as part of a program of short plays dealing with Asian American identity, presented at the Joseph Papp Public Theatre. Six years later, the same Off-Broadway theatre presented *The Great Helmsman*, a comedy about two women who are debating who will be chosen to spend the night with Chairman Mao Zedong. *A Very DNA Reunion*, dealing with the imprecise science of DNA technology, premiered as part of Chicago's Silk Road Theatre Project on March 8, 2010.

The untiring Hwang joined Linda Woolverton and Robert Falls in penning the libretto of *Aida*, a rock musical based on the Italian-language opera by Giuseppe Verdi. The musical, produced by Disney Theatrical, with a score by Elton John and lyrics by Tim Rice, premiered at Broadway's Palace Theatre on March 23, 2003. It was nominated for five Tony Awards and ran for 1852 performances, yielding an album with the original cast. In 2001, Hwang revised the book of Rodgers & Hammerstein's 1958 *Flower Drum Song*, about Wang Ta, the son of wealthy refugees from China residing in San Francisco's Chinatown, torn between his Chinese roots and assimilation into American culture. Following a tryout in Los Angeles, the musical came to Broadway in 2002, received mostly poor reviews and closed after six months.

Hwang wrote the book, to music and lyrics by Phil Collins, of *Tarzan*, based on the 1912 Edgar Rice Burroughs story and the 1999 Disney animated film. After six weeks of previews, the musical officially opened at Broadway's Richard Rodgers Theatre on May 10, 2006. Despite mediocre reviews and poor ticket sales, *Tarzan* managed to keep its doors open for a run of 486 performances.

Hwang collaborated with Korean composer Unsak Chin on an operatic rendition of Lewis Carroll's *Alice's Adventures in Wonderland* and *Through the Looking Glass*. *Alice in Wonderland* had its world premiere at the Bavarian State Opera on June 30, 2007, as part of the Munich Opera Festival. Teamed with Canadian composer Howard Shore, Hwang wrote the libretto of *The Fly*, an opera loosely based on David Cronenberg's 1986 film about a misguided, horrific scientific experiment. *The Fly* was commissioned by the Théâtre du Châtelet in Paris where it opened on July 2, 2008.

For television, Hwang co-wrote with Frederic Kimball the special *Blind Alley* (1985), the story of two people, once linked by an interracial marriage, setting up their daughter's wedding. *The Monkey King* (2001), also known as

The Lost Empire, is a four-hour television miniseries in which an American businessman encounters a beautiful, mystical Chinese lady who transports him to the ancient Chinese underworld.

The protagonist of the feature film *Golden Gate* (1994) is a 1950s G-Man (portrayed by Matt Dillon) who pursues a Communist ring in San Francisco. The trail leads him to a young Chinese-American woman (played by Joan Chen) whose father he helped to put in prison. *Possession* (2002), co-scripted by Hwang with Laura Jones and Neil LaBute, based on a novel by A.S. Byatt, is a puzzle-drama about two scholars, an impulsive American man (portrayed by Aaron Eckhart) and a cool British woman (Gwyneth Paltrow) who investigate an affair between two renowned fictional poets of the mid-1800s. LaBute directed.

In 2014, a year in which Hwang joined the playwriting faculty of the Columbia University School of the Arts, two new Hwang plays premiered Off Broadway — *Kung Fu*, about the life of Bruce Lee, at the Signature Theatre, and *Cain and Abel*, a retelling of the Bible story, at the Flea Theater.

Wikipedia relates that in November 2015, Hwang was the victim of a stabbing near his home in Fort Greene, Brooklyn. The assailant stabbed Hwang in the neck, severing his vertebral artery, and fled from the scene. Hwang was seriously injured and underwent surgery before being discharged from the hospital. The attack appeared to be random, and the attacker was never found.

M. Butterfly remains David Henry Hwang's most popular and critical success. He is acknowledged as the preeminent Asian American dramatist in the United States. He sits on the boards of the Dramatists Guild, Young Playwrights Inc., and the Museum of Chinese in the Americas. From 1994 to 2001, he served by appointment of President Bill Clinton on the President's Committee on the Arts and the Humanities.

Acting Edition: Dramatists Play Service.

Awards and Honors: In 1988, *M. Butterfly* received a Tony Award and a Drama Desk Award for Best Play. The play was nominated for a 1989 Pulitzer Prize for Drama. David Henry Hwang has received numerous grants, including fellowships from the Guggenheim and Rockefeller Foundations, and the New York State Council on the Arts. He has been honored with awards from the Asian American Legal Defense and Education Fund, the Association for Asian Pacific American Artists, the Organization of Chinese Americans, the Media Action Network for Asian Americans, the Center for Migration Studies, the Asian American Resource Workshop, and The China Institute. Hwang holds an honorary degree from Columbia College, Chicago, Illinois. In 1998, the nation's oldest Asian American theatre company, East West Players of Los Angeles, christened its new main stage The David Henry Hwang Theatre. Hwang is the recipient of the 2012 Steinberg Award ($200,000) for playwriting, the most generous prize in theater.

NOTES

1. Bernard Bouriscot confessed to having passed at least 150 classified documents to Shi Pei Pu.
2. *New York Times*, March 21, 1988.
3. *New York Post*, March 21, 1988.
4. *Wall Street Journal*, March 22, 1988.
5. *Daily News*, April 10, 1988.
6. *Newsweek*, April 4, 1988.
7. *WABC-TV7.*
8. *New York Times*, October 28, 2011.

A Few Good Men (1989)

Aaron Sorkin (United States, 1961-)

The military courtroom drama by a novice playwright, Aaron Sorkin, began its artistic incubation at the University of Virginia in Charlottesville, then moved to the Kennedy Center in Washington, D.C., before playing on Broadway for 497 performances. *A Few Good Men* reportedly brought twenty-eight-year-old Sorkin a six-figure deal with movie producer David (*Jaws*) Brown.

The action of *A Few Good Men* takes place in two diverse settings: Washington, D.C., and the U.S. Naval Base in Guantanamo Bay, Cuba. The time: summer, 1986. Marine Lance Corporal Harold W. Dawson and Private First Class Louden Downey have been charged with conspiracy to commit murder, murder in the second degree, and conduct unbecoming a U.S. Marine. The victim, William Santiago, was an unpopular private in their platoon. Assigned to defend Dawson and Downey is Lieutenant Daniel A. Kaffee, a callow Harvard Law School graduate, who prefers playing baseball to pursuing the case.

Prodded by Lt. Commander Joanne Galloway ("Lieutenant, would you feel very insulted if I recommend to your supervisor that he assign different counsel?"), Kaffee discovers that Santiago had written to his senator for help, describing how he was dizzy and nauseated during a PT (Physical Training) run, had fallen behind when going down a rocky hill, and was deliberately pushed down the hill by his sergeant. He was put in remedial physical training and punished by filling sandbags every day after standing his post on the fence line. He is asking the senator to help in a transfer out of the RSC (rifle security company).

It seems that Santiago has penned eleven similar letters and put in for transfer six times. That triggered the ire of his commanders. Santiago, considered a traitor to the Marine Corps motto "Unit, Corps, God, Country," was placed on "Code Red" - a form of hazing-like discipline that befalls enlisted men who don't measure up to standard. Dawson and Downey stuffed a rag down Santiago's throat, accidentally suffocating him. The thrust of Kaffee's defense case is that the two Marines are fall guys willing to go to jail; higher-ups, condoning and instigating brutal treatment of men who don't fit the mold, are the real culprits.

In court, Kaffee gradually sheds his neophyte image when pitted against rigid, flag-waving Lieutenant Colonel Nathan Jessup, the formidable base commander, who barks at Kaffee: "We live in a world that has walls. And those walls have to be guarded by men with guns. Who's gonna do it? You? I have a greater responsibility than you can possibly fathom." Jessup looms larger than life in the courtroom but the reflection is shattered when Kaffee maintains that Jessup ordered the Code Red on Santiago and when it went awry, he signed a phony transfer order for Santiago. Kaffee submits Defense Exhibit A, the Tower Chief's log for Naval Air Station, NAVBASE, Guantanamo Bay, Cuba. It lists incoming and outgoing flights for Thursday, July 7 and Friday, July 8, and the lawyer points out that the logbook was forged to show that Santiago could not have left yet because on those dates no passenger-capable flights left the base.

Kaffee opens the logbook and crosses to Jessup. "Is that your signature?" he asks. Jessup nods, "That's my signature" and reluctantly admits that he ordered the Code Red against Santiago. The case against Dawson and Downey is dismissed while Jessup is placed under arrest. He makes a quick move toward Kaffee, but is grabbed by MPs who pull him back.

Jessup: I'm gonna tear your eyes right outta your head and piss in your skull! You fucked with the wrong Marine! All you did here today was weaken the country… You put people in danger. Sweet dreams, son.

Kaffee: Don't call me son. I'm a lawyer. An officer of the United States Navy. And you're under arrest, you son of a bitch. (To the MPs) The witness is excused.

* * *

While not in the same league with Herman Wouk's *The Caine Mutiny Court Martial, A Few Good Men*, which opened at the Music Box Theatre on November 15, 1989, proved to be popular with critics and audiences. Clive Barnes declared it "A triumphant example of a now fashionably outmoded courtroom drama that sizzles with fun and entertainment."[1] Linda Winer agreed: "People who like courtroom dramas eat them like popcorn, and chances are, people like them are going to gobble *A Few Good Men* as if it were a gourmet brand."[2] Edwin Wilson stated: "Mr. Sorkin not only knows how to set up a scene, he has a sharp sense of humor, and he is greatly aided by director Don Scardino, who puts the cast members through their paces with a military precision that even the gung-ho colonel would have admired."[3]

However, William A Henry III suggested that the play "suffers from bad timing" in view of "the flood tide of change in the Communist world that makes the military appear less vital."[4] Frank Rich found *A Few Good Men* "too predictable to satisfy as a courtroom entertainment, and its attempt to tie its plot to some larger moral issue, in the manner of Charles Fuller's *Soldier's Play,* is lightweight."[5] Otis L. Guernsey, Jr. and Jeffrey Sweet opined that

"*A Few Good Men* puts on the airs of being a play about issues... but what it really is about is giving actors the opportunity to play their favorite scenes from old movies."[6]

The motion picture adaptation that made young Sorkin a rich man was shot in 1992 by director Rob Reiner. Jack Nicholson is mesmerizing as Commander Jessup; Kevin Bacon is eerily intense as Jack Ross, a fanatic captain; Tom Cruise and Demi Moore are solid as attorneys Kaffee and Galloway.

In 2005, Sorkin revised the play for a revival at London's Theatre Royal Haymarket, directed by David Esbjornson, with Rob Lowe as Attorney Kaffee. Staged by Kenne Guillory, *A Few Good Men* was presented in March 2012 at the Sky Lounge, North Hollywood, California, squeezing the large cast into a small, black-box theatre.

* * *

Aaron Sorkin was born in Manhattan to affluent Jewish parents and was raised in the wealthy suburb of Scarsdale, New York. He attended Scarsdale High School where he became involved in the drama club. His interest in theater was whetted when his parents took him to see such Broadway shows as *Who's Afraid of Virginia Woolf?* and *That Championship Season.*

In 1979 Sorkin enrolled at Syracuse University. He graduated in 1983 with a BA degree in musical theatre. He moved to New York City where he pursued an acting career while supporting himself driving a limousine, delivering singing telegrams, and handing out promotional fliers. It is said that one weekend, while house sitting at a friend's place, he found an electric typewriter, started typing, felt exhilarated, and from then on dedicated his life to writing. He sent his first play, *Removing All Doubt*, to his Syracuse theater teacher, Arthur Storch, who was impressed and staged the play at the university. Sorkin's second play, the one-act *Hidden in This Picture*, a Hollywood satire, was presented at Off-Off-Broadway's West Bank Café in 1988, and he developed it into a full-length play called *Making Movies. Making Movies* debuted in 1990 at Off-Broadway's Promenade Theatre, directed by Don Scardino.

Sorkin got the idea for writing *A Few Good Men* from a phone conversation with his sister Deborah, who had graduated from Boston University's Law School and signed up with the U.S. Navy Judge Advocate General's Corps. She was on her way to Guantanamo Bay to defend a group of Marines who had come close to killing a fellow Marine in a hazing ordered by a superior officer. "I wrote [*A Few Good Men*] on cocktail napkins during the first act of Broadway shows where I was serving as a bartender," recalls Sorkin in an interview with broadcast journalist Charlie Rose on August 13, 2003.[7]

Following the success of the courtroom drama on Broadway, Sorkin wrote several drafts of the screenplay with veteran author William Goldman serving as his mentor. Goldman also submitted to Sorkin a story premise to be developed into the script that became *Malice*, a medical thriller released in 1993, featuring Alec Baldwin, Nicole Kidman, Bill Pullman, George C. Scott, and Anne Bancroft. Two years later, Goldman worked as a creative consultant on Sorkin's third screenplay, *The American President*, in which the widowed President of the United States (played by Michael Douglas) is attracted to a lobbyist (Annette Bening) and decides to pursue her despite the advice of his political aides. During the 1990s, Sorkin served, uncredited, as a script doctor on *Schindler's List* (1993), *The Rock* (1996), and *Bulworth* (1998).

Sorkin went on to create *Sports Night* for ABC-TV, a comedy series about the behind-the-scenes happenings on a sports show. Although critically acclaimed, the 1998 show was cancelled after two seasons due to its low ratings. However, Sorkin's next television endeavor, *The West Wing*, depicting fictional life and politics in the White House, was honored with nine Emmy Awards for its season debut in 1999 and became a hit series on NBC.[8]

In 2001, Sorkin was arrested at Burbank Airport for possession of marijuana and crack cocaine. He was ordered by a judge to attend a drug diversion program. His drug addiction was widely publicized. Recovered, Sorkin created *Studio 60 on Sunset Strip*. Describing it as having "autobiographical elements," it was a 2006 show that began with high expectations but fizzled mid-season. A year later, Sorkin scripted the movie *Charlie Wilson's War*, about the Texas congressman Charles Wilson who funded the CIA's secret campaign against the former Soviet Union in Afghanistan.

After more than a decade away from the theater, Sorkin adapted for the stage his screenplay *The Farnsworth Invention*, a drama centered on the bitter conflict that pitted Philo T. Farnsworth, a boy genius who invented television as a high school student in 1927, against David Sarnoff, head of the Radio Corporation of America. The play was presented by the La Jolla Playhouse in San Diego, California from February 20 through March 25, 2007. A subsequent presentation at the Music Box Theatre on Broadway had to surmount a stagehand strike and finally opened on December 3, 2007. It closed on March 2, 2008. Later that year Sorkin undertook to adapt for the movies the novel *The Accidental Billionaire* by Ben Mezrich, about the founding of Facebook. The film was released on October 1, 2010, under the title *The Social Network*, and Sorkin crossed the country to promote it through a series of screenings and interviews. Nicole Sperling of the *Los Angeles Times* spent two evenings with Sorkin and wrote: "The 49-year-old screenwriter behind such television shows and movies as The *West Wing*, *A Few Good Men* and this year's *The Social Network* is a complicated mix of humility and egoism – at once a self-depreciating goofball who struggles with insecurities and a confident titan of his field who recognizes that his name is itself a brand, one that melds fiction and reality into whip-smart dialogue delivered at breakneck speed."[9]

A triple threat, Sorkin continues to tackle theater projects, movies, and television – *To Kill a Mockingbird* (2018), Shubert Theatre; *Camelot* (2022) Vivian Beaumont Theatre, both on Broadway; the screenplays of the features *Moneyball* (2011), *Steve Jobs* (2015), *Molly's Game* (2017), *The Trial of the Chicago 7* (2020), *Being the Ricardos* (2021); and the television shows *The Newsroom* (2012), *A West Wing Special to Benefit When We All Vote* (2020).

Acting Edition: Samuel French, Inc.

Awards and Honors: Aaron Sorkin won a 1999 Emmy for Writing, Drama Series – *The West Wing*; a Peabody Award in 2000 for *The West Wing*; a National Society of Film Critics Award, a Golden Globe Award, a BAFTA Award, and an Academy Award for Best Adapted Screenplay – *The Social Network* (2010); a New York Film Critics Circle Award for Best Screenplay, in collaboration with Steven Zaillian, and a nomination for an Oscar – *Moneyball* (2011).

NOTES

1. *New York Post,* November 16, 1989.
2. *New York Newsday,* November 16, 1989.
3. *The Wall Street Journal,* November 17, 1989.
4. *Time Magazine,* November 27, 1989.
5. *New York Times,* November 16, 1989.
6. Otis L. Guerney, Jr. Ed., *The Best Plays of 1989-1990* (New York: Applause, 1990), 23.
7. Thomas Fahy, *Considering Aaron Sorkin* (Jefferson, North Carolina: McFarland & Company, 2005), 1.
8. A detailed analysis of the television series *The West Wing* is provided in *Mr. Sorkin Goes to Washington* by Melissa Crawley (Jefferson, North Carolina: McFarland & Company, 2006).
9. *Los Angeles Times,* December 9, 2010.

The Laramie Project (2000)

Moisés Kaufman (Venezuela-born American, 1963-) and The Members of Tectonic Theatre Project

A new dramatic form arose during the 1950s and 1960s: the political docudrama. Playwrights in various countries took it upon themselves to examine official documents and court records of historical events and incorporated their findings, sometimes verbatim, into theatrical fare. In England, Ludovic Kennedy wrote *Murder Story* (1954), dramatizing the real-life case known as the Croydon Rooftop Murder: Nineteen-year-old Derek Bentley and sixteen-year-old Christopher Craig exchanged bullets with the police on the premises of a Croydon factory. Craig shot and killed a policeman while trying to escape over a rooftop. The two boys were tried and convicted of murder. Craig, being underage, was sentenced to prison. Bentley was sentenced to death. Playwright Kennedy was deeply affected by the notion that the murderer should survive while his accomplice, who was not carrying a gun that fateful night, would be executed. The case inspired Kennedy to write *Murder Story* as a protest against capital punishment.

In the United States, Saul Levitt based his play *The Andersonville Trial* (1959) on the official records of the 1865 trial of Henry Wirz, commandant of the most notorious Confederate prison-of-war stockade. The courtroom drama raises the issue of passive moral conviction among military men who blindly obey the inhuman orders of their superiors. *Sequel to a Verdict* (1962) by Philip Dunning conjures up a case reminiscent of the Charles Lindburgh kidnapping tragedy.

In Germany, Rolf Hochhuth's *The Deputy* (1963) questions the failure of Pope Pius XII to speak out against the Nazi slaughter of Jews; Peter Weiss re-creates the horrific events at the Auschwitz concentration camp in *The Investigation* (1965); and Heinar Kipphardt's *In the Matter of J. Robert Oppenheimer* (1964) re-examines the hysterical era of McCarthyism when in 1954, Dr. Oppenheimer, "the father of the atomic bomb," was summoned to a congressional hearing regarding his security clearance.

Donald Freed's *Inquest* (1970) is concerned with the controversial Cold War trial and execution of Julius and Ethel Rosenberg, who were found guilty of delivering atomic secrets to the Soviet Union. *The Trial of the Catonsville Nine* (1971) was penned by Daniel Berrigan, a Catholic priest who was one of the seven men and two women who, at the height of Vietnam War, entered the draft board in Catonsville, Maryland, and set 378 recruitment files on fire with homemade napalm. The nine were arrested, convicted, and sentenced to prison terms ranging from two to three-and-a-half years. Eric Bentley's *Are You Now Or Have You Ever Been?* (1972) is centered on the 1950's House Un American Activities Committee hearings, in which figures from the world of show business were subpoenaed to testify about their loyalty as Americans and asked to name any and all communists in the industry. Assembled directly from the transcripts of the hearings, the play uses the actual words spoken by Lillian Hellman, Elia Kazan, and Jerome Robbins, among others.

The Biko Inquest (1978), by Englishmen Norman Felton and Jon Blair, dramatizes the transcripts of the inquest into the 1977 death of South African activist Stephen Biko in a jail cell on September 12, 1977. Five police officers were accused of killing Biko. Emily Mann based *Execution of Justice* (1984) on the court records and her own investigation regarding the 1978 double-barreled killing of San Francisco's Mayor George Moscone and gay Supervisor Harvey Milk by Dan White, a former member of the city's Board of Supervisors.

New York's Tectonic Theatre Project, dedicated to experimentation with form and structure in contemporary drama, went a step further. With Artistic Director Moisés Kaufman at the helm, in 1998 company members traveled to Laramie, Wyoming, to interview townspeople regarding the murder of Matthew Shepard. On October 7, 1998, after midnight, Shepard, a gay student at the University of Wyoming in Laramie, met two local men, Aaron McKinney and Russell Henderson, at the popular Fireside Lounge and agreed to join them for a car ride. The duo robbed, pistol-whipped and tortured Shepard, tying him to a fence in a remote, rural area, and left him to die. Shepard was discovered eighteen hours later by a cyclist. He never regained consciousness and remained on full life support at the Poudre Valley Hospital in Fort Collins, Colorado until he was pronounced dead at 12:53 a.m. on October 12, 1998. McKinney and Russell were arrested shortly thereafter. The police found a bloody gun and Shepard's shoes and wallet in their truck. Both were sentenced to two consecutive life terms. The Shepard murder brought national and international attention to hate crime motivated by homophobia and affected legislation at the state and federal levels.

"The idea of *The Laramie Project* originated in my desire to learn more about why Matthew Shepard was murdered," wrote Moisés Kaufman in an introduction to the acting edition of the play, "about what happened that night, about the town of Laramie. The idea of listening to the citizens talk really interested me. How is Laramie different from the rest of the country, and how is it similar?" [1]

Four weeks after the homicide of Matthew Shepard, nine members of the Tectonic Theatre Project descended on Laramie. They returned to the town many times over the course of the next year and a half and conducted more than 200 interviews. By editing their copious notes, a play emerged. "The experience of working on *The Laramie Project*," stated Kaufman, "has been one of great sadness, great beauty, and, perhaps most important, great revelations – about our nation, about our ideas, about ourselves." [2]

The Laramie Project is divided into three acts; each in turn is divided into episodic "moments." The curtain rises on a Narrator introducing members of Tectonic Theatre as they begin a series of interviews with Laramie residents. Detective Sergeant Hing of the local police department relates that Wyoming is "one of the largest states in the country, and the least populated." Eileen Engen, a rancher, and Doc O'Connor, a limousine driver, speak of the pleasant environment. Philip Dubois, President of the University of Wyoming; Rebecca Hilliker, head of the theatre department; Zackie Salmon, a college administrator; and student Jedadiah Schultz are united in praising Laramie – population 26,687 – as "a beautiful town, secluded enough that you can have your own identity… A town with a personality that most larger cities are stripped of."

"As far as the gay issue," says seventy-year-old Marge Murray, "Laramie is live and let live." Doc O'Connor agrees: "There's more gay people in Wyoming than meets the eye… And I don't think Wyoming people give a damn one way or another if you're gay or straight." Catherine Connolly, a professor at the university, reveals that she was "the first 'out' lesbian or gay faculty member on campus. And that was in 1992."

After absorbing the background information, the actor-interviewers visited the Fireside Lounge, the last place Shepard was seen alive. The Fireside had several pool tables and a stage area for karaoke. The owner, Matt Mickelson, and the bartender, Matt Galloway, relate that on the fateful night, at 10:30 p.m., Matthew Shepard showed up, alone, sat down and ordered his usual beer, Heineken. He did not seem to be looking for anyone; he just enjoyed his drink and the atmosphere. At approximately 11:45 p.m., Aaron McKinney and Russell Henderson came in, "stone-faced, dirty, grungy, rude." They walked up to the bar and paid for a pitcher with dimes and quarters. They took the pitcher into the pool room and kept to themselves. After a while, they returned to the main room and were seen talking to Shepard. Soon Aaron, Russell and Matthew left together. Shadow, an African-American musician who was the establishment's DJ, saw them enter a small black truck. The three sat in the front seat with Matthew in the middle.

Aaron Kreifels, a university student, tells the interviewers that on Wednesday at 5:00 p.m. he left his dorm for a relaxing bicycle ride. "God wanted me to find him," says Kreifels, "because there's no way that I was going to go that way." He found himself in "deep-ass sand" and suddenly noticed something lying by a fence. At first, he thought it was a scarecrow but getting closer noticed the hair and realized that the chest was going up and down. He ran to the nearest house as fast as he could and dialed 911 for the police.

Officer Reggi Fluty found Matthew tied to a fence with a thin white rope, covered in dried blood and barely breathing. His head was distorted and there was "a real harsh head wound." Matthew's shoes were missing.

Dr. Cantway, who worked the emergency room at Laramie's Ivinson Memorial Hospital the night Shepard was brought in, said that he was horrified by the fact that such severe injuries, "the kind that come from a car going down a hill at eighty miles an hour," were inflicted "from someone doing this to another person." Dr. Cantway added that "strangely," twenty minutes before Matthew was carried in, Aaron McKinney arrived with his girlfriend. Two days later Dr. Cantway found out the connection between Matthew and Aaron. "I was very struck!" exclaimed the doctor. "They were two kids! They were both my patients and they were two kids. I took care of both of them… For a brief moment I wondered if this is how God feels when he looks down at us. How we are all his kids… And I felt a great deal of compassion – for both of them."

The second act deals with the reactions of the Laramie residents as word spread about what was generally perceived as "a hate crime." During an arraignment, the judge summarized the essential facts of the case: The defendants, Aaron James McKinney and Russell Arthur Henderson, met Matthew Shepard at the Fireside Bar. After Mr. Shepard confided that he was gay, the subjects lured him into leaving with them in their vehicle and drove to a remote area. Both subjects tied their victim to a fence, robbed him, tortured him, and beat him. Later, officers of the Laramie Police Department found Shepard's credit card and shoes inside the pickup. "Said defendants left the victim begging for his life," said the judge.

Newspersons announced that McKinney and Henderson came from the poor side of town. Both were from broken homes and as teenagers had had run-ins with the law. They lived in trailer parks and scratched out a living working at fast-food restaurants and fixing roofs. Both pleaded not guilty to the charges.

On Monday, October 12, 1998, at 12:53 a.m., Matthew Shepard died. His family was at his bedside.

The third act begins on the day of the funeral. Matt Galloway, the bartender at the Fireside, tells the interviewers that despite a heavy snowstorm, thousands of people dressed in black, carrying umbrellas, attended the local churches and joined in prayer.

In court, Russell Henderson changed his "not guilty" plea to "guilty." He was sentenced "to serve a period of imprisonment for the term of your natural life" for the felony of murder with robbery, and a second period of life imprisonment for kidnapping – both to run consecutively.

The trial of Aaron McKinney commenced a year later. The prosecution played a tape recording of his confession during a police interrogation. "Some kid wanted a ride," said McKinney. "... [A] queer dude... we drove out past Wal-Mart... he starts grabbing my leg and grabbing my genitals... I beat him up pretty bad... with my fist. My pistol. The butt of the gun... I had a few beers and I don't know... it was like somebody else doing it..." The jury found McKinney guilty of kidnapping, aggravated robbery, and second-degree murder, not guilty of premeditated first-degree murder.

McKinney's defense team approached Matthew Shepard's parents, Dennis and Judy Shepard, and pleaded for their client's life. Dennis Shepard made a statement in court, announcing that he's been comforted by the fact that "Matt's beating, hospitalization, and funeral focused world-wide attention on hate. Good is coming out of evil... This is the time to begin the healing process. To show mercy to someone who refused to show any mercy, Mr. McKinney, I am going to grant you life, as hard as it is for me to do so, because of Matthew... May you have a long life, and may you thank Matthew every day for it."

* * *

The Laramie Project premiered at the Denver Center Theatre on February 26, 2000, ran for sixteen performances, and on May 18 moved to New York's Union Square Theatre, where it ran for 126 more. Critic Ben Brantley of the *New York Times* asserted that "while running two and a half hours with two intermissions, *The Laramie Project* sustains its emotional hold. As Mr. Kaufman demonstrated with *Gross Indecency*,[3] he has a remarkable gift for giving a compelling theatrical flow to journalistic and historical material... The evening itself has the feeling of those candlelight vigils. There is the same sense of a stately procession through which swims a stirring medley of emotions: anger, sorrow, bewilderment and, most poignantly, a defiant glimmer of hope."[4]

In November 2000, Kaufman took his company to Laramie, Wyoming to perform the play there. In March of 2002 Kaufman directed a television adaptation of *TheLaramie Project* for HBO, remaining faithful to the interview format of the play, but the casting of many well-known actors (including Steve Buscemi, Peter Fonda, and Laura Linney) in the cameo roles of Laramie townspeople, conflicted with the documentary, real-life aura of the material.

Since then, the play has been mounted more than 2,000 times by high schools, colleges, and community theatres across the United States, and by professional theatres in Canada, England, Ireland, Australia, and New Zealand. A revival was presented by the Promenade Players of Santa Monica, California, March 4-March 19, 2011. Several high school productions, in cities such as Yakima, Washington, Burbank, California, and Surrey, British Columbia, have been banned. Amid concerns from parents, who argued that the play's content was inappropriate for high school students, the Catholic Notre Dame High School in Lawrenceville, New Jersey, cancelled its production of *The Laramie Project* in March 2012, a decision that led to even more controversy among some of the students, staff members and alumni.

Ten years after Matthew Shepard's murder, members of the Tectonic Theatre Project returned to Laramie and conducted follow-up interviews with local residents to explore the long-term impact of the case. According to Moisés Kaufman, "Laramie has changed in some ways. The city council passed a bias crime ordinance that tracks such crimes, though it does not include penalties for them… Several residents say they came out publicly as gay… The university hosts a four-day Shepard Symposium for local justice each spring… And yet, to the bewilderment of some people here, there is no memorial to Mr. Shepard in Laramie. The long fence has been torn down where he lay dying for 18 hours on October 7, 1998. There is no marker. Wild grass blows in the wind. The Fireside tavern is also gone… There is no longer a bar in town where gays, jocks, foreign students and cowboys mix together." [5]

The interviews were collated into an eighty-minute companion piece, *The Laramie Project: Ten Years Later*, which debuted as a stage reading at more than forty theatres across the nation – including La Jolla Playhouse in California; Broad Stage in Santa Monica, California; Arena Stage in Washington, D.C.; Seattle Repertory Theatre; Berkeley Repertory Theatre; Alice Tully Hall at Lincoln Center, Manhattan; University of Arizona in Tucson; and University of Wyoming in Laramie – on October 12, 2009, the eleventh anniversary of Shepard's death. The sequel was also staged overseas in Spain, Australia, and Hong Kong.

Boston's Emerson College produced both *The Laramie Project* and *The Laramie Project: Ten Years Later* in its 2010-2011 season. [6]

* * *

Born and raised in Caracas, Venezuela, Moisés Kaufman is of Romanian and Ukrainian Jewish descent. He moved to New York in 1987, was awarded a Guggenheim Fellowship in 2002, and shortly thereafter founded the Tectonic Theatre Project, a company dedicated to experimentation with language and form in contemporary drama.

Among the plays that Kaufman wrote and developed at the Tectonic was *33 Variations,* which focuses on the latter period of Ludwig von Beethoven's life. It premiered at the Arena Stage in Washington, D.C. in 2007, ran at San Diego's La Jolla Playhouse in 2008, and presented on Broadway at the Eugene O'Neill Theatre, with Jane Fonda, in 2009. Kaufman's *Gross Indecency* covers the 1890s trials of Oscar Wilde, accused of homosexual sodomy with Lord Alfred Douglas. It debuted at Off Broadway's Greenwich House in February 1997, subsequently moved to the Minetta Lane Theatre, and had two stagings in Los Angeles, California, one at Mark Taper Forum in 1998, the other at the Electric Theatre in 2009.

Doug Wright's *I Am My Own Wife*, a one man play that explores the life of Charlotte von Mahlsdorf, a transvestite who survived both the Nazi and Communist governments in East Berlin, was directed by Kaufman for Off Broadway's Playwrights Horizons in 2003. It was transferred to the Lyceum Theatre later that year, making this Kaufman's Broadway directorial debut, and was one of *Time* magazine's Ten Best Plays of the Year. Kaufman's next major assignment was the staging of *Bengal Tiger at the Baghdad Zoo*, an allegorical drama by Rajiv Joseph about a tiger that haunts the streets of present-day Baghdad seeking the meaning of life. Living characters interact with the dead as the war explodes around them. The play debuted at the Kirk Douglas Theatre in Culver City, California in 2009, and subsequently ran at the Mark Forum in Los Angeles. A Pulitzer Prize finalist, it came to Broadway's Richard Rodgers Theatre in 2011, starring Robin Williams in the title role. Critic Charles Isherwood of the *New York Times* wrote that the production was "directed with gorgeous finesse by Moisés Kaufman."[7]

Other plays staged by Kaufman include *One Arm* (2004), based on an unproduced screenplay by Tennessee Williams; *Master Class* (2004), with Rita Moreno; Oscar Wilde's *Lady Windermere's Fan* (2005); and *Macbeth* (2006), featuring Liev Schreiber.

In 2006, Kaufman directed for TV's *The L Word* the episode "Lead, Follow, or Get Out of the Way", and in 2007 the episode "Lesson Number One." In 2010, he was nominated for the New York Drama Desk Award for Outstanding Director of the play *Bengal Tiger at the Baghdad Zoo* by Rajiv Joseph.

Acting Edition: Vintage Books.

Awards and Honors: The 2000 Off-Broadway production of *The Laramie Project* was nominated for the Drama Desk Award as a Unique Theatrical Experience. It won the Lucille Lortel Award for Best Play, the Outer Critics Circle Award for Best Off-Broadway Play, the Los Angeles Garland Award for Best Play, the Florida Carbonell Award for Best Play, the Bay Area Theatre Critics Circle Award for direction, and the Joe A. Callaway Award for Direction — endorsed by Kaufman's peers in the Society of Stage Directors and Choreographers. Kaufman's 2002 television adaptation of *The Laramie Proj-*

ect for HBO won the National Board of Review Award, the Humanities Prize, and a Special Mention for Best First Film at the Berlin Film Festival. The film also earned Kaufman two Emmy Award nominations for Best Writer and Best Director. In 1997, Kaufman received a Tony Award nomination for Best Direction of the play *I Am My Own Wife*. In 1999, he was named Artist of the Year by Venezuela's Casa del Artista. Ten years later, Kaufman's play *33 Variations* was nominated for a Tony Award for Best Play.

NOTES

1. Moisés Kaufman, *The Laramie Project* (New York: Vintage Books, 2001), vi.
2. *Ibid*, vii.
3. The play *Gross Indecency* (1997) by Moisés Kaufman focuses on the trials of Oscar Wilde at the end of the nineteenth century. The famed author was prosecuted under Section 11 of the Criminal Law Amendment Act of 1886, which had made "acts of gross indecency" between men a criminal offense.
4. *New York Times*, May 19, 2000.
5. *New York Times*, September 17, 2008.
6. The Matthew Shepard and James Byrd, Jr. Hate Crime Prevention Act, also known as the Matthew Shepard Act, is an American Act of Congress, passed on October 22, 2009, and signed into law by President Barack Obama on October 28, 2009. The measure expands the 1969 United States federal hate-crime law to include crimes motivated by a victim's actual or perceived gender, sexual orientation, gender identity, or disability.
7. *New York Times*, March 31, 2011.

II. The Trial Occurs Off Stage

The Living Corpse (c. 1900)

Leo Tolstoy (Russia, 1828-1910)

Tolstoy penned *The Living Corpse*, a drama founded on an actual court case, around 1900, but it was published and performed only after his death. The central character of the play, Fedor Protasov, is tormented by the belief that his wife, Liza, has not been at peace since choosing him over his rival for her hand, Victor Karenin. He wants to kill himself but doesn't have the nerve, and he runs away from home. After some time, his wife presumes Protasov dead and marries Karenin. When Protasov is discovered, Liza is charged with bigamy, accused of arranging her husband's disappearance. Protasov shows up in court to testify. When the judge rules that his wife must either give up her new husband, or be exiled to Siberia, Protasov shoots himself. Hysterically, Liza declares that it is Postasov whom she always loved.

The Living Corpse premiered at the Moscow Art Theater in 1911, co-directed by Vladimir Nemirovich-Danchenko and Constantin Stanislavski. It soon was translated into many languages and played in Berlin, Vienna, and Paris. The English-language premiere took place in London on December 6, 1912, under the title *The Man Who was dead*, a production by the Literary Theater Society helmed by A. Andreev, a guest director from Belgrade.

The play's first performance in the United States was a 1911 Yiddish-language production in New York, directed by and starring Jacob Adler, in a translation by Leon Kobrin. The show ran for four months and has been credited with reviving the fortunes of serious Yiddish-language theater in New York, after a period of six years in which lighter fare had dominated. After also playing in New York in a German-language production in 1916, the drama finally was performed on Broadway in English in 1918, under the title *Redemption*. Arthur Hopkins directed. John Barrymore played the lead role of Protasov.

The Red Robe (1900)

Eugene Brieux (France, 1858-1932)

"This play has an astounding theatrical force as it moves relentlessly to picture the perversion of justice by ambition, "writes theatre connoisseur Joseph T. Shipley in his *Guide to Great Plays*. "*The Red Robe* discloses the manner in which unscrupulous men in legal posts can bring ruin upon a family... Of the continuing dangers to justice in the ambitious designs of its supposed guardians, *The Red Robe* is a stirring dramatic picture."[1]

The Red Robe curtain rises on the drawing room of M. Vagret, a district attorney in provincial France. There, Mme. Vagret and her daughter, Bertha, are anxiously reading aloud the headlines of the local papers: "The Irissary Crime: Murderer still at Large!" and "Justice Asleep!"

Mme. Vagret bemoans the fact that the papers are sharply criticizing her husband, a prosecution attorney "in a court of the third class, just because he has never known how to play politics."

Bertha interjects, "Father is going to receive his promotion to a judgeship almost any day." But Mme. Vagret displays the red robe of a judge, which she bought a few years ago for her husband, only to be disappointed when he was bypassed. Sadly, she sends it to be stored with "some more moth balls," and all because of "this good-for-nothing murderer who refuses to be caught!"

Later that morning, Delorme, Vagret's assistant, arrives to inform Vagret that the tramp who is their only suspect in the very crime dominating the news — the slaying of an old man, M. Goyetche – has just been cleared and released. Delorme requests to be replaced— "The daily attacks in the newspaper are driving me mad...Criminal cases aren't tried nowadays by court but by the newspapers."

The Vagrets must now welcome dinner guests, one of whom is assistant prosecutor Mouzon, "forty years of age, moustached, handsome, energetic, suave." Despite the pretense of social ease, those present are all aware that M. Vagret is suffering official disfavor for his failure to secure convictions in three recent trials.

Mouzon asserts that "the Irissary murderer is not a tramp... this tramp, if there was one, would have eaten and drunk at the scene of the murder, either before or after the deed, but he didn't eat or drink...There is wine there, bread, food of various kinds, but he leaves without touching anything! Is that like a tramp? No! ...And why, above all else, does this tramp steal family papers which will give him away to the first policeman he meets? No, gentlemen, the criminal is not a tramp… You must look among those who would profit by the victim's death—relatives, friends, or debtors."

The dinner guests are impressed. Vagret assigns Mouzon to take charge of the case. Mouzon promises that "within three days the murderer will be under lock and key."

The second act takes place in the private office of Mouzon, now an examining magistrate. A new suspect is in custody – Jean-Pierre Etchepare – who has made it no secret around town that he believes himself to have been swindled by the dead man. There are even witnesses who will testify having heard him angrily threaten Goyetche.

"I didn't kill him!" protests Etchepare."I didn't leave my house!"

Mouzon summons the suspect's wife, Yanetta, who confirms her husband's alibi. But she is shocked at what comes next, for the zealous magistrate has a surprise to spring on her: "There was a girl in your name who once served a month's sentence in Paris for complicity in a case of theft," he announces, confident that she has long believed her past well buried.

Yanetta pleads with Mouzon not to expose this to her husband: "He'd go away, Sir, he'd leave me for good—he'd take the children with him…" Ignoring her desperate entreaties, Mouzon orders the couple arrested. As she is dragged out, Yanetta denounces him: "Butcher! Coward! Judas! … The poorer people are, the worse you treat them!"

The third act unrolls in Vagret's office. He enters, obviously troubled. Because of new information, he has decided to do "what any man of honor ought to do" – advise the jury of his skepticism about Etchepare's guilt.

The last act is set again in Mouzon's office. We learn that the trial ended in an acquittal. Vagret now reprimands Mouzon for having introduced the irrelevant but personally damaging information about Etchepare's wife. "You did a villainous thing," he tells his colleague.

Yanetta pleads with her husband to forgive her. "Never, never," he says. For ten years he has lived with a wretch, a liar, a thief. A Basque never pardons such sins. Demoralized, she agrees to let him take the children, begging only that he never reveal anything of their mother's indiscretion. In despair Yanetta accuses Mouzon of ruining her life.

Mouzon shrugs: "An officer of the law is not responsible."

Yanetta, now serving as the author's mouthpiece, proclaims: "Oh, you're not responsible? Then you can, whenever you feel like it, you can arrest people on a shadow of suspicion…you can shame and dishonor whole families, torture the unhappy, dig into their lives, parade their misfortunes, bring to light faults that are forgotten and paid for, faults that go back years. By your cunning, your tricks, your lies and your cruelty you can send a man to the foot of the scaffold, and what is worse, rob a mother of her little ones. And after that, like Pontius Pilate, you can say and you can really believe you're not responsible? Perhaps you're not responsible in the eyes of the law, as you say, but before Justice itself, before the Justice of decent people, before God's Justice, I swear to you, you are responsible; and that's why I'm going to demand a settlement!"

She draws closer to his desk where her hand accidently brushes against a paper knife. As Mouzon begins dismissively to examine files, Yanetta lashes out again: "Of an innocent man you almost made a convict, and of an honest woman, a mother, you make a criminal!" Suddenly aware of the power of the knife now clutched in her hand, she raises it — and, as if compelled by a force beyond her consciousness, strikes him vigorously in the chest. Curtain.

* * *

La Robe Rouge premiered at the Theatre du Vaudeville, in Paris, on March 15, 1900, running for sixty-four performances. Revived at the Theatre Francais on September 23, 1909, it played twenty-one times. Gabrielle Rejane, who appeared as Yanetta, took the production to London's Imperial Theatre on April 6, 1902, for a run of three performances, and later to New York's Lyric Theatre, where it ran, in the French original, from November 14 to December 3, 1904. The *New York Times* found the play to be a "powerful and intellectual arraignment of French law and lawyers... Mr. Brieux has the very rare combination of being at once a master of thought and of the drama. *La Robe Rouge* shows him at his best and most sympathetic." The critic lauded Rejane— "In feature and bearing Rejane was absolutely, remorselessly real."[2]

An English adaptation of *La Robe Rouge* by Bernard Miall, called *The Arm of the Law*, opened at London's Garrick Theatre on February 16, 1904, running seventy-eight performances, with Arthur Bourchier portraying Mouzon and Violet Vanbrugh playing Yanetta. The same leading actors appeared at the Garrick for one matinee on May 25, 1909. Bourchier once again appeared as Mouzon at His Majesty's Theatre on March 25, 1916, for thirty-two performances.

The first American English-language production of *La Robe Rouge*, now called *The Letter of the Law*, opened in Yonkers, New York, on January 14, 1920, and moved to Manhattan's Criterion Theatre on February 23, 1920, for eighty-nine performances. Lionel Barrymore, as Mouzon, won kind words from Alexander Woollcott for "a performance of consummate skill which he gives in an undistinguished and untempting part," while Doris Rankin was deemed by the critic an "indefensible choice for the crucial role of Yanetta—a part which cruelly overtaxes her strength as an actress."[3] *The New York World* stated, "This is a potent example of the good use to which the dramatic stage can be put when it raises its voice against social wrong."[4]

Homer Saint-Gaudens, who translated, adapted, and staged *The Letter of the Law*, took the liberty of changing the ending. In his version, Yanetta strikes Mouzon firmly and intentionally in the breast, quickly withdrawing the dagger. As Mouzon staggers towards her, almost touching her, he grabs the weapon, lunges, then falls dead in front of his desk. Slowly, Yanetta goes out .Moments later, a group of Mouzon's colleagues enters and sees the corpse. Exclaims one of them: "Dead! And the knife still in his hand! Killed himself on the eve of getting the red robe." The associates begin to discuss the now-pending bench vacancy, each claiming a right to it. As they exit, quarreling, one of them remains behind, standing over the body and staring at it, while the curtain falls.

The Red Robe was stripped of its French milieu in a 1956 adaptation by Randolph Goodman, who shifted the locale to the town of Whitfield, Mississippi. The plot parallels the Brieux play in nearly every aspect—but now the injustices to which we are witness are misprisions in the American system of law. Racial prejudice is the theme as ambitious politicians, judges, lawyers, and sheriffs engage in an unscrupulous conspiracy to convict an innocent Black man of murder.

***

Eugene Brieux, the son of a carpenter, rose above ordinary schooling through voracious reading and the study of Latin and Greek. He began to pen plays as a mere boy. When he had just turned twenty, his first play, *Bernard Palissy*, a one act in verse, was presented in Paris for a single performance. While supporting himself as a journalist, young Eugene continued to write for the stage. With Andre Antoine as his mentor and director, Brieux soon made his name with such comedies as *Blanchette* (1892) and *Les Trois Filles de M. Dupont (The Three Daughters of Mr. Dupont,* 1897*)*.

Plays by Brieux that contain criminal elements include the early *La Fille de Durame,* (*Durame's Daughter*, 1890), about a bandit who protects his daughter without revealing their true relationship; *L'Engrenage,* (*The Machine*, 1894), in which a small-town manufacturer, Remoussin, is persuaded to enter politics, then degenerates into corrupt practices, accepts bribes, and comes crashing down when the scandal is published. It is only when Remoussin returns the money, acknowledges his misdeeds, and resigns his post, that he can hold up his head once more as an honest man.[5]

Resultat Des Courses! (Racing results, 1898), depicts a Parisian bronze-worker, Chantaud, who, overcome by gambling fever, embezzles from his employer, is fired from his job, cannot get employment without references, drifts from bad to worse, and is eventually arrested as a vagabond.

Maternité (Maternity, 1903) spotlights a failed, fatal abortion which triggers a trial for child murder. In *Simone* (1908), a wife is murdered by her husband, and the secret is kept from their daughter for many years. In

L'Avocat (The Lawyer, 1922) an attorney, Edmund De Verron, is asked to defend Louise, his childhood sweetheart, after she is accused of killing her husband. Edmund becomes convinced that Louise is guilty of the crime but discovers that she committed the murder in order to stop her jealous spouse from shooting the man she loves—the attorney himself. Edmund obtains her acquittal, but the dark deed causes a chasm between them.

P.V. Thomas, in his study *The Plays of Eugene Brieux*, concludes that the playwright's "body of work herein considered is sufficient to establish his reputation, his career is a remarkable and an honorable one; it seems perfectly safe to say that one of the plays, at least, *La Robe Rouge,* is as good as anything in the dramatic production of contemporary France."[6] It may seem excessive today, but George Bernard Shaw declared that "After the death of Ibsen, Brieux confronted Europe as the most important dramatist west of Russia," and that "he is incomparably the greatest writer France has produced since Moliere ... a ruthless revealer of hidden truth and a mighty destroyer of idols."[7] Shaw's wife, in fact, was the translator of two Brieux plays, *Maternity* and *Woman On Her Own (La Femme Seule).*

Brieux was a social reformer who used the theater as his pulpit. In an interview in the *New York Times*, he declared: "I consider that the drama, like other forms of literature, may legitimately be used as an instrument for the amelioration of social conditions... My life's work is to use the theater in an endeavor to better the conditions, and my sincere wish, my greatest wish is that at the end of my life there may be a little less suffering on this earth."[8]

Time, however, has not been kind to his legacy. Notes one scholar, Albert E. Kalson, "To Brieux's credit, his works may well have played a part in social reforms of the period," yet, "as a dramatist he is remembered as an awkwardly moralizing clinician and outdated reformer."[9]

Awards and Honors: Eugene Brieux was named a commander of the Legion of Honor, and elected to the Academie Francaise in 1910.

NOTES

1. Joseph T. Shipley, *Guide to Great Plays* (Washington, DC: Public Affairs Press, 1956), 121-122.
2. *New York Times*, November 15, 1904.
3. *New York Times*, February 24, 1920.
4. *New York World*, February 24, 1920.
5. The theme of a naïve country man losing his integrity to big-city political machinery, leading to self-realization and mia culpa redemption, will

reappear during the decade in George Broadhurst's *The Man of the Hour*, 1906, and Clyde Fitch's *The City*, 1909.

6. P.V. Thomas, *The Plays of Eugene Brieux* (London: A.C. Fifield, 1913), 112.
7. George Bernard Shaw, preface to *Three Plays by Brieux* (London: Jonathan Cape, 1911), ix, xxvii.
8. *New York Times*, November 15, 1914.
9. Frank N. Magill, ed., *Critical Survey of Drama: Foreign Language Series* (Englewood Cliffs, New Jersey: Salem Press, 1986), 247.

The Witching Hour (1907)

Augustus Thomas (United States, 1857-1934)

Mysticism and murder are wed in *The Witching Hour* by Augustus Thomas, a prominent playwright at the turn of the twentieth century. The dramatic use of hypnotism and telepathy is said to have been inspired by Thomas's acquaintance with then celebrated mind reader Washington Irving Bishop. Thomas added these elements to an earlier one-act play, *A Constitutional Point*, in which a mother begs for leniency for a son convicted of a crime, and came up with the four-act *The Witching Hour*.

The play opens at the Louisville, Kentucky home of Jack Brookfield, a professional gambler who likes to bestow his hospitality on high-stakes players. Among the guests are Jack's sister, Alice Campbell, and her daughter, Viola, Mrs. Helen Whipple, a former flame of Jack's, and her son, Clay, who is in love with Viola. There is also Frank Hardmuth, an ambitious assistant district attorney.

Hardmuth, too, is interested in Viola. But when he tells Brookfield he wishes to marry her, her uncle objects: "She's only nineteen, you know… You're thirty-five." But, in fact, there is more to his reluctance than the simple matter of age difference. Jack believes that Hardmuth is not as upright as he seems and may be implicated in the recent murder of the state's governor.

During the course of the evening, a latecomer, Justice Prentice, discusses with Brookfield the topic of mind-reading, telling him he perceives him to have "a strong hypnotic ability." Later, Clay Whipple reacts superstitiously to the cat's eye worn by Tom Denning, a gambler who's had too much to drink. Together with Hardmuth, Denning teases the younger man, waving the stickpin in his face. As they continue to mock him, Clay grows more and more agitated. "Don't! I tell you, don't!" he pleads. But they ignore him. Frenzied, Clay picks up a paper knife from the desk and blindly strikes out, stabbing Denning. "I didn't mean to hurt him!" cries Clay, "Really, I didn't mean that!"

Nonetheless, his tormentor is dead.

Act two opens several months later in the Washington, D.C. home of Justice Prentice. Jack Brookfield arrives with Viola and Helen, thanking their host for the books he has sent him on thought transference. He describes the experiments he has begun to make with mesmerism, hypnotism, and clairvoyance.

Helen now shows them a letter revealing that her mother, Clay's grandmother, also had a pathological fear of cat's eye stones, an aversion inherited by her son. "It was insanity… He is not a murderer… but they have sentenced him… he—is to die." Judge Prentice promises to help when the case goes to the appeal court.

Back in Kentucky, Brookfield continues his esoteric studies and experiments. It is at this juncture that Hardmuth, now the district attorney, arrives to complain that Jack has been spreading lies about his involvement in Governor Scovill's killing. Jack responds not just by asserting that Hardmuth had indeed been the instigator of this political murder — which benefited his own career — but by taunting him with having pursued the death penalty for Clay as a way of removing a rival for Viola's affections.

Enraged, Hardmuth thrusts a gun against Brookfield's chest.

"Stop!" orders Jack, fixing his gaze upon his adversary. "You can't shoot that gun. You can't pull the trigger… You can't even hold the gun." His is exerting his psychic mastery over his visitor's will. Hardmuth drops the weapon.

Clay is acquitted. The play's twist comes in the last act when Jack allows Hardmuth to escape. "Long before Scovill was killed I thought he deserved killing and I thought it could be done just as it was done," he tells Helen. "I never breathed a word of it to a living soul, but Hardmuth planned it exactly as I dreamed it—and by God, a guilty thought is almost as criminal as a guilty deed." He confesses to her that, in some strange way, he's "always had a considerable influence" over Hardmuth and so must bear some of the blame for his actions. Helen promises to help Jack "to the limit."

* * *

Following a tryout engagement in Providence, Rhode Island, *The Witching Hour* opened at New York's Hackett Theatre on November 18, 1907, running 212 performances, with a second company soon taking it on the road successfully. The *New York Times* critic pronounced it "a really remarkable play," citing its "qualities of suspense, of ingenious complication and dexterous working out." He also went so far as to say that, of the other plays then running in the city, only one could be mentioned in the same breath — Henry Bernstein's hit, *The Thief*."[1]

In a follow-up piece, the *New York Times* reviewer goes on to state, "It is as ingeniously put together as a Chinese puzzle, and yet one is never in the position to say that the incident has been derived merely to create a suspense or to develop a surprise."[2] Among the cast, he singled out John Mason, as Jack Brookfield, and Russ Whytal, playing Justice Prentice.

The Witching Hour was transferred to the silent screen in 1916 and 1921 and remade as a talkie in 1934. A Broadway Television Theatre's production of the play was shown on May 12, 1953.

* * *

Augustus Thomas's father was the director of the St. Charles Theatre in New Orleans, and Thomas grew up in backstage atmosphere. He began writing plays at the age of fourteen, and by the time he was seventeen, he had established an amateur company. Before turning to full-time playwriting, Thomas was a page in the Forty-first Congress, the freight manager of several railroads, a reporter in St. Louis and New York, and editor of the *Kansas City Mirror*. His sixty-five scripts— one-acts, full-lengths and dramatizations of other sources— include other melodramas tinged with psychic phenomena: *Reckless Temple* (1890), *The Jucklins* (1897), *Harvest Moon* (1909), *As A Man Thinks* (1911), and *The Soul Machine* (1915).

Among Thomas's plays with crime or mystery themes are *Edith's Burglar* (1883), an early one-act adapted from a story by Frances Hodgson Burnett and later expanded into *The Burglar* (1897), which relates the influence of a little girl on a crook who mends his ways, and *Nemesis* (1921), in which a jealous husband stabs his faithless wife and pins the killing on her sculptor lover by securing, in clay, his fingerprints which he plants on the murder weapon–a nail file. *The Copperhead* (1918), based on a novelette by Frederick Landis, is a spy story set during the Civil War.

Thomas also injected suspense and mystery elements into a series of historical melodramas: *Alabama* (1890), *In Missouri* (1893), *Arizona* (1900), *Colorado* (1901), *Soldiers of Fortune* (1902, from a story by Richard Harding Davis), *The Ranger* (1907), *Rio Grande* (1916), and *Palmy Days* (1919).

Active in professional theatrical organizations, Thomas was president of the American Dramatists Association (1906-1911), president of the National Institute of Arts and Letters (1914-1915), and executive chairman of the Producing Managers Association (1922-1925). His autobiography, *The Print of My Remembrance,* was published in 1922.

In a critical study of Thomas's career, Ronald J. Davis asserts that unlike the customary blood-and-thunder melodramas of the era, "Thomas's plots are usually background for character and period studies. Action is subdued, situations and traditional climaxes are scarce, and curtains usually fall during quiet moments when a character's emotions rage within… Though his plays lack the universality that would lead to their effective staging today, they were instrumental in the evolution of the American drama from unrefined melodrama imitating foreign plays to skillfully constructed theme plays, American in subject and technique."[3]

Awards and Honors*:* *The Witching Hour* was a top-ten selection in *The Best Plays of 1899- 1909* ("It proved one of those lucky dramas to which fascinated adherents return again and again… It easily ran out the season in New York and was played for two or three seasons on tour").[4] In 1913, Augustus Thomas was awarded an American Academy of Arts and Letters Gold Medal.

NOTES

1. *New York Times,* November 21, 1907.
2. *New York Times,* November 24, 1907
3. Ronald J. Davis, *Augustus Thomas* (Boston: Twayne Publishers, 1984), 52, 125.
4. Burns Mantle and Garrison P. Sherwood, eds. *The Best Plays of 1899-1909* (New York: Dodd, Mead and Company, 1944), 272-273.

The Witness for the Defense (1911)

A.E.W. Mason (England, 1865-1948)

The setting for the first act of *The Witness for the Defense* is colonial India, in the head tent of a camp presided over by Stephen Ballantyne, an English sahib who obviously takes pleasure in drinking and abusing his wife, Stella. Ballantyne is armed and alert to the possibility of intruders bent on stealing an incriminating photograph he possesses. Into this volatile situation walks Henry Thresk, the man — though her husband does not know this — whom Stella once loved and would have married, had her family not pressured her to become Mrs. Ballantyne.

Ballantyne tells Thresk the story of the "compromising picture" and of the desperate men anxious to retrieve it, explaining that it must be carried for safekeeping back to London, where "the big-wigs at the India office" will know what to do with it. Thresk agrees to help by taking the photograph away with him.

After her former lover has made his exit, accompanied by Ballantyne, Stella begins to load her rifle. Upon re-entering, her husband taunts her, "Why don't you shoot yourself and rid me of a fool?" The first-act curtain falls as Stella points the weapon at him.

The second act finds Stella back in England, settled in a Sussex village and being courted by the respectable Richard Hazlewood. But word somehow gets out that, back in India, she had been charged with the murder of her husband, and acquitted, and this news turns Stella into "the curiosity, the freak" of Little Beding. Such attention does not please Richard's conventional family, and one of his uncles, a well-known solicitor, becomes interested enough in the Indian trial to study reports of it. Noticing that the crucial witness in the Ballantyne case, the one "whose evidence made the acquittal certain," is a barrister of his acquaintance, he suggests they invite him for the weekend. "I should very much like to put a question or two to Thresk," Richard's aunt says, approving of her husband's plan.

Thresk accepts, and agrees to review for them the events of the Indian courtroom, beginning with the fact that the prosecution had relied upon Stephen Ballantyne's reputation as a drunkard. He had "humiliated his wife in public and beat her in private. She went in terror of him… perhaps in a panic, very likely under extreme provocation, she seized the rook-rifle and put an end to the whole business."

Thresk goes on to say that the strategy of Stella's counsel had initially been to mount a plea of self-defense. However, his tactics had shifted upon the arrival of Thresk, who showed up to testify about the danger Ballantyne was in. Thresk had heard Ballantyne talk about the ruthless criminals bent on robbing him that very night.

Stella's acquittal followed this revelation.

Now Stella, with her future at stake, decides to risk everything. She confesses to Richard that, in fact, she did kill her husband, though her original thought had been to commit suicide. Remembering the scene, she describes how "he ran at me with his fist raised. I recoiled—he frightened me—and then, before he reached me—yes! . . . And then he fell and lay quite still."

Fearful that knowing the truth will cause Richard to leave her, instead — to her relief — she hears him loyally inform his father: "Stella has been trying to tell me something—often during the last weeks. I knew what it was… I knew very well."

* * *

When *The Witness for the Defense* premiered at London's St. James's Theatre on February 1, 1911, Act 1 ended with the killing of Stephen Ballantyne by his long-suffering wife, Stella. Following a run of 151 performances and a UK tour, the play crossed the Atlantic to the United States. During a three-month tryout period in the principal cities of the West and South, the shooting was eliminated; in the version that headed to Broadway, the first-act curtain descended, with thrilling suspense, upon a silent tableau of husband, wife and rifle.

The morning after it opened at the Empire Theatre in New York on December 4, 1911, the *New York Times* reviewer wrote: "Mr. Mason seems rather given to repetitions and postponements. There are many times when the storytelling seems to be starting at the end and working backwards..."[1] Yet, these reservations aside, he went on to praise the performance of Ethel Barrymore as Stella.

The Witness for the Defense ran for sixty-four performances. In 1913, Mason novelized the play, and in 1919 it was filmed by Paramount with Elsie Ferguson.

* * *

Born in Camberwell, London, Alfred Edward Woodley Mason was a student at Dulwich College and studied literature at Oxford University. Upon joining the Oxford Dramatic Society, he further developed his passion for the stage. Degree in hand, he was hired by a touring repertory company as an actor.

Returning to London, he went to work as a journalist, served as a Liberal member of Parliament, and was encouraged by such friends as Oscar Wilde and Anthony Hope in his writing, which would soon be his full-time occupation. Mason's first novel appeared in 1895, and he went on to publish more than thirty popular potboilers in a variety of genres, the best known of which is the adventure novel *The Four Feathers* (1902). His most enduring hero, however, is M. Hanaud, a detective with the French Sûreté, who made his debut in 1910's *At the Villa Rose* and appeared in four more books. Mason's plays with suspense elements include melodramas taken from his fiction, such as *At the Villa Rose* (1920), *Running Water* (1922), *The House of the Arrow* (1928), and *No Other Tiger* (1928). He died at the age of eighty-three, while at work on a biography of the celebrated seventeenth-century British admiral, Sir Robert Blake.

Acting Edition: Samuel French, Inc. (in manuscript form).

Awards and Honors: *At the Villa Rose* (1910) is included in Howard Haycraft and Ellery Queen's Definitive Library of Detective-Crime-Mystery Fiction.

NOTE

1. *New York Times*, December 5, 1911.

The Shadow (1913)

Eden Phillpotts (England, India-born, 1862-1960).

Following his intensely passionate *The Secret Woman*, Eden Phillpotts came up with another tempestuous drama, *The Shadow*, which likewise takes place among the simple folks of Dartmoor.

In the modest general store owned by Sarah Dunnybrig and her daughter, Hester, villagers discuss the disappearance of much-hated Jacob Waycott. His pony has been found with its neck broken, but the rider has vanished. "He is a very powerful rich man, and yet a very hard man where money's concerned," says Willes Gay, the butcher. "Would sell *The Primroses* off his mother's grave, that man."

Postmaster Thomas Turtle agrees: "He was a great devourer of widow's houses and merciless in his dealings."

A young farmer declares: "Father says if Mr. Waycott be gone dead, he'll hoist up his jubilee flag and go get drunk for joy."

Six months later, the poacher, Saul Coaker, discovers the decomposed body of Waycott at the bottom of an old mine, his skull fractured. Elias Waycott, the victim's nephew and would-be inheritor, is arrested for murder. Postmaster Turtle explains, "He and his old uncle were out, as we all know, and Jacob was heard to threaten Elias and swear to alter his will the very day before he disappeared. And so, Elias had everything to gain by cutting him short. And when he was the gamekeeper in those very woods, and knew every hole and corner, and had a right to be there. And he was there that identical day, and never denied it at the time."

Elias, gentle and educated, was courting Hester Dunnybrig, but the lass married Philip Blanchard, the rough and impassioned butcher's aide. While Elias is being tried, Philip confesses to Hester that he committed the crime: "But then I came to my own affairs and old Jacob stung like an adder and cursed my dead father and said I should have my teeth set on edge with his sour grapes. He goaded me to rage, Hester, and I lost myself and swung my stick and hit him down. Just one crack I gave him and no more. But it done the trick… Not a shadow haunted me, and never has. I went back home along and slept as sound as a saint… I only thought how much sweeter the world would be without that damned rogue in it. 'Twas no more to me than sticking a pig. My business be killing things, ban't it?"

When Elias is convicted on circumstantial evidence, Philip prepares his confession and is about to blow his brains out. However, word comes that

Elias, for love of Hester, made the sacrifice himself: while writing a goodbye letter, he asked the guard for a pen-knife to scratch out a word, and then dashed the weapon in under his ear and cut a vein.

Mournful, Philip still intends to commit suicide: "Shall I go on living among the people and let him rot, without even a stone to tell the world what he was? I be going to die, too, and join him afore the day's cold... I won't take his life. I won't smother and choke under such a fearful gift. Death's a holiday to that."

But Hester argues that Elias sent Philip a "reprieve from his grave... You can't die now. God's willed it and you can't kick against God... Shadows pass—shadows pass, I tell you—they can't hang still for all time. Never a thunder cloud but its darkness pass by... There's no righting wrong in the grave; there's no making good there... You've got to live with me—with me beside you always. That's what he willed—that's what he died for... Live-live-live!"

Philip gazes at her. Then he takes a pistol from his pocket, unloads it, and flings it aside. "I be going to go on living, Hester," he says. The curtain falls.

* * *

The Shadow was first presented by Miss Horniman's renown company at the Gaiety Theatre, in Manchester, on October 6, 1913, directed by Lewis Casson, with Sybil Thorndyke as Hester Dunnybrig. The production moved to London. The *London Times* reviewer called it "a tale of passion and crime," but questioned the "wonderfully eloquent expression" of the rural characters and objected to the "episodic discourses by the members of the 'comic relief'—the doleful butcher, the garrulous mother, and the oracular postmaster."[1]

The Shadow crossed the Atlantic almost a decade later, opening in New York's Klaw Theatre on April 24, 1922, only to be scoffed at by Alexander Woolcott in the *New York Times* as "A drowsy, ambling play" unfolding "in none too convincing form."[2]

NOTES

1. Quoted in *New York Times,* November 30, 1913.
2. *New York Times,* April 25, 1922.

The Letter (1927)

W. Somerset Maugham (England, France-born, 1874-1965)

When writing *The Letter*, W. Somerset Maugham was inspired by the actual case of Ethel Proudlock, an Englishwoman living in Kusla Lumpur, Malaysia, who shot a man who was presumably attempting to rape her. Prouflock's trial for murder "was the sensation of the day, and it was discussed at all the clubs, at all the dinner tables, up and down the peninsula from Singapore to Penang."[1]

As the curtain of *The Letter* rises on a plantation in the Malay Peninsula, Leslie Crosbie empties her six-chamber revolver into the prostrate body of Geoffrey Hammond. She then orders the head boy to get the assistant district attorney, John Withers, and to telephone her husband, Robert.

Sobbing hysterically, Leslie recounts to Robert, Withers, and attorney friend Howard Joyce that Hammond, a family acquaintance, arrived for a visit, kept drinking whiskey, became flirtatious, then suddenly declared his love for her and began to kiss her. His advances became more violent, she says, he seemed like a madman, then when she saw a revolver on the table, she snatched it. She doesn't remember anything else; she heard the shots one after the other.

Crosbie attempts to comfort his wife, telling her that she has done what any woman would have done in her place. Withers states that she behaved magnificently. They all believe that the inevitable official inquiry -the case of R. vs. Crosbie—will clear Leslie of any wrongdoing. It is known that Hammond has been living in his bungalow with a Chinese woman for the last eight months and it will turn public opinion against him.

But just as the trial commences, attorney Joyce learns from his confidential clerk, Ong Chi Seng, that a letter written by Leslie Crosbie was sent to Geoffrey Hammond on the day of his death, urging him to see her. The letter, revealing that Leslie's entire self-defense story is a fabrication, is in the possession of Hammond's mistress, who is willing to sell it for $10,000. Joyce travels to the Chinese quarter of Singapore and purchases the letter from the nameless woman.

The jury finds Leslie not guilty. During a joyful reception at home, Robert hears of the letter and insists on reading it. Cautioned by her husband, Leslie confesses that Geoff Hammond had been her lover for years. Lately he began to change — she heard he was living with a Chinese woman. She sent him a letter, told him she must see him. He came and announced that he was sick and tired of her and never wanted to see her again, so she seized the revolver and "fired and fired till there were no more cartridges." Deeply hurt but indicating that he is willing to forgive Leslie and move on with their lives, Crosbie leaves the room.

Joyce says to Leslie that since she demonstrated courage and strength to do evil, perhaps she will have the courage and the strength to do good. That will be her retribution. Leslie responds tearfully that doing good will not be her retribution. Her retribution is greater, she says, for with all her heart she still loves the man she killed.

* * *

The initial production of *The Letter*—at the Playhouse, London, on February 24, 1927—had a different last sequence. "To avoid tediousness," Maugham replaced Leslie's final confession with a "throwback," in which the climactic confrontation was actually played out. Gladys Cooper and Nigel Bruce enacted the mismatched Crosbies, under Gerald du Maurier's direction. "The play has quickness, variety and strength of attack," dispatched Charles Morgan of the *New York Times*, "but something is missing from it—a spontaneity and depth of feeling, which prevents it from being an important work of art."[2] *The Letter* ran for sixty weeks—including the provinces' tour—becoming one of Maugham's most popular successes in the English theatre.

Transplanted to New York, *The Letter* opened at the Morosco Theatre on September 26, 1927, staged by Guthrie McClintic, with Katherine Cornell and J.W. Austin as the Crosbies. Brook Atkinson, in the *New York Times*, called the play "a bristling, engrossing melodrama," though "perilously thin." The critic admired Maugham's "exotic colors of native life" and saluted Cornell's "vibrant, almost spectrally poignant" impersonation of "the woman in the case, treacherous and brazen," but sadly concluded that "after the final curtain one has a curiously disheartening suspicion that excellent talent in playwriting, acting and directing has been squandered here on pretty meretricious stuff."[3] *The Letter* was delivered during 104 performances, and then toured for the balance of the season.

The first continental performance of *The Letter* took place at the Budapest Vigszinbaz on October 14, 1927, with Mme. Freda Gombaszogi as Leslie. E.B. Jacobi reported that "the piece was very well received" and predicted "a long run."[4]

The Letter bowed in Paris in late October 1929. Phillip Carr, The *Times* reporter in France, announces that the local critics praised the play for "spirited and sustained movement in the development of the plot, as well as picturesque detail in the subsidiary Chinese characters."[5] American revivals of *The Letter* are sparse. Carrie Nye appeared as Leslie at the Studio Arena Theatre, Buffalo, New York, on April 4, 1980, for twenty-seven performances.

Stanley Richards selected *The Letter* for his *Best Mystery and Suspense Plays of the Modern Theatre.* "As in much of the author's work, illusions, stability, and especially fidelity not only can be threatened but more likely torn to revealing shreds in the exotic ambiance of the tropics. And so it was with Leslie Crosbie," writes Richards.[6]

In 1929, Jeanne Eagles, who triumphed in Maugham's *Rain,* played Leslie in a film adaptation of *The Letter,* directed by Jean De Limur. Since it was a transitional period, Paramount Pictures decided to make both a silent and sound version, Paramount also shot a French-language talkie, *La Lettre* (1930), and a Spanish replica, *La Carta* (1931). An Italian film version of *The Letter* was made in 1930, and a German version a year later. Bette Davis enacted Leslie in the atmospheric 1940 Warner Brothers remake—artfully scripted by Howard Koch, tautly directed by William Wyler, hauntingly scored by Max Steiner—wherein a full moon is hovering over the criminal infidelity seeping through the Malay Peninsula. The role of Hammond's Chinese woman, portrayed by Gale Sondergaard, was enlarged here, adding a tense confrontation between the woman and Leslie when they exchange letter and money. A new finale, meant to ensure that crime does not pay, has Leslie walking into the shrubbery knowing that the Chinese woman is waiting for her with a dagger in hand. The film was nominated for seven Academy Awards, including Best Picture, Best Director, and Best Actress, but won none. In 1947, Warner Brothers turned out a pale remake of *The Letter,* titled *The Unfaithful,* directed by Vincent Sherman, with Ann Sheridan in the title role.

Merle Oberon and Walter Huston starred as the Crosbies in a Lux Radio Theatre airing of *The Letter* in 1938. Lucky Strikes Theatre televised *The Letter* in 1950, with Madeleine Carroll. Broadway Television Theatre cast Sylvia Sidney with Gene Raymond in a ninety-minute adaptation. Producers' Showcase presented the play in 1956, featuring Siobhan McKenna, John Mills, Michael Rennie, and Anna May Wong. In 1982, Lee Remick and Jack Thompson appeared in a made-for TV feature.

* * *

William Somerset Maugham graduated in 1897 from St. Thomas' Medical School but instead of pursuing a medical career, he turned to writing. "Maugham felt, after his early struggles and even before he'd achieved fame, that he was born to write, that writing came as naturally to him as swimming to a fish," recounts biographer Jeffrey Meyers. "He loved the actual process of writing, and when the going was good — as it usually was — he couldn't get the words down fast enough... Maugham thought that writing, like drinking, was an easy habit to form and a difficult one to break... Aloof from other people, he immersed himself in his own creations, and his imaginary characters became so vivid that the real world became rather shadowy."[7]

With the publication of the novel *Liza of Lambeth* (1897), Maugham launched a distinctive sixty-five-year writing career. Among his more significant works are the novels *Of Human Bondage* (1915), *The Moon and Sixpence* (1919), *The Painted Veil* (1925), *Cakes and Ale* (1930), *The Narrow Corner* (1932), *Theatre* (1937), and *The Razor's Edge* (1944), as well as the short story collections, *The Trembling of a Leaf* (1921), *The Casuarina Tree* (1926), *Ah King* (1933), and *East and West* (1934). *Ashenden,* or *The British Agent* (1928), based on Maugham's experiences with British Intelligence, is composed of a series of WWI episodes, the torchbearers of realistic, non-romantic spy fiction.

Several of Maugham's novels and short tales contain elements of crime and mystery. During the 1950s, Maugham devoted himself to writing essays and his memoirs. "Maugham's legacy to other writers is an ideal of perfect craftsmanship, and a reassurance that an author can be extremely popular without sacrificing either his intelligence or his culture," writes Michael Wood in an Introduction to *The Letter.*[8]

Maugham penned thirty-two plays between 1902 and 1933. In 1908 he had four productions running simultaneously in London—*Lady Frederick, Jack Straw, Mrs. Dot* and *The Explorer.* His forte was neatly constructed comedies of manners, unfolding in London society, peppered with sardonic commentary on the battle of the sexes. *Our Betters* (1917), *The Circle* (1921), and *The Constant Wife* (1926) are considered to be Maugham's finest efforts. *The Sacred Flame* (1928) presents an argument in favor of euthanasia: a mother feeds her helpless, paralytic son a lethal overdose of sleeping pills to end his suffering. Following the presentation of *Sheppey* in 1933, Maugham surprisingly announces that he was quitting dramaturgy. Regrettably, he was true to his word.

Rain, Maugham's celebrated short story, was adapted to the Broadway stage by John Colton and Clemence Randolph in 1922. *Sadie Thompson,* a musicalization of *Rain* by Howard Dietz and Rouben Mamoulian, came to New York in 1944. During the 1969-1970 season, Sylvester Stallone appeared in a new version, by Ron Link, Off Broadway. The play was the basis for three films, starring Gloria Swanson, Joan Crawford, and Rita Hayworth.

Other stage conversions of Maugham works encompass *The Painting Veil* by Bartlett McCormac (1931), *Theatre* by Guy Bolton (1941), and *Jana,* by S.N. Behrman (1952). *Before the Party,* Rodney Ackland's 1949 adaptation of Maugham's short story of the same name, focuses on a desperate wife who slays her alcoholic husband with a parang.

Many of Maugham's stories have been transformed to the cinema, notably *Sadie Thompson* (1928), *Rain* (1932), *The Painted Veil* (1934), *Of Human Bondage* (1934), *The Moon and the Sixpence* (1942), *The Razor's Edge* (1946), the anthologies *Quartet* (1948) and *Trio* (1950), and the criminous *The Secret Agent* (1936), based on *Ashenden*, directed by Alfred Hitchcock, with John Guilgud in the title role. In addition, there are the movies *The Hour Before Dawn* (1944), a World War II romance-espionage directed by Frank Tuttle; and *A Christmas Holiday* (1944), a Deanna Durbin-Gene Kelly murder yarn directed by Robert Siodmak.

A surge of interest in Maugham's works brought to the screen new versions of *Up at the Villa* (2000), *Being Julia* (2004, adapted from the novel *Theatre*), and *The Painted Veil* (2006).

The series *Somerset Maugham TV Theatre* was broadcast first by CBS-TV, then moved to *NBC-TV*, during 1950 and 1951. In the UK, episodes of *W. Somerset Maugham* were telecast in 1969 and 1970. Many short stories by Maugham were adapted to *Four Star Playhouse*, *Great Mysteries*, and *Tales of the Unexpected.*

Acting Edition: *The Letter* is included in *Great Melodramas*, edited by Robert Saffron (New York: The Macmillan Company, 1966), and in *Best Mystery and Suspense Plays of the Modern Theatre*, edited by Stanley Richards (New York: Dodd, Mead and Company, 1971).

Awards and Honors: Commander, Legion of Honor, 1939; D.L.it. Oxford University, 1957; Fellow, and Companion of Literature, Royal Society of literature, 1961; Honorary Fellow, Library of Congress, Washington, D.C.; Honorary Member, National Institute of Arts and Letters.

NOTES

1. Jeffrey Meyers, *Somerset Maugham: A Life* (New York: Knopf, 2004), 180.
2. *New York Times,* March 3, 1927.
3. *New York Times,* September 27, 1927.
4. *New York Times,* October 30, 1927.
5. *New York Times,* November 17, 1929.
6. Stanley Richards, ed., *Best Mystery and Suspense Plays of the Modern Theatre* (Dodd, Mead and Company, New York, 1971), 265.
7. Jeffrey Meyers, *Somerset Maugham: A Life* (New York: Knopf, 2004), 37.
8. *The Letter* (Arno Press, New York, 1977), xiii.

Gods of the Lightning (1928)

Maxwell Anderson (United States, 1888-1959) and Harold Hickerson (United States, 1896-?)

During the nation's post-World War I red scare, two radicals of Italian descent, shoemaker Nicola Sacco (1891-1927), and fish peddler BartolomeoVanzetti (1888-1927), were indicted for the April 15, 1920, robbery and murder of a paymaster and his guard in Braintree, Massachusetts. They were found guilty despite contradictory evidence, and, after seven years of incarceration, were executed on August 23, 1927.

The cause célèbre, which to this day has spawned charges and counter-charges, debates and investigations, zeroes in on the biases of the period and brazen prosecutorial chicanery. The case fired Maxwell Anderson to pen two plays with the Sacco and Vanzetti case as background – *Gods of the Lightning* (1928), probing the crime and trial, and *Winterset* (1935), depicting an imaginary aftermath, years later, when a son of one of the executed men crusades to clear his father's name.

Set in a mill town on the eastern seaboard, *Gods of the Lightning* begins in Suvorin's grimy restaurant on the ground floor of the Labor Lyceum building. A raucous teamsters meeting is taking place in an adjacent hall. Among the characters that flit in and out are the labor agitators James Macready, fiery and belligerent, and Dante Capraro, gentler and more passive. They have just tussled with the police during a violent protest march. Macready thrusts a revolver into the hands of his fiancé, Rosalie Suvorin, the daughter of the restaurant's proprietor, saying, "Put that away for me, will you, kid?" He claims that a policeman tossed the weapon into his car in order to frame him.

From the street they hear, "Extra! Extra! Paymaster killed! Robbers escape with $28,000 belonging to Northfield Dock Company!" Spiker, a police informer masquerading as an ironworker, calls in the authorities to arrest Macready and Capraro.

Even though district attorney Salter believes that the case against Macready and Capraro is rather thin, political expediency dictates that he charge them as soon as possible. He is relying on Judge Vail, who "has been dead from the neck up for twenty-five years, and from the neck down for about forty."

Salter threatens Mrs. Lubin with exposure of her past as a madam unless she identifies Macready as the man who shot postmaster Kendall, next to the railroad tracks, from his car. Presumably Mrs. Lubin viewed the incident while standing at the front window of her nearby apartment. On the stand, defense attorney Gluckstein rebuts Lubin's testimony by reminding her that a signal tower blocks her view of the street.

Another eyewitness, eighteen-year-old Jerome Bartlett, is cajoled by the district attorney to identify Capraro as the man who escaped from the crime scene in a getaway car. Macready does not help his case when declaring defiantly on the witness stand that he believes the case is rigged, a conspiracy against the working man.

A surprise witness, Michael Suvorin, Rosalie's father, is sworn in and confesses to planning and executing, with a partner named Heine, the murder-robbery of the postmaster: He admits his guilt to save the innocent men. But the district attorney insists that this is a lie concocted to save the defendants.

Both Macready and Capraro are found guilty. Judge Vail pronounces the death sentence.

On the day of execution, the regulars at Suvorin's are hoping, praying—in vain—for the governor's reprieve. When the hands of the clock click midnight, hushed murmurs fill the room. "Don't whisper it! Don't whisper it!" cries Rosalie. "That's what they'll want you to do -whisper it—keep quiet about it—say it never happened—it couldn't happen—two innocent men killed—keep it dark—keep it quiet—No! No! Shout it! They're killing them! — Shout it! Shout it! Cry out! Run and cry! Only—it won't do any good—now." Curtain.

* * *

Gods of the Lightning, produced and staged by Hamilton MacFadden, opened at the Little Theatre on October 24, 1928. Advance reports drove Department of Justice officials to attend the premiere and take notes. The *New York Times* critic found it to be "a strong, harrowing drama,"[1] and complimented the performances of Charles Bickford as Macready, Horace Braham as Capraro, Leo Bulgakov as Suvorin, and—most notably—Sylvia Sidney as Rosalie. However, the production folded after twenty-nine showings.

Unfazed by its vigorous demands, a semi-professional troupe, Actor's Theatre, revived *Gods of the Lightning* at Off-Broadway's Provincetown Playhouse in February 1931. Among the promising young thespians were Robert Lewis and Sanford Meisner, both destined to play an important role in the development of the American theater.

Equity Library Theatre produced *Gods of the Lightning* on November 4, 1961, for ten performances. Theatre scholar Joseph T. Shipley viewed the work as "a rousing piece of propaganda. Like most propaganda, however, the play appeals only to those already convinced of the soundness of the cause it champions... There is, nevertheless, enough sound theatre in *Gods of the Lightning* to make it a forceful dramatic study of the powers-that-be destroying opposition through legal murder."[2]

* * *

James Maxwell Anderson's distinguished career is strewn with plays incorporating criminous elements, in both contemporary and historical settings: *White Desert* (1923), his first produced venture, is the tragic story of a lonely woman in the North Dakota prairies who is shot to death by a jealous husband; *Outside Looking In* (1925), based on Jim Tully's autobiographical *Beggars of Life,* is a picaresque comedy populated with rowdy hobos and tramps who live by their own code of the road; *Buccaneer*, (1925), written with Laurence Stallings , shows how Henry Morgan of the British navy turns pirate, later pardoned and knighted by King Charles II.

Webs of palace intrigue are the core of the Tudor trilogy *Elizabeth the Queen* (1930), *Mary of Scotland* (1933), and *Anne of the Thousand Days* (1948), as well as the period drama *Richard and Anne* (1955), inspired by Josephine Tey's 1951 novel of historical detection, *The Daughter of Time*, which attempts to clear the reputation of hunchbacked, demonized Richard III.

Both Your Houses (1933) is a study of intrigue, graft and corruption in congressional committees; *High Tor* (1937) is a comic fantasy about a nature-loving youth who refuses to sell his inherited rocky mountain and gets entangled with city slickers, crooked rogues, and bank robbers; *Key Largo (*1939) depicts a Loyalist Spanish crusader, who left his comrades behind, redeeming himself when clashing with ruthless gangsters in a Florida Keys hotel; *Lost in the Stars* (1949), based on Alan Paton's novel, *Cry the Beloved Country*, with a score by Kurt Weill, is the epic saga of a Black parson whose son murders a British planter's son, unfolding against the background of racial animosities in South Africa. In *Barefoot in Athens* (1951), Socrates goes on trial for his life, charged by zealots for corrupting the minds of youth. *Bad Seed* (1954), adapted from the William March novel, is a shocker about inherited evil; *The Day the Money Stopped* (1958), cowritten with Brendan Gill, based on his novel, is about the black sheep of a respectable Connecticut family who resorts to blackmail when left out of his father's will.

Between 1924 and 1958, Anderson also penned a potpourri of non-crime plays—tragedies, dramas, comedies, fantasies, and musicals—some in verse, others in prose; some historical, others contemporary; some hitting the theatrical jackpot, others fizzling fast — all devoted by him "to the exaltation of the spirit of man."

The artists who mounted Maxwell Anderson's plays throughout thirty-five years of productivity represent the who's who of Broadway—directors Arthur Hopkins, Guthrie McClintic, George Cukor, Lee Strasberg, Worthington Miner, John Houseman, Joshua Logan, Harold Clurman, Margo Jones, H. C. Potter, and Reginald Denham; designers Jo Mielziner, Lee Simonson, Robert Edmond Jones, Howard Bay, Boris Aronson, and George Jenkins; actors James Cagney, Ruth Gordon, Humphrey Bogart, Luther and Stella Adler, Franchot Tone, Paul Muni, Jose Ferrer, Uta Hagen, Alfred Lunt, Lynn Fontanne, Helen Hayes, Katharine Cornell, Burgess Meredith, Peggy Ashcroft, Hume Cronyn, Lillian Gish, Edmund O'Brien, Walter Huston, Karl Malden, Lotte Lenya, Marlon Brando, Ingrid Bergman, Rex Harrison, Nancy Kelly, Richard Basehart, and Viveca Lindfors.

Several of Anderson's plays were adapted to the screen: *Winterset* (1936); *Elizabeth the Queen*, filmed as *The Private Lives of Elizabeth and Essex* (1939); *Knickerbocker Holiday* (1944); *Joan of Lorraine*, retitled *Joan of Arc* (1948); *Key Largo* (1948); *Anne of the Thousand Days* (1969); *The Bad Seed* (1956); *Lost in the Stars* (1974).

Anderson scripted a television version of *A Christmas Carol* (1954) from the story by Charles Dickens, a few radio plays between 1937-1944, and, with others, the motion pictures *All Quiet on the Western Front* (1930), *We Live Again* (1934), *So Red the Rose* (1935), *Joan of Arc* (1948), and *The Wrong Man* (1957).

The prolific author also wrote the verse volumes, *You Who Have Dreams* (1925) and *Notes on a Dream* (1971) as well as the nonfiction *The Essence of Tragedy* (1939), *The Bases of Artistic Creation*, with Rhys Carpenter and Roy Harris (1942), and *Off Broadway* (1947). In 1938, he joined S. N. Behrman, Sidney Howard, Elmer Rice, Robert Sherwood, and John Wharton to form the Playwrights' Company.

The *New York Times* obituary of March 1, 1959, noted that Anderson "looked upon the theatre as the central artistic symbol of the struggle of good and evil within men. Set a man on the stage, he once said, and you know instantly where he stands morally with the race. The theatre to Mr. Anderson… was an affirmation also that men have within themselves the beasts from which they descend and the God toward which they climb."[3]

Awards and Honors: Pulitzer Prize—*Both Your Houses*, 1933. New York Drama Critics' Circle Award—*Winterset* (1935-1936), *High Tor* (1936-1937). Top-ten selections in the *Best Plays* yearbook—*What Price Glory?* (1924-1925), *Saturday's Children* (1926-1927), *Gypsy* (1928-1929), *Elizabeth the Queen* (1930-1931), *Both Your Houses* (1932-1933), *Mary of Scotland* (1933-1934, *Valley Forge* (1934-1935), *Winterset* (1935-1936), *High Tor* (1936-1937), *The Star-Wagon* (1937-1938), *Key Largo* (1939-1940), *Candle in the Wind*

(1941-1942), *The Eve of St. Mark* (1942-1943), *Storm Operation* (1943-1944), *Joan of Lorraine* (1946-1947), *Anne of the Thousand Days* (1948-1949), *Lost in the Stars* (1949-1950), *Barefoot in Athens* (1951-1952), *Bad Seed* (1954-1955). Nineteen *Best Play* entries put Anderson ahead of George S. Kaufman, who has had fifteen, and Eugene O'Neill, who has had eight. American Academy of Arts and Letters Gold Medal, 1954.

NOTES

1. *New York Times*, October 25, 1928.
2. Joseph T. Shipley, *Guide to Great Plays* (Washington, D.C.: Public Affairs Press, 1956), 25.
3. *New York Times,* March 1, 1959.

Winterset (1935)

Maxwell Anderson (United States, 1888-1959)

Maxwell Anderson, champion of lost causes and crusader for justice, returns to the Sacco-Vanzetti case, which had previously inspired his *Gods of the Lightning* (1928).

Winterset, arguably Anderson's finest achievement in poetic drama, offers an imaginative aftermath to the case. It is set thirteen years after the trial. Bartolomeo (Mio) Romagna, the son of an Italian-American radical wrongly executed, arrives on the East River waterfront in search of Garth Esdras, a witness to the murder who can clear his father's name. Also roaming the alleys are Trock Estrella, the actual killer; his henchman Shadow; Judge Gaunt, who had handed down the verdict, cracking beneath the pressure of conscience; and various vagrants, sailors, and ladies of the night.

Nearby, in a grimy tenement apartment, Garth, his father Rabbi Esdras, and teenage sister Miriamne, are preparing for their Sabbath dinner, when Trock and his men suddenly throw open the door. Trock asks Garth if he has turned state's evidence, but Garth denies it, reminding the gangster that the case was closed. Trock warns Garth to stay home and keep mum.

Garth confesses to his family that he was once a member of a gang and party to a bank robbery. He saw Trock Estrella shoot a paymaster. Afraid for his life, he never mentioned it.

Mio and Miriamne meet at a pier of Brooklyn Bridge and fall in love. Miriamne pleads with Mio to take her away from this gloomy environment. Somewhere, she says, there must be a sunny place for the two of them. But Mio remains steadfast in his quest, vowing that nothing will stir him away from the path of clearing his father's name.

Trock, afflicted with lung cancer and given but six months to live, sends his bodyguards after an insurgent Shadow to protect his turf. Mio confronts Trock, declaring that even though his father and Shadow are dead, they cannot be kept down; they, and all the other Trock victims, will rise up against him with their heads shot off and their entrails dragging. Trock loses his equanimity and when Mio accuses him of killing the paymaster, he retorts that it was not him but Shadow who shot the man. "Now I know!" exclaims Mio, "Now I know!"

Mariamne implores Mio for her brother. Garth has been punished enough, she says, his life has been torment to him. Love wins. When Mio has a chance to call the police and vindicate his father, he relents. He tells

Miriamne that he has lost his taste for revenge, that he is waking from a long trauma of hate.

"Mio of *Winterset*, emotionally crippled by lust for revenge, becomes a complete person only when he accepts love," concludes Barbara M. Perkins.[1] But it is too late for the Romeo and Juliet of the tenements. A burst of machine gun bullets hit Mio fatally, and when Miriamne, in anguish, calls out, "You! There! You in the shadows—You killed him to silence him! But I'm not silenced!," the deadly weapon speaks again. Miriamne sinks to her knees, crawls toward Mio, and dies next to him. Esdras and Garth mourn over the young bodies when the curtain comes down.

* * *

Winterset opened at the Martin Beck Theatre on September 25, 1935, to contradictory reviews. Enthusiastic supporters included Brooks Atkinson who felt that "*Winterset* lives on a plane of high thinking, deep emotion and eloquent writing. It is packed with terror. It is a courageous poem to justice and integrity. In short, it is beautiful."[2] Gilbert Gabriel applauded the "fiercely living verse, cramming its classic form with phrases of extraordinary color and high temperature."[3] Richard Lockridge admired "a poetic tragedy of sullen beauty;"[4] And John Mason Brown said, "I can no longer deny—or resist—the strange and fascinating spell which Mr. Anderson's drama is able to cast over those who sit before it."[5]

Among the naysayers were Percy Hammond who called it "a murky drama;"[6] Robert Garland who found it to be "a murder melodrama in masquerade, a gun-and-gangster thriller with poetic aspirations;"[7] and John Anderson who complained that there was but "one superlative scene in the second act... the rest of the evening lost in articulate emptiness."[8]

There was unanimous acclaim for the staging by Guthrie McClintic; the settings by Jo Mielziner; and the performances of Burgess Meredith as Mio, Margo as Miriamne, and Eduardo Cianelli as Trock. All three were recruited to repeat their roles in a 1936 movie version. *Winterset* ran 179 performances, returning, with some cast changes, for sixteen more.

Equity Library Theatre brought back *Winterset* in 1952, and Yale University in 1959. The American Revival Company produced, with special permission by Mrs. Gilda Andersom, the American Revival Company produced, under Amnon Kabatchnik's direction, with set design by Richard Bianchi, an Off-Broadway resurrection at the Jan Hus Playhouse on February 9, 1966, for thirty performances. Herbert Kupferberg, asserted, "*Winterset* still manages to be an affecting drama of people seeking justice in an unjust world... how many plays can evoke the same warmth, a warmth which has not yet died out."[9] Richard Watts Jr. wrote that Anderson's "lyric tragedy based on memories of the famous Sacco and Vanzetti case proved to be still a social melodrama of considerable intensity and power."[10] William Glover concurred: "Still grips because of sinewy writing and the dateless tensions invoked."[11] *Cue Magazine* appreciated "an authentic, powerful revival of Anderson's tale of a young man's passion to avenge his father's unjust death."[12]

However, Stanley Kauffmann lamented, "I thought it poor when I saw it 31 years ago, and I think it poor now."[13] Jack Thompson concluded, "the play has definitely aged" and "the revival lacks spark."[14]

The Traveling Puerto Rican Company presented a slightly modified version of *Winterset* at the Carver Amphitheatre on July 22, 1969, launching a tour of twenty-five performances in Manhattan, Brooklyn, the Bronx, and Queens. Ramon Gordon directed a cast of twenty, headed by Miriam Colon, Chico Martinez, Muni Seroff, and Wendell Phillips. The Jean Cocteau Repertory tackled the free verse play at the Bouverie Lane Theatre on April 22, 1999, under the direction of Eve Adamson, eliciting from Wilborn Hampton the endorsement, "a stark yet gripping revival that makes a strong case for giving Anderson more serious attention."[15]

Joseph T. Shipley states, "*Winterset* saw beyond the immediate facts of that wrong into the larger issues of faith, justice, and integrity. When the sin of their father is visited upon the sons and daughters of *Winterset*, Anderson achieves, not the flare of indignation that was his *Gods of the Lightning*, but the even flame of steadfastness and truth. Even his verse is ennobled by the depth and fullness of his perception. His language is at his simplest, most effective, and most beautiful."[16]

* * *

Additional plays inspired by the Sacco-Vanzetti case include *The Advocate* by Robert Noah (1963); *Sacco-Vanzetti* with book and lyrics by Armand Aulicino, music by Frank Gaskin (1969); and *Sacco and Vanzetti* by Marketta Kimbrell (1976). The cause célèbre also serves as a catalyst in the college comedy, *The Male Animal,* by James Thurber and Elliott Nugen (1940).

Acting Edition: Dramatists Play Service.

Awards and Honors: The first New York Drama Critics Circle Award, 1935-1936. A top-ten selection in *The Best Plays of 1935-1936* ("The play is written in that inspiring verse which gave so much beauty and eloquence to *Elizabeth the Queen* and *Mary of Scotland*").[17]

NOTES

1. James Vinson, ed., *Great Writers of the English Language: Dramatists* (New York: St. Martin's Press, 1979), 12.
2. *New York Times*, September 26, 1935.
3. *The New American*, September 26, 1935.
4. *New York Sun*, September 26, 1935.
5. *New York Post*, September 26, 1935.
6. *New York Herald Tribune*, September 26, 1935.
7. *New York World-Telegraph*, September 26, 1935.
8. *New York Journal-American*, September 26, 1935.
9. *New York Herald Tribune*, February 10, 1966.
10. *New York Post*, February 10, 1966.
11. *Associated Press*, February 10, 1966.
12. *Cue Magazine*, February 19, 1966, p. 16.
13. *New York Times*, February 10, 1966.
14. *New York Journal-American*, February 10, 1966.
15. *New York Times*, April 23, 1999.
16. Joseph T. Shipley, *The Crown Guide to the World's Great Plays* (New York: Crown, 1956; revised and updated, 1984), 19.
17. Burns Mantle, ed., *the Best Plays of 1935-1936* (New York: Dodd, Mead and Company, 1936), 32.

The Winslow Boy (1946)

Terence Rattigan (England, 1911-1977)

Ronnie Winslow, a thirteen-year-old cadet at an English naval academy, is accused of stealing and cashing a five-shilling postal order. He is expelled. Ronnie's father, a stern banker, believes the boy's pleas of innocence and wages a stubborn struggle to clear his name. The father withstands the scorn of neighbors and the objection of other family members to pursue the case. It becomes a national issue, debated in Parliament, with the Winslow boy eventually defeating the Crown.

The Winslow Boy is based on the real life case of George Archer-Shee, which caused a furor in England prior to World War I. There were those who pooh-poohed it as an idiotic crusade, but others hailed the "cause célèbre" as a milestone step in protecting the honor and rights of the individual.

Stated Rattigan, "In *The Winslow Boy*, the drama of injustice and of a little man's dedication to setting things right, seems to have more pathos and validity just because it involved an inconsequential individual."[1]

Rattigan keeps the tumult and the fireworks at the House of Lords off-stage. The action of the play, extending over two years, takes place entirely in the drawing room of the Winslow home in Kensington. There is a great deal of exposition while relating the mushrooming events, but the playwright leisurely and confidently keeps things moving forward to a suspenseful and heartwarming climax.

The Winslow family is vividly portrayed, and its sacrifices are touching—the father, Arthur, loses his health and his money; Ronnie's brother, Dickie, must forgo a college education; his sister, Catherine, is jilted by her fiancé; the mother, Grace, almost yields to the mounting pressures, and comes close to abandoning her loyalty.

It is Sir Robert Morton (in real life—Sir Edward Carson), one of the most famous attorneys in Britain, who takes it upon himself to fight the Admiralty, the government bureaucracy, and the political establishment, declaring: "Let Right Be Done".

When Sir Robert brings the news of Ronnie's complete vindication, Arthur Winslow prepares to meet with the frenzied press. He is not sure what to say – happy to have lived long enough to have seen justice done to his son? Or, this victory is not his; it is the people who have triumphed? Winslow does not want to seem pretentious. He will merely declare what he really feels: "Thank God we beat 'em."

* * *

The Winslow Boy was first produced, for a short run, at the Theatre Royal in Brighton, on February 25, 1946. On May 23 the play was presented at the Lyric Theatre in London, under the direction of Glen Byam Shaw. John Gielgud and Eric Portman rejected the role of Sir Morton because they thought it too minor—the barrister does not appear until the tag end of the second act. Finally, Emlyn Williams undertook the part. The Lord Chamberlain insisted that the program include a note: "This play is based on a famous case, but the characters are all fictitious".

The critics were divided. Elpseth Grant felt that "In *The Winslow Boy*… Terence Rattigan for the first time does full justice to himself as a serious dramatist,"[2] while J.C. Trewin wrote, "It is, in effect, a Petition of Right, a plea for the liberty of the individual: Mr. Rattigan has vigorously wedded doctrine and drama,"[3] and Paul Dehn commented, "This play is completely real. Mr. Rattigan's writing makes no empty gesture to the gallery."[4]

Among the skeptics was Ernest Betts: "It does not quite live up to the story that thrilled the country in 1908."[5] And the *Daily Mirror* wrote, "The theme of individual liberty ought to be enough for any dramatist, but Mr. Rattigan was not to be denied his clichés."[6]

The Winslow Boy remained at the Lyric for 478 performances before embarking on a provincial tour and crossing the Atlantic to anchor at the Empire Theatre in New York City, on October 29, 1947. Here, too, the reception was mixed. Howard Barnes like it: "A richly satisfying drama. In it the author has dramatized a celebrated defense of individual rights with deep feeling, humor and passion."[7] So did Robert Coleman: "It is a play notable for integrity, honesty and decent emotions. It is a production notable for uniformly fine acting. It is a tribute to justice, something all too often lacking on parts of this globe today."[8] Ward Morehouse called it "A play of force and dignity,"[9] and William Hawkins wrote, "It is a shrewd play, compelling, suspenseful and inspiring."[10] Richard Watts, Jr. complimented the playwright: "It is to Mr. Rattigan's credit that he makes it not only effective dramatically but gives it a completely credible air of gallantry."[11]

On the other side, Brooks Atkinson expressed his disappointment: "For it is disillusioning to discover that Mr. Rattigan is only a practicing playwright when the occasion calls for an artist… Mr. Rattigan's hackneyed technique very nearly conquers his convictions in his anti-climactic conclusion".[12] Louis Kronenberger theorized that "like Noel Coward, Mr. Rattigan often thinks he is being serious when he is only being sentimental; and his keenly-developed sense of theatre makes him unable to resist anything—relevant or irrelevant, high-pitched or low-pitched—that he suspects may get across."[13] John Chapman raspberried the play: "Being a newspaper reader, I have long been aware that Britain has been having little in the way of food, clothing, tobacco and American money. And it can't be having very much in the way of shows either, if *The Winslow Boy* can have had—as it really did—a long West End run and the British equivalent of the Pulitzer Prize, the Ellen Terry Award…it is just about as exciting as watching aillow fight."[14] In an extraordinary reversal, Chapman selected *The Winslow Boy* as one of the ten best plays of 1947 to 1948: "On first viewing I found it less absorbing than did most," conceded Chapman, "but on subsequent readings I discovered its sound workmanship."[15]

The Winslow Boy had a respectable New York run of 215 performances. The play was revived by the Alley Theatre in Houston, Texas (1961); the Barter Theatre in Abington, Virginia (1969); and The Roundabout Theatre Company in Manhattan (1980). Kenneth More portrayed Sir Robert Morton in a 1970 London replica that raised its curtains for 243 performances. Successful productions of *The Winslow* Boy were mounted in France, Germany, Switzerland, Czechoslovakia, Hungary, Greece, Australia, South Africa, Israel, and the Scandinavian countries.

"Few caught the relationship of Rattigan's plot to that of a thriller," observes Holly Hill in her doctoral dissertation. "*The Winslow Boy* is technically a domestic drama, but by posing questions from the moment the curtain rises: Why is Ronnie upset? What will Arthur do when he finds out? Will Sir Robert take the case? Will the petition be endorsed? — Rattigan makes the issue of 'Will right be done?' as theatrical as any variant of Whodunit. He does more than this, however, for he combines the mounting suspense of a thriller plot with serious moral concerns."[16]

A glowing British movie version, in 1948, scripted by Rattigan and Anatole de Grunwald, directed by Anthony Asquith, starred Robert Donat as the defending barrister and Cedric Hardwicke as the beleaguered father. While in the play the actual trial is never seen, the motion picture boasts a superior debate sequence in the House of Lords. David Mamet, the enfant terrible of stage and screen, scripted and directed a surprisingly tame remake in 1999, with Jeremy Northam as Sir Robert, Nigel Hawthorne as Arthur Winslow, and Rebecca Pidgeon as Catherine.

The Winslow Boy was televised in England thrice: Peter Cushing portrayed Sir Robert in 1958; Emlyn Williams repeated his stage performance as Sir Robert in 1961; Alan Badel enacted the role in 1977. In the U.S., *The Winslow Boy* was presented by *Du Pont Show of the Month* on November 13, 1958, featuring Frederic March, Florence Eldridge and Siobhan McKenna as Arthur, Grace and Catherine Winslow, respectively, with Noel William portraying Sir Robert. *The Archer-Shee Case* was televised by *TV Reader's Digest*, ABC, on October 31, 1955, with Cedric Hardwicke as the father and Henry Daniell as Sir Edward Carson.

Acting Edition: Dramatists Play Service.

Awards and Honors: Ellen Terry Award, 1947; New York Drama Critics Circle Award as Best Foreign Play, 1947-1948; a top-ten selection in *The Best Plays of 1947-1948*. Other Ratigan top-ten entries in the Burns Mantle yearbook: *O Mistress Mine*, 1945-1946, and *Separate Tables*, 1956-1957. Commander, Order of the British Empire (C.B.E.), 1958. Knighted, 1971.

NOTES

1. Harry Hyams interview, *Theatre Arts*, November 1956.
2. *Daily Sketch*, London, May 24, 1946.
3. *Observer*, London, May 26, 1946.
4. *Sunday Chronicle*, London, May 28, 1946.
5. *DailyExpress*, London, May 24, 1946.
6. *Daily Mirror*, London, May 30, 1946.
7. *New York Herald Tribune*, October 30, 1947.
8. *Daily Mirror*, New York, October 30, 1947.
9. *The Sun*, New York, October 30, 1947.
10. *New York World Telegram*, October 30, 1947.
11. *New York Post*, October 30, 1947.
12. *New York Times*, October 30, 1947.
13. *PM Exclusive*, New York, October 31, 1947.
14. *Daily News*, New York, October 30, 1947.
15. John Chapman, ed., *The Best Plays of 1947-1948* (New York: Dodd, Mead and Company, 1948), 8.
16. Holly Hill, *A CriticalAnalysis of the Plays of Terence Rattigan* (a dissertation submitted to the Graduate Faculty in Theatre, The City University of New York, 1977), 126.

The Gioconda Smile (1948)

Aldous Huxley (England, 1894-1963)

Jealousy, murder, a frame-up, and a nick-of-time confession are the ingredients of *The Gioconda Smile*, a grim psychological melodrama peppered with social overtones of guilt and punishment.

The Gioconda Smile was first penned by Huxley as a short story included in his masterful collection *Mortal Coils* (1922), then adapted by him to the screen in 1947 as *A Woman's Vengeance*, a notable achievement directed by Zoltan Korda. Huxley later developed *Gioconda* as a play.

Janet Spence, middle-aged and neurotic, poisons the invalid wife of Henry Hutton, a wealthy squire, in the belief that he will marry her. When instead he weds a younger rival, Doris Mead, Spence provides testimony designed to send the innocent man to the gallows.

The Gioconda Smile is somewhat heavy-handed. Scattered philosophical tidbits crowd the plot — "Cynicism is simply confession without repentance;" "The richer people are, the more they value money" — as do verse quotations from Shelley and Shakespeare. However, the last act, taking place on the night of Hutton's execution, is tense and memorable. Dr. James Libbard, the family physician, is convinced of Janet's' guilt, but his efforts to elicit a confession are blocked by the twisted woman, the Mona Lisa of the narrative. Spence is unaware that the doctor has advanced her living room's clock by one hour.

Dr. Libbard draws Spence's attention to the clock. It marks two minutes to eight, zero hour. Spence muses that everything must be ready on the scaffold - the rope, the straps. The warden and the chaplain are probably walking along the corridor, approaching Hutton's cell, unlocking it. And it is all because of a twenty-two-year-old woman, says Spence bitterly, because of her mouth, because of her skin. It isn't fair.

The clock strikes eight. Janet moans and collapses into an armchair. Dr. Libbard soothes her, saying that it is all over, she can go to sleep now. He rolls up her sleeve, dips a piece of cotton wool in a small bowl, rubs the inside of Janet's forearm, and asks quietly how she got Doris Mead to take the poison. Exhausted by tension and pangs of remorse, Spence says, "I put it in her coffee."

Dr. Libbard does the injection, tells Spence that she can sleep now, replaces the syringe on a tray, takes another piece of cotton wool, wipes her arm, and watches her intently for a few minutes to make sure she is asleep. He calls for the nurse to dial Whitehall four-six-five-six, takes the telephone receiver from her, and asks for the Home Secretary: "it's Dr. James Libbard speaking. He is expecting me to call him before seven-thirty… Connected with the Hutton case. Extremely urgent… Thank you. I'll wait." Curtain.

* * *

The Gioconda Smile premiered at the New Theatre, London, on June 3, 1948, with Clive Brook as Henry Hutton, Pamela Brown as Janet Spence, and Noel Howlett as Dr. Libbard. The reception was warm enough (296 performances) to warrant several follow-up productions on the continent. The play crossed the Atlantic and opened in New York's Lyceum Theatre on October 7, 1950, with Basil Rathbone, Valerie Taylor and George Relph. Shepard Traube, the Hitchcockian director of several Broadway suspense melodramas, helmed his company "with relish." Critic John Chapman said, "It is easy to see why Mr. Traube has brought us *The Gioconda Smile*, for it was he who presented the memorable *Angel Street*. The two plays are alike in the tension which grows while justice plugs along in its determined English fashion. And like its superior predecessor, *The Gioconda Smile* is not a whodunit.There is no tricky concealment of fact or circumstance from the audience. The suspense comes from waiting for justice to come to the proper conclusion – and hoping that it will arrive there in time."[1]

William Hawkins theorized: "what lifts this play well out of the thriller class, is that the events develop and illuminate the characters, but the people are never made into accommodations of the plot. They have a life of their own and this brings the performance a lot of subtle tension… There is a mechanical trick with a clock, toward the end, that seems obvious but is utterly absorbing. The final confession comes within about 90 seconds of the final curtain."[2]

Other critics were less obliging. "Aldous Huxley has created a curiously disappointing liaison between metaphysics and melodrama," lamented Howard Barnes. "On the whole it is neither arresting nor profound… *The Gioconda Smile* is literate and well served by the performing and the staging, but it is a limp melodrama."[3] Brooks Atkinson stated in his opening remarks that "although Aldous Huxley is a professional man of letters, he is an amateur on the stage… Despite the effectiveness of the basic story, Mr. Huxley has written a cluttered drama that alternates between hokum and pretentiousness."[4] Robert Coleman found it "hard to believe that the Huxley who fascinated us with *Limbo*, *Chrome Yellow* and other works could also have penned so undistinguished a script as this."[5]

The Gioconda Smile was wiped off at the Lyceum after forty-one performances. The play will probably remain a footnote in the legacy of the author who composed the prophetic novel *Brave New World* (1932), the savage doomsday science-fictional *Ape and Essence* (1948), and the examination of demonic possession among French nuns during the reign of Louis XIII in *The Devils of Loudun* (1952).

Acting Edition: Samuel French, Inc.

NOTES

1. *Daily News*, October 9, 1950.
2. *New York World-Telegram*, October 9, 1950.
3. *New York Herald Tribune*, October 9, 1950.
4. *New York Times*, October 9, 1950.
5. *Daily Mirror*, October 9, 1950.

Requiem for a Nun (1951)

William Faulkner (United States, 1897-1962)

Temple Drake is back. The depraved heroine of *Sanctuary*, William Faulkner's sensational novel, has returned, eight years older but not much wiser, in *Requiem for a Nun.*

Sanctuary (1931), which made Faulkner famous, is a Gothic thriller about a maiden-coed, Temple Drake, who is kidnapped and raped by the sadistic gangster Vitelli, nicknamed Popeye, who then sets her up in a Memphis whorehouse. Popeye arranges for a young thug, Alabama Red, to be Temple's lover so he can watch their lovemaking. Temple Drake becomes thoroughly perverted, joining an evil environment peopled with prostitutes, moonshiners, and mobsters. Interwoven within the lurid proceedings are a murder, a trial, and a mob lynching. Eventually, Temple is rescued by Gowan Stevens, a fellow student, who reappears with her in *Requiem for a Nun* as her husband and father of their two children.

Requiem for a Nun, the horror sequel, is part prose and part drama, peppered with long, didactic stage instructions. Nancy Mannigoe, a Black woman with an even disposition, until recently a domestic servant, stands trial at a Mississippi courthouse for smothering an infant in its cradle. She is found guilty and sentenced to death by hanging.

The action shifts to Gowan and Temple Stevens' living room. It is their six-month-old baby girl who was suffocated by the nanny. The Stevens are planning to leave the next day on an extended trip to California and Hawaii. Gavin Stevens, their lawyer and Gowan's uncle, corners Temple, inquiring about a man who was there the night her daughter was killed.

But Temple avoids any explanation and leaves with Gowan and their son, Bucky. Four months later, a note from Gavin reminding her that there's only a week until the nanny will be hanged, brings the Stevens family back. Temple reluctantly agrees to approach the governor with a plea for clemency. Temple reveals to the governor that Alabama Red's younger brother, Pete, has been blackmailing her over sleazy letters she wrote during a dark past. The devil in Temple took over and she fell for Pete, "a hard and ruthless man, so impeccable in amorality."

Nancy Mannigoe, a former drug addict and prostitute, now the maid, nanny and confidante, discovered that Temple had reneged on the plan to exchange money and jewels from her husband's strongbox for the incriminating letters.

A harrowing flashback takes us to Temple's private sitting room, where she and Pete contemplate eloping. When Pete goes to the car, Nancy confronts Temple, urging her to think of her two little children. Temple is not swayed; nothing will stop her, money or no money, children or no children.

Nancy crosses quietly toward the nursery, picking up a milk bottle from the table as she passes. She stops by the door, looks at Temple with a strange expression, and says, "I tried everything I knowed, you can see that," and exits.

Temple finishes her packing when Nancy emerges from the nursery, without the milk bottle, striding toward the kitchen.

Temple picks up a blanket and heads for the nursery. After a second or two, she screams, the lights fade, and the action returns to the governor's Office.

The governor does not grant a pardon, but Temple realizes that Nancy, "the murderess, the nigger, the dope-fiend whore," sacrificed her life in order to save her, Temple, from abandoning her husband and child, running away with another man to a new chapter of hellish existence.

Temple and Gavin visit Nancy in jail a few hours before the scheduled execution. Calm and serene, ready to go to the gallows, Nancy asks Temple to trust in God: "Believe."

With a new sense of redemption, Temple walks steadily toward the exit. She goes out. The door closes with a clang.

* * *

The world premiere of a German version of *Requiem for a Nun* took place at the Grand Theatre of Zurich in 1951, directed by the Austrian Leopold Lindtberg. The show's success spawned *Requiem* productions in fourteen other countries on the Continent. Albert Camus translated and adapted the play for a Paris presentation in September 1956. The critics cheered. Jean Guignebat in *Liberation* wrote that "Mr. Faulkner's work could by its plot have been just another crime story but is a tragedy in the classic sense of the word in its intensity, nobility, simplicity of language and terseness of style."[1] Jean-Jacques Gautier in *Figaro* found the play "a mixture of Dostoyevsky and Tolstoy retouched by Protestantism plus a dash of psychoanalysis."[2] Guy Verdot of *Franc Tireur* saw Temple Drake as "an Antigone of evil, her husband being the antique chorus of Greek tragedy."[3]

Requiem for a Nun opened at London's Court Theatre on November 26, 1957, winning kudos for Ruth Ford's Temple Drake, Zachary Scott's Gavin Stevens, and Bertice Reading's Nancy Mannigoe, running for thirty performances. The three thespians crossed the Atlantic in a Tony Richardson production designed by Motley, anchoring at Broadway's John Golden Theatre on January 30, 1959. The reviewers were divided.

Walter Kerr recommended the play "for those who are willing to risk a calculated, somewhat over-written, but wholly valid experiment."[4] Frank Aston declared, "It proves how harsh, raw and stunning the mature theater can be."[5] Brooks Atkinson stated, "The slow, dark flow of dialogue is characteristic of Mr. Faulkner, who listens to a distant drum. As a man of feeling and insight, he is entitled to his own method."[6]

The naysayers included John Chapman, who wrote, "It is a murky and sordid affair which exhibits the famed Mississippi littérateur as a tyro at writing for the stage… much of what Faulkner wants to relate happens offstage, and much of what he relates should have happened offstage,"[7] and Robert Coleman, who claimed that "*Requiem* is long on talk and short on genuine action. Its people are difficult to accept. Even the script's resolution seems to have been tacked on."[8] A few aisle men had mixed emotions; Richard Watts Jr. praised "the dark and brooding moral intensity of the distinguished novelist's concern with sin and atonement" but regretted "Mr. Faulkner's lack of experience as a dramatist;"[9] John McClain believed "it is a work of great power and nobility… but, sad to say, it fails as an entity to evoke the deep emotional reaction for which it strives."[10] *Requiem for a Nun* ran for forty-three performances.

Miriam Hopkins played the title role in the movie version of *Sanctuary*, *The Story of Temple Drake* (1933), directed by Stephen Roberts.[11] Lee Remick portrayed Temple in the remake of *Sanctuary* (1961), helmed by Tony Richardson. Ursula Lingen enacted Temple in *Requiem für eine Nonne*, presented on West Germany's television in 1965.

* * *

Born in 1897 in New Albany, Mississippi, William Cuthbert Falkner (later Faulkner) never graduated from high school and never received a college degree. He worked as an assistant bookkeeper at his grandfather's bank in Oxford, Mississippi, as an employee of the Winchester Repeating Arms Company in New Haven, Connecticut, and as a cadet in the Royal Air Force in Canada. When he tried to join the U.S. Army Air Force, he was turned down because he was only five feet, six inches tall.

In 1919, Faulkner enrolled at the University of Mississippi at Oxford, where he contributed poems and short stories to the campus newspaper, *The Mississippian*, and helped found a dramatic club. At the university he wrote a one-act play, *The Marionettes*, a sensuous fable in which Pierrot, hero of French pantomime, is dreaming of seducing the beautiful Marietta.

In 1924, Faulkner published his first book of poetry, *The Marble Faun*. The following year he moved to New Orleans and wrote essays and sketches for the literary magazine *The Double Dealer*. In 1926, Faulkner's first novel was published, *Soldiers' Pay*, incorporating the experiences he encountered when in the RAF. With 1929's *The Sound and the Fury*, considered one of the most important novels of the twentieth century, he began his series about life in a fictional Mississippi county, Yoknapatawpha.

Faulkner was a voracious reader of suspense fiction and an admirer of Carr, Christie, Queen, Sayers, and Stout. He incorporated criminous elements not only in *Sanctuary* and *Requiem for a Nun* but also in other tales of the South. "Uncle" Gavin Stevens saves a Black man framed for murder in *Intruder in the Dust* (1948, filmed 1949) and is the shrewd country lawyer of six detective stories in *Knight's Gambit* (1949), a volume also containing a 1930 mystery, "Smoke," and "An Error in Chemistry," which won second place in the *Ellery Queen Mystery Magazine* contest in 1946. Faulkner's novel *Light in August* (1933) hinges on a brutal murder motivated by a broken relationship and culminates with the lynching of the killer by a violent community mob. According to C. Hugh Holman in *Twentieth Century Crime and Mystery Writers*, Faulkner's *Absalom, Absalom!* (1936) utilizes "the double plot and time structure of the detective story to give form to a serious inquiry into the meaning of southern history and the reliability of history itself… *Absalom, Absalom!* has a past plot, dealing with the violent career of Thomas Sutpen, before, during, and after the Civil War."[12] The forward action of the novel is concerned with two characters, neither of whom had ever seen Sutpen, who are attempting to piece Sutpen's history together from the recollections of others, fragments of letters, and similar clues.

One of America's greatest novelists, Faulkner also penned *Soldier's Pay* (1926), *Mosquitoes* (1927), *Sartoris* (1929), *As I Lay Dying* (1930), *Pylon* (1935, filmed 1958 as *The Tarnished Angels*), *The Unvanquished* (1938), *The Wild Palms* (1939), *The Hamlet* (1940, filmed 1958 as *The Long, Hot Summer*), *Go Down, Moses* (1942), *A Fable* (1954), *The Town* (1957), *The Mansion* (1959), and *The Reivers* (1961, filmed 1969).

Faulkner's output also boasts fifteen collections of short stories, six books of verse, and a dozen volumes of nonfiction, letters and interviews. An important anthology is *The Portable Faulkner* (1946), edited by Malcolm Crowley.

As a screenwriter, Faulkner contributed to the movie versions of Ernest Hemingway's *To Have and Have Not* (1944) and Raymond Chandler's *The Big Sleep* (1946), both directed by Howard Hawks, and starring Humphrey Bogart and Lauren Bacall. Faulkner collaborated on the screenplays of the war movies *Today We Live* (1933), *The Road to Glory* (1936), *Air Force* (1943), and *God Is My Co-Pilot* (1945), as well as the espionage thrillers *Background to Danger* and *Northern Pursuit* (both in 1943), and the suspense melodramas *Fog Over London*, based on the play *The Amazing Dr. Clitterhouse* By Lyndon Barré, and *Escape in the Desert*, loosely based on the play *The Petrified Forest* by Robert E. Sherwood (both in 1944).

Though uncredited, highlights of Faulkner's Hollywood career include *Gunga Din* (1939), George Stevens' rollicking action-adventure; *Drums Along the Mohawk* (1939), John Ford's Revolutionary War saga; *The Southerner* (1945), Jean Renoir's drama about the tribulations of a poor farming family; and *Mildred Pierce* (1945), adapted from James M. Cain's novel, directed by Michael Curtiz and starring Joan Crawford in her Oscar-winning role as an ambitious waitress who finds success in business but loses all when she shoots to death her fickle husband.

In his book *Faulkner and Film,* Bruce F. Kawin, a former professor of English and film at the University of Colorado at Boulder, analyses an original screenplay by Faulkner, *Dreadful Hollow*, written in the late 1940s for director Howard Hawks but never produced. Kawin believes that *Dreadful Hollow* "is so genuinely frightening and so profoundly humanist that it demands comparison with the best of the genre: with *Vampyr*, *Nosferatu*, *Cat People*, *Isle of the Dead*, *The Wolf Man*, *The Black Cat*, and the like."[13] *Dreadful Hollow* is the story of an English girl, Jillian Dare, who has been engaged as a companion to the elderly Countess Czerner in a small town located 204 miles from London. The countess's niece, Vera, is a young, reckless, sensuous woman. Jillian learns to her horror that the countess is Vera, a vampire rejuvenated with the blood of little children.

Tomorrow, adapted by Horton Foote from a story by Faulkner for television's Playhouse 90 in 1961, depicts a member of the jury casting a sole vote against the acquittal of a father accused of killing the wild young man who, while running off with his daughter, drew a gun. A lawyer discovers that the juror was the boy's adopted father who still believed in the boy he raised.

Acting Edition: Vintage Books.

Awards and Honors: A top-ten selection in *The Best Plays of 1958-1959.*

William Faulkner was elected to the National Institute of Arts and Letters in 1939; awarded the Nobel Prize for Literature, 1949; Howells Medal, 1950; National Book Award, 1951, 1955; Pulitzer Prize, 1955, 1963; American Academy of Arts and Letters Gold Medal, 1962. The annual PEN/Faulkner Award for Fiction is the largest peer-juried prize for fiction in the United States.

Faulkner's *Intruder in the Dust* (1948) is an entry in the Howard Haycraft-Ellery Queen Definitive Library of Detective-Crime-Mystery Fiction. *Knight's Gambit* (1949) is an entry in *Queen's Quorum: A History of the Detective-Crime Short Story as Revealed by the 106 Most Important Books Published in this Field since 1845.*

NOTES

1. Quoted in the *New York Times*, September 24, 1956.
2. Quoted in the *New York Times*. September 24, 1956.
3. Quoted in the *New York Times*, September 24, 1956.
4. *New York Herald Tribune*, January 31, 1959.
5. *New York World-Telegram*, January 31, 1959.
6. *New York Times*, January 31, 1959.
7. *Daily News*, January 31, 1959.
8. *Daily Mirror*, January 31, 1959.
9. *New York Post*, February 1, 1959.
10. *New York Journal-American*, January 31, 1959.
11. The 1933 movie version of *Sanctuary, The Story of Temple Drake* caused an uproar and led to the strengthening of the rules of the Production Code. The film's audio was digitally restored in 2010.
12. John M. Reilly, ed., *Twentieth Century Crime and Mystery Writers*, 2nd ed. (New York: St. Martin's Press, 1985), 307.
13. Bruce F. Kawin, *Faulkner and Film* (New York: Frederick Unger, 1977), 137.

III. Interrogation

Following are several plays that feature an interrogation by the authorities which may or not lead to an indictment and trial.

The Third Degree (1909)

Charles Klein (United States, England-born, 1867-1915)

"Innocent until proven guilty" is the ruling principle of the American judicial system. But in *The Third Degree*, the England-born Charles Klein spotlights the official perversion of this precept. Howard Jeffries, an unhappy young man who was in the wrong place at the wrong time, confesses to murder after enduring a "third-degree" questioning.

Disowned by his family for having married an ex-convict's daughter, Howard is desperate enough to ask Robert Underwood, an antiques dealer and an old friend of his stepmother's, for a loan. Underwood, who himself is facing imminent exposure for financial misdealing, is harboring suicidal thoughts. He turns down Howard's request for money but says nothing of his own problems. In despair, Howard falls into a drunken stupor on Underwood's sofa. The doorbell rings. Underwood draws a screen around the couch where Howard is sleeping and then admits the young man's stepmother, Alicia. She has rushed over in hopes of preventing Underwood from taking his own life.

When the curtain rises on Scene II, Captain Clinton of the New York Police has been grilling Howard for seven hours, accusing him of shooting Underwood, whose corpse lies in the next room: "He was found on the floor, dead—you pretended you'd been drinking—that door was locked... The motive is clear—you came for money—were refused—there was a quarrel and you did the trick—Howard Jeffries—you shot Robert Underwood, and you shot him with this pistol."

Approaching mental and physical collapse, Howard admits that he killed Underwood. Sure of his innocence, his distraught wife, Annie, goes to plead with the very father-in-law who disinherited his son over his marriage to her, begging him to hire a top attorney he knows well to take on Howard's defense. The senior Jeffries agrees under the condition that if he does so, she must divorce his son and leave the country.

Annie refuses to make such a bargain and approaches the lawyer, Richard Brewster, on her own. After hearing her emotional appeal, he agrees to represent her husband, even knowing that Howard's father, his longtime client, has chosen not to stand by his son.

Clinton, the police captain who secured Howard's confession, mocks the lawyer's claim that the statement was coerced. Brewster insists that Clinton has been grandstanding to the newspapers on the basis of a dubious admission of guilt. As public sentiment goes against her stepson, the elder Mrs. Jeffries decides to put aside her fears of scandal and do the right thing.

She reveals the final note she received from Robert Underwood, a spurned lover's farewell message that sent her rushing to his apartment that night: "You have forbidden me to see you again … I shall be found dead to-morrow morning."

To the humiliation of Captain Clinton, Underwood's body is submitted to further forensic examination and reclassified a suicide. Howard's father welcomes his son and daughter-in-law into the family, while Richard Brewster proposes to Howard that he come to study law in his office.

* * *

The Third Degree, which premiered at the Hudson Theatre on February 1, 1909, took its melodramatic intensity from the extralegal practice of brutal police interrogations that produced "confessions" extracted, too often, from browbeaten suspects. Staged by the author, who had already more than a dozen plays to his credit, it ran for 167 performances. Initially, the *New York Times* found the play "grippingly, convincingly real," [1] while a second *Times* piece declared that the playwright had "expressed himself with directness, fearlessness, and skill."[2]

Three years later, now titled *Find the Woman*, Klein's stage thriller crossed the ocean to London, opening on June 17, 1912, at the Garrick Theatre to a standing ovation. The reviews were lukewarm. "The usual naïve American mixture of sentiment and violent action," was the verdict of *The Daily News*.[3] Calling the dialogue "bold," the *Daily Express* dismissed the characters as "conventional and superficial."[4]

The Third Degree was novelized by Arthur Hornblow in 1909. It was filmed three times as a silent feature: in 1913, with Klein writing the scenario; in 1919, featuring Hedda Hopper as Alicia Jeffries; and in 1926, under the helm of Michael Curtiz, with added scenes of past events which led to the opening sequence of the play.

* * *

Born in London and educated at North London College, Charles Klein was one of four brothers, all of whom had careers in the performing arts. Having acted in amateur theatre companies, he found his métier as a dramatist after moving to the United States in 1883.

Klein was among the few prolific playwrights with hit plays running simultaneously in New York and on tour at the dawn of the twentieth century. Besides *The Third Degree*, Klein's plays with suspense themes are: *The District Attorney* (1895, co-written with Harrison Grey Fiske), portraying corrupt politicians; *Dr.Belgraff*(1897), treating hypnotism and murder; *The Cipher Code*, (1901), dealing with the theft of a presidential letter; *The Lion and the Mouse* (1905), telling the story of an honest judge targeted for ruin; *The Next of Kin* (1909), showing a heiress in peril; *The Gamblers* (1910), about high-flying bankers; *The Ne'er-do-well* (1912, based on a novel be Rex Beach), whereby a married woman's lover is accused of murdering her husband.; *Potash and Perlmutter* (1913, co-written with Montague Glass), spotlighting a murder committed at a tailoring establishment; *The Money Makers* (1914), about an unscrupulous multi-millionaire; and *The Guilty One* (1916, co-written with Ruth Helen Davis and based on a novel by François Coppée), a courtroom drama in which the accused on trial for murder turns out to be the illegitimate daughter of the prosecuting attorney.

Klein was a passenger on the RMS *Lusitania* in May 1915 and perished when the liner was torpedoed by a German submarine.

NOTES

1. *New York Times*, February 2, 1909.
2. *New York Times*, February 7, 1909.
3. Quoted in the *New York Times*, June 18, 1912.
4. Quoted in the *New York Times*, June 18, 1912.

Darkness at Noon (1951)

Sidney Kingsley (United States, 1906-1995)

Generally acknowledged as Arthur Koestler's masterpiece, the 1940 novel *Darkness at Noon* is based on the Stalinist purges of the 1930s. Playwright Sidney Kingsley had optioned to dramatize the novel in the summer of 1949 and set to work on the play at once. According to Michael Scammell in the biography *Koestler*, the relationship between Koestler and Kingsley soured when Koestler "worried that the American wasn't capturing the nuances of the way communists talked to one another," and Kingsley allegedly completed the script without consultations. Writes Scammell, "Eventually Koestler wrote to Kingsley to say he wanted 'no share in the artistic responsibility of this play. Whether it is good or bad, it must be your burden.'" The conflict led to a suit by Koestler, but in 1952 a New York Arbitration Tribunal faulted him "for manifesting a 'strange apathy' toward the play in its formative stage by refusingto comment on the text when Kingsley was working on it"[1]

In the play adaptation, Sidney Kingsley confined much of the grim action to a Russian prison. One of the inmates, a Communist commissar named Rubashov, a former member of the Central Committee, demands to know the specific accusations against him. Ivanoff, the compound's warden and a former comrade of Rubashov, wants the prisoner to admit that he had been part of a plot to assassinate "the leader" but broke with the rebels when he perceived their aim. A confession would result in a few years of jail instead of a death sentence.

Rubashov refuses to admit to the trumped-up charges. For weeks, Ivanoff tries to break his spirit. Gletkin, a young interrogator, suggests that the warden turn Rubashov over to him, so that he may strong-arm a confession. "I know how to handle these old timers," he grins.

In a solitary cell, where the only communication with other prisoners is through tapping on the granite walls, Rubashov recalls the experiences that led to his arrest. Via flashbacks we learn that his beloved Luba and several close friends have been sacrificed to the will of the party with his complicity.

Rubashov concludes that no ends can justify these means, and he chooses to go to his death. It is "the tragedy of an idealist who saw his ideals grow sour, of a mighty dream that devoured its dreamers," concluded Richard Watts Jr. in the *New York Post*.[2] "What Rubashov failed to see," theorized

Robert Coleman in the *Daily Mirror*, "was that Marxist revolution inevitably consumes its more sensitive, intelligent and visionary leaders; that the goons, the strong-arm boys, take over and perpetuate a reign of terror."[3]

* * *

Following a successful tryout in Philadelphia's Forrest Theatre, *Darkness at Noon* reached Manhattan's Alvin Theatre on January 13, 1951. The majority of the critics showered the play with praise. "A vital and compelling drama…a singular tour de force," declared Howard Barnes.[4] "Mr. Kingsley's work, both as a dramatist and director, is clean, strong and brilliant," stated John Chapman.[5] "This is a stark and uncompromising exposition of life behind the Iron Curtain and one leaves the theatre with a prayer of thanks for the fact that it can't happen here", asserted John McClain.[6]

Brooks Atkinson was among the naysayers: "*Darkness at Noon* works as a pungent, spectacular melodrama of a popular theme. But is lacks the wild, evil music that made Mr. Koetsler's novel so piercing and so memorable."[7] Hobe Morrison vehemently attacked the play, predicting "slight box office prospects,"[8] but *Darkness at Noon* held audiences spellbound for 186 performances. Not surprisingly, the most vitriolic review by Bob Lauter was published in the *New York Daily Worker*, the official newspaper of the United States Communist Party: "A rather dull and pompous spectacle, but a dangerous one… *Darkness at Noon* is an attempt to justify the sniveling cowardice, the colossal duplicity, and the utter moral bankruptcy of Koetsler's heroes: Trotskyite criminals. "[9]

Detouring from Hollywood to New York, Claude Rains, in the role of Rubashov, won applause ("superb," "sensitive," "memorable") and a Tony Award as Best Actor.[10] Also complimented were Alexander Scourby as Ivanoff, Walter J. (later Jack) Palance as Gletkin, Kim Hunter as Luba, and Phillip Coolidge as Prisoner 402.

In 1955, NBCTV's Producers Showcase presented *Darkness at Noon* in an adaptation by Robert Alan Arthur, directed by Delbert Mann, starring Lee J. Cobb.

* * *

Born in New York City in 1906, Sidney Kingsley studied at Cornell University in Ithaca, New York, where he wrote one-act plays for the drama club. He began his professional career as an actor with the Group Theatre. In 1933, the company produced his play *Men in White*, which deals with professional and personal dilemmas in the life of hospital doctors. The first in a series of plays by Kingsley that are committed to social or ideological causes, *Men in White* won the Pulitzer Prize and was filmed in 1934. *Dead End* (1935, filmed 1937) picures the slums of downtown New York as a breeding ground for juvenile crime. *Ten Million Ghosts* (1936), a multimedia venture incorporating motion pictures, lambasts the manufacturin of munitions. *The World We Make* (1939) is about a mentally unbalanced girl, an escapee from a sanatoriom, who manages to heal herself when she finds love and realizes that she is needed. *The Patriots* (1943), a Drama Critics Circle Award recipient, pits Thomas Jefferson against Alexander Hamilton in search of democracy during America's infancy.

In the late 1940s, many of the members of the Group Theatre were investigated by the House Un-American Activities Committee. Kingsley, who had penned scripts in Hollywood, was among those blacklisted. He returned to New York to write for the theater. *Detective Story* (1949, filmed 1951) has a fanatical crime-fighting police detective use third-degree tacticts, electing to be judge as well as sleuth, and destroying himself in the process. *Lunatics and Lovers* (1954) is a frenzied farce zipping through a Broadway hotel suite, populated with crooks, cops, and ladies of the night. *Night Life* (1962) presents a microcosm of society's ills unfolding in a Manhattan key club.

* * *

Arthur Koestler was born on Budapest, Hungary, in 1905, to a well-to-do Jewish family. In 1922, he enrolled at the University of Vienna, where he became a passionate Zionist and, forsaking his education, left for Palestine. He lived for a while in a kibbutz and kept moving, penniless, to Tel Aviv, Haifa, and Jerusalem. Koestler proved to be a versatile journalist, and in 1929 he returned to Europe as a correspondent for a German newspaper. Two years later he joined the Communist Party but left it after the Spanish Civil War and the Moscow purges of the 1930s. During World War II, Koestner was among the first to denounce the Nazi regime, was detained by the French authorities for several months as a resident alien, joined the Foreign Legion, and eventually escaped to England. He served in the British army and became a British subject in 1945. A life fraught with danger behind him, from then on he deicated himself to writing and lecturing, basing his works of fiction on his own experiences, often interweaving psychology with politics. His topics were varied and sometimes controversial, including mysticism, telepathy, the paranormal, euthanasia, Darwinism, the drug culture, capital punishment, and nuclear disarmament. He also wrote scathingly about the Soviet Union and published a four-volume autobiography. His only play, a fantasy called *Twilight Bar*, was produced by Jean Vilar's theatre in Paris in 1946.

Fluent in many languages, Koestler wrote his novel *The Gladiators* (1939), on the revolt Spartacus against Rome, in Hungarian; *Darkness at*

Noon (1940) in German; and *Arrival and Departure* (1943), about a neurotic Communist intellectual, in English. He penned articles in English and French, and sketches in Hebrew for Tel Aviv's satirical cabaret HaMatateh (the Broom).

Known as a ladies' man, Koestler had three wives and a fleeting affair with Simone de Beauvoir. In 1983, suffering from Parkinson's disease and leukemia, he took his own life by swallowing an overdose of drugs. His third wife, Cynthia, died with him in a double suicide.

Acting Edition: Samuel French, Inc.
Awards and Honors: New York Drama Critics Circle Award: Best Play of 1950-51. A top-ten selection in *The Best Plays of 1950-1951* ("A strong and striking drama.")[11] Other Sidney Kingsley top-ten selections in the Best Plays yearbook: *Men in White* (1933-1934), *Dead End* (1935-1936), *The World We Make* (1939-1940), *The Patriots* (1942-1943), and *Detective Story* (1948-1949). Kingsley served as president of the Dramatists Guild of America and was elected to the Theatre Hall of Fame in 1983.

Arthur Koestler received the Sonning Prize from the University of Copenhagen and an honorary doctorate from Queen's University, Ontario, in 1968. He was appointed CBE (Commander of the Order of the British Empire) in 1972.

NOTES

1. Michael Scammell, *Koestler* (New York: Random House, 2009), 375, 401.
2. *New York Post*, January 15, 1951.
3. *Daily Mirror*, January 15, 1951.
4. *New York Herald Tribune*, January 15, 1951.
5. *Daily News*, January 15, 1951.
6. *New York Journal-American*, January 15, 1951.
7. *New York Times*, January 15, 1951.
8. Nina Couch, ed., *Sidney Kingsley: Five Prizewinning Plays* (Columbus: Ohio State University Press, 1995), xxxii.
9. Couch, *Sidney Kingsley*, xxxi.
10. London-born William Claude Rains (1889-1967) appeared in West End plays and was a teacher at the Royal Academy of Dramatic Arts (where his best-known students were Laurence Olivier and John Gielgud), before migrating to America and becoming a renowned character actor. His silky, polished voice was a major asset for his "criminal" career in the movies: mad scientist Jack Griffin in *The Invisible Man* (1933); jealous, murderous lawyer Lee Gentry in *Crime without Passion* (1934);

villainous uncle, John Jasper, in *The Mystery of Edwin Drood* (1935); Maximus, a phony music-hall mind reader in *The Clairvoyant* (1935); malicious Marquis Don Luis in *Anthony Adverse* (1936); power-hungry Earl of Hertford in *The Prince and the Pauper* (1937); Prince John in *The Adventures of Robin Hood* (1938); Don Jose Alvarez de Cordoba in *The Sea Hawk* (1940); corrupt senator Joseph Harrison Payne in *Mr. Smith Goes to Washington* (1939); the title role in *The Phantom of the Opera* (1943); Alexander Sebastian, member of a Nazi spy ring, in *Notorious* (1946); sadistic composer Alexander Hollenius in *Deception* (1946); Victor Grandison, a radio personality with blood on his hands, in *The Unsuspected* (1947); Arthur Martinage, the Machiavellian director of a South African mining company, in *Rope of Sand* (1949); Frederic Lannington, a sneering spouse who is done with, in *Where Danger Lives* (1950); Skalder, the captain of a Nazi supply ship in *Sealed Cargo* (1951); Kees Popinga, an embezzling clerk, in *The Paris Express*, aka *The Man Who Watched Trains Go By* (1953); an international thief, Aristedes Mavros, in *Lisbon* (1956). Rains was nominated four times for Best Supporting Actor Oscar, notably for the role of Inspector Louis Renault in *Casablanca* (1942), but won none. Detailed information about Claude Rains career on stage and in the cinema can be found in *Claude Rains: An Actor's Voice* by David J. Skal (Lexington: University Press of Kentucky, 2008).

11. John Chapman, ed., *The Best Plays of 1950-1951* (New York: Dodd, Mead, 1951), 72.

The Prisoner (1954)

Bridget Boland (England, 1913-1988)

Bridget Boland's psychological drama *The Prisoner* is inspired by the plight of Catholic Cardinal Jósef Mindszenty (1892-1975), an opponent of fascism and communism. On September 16, 1945, Pope Pius XII appointed Mindszenty as Cardinal of Hungary. The Communist regime maintained that church schools were anti-democratic and in 1948 proposed the nationalization of all Catholic schools. Cardinal Mindszenty crusaded against the plan and was arrested. He was charged with treason and was sentenced to life imprisonment. Following the 1956 revolution, Mindszenty was freed.

The Prisoner unfolds on a gloomy set divided into an interrogation room and the prisoner's cell, both furnished only with essentials – a desk, two chairs, a file cabinet in the interrogation room; a chair, table and a bench covered with a blanket in the cell. There are high, barred windows in both rooms. An overhead light is always on.

The curtain rises on a Warden, a stocky man who sporadically sniffs loudly and unpleasantly, ushering in the Prisoner, a man of middle-age and "considerable pride of bearing," dressed in the cassock of a Roman Catholic cardinal.

Enter the Interrogator, who represents the totalitarian government. He too is middle-aged, exhibiting "a genuinely pleasant manner." He is followed by the Secretary, a bustling, self-important man who puts some papers on the desk. At first, the give-and-take between Interrogator and Prisoner is amicable. The Prisoner remembers the Interrogator as a young, brilliant barrister, expert at cross-examination. He appreciates the Interrogator's background – a lawyer and a doctor, a gentleman from a noble family. The Interrogator asks His Eminence to relax. He has deep personal respect for the priest as a World War II Resistance hero.

The Prisoner warns the Interrogator that he has already gone through a similar experience with the Gestapo and that he is difficult to trap and impossible to persuade. He is also inured to most physical pain. The Interrogator assures him that no "racks and thumbscrews" will be used, as a confession from a broken body "seldom looks really spontaneous."

He offers the Prisoner water, but The Cardinal rejects it for fear it is contaminated with a "truth drug." The Interrogator declares that neither drugs nor torture will be used. Theirs is a mental duel. He is intent on finding the Prisoner's "human weakness, the chink in the plate of armour" that will destroy his record as a national hero. He is seeking a conversion, an open confession made in public.

The Interrogator pooh-poohs the previous attempts by the newly formed government to trap The Cardinal by planting photographs of a secret arsenal in his cathedral crypt, and microphones under the rim of his desk. This will be a chess game, between two worthy opponents.

Deprived of sleep, the Prisoner holds on. A coffin is brought to his cell. He is ordered to lift the lid and to his horror sees his mother. It turns out that she is still alive but is sick with cancer. It was a shock tactic, but it does not break the spirit of the Cardinal.

It is the Interrogator who begins to show the strain of the encounter. But eventually, after the relentless and calculated pressure of questioning, he discovers his antagonist's one vulnerable spot – the cardinal's deep sense of personal guilt for a life built on pride. Playing on that, the Interrogator twists and confuses the Prisoner into a confession, charging that he does not love his fellow men and never had any love for God; that he has become a priest for his own glory; that he betrayed his country during the war; that he led a life of lies.

In the final scene the Prisoner is given an elaborate breakfast, which he believes is his last meal before being hung. The Interrogator arrives with the news that his sentence has been commuted. The government does not want him to become a martyr. "I had counted on execution, this is the heavier sentence," laments the Prisoner. The Interrogator produces a revolver from an inner pocket. He offers to shoot the Prisoner with the excuse of fending off an attack. But the Prisoner rejects this form of escape; he has accepted a future of being branded "like Cain."

The Interrogator relates that he is resigning his post at the Ministry of Justice. His encounter with the Prisoner has destroyed his belief in what he has been doing; he realizes that he has ruined something more noble than his own cause.

* * *

Staged by Peter Glenville, *The Prisoner* premiered at the Lyceum Theatre in Edinburgh, Scotland, on March 1, 1954, and moved to London's Globe Theatre six weeks later. Alec Guinness and Noel Willman portrayed the Prisoner and the Interrogator, respectively. Wilfrid Lawson and Richard Easton played the chief wardens. *Theatre World Annual* wrote: "There are snatches of grim humour in Bridget Boland's play, but one is left with a feeling of almost unbearable intensity."[1] The drama ran for sixty performances.

The following year, Boland adapted her play to the screen, with Glenville making his debut as a film director and Guinness reprising his role as the Prisoner. Jack Hawkins played the Interrogator and Wilfrid Lawson portrayed the Warden. Deemed too controversial, *The Prisoner* was banned from the Cannes and Venice Film Festivals.[2]

In 1963, *The Prisoner* was presented on British television, featuring Alan Badel as The Cardinal and Patrick McGoohan as the Interrogator.

* * *

London-born Bridget Boland was educated at Oxford University, where she received her BA, with honors, in 1935. During World War II she became senior commander in the Auxiliary Territorial Force. In addition to *The Prisoner*, Boland penned several plays for the West End during the 1940s and 1950s, notably *Cockpit* (1948), a drama about displaced persons in post-war Europe that utilized several Continental languages and was staged in an unconventional manner at the time, breaking through the Fourth Wall and spilling into the auditorium to involve the audience.

Boland made an important contribution to suspense cinema when in 1940 she co-scripted, with A.R. Rawlinson, the movie version of Patrick Hamilton's play *Gaslight*, starring Anton Walbrook as Mr. Manningham, a dastardly husband who attempts to drive his wife Bella, portrayed by Diana Wynyard, out of her mind.

Boland collaborated on the screenplays of *This England* (1941); *War and Peace* (1956), from the novel by Leo Tolstoy; *Damon and Pythias* (1962); and *Anne of the Thousand Days* (1969), from the play by Maxwell Anderson. Boland was also the author of the radio play *Sheba* (1954) and the teleplay *Beautiful Forever* (1965).

Acting Edition: Dramatists Play Service.

Awards and Honors: Bridget Boland was conominee, in 1969, for an award from the Writers Guild and for an Academy Award for best screenplay for *Anne of the Thousand Days*.

NOTES

1. *Theatre World Annual*, 1954.
2. An earlier motion picture, *Guilty of Treason* (1950), is based on the tumultuous life of Cardinal Josef Mindszenty. The movie was scripted by Emmet Lavery, directed by Felix Feist, and featured Charles Bickford as the cardinal.

A Shot in the Dark (1961)

Marcel Achard (France, 1899-1974)

Paul Sevigne, a young, idealistic examining magistrate who has just been promoted to a post in Paris, is assigned his first case—seemingly a cut-and-dried murder. The prime suspect, Josefa Lantenay, is a sexy parlor maid who was found unconscious, nude, and clutching a gun alongside her dead lover, the chauffeur. Since their employer, Benjamin Beaurevers, is a powerful banker, Sevigne is pressed by his superiors to "get a confession from the girl—a short one, if possible, and you'll be home in time for an early dinner."

But as the investigation of *A Shot in the Dark* progresses, Sevigne concludes that the earthy, guileless, babbling Josefa could not have committed the crime. There is a curious naiveté about the girl who readily admits to a summer affair with the Spanish chauffeur, Miguel Ostos ("The heat, you know, and to tell you the truth, I wasn't wearing very much. I mean, underneath"), to discarding Miguel for another man, and to devoutly protecting her latest lover, who is Monsieur Beaurevers, no less.

"If she talks long enough—the idiot!" says Sevigne, "She'll chatter herself right up the steps to the guillotine."

Against all odds and despite objections from despotic chief prosecutor, Lablache, jaded court clerk Morestan, and his petulant bride, Antoinette, Sevigne persists in unraveling the naughtiness of an aristocratic Parisian household. He interrogates the pompous Beaurevers, who took an instant dislike to the victim for being taller than himself, then swings the pendulum of suspicion toward the banker's arrogant wife, Dominique, "who descended in direct line from Attila the Hun," and who, it turns out, shot Miguel in the dark believing it was her husband carousing with the maid. If it weren't for that mistake, "my wife would now be a rich, beautiful, young widow, free to marry her lover, Monsieur de Bennoit," muses Beaurevers. "He and my wife were inseparable due to their mutual passion for horses—or so I thought. Now I remember how many times, when they came back from the trails, they were exhausted, and the horses were fresh."

Josefa offers to pay Sevigne for having rescued her in the only way she knows how, but he shyly declines. In parting, she promises to mend her ways—get "a good job" and make "a nice fellow happy."

* * *

Marcel Achard's *L'Idiote* premiered in September 1960 at the Theatre Antoine, Paris, achieving reclame with Annie Gerardo as Josefa and Jean-Pierre Cassel as Sevigne. "M. Achard's method is light and ironic. His piece is meant for laughs, and it gets them, " dispatched the *New York Times* correspondent.[1] Following a U. S. tryout (during which Joel Thomas took over the role of Benjamin Beaurevers for the late Donald Cook, only to be replaced by Walter Matthau), an adaptation by Harry Kurnitz, called *A Shot in the Dark*, directed by Harold Clubman, opened on October 18, 1961, and ran for 389 performances at the Booth Theatre.

The reviewers adored Julie Harris's "flamboyant" impersonation of Josefa, admired Walter Matthau's "disdainful banker," praised William Shatner's "vulnerable judge," and complimented Diana van der Vlis's "wholesome" young wife, Gene Saks's "deadpan" court clerk, and Louise Troy's "haughty" Dominique.

But the critics were split regarding the brew of infidelities and crimes. "A saucy and classy little French-American sex comedy," declared John Chapman.[2] "It is written with humor, dramatic effectiveness, emotional force and deft expertness," gushed Richard Watts Jr.[3] "Whether Achard is the French Kurnitz or Kurnitz the American Achard doesn't really matter. With *A Shotin theDark* the two have hit the target," stated Norman Nadel.[4]

The naysayers were Howard Taubman, who found that "The light, tasty soufflé rises only a little,"[5] and Robert Coleman, who claimed that "The result is hit-and-miss."[6]

Judi Dench was cast as Josefa in a subsequent London production. *L'Idiote* was revived in Paris with great success during the 1970-1971 season. In the mid 1990s, the play still proved its bittersweet potency when presented by Vintage Theatre in Elmira, Corning, and Ithaca, New York. A 1964 movie version, scripted by director Blake Edwards and William Peter Blatty, evolved into the second Inspector Clouseau-Peter Sellers comedy, preserving from the original play one motif only—the great detective is out to prove the innocence of Elke Sommer in a murder case despite all evidence to the contrary.

* * *

Prior to his theatre and film career, Harry Kurnitz (1909-1968) wrote several detective novels under the nom de plume of Marco Page. His first mystery, *Fast Company* (1937), depicts murder in the world of rare books; it won Dodd, Mead's Red Badge Award. In *The Shadowy Third* (1946), the theft of a Stradivarius violin leads to bloodshed. Murder strikes during an investigation of art forgery in *Reclining Figure* (1952) and during the making of a criminous movie in *Invasion of Privacy* (1955). Adapting *Reclining Figure* for the stage, Kurnitz kept—lightheartedly—the element of skullduggery swirling around a faked Renoir but eliminated the gore. Emphasis was placed on a romantic attachment between an idealistic art dealer and the spunky daughter of an eccentric collector. *Reclining Figure* opened at the Lyceum theatre on October 7, 1954, and ran for 116 performances.

Other Broadway offerings by Kurnitz include *Once More, With Feeling*, a farcical assault on the realm of music (National Theatre, October 21, 1958—263 performances), and the book of the musical *The Girl Who Came to Supper*, based on Terence Rattigan's *The Sleeping Prince*, with music and lyrics by Noel Coward (Broadway Theatre, December 8, 1963—112 performances).

Kurnitz converted his debut novel, *Fast Company*, to an MGM movie in 1938, the first in a series of rare-book hijinks—*Fast and Loose* (1939) and *Fast and Furious* (1939). Since then, he wrote, often in collaboration, numerous screenplays, including the genre's *The Shadow of the Thin Man* (1941), *The Thin Man goes Home* (1944), *The Web* (1947), *Witness for the Prosecution* (1957), and *How to Steal a Million* (1966).

Kurnitz also penned a Bob Hope spy yarn, *They Got Me Covered* (1942), and a Danny Kaye satire on Russian bureaucracy, a musical adaptation of Gogol's play *The Inspector General* (1949).

The screenwriter's versatility is amply demonstrated in such varied fare as the army comedy *See Here, Private Hargrove* (1944), the fantasy *One Touch of Venus* (1948), the swashbuckling *The Adventure of Don Juan* (1949), the East-West political *The Man Between* (1954), the biblical *Land of the Pharaohs* (1956), and the cinematization of his own battle-of-the-sexes play, *Once More, With Feeling* (1962).

* * *

The career of the French dramatist and screenwriter Marcel Achard (pseudonym of Marcel-Auguste Ferreol, 1899-1974) spans the early 1920s to the end of the 1950s. His first play, *Voullez-vous jouer avec mod?* (1923), a poetic commedia dell'arte about circus clowns, was presented Off Broadway at the York Playhouse on April 30, 1959, in a musical adaptation by Tamara Geva and Haila Stoddard, entitled *Come Play With Me*, for four performances. Other American productions of Achard plays include *Domino* (1932), depicting the misadventures of a jealous husband, translated into English by Grace George and shown—with Achard attending as a guest of honor—at Atlantic City's Apollo Theatre during the first week of August, 1932, then transferred to the Playhouse in New York on August 16 for seven performances; *Jean De La Lune* (*The Dreamer*, 1929), a comic fantasy, presented by the French Theatre of New York at the Barbizon Plaza Theatre on December 13, 1937, for a limited run; *Aupres de ma blonde* (1947), adapted by S. N. Behrman under the title *I Know My Love*, starring the Lunts as a couple celebrating their silver anniversary, reminiscing about their life together (Shubert Theatre, November 2, 1949—246 performances); and *Palate* (1957), about a heel and his fall guy, adapted by Irwin Shaw (Henry Miller's Theatre, October 28, 1958—seven performances; a subsequent London production, in 1960, was called *Rollo*).

Among Achard's thirty-some plays, the more fashionable efforts were *La vie est belle* (*The Most Beautiful Life*,1928); *La belle mariniere* (*The Beautiful Barge Woman*,1929); *La femme en blanc* (*The Woman in White*, 1933); *Petrus* (1933), in which a chorus girl is accused of killing her lover, but is cleared; *Le Corseire* (*the Corsair*, 1938); *Adam*,1938); *Les Compagnans de la Marjolaine* (*The Companions of Marjolaine*, 1952).

In 1950, Achard adapted into French Mary Chase's *Harvey*, and in 1957 he wrote the musical *La Petite Lill* for Edith Piaf.

Achard penned thirty-seven screenplays, mostly in collaboration, notably *La Veuve joyeuse*, a version of *The Merry Widow* (1934); *Mayerling* (1936); *Mademoiselle Doctor* (1937); *Orage* (1938); *Felicie Mantevil* (1942); *Mademoiselle X* (1945); *Madame de ...* (1953); and *Sophie et le crime* (1955).

Among his directors were Ernst Lubitch, Anatole Litvak, Julien Devivier, Max Ophuls, and Marcel Carne.

"Without considering too seriously the larger political and social aspects of life, but with a tolerance and humanist spirit, Achard gives us play after play based on the joy of life and of love," writes Karel Tobey.[7]

Acting Edition: Samuel French, Inc.

Awards and Honors: Marcel Achard—Member, Academie Francaise, 1959; Officer, Legion of Honor. Tony Award—Walter Matthau as Benjamin Beaurevers, Best Supporting Actor.

NOTES

1. *New York Times*, September 26, 1960.
2. *Daily News*, October 19, 1961.
3. *New York Post*, October 19, 1961.
4. *New York World-Telegram*, October 19, 1961.
5. *New York Times*, October 19, 1961.
6. *New York Mirror*, October 19, 1961.
7. *The International Dictionary of Films and Filmmakers, volume 4, Writers and Production Artists* (Chicago: St. James Press, 1987), 1.

In the Matter of J. Robert Oppenheimer (1964)

Heinar Kipphardt (Germany, 1922-1982)

A new dramatic trend arose in Germany during the 1960s – the political docudrama. Associated primarily with Rolf Hochhuth, Peter Weiss and Heinar Kipphardt, the playwrights examined recent historical events by using official documents and court records. Hochhuth's *The Deputy* (1963) questions the failure of Pope Pius XII to speak out against the Nazi slaughter of Jews. In *The Investigation* (1965), Weiss re-creates the horrific events at the Auschwitz concentration camp. Kipphardt's *In the Matter of J. Robert Oppenheimer* (1964) goes back to the hysterical era of McCarthyism when in 1954 J. Robert Oppenheimer, "the father of the atomic bomb," was summoned to a congressional hearing regarding his security clearance.

Kipphardt sifted through 3,000 typewritten pages before condensing the records about Oppenheimer into a two-act, three-hour play. In an introduction to the published edition of *In the Matter of J. Robert Oppenheimer*, Kipphardt states that he deliberately confined himself to drawing upon historical data for the facts presented. "The author exercised his freedom only in the selection, the arrangement, formulation, and condensation of the material," he wrote.[1]

"Films and slides are utilized in this production as documentation of real events and a continuing reminder of this as fact," writes Gordon Davidson, who staged the play's initial U.S. productions in both Los Angeles and New York. "The action on the stage is merely an abstraction of ideas embodied in human behavior; the film is a shadow of reality; the actor on stage is the three-dimensional existence of illusion. The play answers no questions, rather it begs the question and poses problems with which the audience itself must wrestle."[2]

The time: April 12-May 6, 1954. The place: Room 2022, Building T3, Atomic Energy Commission, Washington, D.C. The room, "a small ugly office," has been temporarily furnished for the purpose of the investigation. On a raised platform, back center, is a table surrounded by three black leather armchairs for the members of the Personnel Security Board – Gordon Gray, Chairman, Ward Evans and Thomas Morgan. In front of the platform, floor level, the stenographers are seated with their equipment. At a table on the right, Roger Robb and C.A. Rolander, counselors for the Atomic Energy Commission, are busying themselves with stacks of documents. Opposite are

Lloyd Garrison and Herbert Marks, Oppenheimer's attorneys. There is an old leather sofa in the corner. A swivel chair for witnesses is also prominent.

As the lights fade up, a huge picture of Joseph McCarthy is projected on white screens at the back of the stage. J. Robert Oppenheimer enters the room by a side door. An official leads him to the sofa. He sets down his smoking paraphernalia, steps forward, and introduces himself to the audience as a "Professor of Physics at Princeton, formerly Director of the Atomic Weapons Laboratories at Los Alamos." He explains that he has been summoned to answer questions put to him by a Personnel Security Board concerning his views, his associations, his actions, and the suspicion that he has been disloyal.

Chairman Gray announces that "this is not a trial" and "shall be strictly confidential." Counsel Robb begins the interrogation. Oppenheimer denies that he had a major part in the decision to drop the A-bomb on Japan – that was "a political decision," not his. Once the decision was made, however, he advised on the choice of targets (photographs of several Japanese cities are projected on the background screens). After the bombing of Hiroshima, he had "terrible moral scruples" but believes that by bringing the war to an end as soon as possible many lives were saved.

Roger Robb steps forward and reports that the FBI suspected that Oppenheimer was "probably a camouflaged Soviet agent," which caused President Eisenhower to order "an impenetrable wall between Oppenheimer and all government secrets." It is in the sphere of energy, says Robb, "we came across the new type of traitor – the traitor for ideological, ethical motives."

The text "Guilty Through Association" is projected on the wall screens, and the following interrogation focuses on Oppenheimer's wife, who was first married to a Communist, and his brother Frank, who was a member of the Communist Party until 1941. Oppenheimer's former fiancée, Dr. Jean Tatlock, was also a member of the Party on an "on again, off again" basis. Interrogator Robb presses the point that Oppenheimer, the man responsible for the atomic weapons project in Los Alamos, spent the night with a female Communist. Oppenheimer responds that Tatlock came to him at a time of severe emotional crisis and a few days later committed suicide.

The board's only scientist, Professor Ward Evans, comes forward and declares to the audience that he is disturbed by both queries. He believes that they are humiliating to a scientist. He is also incensed by the State's increasing control over scientists, demanding their conformity.

The industrialist on the panel, Thomas Morgan, asks Oppenheimer if he was aware that in 1943 the Communist Party was an instrument of espionage in the United States. Oppenheimer answers in the negative; at the time the Russians were lauded allies who had just beaten Hitler at Stalingrad. C.A. Rolander, a security expert and Robb's associate, insists that the issue is whether Oppenheimer is a security risk today, when the enemy is not Nazi Germany but Communist Russia. Rolander questions Oppenheimer about his recommendation of physicians with left-wing views for employment at Berkeley and Los Alamos. Yes, admits Oppenheimer, a few of his pupils were in fact Communists but his endorsement of them was purely professional, as they were good scientists.

Professor Evans cannot understand why so many physicists are attracted to radical political ideas. It's because they are open minded and don't have pre-conceived notions, says Oppenheimer. They want to probe into things that don't work and ask why hunger, joblessness, and cruelty persist.

The tenth day of the hearing is Oppenheimer's fiftieth birthday. Projected on the hangings is the text "Is there such a thing as hundred-percent security?"

Major Nicholas Radzi, a security officer specializing in counter espionage, is called to the witness stand. Radzi testifies that in 1943 he was assigned to investigate a possible case of espionage at the University of California at Berkeley. It seemed strange, said Radzi, that everybody they suspected had some sort of connection to Dr. Oppenheimer. He recommended to his superiors at the Pentagon that Oppenheimer be completely removed from any employment by the United States government, but his recommendation was rejected. Dr. Evans asks Radzi whether, with reference to a secret war project, it is possible to achieve 100 percent security. No, Radzi admits, but 95 percent would be possible if scientists would cooperate. Says Radzi: "If we want to defend our freedom successfully, we must be prepared to forego some of our personal liberty."

John Landsdale, a former security officer, is questioned by Garrison, one of Oppenheimer's attorneys. Landsdale's conclusion is the opposite of Radzi's; he believes that the hysteria over Communism is a danger to democracy. Landsdale has no doubt that Oppenheimer should regain his clearance no matter what the FBI reports said.

In Act II, the panel shifts focus to the matter of the hydrogen bomb. Dr. Oppenheimer was widely criticized for delaying the development of the hydrogen bomb in a manner which allowed the USSR to gain ground on the United States in the nuclear arms race. Projected on the background screens is an October 31, 1952, test explosion of the first hydrogen bomb in the Pacific (the isle of Elugelab disappeared within ten minutes) and an August 8, 1953, test explosion of the first Russian hydrogen bomb (alleged to be superior to the American model).

Chairman Gray announces that their secret hearing has been leaked to the *New York Times* and the case of Dr. J. Robert Oppenheimer "dominates the headlines and public discussion all over America."

Questioned by Robb and Rolander, the counsels for the commission, Oppenheimer tells of his "terrible scruples" after Hiroshima and his fear that in a third world war the awesome weapon of a hydrogen bomb will destroy 98 percent of humankind. When the president made the decision to produce it, he helped only as an adviser. It was Dr. Edward Teller who earned the soubriquet "father of the hydrogen bomb."

Dr. Teller is called and sworn in as a witness. In 1945, he wanted to develop a hydrogen bomb, says Teller, but Dr. Oppenheimer did not warm up to the idea. Teller realized that a U.S. hydrogen program would have to take place without Oppenheimer's contribution. No, Teller wouldn't take away Oppenheimer's clearance, but he personally would feel more secure if the vital interests of this country did not rest in his hands. Oppenheimer and Teller look at each other momentarily, and after a slight hesitation Oppenheimer rejects an offer to question Dr. Teller.

The next two witnesses provide contradicting testimonies. David Griggs, chief scientist of the Air Force, believes that Oppenheimer led a silent conspiracy among prominent scientists against the development of the hydrogen bomb. Isador Isaac Rabi, professor of physics at Columbia University, supports Oppenheimer in every way and calls him "the most loyal person I know, including myself."

On the morning of May 6, 1954, the commission concludes the interrogation of forty witnesses. Ward Evans, in his *Minority Report*, announces his complete confidence in Dr. Oppenheimer's loyalty, and sees no reason why his security clearance should be revoked. Chairman Gordon Gray reads the board's majority decision. He and Thomas Morgan find "no indication of disloyalty" but are concerned about Dr. Oppenheimer's "ambiguous and disquieting" attitude toward the development of the hydrogen bomb. Therefore, Dr. Oppenheimer can no longer enjoy "the unreserved confidence of the government and the Atomic Energy Commission." He does not receive security clearance.

Oppenheimer rises to his feet and requests that the Atomic Energy Commissionre view the decision, although he vows never to work on war projects again as it is "the work of the devil."

* * *

The world premiere of *In der Sache J. Robert Oppenheimer* took place at West Berlin's Freie Volksbühne in 1964 under the direction of Erwin Piscator (1893-1966), innovator of the epic theatre and master of the documentary drama. [3] The play performed all over Europe and reached London on October 17, 1966, running for seventy-six performances at the Hampstead Theatre Club. Translated by Ruth Spiers, *In the Matter of J. Robert Oppenheimer* was first produced in America on May 24, 1968, by Los Angeles's Center Theater Group at the Mark Taper Forum. Gordon Davidson directed a cast headed by Joseph Wiseman in the role of Dr. Oppenheimer. The *New York Times* reported that "the first-night audience and critics alike found it distinguished treatment of essentially undramatic material."[4] Critic Walter Kerr provided a second opinion in the *Times*, in which he praised a performance "spare, dry, controlled, quietly intelligent," but at the final curtain remained unclear as to what has been real-life documentation and what has been manipulated by the playwright: "We are not truly certain what we have seen, how responsible or how manipulated the ending has been, how representative the residue may be taken to be."[5] *In the Matter of J. Robert Oppenheimer* ran at the seven-hundred-seat Mark Taper for seven weeks to sold-out houses and was taken to New York, where it was hosted by the Repertory Theater of Lincoln Center on March 6, 1969.

Most of the morning-after reviews were laudatory. "It is a talkative, stimulating and intellectually engaging evening," wrote Clive Barnes. "It is good to have a play in town that offers a little nourishment for thought and discussion." Richard Watts Jr. raved: "The documentary drama by Heinar Kipphardt... is intellectually interesting and astonishingly engrossing theatrically, and it is being given a brilliant production filled with stunningly effective performances."[7] Martin Gottfried asserted that the play "is as important as theatre can get," and applauded the "cohesive" direction by Gordon Davidson as well as the "excellent frigid-warm courtroom set" designed by Peter Wexler.[8]

The television critics were less enthusiastic. Leonard Harris of *WCBS-TV2* complained of "imbalance. It stacks the deck in favor of Oppenheimer and against McCarthy witch-hunts... You can tell the good guys from the bad guys without a program, and there was more to the Oppenheimer affair than that."[9] Edwin Newman of *NBC-TV4* frowned: "It's an interesting work, though not a gripping one... The play in its nature can have no surprises. The story is known. Also, it has no climax. It merely subsides at the end."[10]

The cast was received with kudos, notably Eduard Franz as Ward Evans, the sympathetic member of the board; Philip Bosco as Gordon Gray, the skeptical chairman; and Herbert Berghoff as Edward Teller, the opposing scientist. Joseph Wiseman, in the role of Dr. Oppenheimer, garnered unanimous praise. "A fine choice," "Altogether superb," "Calmly dominates the evening," wrote the critics.[11]

In the Matter of J. Robert Oppenheimer ran for sixty-four performances. The play returned to Lincoln Center on June 26, 1969, with Paul Sparer portraying Dr. Oppenheimer, for 108 showings. On October 13, 1969, it began a tour at the National Theatre in Washington, D.C. and closed in San Francisco on January 10, 1970. The Seattle Repertory Theatre of Seattle, Washington, included *In the Matter of J. Robert Oppenheimer* in its 1969-1970 season. Almost four decades later, in 2006, the play was mounted by Off Broadway's

Keen Company, a troupe dedicated to plays that are "generous in spirit" and are "saying anything optimistic or positive about humanity."

Other playwrights to tackle the Oppenheimer saga are Joseph Boskin – *The Oppenheimer Affair* (1968), and Carson Kreitzer — *The Love Song of J. Robert Oppenheimer* (2004).

Produced by England's BBC-TV in 1980, *Oppenheimer: Father of the Atomic Bomb,* a seven-episode mini-series, featured Sam Waterston as the physicist and David Suchet as his nemesis Edward Teller. A year later, the documentary *The Day After Trinity* covered scientists involved in the creation and testing of the first atomic bomb, including J. Robert Oppenheimer as himself. In 2005, *Doctor Atomic*, John Adams' operatic treatment of J. Robert Oppenheimer and his wife Kitty, premiered in San Francisco under the direction of Peter Sellars. A slightly revised version was presented by Lyric Opera of Chicago in 2007 and the following year by New York's Metropolitan Opera. Gerald Finley starred in the title role. *Doctor Atomic* follows the last twenty-four hours in the creation of the atom bomb at Los Alamos, New Mexico. Made by ITVS in 2008, *Wonders Are Many: The Making of Doctor Atomic* traces the creation of the opera. A television documentary, *The Trials of J. Robert Oppenheimer*, a two-hour brew of archive footage, interviews and dramatization, was aired by PBS on January 26, 2009. In 2010, film director Lucy Walker mixed newsreel footage, graphics and interviews with scientists and politicians in the documentary *Countdown to Zero*, a disturbing testament to the horrors of the nuclear bomb. Included is a haunting clip of J. Robert Oppenheimer emoting his mea culpa, "Now I have become Death, the destroyer of worlds."

* * *

Heinar Mauritius Kipphardt was born in Heidersdrof, Upper Silesia, Germany, in 1922. When he was eleven years old, his father, a dentist, was sentenced to five years in the Dürrgoy concentration camp for expressing anti-Nazi views. During World War II, Kipphardt served in the German army, by then in full retreat before the Russian advance. Both experiences impacted him profoundly and his politics became radically left-wing.

Kipphardt studied medicine in Düsseldorf and practiced as an MD, but he shifted his career direction in 1950, becoming literary adviser and chief dramatist for the Deutsches Theater in East Berlin. In 1959 he moved to West Berlin and served in a similar capacity at the Munich Kammerspiele (Intimate Theatre). Kipphardt's first major play, *Der Hund des Generals* (*The General's Dog*, 1962), deals with inhumane treatment of infantry men by the generals. A sentry accidently shoots the general's favorite dog. The general gets so angry that he sends an entire company to an untenable position where they are completely wiped out. *Joel Brand* (1964) and *Bruder Eichmann* (*BrotherEichmann*, produced posthumously in 1983) focus on the genocide of the Jews in Nazi Germany. Kipphardt adapted *Joel Brand* and *Bruder Eichmann* to television and penned for German TV two versions of *In the Matter of J. Robert Oppenheimer.*

Acting Edition: Hill and Wang.

Awards and Honors: A top-ten selection in *The Best Plays of 1968-1969.* Heinar Kipphardt was the recipient of the East German national prize, 1953; Schiller Memorial prize, 1962; Gerhart Hauptmann prize, 1964; Adolf Grimme prize, 1965; German Academy of Representational Arts television prize, 1975; Society of German Doctors film prize, 1976; Prix Italia, 1976; and Bremen Literature prize, 1977.

NOTES

1. Heinar Kipphardt, *In the Matter of J. Robert Oppenheimer* (New York: Hill & Wang, 1968), 5.
2. Otis L. Guernsey Jr., ed., *The Best Plays of 1968-1969* (New York: Dodd, Mead, 1969), 235.
3. A year earlier, in 1963, Erwin Piscator staged in Berlin the controversial political drama *The Deputy* by RolfHochhuth. Piscator was one of the first directors to use film strips in conjunction with live actors. His influence was apparent in the work of Joan Littlewood at Theatre Workshop in England and in that of the Living Theatre in the United States.
4. *New York Times*, May 27, 1968.
5. *New York Times*, June 9, 1968.
6. *New York Times*, March 7, 1969.
7. *New York Post*, March 7, 1969.
8. *Women's Wear Daily*, March 7, 1969.
9. *WCBS-TV2*, March 6, 1969.
10. *NBC-TV4*, March 6, 1969.
11. Born 1918 in Montreal, Quebec, Canada, Joseph Wiseman began acting in summer stock as a teenager and made his Broadway debut playing a bit part in Robert E. Sherwood's *Abe Lincoln in Illinois*. During the 1940s he enacted feature roles in Maxwell Anderson's *Candles in the Wind* and *Joan of Loraine*, William Shakespeare's *Antony and Cleopatra*, and Sidney Kingsley's *Detective Story*. His other Broadway credits include appearances in Jean Anouilh' *The Lark*, Arthur Miller's *Incident at Vichy*, and revivals of Clifford Odets' *Golden Boy* and Paddy Chayefsky's *The*

Tenth Man. In Hollywood, Wiseman made a dozen movies, including *Detective Story* (1951), *Viva Zapata!* (1952), *Les Miserables* (1952), *The Garment Jungle* (1957) and *The Unforgiven* (1960), before playing the role he is most remembered for, the sinister title character in *Dr. No* (1962), the first James Bond movie. "I had no idea it would achieve the success it did," Wiseman told the *Los Angeles Times* in 1992. "As far as I was concerned, I thought it might be just another grade-B Charlie Chan mystery." On television, Wiseman played the recurring role of crime boss Manny Weisbord in the 1980s series *Crime Story*. Over the years he was featured on series such as *Danger, Suspense, Justice, On Trial, The Untouchables, The Streets of San Francisco*, and *Law & Order*. In 2001, Wiseman returned to Broadway in a production of Abby Mann's *Judgment at Nuremberg*. He died at his home in Manhattan in 2009. His daughter, Martha, said that Wiseman viewed *Dr. No* with disdain. "He was horrified in later life because that's what he was remembered for. Stage acting was what he wanted to be remembered for." *Los Angeles Times*, October 21, 2009.

Agnes of God (1980)

John Pielmeier (United States, 1949-)

Martha Livingston, a court-appointed psychiatrist, is assigned to determine the sanity of a young nun, Agnes, accused of strangling her own newly born baby with its umbilical cord and discarding the body into the convent's wastebasket. Who fathered the child and who actually killed it are among the key investigative queries of *Agnes of God.*

On the stark, bare stage, a clash develops between the cynical chain-smoking psychiatrist – an atheist, ex-Catholic – and the formidable, miracle-prone Mother Superior, Miriam Ruth, who insists that Agnes knows nothing about sex and birth and "hasn't been troubled, except by God." Livingston accuses Ruth of killing the baby herself, to avoid a scandal. The Mother Superior claims that while she did assist in the birth, she was panicked by "so much blood," and left to get help. At that point, she says, both mother and baby were alive.

Through hypnotic interrogation, Livingston elicits from Agnes details of a tortured childhood warped by a sadistic mother, an abusive upbringing that has affected her ability to think rationally. The simple-minded, haunted nun confesses to the killing, saying it was done to "save" the baby girl and "give her back to God." The siring of the infant remains an enigma—could it have been God's, or that of a visiting priest, or a local field hand? All three women — Agnes, Livingston, and Miriam Ruth — are forced to face some harsh realities in their own lives, and to examine their common faith.

* * *

Agnes of God was baptized as a stage reading at the O'Neill Theatre Center in Waterford, Connecticut on July 26, 1979, under the direction of Robert Allan Ackerman. Doctor Martha Livingston was portrayed by Jo Henderson, Mother Miriam Ruth by Jacqueline Brooks, Sister Agnes by Dianne Wiest. The first fully mounted production of *Agnes of God* opened on March 9, 1980, at the Actors Theatre of Louisville, directed by Walton Jones, with Adale O'Brien, Anne Pitoniak, and Mia Dillon. It was then presented at Center Stage, Baltimore, Maryland; Stage West, Springfield, Massachusetts; Old Globe Theatre, San Diego, California; GeVa Theatre, Rochester, New York; and Players State Theatre, Coconut Grove, Florida.

The drama's Broadway debut took place at the Music Box Theatre on March 30, 1982, staged by Michael Lindsay-Hogg, featuring Elizabeth Ashley, Geraldine Page, and Amanda Plummer. The New York critics hailed the three stars but condemned the play: "While *Agnes of God* aspired to be both a chilling thriller and a stirring reaffirmation of the power of faith, it fails on both counts," wrote Frank Rich[1]; "Cleverly executed blood and guts evening in the theatre with aspirations beyond dramatic butchery. However, with so much theological musing, there is less in this than meets the sky," sighed Clive Barnes. [2] "A good deal of mumbo-jumbo obscuring the central issues, which has to do with faith and miracles," sniffed Douglas Watt. [3] "Uninteresting, un-fascinating play… overwrought and under wrought," scowled Dennis Cunningham. [4] "For all its pretensions to serious analysis of psychological vs. ecclesiastic dogmas, *Agnes of God* amounts to little more than old-fashioned sensational melodrama," objected John Beaufort. [5] "If *Agnes of God* just fails as an example of the playwright's craft it shines as a demonstration of three actresses' seductive art," opined Richard Corliss. [6]

However, Ron Cohen of *Women's Wear Daily* found *Agnes of God* "a theatrical event" and complimented playwright Pielmeier: "His writing is taut, his scenes bristle with conflict and his dialogue has occasional eloquence as well as clarity." [7]

A sort of miracle occurred when *Agnes of God* overcame the mostly negative reception, running heftily for 599 performances and a selling to the movies. The 1985 motion picture version, scripted by Pielmeier and directed by Norman Jewison, starred Jane Fonda, Anne Bancroft, and Meg Tilly in the three tour-de-force roles. The play was also released as an audiobook, performed by Barbara Bain and Emily Bergl, Los Angeles Theatre Works, in 2001.

* * *

Born in Altoona,Pennsylvania, in 1949, John Pielmeier earned a BA degree from the Catholic University of America in 1970 and an MFA degree from the Pennsylvania State University in 1978. He began his career as an actor, affiliated with the repertory companies of the Actors Theatre of Louisville, Kentucky; the Guthrie Theatre, Minneapolis, Minnesota; Milwaukee Rep; Alaska Rep; Baltimore's Center Stage; and the Eugene O'Neill National Playwrights' Conference, Waterford, Connecticut, where, in a shift to playwriting, he introduced *Agnes of God*.

During the 1980s, Pielmeier penned two other Broadway ventures. The drama *The Boys of Winter* (Biltmore Theatre, December 1, 1985 — nine performances) cast Matt Dillon and Wesley Snipes as members of a Marine Unit on a dangerous mission during the Vietnam War. The thriller *Slight of*

Hand (Cort Theatre, May 3, 1987 — nine performances) depicts a small-time magician (played by Harry Groener) with a perchant for practical jokes.

Among Pielmeier's additional plays are *Jass,* presented as a stage reading at the Actors' Studio in May 1980, The New Dramatists in June 1981, and The O'Neill Theatre Center during the summer of 1985; *Chapter Twelve – The Frog,* February 1981, and the one-act *Cheek to Cheek,* November 1983 – both at the Actors' Theatre of Louisville; *Courage,* a one-man show looking into the intimate life of J.M. Barrie, also at the Actors' Theatre of Louisville in 1983 and Off-Off Broadway the following year; *Courage, Short Places,* and *Steeple Chase* Off-Off Broadway during 1984-1989; *Impassioned Embraces* at the Repertory Theatre of St. Louis, January 1989; *Will,* September 1991, and *Voices in the Dark,* October 1994, both at Seattle's Contemporary Theatre; *Voices in the Dark,* with Judith Ivey starring as a radio talk show host who is menaced by a mysterious caller, made it to Broadway's Longacre Theatre on August 12, 1999, running for sixty-eight performances; the book for a musicalization of *Young Rube* at the Repertory Theatre of St. Louis, September 1993; and *Slow Dance with a Hot Pickup,* a musical that went through a number of workshops, then premiered at the Barnstormers Theatre in Tamworth, New Hampshire in 2007. Also in 2007, Pielmeier's play *Madonna and Child* was read at the New Harmony Conference.

2021 proved to be a banner year for Pielmeier. He adapted his 2017 best-selling novel, *Hook's Tale*, for the stage and it premiered at Houston's Stages Theatre. His musical *Fathers and Sons*, teamed with Matty Selman, based on the life of Maria Montessori, was workshopped at the University of Evansville. And his play *Marlowe! Goethe! Faust!,* mixing two interpretations of the Faust legend with the lives of Christopher Marlowe and Johann Wolfgang von Goethe, had its world premiere at the Denizen Theatre, New Paltz, New York.

A stage adaptation by Pielmeier of William Peter Blatty's novel *The Exorcist* was produced at London's Phoenix Theatre in the West End in 2017 to rave reviews, toured the U.K., and is under option for Broadway.

Pielmeier has written and produced more than twenty-five movies for television, some with collaborators, including *Sins of the Father*; *The Stranger Within*; *The Last P.O.W.*; *The Shell Seekers*; *Through the Eyes of a Killer*; *Original Sins*; *Forbidden Territory*; a new adaptation of *Flowers for Algernon*; *Living with the Dead*, a miniseries; the critically acclaimed *Hitler:The Rise of Evil*; and the hit miniseries *The Capture of the Green River Killer*. His adaptations of two Patricia Cornwell mysteries, *At Risk* and *The Front*, aired on Lifetime in April 2010, and his treatment of *The Pillars of the Earth*, an eight-hour series based on Ken Follett's novel, aired throughout the world beginning in July 2010, while his eight-hour adaptation of Follett's *World Without End*, a sequel to *Pillars*, premiered in the autumn of 2012. Pielmeier's television film, *The Long Island Serial Killer: A Mother's Hunt For Justice*, was broadcast in February 2021.

Pielmeier is a member of the Dramatists Guild, the Writers Guild of America East, Actors Equity, and Screen Actors Guild. He has been a guest lecturer at Carnegie Mellon University, Penn State, and the University of Vermont.

Acting Edition: Samuel French, Inc.

Awards and Honors: *Agnes of God* was a top-ten selection in *The Best Plays of 1981*-1982—"certainly one of the highlights of the season." [8] Tony Award,1982; Amanda Plummer, Outstanding Featured Actress in the title role, Drama Desk Award, 1982. For his 1985 screenplay of *Agnes of God*, John Pielmeier earned a Writers Guild of America nomination for Best Screenplay Based on Material from Another Medium. Pielmeier's *Voices in the Dark* won the 1999 Edgar Award for Best Play. In 2003, Pielmeier was inducted into the Blair County, Pennsylvania Arts Hall of Fame. His musical *Slow Dance with a Hot Pickup* garnered four 2007 New Hampshire Theatre Awards, including Best New Play and Best Production of a Musical. For his 1983 television movie, *Choices of the Heart*, about slain American missionaries in El Salvador, pielmeier received a Christopher Award, the Humanities Award, a Writers Guild of America nomination for Best Teleplay, and an Honorary Doctorate of Letters from St. Edward's University in Austin, Texas. *The Capture of the Green River Killer*, a miniseries, was named by *Variety* as the Best Television Movie of 2008.

NOTES

1. *New York Times,* March 31, 1982.
2. *New York Post,* March 31, 1982.
3. *Daily News,* March 31, 1982.
4. *WCBS-TV2*, March 30, 1982.
5. *The Christian Science Monitor,* April 19, 1982.
6. *Time Magazine,* April 12, 1982.
7. *Women's Wear Daily,* March 31, 1982.
8. Otis L. Guerney Jr., Ed., *The Best Plays of 1981-1982,* (New York: Dodd, Mead, 1982), 14.

Death and the Maiden (1991)

Ariel Dorfman (United States, Argentina-born, 1942-)

Born in Buenos Aires, Argentina, Ariel Dorfman is a Chilean novelist and playwright who was persecuted by the regime of Augusto Pinochet and forced into exile in the United States. In 1991, Dorfman composed a play carved from his experiences, set in "a country that is probably Chile but could be any country that has given itself a democratic government just after a long period of dictatorship."

Death and the Maiden is the story of Paulina Salas, a South American married to a prominent lawyer, Gerardo Escobar, who has recently been appointed by the new president of the republic to head a commission investigating human rights violations.

On his way to their beach home, Gerardo has a flat tire. Doctor Roberto Mirnada stops to help. Gerardo invites the Good Samaritan to spend the night. Upon hearing the doctor's voice, Paulina believes that he is the man who raped and tortured her fifteen years earlier as she lay blindfolded in a military detention center. While the household is asleep, Paulina slips into Roberto's bedroom, hits him with a blunt instrument, binds him to a chair, and gags him with her panties. Then, at gun point, she orders her shocked husband to serve as the doctor's defense attorney in "a trial."

Roberto vehemently denies that he was the doctor-torturer: "I'm a quiet man. Anyone can see that I'm incapable of violence." But Paulina draws from him a few tidbits of information – "small lies, small variations" – that could only have been known to her true torturer. She also finds in his car a cassette of Schubert's "Death and the Maiden," the quartet that played in the background when she was degraded.

Just as Paulina aims her gun at Roberto, a giant mirror descends, forcing the members of the audience to look at themselves. A final scene, occurring several months later, has Paulina and Gerardo attending a concert. Roberto enters, and, based on a stage instruction, he may or may not be an illusion in Paulina's head. The instruments are tested and tuned. Then "Death and the Maiden" begins. Paulina and Roberto lock eyes for a moment.The music plays as the curtain falls.

* * *

In an afterword to the acting edition of *Death and the Maiden*, playwright Dorfman enumerates the "sort of questions" that triggered the writing of his play: "How can those who tortured and those who were tortured coexist in the same land? How to heal a country that has been traumatized by repression if the fear to speak out is still omnipresent everywhere? And how do you reach the truth if lying has become a habit? ... I felt that *Death and the Maiden* touched upon a tragedy in an almost Aristotelian sense, a work of art that might help a collective to purge itself, through pity and terror, in other words to force the spectators to confront those predicaments that, if not brought into the light of day, could lead to their ruin."[1]

Death and the Maiden began as a reading at the Institute for Contemporary Art in London on November 30, 1990. A workshop production was staged in Santiago, Chile, on March 10, 1991. The play had an acclaimed world premiere at London's Royal Court Upstairs on July 9, 1991. Later that year, on November 4, it moved to the Mainstage at The Royal Court with the same cast (Juliet Stevenson, Bill Paterson, Michael Byrne) and director (Lindsay Posner), winning the Sir Laurence Olivier Award for Best Play of the season.

The American opening of *Death and the Maiden* took place at the Brooks Atkinson Theatre in New York on March 17, 1992, under the direction of Mike Nichols, featuring Glenn Close as Paulina, Richard Dreyfuss as Geraldo, and Gene Hackman as Roberto. The reception by the critics was split. "A good strong mainstream melodrama," wrote Clive Barnes. "[a] play that on its own modest terms possesses thrills, spills and passion."[2] Edwin Wilson believed that "Mr. Dorfman's challenging play is both a political document and a psychological thriller."[3] Linda Winer found *Death and the Maiden* "engrossing, moderately suspenseful, meticulously produced."[4]

On the other hand, Jack Roll complained that by concentrating on the problem, whether Paulina has the right man, the play turned into a whodunit, undercutting "what should be its most agonizing question: how could a civilized human being become an evil monster in an oppressive regime?"[5] Two *Daily News* reviewers pointed accusing fingers at *Death and the Maiden*: Howard Kissel wrote, "I had trouble taking what happened on stage seriously. I kept imaging I was watching parlor games in Beverly Hills."[6] Likewise, Doug Watt stated, "There's precious little intellectual content in this disappointing evening."[7]

The production elements, too, earned A's and F's. "Under Mike Nichols' riveting direction, the superb cast maintains the piano-string tautness and menacing situation," applauded John Beaufort.[8] "Mike Nichols' staging, alas, is too ornate and stately, its pace slowed by pregnant pauses and suspense-draining scene changes. Moreover, the actors seem weirdly naturalistic for so polemic a text," lamented William A. Henry III.[9] Nonetheless,

Glenn Close won the 1991-1992 Tony Award for Best Actress; years later, in a televised Actor's Studio session, she said that the role of Paulina was "the hardest thing I ever had to do."[10]

Star power kept *Death and the Maiden* on the boards for 159 performances. The Mark Taper Forum of Los Angeles presented *Death and the Maiden* in 1994, starring Jimmy Smits, Wanda de Jesus and Thomas Milian. That same year, a movie version, co-written by Dorfman, directed by Roman Polanski and starring Sigourney Weaver as Paulina, Ben Kingsley as Roberto, and Stuart Wilson as Geraldo, kept the tense proceedings confined to a secluded beach house. Dorfman also penned the libretto for an opera version that had its world premiere at Sweden's Malmo Opera House in September 2008.

* * *

Vladimiro Ariel Dorfman was born in Buenos Aires on May 6, 1942, the son of a prominent Argentine professor of economics and a literature teacher. At the age of two, his family was forced to flee to the United States because of his father's opposition to the Argentine government of Juan Peron. In 1954, during the McCarthy era, the Dorfmans moved to Chile. Dorfman was determined to become a writer as a youth. He attended the University of Chile and became a Chilean citizen in 1967. From 1968 to 1969, he attended graduate school at the University of California at Berkeley. His thesis on the absurd in plays by Harold Pinter, who he befriended years later, was published in 1968.

During 1970-1973, Dorfman served as a cultural advisor to President Salvador Allende. After the 1973 coup by Chilean General Augusto Pinochet, Dorfman was forced to leave the country and moved between Paris, Amsterdam and Washington, D.C. Since 1985 he has taught at Duke University in Durham, North Carolina, where he is currently a professor of literature and Latin American Studies. Since the restoration of democracy in Chile in 1990, he has divided his time between Santiago and the United States, where he became a citizen in 2004.

Dorfman has been a human rights activist for many years, and has addressed the General Assembly of the United Nations and other forums on social issues. His plays, novels, short stories, essays, and poems often deal with the horrors of tyranny. His plays have been translated into more than forty languages and performed in more than 100 countries. *Widows*, a political allegory that Dorfman adapted from his 1983 novel, is the poignant story of a group of black-clad peasant women whose husbands "disappeared" into the maw of a military junta. While washing laundry by the river, the women discover a man's faceless corpse floating to the surface. A struggle ensues: each of the women believes the man to be her missing husband. *Widows* first played at the Mark Taper Forum, Los Angeles, California in 1991 and reached New York's 59E59 Theatre in 2008. Critic Charles Isherwood pointed out that "Mr. Dorfman's compassion for the suffering of the women is palpable, as is his contempt for the brutal tactics of the military men." But, added Isherwood, "He has failed to translate his moral and emotional responses to these historically inspired events into compelling or even convincingly truthful drama."[11]

In Dorfman's *Reader*, a dedicated censor, Daniel Lucas, receives an unfinished novel and finds in it a description of his own past crimes. The play received its world premiere at the Traverse Theatre during 1995's Edinburgh Fringe Festival. Atypical of other Dorfman's works, *Who's Who* is a murder mystery farce that unfolds in Hollywood during a terrorist plot. It premiered at Germany's Frankfurt Schauspielhaus in 1998. That same year, also in Germany, *Mascara* opened at the Bonn Schauspielhaus. A psychological thriller about a man whose invisibility allows him to take incriminating photographs, *Mascara* was dramatized by Dorfman from his 1988 novel in collaboration with his son Rodrigo.

Speak Truth to Power: Voices from Beyond the Dark is based on a book written by Kerry Kennedy, featuring interviews with human rights champions who overcame overwhelming odds against authoritarian rulers. The play was first presented at the Kennedy Center in Washington, D.C., in 2000 and subsequently aired on PBS as part of its Great Performances series. Directed by Gregory Mosher, it starred Sigourney Weaver, Kevin Kline, Alec Baldwin, and John Malkovich. Since then, *Speak Truth to Power* has been performed across America and around the world. On November 2, 2006, the play was presented in the Middle East for the first time as part of a red-carpet Gala Dinner charity event at the Qatar National Theatre.

The Other Side, an anti-war play first shown at the New National Theatre in Tokyo, Japan, in 2004, reached New York's City Center Stage on December 13, 2005. It tells of an old couple residing near the border of two fighting countries, passing their days confirming the identity of dead bodies and burying them. "In *The Other Side*, Mr. Dorfman has set out to denounce the cruelty of global feuds fired by nationalism and ethnic prejudice," wrote critic Charles Isherwood. "But he expresses this unexceptional sentiment in the form of a ponderous comedy-drama that could itself be accused of a human-right violation, albeit a minor one: the wholesale waste of two first-rate actors [John Cullum and Rosemary Harris]."[12]

Inspired by Dante's epic poem *The Divine Comedy* and reminiscent of Jean-Paul Sartre's *No Exit*, Dorfman's *Purgatorio* features a Man and a Woman who, in their afterlife, interrogate one another while groping for forgiveness and contrition. The play had a workshop production at the Theatre Studies Department of Duke University in February 2005 and later that year was produced by the Seattle Rep. Arcola Theatre in London's West End presented *Purgatorio* in 2008. The Hoy Polloy Theatre of Brunswick, Australia, mounted it in 2009.

Picasso's Closet, a counterfactual history in which the influential artist is murdered by the Nazis, had its premiere at Theatre J in Washington, D.C. in 2006. Dorfman wrote the book and Eric Woolfson the music of *Dancing Shadows*, wherein an imaginary village is devastated during a war. The musical was first presented at the Seoul Center Opera House, South Korea, in 2007.

For England's BBC-TV, Dorfman and his son Rodrigo scripted *Prisoners in Time* (1995), in which a tormented ex-prisoner of war and the mea-culpa Japanese man who tortured him meet face to face, each hoping to find redemption and peace. Dorfman's 1998's *Heading South, Looking North: A Bilingual Journey*, an account of his life of exile and bicultural roots, was the source of a feature-length documentary, *A Promise to the Dead*, which had its world premiere at the 2007 Toronto International Film Festival. The footage included glimpses of Salvador Allende, Hugo Chávez, Augusto Pinochet, Henry Kissinger, Richard Nixon – and Ariel Dorfman himself. Dorfman borrowed elements from the old classic *The Hands of Orlac*[13] when concocting the feature *Blood and Honey* (2010), a surreal murder thriller: a Taiwanese concert pianist, who had a heart transplant, is experiencing terrifying nightmares and decides to track down the identity of the donor. She discovers that she was given the heart of a murderer.

Acting Edition: Penguin Plays; Samuel French, Inc.

Awards and Honors: *Death and the Maiden* won the 1992 Laurence Olivier Theatre Award for Best Play. Ariel Dorfman's first novel, *Hard Rain* (1973), won the Sudamericana Award. Dorfman received the Lowell Thomas Award for his travel book, *Desert Memories* (2004). Dorfman and his son, Rodrigo, garnered a Writer's Guild of Great Britain Award for *Prisoners in Time* (1996). *Dancing Shadows*, Dorfman's musical in collaboration with composer Eric Woolfson, won five Korean "Tony" awards (2007). Dorfman won two Kennedy Center Theatre Awards for his plays *Reader* and *Widows*. In July 2010 he had the honor of delivering the Nelson Mandela Lecture in South Africa. He is a member of *L'Académie Universelle des Cultures* in Paris, and the American Academy of Arts and Sciences.

NOTES

1. Ariel Dorfman, *Death and the Maiden* (New York: Penguin Books, 1992), 73-74.

2. *New York Post*, March 18, 1992.
3. *Wall Street Journal*, March 24, 1992.
4. *New York Newsday*, March 18, 1992.
5. *Newsweek Magazine*, March 30, 1992.
6. *Daily News*, March 18, 1992.
7. *Daily News*, March 27, 1992.
8. *Christian Science Monitor*, March 27, 1992.
9. *Time Magazine*, March 30, 1992.
10. *Inside the Actor's Studio*, TV's *Bravo*, June 29, 1997.
11. *New York Times*, January 21, 2008.
12. *New York Times*, December 14, 2005.
13. *Les Mains d'Orlac* (*The Hands of Orlac*), a 1920 French novel by Maurice Renard, is the story of a famous pianist whose hands are crushed in a train wreck. A Parisian surgeon attaches the limbs of a murderer – with fatal results. *The Hands of Orlac* was the basis for a German expressionistic film in 1924, with Conrad Veidt in the role of Paul Orlac; a 1935 American remake, titled *Mad Love*, featuring Colin Clive as the injured pianist and Peter Lorre as a deranged surgeon; and a 1960 British feature, starring Mel Ferrer and Christopher Lee.

IV. Lawyers and Judges Out of Court

The Woman in the Case (1905)

Clyde Fitch (United States, 1865-1909)

Clyde Fitch may have been inspired by the real-life case of Nan Patterson, whose death was never definitely declared a suicide or a murder, when he wrote *The Woman in the Case.*

The first act is set during a Manhattan dinner party three months after the wedding of man-about-town Julian Rolfe to socialite Margaret Hughes. The guests include their three bridesmaids.The mood of the evening is clouded by the recent murder of Philip Long, the best man.

Margaret's mother enters clutching an evening paper that trumpets the claims of a notorious vamp, Claire Forster, boasting publicly of an affair with Julian. As proof, she has offered to produce love letters from him. Julian denies any current relationship with Claire Forster, but he does admit that she was his mistress before he met Margaret. Philip Long, his best man, then fell under Claire's spell. Julian describes how he warned his friend away from her and succeeded in preventing Philip from proposing to Claire.

At that moment, the police interrupt the evening with a warrant for Julian's arrest for the murder of Phillip Long. Margaret clings to her husband as he is taken away.

Act 2 takes place in the visitors' room at the Tombs, the city jail. While they are waiting for Julian, George Thompson, a lawyer friend, discloses that the incriminating letters Claire possesses are dated only a few days before the murder. Margaret is convinced they are forged.

When the prisoner is brought in, Thompson expresses concern about the accumulation of "strong circumstantial proof" against Julian, mainly the fact that following his encounter with Philip that night he did not go straight home. "My brain was on fire," explains Julian."I had to walk it off in the cool of night. I walked for two hours in the park."

Once Julian is returned to his cell, Margaret tells Thompson of her plan to clear her husband: she intends to rent a flat in the same building as Claire Forster and worm her way into the woman's confidence. "I'll powder and paint and dye my hair. I'll live her life with her, whatever it is. And then, what a reward if, at the end, with you hidden somewhere as witness, I get the true story from her lips! ... I mean to choke out of her the truth."

Act 3 unfolds in Margaret's new apartment on West 52nd Street, two months later. Calling herself Mrs. Darcy, she has convincingly changed her appearance, voice, and demeanor. She anxiously tells Thompson that "tonight is my last chance," for Julian's is due in court the next day. According to her plan, Thompson and Inspector Williams, the policeman investigating the murder, are hidden in an adjoining room where they will be able to hear the women's conversation.

Plying her guest with wine, Margaret works the chit-chat around to a discussion of the night of Philip's death, soliciting from Claire the sudden, inadvertent confession that Philip Long, in fact, had committed suicide. Admits Claire, " I saw his hand go behind his back, but I didn't dream! 'My life's rotten anyway,' he said 'and I'm going to end it!' And before I could stop him, he'd shot himself!" She blames Julian for breaking her relationship with Philip and causing his death.

Unable to contain herself, Margaret reveals her true identity: "You fiend! I am his wife! Do you understand? His wife! Julian Rolfe's wife! And he's free! Do you hear me, free!"

* * *

The Woman in the Case introduces various elements that later became hallmarks of detective fiction: the innocent party entrapped by circumstantial evidence as a murder suspect; the lack of an alibi; an intense quarrel between the suspect and the victim prior to the discovery of the body; and the sharp cross-examination of the suspect before the attorney for the defense agrees to take on the case (this device was embellished years later by J.B. Priestley in *The Winslow Boy* and by Agatha Christie in *Witness for the Prosecution*).

After a preview in Rochester, New York, at the Lyceum Theatre on January 28, 1905, *The Woman in the Case* opened two days later at Broadway's Herald Square Theatre. Blanche Walsh took the lead role of Margaret Rolfe, while Robert Drouet played her husband, Julian. The *New York Times* proclaimed it a "play of exceptional interest. It is unquestionably Mr. Fitch's most virile and vital contribution to the theatre since *The Climbers*."[1] In a follow-up piece, the *Times* pointed out that by "avoiding the clap-trap sensationalism in this newest play, Mr. Fitch has revealed much ingenuity... the result is a quivering slice of life, gruesome but truthfully effective."[2] It ran for eighty-nine performances, reopening four years later at the Madison Square Garden, starring Violet Vanbrugh.

A silent photoplay, in 1916, featured Pauline Frederick and Alan Hale. Betty Compson and William P. Carleton appeared as the Rolfes in a 1922 remake entitled *The Law and the Woman*. A talkie version, *The Wiser Sex* (1932), starring Claudette Colbert and Melvyn Douglas, took many liberties with the original material, juxtaposing the suicide with a double murder.

* * *

Arguably the finest American playwright at the turn of the twentieth century, and certainly the most successful, William Clyde Fitch – a graduate of Amherst College, 1886, where his effeminate demeanor won him major women's roles in the dramatic club – launched a prolific career with *Beau Brummel*, an 1890 smash hit penned for Richard Mansfield. A play of fictionalized history and court intrigue, it was revived in New York in 1894, 1900, 1905, 1906, 1907, and 1917 and filmed in 1924 with John Barrymore and thirty years later with Stewart Granger.

Many of Clyde Fitch's plays rely on suspense for their dramatic impact. Among these are *Nathan Hale* (1899), an account of the Revolutionary War-era schoolmaster who became a patriotic spy, and *Barbara Frietchie* (1899), a Civil War drama in which the eponymous heroine is gunned down on the balcony while waving the Union flag. *The Cowboy and the Lady* (1899), *The Marriage Game* (1901), and *The City* (1909) all feature murders, while *Major André* (1903) tells us about the capture, imprisonment, and execution of a British spy during the American Revolution.

Over the course of his nineteen-year career, Fitch wrote fifty-six plays, thirty-six of them original and the remainder translations or adaptations of foreign dramatic works or novels. In 1901 alone, he had six plays running on Broadway. The royalties from such a relentless output made him "the first millionaire dramatist in America."[3] Gradually, Fitch took on more and more responsibility for his productions, eventually even directing his own work for the stage.

However, in the end, what he will be remembered for are "his studies of human characters who are endowed with a shining virtue or possessed by one absorbing vice… The emotions are universal, too, recognizable to all humanity, which accounts for the international success of *The Truth* [a play that treats the subject of pathological lying] and *The Woman in the Case*."[4]

Awards and Honors: Clyde Fitch's *Barbara Frietchie* and *The Climbers* were both top-ten selections in Burns Mantle's *The Best Plays of 1899-1909* (Burns Mantle and Garrison P. Sherwood, eds., New York: Dodd, Mead and Company, 1944).

NOTES

1. *New York Times*, January 31, 1905.
2. *New York Times*, February 5, 1905.
3. Mark Hawkins-Dady, ed., *International Dictionary of Theatre: Playwrights* (Detroit: St. James Press,1994), 323.
4. Arthur Dobson Quinn, *A History of the American Drama: From the Civil War to the Present Day* (New York: Appleton-Century-Crofts, Inc., 1936), 294-95.

At Bay (1913)

George Scarborough (United States, 1875-1951)

George Scarborough's *At Bay* centers on Aline Graham, daughter of the U.S. District Attorney, who hides a skeleton in her closet. She is secretly marriage to Tom Woolworth, a foreign correspondent, who deserted her. A shady Washington, D.C. lawyer, Judson Flagg, gets hold of a letter written by Aline to Woolworth, signed "your wife in a secret." Aline finds herself "at bay" when Flagg summons her to his office and demands one thousand dollars for the letter. "I haven't that much money… This is blackmail!" Aline says. She tosses a few bills on his desk and offers him an emerald brooch.

Flagg suggests that there is another way to secure the letter— "You are very pretty, my dear… we could be friends." As Aline retreats toward the door, Flagg seizes her roughly. A struggle ensues. Flagg pinions Aline's left hand but she manages to strike him on the forehead with the base of a paper knife. When Flagg proceeds to attack her, Aline plunges the sharp point into his breast. The lawyer staggers backward, pulling out the weapon. Wounded, he grabs Aline's brooch and pushes a button that activates a hidden flash camera.

Later, Flagg's body is found sprawled across the desk. A soldier of fortune, Captain Lawrence Holbrook joins his friend Robert Dempster, Chief of the U.S. Secret Service, to investigate the case. Upon entering the victim's office, the captain smells smoke in the air—and perfume. He finds a brooch held in Flagg's clenched hand and hides it in his pocket, for he recognizes that the ornament belongs to Aline Graham, the woman he loves. Holbrook smuggles out the incriminating letter and the camera plate, later admitting to Chief Dempster that he has destroyed evidence.

The chief has to arrest him for accessory to murder, albeit after the fact.

The chief interrogates Aline and gives orders to lock her up when the medical examiner, Francis Elliott, who had been hired by Holbrook to attend the autopsy, arrives with the announcement, "Nobody killed Flagg… the man died of cardiac weakness."

Chief: But that stab with a paper file?

Doctor: Only a glancing and superficial wound. Death was due to excitement—rupture of the heart.

Aline tells Holbrook that her "secret marriage" was but "a mockery arranged by a scoundrel." With a convenient wind-down coincidence, the captain relates to her that Tom Woolworth is "as dead as mackerel. Dead as a door nail… I buried him… I held his hand when he died."

Holbrook assures the family priest, Father Shannon, that his services will be needed tomorrow and takes Aline in his arms. Curtain.

* * *

At Bay tried out at the Belasco Theatre, Washington, D.C., on September 22, 1913, then opened in Manhattan's Thirty-Ninth Street Theatre on October 7 to mostly positive reviews: "If you want real suspense in a play and plenty of thrills—in short, a good genuine melodrama—go and enjoy *At Bay.*"[1] "Mr. Scarborough's play is an unusual achievement in view of his short experience… It is a clean melodrama"[2] "The subsequent developments were of a kind to create and prolong suspense—to give one, too, that tremulous feeling along the spine which, in the theatre, represents a certain kind of pleasure;"[3] "*At Bay* proves that George Scarborough is not a sensationalist but a dramatist."[4] The lone dissenting opinion was that of the *Evening World* critic who opined that the play "causes more wonder than thrills."[5] *At Bay* ran for 119 performances, was novelized by Page Philips in 1914, and filmed—as a fifty-minute silent feature—a year later.

A few months prior to the premiere of *At Bay*, on August 14, 1913, George Scarborough's *The Lure* opened at Maxine Elliott's Theatre to heated controversy. Publicized as "the red light play," *The Lure* is a white slave drama about an innocent working girl cunningly drawn, by dastardly villains, into a house of ill repute. Fighting to preserve her honor, the girl is saved in the nick of time by her Secret Service lover. The police ordered *The Lure* closed and the producers put under an arrest warrant until a grand jury and the deputy police commissioner attended a closed performance on September 11, 1913. The play was allowed to reopen on September 26, with revisions in the scenes depicting the "imprisoned girls."

Interviewed by columnist Archie Bell in the *Green Book Magazine*, Scarborough said, "I regret the police interference in the matter, for while some people may think that it was good for the play from the publicity point of view, I believe that it was bad. It gave people the wrong impression. My play was truth, plain, unvarnished truth, and it should have succeeded on its own merits without any assistance from the police."[6] *The Lure* ran for 132 performances.

Scarborough's *The Last Resort* (1914) focuses on a crusading lawyer who tangles with corrupt corporation leaders with the aid of a crusading newspaperwoman. The *New York Times* praised the play for breaking new dramaturgical grounds: "The old melodrama with its trustful, clinging heroine is gone. Gone is the old-style villain, black moustache, cigarette, curses and all. And in their place is the modern heroine, an enterprising reporter in this case, who has kept all the charm of the old one and added to it the ingenuity and resourcefulness that used to belong to the adventuress while matched against her who is the new villain, political boss and corporation lawyer."[7]

But Scarborough returned to unabashed melodrama in *The Heart of Wetona* (1916), the story of an Indian maiden deflowered by a white man and the vengeful Comanches who track him down.

The Son-Daughter (1919), co-written with David Belasco, pictures the saga of Lien Wha, the daughter of an influential Chinese merchant in New York, who strangles a wicked imperialistic spy and escapes into the arms of her lover—none other than the son of the revolutionary leader in China.

The Mad Dog (1921) is "a hot violent and smoky melodrama,"[8] about a fugitive from the Colorado State penitentiary making his way toward the Mexican border.

Co-written with Scarborough's wife, Annette Westbay, *The Heaven Trappers* (1927) is a comedy-drama about two scoundrels and their female cohort, who disguise themselves as traveling prophets in order to invade the territory of moonshine distillers.

Several years later, Scarborough's *Bad Babies* was raided twice by the police at San Francisco's Capitol Theatre for utilizing a very young cast enacting schoolboy and schoolgirl delinquents and harlots. The notoriety brought the play eight weeks of full houses. Scarborough's career had come full circle since police involvement with his very first steamy play, *The Lure*, in 1913.

Scarborough carved for himself a lucrative career in Hollywood, where he wrote silent films and early talkies for Fox Film Corporation. Many of his movies were crime-ridden. *The Final Judgment* (1915) had Ethel Barrymore portraying an actress who comes to the rescue of her husband, a young district attorney, suspected of homicide. *Cupid's Roundup* (1918) is a Western adventure about a cowboy who exposes a band of cattle rustlers and is accused of murder—Tom Mix's first starring role in a feature film. In *Under the Yoke* (1918), Theda Bara enacts an attractive Spanish woman, settled in the Philippines, who inadvertently causes the assassination of her father. *Her One Mistake* (1918) is the story of a wealthy heiress who falls in love with a brigand but stabs him to death when he attacks her. Master crooks, German spies, and Secret Service agents chase after the designs of a new aeroplane in *Luck and Pluck* (1919). The daughter of a reformed criminal becomes engaged to a district attorney in *Lovebound* (1923), but finds her happiness in jeopardy when forced to participate in a jewel robbery by her father's erstwhile accomplice; *The Locked Door* (1929), adapted to the screen from Channing Pollock's play, depicts the dilemma of a married woman, played by Barbara Stanwyck, who is found enclosed in a room with the dead body of a former beau.

NOTES

1. *The Evening Telegram,* October 8, 1913.
2. *The Sun,* October 8, 1913.
3. *New York Times,* October 8, 1913.
4. *Evening Sun,* October 8, 1913.
5. *Evening World,* October 8, 1913.
6. *Green Book Magazine,* January 1914.
7. *New York Times,* March 3, 1914.
8. *New York Times,* November 9, 1921.

The Law of the Land (1914)

George Broadhurst (United States, England-born, 1866-1952)

The action of *The Law of the Land* begins in the study of Robert Harding, a prominent lawyer. Through a conversation between Harding's private secretary, Arthur Brockland, and his butler, Chetwoode, we learn that their employer possesses "the devil of a temper" and is extremely hard on his wife, Margaret.

Robert Harding arrives home, summons Margaret, and admonishes her for rekindling a relationship with former flame Geoffrey Morton, a famous global engineer who has recently returned from abroad. "The mountain he tunneled in Syria, the bridge he built in China, the marvelous dam he has just constructed in Africa," sneers Harding. Margaret admits to receiving a note from Morton. Fuming, her husband advances menacingly, but at this moment Brookland enters: "Mr. Harding! … I can't stand to see a lady insulted like this. I really can't."

Harding retorts: "Then let me tell you that you don't *have* to stand it. You quit now, this minute. You're discharged… Get out."

Says Brockland: "I really couldn't leave your wife alone with you."

Harding gasps with rage. He strikes Brockland and a struggle ensues with the secretary getting the worst of it. Margaret thanks Brockland, and he goes.

Geoffrey Morton is admitted and accuses Harding of spreading nasty rumors about him. The Hardings' nine-year-old son, Bennie, enters in his pajamas, blinking sleepily. "Uncle Geoffrey!" cries the child and embraces the visitor.

Harding scoffs: "Ben, why didn't you speak to me when you came in? … Why haven't I seen this month's report from school?" On the heels of a temperamental outburst, Harding snatches a whip from the wall and orders Bennie into the next room. A crack of the whip is heard, followed by shrieks: "Don't papa, don't—please don't."

Morton utters "I can't stand it," exits, and there are sounds of a scuffle. Morton reenters carrying the whip and throws it across the room.

Harding, too, returns as his wife rushes off: "I'm coming, Bennie. I'm coming."

Harding: Well, I've learned what I wanted to know. He isn't *my* son. He's yours.

Morton: It's a lie.
Harding: It's the truth, but it never came to me till I saw the three of you there together… Then it came to me like a flash.

Morton continues to deny Harding's speculation but Margaret enters saying, "Yes, it is the truth… What's the use of denying it any longer. Why continue this life of deception and horror?" Morton intends to leave the house with Margaret and Bennie, but Harding insists that the boy remain with him, declaring, "There will be no divorce—even now—that I know." Reluctantly, Morton exits, promising Margaret, "You'll hear from me in the morning."

Left alone with his wife, Harding taunts Margaret by threatening to expose the brewing scandal to the "scavengers of the press": "How they will revel in it… Can you see the headlines! And the photographs—on the front page—photographs of you—and the boy! By God, I'll make your name—and the boy's—a by-word through the country—and then I'll kick you out—both of you—into the streets—and even then, you won't be able to marry Morton and your son will still be just what he is today. It's the law of the land!"

He picks up the whip: "I'll trash the boy till he won't be able to stand."

Margaret takes a pistol from a desk drawer and backs toward the door: "Put that down! … Put it down—or I'll shoot."

Harding laughs and lunges toward her. Margaret fires and Harding falls. She gasps with horror. Brockland rushes in, realizes the situation, removes the revolver from Margaret's hand, and, kneeling, lays it near the arm of the dead man. The curtain falls.

Act 2 unfolds in the dining room. Brockland soothes Margaret, "They're sure to think its suicide… We're perfectly safe… We'll let everything be discovered naturally… First of all, in a casual way we'll arrange to send Chetwoode to your husb…—to his—bedroom."

The butler is told to fetch Harding for breakfast. He returns agitated, declaring, "Your husband—he's dead… For hours… He shot himself through the heart." Brockland hurries off. Margaret sends Chetwoode to fetch the family physician, Dr. Whittridge.

Brockland returns: "Something extraordinary—something unbelievable—has happened… I found him lying on the floor as we had left him—but the revolver was in his hand!" Margaret exclaims: "But you placed it on the floor… Then how could it get—how could—it's incredible—impossible! Perhaps he wasn't dead… Perhaps he recovered consciousness…"

Brockland says with conviction: "He was dead. I'd swear to it."

Margaret whispers: "Then someone must have been in that room—someone knows." Chetwoode returns, admitting that he was the one who found the body and placed the revolver in the victim's hand to make it appear like suicide.

Geoffrey Morton and Dr. Whittridge arrive on the scene and are told that Harding committed suicide. Morton theorizes that Harding must have gone into "a fit of his uncontrollable temper—a second or two of madness—and then—it was done."

Captain Pritchard, a hard-boiled lawman, requests that Dr. Whittridge examine the body closely: "Notice particularly the direction of the wound and the absence of powder marks." The doctor concludes that the wound was not self-inflicted. Captain Pritchard asks Brockland and Chetwoode if they had heard a shot last night, grills both fiercely, accuses them of lying, and saber-rattles about making an arrest.

The third act takes place in Margaret's room, where she describes to Morton the horrors of last night, relating how the sympathetic Brockland and Chetwoode conspired to help her. "If you confess the entire truth," says Morton, "the jury would either acquit you or disagree. No twelve men in this country would unanimously condemn a woman who did what she thought was right to protect her child."

Still, concerned that the proceedings might scar Bennie for life, Geoffrey offers to undertake the blame upon himself: "They know I came here last night… We quarreled, and I shot him… The murder will be fastened on me, and neither Bennie nor you will be brought into it in any way… He belongs to me just as much as he belongs to you, and no one shall spoil his life while I can help it… He is my son, my own flesh and blood, and I won't let anyone, not even you, come between me and my right to save him!"

The last act reverts back to Robert Harding's study. A softer, more benevolent investigator has taken over the case—Inspector Cochrane. His wife has just had twins— "both boys, weighed eight pounds apiece, too," he declares. "I've always wanted kids! And we've been married seven years, and until now we didn't have even a hope! I'll be good to 'em, too. I've got no use for a man who isn't kind to kids and animals. Any man who would abuse a horse, a dog or a child, must have something wrong with him. That's one thing I can't stand for."

The inspector studies the murder gun and mumbles, "Finger marks." He sends an officer to get the prints of all the men in the house. He then produces an ornament that had fallen from the evening gown worn by Margaret the previous night: "It was found in this room this morning and maids don't wear things like these." The Inspector elicits from Margaret details about the flogging of Bennie.

"The skunk!" growls Cochrane. "The dirty skunk! … His own father! What do you think of that! … He must have been a fine man!"

Margaret emotes: "He was terrible! I couldn't begin to tell you the indignities—the cruelties—I've suffered, but I bore them all for the sake of the boy!"

Morton intervenes and confesses to the shooting, but Margaret cannot accept the sacrifice: "Inspector, he didn't kill him. I did... I'm the one who killed him and I'm the one who must pay! (She points at the whip) My husband picked it up and said he would trash Bennie again... I pleaded with him, but he only laughed. So I took the revolver... He came toward me—and then—and then –"

Cochrane interjects: "I know the rest! You dropped the gun, it was discharged by accident and shot him through the heart! ... Then you got frightened, went away, and later your butler came up and, thinking to help you out, put the gun in his hand. It's as plain as day! ... There were no witnesses. It happened that way and that's all there is to it."

The phone rings. Cochrane picks it up: "That's probably for me. Hello! How are you, Coroner? (Pause) It was an accident, that's all. (Pause) How long will that be? Then I'll wait. I want to tell you about the kids. (Pause) Yes, they're doing fine—both of 'em! And the grips they have! One of 'em this morning took hold of my finger...he held onto it as if he would never let go... I didn't know a kid could have a grip like that..." Curtain.

* * *

The Law of the Land opened at the Forty-Eighth Street Theatre in New York on September 30, 1914, co-staged by Edward Elsner and the author, and ran for 221 performances. "Grim melodrama — often painfully tense," blazed the *New York Times*. "In this, George Broadhurst's appeal to his audience is more in the nature of a knife thrust in, turned, and then slowly, slowly drawn out."[1] Julia Dean won high praise for her portrayal of the long-suffering wife, as did Walter Craven in the role of the humane police inspector.

Scripted and directed by Maurice Tourneur, *The Law of the Land* was filmed as a silent feature in 1917.

Acting Edition: Samuel French, Inc. (in manuscript form).

NOTE

1. *New York Times*, October 1, 1914.

The Cat and the Canary (1922)

John Willard (United States, 1885-1942)

The wind is howling, the will is read at the stroke of midnight, and the heiress is stalked by an unknown killer in the cobwebbed Glencliff Manor on the Hudson.

The Cat and the Canary inherited the mantle of *The Bat* as America's classic mystery-comedy, famed for its ingenious use of secret panels and sliding doors. It is the granddaddy of all "old dark house" thrillers.

Author John Willard learned the techniques of blood-and-thunder melodrama while an actor. Among the roles he depicted on Broadway was Detective Sergeant Cassidy in Bayard Veiller's *Within the Law* (1912). In his *The Cat and the Canary*, which opened at the National Theatre on February 7, 1922, Willard portrayed Harry Blythe, one of six relatives who gather at the isolated mansion of Cyrus Ganby West, on the twentieth anniversary of West's passing, to hear family lawyer Roger Crosby read his last testament.

Lovely Annabelle West is named the sole inheritor of "money, bonds, securities, estate, real and otherwise." But the will of her eccentric uncle, who feared a streak of insanity in the family, contains a codicil:"In the event of the death of the beneficiary, or if he or she be proved to be of unsound mind, or if it be proved in a court of law that the said beneficiary is not competent to properly handle the estate, then my executor will open the envelope marked '3' and declare the next heir."

The lawyer realizes that the seal of the "envelope marked '3'" has been broken and is convinced that Annabelle is in danger. When Annabelle just laughs at his overprotectiveness he tries to explain, and as he does so, a panel in the wall opens noiselessly and a hand comes through, clutching Crosby by the throat and dragging him off.

Annabelle, who has been perusing a book, looks up and finds herself alone.

When she relates to her relatives that Crosby has disappeared into thin air, they begin to doubt her mental stability. The elusive next heir spends the rest of the night stalking Annabelle in an attempt to frighten the wits out of her. A claw-like hand appears from nowhere, a monstrous figure lurks in the shadows, and Crosby's body topples out of a closet, wreaking havoc on the girl's composure.

Who is the mysterious "Cat?" Is it the West Indies housekeeper, "Mammy" Pleasant, who claims that "there's a evil spirit working around this house?" Is it the sullen adventurer, Harry Blythe? The romantic poet, Charles Wilder? The indecisive veterinarian, Paul Jones? ("I have felt better—but on the other hand, I have felt worse.") The psychic, Susan Sillsby? ("I know it, just as sure as I'm standing on this spot, that something is going to happen. Something terrible.") The mousy Cicely Young? Or is it the "homicidal maniac" who escaped earlier that day from Fairview, a nearby asylum?

In a frenetic climax, nice-guy Charlie Wilder is unmasked as the culprit, and it is bumbling Paul Jones who saves Annabelle in the nick of time. When Charlie is carted away, Paul meekly turns to Annabelle: "I thought—that is, I got to thinking, after what you'd been through tonight that maybe you wouldn't be so nervous if you were to wake up suddenly and found me your husband. "They embrace as the curtain falls.

* * *

The Cat and the Canary was welcomed by Alexander Woollcott: "The National Theatre has gone in for melodrama in the manner of Mary Roberts Rinehart—spooky melodrama, with a lot of quaking people cooped up in a shadowy old house, while doors are opened by unseen hands, strangled cries are heard in the darkness and murdered men pitch headlong into the room from behind secret panels… It is the handiwork of John Willard who has turned out a creepy young thriller, nicely calculated to make every hair on your head rise and remain standing from 8.30 till nearly 11."[1]

Florence Eldridge as Annabelle and Henry Hull as Paul found themselves in a mega hit that ran 349 performances, spawned numerous stock productions, and was adapted several times to the screen.

The Cat and the Canary was presented at London's Shaftesbury Theatre on October 31, 1922, running 101 performances, and was revived at the Regent Theatre, London, in 1927, for 14 evenings.

In 1937, *The Cat and the Canary* came back to Broadway for nine performances. Brooks Atkinson believed that "the tricks of *The Cat and the Canary* are now off the old hat remainder counter. Nothing ages quite so rapidly as a barnstorming thriller."[2]

However, when the Whodunit Company assigned me to get *The Cat* out of the bag again at Off-Broadway's Stage 73 in 1965, the majority of New York critics gave the play a new lease on life. "*The Cat and the Canary* still can make that little shiver run up and down the spine," wrote Richard P. Cook;[3] "There's warmth and humor and an immaculate sense of timing that scatters the chills, thrills and suspense into the audience," stated Judith Crist;[4] "*The Cat and the Canary* is scary and fun, and should be required theatre every Halloween," chirped W.M.H. van Okker.[5] The reviewers praised the cast which included Adale O'Brien as Annabelle, Tom Wheatley as Paul, Helen

Martin as the superstitious maid, and Abe Vigoda—prior to his migration to the West Coast for *Barney Miller* and *Fish*—as Hendricks, a menacing sanatorium guard. The play ran for 143 performances, during which I had a grand time eavesdropping in the lobby for the squeals and cackles of the audience.[6]

The Cat and the Canary resurged in 1979, first on February 15 at the Halcyon Repertory Company, Chicago, Illinois, where lawyer Roger Crosby changed genders and became Regina Crosby. Later that year it was performed by two Off Broadway companies in New York, the Impossible Ragtime Theatre, which updaed the proceedings from the 1920s to the 1970s, and Manhattan Punch Line, which used a new adaptation by Roderick Cook.

The Cook version follows the Willard original closely but there are two innovations: Instead of a menacing West Indies housekeeper there is a pixie Irish one, Pegeen ni Houlihan, "a wizened old crone with haunted eyes." And Hendricks, the asylum guard, is in cahoots with the murderer, Charlie Wilder, and insists on being paid at once.

The Cat and the Canary came back to Off Broadway's Village Performers Theatre on July 17, 1985. Reviewer Michael Sommers sniffed at "lack of finesse in the directing department (plus miscasting)" but concluded, "Still, the play's the thing, and this particular one really works after all these years."[7]

Willard novelized the play in 1927 (published by *Readers Library*). That same year, director Paul Leni, a newcomer from Germany, peppered his silent movie version of *The Cat and the Canary* with expressionistic touches—credit cards shifted by cat's paws, the image of Cyrus West dying amidst gigantic medicine bottles, white curtains blowing in the wind along dark corridors. Laura LaPlante played the besieged Annabelle alongside nimble Creighton Hale as Paul.[8] In January 2023, the Museum of Modern Arts chose the movie for preservation and exhibition,

A 1930 talkie remake, titled *The Cat Creeps*, was co-directed by Willard and Rupert Julian who cast Helen Twelvetrees and Raymond Hackett. Bob Hope and Paulette Goddard starred in a 1939 rendition directed by Elliott Nugent. *The Cat* meowed again in a 1978 British version directed by Radley Metzger, featuring Honor Blackman and Michael Callan.

Mexico had its own film adaptation—*La voluntad del muerto*—in 1940. Swedish television presented *Katten och kanariefagelin* in 1961.

* * *

John A. Willard continued to pen mystery thrillers—with diminishing returns. *The Green Beatle* (1924) is set in San Francisco's Chinatown. The proprietor of a curio shop, sinister Chang Hong, leashes his revenge on the American who, years earlier, raped his beloved Suey-Yen in Shanghai.

Fog (1927) begins on a deserted Long Island wharf and continues aboard an old schooner. There is a formal yacht party, but the host does not show up.The festive mood changes dramatically when three of the guests are thrown overboard. Some trick disappearances, a time bomb set to explode in five minutes, and the actual rocking of the boat on stage yielded sporadic suspense. Scripted by Willard, *Fog* was filmed in 1929 under the title *Black Waters* and was Great Britain's first "all-talkie."

In *Adventure* (1928), soldier of fortune Michael O'Shane comes to the rescue of Dolores Hampton in New York's Central Park and follows the girl to her father's cattle ranch in Wyoming, where he protects the grazing range from marauding sheep growers, shoots bad guy Angel Evans, and wins the heart of Dolores.

Willard's last play, *The Murder Game*, opened in Sharon, Connecticut in 1937, but failed to reach Broadway, leaving *The Cat and the Canary* the playwright's sole claim to fame.

* * *

According to the *Encyclopedia of Mystery and Detection*, John A. Willard, who was born in San Francisco, "tried his hand at being a gold miner, reporter, cowboy, art student, aviator and actor before becoming a pilot in France during World War I… Willard got the idea for his most famous work, *The Cat and the Canary*, while flying bombing missions in France."[9]

As an actor, Willard had a robust Broadway career that began in 1912 and lasted until 1938. He was featured in *Making Good* by Owen Davis (1912), *Within the Law* by Bayard Veiller (1912), *The Son-Daughter* by George Scarborough and David Belasco (1919), Gilbert and Sullivan's *The Mikado* (1925) and *The Pirates of Penzance* (1936), Shakespeare's *Julius Caesar* (1937), and Thomas Dekker's *The Shoemaker's Holiday* (1938).

Willard's contributions to the silver screen include the portrayal of Inspector Gregson in *Sherlock Holmes* (1922), alongside John Barrymore's Great Detective, and the co-scripting of *The Mask of Fu Manchu* (1932) from a Sax Rohmer thriller, with Boris Karloff as the Oriental arch-villain, Myrna Loy as his sadistic daughter, and Lewis Stone as Scotland Yard's Nayland Smith.

Acting Edition: Samuel French, Inc.

NOTES

1. *New York Times*, February 8, 1922.

2. *New York Times*, June 15, 1937.
3. *Wall Street Journal,* January 6, 1965.
4. *New York Herald Tribune*, January 5, 1965.
5. *The Villager*, January 7, 1965.
6. The sets of the show were shipped to Israel for a copycat production (in a Hebrew translation), which opened in Tel-Aviv and ran outside the city. The Israeli public was puzzled by the content and style of this old-fashioned American melodrama and the endeavor did not fly.
7. *Back Stage*, August 30, 1985.
8. Director Leni and his star La Plante also collaborated in 1929 on the silent thriller *The Last Warning.* Leni (1885-1929), a German filmmaker, was invited to Hollywood on the strength of his expressionistic horror film, *Waxworks* (1924). In addition to *The Cat and the Canary* and *The Last Warning,* Leni's U.S. movies include: *The Chinese Parrot* (1927), with Sojin Kamiyama playing Police Inspector Charlie Chan; and *The Man Who Laughs* (1928), casting countryman Conrad Veidt in the role of Victor Hugo's carnival freak. Leni died prematurely, at the age of forty-four, of blood poisoning.
9. Chris Steinbrunner and Otto Penzler, ed., *Encyclopedia of Mystery and Detection* (New York: McGraw-Hill Book Company, 1976), 420.

The Leavenworth Case (1936)

Basil Ring, pseudonym for Wilbur Braun (United States, 1896-1968)

Anna Katharine Green (1846-1935) is "variously regarded as the 'mother, grandmother, and godmother of the detective story' because of her authorship of *The Leavenworth Case* (1878)—usually considered to be the first detective novel written by a woman."[1] The novel introduced an early series investigator, Ebenezer Gryce of the New York police force, a hardworking prober sans the flamboyancy and eccentricity of other literary sleuths of the era. (Gryce, brought to life nine years before Sherlock Holmes, will continue to be the stolid detective of ten additional books, all—alas—tossed aside today).

Michele Slung, in *Twentieth Century Crime and Mystery Writers*, wrote that *The Leavenworth Case* "makes use of a number of devices that were to become staples of the genre: a map of the scene of the crime, lists of deductions and possibilities, headlines to show the developments of the case. The young lawyer-narrator, a foreshadowing of the amorous susceptibilities of Watson and Hastings, falls in love with one of the comely suspects."[2]

The Leavenworth Case is also a torchbearer of the body-in-the-library subgenre. Horatio Leavenworth, an eccentric Fifth Avenue millionaire, about to sign a new will, is found seated at his library desk with a bullet hole in his head, an apparent suicide. A ballistics report, medical evidence, and a coroner's inquiry are integrated into the proceedings.

Gryce concludes and scores of future disciples would echo: "We have no common villainy to deal with here; genius has been at work." The mansion doors have been locked for the night and the windows shuttered, so it appears that this is an inside job, perpetrated by a member of the household. But who?

The Leavenworth Case became an immediate success and has been reprinted sporadically—in hard and soft covers—throughout the twentieth century. S. S. Van Dine, creator of Philo Vance, himself a best-selling author, introduced a 1934 publication of *The Leavenworth Case* as "one of the great classics of this type of fiction… the style of the book, the convincing logic and its sense of reality, give it an undeniable distinction. Not only is it highly interesting and entertaining for the average reader, but it contains qualities of careful ratiocination and painstaking workmanship which many of the modern writers of detective stories would do well to emulate."[3]

While the novel still survives, an 1891 play adaptation of *The Leavenworth Case,* by Anna Katharine Green, is all but forgotten. A *New York Times* dispatcher called it "a careful dramatization" of the original work, "strong and thrilling story," but complained that the "incidents too strongly border on the awful and tend to harrow up the feelings of an audience."[4] The play version of *The Leavenworth Case* depicts the actual shooting of Horatio Leavenworth at the end of Act I and the audience is privy to the identity of the murderer throughout the investigation.

In 1936, *The Leavenworth Case* was incarnated by Wilbur Braun, under the pen name Basil Ring, as a mystery play in a prologue and three acts. While the Green novel begins with Mr. Leavenworth's private secretary visiting the law offices of Veeley, Carr & Raymond to report the murder of his employer, the Ring dramatization opens with an early morning domestic scene at the Leavenworth home, during which we are introduced to various household figures who will soon play important roles in the saga of a double murder: the tall, powerfully built butler, Thomas Dougherty; the pert, rosy-cheeked maid, Molly O'Flannigan; the stout, Irish cook, Kate Malone; the clean-shaven, genteel secretary, Trueman Harwell; and the two mistresses of the manor—Eleanore, Horatio Leavenworth's adopted niece, a tall, willowy girl in her early twenties; and Mary, her cousin, a dainty, exceptionally beautiful maiden of twenty-one. Through the gossipy servants we learn that there is a coldness between the cousins, and that one of the staff, Hannah Chester, a diminutive girl in her late teens, did not come home last night.

A young lawyer, Everett Raymond, arrives carrying a briefcase. Raymond informs Harwell that he is a junior member of the firm, summoned by Leavenworth. When they knock on the locked door of the study, there is no response. With mounting concern, Raymond calls police headquarters.

Ebenezer Gryce—here called "Chief of Inspectors"—arrives on the scene and with him his vivacious assistant Sally Burke, an addition to the novel's original gallery of characters. The body of Horatio Leavenworth is discovered, the key is missing, and there is no gun in the room.

Gryce grills the residents one by one. Thomas the butler asserts that he locked all doors and windows, and that even as a light sleeper he did not hear anything during the night; secretary Trueman relates that Mr. Leavenworth's demeanor was nothing out of the ordinary; and Kate, the cook, declares that she would like to get her hands "on the spalpeen what shot off that gun jist for tin seconds."

Suspicion mounts against Eleanore, when it becomes known that she is an expert marksman, and when the missing key is found in the drawer of her dressing table. Eleanore stammers that she cannot explain it and swears that she didn't kill her uncle. During her protestations, the first act curtain descends.

Smitten with Eleanore, Everett Raymond springs on her a proposal of marriage and assures her that he will relieve her of suspicion by unmasking the true murderer.

The plot thickens when the maid, Hannah Chester, is found dead in a secret passageway behind a paneled library bookcase. Gryce theorizes that Hannah knew who murdered Horatio Leavenworth and must have signed her own death warrant by confronting the culprit. The pendulum of apprehension tilts toward Mary—she is the heiress of the Leavenworth fortune, and the murdered maid's handkerchief is found among Mary's soiled linens.

In a climax which would become characteristic of detective fiction, Gryce assembles all the suspects. He faces Mary and accuses her of murdering her uncle. Trueman Harwell jumps up and reveals that he approached Leavenworth, told him of his high regard for Mary, and asked him for her hand in marriage. Leavenworth laughed, derided Harwell, and ordered him to leave the house and never return. Harwell saw red, opened a drawer, procured a revolver, and fired it straight at Leavenworth's head. He then hurriedly left the room and locked the door. He met Hannah Chester coming down the hall with a candle in her hand. She saw him; he had to silence her.

Harwell suddenly rushes out, but Gryce soothes everybody, explaining that four of his men are waiting for Harwell outside the door of the house. Oh, yes, he knew all along that Harwell was guilty. He accused Mary to wring a confession from the real murderer.

Regrettably, Gryce never explains how he came to the conclusion that Harwell was the guilty party. While most of *The Leavenworth Case* unfolds in a straightforward, cohesive manner, the adapter, bowing to traditions of the time, could not resist such embellishments as a door opening quietly for an unknown eavesdropper, the sudden sliding of a secret panel, a long arm creeping along the wall for the switch, and the lights going out at opportune moments. Broad humor is supplied by the feisty Irish cook, the snoopy assistant sleuth, and detective Gryce himself when he becomes afflicted with gout.

Wilbur Braun's *The Leavenworth Case* was presented at Off Broadway's Cherry Lane Theatre in May 1944.

* * *

A 1923 silent motion picture, scripted by Eve Stuyvesant, directed by Charles Giblyn, and distributed by Vitagraph, eliminated the character of Detective Gryce and had Raymond, the family lawyer, solve the mystery.

In 1936, Republic Pictures financed a talkie of *The Leavenworth case*, with a scenario by Albert Demond and Sidney Sutherland, directed by Lewis D. Collins. Here, secretary Trueman Harwell becomes a doctor enamored with Gloria Leavenworth, now the wife of stockbroker Silas Leavenworth –

killing him with the aid of a monkey, "Jocko," trained to turn on the gas in Leavenworth's room.

A second rendition was filmed for release in Great Britain where censors objected to the depiction of a doctor as a murderer; the culprit turns out to be Silas's spinster sister, Phoebe, who considered Leavenworth a thief and a blackguard. The investigators in both versions (shot at the same time with only the opening and ending sequences differing) were police detectives Bob Gryce (portrayed by Norman Foster) and O'Malley (Warren Hymer).

* * *

Anna Katharine Green was the daughter of a well-known defense lawyer whose cases provided "raw material" for her books. Anna's ambition was to write poetry. She penned a volume of verse, *The Defense of the Bride and Other Poems* (1882), and a blank verse tragedy, *Risifi's Daughter* (1886). In this play, Prince Osaldi of Florentine, having lost his assets, consents to the betrothal of his elder son Giovanni to Ginevra, daughter of Risifi, a wealthy merchant. But Ginevra is in love with Camillo, Giovanni's younger brother. Risifi insists that his daughter marry the heir of the prince, the older Giovanni, who, smitten with the maiden, loving his brother, and intent on saving the family from ruin, commits suicide.

Catherine Ross Nickerson, in *The Web of Iniquity*, relates that "The actual writing of *The Leavenworth Case* was itself a matter of domestic secrecy… the idea for the story came to her in a dream: 'It is so passionate, so strong, so subtle, so dread, dark, and heart-rending it ought to be written with fire and blood'… James Green encouraged his daughter to write poetry but strongly disapproved of the idea of novel writing. Therefore, Green wrote *The Leavenworth Case* in secret, confiding only in her stepmother, and showing the manuscript to her father only after it was completed."[5]

Following the windfall of *The Leavenworth Case*, Green continued to produce a long line of detective novels and short stories. In addition to Gryce, she created two other sleuths, both women, described by Michele Slung as "the elderly and excessively nosy Miss Amelia Butterworth," and "a dainty girl detective" named Viola Strange, whose cases are chronicled in *The Golden Slipper and Other Problems* (1915). "Both can be seen as prototypes," writes Slung. "Miss Butterworth for the Jane Marples and Maud Silvers, and Violet Strange for the Nancy Drews."[6]

* * *

Wilbur Braun utilized fifty-five nom de plumes for his prolific output of mystery plays, melodramas, comedies, and adaptations. Under his own name, he published plays as diverse as *After Wimpole Street* (1935), "a comedy drama based on the married life of Elizabeth Barrett and Robert Browning;" *The Adventures of Tom Sawyer* (1936), "an ageless comedy for children and grownups alike, based on Samuel L. Clemens' celebrated novel;" *Curse You, Jack Dalton!* (1936), a parody of the old-fashioned melodrama, pitting the poor but virtuous Bertha Blair against the dastardly, mustached Egbert Van Horn; and *Murdered Alive!* (1934), a wild romp boasting a collage of melodramatic devices: weird happenings within an upper-class estate during a stormy night, the reading of a will at midnight, secret panels, lights going off, screams galore by the female members of the cast, a buffoonish detective, a broad-comedy maid, and a surprise ending—the presumed victim, the head of the household whose estate is coveted by vulturous relatives, is not dead after all.

Murder In Hollywood (1935), a lighthearted treatment of Tinseltown during the 1930s, incorporates a tough female director with megaphone in hand; tall, dark and handsome movie heart-throbs; glamorous, competing screen queens; a silly studio detective who boasts, "I've got a reputation for bein' the best sleuth in Hollywood;" and a naïve Kansas girl who arrives on the scene "to star in movin' pitchures," but instead ends up solving the murder of a womanizing leading man.

Find the Woman! (1935), subtitled "A Mystery Farce in Three Acts," pictures the misadventures of a group of tenants at Miss Hannah Welcome's boarding house confronted with Russian spies, buffoonish lawmen, and Secret Service agents. The title villain of *The White Phantom* (1935) is a notorious lawbreaker. However, the strange apparition covered entirely by a large white sheet, flitting in and out leaving behind poison letters for the female resident of the Kinsley manor, is a pretender revealed at the denouement to be the real estate agent who has designs regarding the property. *The Tiger's Claw* (1936) is composed of a similar plot line, which has the new tenant of a leased lonely house warned to "leave at once or you'll never live until morning," an identical sound track (deep moans, bloodcurdling screams, mocking laughter, shrill telephone rings), and the same gallery of characters (garrulous women, henpecked men, wide-eyed teens, and an incompetent policeman) except that the villain of the piece, The Tiger, hovers in the background donning a black hooded robe.

As "Ned Albert," Braun dramatized *East Lynne* (1941), the daddy of all "meller drammers" inspired by Mrs. Henry Wood's 1861 novel, as well as the hillbilly comedies *Comin' Round the Mountain* (1938) and *Shotgun Wedding* (1952).

"Orville Snapp" was the name above the title of *The Haunted High School* (1939), in which the pupils of Eagle High solve a series of unexplained accidents, and *Murder Mansion* (1942), wherein lovely Carlotta Cramer inherits a lonely old mansion off the coast of Maine only to learn that it has been the scene of several murders. "Raymond Dumkey" hatched *The House Nobody Lived In* (1947), a haunted house yarn complete with a ghost, a murder, a bogus investigator, and a fearful colored maid. "Walter Blake" populated a summer home with a dozen offbeat people in *The Foolproof Murder* (1947), "a mirth-filled mystery comedy in three acts." Detective Criss Cross is on the prowl unearthing imaginary clues, collaring innocent suspects, and discovering dead bodies which turn out to be very much alive. "Edwin F. Hornung's" *Your Time Is Up* (1949) depicts the murder of a notorious gambler and the disappearance of a famous radio broadcaster.

"Alice Chadwick" is the alias attached to an interesting line of adaptations from popular novels: *Anne of Green Gables* (1937), from the 1908 novel by L. M. Montgomery; *The Trail of the Lonesome Pine* (1937), from the 1908 novel by John Fox, Jr.; *Tish* (1939), from the 1916 short stories by Mary Roberts Rinehart; *Great Expectations* (1948), from the 1860-1861 novel by Charles Dickens; and *Pudd'nhead Wilson* (1958), from Mark Twain's 1894 novel. "Chadwicke" also penned, in 1956, *Davy Crocket*, "a robust comedy drama in three acts based on the life of America's heroic young backwoodsman."

Under the pseudonym "Stephen Bristol," Braun brought to the stage "Flashgun Casey," a hard-knuckled sleuth created by George Harmon Coxe for the pulp magazines. The hero of novels, movies, radio and television, Jack Casey's only theatrical appearance is in *Crime Photographer* (1950). On assignment for the fictitious *Boston Express*, Casey locks horns with an arch-villain called "The Chief."

Acting Edition: Samuel French, Inc. (in manuscript form).

Awards and Honors: Anna Katharine Green's novel *The Leavenworth Case* (1878) was selected by Howard Haycraft and Ellery Queen for inclusion in the *Haycraft-Queen Definitive Library of Detective-Crime-Mystery Fiction*.

NOTES

1. Chris Steinbrunner and Otto Penzler, eds., *Encyclopedia of Mystery and Detection* (New York: McGraw-Hill Book Company, 1976), 173.
2. John M. Reilly, ed., *Twentieth Century Crime and Mystery Writers* (New York: St. Martin's Press, 1980), 696.
3. Anna Katharine Green, *The Leavenworth Case* (New York: G.P. Putnam's Sons, 1934), viii.
4. *New York Times*, September 20, 1891.

5. Catherine Ross Nickerson, *The Web of Iniquity* (Durham, North Carolina: Duke University Press, 1998), 70.
6. John M. Reilly, ed., *Twentieth Century Crime and Mystery Writers* (New York: St. Martin's Press, 1980), 697.

Hanging Judge (1952)

Raymond Massey (United States, Canada-born, 1896-1983)

The tables have turned on the title character of Raymond Massey's *Hanging Judge*. Sir Francis Brittain, a ruthless High Court jurist, finds himself accused of fatally poisoning a blackmailer.

The action of the play takes place over a period of four months in England during the time between the First and Second World Wars.

The curtain rises on a small insert showing the judge's bench of a London criminal court. Sir Brittain, in scarlet robes and a wig, addresses an unseen Jury: "Now, members of the jury, you must ask yourselves if it is reasonable to suppose that an innocent man could have acted in this manner... could have disposed of the girl's body in such a callous, brutish manner... by weighting it with stones and dropping it in the canal."

In a prison's death-row cell, three men are seated at a table playing poker. Two of them, Bill and Bert, are wardens, while the third, Harry Gosling, is a young man about twenty-years-old, due to be hanged this very night. Gosling is a card sharp. He shows the card players some tricks, dealing to the elder warden a full house, to the young one a flush, and to himself four aces. "I learned all that from my brother, when I was a kid," he relates.

John Teal, Gosling's older half-brother by a different father, has just arrived from America and is allowed by the governor to visit the condemned man. Teal is shabbily dressed but is described as having "a touch of distinction about him." Gosling grasps his brother's hand and says, "Jack, I didn't do it. Before God, I didn't." Teal assures him that he does not doubt his innocence. Gosling confides that his pregnant girlfriend, Rose, became very agitated when he said he couldn't marry her because he had no money. Rose grabbed a knife which was on the table and stuck it in her heart three times before he could move. "She just dropped and she was dead," says Gosling. Panicky, he did the wrong thing and threw the body in the river. In court, the prosecutor got him twisted up, and the judge was worse, constantly stopping his lawyer and emphasizing to the jury that Gosling is a "depraved" man, that there are no extenuating circumstances, and that they are not to be swayed by emotion.

The Governor of the prisons arrives with the bad news that the final appeal was rejected. Gosling's counsel, Sir Keith Nottingham, "a handsome, rugged man of middle age," enters and says, "We've done everything we possibly could, Harry, but we failed… You've got to try to be brave." Gosling blubbers that he never hurt anybody, that the judge knew he wasn't guilty, that the judge is the real murderer, "killing me for his fun."

John Teal embraces his brother, telling him that he thought he would go first "for I can't last long." Before he too dies, declares Teal, he has "a job" to do.

The following evening, at the Adelphi Club, Gilbert West, an aggressive Member of Parliament, tells Sir Francis Brittain, a tight-lipped man in his sixties, that Harry Gosling stuck to his innocence to the end. Over whiskey and soda, Brittain scorns counselor Nottingham: "He chose the wrong profession – the stage is his métier, Drury Lane melodrama… The purpose of a penal code is to punish – to deter others from crime."

Several members of the club express their surprise that Gosling was not awarded a reprieve. In a corner, Sir George Sidney, a bluff, witty man of forty-eight, a product of Eton, converses with Colonel George Archer, a former chief of police in Singapore, now appointed Chief of the Norfolk Constabulary. Archer has recently returned from the Orient and is glad to meet Sir George, who, he says, "is quite a detective." Sir George was helpful to Archer in the capture of a drug smuggling ring. Sir Keith Nottingham joins them and Sidney introduces him to Archer, "a friend and a fellow sleuth; I the infallible Holmes and he is the dogged Inspector Lestrade." The conversation turns to Judge Brittain. Nottingham says heatedly, "Brittain was trying me – not Gosling! He hates me!"

John Teal enters and asks to speak with Judge Brittain. Teal tells the judge that he knows all about his double-life existence. He is aware of the judge's alias as John Willoughby and of his farmhouse at Moxton in Norfolk. In hushed tones, Brittain suggests that they meet next Friday evening at the farmhouse.

The action shifts to Brittain's retreat in Norfolk. The area folk know him as John Willoughby. Mary Reddish, "a plump, pretty country woman in her thirties," enters and is greeted warmly by the judge. They kiss, and Mary complains that it has been eight weeks since he came home. She assures Brittain that she hasn't told her father, or anyone else, of their "little understanding."

He is sending her home early tonight, the judge says, because of a pending visit by a man whom he must see alone. After Mary's departure, he takes a folded paper from his pocket and pours the contents into a glass of brandy.

John Teal knocks on the door and walks in nervously. He reminds Brittain of his mother, Mabel Teal, who thirty years ago was the judge's lover, and declares, "I am your son, Brittain!" He exhibits to the judge a batch of letters to prove his claim, but Brittain, calmly, announces that he is well able to handle blackmailers and threatens to call the police. Teal becomes agitated, raves that he has only months to live, but still has time to ruin Brittain and his "mess of dignity." He falls into a chair, trembling with a paroxysm of pain. The judge offers Teal a glass of Brandy and he gulps it down. He is seized with violent convulsions, crumples in agony, and falls to the floor, the glass rolling away.

Brittain stares at Teal in horror, then slowly crosses to the telephone, lifts the receiver, but rapidly replaces it. He goes to the body, realizes that Teal is dead, and removes the letters from a pocket. He throws them into the fireplace and lights a match as the curtain falls.

The second act unfolds at the Adelphi Club. Brittain relates to Sir Ronald Pond, "a dapper, little man of fifty-five," that he was on a walking trip in Scotland, but had to curtail the venture because the mist became intolerable. Pond, an admirer of the John Thorndike detective stories,[1] tells the judge of the buzz generated by a body found in the well of a farmhouse at Moxton. Brittain teases him, and they exit for lunch.

Colonel Archer joins George Sidney and confides that he was assigned to the Norfolk case. It's pretty clear, says Archer, that a murder was committed; the prime suspect is the missing Willoughby, and nobody knows much about him. He seems to be in his sixties; he bought a converted farmhouse about two years ago and used it during holiday periods; he had announced that he was a schoolteacher from the Midlands; his presence at Moxton tallies with school vacations; none of the gentry knew him personally, and only a few by sight; he had a rather unsavory reputation: a former maid complained that he wanted amorous acquiescence in addition to culinary skills.

Archer tells Sidney that John Teal's body was found in the well in Willoughby's garden two days ago. A police surgeon reports that it definitely wasn't drowning. The post mortem conclusions are due soon. Archer pulls an envelope from his pocket and produces several photostatic copies of letters. "They were found in a sort of secret pocket sewed up in Teal's coat under the left armpit," says Archer, adding that the papers were tucked in an oil skin wallet and are not badly spoiled. Among them was a birth certificate of thirty-five years ago, "November 30, 1899," with the names of the parents: "Frances Mabel Teal – John Willoughby." In the letters, "J.W." repudiates all responsibility of "your unfortunate condition."

A Moxton constable, Sergeant Scotton, arrives to provide a description of Willoughby as "a rather flabby, truculent chap in his middle sixties, who gives the impression that he was used to having authority." Willoughby was tracked to the Charing Cross Station, but no further than that. Judge Brittain enters and peruses the Bradshaw timetable. Sidney introduces him to Colonel Archer. Sergeant Scotton gazes at Brittain, and the judge, coolly, explains that of course he is John Willoughby, a name which he used to insure privacy during his "leisure time." "Good God!" Exclaims Sidney.

Archer asks Brittain to accompany him to Scotland Yard for questioning. Brittain requests to consult with his solicitor, Sir Reginald Pond, who is in the club's dining room. As Brittain departs, Sidney warns Archer that Pond "is about the most slippery lawyer in this country… I'll lay you five to one that at this moment he is telephoning the Home Office to get this affair hushed up." And true enough, a phone call comes from the Commissioner of the Metropolitan Police with an instruction that "on no account is Judge Brittain to be taken to Scotland Yard." Archer gets another phone call and informs Sidney that the post mortem shows that Teal died of cyanide poisoning.

Sidney calls the *Evening Globe* and sets an immediate appointment with the editor, Lord Bradenham. Soon a stop-press edition of the paper arrives in the club, with a blazing headline: "The missing man Willoughby in the body-in-the-well case has been identified as Sir Francis Brittain, the High Court Judge."

The pace of the proceedings accelerates. At the Adelphie Club, members are astounded by the fact that a High Court Judge has been subjected to prosecution on a capital charge. Solicitor Pond urges Brittain to leave the country via a midnight plane, but the judge refuses; he intends to give himself up and trust the law of England to find him innocent.

In the jury room at the Norwich Hall of Assize, the jurors express opinions pro and con, mostly con. Juror No. 6 believes that the case against the defendant is "strong," Juror No. 2 opines that the "defense fellow is a trifle too smooth," and Juror No. 5 pronounces his disdain of the "old buzzard" on trial.

In a small room in the Norwich jail, Brittain, tense and haggard, theorizes to Solicitor Pond that Teal committed suicide. He saw Teal die when drinking a glass of brandy, with the powder in it. Long afterwards, he dragged the body out to the well. Pond believes that this revelation will throw his defense "out the window," but Brittain insists that "the truth can never convict an innocent man – in this country, under the law of England!"

At the Adelphi Club, George Sidney, who intensely followed the trial, surprises all by suddenly exclaiming that Brittain is innocent. Yes, on account of him the judge is on the dock, but he has a change of heart. He does not believe that a guilty man would say, 'I never saw him take any poison and I was watching all the time'! Like everyone else, Sidney refused to believe Brittain's statement that he put in the victim's brandy an innocent headache medicine; the police searched the judge's London house and found none. But last night, with doubts percolating in his mind, he looked up Henry Passmore, "a stupid ass" of a manservant, and solicited from him the information that in a routine clean-up he threw out "some old medicines" – a week before Brittain left for Moxton the last time.

Mr. Justice Parkinson, in scarlet robes and wig, addresses an unseen jury and points out that Passmore's testimony regarding medication in powdered form, stored at Judge Brittain's home, is an element to be considered in their discussions. In the jury room, juror No. 6 asserts that the late John Teal, who couldn't have lived long anyway, may have committed suicide in a manner that will incriminate the judge. But the other jurors insist that an innocent man would not have thrown the body into the well and then disappear into his perfectly good hiding place – his real identity. Juror No. 6 bows under pressure, and the Foreman says with satisfaction, "That makes it complete. The verdict is 'guilty as charged.'"

The last scene takes place at the office of the Governor of Norwich Gaol. George Sidney reveals to the Governor, a retired army officer, that the Home Office received a letter written by John Teal, confessing that he was about to kill himself by swallowing cyanide at Brittain's country home, and describing how he would leave evidence proving that Brittain had poisoned him. Teal sent the letter to a friend in America to be forwarded back to England three months later. It came to light three days before the hanging! In the letter, Teal states, "I want Brittain to suffer, not to die. That's too easy."

The Governor tells Sidney that since the refusal of his appeal, Brittain has gone to pieces. He sends for the prisoner. Wardens bring in Brittain, dressed in prison denim clothes and looking very old. Sidney tells Brittain that his innocence has been established and that a Royal Pardon has been granted to him. But the former judge does not seem to comprehend, and keeps mumbling incoherently, with broken sentences, that both the jury and the Court of Criminal Appeal cannot be wrong … so he must have done it. He can't remember… he doesn't think so… but he has had judgment!

* * *

Hanging Judge was adapted to the stage by Raymond Massey from a 1948 novel, *Let Him Have Judgment* (U.S. title, *Hanging Judge*), by the British mystery writer Bruce Hamilton. The play opened at London's New Theatre on September 23, 1952, starring Godfrey Tearle as Sir Francis Brittain,[2] and ran for ninety-four performances. Famed filmmaker Michael Powell directed.

Born August 30, 1896, in Toronto, Canada, to affluent parents, Raymond Massey developed an interest in theater when a student at Appleby College in Oakville, Ontario. He continued to enroll in acting classes at the University of Toronto and at Oxford University, England. During World War I he enlisted in the Canadian Field Artillery and while on duty appeared in an army minstrel show. Wounded in France, Massey returned home, but instead of joining the family business of making agricultural equipment, as expected of him, he decided to pursue a career in the theater.

Massey's stage debut took place in a 1922 British production of Eugene O'Neill's *In the Zone*. During the 1920s, he established himself in London as a leading classical actor. In 1931, while playing Hamlet on Broadway, he was offered the role of Sherlock Holmes in a British film based on Arthur Conan Doyle's 1910 play version of *The Speckled Band*. He made his first Hollywood picture in 1932's classic *The Old Dark House* and returned to England, playing major roles for producer Alexander Korda (*The Scarlet Pimpernel*, 1935; *Things to Come*, 1936; *The Drum*, 1938) and director Michael Powell (*49th Parallel*, 1941; *A Matter of Life and* Death, 1946; *The Queen's Guards*, 1961).

In 1938, Massey appeared on Broadway in his signature role: Abraham Lincoln, in Robert E. Sherwood's Pulitzer Prize-winning play, *Abe Lincoln in Illinois*, a part he repeated in the 1940 movie version. A wide variety of film characterizations followed, notably fierce abolitionist John Brown in Michael Curtiz's *Santa Fe Trail* (1940), murderous Jonathan Brewster in Frank Capra's *Arsenic and Old Lace* (1941), steely Nazi Major Otto Baumeister in Raoul Walsh's *Desperate Journey* (1943), victimized Brigadier General Ezra Mannon in Dudley Nichols's *Mourning Becomes Electra* (1947), powerful newspaper mogul Gail Wynand in King Vidor's *The Fountainhead* (1949), and the deeply religious Adam Trask in Elia Kazan's *East of Eden* (1955).

On television, Massey played Dr. Gillespie in the NBC series *Dr. Kildare* (1961-1966).

Massey became a naturalized citizen of the United States in 1944. In his witty autobiographies, *When I Was Young* (1976) and *A Hundred lives* (1979), he tells the story of his three marriages and two children, Anna Massey and Daniel Massey, who followed him into acting.

Raymond Massey died of pneumonia in 1983 and is buried in Beaverdale Memorial Park in New Haven, Connecticut.

Englishman Bruce Hamilton (1900-1974) was educated at Westminster and University College, London. He spent much of his adult life as a teacher of history in Barbados, and he served as president of the Barbados Arts Council in 1958-1959. Hamilton was the author of ten well-regarded detective novels. The first, *Hue and Cry* (1931), is the story of a provincial footballer who kills the sadistic chairman of his club and escapes to London. The last, *Too Much of Water* (1958), depicts several murders on an ocean liner bound for Barbados.

Bruce was the older brother of Patrick Hamilton (1904-1962), author of the milestone stage thrillers *Rope* (1929) and *Gas Light*, aka *Angel Street* (1939). Bruce wrote a memoir of Patrick, *The Light Went Out*, in 1972.

Awards and Honors: Raymond Massey was an Academy Award nominee for Best Actor in *Abe Lincoln in Illinois* (1940).

NOTES

1. A forensic scientist and lawyer, Dr. John Evelyn Thorndyke is considered the premier medico-legal detective in the annals of the genre. Thorndyke was created by R. (Robert) Austin Freeman (1862-1943), an English physician and mystery writer, who in his short-story collection, *The Singing Bone* (1912), introduced the "inverted" motif, wherein the reader is a witness to the crime, and the interest centers not on the identity of the culprit, but on how he will be apprehended. Thorndyke made his debut in the 1907 novel *The Red Thumb Mark*, and until 1942 was the scientific sleuth of twenty-two novels and six short-story collections.
2. American-born Godfrey Tearle (1884-1953) became a noted Shakespearean actor on the British stage, appearing, among others, in the title roles of *Macbeth*, *Othello*, and *Henry V*. His memorable screen part was that of Professor Jordan, a respectable country squire whose missing finger unmasks him as an enemy agent, in Alfred Hitchcock's *The 39 Steps* (1935).

A Case for Mason (1967)

William McCleery (United States, 1911-2000)

The world's most renowned literary attorney, Perry Mason, is the hero of more than eighty novels, scores of radio programs, a half-dozen movies, and two television series. On stage, he defended a client only once, in *A Case for Mason*, dramatized by William McCleery in 1967.

The play springs from Erle Stanley Gardner's *The Case of the Fiery Fingers* (1951). In addition to Perry Mason, McCleery recruited the characters of Della Street, the lawyer's highly efficient, wise-cracking secretary; LAPD's Lieutenant Arthur Tragg, an intelligent, fair-minded adversary; and Sergeant Holcomb, a tough, two-fisted cop.

A Case for Mason takes place in the study of Bryan Bain's house on the outskirts of a California city. Bain, a best-selling author of popular fiction, is having a difficult time writing a different kind of novel, one that focuses less on action and more on character.

Bain's young live-in assistant, Nellie Conway, is intense and supportive. His middle-aged housekeeper, Victoria Braxton, is devoted and exacting. But the household is not happy, for Bain's second wife, Elizabeth, is shrewishly domineering. Sensing that Nellie is interested in her husband, Elizabeth accuses the assistant of stealing family jewelry.

Bain asks Perry Mason to look into the matter. Secretary Della convinces Perry to take on the trivial case, so that he will get out of the office and keep away "from those ringing telephones" and "those clients with the life and death emergencies."

By the end of the first act, the insignificant assignment turns into a murder case. Mrs. Bain is found dead in her bed and the family physician, Dr. Keener, decrees that she was poisoned.

Lieutenant Tragg and Sergeant Holcomb believe that Nellie, in love with her employer, lethally drugged Mrs. Bain's milk. Perry Mason disagrees. To the chagrin of the law officers, Nellie turns out to be innocent. For a while it seems that the husband, Bryan, is the culprit, but Mason sets up a trap by secretly switching on the house intercom and eavesdropping on an incriminating confession by the housekeeper, Victoria. When Mason confronts her, Victoria admits to poisoning both of Bain's wives. She insists that the two Mrs. Bains married Bryan for his name and fortune, then made his life miserable. Now that they are both gone, he will be free to write "his beautiful books."

A Case for Mason clones some key elements from *Speaking of Murder* (1956) by Audrey and William Roos. In both plays the malefactor is a housekeeper obsessively in love with her employer, who murdered his first wife, then targets the second for extinction.

Not entirely convincing, and less than stylish, *A Case For Mason* is nevertheless breezy and diverting, retaining the premise of a seemingly airtight case against an innocent party, the rescue legalities by Perry Mason, and the climactic unmasking of the real culprit.

* * *

Perry Mason made his debut in Erle Stanley Gardner's *The Case of the Velvet Claws* (1933). He utilized his legal prowess in eighty-two novels, all published by William Morrow and Company, New York, and many printed simultaneously in Toronto, followed by numerous foreign editions. A few Mason cases went to press after the author's death in 1970.

The Perry Mason books became enormous best sellers, making the author a champion among mystery writers. E.H. Mundell's *Erle Stanley Gardner: A Checklist* asserts that "It is probable that Gardner has been read by more people than any fiction writer who ever wrote."[1]

Chris Steinbrunner and Otto Penzler's *Encyclopedia of Mystery and Detection* states that "Internal evidence in the Mason series indicates that the lawyer was born in 1891. He is described as a big man, but he is not heavy. Although he says that he has no time for sports or exercise, he remains fit and performs well in situations involving physical danger. He has long legs, broad shoulders, and piercing eyes in a rugged face. His thick, wavy hair and excellent speaking voice make him attractive to many women."[2]

However, the public image of Perry Mason is that of burly Raymond Burr, who early in his film career was cast as a villain in the Marx Brothers' *Love Happy* (1950), Raymond Chandler's *The Blue Gardenia* (1953), and Alfred Hitchcock's *Rear Window* (1954), but then was chosen to play Perry Mason in the long running CBS television program (1957-1966).

According to *The Perry Mason TV Show Book* by Brian Kelleher and Diana Merrill,"One of the secrets of the Mason show was that, unlike other television mysteries of the time, the scripts concentrated less on the actual murder and more on looking for the clues and solving the case. In most other similar shows, the execution of the murder was the focal point, and the sequence of putting the clues together was secondary."[3]

Kelleher and Merrill relate, "Like *Alfred Hitchcock Presents*, another popular series running at the time, each Mason show had a last-minute twist ending. However, unlike homicides presented on Hitchcock's thrillers, the real murderer was never revealed on *Perry Mason* until the very last moment.

This was in part to sustain the element of surprise that was critically needed for the show, especially since the viewer knew that Mason's clients weren't going to get convicted."[4]

The New Adventures of Perry Mason, presented by CBS-TV in 1973, failed to ignite interest and was off the air by February 1974. In 1985, and until his death in 1993, Raymond Burr reemerged as Perry Mason in occasional two-hour made-for-television movies.

Perry Mason's career was less illustrious on the big screen. In the 1930s he was featured in six Warner Brothers motion pictures, all failures. Debonair Warren William portrayed the crusading lawyer in four of them; he was succeeded by Ricardo Cortez and Donald Woods.

On radio, Mason defended innocent clients in a fifteen-minute CBS program that ran daily from 1943 to 1955. He was also the knight-in-shining-armor of a comic strip during 1950-1952.

* * *

Erle Stanley Gardner was born in 1889 in the small town of Malden, Massachusetts, to parents who were proud to be of Mayflower stock. The family moved to California for business reasons: the company for which Gardner's father worked had gold mining interests there. Gardner's free-wheeling spirit got him suspended from the Orville Union High School when he drew a professor's caricature in the school's paper and on the front of the school's building.

Gardner enrolled at Valparaiso University in Indiana to study law but following a boxing encounter with a professor left town hurriedly by train. From then on, he studied the law in lawyers' offices and by reading legal cases for an average of fifty hours a week for three years. He passed his bar examination in 1911. During the next ten years he practiced law as a junior partner for several well-known defense attorneys. His clients were mainly penniless Mexicans and Chinese.

In 1925, in order to supplement his income, Gardner took a stab at writing. He chose a pen name, Charles M. Green, and sent stories to pulp magazines. "I started in collecting rejection slips on a wholesale basis. My stories were terrible," said Gardner years later. "Every time I got a rejection slip, in place of getting discouraged I got mad."[5] His breakthrough came in 1923 with a novelette, *The Shrieking Skeleton*, which he submitted to *Black Mask*, home of Carroll John Daly, Frederick Nebel, Dashiell Hammett, and other hard-boiled writers. *The Shrieking Skeleton* is the story of a renowned scientist, Doctor Potter, who is murdered by his Japanese butler, Kumi, to avenge his sister, whom Potter had seduced. Alva Johnston relates in her study *The Case of Erle Stanley Gardner* that the manuscript was initially returned to Gardner with an attached note by circulating manager P.C. Cody: "This is the most puerile story I have ever read. The plot has whiskers like Spanish moss on a Southern live oak, and the characters talk like a dictionary." Gardner went back to his typewriter and "rewrote *The Shrieking Skeleton* until he had stone bruises on his fingertips.... In its final version, *The Shrieking Skeleton* was not only accepted by *Black Mask* but was made the leading story in the issue of December 15, 1923. Erle received a check for $140, a cent a word for 14,400 words, and he was the proudest man in Southern California."[6]

Gardner's first success came with the creation of a series detective, Speed Dash, a "human fly" who would climb a building to enter a room containing evidence and, blessed with a photographic mind, would memorize the room in the blink of a tenth of a second. Other early pulp heroes were Lester Leith, a confidence man who steals money from criminals; the lawyers Ken Corning and Peter Wennick; Ed Jenkins, the Phantom Crook; and Sidney Zoom and his police dog, Rip.

Gardner soon realized that his most valuable asset was his legal background. His initial Perry Mason novels, *Reasonable Doubt* (published under the title *The Case of the Velvet Claws*) and *Silent Verdict* (published as *The Case of the Sulky Girl*) were rejected by several publishers but eventually accepted by William Morrow and Company, the firm that subsequently published the first editions of all his books. Other popular sleuths created by Gardner are small-town district attorney Douglas Selby and, under the pseudonym A.A. Fair, the team of private eyes Bertha Cool and Donald Lam in a series distinguished by bright, humorous dialogue.

In the 1960s, concerned about recent trends in American literature, Gardner told the *New York Times*, "I have always aimed my fiction at the masses who constitute the solid backbone of America. I have tried to keep faith with the American family. In a day when the prevailing mystery story trends are toward sex, sadism and seduction, I try to base my stories on speed, situation and suspense."[7]

Popular culture scholar Francis M. Nevins called Gardner "one of the great natural storytellers," a writer who left behind "over a quarter of a century of rich creative work which will be read and reprinted and reread as long as the art of storytelling is cherished."[8]

* * *

William McCleery was born in 1911 in Hastings, Nebraska. He entered the University of Nebraska when he was just fifteen years old. It is reported that his mother, a musician, financed his college education by playing the piano and the organ for a movie house in Hastings. At nineteen, McCleery was a cub reporter for the *Omaha World-Herald*. After graduation in 1931, he traveled to New York.

McCleery held editorial positions with the Associated Press, Hearst newspapers, *Life* magazine, *P.M.*, and *Ladies Home Journal*. As an editor, McCleery was affiliated with Princeton University in the years 1963-1997; he founded *University: A Princeton Quarterly*, edited the book *The Human Nature of a University* (1969), compiled *Conversations on the Character of Princeton* (1986), and penned *The Story of a Campaign for Princeton 1981-1986*.

McCleery served as a member of the board of directors of Princeton's McCarter Theatre, and he was theatre reviewer for the Princeton area's *Town Topics* during 1970-1998.

McCleery had two comedies produced on Broadway. *Hope for the Best* (Fulton Theatre, April 23, 1945 – 117 performances) starred Franchot Tone as a popular gossip columnist, Michael Jordan, who wishes to shift gears and write more meaningful material. He is aided by young, sympathetic Lucille Daily, played by Jane Wyatt, and they get attached in more ways than one. *Parlor Story* (Biltmore Theatre, March 4, 1947 – twenty-three performances) is the story of a former newspaperman, Charles Burnett, portrayed by Walter Abel, who has accepted a professorship on the faculty of a Missouri university and strives to become its president. Burnett is foiled by the plotting of the paper's editor, who wants him back.

Other plays by McCleery include the university-town comedy *Good Housekeeping*, which in 1949 was previewed on the road with Helen Hayes and her eighteen-year-old daughter, Mary MacArthur, but had to be cancelled due to the sudden death of Mary from polio. *The Lady Chooses* premiered in 1954 at the Westport Country Playhouse in Westport, Connecticut, featuring Faye Emerson as an idealistic, somewhat naïve woman who unwittingly gets entangled in shady political maneuvers. An adaptation of the 1958 Peter DeVries novel *A Mackerel Plaza*, the story of a widowed clergyman who plans to remarry, was a failed pre-Broadway tryout but is regularly performed by amateur theatrical groups. *Good Morning, Miss Dove*, based on the 1954 bestselling novel by Frances Gray Patton and given its first production by the Peterborough Players in Peterborough, New Hampshire in 1962, focuses on a strict yet beloved New England schoolteacher. Patricia Clark, the attractive thirtysomething editor of a top New York magazine, must choose between true love and career ambitions in the comedy *Hardesty Park*. *Match Play*, set in a contemporary newspaper publisher's office. It was produced posthumously at McCleery's alma mater, the University of Nebraska-Lincoln.

Acting Edition: Samuel French, Inc. (in manuscript form).

Awards and Honors: In 1944, Erle Stanley Gardner was awarded a Pocket Books Gertrude as a member of the Million Copy Club. A few years later he received a larger Gold Gertrude as a member of the Five Million Copy Club. In the mid-fifties he had passed the fifty million mark and was given a special scroll. Gardner's *Court of Last Resort* won the Mystery Writers of America Edgar Award for Best Fact Crime in 1953, and he received a Grand Master Award from MWA in 1962. He was made an honorary alumnus of Kansas City University in 1955 and granted an honorary L.L.D by McGeorge College of Law, Sacramento, California, in 1956.

In 2009, the U.S. Postal Service initiated a set of stamps honoring television icons, including Perry Mason.

NOTES

1. E.H. Mundell, *Erle Stanley Gardner: A Checklist* (Kent, Ohio: Kent State University Press,1968), introduction, n.p.
2. Chris Steinbrunner and Otto Penzler, *Encyclopedia of Mystery and Detection* (New York: McGraw-Hill, 1976), 280.
3. Brian Kelleher and Diana Merill, *The Perry Mason TV Show Book* (New York: St. Martin's Press, 1987), 16.
4. Brian Kelleher and Diana Merrill, *The Perry Mason TV Show Book*, 16.
5. Dorothy B. Hughes, *Erle Stanley Gardner: The Case of the Real Perry Mason* (New York: Morrow, 1978), 77.
6. Alva Johnston, *The Case of Erle Stanley Gardner* (New York: Morrow, 1947), 25-27.
7. Chris Steinbrunner and Otto Penzler, *Encyclopedia of Mystery and Detection*, 165.
8. Chris Steinbrunner and Otto Penzler, *Encyclopedia of Mystery and Detection*, 166.

Curse of the Werewolf (1990)

Tim Kelly (United States, 1931-1998)

The stylistic approach to Tim Kelly's *Curse of the Werewolf* is earmarked by the play's sub-title: "A Hair-raising Comedy Spoof in Two Acts." Kelly, a prolific playwright, recommends that "this spoof of werewolf films should be played very broadly, getting all the laughs it can. However, it will be much funnier if the actors perform the play as if the plot were genuinely serious. This way the absurd situations, bizarre personalities and non-stop action will be hilarious."[1]

The action of the play unfolds in the sitting room of Gargoyle House, a spooky castle on a lonely New England Island. "Everything about the almost medieval room suggests mystery and dark deeds," confides the playwright. "It's gloomy and forbidding – a place where no sane person would care to stay for any length of time."[2] Prominent among the furnishings in an old grandfather clock.

Prior to the lifting of the curtain, "frightening mood music" is heard – like the soundtrack from a classic monster movie. Gradually it fades, to be replaced by the spine-chilling howl of a wolf.

At rise, the sitting room is in shadows. Some dim light comes from a fireplace' burning log. The drapes are drawn apart at the French doors and a shaft of moonlight is glimpsed in the garden, "where puffs of fog rise like deadly vapors." Suddenly – something has leaped into sight at the French doors. Is it human? Is it animal? We manage to get a brief look – bushy beard, furry hands, wild hair.

Enters Mrs. Grimm, the castle's housekeeper. She wears a floor-length black dress, and her hair style is severe. There's a leather belt around her waist and from the belt dangles a ring of keys. Her face is dusted with white powder and her lips are dark. "This odd makeup gives her a somewhat ghoulish effect," chirps the playwright.[3]

A sound of knocking echoes from the front door. Mrs. Grimm exits Up Center, into the hallway. The stage is empty for a moment, then Little Messalina enters, "a thoroughly nasty child; mean, willful, uncaring, probably vicious... Although she projects the image of a ten-year old, she is obviously much older, maybe 14-16. Our first impression is that she's a mental case."[4]

Little Messalina crosses Down Center, looks at the audience with a hateful expression on her face, and sings:

Three blind mice, three blind mice,
See how they run! See how they run!
They all ran after the farmer's wife,
Who cut off their tails with a carving knife.
Did you ever see such a sight in your life
As three blind mice.

The little girl sticks out her tongue, pouts, and leaves. Mrs. Grimm reenters, followed by Joan Tarbuckle, an executive type, capable and self-assured. She carries an attaché case, which she sets on a desk, then produces a compact mirror and checks her coiffure.

Algernon Snipes, master of Gargoyle House, enters. A note in the published script states: "The actor who portrays Algernon will also play his identical twin brother, Colonel Snipe. Algernon bears quite a resemblance to the werewolf we saw briefly at the French doors. Beard, wild hair, no furry hands. He wears a dressing gown and cap, spectacles. He's very arthritic and moves bent over, with the aid of two canes. The effect is of a spider or land crab walking." Algernon moves slowly to the sofa and sits.

Algernon: You've found Boris?

Tarbuckle: I wish I had good news for you, Mr. Snipes.

Algernon: That, I take it, means that you haven't found my nephew.

Tarbuckle: As you know, I've had private detectives on the case. I've advertised. Your sister's son has dropped from the face of the earth. I shall, of course, continue to search.

Cautiously, housekeeper Grimm steps into view, Down Right, eavesdropping. She hears Algernon asking to see his second, revised will, and observes Tarbuckle fishing a legal document from her attaché case. Algernon flips a few pages and decrees that he'll keep the will with him. Tarbuckle reports that the government bonds purchased by Algernon are doing exceptionally well, picks up her case, and leaves.

Thinking he's alone, Algernon drops the canes, crosses sprightly to the grandfather clock, turns the key to open it, and tucks the will inside. Mrs. Grimm observes all when suddenly her son, Humphrey, a humped, weird young handyman staggers in through the French doors. He wears gardening gloves.

Humphrey asks about the visitor and Algernon tells him that Miss Tarbuckle went back to the mainland. The handyman places a finger on one eye and says, "Humphrey sees things. I don't want harm to come to you. You are Humphrey's friend." He seizes Algernon's hand and, slobbering, rubs it against his cheek, then bites it. Algernon whacks at poor Humphrey, who whimpers like a kicked dog and limps into the fog. Soon from the grounds comes the terrifying wolf's howl. "I'll put a stop to this," rasps Algernon.

"Whoever you are, you've met your match in Algernon Snipes!" He gets the canes and holds them together to make a club. Gripping his weapon tightly, he strides through the French doors and off. After a pause we hear the sounds of a terrible struggle: howls, barks, growls, integrated with Algernon's voice, "Monster! Beast! Go back! Back, I say! Let go! Auuuuuuuuuugh!"

Algernon stumbles back into the room. His hands are at his throat. Breathing heavily, he makes it to the sofa and collapses. Mrs. Grimm comes out from her hiding place, moves toward him, and says in alarm, "Mr. Snipes, sir. What has happened?" Algernon whispers, "It's come back. The curse, the curse. The curse of the werewolf!" He pulls away his hands and we see that his throat has been savaged. Mrs. Grimm gasps. Algernon dies. From the fog comes another howl, and another, as the lights fade for the end of scene one.

Scene 2 transpires a week later. Hushabye, a gossipy neighbor, arrives on the scene to provide comic relief. She confides to Mrs. Grimm her suspicion that Little Messalina had murdered Algernon Snipes. "The girl is a murderess if ever I saw one," she states. "I know the type. I don't think Little Messalina is a child. I think she's a tall midget – and a mean one." The new governess, Connie Pigeon, enters – a pretty young woman with a pleasant personality. She is followed by Buzz Halliburton, Algernon's nephew, an entertainer whose act partner is a penguin named Admiral Byrd. He carries the penguin in a small pet box and hands Mrs. Grimm a card: "Halliburton and Byrd. Available for kiddie parties. Now appearing Circus Stupido."

Buzz, whose real name is Boris, says that his uncle has sent for him. He has never met him. Hushabye informs him that Algernon was murdered a week ago. "Died right there on the sofa," she declares. "Throat tore out. Messy." Instinctively, Connie and Buzz grab for their throats. Hushabye advises Connie to think twice about taking the governess job and exits.

Little Messalina enters. Buzz introduces himself to her and she stamps on his instep. The girl then takes Connie by the hand and leads her out to feed the Venus-flytrap and the baby piranha. Mrs. Grimm explains to Buzz that Little Messalina is his late uncle's ward. She points at a portrait on the wall and tells Buzz that this is his ancestor Harry Snipes, who was driven out of Scotland and made this island his sanctuary. Gambling debts? asks Buzz. No, answers Mrs. Grimm, Sir Harry was a werewolf. "If that's true," laughs Buzz, "they ought to call him Sir Hairy."

A married couple now joins the gallery of characters – Colonel Snipes, twin brother of Algernon Snipes, a gung-ho soldier-of-fortune, and his wife Veronica, a femme fatale. To the chagrin of Connie, Veronica flirts outrageously with Buzz, who is mesmerized by her. The plot thickens when attorney Joan Tarbuckle arrives with an unexpected guest, whom she introduces as Boris Halliburton.

Buzz: I'm Boris Halliburton.

Boris: I'm Boris Halliburton.
Colonel Snipes: Two Boris Halliburtons?
Veronica: Someone's an impostor.

Sheriff Birdsong arrives through the garden. Injects the playwright: "In a bygone era this lawman would be referred to as a 'dumb flatfoot.' Anything but the simplest case is beyond him. He wears a raincoat, holds a flashlight."[5] The sheriff asks Buzz if he has any ideas who'd want to murder his uncle. Buzz explains that his mother was Uncle Algernon's sister and that he never met this side of the family until today.

Tarbuckle enters carrying her attache case and sits at the desk. She is followed by Colonel Snipes, who impatiently asks Mrs. Grimm to get "the others" for the reading of the will. His wife Veronica, Little Messalina, the boy Humphrey, and the newly arrived Boris enter and scatter in the room. Connie sits aside by the fireplace. Mrs. Grimm stands in the hallway. The sheriff leans against the French doors. Tarbuckle produces the will from the case just as the lights flicker, a thunder rumbles, a lightning flashes.

Tarbuckle proclaims that Mrs. Grimm gets a five hundred dollar saving bond ("How generous," she says sourly); Humphrey receives Mr. Snipes' old suits and a Lionel train set ("Train set. Good," he chuckles happily); Little Messalina's expenses will be paid until she is twenty-one; the bulk of the estate – Gargoyle House, the land, stocks, bonds, et cetera – is left entirely to Boris (Buzz and Boris: "I'm rich!"); Colonel Snipes and his wife Veronica get "the boot. Cipher, zero, zilch" ("I don't want the boot," whines Veronica, "I want the booty.") The Colonel rebukes her for "making a spectacle" of herself, declares that he is a soldier who knows how to take the disappointing news on the chin, and marches to the study to sulk. Tarbuckle finishes her reading with an unusual proviso, "If, at any time, Boris Halliburton shows any sign of severe mental deterioration, they will be null and void," a caveat borrowed from the classic 1922 melodrama *The Cat and the Canary*.

Mrs. Grimm announces that dinner is served and invites the sheriff to join. There is a general exit with the exception of Buzz and Boris. With thunders and flashes of lightning in the background, the two men meet face to face.

Boris : You're going to end up behind bars.
Buzz: One of us is.

Connie calls for Buzz off stage and he exits. The howl of a wolf draws Boris's attention to the garden in time to catch a brief glimpse of fiery red eyes receding into the night.[6] Boris moves to the French doors. Foolishly, he steps onto the grounds. We now audit the same sort of struggle we heard at the end of Scene One – howls, barks, growls, the gnashing of canine teeth, and the snapping of jaws. Boris stumbles back into the sitting room, tips over a chair, and hits the floor with a thud.

Excited voices come from off stage. Sheriff Birdsong enters, followed by Buzz and Connie. At the sight of the open French doors, the sheriff draws a revolver. They see the body of Boris. The sheriff goes down on one knee and says, "Like Algernon Snipes. Nipped at the throat." Mrs. Grimm steps in and croaks with dread," You fools. Don't any of you understand?" She points to the portrait. "He's come back, Sir Harry." From outside the house comes another howl. The lights fade out, leaving an afterglow on the weird portrait of Sir Harry Snipes.

The curtain rises on Act 2. The body of Boris has been removed to a freezer. Lawyer Tarbuckle wants to leave for the mainland, but sheriff Birdsong objects: "No one is leaving the island." Tarbuckle asks if she's a suspect and Birdsong retorts, "Everyone's a suspect." Colonel Snipes suggests that Humphrey is a natural suspect – "The boy is morbid." Tarbuckle concurs: "Humphrey is capable of anything." The lawyer adds that she had tracked Boris down in Canada and she is certain that the dead man was the nephew of Algernon Snipes, which means that Buzz Halliburton is an imposter. The sheriff exits to pursue his investigation elsewhere, leaving Colonel Snipes and Tarbuckle alone. They are not aware that the portrait of Sir Harry slowly opens as if it were a door and Mrs. Grimm is behind it, eavesdropping. She learns that the Colonel and the lawyer were in cahoots to gain possession of the estate. Boris was brought in for that purpose and would have been paid off. Colonel Snipes suggests that they get rid of the penguin trainer, for he's the only one who stands between him and the estate.

Mrs. Grimm closes the portrait. Connie sends Little Messalina to her room, suggesting that she read *Nicholas Nickleby* before she goes to bed. "I like murder stories," says the child.

Buzz corners Connie in the sitting room with the notion that whoever killed the other Boris was after him. Connie theorizes that it could have been the Colonel – "He was going to get everything before Algernon Snipes changed his mind." Buzz believes that the murderer could have been Veronica – "She's come up empty-handed. I'm the only thing that stands between a fortune and her greedy little paws. Hands, I mean hands."

Connie leaves to see how Little Messalina is getting on. A thunder rumbles. The lights flicker and dim. Buzz goes to the desk, opens a drawer, and brings out the will. "Better have another look," he mumbles to himself. As he reads aloud a portion of the document, a pair of large, furry hands push through the drapes and attempt to grab him. He steps away and the hands withdraw. Buzz flips a page, backsteps to the drapes and again, the large, furry hands reach to grab him. He moves away in the nick of time.

Sheriff Birdsong enters through the front door. He gathers all "the suspects" for a round of questions and is surprised to learn that the lawyer, Miss Tarbuckle, is not to be found. The sound of the grandfather clock striking gets everyone's attention. "Why, that clock hasn't worked for years," says Mrs. Grimm. Birdsong draws his revolver and cautiously, step by step, approaches the clock. Just as he is about to reach it, the lower portion snaps open, revealing the body of Tarbuckle within.

However, the lawyer is not dead. In the next scene she appears with a wide bandage around her head and demands that the sheriff arrest Colonel Snipes. "He killed Algernon. He killed Boris. He tried to kill me," she says furiously. Nor was Boris dead. He suddenly stumbles in, hand to his throat, shivering. He points to Tarbuckle: "She hired me to impersonate Halliburton, all right. Only she didn't tell me she was going to k-k-k-k-kill me. I've spent the last hours banging on that freezer door."

The sheriff orders Boris, Tarbuckle, and Colonel Snipes to raise their hands and leave through the hallway. He walks behind them, revolver in hand. Veronica tells the audience, "I never pick a winner," and exits Down Left. Mrs. Grimm reveals to Buzz and Connie that long ago, when she was in his employ, she and Algernon Snipes fell in love and were married on his yacht, officiated by the captain. But soon Algernon denied they were ever married and when she had a baby, he refused to acknowledge the child. "Then Humphrey is your cousin," says Connie to Buzz. "That would mean that Humphrey is the true heir... Buzz, you've come up empty-handed." Mrs. Grimm relates her belief that the master was grooming Little Messalina to be Humphrey's wife.

Buzz, entirely relieved, comments: "Know the best part? There never was a werewolf." He asks Humphrey to take off his gloves. The boy removes a glove and with a smile lifts his hand to full audience view. There, in bold outline, is the mark of a pentagram. Humphrey laughs hee, hee, hee, and lopes off. His mother hurries after him.

Connie: What a night! Imagine, Humphrey and Little Messalina.

Buzz: They'll make a lovely couple. (*Romantically*) Tell you what, Connie. Maybe you and I should get married. We could spend our honeymoon here at Gargoyle House. (*Out to the audience*) Only kidding.

Humphrey howls from offstage as the curtain descends.

* * *

Tim Kelly (1931-1998) was born in Saugus, Massachusetts, a small New England town near Boston. At the age of twelve, he got a $50 check for a story he wrote about a dog that went to war, published in the *Victorian*. As an adolescent, Kelly was attracted to the low-key horror films produced by Val Lewton (*Cat People*, *I Walked with a Zombie*, *The Body Snatcher*), and to the imaginative works of Edgar Rice Burroughs and L. Frank Baum. Impressed by the plays of Arthur Miller and Tennessee Williams, he began to write for the stage. Kelly attended Emerson College in Boston and earned an M.F.A. in playwriting at the Yale School of Drama.

Kelly's first play, *Widow's Walk*, "A Mystery Thriller in Three Acts," was published in 1963. Since then, with more than 200 plays to his credit, Kelly has become the unsung hero of America's hinterland theatres. While his works are rarely produced in New York, they are constantly performed across the U.S. by such notable companies as the Studio Ensemble Theatre, Royal Court Rep, Los Angeles Actor's Theatre, The Aspen Playwright's Festival, and the Seattle Repertory Company.

The plays, published under several pseudonyms, cover a wide range of genres: whodunit, true crime, horror, science fiction, adventure, western, melodrama, youth plays, and children's plays. Kelly's heroes include Sherlock Holmes, Robin Hood, and Hawkshaw the Detective, while the villains are Dracula, Frankenstein, The Wolfman, the Zombie, The Invisible Man, Sweeney Todd, Jack the Ripper, and Dr. Jekyll and Mr. Hyde. Kelly adapted to the stage works by Victor Hugo, Alexandre Dumas, Sheridan LeFanu, Charles Dickens, Wilkie Collins, Robert Louis Stevenson, H.G. Wells, Oscar Wilde, Mark Twain, Edgar Allan Poe, and Edgar Wallace – interweaving horrific elements with sly humor.

Kelly recreated the world's foremost consulting detective in the one-act *The Last of Sherlock Holmes* (1970), *Sherlock Holmes Meets the Phantom* (1975), and *Beast of the Baskervilles* (1984); the full-length *The Hound of the Baskervilles* (1976), *Sherlock Holmes* (1977), and *The Adventure of the Speckled Band* (1981); and the musical *Sherlock Holmes and the Giant Rat of Sumatra* (1987). Named after the famous sleuth, Shirley Holmes, a young coed, is the heroine of Kelly's *If Sherlock Holmes Were a Woman* (1969). Kelly's *the Adventure of the Clouded Crystal* (1982) deals with a stormy relationship between Sir Arthur Conan Doyle and magician Harry Houdini.

For younger audiences, Kelly spotlighted Alice-in-Wonderland, Cinderella, Tom Sawyer, the Three Musketeers, the Wizard of Oz – and Zorro.

Kelly died on December 7, 1998, after suffering a brain hemorrhage in his Hollywood, California home. He was cremated, per his request.

Acting Edition: The Dramatic Publishing Company, 1990.

Awards and Honors: Boston's Emerson College has twice honored Tim Kelly for his "Contributions to the Field of Playwriting." In 1991, Kelly beat more than 300 entries to win the Elmira College Original Playwriting Contest with his blood-and-thunder drama *Crimes at the Old Brewery*. The play, depicting the squalor of Manhattan's Five Points during the 1850s, premiered, under my direction, at the college's Emerson Theatre on March 7, 1991.

NOTES

1. Tim Kelly, *Curse of the Werewolf* (Woodstock, Illinois: The Dramatic Publishing Company, MCMXC), unpaginated.
2. *Ibid*, 7.
3. *Ibid*, 8.
4. *Ibid*, 8.
5. *Ibid*, 35.
6. A Production Note explains the special effect of the "fiery red eyes" at the window: "A stage crew member dressed in black, black hood over the face, gloves, holds two small flashlights with red bulbs and moves them together up and down, side to side. These 'pinpoints' represent the 'eyes of the werewolf.' Another method is to have a black can with two holes cut into it, red gel over the holes and a flashlight inside."

V. Jury Room

The Woman on the Jury (1923)

Bernard K. Burns (United States, 1881-1937)

Betty Brown, alert, intelligent and well bred, makes the mistake of trusting George Wayne, a thirty-eight-year-old successful businessman from New York. She believes his declaration of love and agrees to a tryst at his remote summer cottage in the mountains of Vermont. Come September, Betty has a rude awakening when Wayne offers her $20,000 for a trip to Europe. "So as far as you are concerned, this is just an ordinary common affair?" she shakily asks.

After initial attempts to soothe her, Wayne confesses that there is another girl in the picture who "has certain expectations."

Betty calls Wayne a "flesh hunter," derides him for promising her "love as enduring as the mountains" and a future in "a Peter Pan house," and orders him out. As Wayne leaves for his car, Betty seizes a pistol and fires two shots through the door. It would seem that the bullets could not have missed Wayne, but following a tense moment, the sound of the motor is heard fading away.

The action now shifts from the dramatic prologue of *The Woman on the Jury* to a Manhattan courtroom, three years later. Grace Pierce is on trial for killing James Montgomery. Betty Brown, now Mrs. Masters, is on the jury, and so is her husband, Fred. On the witness stand, Mrs. Pierce, the widowed mother of the defendant, testifies that she believed Montgomery to have been her daughter's husband - "One night I got a telegram from Albany.It said they were on their way to New York to be married…"

The night Montgomery was killed there was a quarrel in the bedroom. Mrs. Pierce testifies that she heard him tell Grace, "I'm ready to quit the whole damn affair right now… I'm through. Now if you don't try to make trouble, I'll fix you up with money enough, but if you do start trouble all the lawyers in New York won't get you a damn cent!" Mrs. Pierce describes an escalating wrangle: "… and then my daughter threw herself at him, struck him in the face, and pushed him toward the door. I tried to get between them. There was a struggle and… and…" The shot was fired, and Montgomery is killed by his own pistol.

The defendant takes the stand and is sworn in by the clerk. With an emotional outburst, Grace relates that she understood Montgomery planned to marry her in spite of his claim that "complications" stood in the way — "and if I loved him, I would trust him… that a thousand ceremonies couldn't make us love each other more… he had said that love should be as free and innocent as Peter Pan."

Juror number 5, Betty Masters, rises and asks if that was the exact expression used by James Montgomery. "Yes," says the defendant, who then continues her testimony by informing the court she knew Montgomery was living with a woman in Vermont: "I employed a detective, Thomas McGuire."

On the stand, McGuire reports that Montgomery had a liaison with another woman in a cottage on the top of Baldhead Mountain, and that he was known to that community there by the name of Wayne. Mrs. Pierce asks to give testimony, and declares: "I love my daughter… I have given all my life to her… I shot James Montgomery."

The defendant, hysterically, shouts: "Mother! She didn't. I did! I did! I killed him!"

Mrs. Pierce insists: "He had his hands on my daughter's throat. I rushed to help her. I felt the weight of the pistol in his overcoat pocket. I drew it from his pocket, pressed it against him and fired. He fell. My daughter fainted."

Prosecutor Emmett offers her the pistol and asks that she go slowly through every movement of securing the weapon and firing it. Mrs. Pierce does as directed but fails to release the safety catch of the automatic. When the defendant is required to repeat the motion and she too neglects to shift the safety catch, Emmett denounces her for astutely falsifying the demonstration. In his summation, Emmett accuses Grace Pierce of being "fully and equally responsible for the immoral unlawful situation which brewed this cold-blooded murder… Behind murder there are strong motives and passions… and the strongest of these is the murderous, merciless jealousy of the woman who is replaced by another woman… It was not mother love that pulled the trigger on this gun, but the jealousy of this mistress — it was the hand of the woman scorned."

Defense Attorney Nellis reminds the ladies and gentlemen of the jury that it is their duty to find Miss Pierce guilty beyond all reasonable doubt and suggests that "in the blind struggle with the defendant, Montgomery shot himself."

In the jury room, it soon becomes evident that the vote is eleven to one for conviction. The holdout, Betty, states categorically, "I'll sit here—well, to use a man's expression—I'll sit here 'til Hell freezes over before I will vote a death penalty against that poor girl… when a woman, goaded to insanity by a beast of a man, suddenly finds a weapon in her hands and in an insane impulse uses it, she is not a downright murderer."

One of the jurors, Otto Schmidt, a phlegmatic, comfortable fellow who is his wife's errand boy in a delicatessen store, sighs: "Do you think you know more than the whole bunch of us men? Women shouldn't be on juries—that's a man's work."

The foreman of the jury, John Gerrity, a vigorous, aggressive Irish-American, is disgusted: "One for acquittal, eleven for conviction… Women on the jury— it's a hell of a place for a woman!"

Betty holds out for two days and nights. Finally, realizing that there is no other way to convince her fellow jurors, Betty, though jeopardizing her blissful marriage, confides her illicit relationship with George Wayne, alias James Montgomery, and her impulsive reaction at the moment her lover "struck her a terrible blow that shattered her." For the first time in her life, says Betty, her finger closed on the trigger of a gun and sent two shots through the door that he had just closed behind him – "And the way that I shot Montgomery is the way that girl out there shot him—in a blind unknowing impulse—if she shot him at all… Please, please, give me this girl's life!"

Betty collapses in her chair and cries audibly. The men are visibly touched. They pass the ballot box and call for the bailiff. Before leaving the jury room they solemnly swear that no mention of Betty's confession will ever pass their lips. They deliver in court the verdict "not guilty" and Grace is discharged. Mr. Masters, admittedly "shocked and dazed," embraces his wife, vowing to forget her past indiscretion "the moment we pass that door."

* * *

The Woman on the Jury premiered at the Eltinge Theatre, New York, on August 15, 1923, under the direction of Lester Lonergan, running seventy-seven performances. The *New York Times* found the play "quite frankly conceived as melodrama," but complimented playwright Burns for handling a novel situation "in a mainly skillful manner." The reviewer applauded Mary Newcomb's "quiet and effective art" in the role of Betty Brown-Masters.[1]

The Woman on the Jury was filmed twice by First National Pictures: a 1924 silent version with Sylvia Breamer in the title role, and a 1929 talkie, retitled *The Love Racket*, featuring Dorothy Mackaill.[2]

* * *

Bernard K. Burns is the author of two unorthodox plays. *Tread of Men* (1924) begins in a French graveyard where the ghosts of fallen soldiers rise and travel to visit their families in upstate New York, the English countryside, and Berlin, respectively. *Ticker Tape* (1934) tells several stories hinged on the same source—the stock market crash of 1929. Some of the drama's quick twenty-eight scenes unfold in the boardroom of a broker's office. A continuous blend of tickers, telegraph instruments, typewriters, and newspaper presses click and clack in the background.

NOTES

1. *New York Times*, August 16, 1923.
2. The gambit of pitting a sole dissenting juror against the other eleven who are eventually persuaded to shift position would be utilized in Fred Ballard's *Ladies of the Jury* (1929) and Reginald Rose's *Twelve Angry Men* (1952).

Ladies of the Jury (1929)

Fred Ballard (United States, 1885-1957)

Most of the action of *Ladies of the Jury* takes place in a Rosedale, New Jersey jury room, where the panel of twelve men and women deliberates the case of Yvette Yvet Gordon, an ex-chorus girl charged with the murder of her rich, elderly husband.

When the jurors commence to weigh the evidence, eleven members of the panel vote guilty, with one holdout—Mrs. Livingston Baldwin Crane, a middle-aged, high-society matron. Similar to the later *Twelve Angry Men* (1954), *Ladies of the Jury* depicts how the sole dissenter manages, step by step, to shift the opinion of the others to not guilty.

However, while the jurors of the Reginald Rose play didactyly analyze the pros and cons of their homicide case, bringing forth diverse opinions coated with social connotations, there is hardly any discussion of testimony or issues among the "Ladies of the Jury." Instead, Crane swings them over to her side with beguiling charm and disarming bribes: she orders hot food for the sequestered group; distributes silk pajamas and robes for an overnight stay; compliments the artistic merits of a poet and a ukulele player; and offers another jurist the position of cook in her household.

An inherent weakness in the play lies in the fact that Crane does not have any evidence to support her stand. She is guided exclusively by intuition: "But there was nothing whatever in Mrs. Gordon's appearance that would suggest a murderess… I am absolutely convinced of Mrs. Gordon's innocence."

Crane admonishes the jurors for being "taken in" by the prosecuting attorney's "cheap harangue" and by his star witness, the Gordon's maid, Evelyn Snow, "a particularly obvious adventuress." Alternatively, the sly Mrs. Crane flatters the group— "Who could ask for more charming company than our scintillating friends gathered here."

Finally, on the 124th ballot, the twelve members of the jury turned in a unanimous vote of not guilty.

* * *

Any misgivings regarding Crane's methods of influence were dissipated by then-First Lady of American theatre, Mrs. Minnie Maddern Fiske. When *Ladies of the Jury* opened at Erlanger's Theatre on October 21, 1929, the *New*

York Times critic praised Fiske's "gay and bubbling performance ... she plays with great spirit and zest, but she also brings out shadings and nuances of character not to be discerned in the general run of comedy... With this particular First Actress in charge, Mr. Ballard's new comedy becomes a good-natured piece of fooling which last night's audience found hilariously funny."[1]

The *New York Sun* stated that "Mrs. Fiske and *Ladies of the Jury* are a very happy combination. She has had much loftier vehicles for her great talents, but few more entertaining ones."[2] "It was all most laughable," chirped the *Herald Tribune*," just another of Mrs. Fiske's little and jovial frolics."[3] The *Brooklyn Daily Eagle* dissented:"It is all very lively high school fun, a riot for a stock company, not worthy material for a Mrs. Fiske."[4] *Ladies of the Jury* ran for eighty-eight performances.

The play was transferred to the screen twice by RKO Radio Pictures. In 1932, Edna May Oliver starred as Mrs. Crane, and Jill Esmond as Mrs. Gordon. This version climaxed in the jury's visit to the scene of the crime. In 1937, retitled *We're on the Jury*, Helen Broderick and Colleen Clare starred, with comic Victor Moore enacting the foreman of the jury, disrupting the proceedings and aggravating the judge, played by Robert McWade in both versions.

Acting Edition: Samuel French, Inc.

NOTES

1. *New York Times*, October 22, 1929.
2. *New York Sun*, October 22, 1929.
3. *New York Herald Tribune*, October 22, 1929.
4. *Brooklyn Daily Eagle*, October 22, 1929.

Twelve Angry Men (1954)

Reginald Rose (United States, 1920-2002)

The best known jury play is arguably Reginald Rose's *Twelve Angry Men*, adapted from CBS's Studio One teleplay of 1954.

The entire action unfurls in a stuffy jury room, where twelve jurors, all white males from varied rungs of society, are debating the case of a slum Black youth charged with the stabbing murder of his father. The verdict must be unanimous. The characters are unnamed. The jurorrs are identified merely by number.

After a short discussion, eleven jurors vote guilty, but juror number 8 is doubtful and insists on reviewing the witnesses' testimonies. Juror number 3 brings up the fact that early in the evening of the murder, an old neighbor heard the kid and his father quarreling. Juror number 10 reminds all that a woman across the street testified that she saw the actual killing from her window. Juror number 7 recounts the checkered past of the accused – stealing, mugging, reform school at fifteen. Juror number 3 clings to the fact that the kid bought "a cute little switch knife."

Number 8 asks the guard to bring the murder weapon. It is an oddly designed weapon, but number 8 reaches into his pocket and withdraws an identical switch blade. He then goes step by step through the various strands of evidence and one by one the jurors change their minds. Upon illustrating that the five-feet-eight-inches-tall kid could not have stabbed his six-foot-two-inches father downward, and upon the realization that the woman across the street would not have worn her bifocals when going to bed, the jurors unanimously are convinced that "there is reasonable doubt."

* * *

In 1964, Leo Genn appeared as juror number 8 on the London stage, directed by Margaret Webster. Harold Pinter helmed a production of the play, which opened at the Bristol Old Vic on March 7, 1996, featuring Kevin Whately as Juror number 8 and E.G. Marshall as the Voice of the Judge. The show transferred to the the Comedy Theatre in London later that year. Many theatrical productions followed, including one in a Hebrew translation offered by Israel's Habimah National Theatre in the dawn of the twenty first century. In 2003, the British producer/director Guy Masterson staged an all comedian revival, with Owen O'Neill as Juror 8, offering it during the Edinburgh Fringe Festival, garneing critical acclaim. The Roundabout Theatre Company of New York presented *Twelve Angry Men* in 2004, under the direction of Scott Ellis, with Boyd Gaines as Juror 8, Philip Bosco as Juror 3, and Robert Prosky as the Voice of the Judge, for a run of 228 performances. Prosky appeared as Juror 3 in a Washington D.C. production of the show, opposite Roy scheider as Juror 8, and Rene Auberjonnois as Juror 5. Richard Thomas starred as Juror 8 in a 2007 national tour. That same year, Los Angeles Theatre Works mounted a production of the play that was later recorded as an audiobook.

The Dramatic Publishing Company published the play version, by Sherman L. Sergel, in 2008. The George Street Playhouse in New Brunswick, New Jersey, revived *Twelve Angry Men* from March 13 to April 8, 2012, with Jack Klugman as Juror number 9. Directed by Christopker Haydon, a London West End production opened in November 2013, running until March 1, 2014 at the Garrick Theatre. In 2014, Independent Theatre Pakistan performed an adaptation of *Twelve Angry Men* at Alhamra Arts Council, Lahore, directed by Azeem Hamid. [1]

Acting Edition: The Dramatic Publishing Company.

NOTE

1. The 1954 television production of *Twelve Angry Men* for CBS Studio One starred Norman Fell as Juror number 1, Franchot Tone as Juror number 3, Walter Abel as Juror number 4, and Robert Cummings as Juror number 8. In 1957, Sidney Lumet directed a stellar cast, headed by Henry Fonda and Lee J. Cobb, in a definitive motion picture version of *Twelve Angry Men*. It was nominated for three Academy Awards: Best Picture, Best Director, and Best Adapted Screenplay. Forty years later, William Friedkin helmed a remake that starred Jack Lemmon, George C. Scott, James Gandolfini, William Petersen, Tony Danza, Hume Cronin, and Ossie Davis. In 2007, Russian director Nikita Mikhalkov filmed an updated version, called *12*, featuring Sergey Makovetsky and Sergey Garmash. In *12*, the jury is sequestered in an unused school gymnasium to decide the fate of a Chechen boy accused of murdering his adoptive Russian father. The movie was nominated for an Oscar as best foreign language film.

Twelve Angry Women (1977)

Reginald Rose (United States, 1920-2002)

In the mid-1970s, Sherman L. Sergel adapted the original TV show for an all-female cast and coined it *Twelve Angry Women.* In this version too, the entire action takes place in a stuffy jury room where twelve jurors, all white females from varied sections of society, are debating the case of a Black youth from the slums who has been charged with the stabbing death of his father. A failure to reach a unanimous verdict will result in a mistrial. A guilty verdict will be accompanied by a mandatory death sentence.

Sergel provides a character description of the jurors in the published acting edition of *Twelve Angry Women*: The Foreman is "a small, pretty woman who is impressed with the authority she has and handles herself quite formally. She is not overly bright but dogged." Juror number 2 is "a meek, hesitant woman who finds it difficult to maintain any opinion of her own. She is easily swayed." Juror number 3 is "a very strong, forceful, extremely opinionated woman, within whom can be detected a streak of sadism." Juror number 4 "seems to be a woman of wealth and position, and a practiced speaker who presents herself well at all times. Her only concern is with the facts of this case." Juror number 5 is "a naïve, very frightened young woman who finds it difficult to speak up when her elders have the floor." Juror number 6 is "an honest but dull-witted woman who comes upon her decisions slowly and carefully." Juror number 7 is "a loud, flashy, glad-handing woman who works in a department store and has more important things to do than sit on a jury. She is quick-tempered, a bully and, of course, a coward." Juror number 8 is "a quiet, thoughtful, gentle woman – a woman who sees all sides of every question and constantly seeks the truth. She is a woman of strength tempered with compassion." Juror number 9 is "a mild, gentle old woman, long since defeated by life and now merely waiting to die." Juror number 10 is "an angry, bitter woman – a woman who antagonizes almost at sight. She is also a bigot who places no value on any human life save her own." Juror number 11 is "a refugee from Europe, who came to this country in 1941. She speaks with an accent and is ashamed, humble, almost subservient to the people around her." Juror number 12 is "a slick, bright advertising woman who thinks of human beings in terms of percentages, graphs and polls, and has no real understanding of people."

The Guard is a bit part – "She can be a policewoman, of any age."

After a short discussion, eleven jurors vote guilty, but juror number 8 is doubtful and insists on reviewing the witnesses' testimonies. Not unlike *Twelve Angry Men*, Juror number 3 brings up the fact that early on the evening of the murder, an old neighbor heard the kid and his father quarreling; Juror number 10 reminds all that a woman across the street testified that she saw the actual killing from her window; Juror number 7 recounts the checkered past of the accused – stealing, mugging, reform school at fifteen; and Juror number 3 points out that after the encounter with his father, the kid went to a neighborhood store and bought a switch blade.

Number 8 asks the guard to bring in the murder weapon. It is an oddly designed knife, but number 8 reaches into her purse and withdraws an identical one. She then goes step by step through the various strands of evidence and one by one the jurors change their minds. Upon illustrating that a five-foot-eight-inch-tall kid could not have stabbed his six-foot-two-father downward, and upon the realization that the woman across the street would not have worn her bifocals when going to bed, the jurors are unanimously convinced that "there is reasonable doubt."

While *Twelve Angry Men* made it to Broadway, played around the world, and was successfully adapted to the silver screen, *Twelve Angry Women* has only been produced by community theatres, high schools and colleges on both shores of the Atlantic. The Monroe Theatre Guild of Monroe, Wisconsin, presented the female version at the Monroe Junior High Auditorium on February 17, 18, 19, 1977. During the first decade of the twenty-first century, *Twelve Angry Women* was mounted by Texas Christian University, Fort Worth, Texas (2003); Swindon's Old Town Theatre Company, Swindon Wilts, England (2004); The Theatre of Western Springs, Western Springs, Illinois (2005); Branch River Theatre, Marlborough, New Hampshire (2008); Manhattan Theatre Source, New York (2008); Hollywood Fight Club Theatre, Hollywood, California (2009); The University of Hartford, Hartford, Connecticut (2009); Unitarian Universalist Church, Bloomington, Indiana (2009); Convent of the Sacred Heart, Greenwich, Connecticut (2010); McLean High School, McLean, Virginia (2010); Perrysburg Area Arts Council, Perrysburg, Ohio (2011); Newman High School Drama Department, Newman, Georgia (2011); Seattle Pacific University, Seattle, Washington (2011); and Gloucester County Institute of Technology, New Jersey (2012).

An all-black cast played the angry women at the Black Arts & Cultural Center, Kalamazoo, Michigan (2009). A mixed troupe of men and women was recruited for *Twelve Angry Jurors*, produced by the Performing Arts Center at Glendale Community College, Glendale, Arizona (2010).

* * *

Born in Manhattan in 1920, Reginald Rose attended Townsend Harris High School and studied at City College from 1937 to 1938 before serving in the U.S. Army during 1942-1946, attaining the rank of first lieutenant. He sold his first teleplay, *Bus to Nowhere*, in 1950 to the live CBS dramatic anthology program Studio One, for which he wrote his breakaway hit *Twelve Angry Men* four years later. The Drama was inspired by a real-life experience: Rose had been a member of the jury on a manslaughter case that involved a furious, eight-hour argument among the jurors.

Rose joined Paddy Chayefsky and Rod Serling in creating thought-provoking dramas during the Golden Age of live television. He wrote for all three major broadcast networks. *Crime in the Street* was shown on ABC's Elgin Hour in 1955. His 1957 pilot *The Defender* launched the series *The Defenders* for CBS.[1] *The Sacco-Vanzetti Story* was presented by NBC's Sunday Showcase in 1960.[2] *Dear Friends* made a splash on CBS Playhouse in 1967.[3] He contributed scripts to Philco Television Playhouse, Alcoa Hour, Playhouse 90, Suspense, and Twilight Zone.

In the mid-1950s, Rose adapted to the screen his three acclaimed teleplays: *Crime in the Streets*, a drama focused on an alienated teen, played by John Cassavetes, who conspires to commit a murder; *Twelve Angry Men*; and *Dino*, a juvenile delinquent tale featuring Sal Mineo. In 1958, Rose penned the screenplays of *Man of the West*, an epic-scale Western starring Gary Cooper as a reformed outlaw, and *The Man in the Net*, a whodunit with Alan Ladd, which Rose adapted from a novel by Patrick Quentin.[4] *Baxter* (1973) spotlights the relationship between a young, lisping boy and his speech therapist, played by Patricia Neal. *The Wild Geese* (1978) is an action yarn – highlighted by the participation of top British actors Richard Burton, Roger Moore, Richard Harris, and Stewart Granger - about mercenaries who rescue a kidnapped African leader. *Somebody Killed Her Husband* (1978) has Farrah Fawcett entangled in a "tepid comedy-mystery-romance," according to movie maven Leonard Maltin.[5]

In the 1980s, Rose scripted *The Sea Wolves*, based on the true story of a retired British cavalry unit undertaking an espionage mission during World War II; *Whose Life Is It Anyway?*, adapted from a play by Brian Clark, about a sculptor, portrayed by Richard Dreyfuss, who is paralyzed from the neck down and argues for his right to die; *The Final Option* (aka *Who Dares Wins*), an account of a British officer's attempt to infiltrate a terrorist gang; and *Wild Geese II*, an adventure sequel in which a gaggle of mercenaries are recruited to spring arch-Nazi Rudolf Hess from Berlin's Spandau prison.

Married twice and the father of six boys, Rose died in 2002 in Norwalk, Connecticut from heart failure. He was 81.

Acting Edition: The Dramatic Publishing Company.

Awards and Honors: Reginald Rose received an Emmy Award for his teleplay and an Oscar nomination for his screenplay of *Twelve Angry Men*. The 1957 motion picture was also nominated for an Academy Award in the categories of Best Picture and Best Director (Sidney Lumet). It won the Golden Bear Award at the Berlin International Film Festival, and in 2007 *Twelve Angry Men* was selected for preservation in the United States National Film Registry by the Library of Congress. The Roundabout production of *Twelve Angry Men* garnered a 2005 Drama Desk Award for Best Revival of a Play and was nominated for a Tony Award in the same category.

NOTES

1. *The Defenders* ran on CBS-TV from 1961 to 1965. The series starred E.G. Marshall and Robert Reed as a father-son team of lawyers who tackle challenging legal cases. Reginald Rose utilized elements from the show for a two-act stage adaptation also called *The Defenders*.
2. Reginald Rose adapted to the stage his teleplay *The Sacco-Vanzetti Story*, about the trial and execution of Italian immigrants Nicola Sacco and Bartolomeo Vanzetti who were accused of murdering two payroll guards in a daylight robbery in April 1920. Under the title *This Agony, This Triumph*, the play was produced in California in 1972.
3. The teleplay *Dear Friends*, in which three couples meet and discuss their problems only to gradually lash out at each other by exposing closet skeletons, was transferred to the stage by Reginald Rose, produced in Edinburgh, Scotland in 1968, and by the Lakewood Little Theatre, Cleveland, Ohio, the following year.
4. Patrick Quentin, Q. Patrick and Jonathan Stagge are the pseudonyms of four authors in a complicated collaboration. The main contributor, Hugh Callingham Wheeler, jointly penned more than thirty highly regarded detective novels, a true-crime paperback original (*The Girl on the Gallows*, 1954), and a collection of criminous tales, *The Ordeal of Mrs. Snow and Other Stories*, for which he won the Mystery Writers of America's Edgar Allan Poe Award in 1963.

   In the 1960s, Wheeler shifted gears to playwriting and had his ups and downs on Broadway. Generally, his dramas and comedies did not fare well: *Big Fish, Little Fish* (ANTA Theatre, March 15, 1961 – 101 performances), is about a small-press editor surrounded by hangers-on. *Look: We've Come Through* (Hudson Theatre, October 25, 1961 – five performances), depicts the developing relationship between a girl-with-a-past and a young man with a homosexual history. *Rich Little Rich Girl*, based on a play by Miguel Mihura and Alvaro de Laiglesia (a pre-Broadway tryout, for two weeks, at the Walnut Street Theatre, Philadelphia, October 26, 1964), is a comedy of murder involving a South American dictator. *Truckload* (Lyceum Theatre, September 6, 1975 – closed after a week of previews) tells of hitch-hiking across the country in trucks.

Wheeler did, however, contribute the libretto for some very successful musicals, winning Tony, Drama Critics Circle, and Drama Desk Awards: *A Little Night Music* (Shubert Theatre, February 25, 1973 – 600 performances), based on the 1955 Ingmar Bergman film, *Smiles of a Summer Night*, about a weekend of romance and sex at a country estate; *Irene* (Minskoff Theatre, March 13, 1973 – 604 performances), an adaptation of a 1919 musical focusing on the behind-the-scenes romance between a fashion designer and his female associate; *Candide* (Chelsea Theatre Center of Brooklyn, December 11, 1973 – forty-eight performances; transferred to the Broadway Theatre, March 10, 1974 – 740 performances), a revised book of the 1956 musical based on Voltaire; *Pacific Overtures* (Winter Garden, January 11, 1976 – 193 performances), additional material to the book by John Weidman regarding Admiral Perry's arrival in 1853 to isolated Japan; and *Sweeney Todd, the Demon Barber of Fleet Street* (UrisTheatre, March 1, 1979 – 557 performances), founded on a version of *Sweeney Todd* by Christopher Bond, concerning a London barber who soothes an ire at society by slitting his customer's throats and consigning them to a pastry cook who then sells them baked in her pies.

For the cinema, Wheeler co-wrote the screenplays for *Five Miles to Midnight* (1962), *Something for Everyone* (1969), *Cabaret* (1972), and *Travels with My Aunt* (1973).

5. *Leonard Maltin's 2012 Movie Guide* (New York: Plume, 2011), 1282.

A Wicked Soul in Cherry Hill (2022)

Words and Music by Matt Schatz (United States, 1978-)

In the fall of 1994, a sensational murder shocked the suburban community of Cherry Hill, New Jersey. The wife of an admired rabbi was found dead at home with a fractured skull, and the ensuing investigation unearthed that Rabbi Fred Neulander had an affair with a Philadelphia radio announcer and hired two hitmen to kill his wife.

Playwright-composer Matt Schatz, who lived for a while in Cherry Hill, has written a play about the sordid affair, utilizing music and lyrics, dispensing almost entirely with spoken dialogue. *A Wicked Soul in Cherry Hill* received its world premiere at The Geffen Playhouse, Los Angeles, on June 30, 2022. Under the direction of Mike Donahue, the audience serves as the jury in the climactic trial.

Much of the action takes place in a reform synagogue. Three actors and three actresses appear in varied roles: the rabbi, the rabbi's wife, the rabbi's son, the rabbi's daughter, the rabbi's mistress, a cantor, a junior rabbi, a hitman, a journalist, and others.

A flashback takes us back to the arrival of the rabbi in 1968 dressed in jeans and introducing himself as "Fred." He hired a cantor who plays the guitar and began to revolutionize the synagogue customs. He also got married to "a dutiful wife" and they had "three beautiful children." The wife established "The Cherry Hill Kosher Cake Company," which became a big success, catering to weddings and holidays. She found herself spending her nights at her workplace, and "it's very rare we're both at home."

The story shifts focus to Woman 3, a radio DJ at W.P.E.N. who marries a co-worker, a secular Jew named Ken, even though he's "two decades her junior." Ken eventually dies of cancer and Woman 3 meets the rabbi to ask if he conducts funerals. "Please call me Fred," says the Rabbi.

Woman 3 sings:

"His eulogy is kind of amazing
One would think he'd known your spouse
And when he is done you know there's not a one
With an eye that is dry in the house."

After a few weeks she gets a call from Fred, offering to take her for coffee. She asks, "How about my place instead?" A meal of bagels, lox, and pickled tomatoes ends with a kiss, and Woman 3 exclaims,

"Suddenly you feel alive
And you're born again at forty-five.
You could say no
But oh
No is no way to survive.

They went through a clandestine affair for two years. She was willing to convert but he said that "rabbis can never ever divorce."

A new member joined the temple, named Len, and "the first thing he mentioned was that he was once in the CIA." Among his past experiences, related Len, was trying to kill Castro twice, and he carried the card of a private detective.

The rabbi engaged Len as s secretary and eventually solicited him to kill his wife. The jolly mood of the play now turns grim. After one failed attempt, Len returns to the rabbi's home carrying an old lead pipe. Fred finds the body on the floor, "blood around her head," and dials 911, "my wife is dead."

Under alarm sounds, all sing:

"There's a scary man out there
And he is out there still
Stalking prey and walking through the streets of Cherry Hill.
We don't know what he looks like
And perhaps we never will.
All we know is that he has an appetite to kill."

Len confessed the deed to a pretty reporter, and she called the authorities. Len and the rabbi were arrested, and the community was shocked. The townies turn to the audience – "Ladies and gentlemen of the jury" – and croon "He wanted more," the tragedy of a rabbi who had "three beautiful children, a dutiful partner, an exemplary temple to lead" – but wanted more.

All men:
He was the pillar of the community.
All Women:
He was the killer of the community.
All Men:
Found on the floor
She was taken too young.
All Women:

What say the jury?
Man 1:
Killer.
Woman 1:
Pillar.
Woman 2:
Killer.
Man 3:
Pillar.
All:
The jury is hung.

Trial 2 took place at the Monmouth County Courthouse. The verdict? Because he played ball, Len got only 14 years; the rabbi was sentenced to life. The community members question:

Why do we recount and recall?
Can't we just forget?
And even better yet
Pretend it never happened at all?

It doesn't take long for them to answer:

But it's in our culture to question
To argue, to kibitz, to fight
And it doesn't matter if you're in a synagogue
Or theater
On each Friday night.[1]

* * *

Upon the opening of *A Wicked Soul in Cherry Hill* at The Geffen Playhouse, Evan Henerson, the online reviewer of *Broadway World*, Los Angeles, raved: "Director Mike Donahue's production on the Geffen's Cates stage is intelligent, well-crafted and downright fun... Through entirely sung-through dialog, we learn about the town, its denizens and character... And, of course, we meet the Rabbi himself. As embodied by Danny Rothman, he's youthful, charming, slightly tweedy and possessed of an easy smile... The characters are to a person, excellent both in their vocal abilities and in their character-swapping versatility. Especially strong are Rivkah Reyes, playing the Rabbi's daughter and a small-paper journalist, and Jill Sobule, who is outstanding as the Rabbi's pragmatic wife and congregation's cantor."[2]

Los Angeles Times' Charles McNulty found *A Wicked Soul* "a charmingly unpretentious production... Neighbors have gathered to contemplate the gravity of the Rabbi's sin, the nature of evil and the lingering shock that a pillar of the community could have been capable of such murderous duplicity... One by one the characters recall where they were when they first heard the news of the murder... This backstory is confusingly rendered. The sudden shifts in time are abrupt and sometimes hard to track. Adding to the blurriness is the way cast members are called upon to play multiple roles... The musical rarely allows us to get to know any of the characters in depth." However, writes McNulty, "[Director] Donahue elicits a laid-back quality from his ensemble that is wry delight... I left the Geffen prepared to declare *A Wicked Soul in Cherry Hill* a hit, with a few qualifications... but as occasionally happens in the life of a critic, when I woke up the next day to write the review, I had second thoughts. Treated as a purely fictional story, the musical is a delight. But a woman was murdered, a family shattered and a community left reeling. Should I really be chuckling over the droll lyrics of kibitzing bystanders?... A musical this much fun shouldn't make you squirm in the morning."[3]

NOTES

1. Other plays that are centered on a community's turmoil include: *Fuenta Ovejune* (c.1614) by Lope de Vega, *An Enemy of the People* (1883) by Henrik Ibsen, *The Treasure* (1907) by Shalom Aleichem, and *The Visit* (1956) by Friedrich Duerrenmatt.
2. *Broadway World*, Los Angeles, July 3, 2022, *broadwayworld.com*
3. *Los Angeles Times*, July 5, 2022.

APPENDIX A

Twentieth Century Courtroom Dramas

I. Plays that unfold in a courtroom – civil, religious, military – or contain a pivotal courtroom scene:

THE LIVING CORPSE (written c. 1900, premiered 1911) by Leo Tolstoy
DANTON (1900) by Romain Rolland
DANTON'S DEATH (1902) by Georg Büchner
OLD SLEUTH (1902) by Hal Reid
SAM HILL JONES (1902) by Hal Reid
RESURRECTION (1903) by Henri Bataille and Michael Morton, adapted from Leo Tolstoy's novel
THE SCALES OF JUSTICE (1903) by John Rinehart
THE SORCERESS (1904) by Victorien Sardou
THE SILVER BOX (1906) by John Galsworthy
MADAME X (1908) by Alexandre Bisson
SWANWHITE (1908) by August Strindberg
JUSTICE (1910) by John Galsworthy
THE CONFESSION (1911) by James Halleck Reid
THE BOSS (1911) by Edward Sheldon (1911)
WITHIN THE LAW (1912) by Bayard Veiller
THE SECRET WOMAN (1912) by Eden Phillpotts
THE MYSTERY OF THE YELLOW ROOM (1912) by Gaston Leroux
THE ADORED ONE aka THE LEGEND OF LEONORA (1913) by J.M. Barrie
ON TRIAL (1914) by Elmer Rice
ROBIN HOOD AND THE PEDLAR (1914) by John Drinkwater
THE WARE CASE (1915) by George Pleydell
THE MAN ON THE BOX (1915) by Grace Livingston Furniss
YOUNG AMERICA (1915) by Fred Ballard
THE GUILTY ONE (1916) by Charles Klein and Ruth Helen Davis
LIGHTNIN' (1918) by Winchell Smith and Frank Bacon
FOR THE DEFENSE (1919) by Elmer Rice
DADDY DUMPLINS (1920) by Rufus King and George Barr McCutcheon
IN THE NIGHT WATCH (1921) by Michael Morton
SAINT JOAN (1923) by George Bernard Shaw

THE ADDING MACHINE (1923) by Elmer Rice
THE WASP (1923) by Thomas Fallon
THE MONGREL (1924) by Elmer Rice, adapted from the German of Herman Bahr
BEGGAR ON HORSEBACK (1924) by George S. Kaufman and Marc Connelly
THE TRIAL OF JESUS (1925) by John Masefield
A HOLY TERROR (1925) by Winchell Smith and George Abbotts
THE ENCHANTED CHRISTMAS TREE (1925) by Percival Wilde
AN AMERICAN TRAGEDY (1926) by Patrick Kearney, based upon the novel by Theodore Dreiser
CAPONSACCHI (1926) by Arthur Goodrich, based upon the poem "The Ring and the Book" by Robert Browning
CHICAGO (1926) by Maureen Dallas Watkins
THE PEARL OF GREAT PRICE (1926) by Robert McLaughlin
THE TRIAL OF MARY DUGAN (1927) by Bayard Veiller
THE BELLAMY TRIAL (1928) by Frances Noyes Hart and Frank E. Carstarph
MACHINAL (1928) by Sophie Treadwell
A FREE SOUL (1928) by Willard Mack
NO OTHER TIGER (1928) by A.E.W. Mason
THE TRIAL OF YOU (1928) by Vere Bennett
POTIPHAR'S WIFE (1928) by Edgar C. Middleton
SCARLET PAGES (1929) by Samuel Shipman and John B. Hymer
THE MOUTHPIECE (1929) by Frank J. Collins
THE EXCEPTION AND THE RULE (1929/1930) by Bertolt Brecht
THE SILENT WITNESS (1930) by Jack de Leon and Jack Celestin
DRAW THE FIRES! (1930) by Ernst Toller
THAT'S THE WOMAN (1930) by Bayard Veiller
CYNARA (1930) by H.M. Harwood and R. Gore Browne
ROOM 349 (1930) by Mark Linder
PRECEDENT (1931) by I.J. Golden
LANDSLIDE (1932) by Ugo Betti
NIGHT COURT (1932) by Mark Hellinger and Charles Beahan
NINE PINE STREET (1933) by John Colton and Carlton Miles
WE, THE PEOPLE (1933) by Elmer Rice
JUDGMENT DAY (1934) by Elmer Rice
A HAT, A COAT, A GLOVE (1934) by William A. Drake, from the German of Wilhelm Speyer
LEGAL MURDER (1934) by Dennis Donoghue
THEY SHALL NOT DIE (1934) by John Wexley
LIBEL! (1934) by Edward Wooll

MURDER TRIAL (1934) by Sidney Bax
HEADLINE (1934) by Arnold Ridley
NIGHT OF JANUARY 16TH (1935) by Ayn Rand
THE UNGUARDED HOUR (1935) by Bernard Merivale
OLD BAILEY (1935) by Campbell Dixon
FOR THE DEFENCE (1935) by John Hastings Turner
THE ELDEST (1935) by Carlton Miles and Eugenie Courtright
WHAT REALLY HAPPENED (1936) by Marie Belloc Lowndes
THE MISSING WITNESS (1936) by James Reach
LAW AND ORDER (1936) by Frederick Burtwell
LAUGHTER IN COURT (1936) by Hugh Mills
MURDER ON ACCOUNT (1936) by Hayden Talbot and Kathlyn Hayden
BLIND MAN'S BUFF (1936) BY Ernst Toller and Denis Johnston
YOUNG MADAME CONTI (1936) by Hubert Griffith and Benn W. Levy
OSCAR WILDE (1936) by Leslie and Sewell Stokes
INJUNCTION GRANTED (1936) by The Editorial Board of the Living Newspaper
THE DEVIL AND DANIEL WEBSTER (1939) by Stephen Vincent Benét
JOHNNY BELINDA (1940) by Elmer Harris
NATIVE SON (1941) by Paul Green and Richard Wright
THE GOOD WOMAN OF SETZUAN (1943) by Bertolt Brecht
PICK-UP GIRL (1944) by Elsa Shelley
THE PURIFICATION (1944) by Tennessee Williams
SIGNATURE (1945) by Elizabeth McFadden
ANGEL (1945) by Mary Hayley Bell
CHRISTOPHER BLAKE (1946) by Moss Hart
THE STORY OF MARY SURRATT (1947) by John Parick
THE TRIAL (1947) by Andre Gide and Jean Louis Barrault, based upon the novel by Franz Kafka
BLIND GODDESS (1947) by Patrick Hastings
THE EXCEPTION AND THE RULE (1947) by Bertolt Brecht
THE CAUCASIAN CHALK CIRCLE (1948) by Bertolt Brecht
ANNE OF THE THOUSAND DAYS (1948) by Maxwell Anderson
THE VIGIL (1948) by Laszlo (Ladislaus) Fodor
LOST IN THE STARS (1949), book and lyrics by Maxwell Anderson, music by Kurt Weill, based upon the novel *Cry, the Beloved Country* by Alan Paton
A PIN TO SEE THE PEEPSHOW (1951) by F. Tennyson Jesse and Harold Marsh Harwood, adapted from Jesse's novel
BAREFOOT IN ATHENS (1951) by Maxwell Anderson
BILLY BUDD (1951) by Louis O. Coxe and Robert Chapman, adapted from the novella by Herman Melville

THE LARK (1952) by Jean Anouilh
THE TRIAL OF MR. PICKWICK (1952) by Stanley Young, based on Charles Dickens' *The Pickwick Papers*
WITNESS FOR THE PROSECUTION (1953) by Agatha Christie
THE CRUCIBLE (1953) by Arthur Miller
THE CAINE MUTINY COURT-MARTIAL (1953), dramatized by Herman Wouk from his Pulitzer Prize novel
CARRINGTON, V.C. (1953) by Dorothy and Campbell Christie
CAN-CAN (1953), book by Abe Burrows, music and lyrics by Cole Porter
HIS AND HERS (1954) by Fay and Michael Kanin
INHERIT THE WIND (1955) by Jerome Lawrence and Robert E. Lee
MAN ON TRIAL (1955) by Diego Fabbri
THE REMARKABLE INCIDENT AT CARSON CORNERS (c 1955) by Reginald Rose and Kristin Sergel
TIME LIMIT! (1956) by Henry Denker and Ralph Berkey
THE PONDER HEART (1956) by Joseph Fields and Jerome Chodorov, adapted from the story by Eudora Welty
COMPULSION (1957), dramatized by Meyer Levin from his novel
THE DEFENDERS (1957) dramatized by Reginald Rose from his television show
BROTHERS IN LAW (1957) by Ted Willis and Henry Cecil
THE RESISTIBLE RISE OF ARTURO UI (1958) by Bertolt Brecht
THE MAN WHO NEVER DIED (1958) by Barrie Stavis
YOU, THE JURY (1958) by James Reach
THE TRIAL OF DIMITRI KARAMAZOV (1958) by Norman Rose, extracted from *The Brothers Karamazov* by Fyodor Mikhailovich Dostoyevsky
THE BLACKS (1959) by Jean Genet
THE LEGEND OF LIZZIE (1959) by Reginald Lawrence
ANATOMY OF A MURDER (1959) by Elihu Winer, adapted from the novel by Robert Traver
RASHOMON (1959) by Fay and Michael Kanin, based upon the stories by Ryunosake Akutagawa
BECKET (1959) by Jean Anouilh
THE ANDERSONVILLE TRIAL (1959) by Saul Levitt
THE TRIAL OF COB AND LEACH (1959) by Christopher Logue
ONE WAY PENDULUM (1959) by N.F. Simpson
LOCK UP YOUR DAUGHTERS (1959), Book by Bernard Miles, Lyrics by Lionel Bart, Music by Laurie Johnson, based upon the novel *Rape Upon Rape* by Henry Fielding
THE TRIAL OF JOAN OF ARC AT ROUEN (1959) by Bertolt Brecht
BETWEEN TWO THIEVES (1960) by Warner Le Roy, adapted from the Italian of Diego Fabbri

THE DEADLY GAME (1960) by James Yaffe, adapted from the novel *Traps* by Friedrich Duerrenmatt
A MAN FOR ALL SEASONS (1960) by Robert Bolt
SETTLED OUT OF COURT (1960) by William Saroyan and Henry Cecil, based on the novel by Cecil
DAUGHTER OF SILENCE (1961), dramatized by Morris L. West from his novel
WE'RE ALL GUILTY (1962) by James Reach
SEQUEL TO A VERDICT (1962) by Philip Dunning
THE GENERAL'S DOG (1962) by Heinar Kipphardt
SWEENEY TODD THE BARBER (1962) by Brian J. Burton
THE ADVOCATE (1963) by Robert Noah
THE SAVAGE PARADE (1963) by Anthony Shaffer
LICENSE TO MURDER (1963) by Elaine Morgan
A CASE OF LIBEL (1963) by Henry Denker, adapted from the book *My Life in Court* by Louis Nizer
A DARKER FLOWER (1963) by Tim Kelly
BLUES FOR MR. CHARLIE (1964) by James Baldwin
INADMISSIBLE EVIDENCE (1964) by John Osborne
HOSTILE WITNESS (1964) by Jack Roffey
HAMP (1964) by John Wilson
THE GENERAL'S DOG (1964) by Heinar Kipphardt
THE INVESTIGATION (1965) by Peter Weiss
ALIBI FOR A JUDGE (1965) by Felicity Douglas, Henry Cecil, and Basil Dawson, adapted from the book by Cecil
DRAT! THE CAT! (1965), book and lyrics by Ira Levin, music by Milton Schafer
JUSTICE IS A WOMAN (1966) by Jack Roffey and Ronald Kinnoch
THE MAN IN THE GLASS BOOTH (1967) by Robert Shaw
FOR THE DEFENSE (1967) by James Reach
THE RIMERS OF ELDRITCH (1967) by Lanford Wilson
ACCORDING TO THE EVIDENCE (1967) by Felicity Douglas, Henry Cecil, and Basil Dawson, adapted from the book by Cecil
THE TRIAL OF LEE HARVEY OSWALD (1967) by Amram Ducovny and Leon Friedman
THE PEOPLE vs. RANCHMAN (1968) BY Megan Terry
IVORY TOWER (1969) by Jerome Weidman and James Yaffe
THE LYONS MAIL (1969), adapted by George Rowell from *The Courier of Lyons* (1854) by Charles Reade
CONDUCT UNBECOMING (1969) by Barry England
A WOMAN NAMED ANNE (1969), adapted by Henry Cecil from his own novel

THE COURT MARTIAL OF BILLY BUDD (1969) by James M. Salem, based upon the novel by Herman Melville
INQUEST (1970) by Donald Freed (aka THE U.S. vs. JULIUS AND ETHEL ROSENBERG)
THE TRIAL (1970) by Steven Berkoff, base upon the novel by Franz Kafka
A VOYAGE ROUND MY FATHER (1970) by John Mortimer
A WOMAN NAMED ANNE (1970) by Henry Cecil
SCRATCH (1971) by Archibald MacLeish, suggested by Stephen Vincent Benet's short story, "The Devil and Daniel Webster"
THE TRIAL OF THE CANTONSVILLE NINE (1971) by Daniel Berrigan and Saul Levitt
THE LOVE SUICIDES AT SCHOFIELD BARRACKS (1972) by Romulus Linney
THE REMARKABLE SUSAN (1973) by Tim Kelly
THE TRIALS OF OSCAR WILDE (1974) by Gyles Brandreth
CHICAGO (1975) book by Fred Ebb and Bob Fosse, lyrics by Fred Ebb, music by John Kander, based on the play by Maurine Dallas Watkins
THE RUNNER STUMBLES (1976) by Milan Stitt
SLY FOX (1976) by Larry Gelbart, based on *Volpone* by Ben Jonson
JACK SHEPPARD (1976) by Ken Campbell
CAUSE CÉLÈBRE (1977) by Terence Ratigan
THE BIKO INQUEST (1978) by Norman Fenton and Jon Blair
BREAKER MORANT (1978) by Kenneth G. Ross
ZOOT SUIT (1978) by Luis Valdez
ESMERALDA AND THE HUNCHBACK OF NOTRE DAME (1978) by Andrew Piotrowski
SWEENEY TODD, THE DEMON BARBER OF FLEET STREET (1979) book by Hugh Wheeler, Music and Lyrics by Stephen Sondheim
NUTS (1980) by Tom Topor
SALT LAKE CITY SKYLINE (1980) by Thomas Babe
THE HISTORY OF THE DEVIL (1980) by Clive Barker
THE NEW TRIAL (1982) by Peter Weiss
EXECUTION OF JUSTICE (1984) by Emily Mann
THE MYSTERY OF EDWIN DROOD (1985) book, lyrics and music by Rupert Holmes, based on the unfinished novel by Charles Dickens
NEVER THE SINNER (1985) by John Logan
THE BOYS OF WINTER (1985) by John Pielmeier
THE FINAL TRIAL OF RICHARD III (1985) by Mary W. Schaller
LES MISÉRABLES (1985) book by Alain Boublil and Claude-Michel Schönberg, music by Schönberg, lyrics by Herbert Kretzmer, based on the novel by Victor Hugo
TO KILL A MOCKINGBIRD (1987) by Christopher Sergel, adapted from the novel by Harper Lee

BEYOND REASONABLE DOUBT (1987) by Jeffrey Archer
M. BUTTERFLY (1988) by David Henry Hwang
MOCK TRIAL (1988) by Romulus Linney
A FEW GOOD MEN (1989) by Aaron Sorkin
THE BACKGROUND (1989) by Jules Tasca, adapted from a story by "Saki"
THE TRIAL OF DR. JEKYLL (1989) by William L. Slout
2 (1990) by Romulus Linney
GREEN FINGERS (1990) by Michael Wilcox
SLAUGHTER ON SECOND STREET (1991) by David Kent
DRACULA IN PARADISE (1991) by Tom Jordan
THE ANASTASIA TRIALS IN THE COURT OF WOMEN (1992) by Carolyn Gage
HAUPTMANN (1992) BY John Logan
HERE COMES THE JUDGE (1992) by Billy St. John
OLEANA (1992) by David Mamet
STARCROSSED: THE TRIAL OF GALILEO (1994), book and lyrics by Keith Levenson and Alexa Junge, music by Jeanine Tesori
STAR WITNESS (1994) by Billy St. John
THE BOYS IN THE BASEMENT (1995) by Karen Houppert and Stephen Nunns
K: IMPRESSIONS OF A TRIAL (1995) by Garland Wright, adapted from Franz Kafka's novel *The Trial*
GREENBORO: A REQUIEM (1996) by Emily Mann
RAGTIME (1997) by E.L. Doctorow
GROSS INDECENCY (1997) by Moisés Kaufman
MOCK TRIAL (1997) by Romulus Linney
AFTERMATH OF A MURDER (1997) by George Singer
JURIS PRUDENCE (1997) by Jason Milligan
GHOST DANCE (1997) by Mark Stein and Frank Condon
THE TRIAL OF ONE SHORTSIGHTD BLACK WOMAN vs. MAMMY LOUISE AND SAFREETA MAE (1998) by Marcia L. Leslie
PARADE (1998) book by Alfred Uhry, lyrics and music by Jason Robert Brown
SHANGHAI MOON (1999) by Charles Busch
KANGAROO COURT (1998) by Nicholas Checker
DIS-ORDER IN THE COURT (1999) by Pat Cook
TO MEET OSCAR WILDE (1999) by Norman Holland
EVERYBODY'S RUBY (1999) by Thulani Davis

* * *

THE ACCUSED (2000) by Jeffrey Archer

THE PERFECT MURDER (2000) by Hugh Janes
THE LARAMIE PROJECT (2000) by Moisés Kaufman
A LESSON BEFORE DYING (2000) by Romulus Linney
COMEDY COURT aka CONTEMPT OF COURT (2000), book by David Landau, music and lyrics by Nikki Stern
JUDGMENT AT NUREMBERG (2001) by Abby Mann
THRILL ME (2003), book, music, and lyrics, by Stephen Dolginoff
HAMLET'S APPEAL (2004), Shakespeare Society
ROMANCE (2005) by David Mamet
DIRECT FROM DEATH ROW THE SCOTTSBORO BOYS (2005) by Mark Stein
THE PEOPLE vs. MONA (2007) by Patricia Miller and Jim Wann
THE LAST DAYS OF JUDAS ISCARIOT (2007) by Stephen Adley Guirgis
COURT-MARTIAL AT FORT DEVENS (2007) by Jeffrey Sweet
THE BIG BAD MUSICAL (2007), book by Alec Strum, music and lyrics by Bill Francoeur
THE TRIAL OF MATA HARI (2008) by Elaine Kendall
THE LIFEBLOOD (2008) by Glyn Maxwell
PRISONER OF THE CROWN (2008) by Richard F. Stockton
THURGOOD (2008) by George Stevens, Jr.
THE PEOPLE vs. MONA (2008), book by Patricia Miller and Jim Wann, music and lyrics by Jim Wann
SHAKESPEARE ON TRIAL (2009) by Anthony Giordano
THE DEEP THROAT SEX SCANDAL (2010) by David Bertolino
SAND IN THE AIR (2011) by Brian Raine
SOUTH OF DELANCEY (2011) by Karen Sommers
8 (2011) by Dustin Lance Black
A TIME TO KILL (2011) by Rupert Holmes, adapted from the novel by John Grisham
THE TRIAL OF FRANKLIN DELANO ROOSEVELT (2011) by Edward Bernstein
MURDER IN THE FIRST (2012) by Dan Gordon
JINGLE JURY (2012), book by Jay Moriarty, music and lyrics by Bill Francoeur
CLARENCE DARROW (2013) by Gary Anderson
THE BEATING (2013) by Mona Deutsch Miller
9 CIRCLES (2013) by Bill Cain
MURDER IN DISGUISE (2013), interactive with the audience
ARGUENDO (2013), created by Elevator Repair Service (ERS) ensemble
ELECTRA (2014), adapted by Steven Sabel and J.P. Rapozo from the play by Euripides
THE WRONG MAN (2014) by Ross Golan

THE BULLPEN (2014) by Joe Assadourian
WIESENTHAL (2014) by Tom Dugan
BEHIND THE BEAUTIFUL FOREVERS (2014) by David Hare, adapted from the book by Katherine Boo
EMMETT, DOWN IN MY HEART (2015) by Clare Coss
FERGUSON (2015) by Phelim McAleer
MOST DANGEROUS MAN IN AMERICA (2015) by Amiri Baraka
DISINHERIT THE WIND (2015) by Matt Chait
MARTIN LUTHER ON TRIAL (2015) by Chris Cragin-Day and Max McLean
ANGEL: A NIGHTMARE OF THE HOLOCAUST (2015) by Samantha Simmonds-Ronceros
DEAD DOG PARK (2016) by Barry Malawer
RIGHT LEFT WITH HEELS (2016) by Sebastian Majewski
ROE (2016) by Lisa Loomer
THE TRIAL OF AN AMERICAN PRESIDENT (2016) by Richard Tarlow
SPINDLE CITY (2016), book, lyrics, and music by Katrina Wood
MARTIN LUTHER ON TRIAL (2016) by Chris Cragin-Day and Max McLean
TRIAL OF FAITH (2016) by Mary Ryzuk
STAR WITNESS (2016) by Billy St. John
TRIAL OF THE WICKED WITCH (2016) by Craig Sodaro
JOAN OF ARC: INTO FIRE (2017), book, music, and lyrics by David Byrne
X; OR, BETTY SHABAZZ v. THE NATION (2017) by Marcus Gardley
ROE (2017) by Lisa Loomer
THE DREYFUS AFFAIR (2017) by Eve Wolf
CHASING JACK (2017) by John S. Anastasi
FUTURE COURT: THE BINDY LIPTON MASSACRE (2018) by David Dickens
TO KILL A MOCKING BIRD (2018) by Aaron Sorkin, adapted from the novel by Harper Lee
THE COURTROOM (2019) by Arian Moayed, based on court transcripts
SOCRATES (2019) by Tim Blake Nelson
THE CENTRAL PARK FIVE (opera, 2019) by Anthony Davis and Richard Wesley
Vs. (2021) by Carl Hancock Rux
GOLDEN SHIELD (2022) by Anchuli Felicia King
JINGLE JURY (2022), book by Jay Moriarty, music and lyrics by Bill Francoeur
WHO KILLED MY FATHER (2023) by Edouard Louis
BERLUSCONI: A NEW MUSICAL (2023) by Ricky Simonds and Simon Vaughan

VARDY v. ROONEY: THE WAGATHA CHRISTIE TRIAL (2023) by Liv Hennessy

II. A trial looms in the background of the proceedings:

THE RED ROBE (1900) by Eugene Brieux
THE WITCHING HOUR (1907) by Augustus Thomas
THE THIRD DEGREE (1909) by Charles Klein
THE WITNESS FOR THE DEFENSE (1911) by A.E.W. Mason
THE SHADOW (1913) by Eden Phillpotts
THE WOMAN WHO WAS ACQUITTED (1919) by André de Lorde
THE ATTORNEY FOR THE DEFENSE (1924) by Eugene G. Hafer
THE LETTER (1927) by W. Somerset Maugham
COQUETTE (1927) by George Abbott and Ann Preston Bridgers
THE FRONT PAGE (1928) by Ben Hecht and Charles MacArthur
GODS OF THE LIGHTNING (1928) by Maxwel Anderson
MIDNIGHT (1930) by Claire and Paul Sifton
THE CHILDREN'S HOUR (1934) by Lillian Hellman
WINTERSET (1935) by Maxwell Anderson
THE DEVIL ON STILTS (1937) by Florence Ryerson and Colin Clements
THE WINSLOW BOY (1946) by Terence Rattigan
THE GIOCONDA SMILE (1948) by Aldous Huxley
REQUIEM FOR A NUN (1951) by William Faulkner
DEAD PIGEON (1953) by Lenard Kantor
THE DOCK BRIEF (1957) by John Mortimer
VOLPONE, or THE FOX (1985), adapted by Gunduz Kalic and Don Campbell from the 1606 comedy by Ben Jonson
LIZZIE! (1993) by Owen Haskell
BUTTERFLY KISS (1994) by Phyllis Nagy
THE SECRET OF CELL BLOCK 7 (1999), book by Kelli Connors, music and lyrics by Cathy Sanborn

* * *

THE STANWAY CASE (2003) by Sam Bobrick
HIS GIRL FRIDAY (2003) by John Guare
FOR ALL TIME (2008) by K.J. Sanchez
RACE (2009) by David Mamet
WHEN WE GO UPON THE SEA (2010) by Lee Blessing
COMPULSION (2010) by Rinne Groff
HELLMAN vs. McCARTHY (2014) by Brian Richard Mori

UNSEAMLY (2014) by Oren Safdie
THE BULLPEN (2015) by Joe Assadourian
WATCHING O.J. (2015) by David McMillan
THE PENITENT (2017) by David Mamet
HOLLYWOOD DIARY (2017) by Octavio Carlin
UNCLE TED (2022) by Dan Wackerman
A WICKED SOUL IN CHERRY HILL (2022) by Matt Schatz

III. Interrogations:

MRS. DANE'S DEFENSE (1900) by Henry Arthur Jones
INTERVIEW (1904) by Octave Mirbeau
ENEMIES (1906) by Maxim Gorky
THE AFFAIR OF POISONS (1907) by Victorien Sardou
THE WITCH (1910), adapted by John Masefield from the Norwegian of H. Wiers-Jenssen
HOPPLA! SUCH IS LIFE! (1927) by Ernst Toller
LIFE OF GALILEO (1943) by Bertolt Brecht
MEN WITHOUT SHADOWS (1946) by Jean-Paul Sartre
MONTSERRAT (1949), adapted by Lillian Hellman from a drama by Emmanuel Robles
THE QUEEN AND THE REBELS (1949) by Ugo Betti
DARKNESS AT NOON (1951) by Sidney Kingsley
THE PRISONER (1954) by Bridget Boland
THE LARK (1955), adapted by Lillian Hellman from Jean Anouilh's *L'Alouette*
THE DOCK BRIEF (1958) by John Mortimer
A SHOT IN THE DARK (1961) by Marcel Achard
THE DEVILS (1961) by John Whiting, adapted from the novel *The Devils of Loudun* by Aldous Huxley
INCIDENT IN VICHI (1964) by Arthur Miller
THE TRIAL OF ANNE OPIE WEHRER AND UNKNOWN ACCOMPLICES FOR CRIMES AGAINST HUMANITY (1968) by Robert Ashley
IN THE MATTER OF J. ROBERT OPPENHEIMER (1968) by Heinar Kipphardt
THE TRIAL (1972) by Anthony Booth
ANSWERS (1972) by Tom Topor
ARE YOU NOW OR HAVE YOU EVER BEEN (1972) by Eric Bentley
THE RECANTATION OF GALILEO GALILEI (1973) BY Eric Bentley
FROM THE MEMOIRS OF PONTIUS PILATE (1976) by Eric Bentley

TIME TO KILL (1979) by Leslie Darbon
AGNES OF GOD (1980) by John Pielmeier
MASTERGATE (1989) by Larry Gelbart
BOBBY GOULD IN HELL (1989) by David Mamet
THE STRANGE CASE OF Dr. JEKYLL AND Mr. HYDE (1990) by Eberle Thomas and Barbara Redmond
DEATH AND THE MAIDEN (1991) by Ariel Dorfman
SPAIN (1993) by Romulus Linney
SCOTLAND ROAD (1993) by Jeffrey Hatcher
AN INTERVIEW (1995) by David Mamet
TAKING SIDES (1995) by Ronald Harwood
THE INTERROGATION OF NATHAN HALE (1995) by David Stanley Ford

* * *

RED DEATH (2001) by Lisa D'Amour
A JURY OF HER PEERS (2002) by Burton Bumgarner
THE PILLOWMAN (2003) by Martin McDonagh
SECURITY (2004) by Israel Horovitz
A PICASSO (2005) by Jeffrey Hatcher
NEW JERUSALEM (2008) by David Ives
THE WHITE CROW: EICHMANN IN JERUSALEM (2009) by Donald Freed
CONVICTION (2010) by Oren Neeman
VERITAS (2010) by Stan Richardson
UNNATURAL ACTS (2011) by Tony Speciale
JANE FONDA IN THE COURT OF PUBLIC OPINION (2011) by Terry Jastrow
OSWALD: THE ACTUAL INTERROGATION (2012) by Dennis Richard
THE ANARCHIST (2012) by David Mamet
THE NORTH POOL (2013) by Rajiv Joseph
THE NETHER (2013) by Jennifer Haley
THE INTERVIEW (2013) by Michael Franco
THE ENGLISH BRIDE (2013) by Lucile Lichtblau
CHOIR BOY (2014) by Tarell Alvin McCraney
TONGUES (2014) by E.A. Primamore
A HUMAN BEING DIED THAT NIGHT (2015) by Nicholas Wright
PIMM'S MISSION (2015) by Christopher Stetson Boal
IS THIS A ROOM (2019) by Tina Satter

IV. Jury Room:

RESURRECTION (1903) by Michael Morton, adapted from the novel by Leo Tolstoy
THE WOMAN ON THE JURY (1923) by Bernard K. Burns
THE JURY OF HER PEERS (1925) by Edward Harry Peple
LADIES OF THE JURY (1929) by Fred Ballard
GOOD MEN AND TRUE (1935) by Brian Marlow and Frank Merlin
JURY'S EVIDENCE (1936) by Jack de Leon and Jack Celestin
LADIES AND GENTLEMEN (1939) by Ben Hecht and Charles MacArthur
SO THE JURY WAS HUNG (1950) by Jack Steele
HANGING JUDGE (1952) by Raymond Massey
TWELVE ANGRY MEN (teleplay aired on CBS's Studio One in 1954; play version published by Samuel French in 1955; Broadway debut, 2004) by Reginald Rose
JURY ROOM (1961) by C.B. Gilford
TWELVE ANGRY WOMEN (1977) by Sherman L. Sergel, adapted from a teleplay by Reginald Rose
JUDGE AND JURY (1994) by Mark Dunn

* * *

PRISONER OF THE CROWN (2008) by Richard F. Stockton
SIX UPSET WOMEN (2015) by A.S. Lipson
TWELVE ANGRY PIGS (2017) by Wade Bradford

V. Lawyers and Judges out of Court:

THE GIRL AND THE JUDGE (1901) by Clyde Fitch
THE LION AND THE MOUSE (1905) by Charles Klein
THE HOUSE OF JUDGES (1907) by Gaston Leroux
AT BAY (1913) by George Scarborough
THE LAST RESORT (1914) by George Scarborough
THE LAW OF THE LAND (1914) by George Broadhurst
AT 9:45 (1919) by Owen Davis
THE UNKNOWN WOMAN (1919) by Willard Mack
THE LAWYER (1922) by Eugene Brieux
THE CAT AND THE CANARY (1922) by John Willard
THE RINGER (1926) by Edgar Wallace
THE MOUTHPIECE (1929) by Frank J. Collins

COUNSELLOR-AT-LAW (1931) by Elmer Rice
LONDON WALL (1931) by John Van Druten
COUNSEL'S OPINION (1932) by Roland Pertwee
JACK O'LANTERN (1932) by James Dawson
THE UNGUARDED HOUR (1935) by Bernard Merivale
THE LEAVENWORTH CASE (1936) by Basil Ring
THE JUDGE (1938) by Jill Craigie and Jeffrey Dell
SEE MY LAWYER (1939) by Richard Maibaum and Harry Clork
THE ZOMBIE (1941) by Robert St. Clair
AND THEN THERE WERE NONE (1943) by Agatha Christie
CORRUPTION IN THE PALACE OF JUSTICE (1945) by Ugo Betti
THE MAGNIFICENT YANKEE (1946) by Emmet Lavery
THE COCKTAIL PARTY (1949) by T.S. Eliot
THE DEEP BLUE SEA (1952) by Terence Rattigan
HANGING JUDGE (1952) by Raymond Massey
CAN-CAN (1953), book by Abe Burrows, music and lyrics by Cole Porter
BROTHERS IN LAW (1957) by Ted Willis and Henry Cecil
PUDD'NHEAD WILSON (1958) by Alice Chadwicke, adapted from the novel by Mark Twain
THE BARGAIN (1961) by Michael Gilbert
SWEENEY TODD THE BARBER (1962), book, music and lyrics by Brian J. Burton
TIME OF HOPE (1963) by Arthur and Violet Ketels, adapted from the novel by C.P. Snow
FEATHERTOP (1963) by Maurice Valency, after a story by Nathaniel Hawthorne
AFTER THE FALL (1964) by Arthur Miller
INADMISSIBLE EVIDENCE (1964) by John Osborne
EAST LYNNE (1965) by Brian J. Burton, adapted from the novel by Mrs. Henry Wood
ALIBI FOR A JUDGE (1965) by Felicity Douglas and Henry Cecil, from the book by Cecil
THE JUDGE (1967) by John Mortimer
A CASE FOR MASON (1967) by William McCleary, based upon characters created by Erle Stanley Gardner
SWEENEY TODD, THE DEMON BARBER OF FLEET STREET (1969) BY Austin Rosser
JEREMY TROY (1969) by Jack Sharkey
A VOYAGE ROUND MY FATHER (1971) by John Mortimer
SWEENEY TODD, THE DEMON BARBER OF FLEET STREET (1973) by Christopher G. Bond

CLARENCE DARROW (1974) by David W. Rintels, adapted from the book *Clarence Darrow for the defense* by Irving Stone
CURTAINS (1975) by Gloria Gonzalez
FIRST MONDAY IN OCTOBER (1978) by Jerome Lawrence and Robert E. Lee
ARISTOCRATS (1979) by Brian Friel
SWEENEY TODD, THE DEMON BARBER OF FLEET STREET (1979), book by Hugh Wheeler, music and lyrics by Stephen Sondheim
GUILTY CONSCIENCE (1980) by Richard Levinson and William Link
THE WOMAN IN BLACK (1987) by Stephen Mallatratt
SCALES OF JUSTICE (1988) by William Kovacsik
THE PERFECT MURDER (1989) by Mike Johnson
CURSE OF THE WEREWOLF (1990) by Tim Kelly
AN INTERVIEW (1995) by David Mamet
'TIL DEATH DO US PART (1997) by Craig Sodaro
LAWYERS (1998) by Henry G. Miller
CLARENCE DARROW TONIGHT (1999) by Laurence Luckinbill

* * *

WHERE'S MY MONEY? (2001) by John Patrick Shanley
PERSONAL EFFECTS (2003) by Douglas Post
TRYING (2004) by Joanna McClelland Glass
SWAMP PIRATE ZOMBIES (2011) by Andrew Ross
DON'T GO GENTLE (2012) by Stephen Belber
DISGRACED (2012) by Ayad Akhtar
MURDER BY TEN (2012) by Eddie McPherson
RED SPEEDO (2013) by Lucas Hnath
CLOSELY RELATED KEYS (2014) by Wendy Graf
INTERMISSION (2014) by Daniel Libman
THE RELIGION THING (2014) by Renee Calarco
RUNNING AWAY FROM THE ONE WITH THE KNIFE (2015) by Aaron Landsman
BUZZER (2015) by Tracey Scott Wilson
THE ORIGINALIST (2015) by John Strand
FULFILLMENT (2015) by Thomas Bradshaw
WOULD YOU STILL LOVE ME IF... (2015) by John S. Anastasi
RED SPEEDO (2016) by Lucas Hnath
A DOG STORY (2016), book by Erich H. Weinberger, music and lyrics by Gayla D. Morgan
TRIAL OF THE WICKED WITCH (2016) by Craig Sodaro

THE PENITENT (2017) by David Mamet
GENTLY DOWN THE STREAM (2017) by Martin Sherman
THE PORTUGUESE KID (2017) by John Patrick Shanley
SKINTIGHT (2018) by Joshua Harmon
THE DARKNESS INSIDE (2018) by Billy W. Boone
A LITTLE LIFE (2018) by Koen Tachelet, adapted from the novel by Hanya Yanagihara
WHITE NOISE (2019) by Suzan-Lori Parks
LUNCH BUNCH (2019) by Sarah Einspanier
SISTERS IN LAW (2019) by Jonathan Shapiro
MsTRIAL (2019) by Dep Kirkland
OBJECTION! DISORDER IN THE COURT! (2020) by Brianna Dehn
THE TRIAL OF EXISTENCE (2021) by Brent Holland
PRIMA FACIE (2023) by Suzie Miller

APPENDIX B

More Jury Room Plays

On October 17, 1939, Helen Hayes, the First Lady of the American stage, became a member of the jury in *Ladies and Gentlemen*, adapted by Charles MacArthur and Ben Hecht from a drama by Hungary's *Ladislaus Bush-Fekete* (Martin Beck Theatre – 105 performances). The ladies and gentlemen of the jury are pondering the fate of a popular novelist accused of causing his wife's death by pushing her from a cliff on Mount Wilson. Miss Scott (Helen Hayes), secretary to a Hollywood movie mogul, and an admirer of the writer's works, insists that he could not have committed the crime. One by one – "Through cajolery, flattery, guile and a dash of sex," according to Sidney B. Whipple in the *New York World Telegram* of October 18, 1939 — she wins the opposing jurors over, while romantically succumbing to the charms of the antagonistic foreman.

* * *

The Jury of Her Peers (copyright 1925), by Edward Harry Peple, is a hilarious satire spotlighting the first ever United States jury composed entirely of women. The jurors, members of the Women's Progressive League, are united in condemning the defendant, handsome William Keets, over a breach of promise he made to young, alluring Catherine Carroll. The feisty jurors are unaware that the lawsuit is a set-up planned by "victim" Carroll, "rascal" Keets and their own respective husbands who have all banded together against them, determined to inflict "a nice little boomerang of ridicule" upon "twelve eager and palpitating juresses and two hair-pulling female attorneyesses." The masculine scheme fails, and the men find themselves in an over-night jail for contempt of court.

* * *

In Mark Dunn's comedy *Judge and Jury*, which opened at the Thirteenth Street Repertory Company in New York City on February 4, 1994, a six-member jury is gathered in a Texan jury room to deliberate the case of a young couple blaming each other for mental cruelty. It is a scorching summer day, and the air-conditioner is out of commission. The three men and three women spend most of the day on gossip and private matters, barely discussing the case at hand. When finally they agree on a verdict — "one dollar to the male plaintiff, nothing for the female defendant" - the bailiff announces that "there's been a settlement" and their services are no longer needed.

APPENDIX C

Twentieth Century Death-Row Plays

Throughout the 20th century there were quite a few plays that ended on death row in European and American prisons. The vaults of Newgate, the scaffoldings of the Tower of London, the batteries of the Bastille, and the cells of Sing Sing were captured on the stage with nerve-wracking effect.

Among the dramas that boasted last-minute hanging, garroting or electrocution are: *Danton's Death* by George Büchner (written, 1835; first produced, 1902); *The Campden Wonder* by John Masefield (1907); *The Valiant* by Holworthy Hall and Robert Middlemass (1920); *Man and the Masses* by Ernst Toller (1924); *An American Tragedy* Patrick Kearney, based on Theodore Dreiser's 1925 novel (1926); *Spellbound* by Frank Vosper (1927); *Machinal* by Sophie Treadwell (1928); *Gods of the Lightning* by Maxwell Anderson (1928); *The Criminal Code* by Martin Flavin (1929); *The Last Mile* by John Wexley (1930); *Smoky Cell* by Edgar Wallace (1930); *Children of Darkness* by Edwin Justus Mayer (1930); *Draw the Fires!* by Ernst Toller (1930); *Midnight* by Claire and Paul Sifton (1930); *Elizabeth the Queen* by Maxwell Anderson (1930); *Two Seconds* by Elliott Lester (1931); *Mary of Scotland* by Maxwell Anderson (1933); *End and Beginning* by John Masefield (1933); *They Shall Not Die* by John Wexley (1934); *The Postman Always Rings Twice* by James M. Cain, dramatized from his 1934 novel (1936); *Leave Her to Heaven* by John Van Druten (1940); *Native Son* by Paul Green and Richard Wright, dramatized from Wright's 1940 novel (1941); *Uncle Harry* by Thomas Job (1942); *Antigone* by Jean Anouilh (1943); *Joan of Lorraine* by Maxwell Anderson (1946); *The Trial* by Andre Gide and Jean-Louis Barrault, based on Franz Kafka's 1925 novel (1947); *Anne of the Thousand Days* by Maxwell Anderson (1948); *Lost in the Stars* by Maxwell Anderson and Kurt Weill, based on the 1948 novel *Cry, the Beloved Country* by Alan Paton (1949); *Deathwatch* by Jean Genet (1949); *Song at the Scaffold* by Emmet Lavery, from the 1933 novel by Baroness Gertrud von le Fort (1949); *Darkness at Noon* by Sidney Kingsley, from the 1940 novel by Arthur Koestler (1951); *Requiem for a Nun* by William Faulkner (1951); *Billy Budd* by Louise O. Coxe and Robert Chapman, from the 1891 novella by Herman Melville (1951); *A Pin to See the Peepshow* by F. Tennyson Jesse and Harold Marsh Harwood, adapted from Jesse's 1934 novel (1951); *Someone Waiting* by Emlyn Williams (1953); *The Crucible* by Arthur Miller (1953); *Murder Story* by Ludovic Kennedy (1954);

The Quare Fellow by Brendan Behan (1954);*Compulsion* by Meyer Levin, dramatized from his 1956 novel (1957); *Dialogues des Carmélites*, music and libretto by Francis Poulence, after a play of the same name by Georges Bemanos (opera, 1957); *The Man Who Never Died* by Barrie Stavis (1958); *Channa Senesh* by Aharon Megged (1958); *Frankenstein* by David Campton, adapted from Mary Shelley's 1818 novel (1959); *A Man for All Seasons* by Robert Bolt (1960); *Gallows Humor* by Jack Richardson (1961); *The Devils* by John Whiting (1961); *The Advocate* by Robert Noah (1963); *The Murder of Maria Marten, or The Red Barn* by Brian J. Burton (1963); *The People vs. Ranchman* by Megan Terry (1967); *The Disposal* by William Inge (1968); *Inquest* by Donald Freed (1970); *The Runner Stumbles* by Milan Stitt (1976); *From the Memoirs of Pontius Pilate* by Eric Bentley (1976); *Breaker Morant* by Kenneth G. Ross (1978); *Hauptmann* by John Logan (1992); *A Lesson Before Dying* by Romulus Linney, based on the 1993 novel of the same name by Ernest J. Gaines (2000); *In the Penal Colony*, music by Philip Glass, libretto by Rudy Wurlitzer, based on a short story of the same name by Franz Kafka (opera, 2000).

Last-minute reprieves occur in *If I Were King* by Justin Huntley McCarthy (1901); *The Cardinal* by Louis N. Parker (1902); *A Working Girl's Wrongs* by Hal Reid (1903); *The Woman in the Case* by Clyde Fitch (1905); *How Hearts Are Broken* by Langdon McCormick (1905); *For a Human Life* by Hal Reid (1906); *The Confession* by James Halleck Reid (1911); *Silence* by Max Marcin (1924); *Beggar on Horseback* by George S. Kaufman and Marc Connelly (1924); *The Threepenny Opera* by Bertolt Brecht and Kurt Weill, adapted from the 1728 play *The Beggar's Opera* by John Gay (1928); *Fast Life* by Samuel Shipman and John B. Hymer (1928); *The Front Page* by Ben Hecht and Charles MacArthur (1928); *Midnight* by Claire and Paul Sifton (1930); *Precedent* by I.J. Golden (1931); *Riddle Me This!* by Daniel N. Rubin (1932); *Chalked Out* by Warden Lewis E. Lawes and Jonathan Finn (1937); *The Gioconda Smile* by Aldous Huxley (1948); *Dial "M" for Murder* by Frederick Knott (1952); *Hanging Judge* by Raymond Massey (1952); *The Prisoner* by Bridget Boland (1964); *The Beggar's Opera* by Václav Havel, adapted from the 1728 play by John Gay (1976); *Amazing Grace* by Michael Cristofer (1995); *Parade*, book by Alfred Uhry, music and lyrics by Jason Robert Brown (1998); *Coyote on a Fence* by Bruce Graham (2000); *Dead Man Walking*, opera, libretto by Terrence McNally, music by Jake Heggie (2000).

* * *

Claude Newman: A Miracle on Death Row by Cathal Gallagher (2005); *Direct from Death Row the Scottsboro Boys* by Mark Stein (2006); *Terre Haute* by Edmund White (2007); *The Exonerated* by Jessica Blank and Erik Jensen